Principles of Management

PRINCIPLES OF MANAGEMENT

Dr. B. S. Moshal

Reader (Retd.), Deptt. of Commerce
Zakir Husain Post Graduate Eve. College
(Delhi University)
Founder Director, D.C.A.S (I.P. University)
Former Visiting Faculty ICAI

Ane Books Pvt. Ltd.

New Delhi ♦ Chennai

Principles of Management

B. S. Moshal

Published by

Ane Books Pvt. Ltd.

4821, Parwana Bhawan, 1st Floor, 24 Ansari Road, Darya Ganj,
New Delhi - 110 002, Tel.: +91(011) 23276843-44, Fax: +91(011) 23276863
e-mail: kapoor@anebooks.com, Website: www.anebooks.com

Branch Office :

- Avantika Niwas, 1st Floor, 19 Doraiswamy Road, T. Nagar,
  Chennai - 600 017, Tel.: +91(044) 28141554, 28141209
  e-mail: anebookschennai@gmail.com, rathinam@anebooks.com

ISBN : 978-81-8052-275-8

Printed at R.K. Offset Process, New Delhi

Dedicated to

my

Parents & Guru

Preface

Management is dynamic and developing discipline. Its application all over the world is as old as human civilization. But it has emerged as distinct academic field only during twentieth century. In the recent past due to rapid diverse, complex and unstructured changes taking place in business environment, the overall role of the manager has become more demanding and challenging. More emphasis is being placed on management of strategic alliances, improvement in productivity, worldwide demand of quality management, management of change, strategic management and ethical and social aspect of business etc.

In changed situations, existing techniques and approaches of management seem to be less effective and inadequate. Thus an application of management theory has to be supplemented by high degree of creativeness and innovativeness and by the use of many other skills on the part of managers. To become more sensible and responsive to the needs of changing environment, the manager have to assume new roles as per the demand of the situation. Apart from traditional role of seeking efficient and effective utilization of resources for achieving organizational objectives the new generation manager has to focus more on transformational leadership, self control, social and ethical implications of decisions, role of economic agent and trustee of resources.

The text of this book has been primarily designed to provide clear understanding of the subject in today's context to the students of managemental and professional managers. Attempts have been made to familiarize them with the latest developments taking place in the theory as well and practice of management.

The subject matter of this book has been organised in and presented through eighteen chapters. The first set of three chapters deals with basic nature and importance of management, elements of managing process, role of manager, an overview of various function areas and historical aspect of evolution of management thoughts. Second set of four chapter contains necessary information on planning process, its importance, types of plans and techniques of planning with reference to corporate planning and strategy formulation. Along with this, latest perspective and complexities of decision making process have been dealt with carefully.

The third group of four chapters has been devoted to organizing process, its nature, importance and elements. Adequate information on departmentation delegation of author and traditional and modern forms of organization, has been furnished. The fourth set of three chapters provides required information on the elements of directing including motivation leadership and communication. The last set of three chapters gives an adequate coverage to controlling function including traditional and modern techniques of controlling, coordination management of change, new trends in management and challenges for the modern managers.

To expose manager and students of management with real life problem situation which may arise in managing process a separate chapter has been devoted on management case study method. It will enhance their decision making abilities, analytical skill and communication skill.

Dr. B.S. Moshal

Acknowledgement

On bringing the book in its existing form, thoroughly revised one, the author is really indebted to many resource persons and authors whose work and experience has been shared. I express my sincere thanks to some of my colleagues for their guidance, help and inspiration including Dr. N.K. Kakkar, Director Maharaja Agrasen Institute of Management Dr. M.S. Chaudhary, Director Surajmal Institute, Dr. M.S. Rawat, Principal D.C.A.C, Dr. R.B Solenki Ambedkar College, Sh. C.S. Pant Dayal Singh College, Dr. N.K. Agrawal, School of Open Learning, Dr. G.C. Kasturi, Rajdhani College, Delhi University.

Suggestions for the improvement of text are always welcome and will be taken care of in the next edition.

DR. B.S. MOSHAL

Acknowledgement

Contents

Chapter 1

Conceptual Framework of Management

Learning Objectives

1. To understand how physical resources are utilised by labourers.
2. To understand the basic theme of management along with various interpretations of this term.
3. To bring out the main features of management.
4. To understand management as a process and its functions as sub-processes.
5. To understand management as a profession, a combination of science and art and distinct from administration.
6. To understand the concept of family management versus professional management, particularly with reference to India.
7. To remember basic management skills and styles used by managers in practice.
8. To understand how management knowledge can be used in every economy and society.

CONCEPT AND MEANING OF MANAGEMENT

The knowledge of management is used for organising and managing the work of people in an organisation. Managers mobilise the efforts and activities of people in the direction of achieving common goals. The knowledge of management has universal application. It is widely used in every society and economy and is needed in every walk of human life. It is more significant and useful for business organisations. Such organisations are economic entities and profit-earning bodies.

They perform economic functions of producing and distributing goods and services for the satisfaction of human needs and wants.

In order to conduct these business activities, both physical and human resources are acquired and used. Physical resources such as land, building, capital, raw material, machines, technology, etc., are of a peculiar nature. They are lifeless and scarce resources. Thus, they need human resources like labour and management to utilise them towards the accomplishment of pre-determined objectives. In the process of acquiring, mobilising and utilising these limited resources for performing economic functions, a group of people commonly known as managers assume an important position and perform a key role. It is only by performing a wide range of activities and functions by these managers that physical resources are used through labour for realising goals.

Thus, in this context generally it is said that management is to get things done by others. It is one of the simplest versions of management. But actually, it is much more than that, involving a number of activities, functions, approaches, skills and knowledge to be used by the manager for managing the affairs of the organisation efficiently.

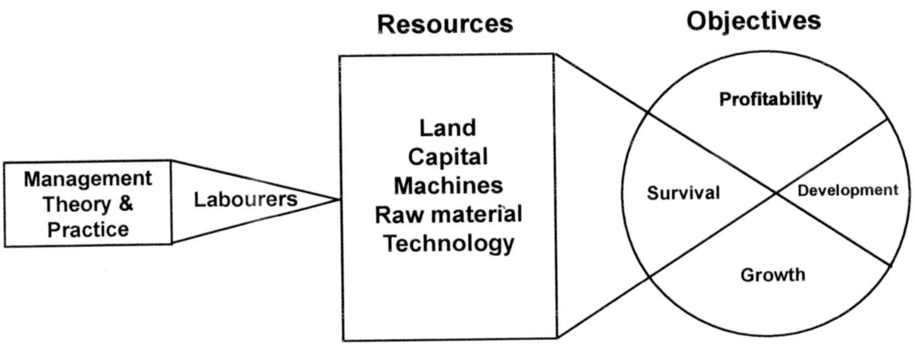

Figure 1.1. Application of management knowledge to achieve objectives of the organisation

Management scientists belonging to different disciplines offer different meanings and interpretations to this term. Economics regards it as one of the important factors of production used for creating wealth but accountants give another interpretation and consider management as a process of analysing and interpreting various facts, data and statementes, especially in relation to profitability and finance soundness. Similarly, behavioural scientists place more emphasis on the human aspect involved in management and treat it as a human and social process.

Not only this, some authors consider management as a set of managerial functions to be performed by a group of individuals known as managers. But others believe that management is a separate discipline or a systematic body of knowledge, consisting of certain principles, generalisations, concepts and rules to be applied in a particular situation for obtaining better results.

To come out from the controversy and sharp differences among various authors regarding the definition and interpretation of management, it is desirable to analyse and view it in a broader perspective in terms of its origin and gradual development. According to F. W. Taylor, who is known as the father of scientific management, "management is an art of knowing what is to be done and seeing that it is done in the best possible manner."

In this definition he has highlighted two basic functions involved in the process of management and these are planning and controlling. As compared to it, a more comprehensive definition has been forwarded by Henri Fayol, the father of modern management. According to Fayol, management is "to forecast, to plan, to organise, to command, to coordinate and to control." In this definition, all basic functions of management have been included.

Similarly, a functional approach has been followed by modern management scientist Peter Drucker. According to him, "management is a system or organ and any system or organ can be defined only by describing and explaining functions performed by it." Lawrence Appley has submitted an oversimplified version of management which makes the purpose and process of it quite clear. According to Appley "management is the accomplishment of results through the efforts of other people. More precisely, McFarland has defined the term 'management' as that process by which managers create, direct, maintain and operate purposive organisation through systematic co-ordinated and co-operative human efforts."

In this definition he has placed more emphasis on the dynamic nature of management in relation to organisation in which group efforts are directed and coordinated for achieving goals. Furthermore, Dale S. Beach has defined it "as a social process entailing responsibility for effective economic planning and regulation of operations of enterprises." According to Beach, in the process of management more responsibility lies on managers for planning and regulating activities of employees who are working in the organisation.

In the words of Kreitner, "management is a process of working with and through others to achieve organisational objectives in a changing environment. Central to this process is the effective and efficient use of limited resources." Kreitner has stressed more on two important variables such as effectiveness and efficiency in relation to the use of resources.

Review and analysis of the above definitions of management makes it clear that every author has tried to define the term 'management' either by placing more emphasis on one of the aspects of it or by adding a new dimension to it. So far, two identical definitions on the basic theme of management have not emerged. It all has resulted in a hazy situation. Moreover two definitions are hardly identical in respect to all relevant and basic elements of management. It is because knowledge of management deals with human behaviour which is very dynamic and complex and cannot be reduced to a formula which leaves scope for authors to interpret it differently. Besides, management is a growing and developing discipline. It has witnessed many drastic changes in its nature and scope, coverage and orientation over the last five decades. All along with technological and social development taking place in society, it has emerged as one of the important branches of social sciences.

Therefore, definitions and interpretations of the term 'management' have virtually become less relevant or outdated in the context of the rapidly changing environment. Historical analysis of developments taking place in this field reveals that during the initial stages of development management was simply considered a way of getting things done by others. This version was further elaborated by many authors like Henri Fayol and others and they developed it as a dynamic process. In the present context, especially on account of a growing need for professionalisation, separation of ownership from management and globalisation of economic activities, a new dimension has been added to it and it has become more popular as strategic management dealing with strengths and weaknesses of organisation and relating them to opportunities and threats arising out of a changing environment.

Basically, management is an integrated set of functions, processes, approaches and other skills to be used for mobilising and utilising resources for achieving predetermined objectives in a changing environment. Particularly in the context of organisations which are man-made systems, management remains an invisible force the chief organ of which directs and coordinates activities of its members to seek common goals.

Management is much more than mere performance of managerial functions of planning, organising, staffing and controlling. To get better results, managers have to be innovative and creative on their part in every sphere of the managing process. They have to use a variety of skills such as human skill, technical skill, communication skills, etc. To be more effective they have the responsibility of creating a conducive internal environment and reconciling with a rapidly changing external environment. Their success largely depends on their capabilities as to how sharply they can visualise the movement of environmental factors and how effectively they use it for optimising results.

In a nutshell, the managing process involves:

1. Performance of management functions, planning, organising, staffing, directing and controlling.
2. Using managerial skills such as conceptual, analytical, administrative, technical and human skills.
3. Carrying out managerial activities such as decision-making, communicating and networking.
4. Creating a congenial internal environment by building strong organisational culture, systems, norms and values.
5. Seeking optimum utilisation of both human as well as physical resources.
6. Scanning the external environment and devising ways to cope with a rapidly changing environment.

The features of management are:

1. Management is a process.
2. Management is a social process.
3. Management is a system of authority.
4. Management is a goal-oriented process.
5. Management is a dynamic process.
6. Management involves effective and efficient utilisation of resources.
7. It is a multi-disciplinary field.
8. It is a critical and vital sub-system of an organisation.
9. It is a full-fledged academic discipline.
10. Management is a combination of science and art.
11. It is all-pervasive.
12. It is an influence process.

The following characteristics may be derived from the definitions of management given above:

(1) Management is a Process

Although the term 'management' has been defined from different angles, the majority of authors believe that it is a process of getting things done by others. In this process, to get things done by others, certain basic functions are to be performed such as planning, organising, staffing, directing and controlling. These functions may also be considered as elements of the management process.

(2) Management is a Social Process

The basic responsibility of every manager is to get things done by others. To discharge this responsibility he has to establish interpersonal relations with the people working under his control. He has to understand their behaviour not only as an individual member but also as a member of a group. To get better results, it is necessary for a manager to understand the personal as well as social needs of the employees so as to motivate them.

(3) Management is a System of Authority

As stated earlier, in the process of management, a number of functions are to be performed by managers. They need to have enough authority and power for it. Without having formal authority they cannot prepare plans and direct and control the activities of subordinates for the accomplishment of predetermined objectives. Managers hold a position in an organisation and authority is vested in that position. So, their position is identified in terms of authority and responsibility given to them.

(4) Management is Goal-oriented

Some authors have viewed management as a sub-system of an organisation thereby directing and coordinating activities of members to seek goals. It is only to achieve these goals that knowledge of management is used. In the absence of these goals, there is little planning, organising, directing and controlling in an organisation. In the words of Kreitner, without organisational objectives the management process is like a trip without a specific destination and would be aimless and wasteful.

(5) Management is a Dynamic Process

Management is no more stereotyped knowledge; rather, it is ever-changing particularly in the context of a changing environment. To maintain survival of the organisation, managers have to work out new relationships, develop new approaches and new ideas so as to cope with the changing environment. By their innovativeness and creativity, they make the organisation capable of converting threats and problems arising out of changing situations into opportunities.

(6) Management Involves Effective and Efficient Utilisation of Resources

To achieve objectives, managers have to integrate physical as well as human resources and utilise them most effectively and efficiently. A proper balance is to be maintained between effectiveness of use which implies use of resources in a right way and efficiency which indicates the ratio between input and output or cost or benefit. In other words, a manager is said to be efficient if he succeeds in containing costs as much as possible and conserves limited resources.

(7) Management is Multi-disciplinary

To seek better results and improved performance in the field of management, concepts, ideas, generalisations and principles of other disciplines are also used. To make superior quality of decisions, the use of statistical devices and mathematical tools has become the style of the manager. Similarly, the use of knowledge of economics, psychology, sociology and anthropology for understanding human behaviour and analysing market forces has become a regular feature of it.

(8) Management is a Critical and Vital Sub-system of an Organisation

Organisations are man-made systems to be operated through individuals by applying management knowledge. Management is a prime mover of the organisation and it is made functional and productive by using management force which is invisible and intangible. Not only this, survival, prosperity, growth and development of the organisation to the larger extent depend on the quality of management knowledge being used by talented professional managers.

(9) Management is a Discipline

Management has emerged as one of the important branches of social sciences. It consists of principles, generalisations, concepts, approaches and rules dealing with human behaviour. Therefore, it is said to be an inexact science or soft science. These principles of management have to be applied to practical situations to get results.

(10) Management is a Combination of Art and Science

Management knowledge exhibits some characteristics of art and some of science. Therefore it is considered a combination of both.

(11) Management is All-pervasive

Management is an universal phenomenon. Its use is not confined to business or other economic activities only. it is equally important in every walk of life. Management knowledge is used in every economy, in every organisation and at every level of organisation. Thus, there is a generic, pervasive and global need to manage limited resources to get maximum benefits.

(12) Management is an Influence Process

To get better results and seek optimum utilisation of all physical resources, managers exercise an influence on the behaviour of people working under their control. There is a need to influence the behaviour of people because physical resources which are lifeless and scarce have to be used through them. In the process of influence, the managers regulate, control, mould and reshape the behaviour of subordinates to make it desirable. In order to exercise influence, he uses his position, competence, authority and resources available at his disposal. By determining and providing various stimuli (rewards and punishment) he motivates and inspires them to behave and act in a desired manner.

Not only the behaviour of people, event, situations or variables are also influenced by him to reconcile with a changing environment. He maintains a vigilant watch on the situation, brings it under his control and sometimes makes it happen by taking suitable strategic measures. The process of influence is bilateral in the sense that on the one hand, managers exert pressure on these and, on the other hand, decisions and actions of managers are influenced by these variables.

In this connection, it is, however, to be noted that managers take proactive and reactive measures to deal with them successfully. Innovative managers, by taking suitable measures try to avert undesirable situations or ensure that it happens in a desired manner. Once an event occurs, by taking damage control action, the ill-effect of these events is reduced to a minimum. Besides, the values of the organisation, its goals, strategies and policies have to be adjusted and made in conformity with the present situation.

Furthermore, management is an integrative and dynamic process. Regular exercise on the part of managers for developing and discovering new ideals, vision, image and relationships has become a well recognised part of their activities. In order to generate these ideas, research work and analysis is undertaken on a regular basis.

Innovativeness and creativity on the part of managers is necessary. The ideas so discovered have to be further processed for ascertaining their feasibility, practicability and suitability for implementation. In brief, the process of management involves interaction with ideas, things, resources, people and goals. It is a process of converting ideas into decisions, decisions into action and action into concrete results and outcome.

MANAGEMENT AS A PROCESS

Management is a process of integrating and utilising physical and human resources to seek objectives. Management is a human and social process which is directed upon individuals to get things done by them. Like other processes, it consists of many actions or activities or functions which are to be carried out in a logical sequence. It is a result-oriented process direction related with the task of determining objectives and developing a suitable course of action to accomplish them more efficiently. It is a continuous process, because it has no definable end. The steps or elements involved in it are to be performed in a continuous cycle. The elements or activities that are performed in this process are also known as functions of management.

This popular approach of describing what managers do in the process is viewed as functional approach. It was developed by Henri Fayol and it became popular because it characterises the management process as a sequence of rational and logical steps. However, Fayol claimed that planning, organising, command, coordination and control were basic and common denominators for all managers in the process of management. But later on due to certain changes taking place in the nature and field of management, the sequence of functions was rearranged by adding some more functions. Finally, it was made as planning, organising, staff, directing and controlling. Brief descriptions of these are as under:

Commonly referred to as a basic management function, planning is a process of determining objectives, developing alternative courses of action and selecting the best course of action for achieving objectives. It is a forward-looking approach which involves futurism and making estimates or projections about the future. In order to visualise the future, the past is analysed. It is related to the present and on the basis of that the future is forecast.

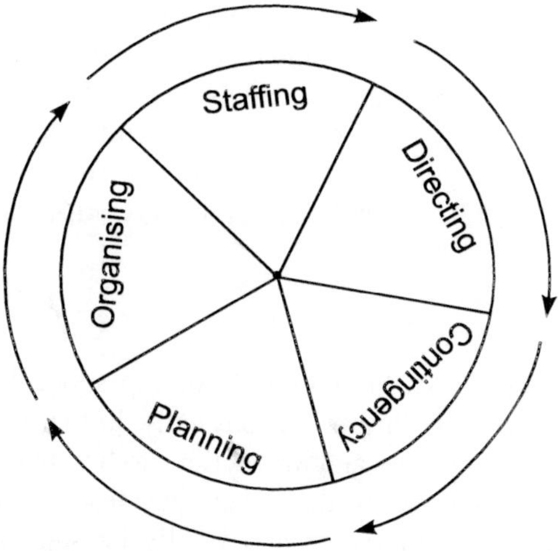

Figure 1.2. Management process and sub-processes planning

Thus, the planning function focuses on the future destination of organisation which provides direction to its activities. In planning, managers decide in advance which is to be done, when, how and by whom. Successful managers visualise even at the time of making plans what problems may probably arise at the time of implementing them.

ORGANISING

Careful organising, like planning, helps in making efficient utilisation of human resources. It is a process of establishing a working relationship among the employees. The various activities are assigned to them, authority is granted to them, and they are brought in the relationship of superior and subordinate. This working relationship brings order and discipline in the organisation. Every employee knows very well who his superior is to command his activities and who is to be commanded by him. Similarly, in organising a process the role and relation as a position of each individual in the organisation is spelt out clearly. Organising may also be considered as a process of integrating, balancing, unifying and coordinating activities of various employees for accomplishing pre-determined objectives. The process of organising also involves the creation of various units or departments, assigning a group of activities to them with enough authority and finally maintaining coordination among them.

STAFFING

Once the structure of an organisation is brought into existence by determining the role and relationship of various positions, these positions have to be manned by individuals. Staffing is a process of determining the quality and quantity of the human force needed for the organisation, making all necessary arrangements for acquiring it through recruitment and selection, maintaining them for a longer period of time by making and implementing suitable personnel policies and finally developing them to the maximum of their capabilities and potential. Thus, the staffing function of management is mainly concerned with manpower planning, recruitment, selection, training and development, compensation and maintaining of human resources in the organisation.

Directing

Directing is a process of helping and guiding subordinates in the direction of achieving objectives of organisation. Basically, in the process of directing, the superior issues necessary orders and instructions to his subordinates regarding the work which has been assigned to them. He educates and guides them regarding various methods of doing the work and finally he supervises the work being performed by them on a regular basis. In the process of directing three elements are involved, namely, communication, motivation and leadership. In brief, for directing the activities of subordinates, two-way communication has to be maintained between them and simultaneously the superior has to motivate the subordinates and provide dynamic leadership to them.

Controlling

Controlling is a process of ensuring that each and every activity has been performed in a planned manner and in conformity with pre-determined standards of performance. It is essentially a process whereby standards of performance are determined for every employee and his actual performance is measured and then compared with these standards, to find out deviations and to take remedial measures to improve performance. So the process of controlling includes all activities, actions, procedures, methods used by managers for bringing actual results nearer and closer to desired results. The process of controlling is not only concerned with improving performance but it also includes all actions and techniques used by the organisation for regulating and controlling the use of resources to achieve planned goals. It also regulates the behaviour of employees to maintain order and discipline among them. It also checks distortions and deviations which may take place in the system to make it more cost-effective.

Some Observations

On the basis of the above discussion on the management process, the following observations can be made:

1. The management process essentially consists of some basic steps which are known as functions or elements or sub-processes of management such as planning, organising, staffing, directing and controlling.
2. These functions or elements of management are primary or basic in nature. These are to be performed by every manager in all situations to get things

done by others. In practice, there are many more other functions which may be derived from these known as subsidiary functions like reporting, budgeting, forecasting, representation, innovations, etc.

3. Planning is a starting point of the management process followed by other functions. Obviously, without planning there is little organising, staffing, directing and controlling. The process of management comes to an end at controlling. Thus, these basic functions of management are to be performed in a definite and logical sequence to get better results.
4. The management process operates through these elements or functions which may also be considered as sub-processes of management. All these sub-processes contribute to the functioning of the management process and get essential strength and power from it.
5. Being sub-processes, all these management functions are closely related, inter-dependent and independent. Although these functions are to be performed by managers independently such as making a plan and designing the organisation, recruitment and selection and exercising control are independent functions. But they are organically or functionally related to each other such as planning paves the way for organising and organising for staffing and other functions and the like. Similarly, all these will have little meaning if not followed by controlling. In other words, if we consider these functions separately and in isolation they are bound to lose their relevance, meaning and importance. Therefore, these can produce the desired results only when they are perceived in totality and considered as a part of the management process.
6. In the process of management, the above-mentioned functions are performed for seeking goals, therefore they are considered as the means of achieving goals. It is because by performing these functions efficiently and in logical sequence better results can be produced.

NATURE OF MANAGEMENT

Besides the above discussion on management, to understand its basic nature precisely it may further be studied and analysed in terms of many of its other aspects such as management as combinations of both art and science, its relation with administration, management as a profession, managerial skills, styles of a manager, etc.

Management is Combination of Art and Science

Management knowledge shows the characteristics of both art and science. In fact, these two disciplines are not mutually exclusive but they are supplementary to each other. Every discipline of art is always backed by science which is basic knowledge of that art. Similarly, every discipline of science is complete only when it is used in practice for solving various kinds of problems faced by a human being in the organisation or in other fields of social life which is more related to an art.

Art basically deals with an application of knowledge, personal skill and know-how in a specific situation for achieving given objectives efficiently. So it is concerned with the best way of doing things and seems to be personalised in nature.

During the initial stages of the development of management, it was considered as an art. It is because at that time there was a jungle of managerial knowledge and it was not codified and systematic. People used to get things done by others in their own way giving an impression to others that whosoever uses it knows the art of using it. This kind of loose and inadequate understanding of management further supported that it is an art. Management can be well understood as an art on the following counts:

Management as an Art

1. It has practical application in a given situation.
2. The experience of a manager is not transferable.
3. It involves the use of creativity and innovativeness.
4. It implies the use of personal judgement, perception and intuition.

Management as a Science

1. Systematic and organised body of knowledge.
2. Developed through observations, research and experiment.
3. Based on relationship of cause and effect.
4. Knowledge of it is transferable.
5. Has universal application.

Management as an Art

1. The knowledge of management like other arts has a practical application. It is capable of being used in specific situations to get better results. In every situation, the manager attempts to solve problems efficiently or make superior quality decisions and realise objectives or targets with minimum effort and resources. He does it only by using management knowledge. The application of management knowledge to some extent is personalised depending on the individual manager. Though knowledge about principles, concepts and generalisations of management remains the same, the manner in which it is used differs from one manager to another.
2. At the same time, continuous application of management knowledge to a practical situation by a manager results in gaining experience on his part. With the passage of time he gains more and more experience which is personal in nature and becomes his possession and which cannot be transferred to others. Therefore, managers having more experience of using the principles of management in practice normally become more efficient in their functioning. They develop more skills and abilities to translate management knowledge into practice.

3. Application of management knowledge also calls for using innovativeness and creativity on the part of managers. On the basis of the fundamentals of managerial knowledge, analytical abilities, farsightedness, etc., the manager can discover new ideas, relationships and more efficient ways of doing things. It is possible only through rigorous research and analysis, creative approach and scientific outlook on the part of managers. Thus, the use of innovativeness and creativity makes it an art.
4. One more reason for considering management as an art is that in many situations, theoretical knowledge of management may not be adequate or relevant for solving problems. It may be due to complexities involved in the problem or size of the problem or it may be the uniqueness of it. In such situations, the manager has to rely more on his past experience, perception, intuition and judgement. He may use the 'rule of thumb' (hit or miss approach) or the trial-and-error method to solve such problems. Added to this, sometimes he may redefine and reformulate the problem by applying creativity and personal experience to get the problem solved. In this way, more use of art is inevitable.

Management as a Science

Management as a science bears the following characteristics:

1. Management is a systematic body of knowledge, consisting of principles, generalisations, approaches and concepts to be applied to practical situations. This knowledge serves as a basis for managers to understand the process of management and the problems involved in it. The manager can manage the situation or organisation in a systematic and scientific manner only if he possesses adequate knowledge of management and its principles. In the words of Peter Drucker, managers need a systematic supply of an organised body of knowledge for taking risky decisions of business enterprises in a complex and rapidly changing technology, economy and society. Organisational and managerial needs, goals and values can come into sharp focus through scientific knowledge.
2. Secondly, the principles, generalisations and concepts of management have been developed and formulated on the basis of observation, research and analysis and experimentation as in the case of principles of other sciences. These principles of management are supported by valid evidence, are precise in nature and more purposeful.
3. Like other scientific principles, management principles are also based on the relationship between cause and effect. They indicate that the same cause under similar circumstances will produce the same effect. For instance, according to the principle of personnel management, if you pay more to workers, they will produce more. Payment made to them serves as an incentive or stimulus which ultimately activates them to produce more. Though these principles have been formulated through observation

and research and analysis, they cannot be compared with the principles of physical science which produce uniform results in similar situations.

4. Management knowledge and its principles are codified and systematised and therefore can be transferred from one to another person and can be taught and learned.
5. Management principles are universally applicable to all types of organisations in every economy. They are generalised in nature and provide general guidelines for managers to use them in practice. The basic nature of management knowledge indicates that like other sciences it is also a combination of both art and science which are not mutually exclusive disciplines. In the words of Robert H. Hilkert "in the area of management, science and art are two sides of the same coin." Thus, one must acquire knowledge of management theory, principles and generalisations to become a manager. It is because this knowledge may help him in understanding and analysing problems and to solve them.

Application of theoretical knowledge in practice for solving problems and making decisions has actually broadened the horizons of management knowledge. It is because by using it repeatedly special skill, experience and competence is developed among managers and every successive problem is solved by them more efficiently. Thus, the process of management involves both science and art. To become a good manager one has to acquire a theoretical knowledge of management and subsequently by using it in practice he has to develop and gain experience from it. Consequently, proper combination of theory as well as personal experience gained by managers may lead to better results.

Management as a Profession

Besides, a combination of art and science, management may also be considered as a quasi-profession because it possesses some characteristics of it. The following criteria of a profession will help in identifying that part of management knowledge which may be considered as a profession:

1. A profession is a body of specialised knowledge consisting of principles, concepts and techniques which are proven, systematic and capable of being applied to practical situations.
2. Since professional knowledge is systematised and codified, it can be acquired and learned through the formal education system and training programmes.
3. A profession emphasises on having a central body or apex body or an association to formulate a code of behaviour for its members. It also prescribes minimum qualifications to obtain entry into the profession to become a member.

4. A profession also calls for rendering competent and specialised services to clients. So the service to clients as well as to society becomes a motive of the professional members.
5. A profession demands a scientific attitude and commitment to discover new ideas on a regular basis to upgrade the existing knowledge of the profession. It is done to improve quality of service and the level of efficiency that is provided to clients.
6. In addition to the above, one more important feature of a profession may be that it also requires that the members exercise restraint and self-discipline, a high degree of objectivity and integrity in the process of providing services to customers. This is done to command respect from them.

Having enumerated and described the various basic characteristics of a profession, one can evaluate and judge whether management is a full-fledged profession or where or what does it lack. So far as the first two characteristics are concerned, management knowledge meets them fully because it has developed as a systematic body of knowledge made up of principles, generalisations and concepts which are codified and applicable in practice. Similarly, due to the nature of management principles and theory, one can acquire management knowledge through formal education imparted by universities and institutions and training provided by business organisations.

Although there have been some attempts to form a central organisation for regulating and controlling the profession, namely, the Indian Management Association, it could not emerge as an apex body with a formal and legal character. Therefore, it could not formulate a code of conduct for practising managers and could not even bring them under its fold as members. Likewise, there is no minimum qualification prescribed either to get entry into the management profession or to become a member of it. In practice, whosoever manages is known as a manager, irrespective of his qualifications.

In respect of other characteristics such as motive, the manager in every situation attempts to produce higher output by using lesser input so as to maintain higher profitability. But in modern times, the manager's responsibility towards society has increased and he is expected to work not only as a representative of the owner but also to represent the interests of customers, employees, financiers, community and society.

Similarly, like in all other professions, he has to strive to discover new ideas, relationships and concepts on a regular basis and to act in a dynamic and innovative manner to cope with the changing environment. Managers are not respected so much as professionals of other streams like doctors, advocates, chartered accountants, etc. This is because no uniform code of conduct has been developed and applied to them.

Thus, management has some features of a professional body of knowledge. But till now it could not acquire the status of a full-fledged profession even in highly developed economies.

Professionalisation of Management

That management is an art, science and profession is not merely an academic statement, but it raises certain issues that are concerned with future development of this branch of knowledge. Management still remains a developing field. Many changes are taking place regularly in terms of its nature, significance, scope, etc. In a modern society, it is occupying a more important position which has ultimately added many new dimensions to it.

In the recent past, on many occasions, society has been challenging the ethical and moral values and bases of management decisions. More emphasis is being placed on the need for professionalisation of management. In detail, the following reasons may be attributed to the growing need of professionalisation of management knowledge:

1. In the more popular form of business organisation, that is, joint stock companies, ownership has been separated from its management and control. This situation has really contributed to the development of management as a profession. Modern managers have to promote and protect the interests of many social groups such as consumers, employees and society as whole, along with the economic motive of earning a profit. To resolve conflicts and integrate and balance contradictory interests, the professional outlook of a manager may help him in a big way.
2. The rapid expansion and growth of universities and other institutions imparting management knowledge and the growing significance of training programmes in business organisations also indicate more professionalisation in the days to come.
3. In a high-tech industrial society, manifold changes have occurred in the role of managers. They have to manage not only various resources, but also knowledge for the benefit of the organisation.
4. In the context of globalisation of economic operations, many strategic areas have been developed which require professional expertise and specialised knowledge such as strategic planning, control and research and development activities and information system, merger, collaboration, etc. Multinational corporations have been attempting to enhance their global market share strictly by adopting a professional outlook and approach towards management of operations.
5. Increased utilisation of specialised management services like consultancy, human resource development, training programmes, etc., that are linked with a scientific attitude and thinking also requires a team of professional managers to handle these areas carefully and efficiently.

Family Management versus Professional Management

Family management implies the management and control of business operations by a group of members belonging to a particular family and by their kith and kin regardless of their knowledge about management. This kind of management practice was very common in India till recently. Even at present many Indian industrial empires remain family managed. It is because top positions in the management hierarchy are occupied by the owners. In a family-managed business, decisions are made, policies are formulated and action programmes are made on the basis of values and beliefs of the family. They are greatly influenced by family interests and business becomes more an extension of the family. Even some disputes and disagreement related to family matters would have a direct reflection in the functioning of the business organisation. There is complete identity among goals, needs and values of business and family especially in small- and medium-sized business organisations.

Family management implies:

1. Management and control by owners or their kith and kin.
2. Business is considered as an extension of the family.
3. Family matters and interests affect the conduct of business.
4. Identity between goals, values and needs of family and the business organisation.
5. Entrepreneurial style of management prevails.
6. Suitable for small and medium sized business organisations.

But in a professionally managed enterprise contrary to family managed, the ownership is separated from management and control. The authority to manage and control business operations is delegated to professionally qualified managers who have required managerial knowledge in their respective areas. Since professional managers do not have an ownership interest and they manage the enterprise independently by taking bold, balanced and factual decisions, essentially professional management implies:

- Induction of professionally qualified managers into the organisation who possess the required basic knowledge of management with formal training in the various key and strategic areas.
- To manage different areas and activities of organisation, relevant specialised modern management knowledge should be applied to specific situations as per requirements. It should also be followed by a scientific approach, thinking and attitude on the part of managers to make superior quality of decisions and to manage the organisation efficiently.
- To get better results and performance, professional managers require to use a combination of theoretical knowledge along with practical experience, which they gain out of repetitive application of management knowledge in practice.

- In addition to these, the style of a modern manager is also marked by a high degree of objectivity, creativity and use of various managerial skills and approaches so as to resolve conflicts and integrate diverse interests.
- Professional managers have a different outlook and approach which is based on the philosophy of the larger interests of the organisation. They also adopt and observe high ethical and moral values and understand the implications of the human side of management in decision making.
- Functional managers consider the organisation as an open adaptive system and introduce dynamism into it to cope with the changing environment, they think and act strategically.

Universality of Principles of Management

Like the principles of other sciences, managerial principles are universally applicable. These principles are a part and parcel of management theory. They explain the relationship between two or more variables. Thus, they are regarded as a fundamental statement or general truth providing guidance to the thoughts and actions of managers. The principles of management have been formulated through rigorous observation, research, analysis and experience of executives. They provide guidelines and ground rules for managers to manage the organisation efficiently. In the words of Peterson, they are "modes of action."

These principles have been developed with respect to several areas and functions of management. Advocates of the classical theory of management relied too much on these principles and they considered them as prescriptive fundamental truth having universal validity and applicability for different situations. It is because these principles are applicable to all types of organisations such as economic, non-economic, social, religious, political, etc., and provide guidance to managers working at different levels. More precisely, in the words of Professor Mugginess, "there exists a systematic body of knowledge that constitutes the core of principles of management that are true in all managerial situations. These principles are applicable whether it is a business organisation, a government organisation, a religious organisation, a social or any other type of organisation. These principles are also true to all levels of management from the foreman to the chief executives." But it should however be noted that these principles of management do not provide readymade stereotype solutions of management problems. Thus, these should be strictly used as guidelines to understand problems and move systematically towards a solution. By using these principles one can improve one's understanding about the problem and get an insight into it.

Similarly, the principles of management are related to human behaviour which is very dynamic and complex and cannot be understood and predicted in all respects correctly. For applying these principles efficiently, all those factors which probably influence working behaviour of an individual should be taken into account. Henri Fayol has made it quite clear that these principles are very flexible and capable of adaptation, and to get the desired results one should know how to use the principles.

In view of the basic nature and limited scope of these principles, modern management scientists do not fully endorse the views expressed by classical theorists. They argue that these principles are merely tentative, flexible and suggestive guides to managers. Since the results produced by the application of these principles differ from one situation to another, they cannot be regarded as a fundamental truth like the principles of the physical sciences.

Sometimes, these principles prove so irrelevant that the practitioner is bound to treat them as half truths or misleading or self-contrary. They do not find proper validation in support of the usefulness of these principles.

Although these principles of management are not absolute, mainly due to the nature of the discipline to which they belong, one should not lose sight of the fact that they form a theoretical body of management knowledge calling upon managers to have the required knowledge and skill to use these principles carefully and efficiently.

Nevertheless, these principles are of crucial importance for managers in understanding problems and conditioning their styles and approaches to solve problems and make decisions. In the words of Terry: "They are capsules of selected management wisdom to be used carefully and discretely."

As stated earlier, management consists of principles, processes, functions and approaches to be used in practice to get results. In modern society, management has become a basic requirement for all organisations irrespective of size, nature and goals and objectives to be pursued by them. It is general, pervasive and global in nature. But these characteristics hold good only with regard to the theoretical part of management.

However, principles, processes, functions and skills of management have universal application. But exact results arising out of their application may differ from situation to situation depending on situational variables, experience of the manager and his level of knowledge.

Thus, many authors consider it as situation-bound. It is because some principles of giving incentive for raising productivity will certainly have different implications and results in different situations. For instance, monetary incentives may prove more effective in Indian organisations for motivating employees, but in a highly developed economy like the U.S.A. employees do not bother for these incentives; rather they are more inclined to other higher order non-monetary incentives such as appreciation, recognition, self-fulfilment, etc.

MANAGERIAL SKILLS

Management is a result-oriented process. To get better results, apart from application of management knowledge, certain abilities are also used by managers. These abilities are known as managerial skills. These abilities include both inherited and acquired ones. These are primarily required for effective implementation of the principles of management. The skills or abilities required to be possessed by managers may be classified as under:

1. Conceptual Skills

It is an ability to visualise the organisation as a whole system and form an image and develop vision in the context of the future environment. By applying these abilities managers successfully coordinate various subsystems and relate them in a meaningful manner with the larger system to seek its smooth functioning. Conceptual skills are used for developing thinking in an abstract term to visualise and understand the future. Managers need these abilities for scanning the changing environment and discovering the various opportunities provided by it and the problems and threats arising out of it and finally relating them to the strengths and weaknesses of the organisation. The conceptual skills also include an ability to determine the overall objectives of organisation by integrating them with sub-objectives and formulating basic strategies for the whole organisation.

2. Analytical Skills

These skills are more related with scientific attitude and thinking on the part of the manager for solving different problems and making decisions. Analytical skills refer to those abilities which are needed by managers for studying the problem in a systematic way, gathering necessary information on its various aspects, and establishing and describing the relationship between two or more variables. These abilities are also used for decomposing a complex and complicated phenomenon into various components to get an insight into it. A manager may become analytical in his approach for judging the performance of his subordinates, solving problems and making decisions.

3. Human Relations or Behavioural Skills

The basic responsibility of every manager is to get things done by others. In this process he needs behavioural skills. These skills refer to those abilities which are needed by the manager to deal with subordinates effectively. To manage them he has to understand their needs, interest and values. He interacts with them to know the general tendencies of human behaviour and factors influencing it. By using behavioural skills he may establish good rapport, warm relationships and conducive inter-personal relations with his subordinates. Human relations skills are also needed to provide a dynamic and effective leadership and build team spirit among employees (Table 1.1).

TABLE 1.1: MANAGERIAL SKILLS

Conceptual skills
* to form an image
* to develop vision
* to integrate and coordinate sub-systems
* to formulate basic plans
* to scan and reconcile with external environment

Analytical skills
* to use a scientific attitude
* to break a problem into components
* to study and solve problems
* to evaluate performance
* to make decisions

Human skills
* to deal with subordinates
* to communicate
* to lead, motivate and guide them
* to look into their needs
* to develop inter-personal relations
* to build team spirit among them

Administrative skills
* to implement decisions and plans
* to mobilise and use resources for them
* to use a practical approach
* to study and work upon ground realities

Technical skills
* to have knowledge of jobs and job content
* to have knowledge of using technology for them
* to train subordinates
* to supervise work performed by them

4. Administrative Skills

Generally, decisions are made at higher levels and have to be got implemented by managers working at lower levels. Managers with the responsibility for the implementation of the decisions require administrative skills. It refers to those abilities which he uses for coordinating various activities, seeking effective utilisation of allotted resources and getting things done by subordinates. This type of skill also includes the ability to be practical or pragmatic, both in thinking and in action. By applying these skills he performs managerial functions taking into account the ground realities of the situation and behaves likes an 'administrative man.'

5. Technical Skills

These skills refer to abilities to use specialised knowledge and proficiency in handling methods, procedures and techniques for doing a specific job. It also includes knowledge about jobs and job content and logical sequence of the procedures needed to perform them.

Such skills are more related with the nature and content of the job and technology to be used to complete it. Technical skills are needed by managers to provide training to their subordinates regarding the use of new techniques and methods and also to provide technical guidance and help to them.

In practice, it is found that conceptual skills are more important for managers working at higher levels and technical skills seem to be more important at lower levels, particularly at the supervisory levels. The reasons are that the supervisor is directly concerned with the various activities and jobs to be assigned to and performed by core workers. He has to help and guide them for using relevant methods and techniques.

Similarly, managers at the top have to have an integrated approach and thinking. They perceive problems in the context of the whole organisation and make such decisions which are in the larger interests of the entire organisation. But other types of skills are equally important for all managers at all levels.

STYLES OF MANAGERS

A manager is a distinct personality and belongs to an elite group and enjoys respect, status and authority. He performs a very complex job which is not marked by certain functions only but it is much more than that.

He has three major inputs, namely things (physical resources), ideas and people. By processing these he produces outputs. He performs a variety of functions as per the demand of the situation. He acts as an entrepreneur, planner, leader, change agent, damage controller, problem solver and handler of conflicting situations.

The style of a manager refers to the manner or way in which he performs managerial functions, plays various roles on the one hand and on the other hand, how he looks at a situation or problem, his reaction to it and how he solves it are all included in his style. The style of a manager is wider in scope covering not only people but also things and ideas.

Managerial style is mainly conditioned by the rank-and-file in the organisation, level of knowledge, skill and abilities, internal and external environment, philosophy and values of the management. In practice, the following styles are exercised by managers:

1. Entrepreneurial Style

If the style of a manager is highly marked by ownership-orientation, that is, the manager behaves more like an owner, it is known as the entrepreneurial style. He makes bold decisions based on his intuition without going through prescribed policies and procedures. He is highly ambitious, enthusiastic, energetic and dominant in his approach. He is a pragmatic and result-oriented person commanding a team of loyal workers. He takes calculated risks to exploit new business ideas and opportunities. His behaviour is more influenced by his emotions and sentiments rather than rationality and intellect. He seeks a high degree of compliance with orders and instructions given by him to the employees. He also expects them to work hard to achieve targets and fires them casually. He may not be very sure about the outcome of his decisions, even then he goes on deciding. He has no set pattern to follow, rather he is unstructured and unsystematic in his approach. He does not respect rules and formalities, rather he moves in a direct manner adopting shortcut methods (Table 1.2).

TABLE 1.2: STYLES OF MANAGERS

Entrepreneurial style

* Manager behaves as an owner
* He takes bold and intuitive decisions
* He is practical and result-oriented
* He is more emotional and sentimental
* He seeks a high degree of compliance of orders and standards
* He is unstructured in his approach
* He likes loyal employees and fires others

Conservative style

* Manager follows principles of classical theory
* He does not interact with external environment
* He maintains continuity and status quo
* He does not risk using new opportunities
* He uses tried and tested plans and methods
* He has simple and easily attainable goals to achieve

Methodical style

* Manager follows scientific approach
* He is methodical and systematic
* He uses mathematical and statistical devices to take decisions
* He interacts with external environment but only to some extent
* He uses those plans and methods which ensure optimum results and a high degree of precision

Quasi-professional style

* Manager is well equipped with knowledge of modern management
* He is dynamic in his approach
* He interacts with external environment
* He uses proactive and reactive measures to cope with change
* He combines rationality with reality
* He takes bold but factual decisions
* He initiates and manages change effectively

2. Conservative Style

This style is usually followed by managers who strongly believe in the classical theory of management. This style is very popular with private and public sector managers in India. Conservative managers prefer to work in a close setting, and do not interact with the outside world much. They strongly believe in slow change, maintaining the status quo, stability and continuity. They do not take risks to implement new opportunities and therefore adopt only those procedures, methods and ways which have been tested and tried by them in the past. Since they are not ambitious, they do not like change and are not dynamic in their approach. They determine simple, quantitative and attainable goals and remain happy with a reasonable performance. In the event of environmental changes, they hide themselves and somehow maintain the survival of the organisation without interfering with them.

3. Methodical Style

Managers who follow this style are generally scientific in their approach. They adopt a scientific attitude and thinking and do not accept anything without reason. They are methodical in the sense that they move systematically and scientifically from one step to another to solve problems and make decisions. They are rational in goal setting and developing a suitable course of action to achieve them. In order to secure a high degree of precision, perfection and optimum performance, they prefer to use mathematical, statistical and engineering devices. They are very orderly in their approach, quit alert about events in the external environment and are capable of coping with changes in an economical manner.

4. Quasi-professional Style

The group of managers who adopt this style of management are by and large well-versed and well-equipped with modern management knowledge. They are quite familiar with modern techniques and devices to be used to solve problems. By using their specialised knowledge and providing a dynamic leadership, they make the organisation capable of coping with a changing environment. They combine rationality with reality to make timely and superior quality decisions. They are cautious and courageous, reactive and proactive and firm and flexible in their approach. They do not leave anything to chance. They maintain stability in the organisation by their firmness and introduce changes by using dynamism. They adopt both types of measures, proactive measures are initiated before the happening of an event and reactive measures are used to control damage after the happening of an event. They are capable of analysing and visualising changes that are likely to occur; they influence them, bring them under control and at the same time, reshape them. Professional managers believe in factual decision-making by rejecting intuition. They become more objective and impartial in a situation.

MANAGEMENT AND ADMINISTRATION

There has been a controversy regarding the interpretation of these two terms among various authors of management. In a real sense, both of them represent systematic integration, mobilisation and utilisation of physical resources and direction of human effort to accomplish predetermined objectives. Nevertheless, some thought may be given to the viewpoints of various authors. Some authors maintain that there is no difference between these two terms and therefore they can be used interchangeably. They believe that if at all there is any difference between management and administration it may perhaps arise out of usage of these terms in practice. The term 'management' is used on connection with the performance of economic activities, while, in non-academic organisations for similar activities the term 'administration' is used. This viewpoint is subscribed to by William Newman, Peter Drucker, etc.

But there is another group of management scientists who believe that there exists a difference between these two terms. They include William Spriegel, R. H. Landsburg ,McFarland, Oliver Sheldon, etc. Those who distinguish between these two are further divided in terms of scope and nature of management and administration. Some of them like Oliver Sheldon, William Schizo and Spriegel feel that administration is wider, more generic and all-inclusive of management. They propagated that administration is the function of determining the general purpose of an enterprise, corporate policies and general plans and procedures to achieve them whereas management is concerned with the execution of policies within the limits set by the administration. In the words of Spriegel "management is essentially an executive function and deals particularly with the active direction of human effort. Administration is largely determinative whereas management is essentially executive."

On the other hand, authors like Kimball and Kimball and other British writers hold the opinion that management is a more comprehensive function than administration. In the words of Kimball and Kimball, management is a wider concept embracing all duties and functions that pertain to imitation of an enterprise and the establishment of all major policies. According to them, administration is concerned with the actual work of executing or carrying out objectives. Thus, according to this view, functions and administration is confined to doing things in a routine manner by using set procedures and norms but management is a dynamic, innovative and creative process.

The foregoing discussion on the two terms 'management' and 'administration' indicates that most American authors consider administration in a broader field including all kinds of managerial activities. In contrast, British authors of management maintain that management refers to a high level of managerial activities such as goal setting, policy formulation, strategy making, etc. and administration is an operative part of it which is concerned with lower order management activities such as implementation of plans and other decisions.

SIGNIFICANCE OF MANAGEMENT

On the basis of the discussion above on management, it can safely be inferred that it is a life-giving element in an organisation. It is because all man-made organisations do require some force to function. In fact, a group of people known as managers provide this force and make the organisation a productive unit. In every group endeavour to seek common goals, management force is used to direct and coordinate activities of the members effectively and efficiently. Management, in this sense, is regarded as a prime mover of an organisation and a critical variable for its survival, growth, prosperity and development. In the context of organisational activities its importance can be outlined as under:

- Management facilitates an efficient accomplishment of predetermined goals. Activities and functions performed by various individuals in the organisation are properly directed and coordinated towards these goals by managers. A team of professional managers can successfully lead, motivate and guide others to make valuable contributions in this regard.
- Management integrates physical as well as human resources for realising objectives. An effective and optimum utilisation of all these resources can be secured by applying managerial knowledge. Managers continuously strive to reduce inefficiency, wastage and spoilage in the use of these resources, thereby enhancing productivity.
- Management remains a critical variable in an organisation. It is because the survival, profitability and growth of an organisation to a large extent depends on a professional approach and the abilities of managers. They provide an effective and dynamic leadership and increase the capabilities of an organisation to cope with a changing environment.
- An application of management knowledge on the one hand results in a proper and effective utilisation of resources and on the other it also helps to reduce the cost of various operations undertaken and performed in an organisation. It is done by economising the entire functioning of the organisation and making production and distribution more cost effective.
- A team of professional managers inducted into an organisation may also help in building a proper congenial internal environment by formulating and implementing a set of suitable managerial policies and strategies. This kind of environment further contributes to higher efficiency and all-round development in the personality of employees.
- Management also integrates personal goals and the interests of employees with that of the organisation. It is crucial to seek maximum cooperation and commitment from the employees to achieve common goals.

Emerging Role of Management in an Economy

The importance of management knowledge is not confined only to business organisations. It remains equally a vital input for the economic development of the country. The rate and pace of economic development of any nation is greatly influenced by the quality and talent of management knowledge used. It is because in every economy resources are scarce and limited and it is only through their effective and efficient utilisation can the rate of economic development be enhanced.

For a faster rate of economic growth, more emphasis is to be laid on the revolution of management knowledge in the country. The development of the required management skills and talent seems to be a key factor for the economic prosperity of a nation, because it is a team of managers known as economic agents of society who create wealth for the country and provide material things needed by its citizens.

In the Indian context, it is evident that despite the availability of huge natural resources and a cheap labour force, economic progress has been far from satisfactory. More so, since independence, the poverty line has been broadened in spite of the introduction and implementation of various programmes for social development. So, to ensure economic growth, various inputs like labour, capital, raw material, technology, etc., require the catalysts of management for optimum results both at the micro as well as the macro level of the economy.

It has also been observed in the past that if the country has all productive resources required for attaining a desired rate of growth, even then expected results can be obtained only by managing these resources efficiently. It has been rightly stressed that good quality of management is an important input not only for the success of a business but for the overall economic development of the country as well.

The Indian economy has witnessed many ups and downs over the last five decades. But despite massive investment in the industrial sector the desired results have not been produced. Since independence, to secure a balanced economic growth, the public sector has been strengthened and promoted in every respect. But due to lack of committed and talented professional managers, it could not help in boosting the growth rate; rather, it has come on the verge of collapse. It is also widely accepted that rapid economic development can take place only when people work together in an organisation with team spirit, devotion and loyalty.

Abundantly available human skills in the country can be profitably used and their contribution can be made more meaningful in the economy only when this resource is properly developed by applying management knowledge. As individuals, Indians are not inferior to anyone but they fail in making a valuable contribution when they work in an organisation. It occurs merely because of poor working environment and work culture which can be improved by inducting qualified professional managers in an organisation.

After the initiation of reforms in the Indian economy and its globalisation which started from 1991, new opportunities as well as challenges and threats are arising out of the changing environment. Indian industries are likely to face cut-throat competitors from giant multinational companies. In this race to get an upper edge, Indian industries have to make their production and distribution system cost-effective by managing them efficiently. In order to seek strategic alliance from outside to obtain the benefit of sophisticated advanced technology, the development and use of the required managerial skills is necessary. It is widely accepted that every developing country in Asia, Africa, the Middle East and Latin America is seriously handicapped by lack of people with a high level of technical and managerial skills. Indian industries, to come to the mark, have to switch over from the old bureaucratic and family management system to a modern management system to compete with multinational corporations.

There are growing expectations among the people of the country that business organisations that are not enjoying huge resources at their disposal have a definite role to play in the economic as well as social development of the country.

The multidimensional role of modern corporate managers may include the following package of strategies and policies:

1. They would combine social rationality with economic rationality while managing the affairs of the organisation. In other words, while making decisions, they should analyse the social, moral and human implications of these decisions and, at any cost, public interest should not be ignored altogether.
2. A sound base of research and development activities should be built so as to maintain innovativeness and creativity in managing business enterprises.
3. They should also be inclined to build the infrastructure necessary for further growth and development of enterprises.
4. Corporate management should also own responsibility to develop the required technical and managerial skills by making meaningful interface with universities and other educational institutions.
5. They should also create an atmosphere of healthy competition which is a basic requirement to increase the efficiency level of the organisation.

SUMMARY

Management has emerged as one of the important branches of the social sciences. An application of it is not required only in the field of business, but it can be profitably used in every sphere of life. It is by using management knowledge that all available physical as well as human resources are utilised for achieving the objectives of the organisation. An individual or group of individuals using this knowledge are known as managers. They perform managerial functions of planning, organising, staffing, directing and controlling to get things done by others. They also use a variety of managerial skills, and carry out many managerial activities so as to seek effective and efficient utilisation of organisational resources. The entire knowledge of management aims at creating a congenial internal environment and balancing it with a rapidly changing external environment. Today's managers can succeed only if they think and act strategically in the broader global perspective. It is because they have to get things done by people belonging to different sub-cultures.

The process approach of management specifies that all the above-mentioned management functions are to be performed in a given sequence. This is because they are organically related to each other. Management knowledge exhibits many characteristics of science as well as of art. Thus, it is better to consider it as a combination of both. On the one hand, it is a systematic and organised body of knowledge that has been developed through observation and research and analysis. On the other hand, it is capable of being used in practice and requires creativity on the part of managers. Similarly, it meets many basic features of a profession, but has yet to acquire the status of a full-fledged profession.

Knowledge of management has a general applicability or universal application. But its effective and efficient use is greatly influenced by the nature of a given situation which may vary. Thus, to be a successful manager, one has to choose a particular style or combination of many managerial styles. Surprisingly enough, the conservative style of management is still being used partially along with a semi-quasi professional style to get better results. Similarly, in many situation, managers behave and act more as entrepreneurs, take calculated risks, overlook prescribed norms and rules and use their intuition in place of intellect.

Management is related to administration. Rather, many authors of management use these two terms interchangeably and make a difference only in the context of a business organisation and civil administration. In addition, others consider management as an all-inclusive and broader than administration. But it is refuted by many other authors who regard administration as more important than management. The controversy is yet to be resolved.

Although management knowledge can profitably be used for managing political, social, educational and other human activities, it is considered more significant in the economic sphere. It is because every economic organisation is formed and functions to seek common goals as efficiently as possible. To achieve these objectives, both human as well as physical resources are mobilised and utilised efficiently. It is all done by a team of self-motivated and committed professional managers by using management knowledge. Proper use of management knowledge may lead to cost reduction and generation of more revenue for the organisation.

It also increases the capability of an organisation to cope with a rapidly changing environment. The management is considered as vital and critical sub-systems of an organisation owe their success to it. It is because all physical resources such as capital, land, building, machine, raw material, etc., are to be utilised by the human force. Thus, at every sphere of the organisation the use of management knowledge paves the way for the efficient use of human force and occupies a central place.

The significance of management knowledge is not confined only to business organisations. It is regarded as an important and strong input for the overall economic development of the country. The pace of economic development to a large extent is conditioned by the quality of managerial talent used therein. In every economy, limited availability of resources demands an efficient use of them. It is possible only by using management knowledge. In view of an important role of management knowledge in the economy, managers are considered as 'captains' or business leaders. It is only on account of their dynamic leadership that business grows and grows. It ultimately generates additional employment opportunities, helps in improving the standard of living and makes the entire economy vibrant.

After the initiation of economic reforms in 1991, the external environment has been changing rapidly and drastically. Indian business organisations are facing cut-throat competition from multinational corporations. It further demands world class managers to manage these Indian organisations. Indian managers have to develop skills and abilities to command resources and operate beyond borders. They have to be more sensitive and have a better understanding of the behaviour of environmental factors. The new breed of managers is expected to be more creative, analytical, with technical expertise, leadership qualities and networking skills. Thus their role is not confined only to the corporate world but the economy of a nation also needs their services and contributions to grow and prosper.

TEST QUESTIONS

1. How do you support the view that management must be defined in terms of effectiveness, co-ordination of resources and objectives?
2. Management is concerned with ideas, things and people. Comment.
3. Management is a process of getting things done by others through planning, organising, staffing, directing and controlling. Comment.
4. Management is a combination of science as well as art. Comment.
5. Professional management is management conducted by professionally qualified managers. Comment.
6. Distinguish between family management and professional management. To what extent has management been professionalized in India?
7. How would you argue that management is valuable for organisational success?
8. What are the special abilities which managers use to perform their task?
9. Good managers are born, not made. Discuss.

10. Write short notes on:
    (a) Quasi-professional management style
    (b) Managerial skill
    (c) Management as an art
    (d) Management as a profession
    (e) Entrepreneurial style of management
    (f) Management process is universally applicable.

OBJECTIVE TYPE QUESTIONS

Which of the following statements are correct and which are incorrect? Give arguments to support your answer.

1. Technical skills are equally important for managers.
2. Effectiveness of business enterprises refers to the degree to which it achieves its objectives.
3. Conceptual skills imply the ability to use tools, procedures and techniques.
4. Professional managers reject intuition and obscurantism as a base of action.
5. Analytical skill implies breaking down a problem into solvable components.
6. Styles of management have more dimensions than styles of leadership.
7. Management styles are not the same as leadership styles.
8. Conservative style of management is very popular with private and public sector managers in India.
9. Conceptual skills are more important for managers at a higher level while technical skills are vital for managers at the supervisory level.
10. The principles of management are half-truths, misleading and self-contradictory.
11. Management knowledge is needed in all organisations at all levels.
12. Management practice is bound by situations.
13. Management does not provide readymade answers for organisational problems.
14. Conservative managers do not feel comfortable with the status quo.
15. Entrepreneurial managers are result oriented and pragmatic.
16. Conceptual skill is required more at the lower level of management.

REFERENCES

Barnard, I. Chester. *The Functions of Executive*. Cambridge, U.S.A.: Harvard University Press, 1933.

Dalton, M. *Men Who Manage*. New York, U.S.A.: John Wiley and Sons, 1959.

Drucker, Peter F. *The Effective Executive*. New York, U.S.A.: Harper & Row, 1967.

Fayol, Henri. *General and Industrial Management.* New York, U.S.A.: Pitman, 1949.

Haynes and Massier. *Management: Analysis, Concept and Cases*. New Delhi, India: Prentice-Hall, 1967.

Koontz, Harold and Weihrich. *Essentials of Management*. New Delhi, India: Tata McGraw-Hill Publishing Company, 2001.

Likert, Rensis. *New Pattern of Management*. New York, U.S.A.: McGraw-Hill, 1967.

McFarland, Dalton. *Management Functions and Practice*. New York, U.S.A.: MacMillan, 1979.

Mittal, K. M. *Social Responsibility of Business: Concept, Areas and Practices*. New Delhi, India: Chanakya Publications, 1988.

Moshal, M. S. *Management: Theory and Practice*. New Delhi, India: Galgotia Publishing Company, 2002.

Stoner, A.F., Freeman, R. Edward, and Gilbert, Daniel R.. *Management*. New Delhi, India: Prentice-Hall of India, 2001.

William and Warren. *The Process of Management*. New Delhi, India: Prentice-Hall of India, 1988.

TIME MANAGEMENT
A Priority-setting Plan

Manage your time better by dividing tasks into four categories:

1. Direct Value: High priority—making a sale, presenting to your staff, writing a report.
2. Indirect Value: What pays off later—learning new skills, setting goals.
3. Necessary Non-value: Things you must do that have no value for you; filling out government forms, taking many phone calls.
4. Unnecessary Non-value: These include things such as writing routine reports that co-workers no longer read.

How to categorise

- ❖ Log your daily activities for at least a week. Review what you did and classify each activity according to the value definitions.
- ❖ List the most important internal and external customers who should get the most of your attention. Then compare your list with your log.

Box continued

Box continued

- Determine how much high-value work you think you are doing for your most important customers.
- Ask those customers to tell you which of your activities they consider to have the highest value.
- Use what you learn to plan your days, weeks and months around the high-value activities those customers have identified.

THE INDIAN MANAGEMENT THEORY

Theory 'I' Management stands for India-centric management practices that should be put into practice for managing Indians. For ages now, the rest of the world has been boasting about its management practices and we have been following them. Perhaps it is high time that that we have our own culture-centric practices which will give our companies more productivity and worker motivation. Theory 'I' management thus is an attempt to take the practical aspects of our culture and put it to work.

The Principles of Theory 'I' Management

Most Indians value bonding emotions, long-term relationships, growth opportunities and commitment. Our cultural roots of tolerance often make us complacent. Excessive corruption in daily life and lack of patriotism at a macro level leaves us morally bankrupt. These principles have been arrived at after a thorough research that we conducted on more than 3,000 managers across the country. The most important revelation from this survey is about the uniqueness of today's Indian psyche.

On the one hand, as expected, research goes to prove our cultural values and a lot of similarities can be drawn with the Japanese value systems. On the other hand, when faced with the fact that everything Indian is so cool outside India, like bhangra and Indipop finding a place in the global pop charts, the IT revolution fuelled by home-grown geeks, our B-school graduates becoming global leaders, NASA with top Indian scientists, it remains a fact that time and again we have failed to perform in India.

It seems that Indians look for the first opportunity to become complacent; something that they are unable to do in the competitive Western world and their 'hire and fire' system. Thus, Indians need an India-centric management theory.

What it Prescribes

Theory 'I' management prescribes solutions at two levels, the Macro and the Micro. The Macro aspects deal with policies to tackle the last principle of "Theory 'I' Management", which is ways to control levels

Box continued

Box continued

of corruption through changes in the judicial system. At a Micro level, Indian leaders have to necessarily increase the element of the human touch in the organisation. It has been found that total job security results in a sense of complacency but too much insecurity can cause an average creative brain to go into a tailspin.

Indian leaders could do well, perhaps, by implement the Theory 'I' Management with the help of Indian leadership techniques which are explained in the *Gita* and *saam, daam, dand* and *bhed* techniques where *saam* stands for dealing with people in a sweet manner, *daam* is bribing or paying money to get one's work done, *dand* means using harsh means to get one's way and *bhed* means creating a division among people to achieve one's target.

In the *Gita,* Lord Krishna talks about three types of people. The *tamasic* or people buried in inertia, the *rajasic* or people performing actions inspired by their egos and the *satvik* or people who perform deeds using their intelligence and inspired by love and compassion. By combining the leadership principles of *saam, daam, dand* and *bhed* with the different types of people described in the *Gita* we can devise a relationship strategy, which suits each category of individual.

In fact, all management books as well as management gurus talk about leadership but nobody talks about 'followership', as the *Gita* does. Perhaps, the only example which comes to my mind as an immediate exception is the army. Knowingly, or by default, the army focuses on followership.

In India, we need to remove the dichotomy existing in our system, where on the one hand we keep on harping about our culture and on the other we overlook this aspect completely when it comes to managing people.

CASE STUDY I
People Express*

The behavioural approach in management, generally based on conclusions drawn from the Hawthorne Experiments, proposes that productivity increases when the workers are recognised as important members of the organisational family. That is what People Express did. Every employee was given a share in the ownership of the company and lifetime employment security was offered to all. People Express became a classic example of organisational success and managerial effectiveness.

Case Study I continued

Case Study I continued

Donald Burr was the founder and chairperson of People Express. He has been credited with building a humane kind of organisation where employees were given a great deal of freedom of operation. Every employee was a part owner of the company. There was no class distinction between managers and workers. Managers helped workers in carrying out their duties, pilots helped out in handling the baggage and passenger comfort was given the top priority. Every employee was given the opportunity and encouraged to know the company well. Even top executives rotated from job to job to learn the major aspects of the business.

People Express was expanding its operations very fast. Within five years of its formation, it acquired Frontier Airlines and because the fifth largest airline in the country. Since the infrastructure and operational resources did not match the fast expansion, People Express experienced its first losses and with it, its managerial style changed. It changed from a participative style of management and a family-type organisation to a more traditional style. Donald Burr took charge of the airline and began dictating policies and it became risky for employees to speak out. One of the ordinal architects of lifetime employment at People Express, Lori Dubose, was fired when she started asking questions and speaking critically about some aspects of the operations. Similarly, another director of the company, Harold Parety, who was told to report to work at 6 a.m. and stay till 9 p.m., irrespective of whether there was enough work for him to do or not felt it to be an insult to his integrity and quit his job and formed his own airline.

Eventually People Express declared bankruptcy because it could not generate enough revenue to meet operating expenses and other debts.

Questions

1. Do you think that the change from participating management style to a more classic one contributed towards the final collapse of People Express? Explain your reasons.
2. Do you think that a particular style of management which is effective when the company is growing is equally effective when the company has grown large?
3. Why do you think Donald Burr changed his managerial style? Was he justified in firing Lori Dubose because she disagreed with his managerial policies?

CASE STUDY II

Bharat Engineering Works Limited

Bharat Engineering Works Limited is a major manufacturer of industrial machinery besides other engineering products. It has enjoyed a considerable market preference for its machinery because of limited competition. Usually there has been more orders than what the company could supply. However, the scenario changed quickly because of the entry of two new competitors in the field with foreign technological collaboration. For the first time, the company faced problems in marketing its products with the usual profit margin. Sensing the likely problem, the Chief Executive appointed Mr. Arvind Kumar as General Manager to direct the operations of the industrial machinery division. Mr. Kumar had a similar assignment abroad before returning to India.

Mr. Kumar had a discussion with the Chief Executive about the nature of the problems being faced by the company so that he could fix his priorities. The Chief Executive advised him to consult various heads of departments to have first-hand information. However, he emphasised that the company lacked an integrated planning system while members of the board of directors insisted on introducing this in several meetings both formally and informally.

After joining as general manager, Mr. Kumar got briefings from the heads of all departments. He asked them to identify the major problems and issues concerning them. The Marketing Manager indicated that in order to achieve higher sales, he needed more sales managers and sales professionals. His main concern was a lack of engineering support to sales and marketing efforts. The company had adequate engineers but they were spread under three separate engineering groups. Sales people had no central organisation which had responsibility to provide sales support. Therefore, some jobs were being done from outside at higher cost with lower quality. Besides, he needed a generous budget for demonstration systems which could be sent on a trial basis to customers to win business.

The Production Manager complained about the old machines and equipment used in manufacturing. Therefore, the cost of production was high but without corresponding quality. While competitors had better equipment and machinery, Bharat Engineering neither replaced its age-old plant nor got it reconditioned. Therefore, to reduce costs, it was essential to automate production lines by installing new equipment.

The Director of Research and Development (R&D) did not have any specific problem and therefore, did not indicate any change. However, a principal scientist in R&D indicated one day that the Director, R&D,

Case Study II continued

Case Study II continued

though very nice in his approach, did not emphasise on short-term research projects which could easily increase production efficiency to the extent of at least two per cent within a very short period. Moreover, such projects did not involve any major capital outlay.

Mr. Kumar was convinced about the management process going on in the division and the type of problems being faced.

Questions

1. Discuss the nature and characteristics of the management process followed in the company.
2. What are the real problems of the Industrial Machinery Division of the company?
3. What steps should be taken by Mr. Kumar to overcome these problems?

—oo(O)oo—

CHAPTER 2

MANAGEMENT PROCESS, ROLES AND FUNCTIONAL AREAS

LEARNING OBJECTIVES

1. To understand the managing process
2. To apply managerial skills
3. To know about managerial roles
4 Knowing about functional areas of management

MANAGING PROCESS AND ITS ELEMENTS

Management is a process of integrating both physical as well as human resources to attain objectives. It is a human and social process directed at individuals to get things done by them. Like other processes, it consists of many actions or activities or functions which are to be carried out in a logical sequence. It is a result-oriented process, directly related with the task of determining objectives and devising ways to accomplish them efficiently.

Management is a continuous process because it has no definable end; and steps or elements involved in it are to be performed in a continuous cycle. The elements or activities which are performed in this process are known as the functions of management. This popular approach describing what managers do in the process, is viewed as a functional approach. It was developed by Henri Fayol and became popular because it characterises the management process as a sequence of rational and logical steps. Fayol claimed that planning, organising, commanding, coordinating and controlling were basic and common denominators for all managers in the process of management. But later, due to certain changes in the nature and field of management, the sequence of functions was re-arranged by adding some more functions and virtually, it was made as planning, organising, staffing, directing and controlling. A brief description of the steps involved in the process of management is given below.

Planning

Commonly referred to as a basic management function, it is a process of determining objectives, developing alternative courses of action and selecting the best course of achieving objectives. It is a forward-looking approach which involves futuristic estimates or projections. To visualise the future, the past is analysed, related to the present and, on its basis, the future is forecast. Thus, the planning function structures the future destination of an organisation which provides direction to its activities. In planning, managers decide in advance what is to be done, when, how and by whom it will be done. Successful managers visualise what problems may arise at the time of implementing plans.

Organising

Careful organising, like planning, helps in making efficient utilisation of human resources. It is a process of establishing working relationships among employees. Various activities are assigned to them, authority is granted to them, and they are brought in the relationship of superior and subordinate. This working relationship brings order and discipline in an organisation. Every employee knows who his superior is and commands his activities and who is to be commanded by him.

Similarly, in the organising process role, the relationship and position of each individual in the organisation is spelt out clearly. Organising may also be considered as a process of integrating, balancing, unifying and co-ordinating activities of various employees to accomplish pre-determined objectives. The process of organising involves the creation of various units or departments, assigning groups of activities to them with enough authority and finally, seeking co-ordinated functioning in the context of the entire organisation.

Staffing

Once the structure of an organisation has been brought into existence by determining the role and relationship of various positions, the next critical stage is manning these with individuals. Staffing is a process of determining the quality and quantity of the human force needed for the organisation, making all necessary arrangements for acquiring it through recruitment and selection, maintaining them for longer periods of time by making and implementing suitable personnel policies and finally, developing their capabilities and potential to the maximum.

Thus, the staffing function of management is mainly concerned with manpower planning, recruitment, selection, training and development, compensation and maintenance of human resources in the organisation.

Directing

Directing is a process of helping and guiding subordinates to achieve the objectives of the organisation. Basically, in the process of directing, the manager issues necessary orders and instructions to subordinates regarding the work assigned to them. He educates and guides them regarding the various methods of doing the work and finally, he supervises the work being performed by them on a regular basis.

In the process of directing, three elements are involved, namely, communication, motivation and leadership. In brief, to direct the activities of subordinates, a two-way communication has to be maintained and simultaneously, the manager has to motivate the subordinates and provide dynamic leadership.

Controlling

Controlling is a process of ensuring that each and every activity has been performed in a planned manner and in conformity with pre-determined standards of performance. It is essentially a process whereby standards of performance are determined for every employee and his actual performance is measured and then compared with these standards, so as to find out deviations and take remedial measures to improve performance.

The process of controlling includes all activities, actions, procedures and methods used by managers to bring about results as near as possible to the desired results. The process of controlling is concerned not only with improving performance but also includes all actions and techniques used by the organisation to regulate the use of resources achieve planned goals. It regulates the working behaviour of employees to maintain order and discipline. It checks distortions and deviations taking place in the system to make it more cost-effective.

The following observations are noteworthy in the process of management:

1. The management process essentially consists of various steps known as functions or elements of management such as planning, organising, staffing, directing and controlling.
2. These functions or elements of management are primary or basic in nature. They are performed by every manager in all situations to get things done by others. In practice, there are numerous other functions known as subsidiary functions like reporting, budgeting, forecasting, representation, innovation, etc.
3. Planning is a starting point of the management process followed by other functions. Without planning, there is little organising, staffing, directing and controlling. The process of management culminates in controlling. The basic functions of management are to be performed in a definite and logical sequence to get better results.
4. The management process operates through these functions which may be considered as sub-processes of management. All these sub-processes

contribute to the functioning of the management process, deriving essential strength and power from it.

5. Being sub-processes, all management functions are closely related, interdependent as well as independent. They are performed by managers independently, for example, making a plan, recruitment, selection and exercising control. But these functions are organically or functionally related to each other. Planning paves the way for organising and staffing. Similarly, all these will have little meaning if not followed by controlling. In other words, if we consider these functions separately and in isolation, they are bound to lose their relevance, meaning and importance. Therefore, the desired results can be produced only when they are perceived in totality and considered as part of the management process.
6. In the process of management, the above-mentioned functions are performed to achieve goals. It is only by performing these functions efficiently and in a logical sequence can better results be obtained from resources, human and material.

Managerial Skills

Management is a result-oriented process. To get better results, apart from application of management knowledge, certain abilities are used by managers. These abilities are known as managerial skills, which may be inherited and acquired. The various skills or abilities required to be possessed by managers may be classified as under:

(i) Conceptual Skills

It is an ability to visualise the organisation as a whole system, form an image and develop a vision of it in the context of the future environment. By applying these abilities, managers successfully co-ordinate various sub-systems and relate them in a meaningful manner with the larger system to seek its smooth functioning.

Conceptual skills are used to develop thinking in an abstract form and to visualise and understand the future. Managers need these abilities to scan the changing environment and discover various opportunities, spot problems and threats arising out of a dynamic situation and, relate them to the strengths and weaknesses of the organisation.

The conceptual skills also include an ability to determine the overall objectives of an organisation by integrating it with sub-objectives and formulating a basic strategy.

(ii) Analytical Skills

These skills are more related with scientific attitude and thinking on the part of managers to solve different problems and take decisions. Analytical skills refer to those abilities which are needed by managers to study the problem in a systematic way, gather necessary information on its various aspects and establish and describe the relationship between two or more variables. These abilities are used to break down complex and complicated phenomena into various components to get an insight into it. A manager may become analytical in his approach for judging the performance of his subordinates, solving problems and making decisions.

(iii) Human Relations or Behavioural Skills

The basic responsibility of every manager is to get things done by others. In this process, he needs behavioural skills. These skills refer to those abilities which are needed by managers to effectively deal with subordinates. To manage, he has to understand their needs, interests and values. He interacts with them, guides, directs, leads and motivates them. In this regard, he is expected to know the general tendencies of human behaviour and factors influencing it. By using behavioural skills, he may establish good rapport, warm relationships and conducive interpersonal relations with his subordinates. Human relations skills are needed to provide a dynamic and effective leadership and build team spirit among employees.

(iv) Administrative Skills

Generally, decisions are made at higher levels and implemented by managers at lower levels, who require administrative skills for it. It refers to abilities used to coordinate various activities, seeking effective utilisation of allocated resources and getting things done by subordinates. This requires pragmatism in thought and action. In applying these skills and performing managerial functions, a manager takes into account the ground realities and behaves like an 'administrative man' with a practical approach.

(v) Technical Skills

These skills refer to specialised knowledge and proficiency in handling methods, procedures and techniques for doing specific jobs. It also includes knowledge about jobs and job content and the logical sequence of procedures needed to perform it. They are related to the nature and content of a job and technology for completing it. Technical skills are needed by managers to provide training to subordinates regarding the use of new techniques and methods and to provide technical guidance and help to them.

Conceptual skills are more important for managers at higher levels and technical skills are useful at lower levels, particularly at the supervisory level. This is so because a supervisor is directly concerned with the various activities and jobs to be assigned to and performed by core workers. Similarly, managers at the top must have an integrated approach. They perceive a problem in the context of the whole organisation and make decisions in the larger interest. However, other types of skills are equally important for all managers at all levels.

Styles of Managers

A manager is a distinct personality, belongs to an elite group, enjoys respect, status, authority and performs a very complex job. A manager uses three basic inputs, namely, things (physical resources), ideas and people. By processing them, he produces outputs and performs a variety of functions as per the demand of the situation. He functions as an entrepreneur, planner, leader, change agent, damage controller, problem solver and handler of conflicting situations.

The style of a manager refers to the manner in which he performs managerial functions; how he looks at a particular problem or situation and plays various roles. It is wide in scope, covering not only people but things and ideas. Managerial style is mainly conditioned by his rank in the organisation, level of knowledge, skill and abilities, internal and external environment, philosophy and values of management.

In practice, the following styles are exercised by managers:

(i) Entrepreneurial Style

If the style of a manager is highly marked by ownership-orientation, that is, the manager behaves more like an owner, it is known as the entrepreneurial style. He takes bold decisions based on intuition without going through prescribed policies and procedures. He is highly ambitious, enthusiastic, energetic and dominant in his approach. He is pragmatic and result-oriented, commanding a team of loyal workers. He takes calculated risks to exploit new business ideas and opportunities.

His behaviour is influenced by his emotions and sentiments rather than rationality and intellect. He seeks a high degree of compliance to orders and instructions given by him to the employees. He also expects them to work hard to achieve targets and fires them casually.

He may not be very sure about the outcome of his decisions, but continues to take them. He has no set pattern to follow, is unstructured and unsystematic in his approach. He does not respect rules and formalities but moves in a direct manner, adopting short-cut methods.

(ii) Conservative Style

This style is usually followed by managers who strongly believe in the classical theory of management. It is very popular with private and public sector managers in India. Conservative managers prefer to work in a close setting, not unduly interacting with the outside world. They strongly believe in slow change, status quo, stability and continuity. They do not take risk for implementing new opportunities and adopt only those procedures, methods and ways that have been tested and tried by them in the past. They do not like change and dynamism in approach. They determine simple, quantitative and attainable goals and are happy with reasonable performance.

In the event of environmental changes, they somehow maintain the survival of the organisation without interfering with the changes.

(iii) Methodical Style

Managers following this style are generally scientific in their approach. They adopt a scientific attitude and thinking and do not accept anything without reason. They are methodical in the sense that they move systematically and scientifically from one step to another to solve problems and make decisions. They are rational in goal-setting and develop a suitable course of action to achieve them. In order to secure a high degree of precision, perfection and optimum performance, they prefer to use mathematical, statistical and engineering devices. They are very orderly in their approach, quite alert about events in the external environment and capable of coping with changes in an economical manner.

(iv) Quasi-professional Style

Managers who adopt this style of management are well-equipped with modern management and familiar with modern techniques and devices. By using their specialised knowledge, they are capable of coping with the changing environment. They combine rationality with reality to make timely and superior quality decisions. They are cautious and courageous, reactive and proactive and firm and flexible in their approach. They do not leave anything to chance. They maintain stability in the organisation by their firmness and introduce changes by using dynamism. They adopt both types of measures to check the occurrence of events; proactive measures are initiated to prevent occurrence of an event and, after the event, reactive measures are used to control the damage. They are capable of analysing and visualising changes which are likely to occur; they influence them, bring them under control and often reshape them. Professional managers believe in factual decision-making; rejecting intuition, they become more objective and impartial to a situation.

Role of Manager in an Organisation

Management is regarded as a critical variable and important input for an organisation. The success and prosperity of an organisation is shaped by the quality of managerial talent and abilities of managers. It is the basic responsibility of managers to get physical resources utilised through employees effectively and efficiently to achieve predetermined objectives.

In this process, the manager performs certain basic functions like planning, organising, staffing, directing and controlling. To get better results, achieve higher efficiency and successful accomplishment of objectives, mere performance of managerial functions is not enough. Much more is required. Managers occupy a position of authority and exercise it to solve problems, take stock of the situation and resolve conflicts and crises.

In the overall functioning of an organisation, especially in a dynamic environment, they cannot remain stereo-type managers, performing managerial functions in a systematic and rational manner. They have to act according to changing situations.

The role of the manager is identified in terms of his position and pattern of behaviour which he is expected to adopt in relation to his subordinates, peers and superiors. A manager moves up vertically to a higher position as his quantum of work-load increases and job content changes. For instance, at the lower level, a manager is more concerned with technical aspects. At a higher level, he has to exercise conceptual skill; the main job is to integrate and coordinate various components or sub-systems of the organisation, as top executives normally do.

A top executive's work is marked by brevity, due to time constraints; fragmentation, because it not always possible to be rational and systematic; and verbal communication, because a lot has to be communicated within a given time schedule. It makes the role and style of functioning of top executives distinct from lower level managers.

During the 70's, Henry Mintzberg and others concluded that apart from performing managerial functions, there are 10 managerial roles which may be identified in relation with the position occupied and behaviour in a given work setting with subordinates, peers and superiors.

Mintzberg identified 10 roles which are common to managers on the basis of a study of the behaviour of executives at work. These roles have been placed in three major groups, namely, interpersonal, informational and decision. It is, however, believed that among these, the interpersonal role is more basic and inclusive because the informational role arises out of it and, both of these give rise to the decision-making role.

1. Interpersonal Roles

In the process of management, the manager needs to interact with subordinates to get things done by them, and also communicates with superiors, peers, trade union leaders, customers, government and other agencies whose interest is involved in the business. Its importance is evident from the fact that a manager spends nearly 80 per cent of his time in interacting with these parties.

Such interactions call for proper knowledge and understanding on the part of the manager about interpersonal behaviour. It helps the manager to establish effective and congenial interpersonal relationships and personal rapport with the parties. Such interactions involve the following three types of interpersonal roles:

(i) Figurehead Role

The manager works in a line of authority. His position is identified in terms of formal authority, responsibility, obligations and relationships. As a symbol of formal authority, he performs various ceremonial duties, for example, receiving visitors, attending weddings of subordinates, signing various documents and delivering speeches and lectures in important social gatherings such as schools, clubs, and other religious places.

These duties and obligations are of a ceremonial nature but are very important for the smooth functioning of the organisation. Managers are not only identified with the success and failure of the organisation, they also represent members of the organisation and outsiders dealing with it.

(ii) Leadership Role

The most important role of the manager is to lead, guide and motivate subordinates and get work done properly. A manager is responsible not only for his own acts but for the activities performed by his subordinates. The leadership qualities of the manager help him to influence the working behaviour of subordinates, contributing to a higher level of efficiency.

(iii) Liaison Role

A manager serves as a connecting link, vertically with superiors and subordinates, and horizontally with other managers at the same level. Outside the organisation, managers have to undertake liaison to assess the external environment to enable the organisation to cope with it. They indulge in power politics to negotiate and compromise with internal and external forces such as trade unions, government and competitors.

2. Informational Role

To preserve and protect the identify of an organisation and to secure its smooth functioning, a manager has to scan the external environment on a regular basis and to deal with outside parties, effectively for which he has to gather a lot of relevant information on various matters concerning the organisation.

The manager plays three important informational roles while managing the operations of an organisation:

(i) Role of Monitor

Managers interact and deal with insiders and outsiders and scan the external environment constantly to get useful information. They collect information on various aspects of the organisation and its environment through reports, informal relations, dealings and liaison work. They are the most well-informed members of their work group. While managing, they monitor every situation very closely and minutely, collect information regarding it and finally, solve it effectively.

(ii) Role of Disseminator

A manager continuously transmits selected information which he has compiled through the role of monitor of his subordinates. He keeps them well-informed regarding any change in the process, structure, policies and other plans of the organisation. Necessary information is disseminated among subordinates by him through formal and informal meetings, memorandums, orders and instructions issued from time to time.

(iii) Role of Spokesperson

A manager acts as a spokesperson of his work group while supplying information to superiors and peers. Similarly, he keeps outside parties well-informed on behalf of the organisation. He negotiates and enters into compromises with internal and external parties.

3. Decision-making Roles

By interacting with insiders and outsiders, a manager gets important information, which he can use to take decisions and solve problems. According to Mintzberg, information is the basic input of decision-making for managers, who play four decision-making roles:

(i) As an Entrepreneur

Managers have a primary responsibility to improve the overall functioning of their respective work units. They act as entrepreneurs, take bold decisions, seek better results from subordinates, initiate required changes and implement them for the betterment of the organisation. To initiate and implement changes, managers have to be dynamic, innovative and creative. They direct efforts towards discovering new product ideas with the active help of employees, examine the economic viability of the ideas and arrange necessary resources for implementation.

(ii) As a Disturbance or Conflict Handler

An organisation is a collective entity with diversity of interests and duality of roles for managers. For example, the owners' group may be interested in high profits whereas employees may seek more benefits in the form of higher wages and better working conditions. In such situations, it is only by applying managerial knowledge and playing the role of conflict handlers, thinking analytically and acting practically, that managers can hope to effectively integrate the interest of employees with the organisation. Similar conflicts may arise with outside parties which would have to be resolved through meetings, negotiations and compromise.

(iii) As a Resource Allocator

To manage the organisation, physical and human resources are mobilised and utilised efficiently by managers to accomplish predetermined objectives. They have to play the role of resource allocators. And, in the case of multiple objectives, they set priorities for allocation of resources. In the life cycle of an organisation, priorities keep changing.

For example, at the initial stages of formation of an organisation, the survival objective gets top priority which may be later superseded by profit. Similar criteria may be adopted by the manager in relation to activities. Some activities may be critical or more important for survival and profitability. Others may be supportive and less important. Managers allocate resources for these activities in accordance with their priorities.

(iv) As a Negotiator

Managers work on behalf of the organisation or work unit and subordinates, not only as spokespersons but as negotiators. They enter into agreements on behalf of the organisation. For example, the personnel manager negotiates with trade unions and representatives of workers. Similarly, the finance manager may negotiate with financial institutions to secure funds at reasonable cost and the purchase manager may be interested in negotiating terms and conditions for purchasing raw material, etc. Sometimes managers negotiate with other members of the organisation for reducing their disagreements about goals and roles. As disputes arise in an organisation, managers take up the role of indicators, negotiators and arbitrators.

Functional Areas of Management

For convenience and obtaining the advantages of specialisation, the activities of an organisation are grouped into various functions. For example, production, finance, personnel, marketing and research and development and numerous other activities are classified as separate groups. These are identified as functional areas of a business organisation. They are also treated as subsystems because the organisation functions through them.

Since theory and the principles of management are applied on these functional areas with equal importance, they have emerged as functional areas of management, as explained below:

1. Production or Operations Management

Production of goods and services undertaken by numerous industries forms an important part of business activities. It is primarily concerned with the conversion of raw materials into finished products through various activities and operations. These are performed in a logical sequence and known as the conversion process.

The term 'production' was earlier linked with factories, where goods of tangible shape, volume, colour and weight are produced. Today, production is used in a general sense as a process through which goods and services are produced. The production function implies bringing together men and machines to produce goods and services to the satisfaction of human needs and wants. Production management also includes management of non-manufacturing or service organisations such as transport, banking, insurance, warehousing, health, education services, etc.

Production management deals with decision-making in relation to the production process so that goods and services of required quality and quantity are produced within a given time schedule and cost. To achieve the objectives, production processes are designed and controlled to maintain the cost effectiveness of the entire production system.

Production functions may be viewed as 'input, output systems' working in an external environment to achieve objectives. The inputs of the production system may be identified as necessary resources such as land, building, capital, machines, material, technology, labour and management. Owing to the conversion of inputs, some outputs are produced in the form of products and services for society. The output may be in the form of finished products, cured patients, serviced customers, delivered goods, etc.

The main objective of a production system is to produce goods and services of required quality and quantity with minimum cost and within a given time schedule and are classified as performance and cost objectives.

Performance objectives imply effective and efficient utilisation of resources, maintaining quality specifications and maximum utilisation of capacity, etc. Cost objectives refer to control of various fixed and variable costs and other visible and invisible costs such as opportunity cost, downtime cost, cost of dissatisfaction, etc. (Figure 2.1)

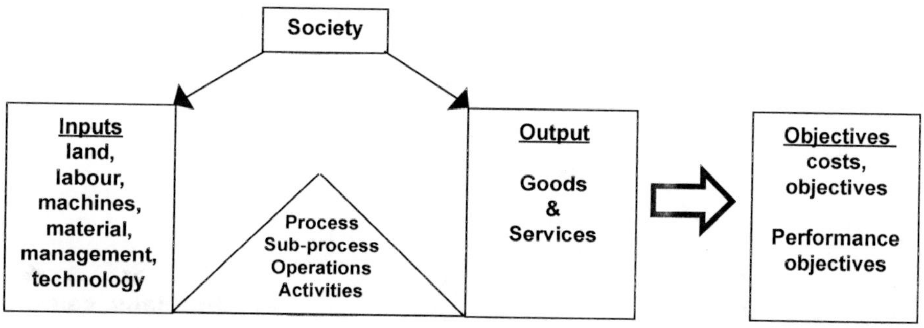

Figure 2.1. Production system

Production operation management is essentially a function of decision-making with regard to the production system to realise predetermined objectives. These decisions may be grouped as under:

(i) Planning Decisions: Designing a production system, including capacity planning, facility location, layout planning, etc.

(ii) Planning the use of a conversion system such as forecasting, scheduling, job shop scheduling, project planning, etc.

(iii) Organising decisions for conversion, structuring of operations, staffing, job and work design, production operation standards and payment system.

(iv) Controlling decisions, monitoring and control of entire conversion process in terms of required quantity, quality specifications, time schedule, inventory control, cost structure and maintenance of the production system.

2. Marketing Management

The functional area of marketing is mainly concerned with the distribution system. Goods and services produced by numerous industries are made available to customers as efficiently as possible. A large number of activities and operations are performed by organisations involved in the distribution system. Thus, planning, organising, staffing, directing and controlling of these operations which are performed in the flow of goods from producers to consumers is regarded as marketing management. It includes the following elements:

(i) Plans and policies of the organisation should be customer-oriented and aim at higher customer satisfaction.

(ii) The main objective of a marketing organisation should be to generate more profitable sales volume by maintaining cost-effectiveness of the marketing system.

(iii) All activities and operations of marketing should be integrated and well-coordinated with other activities of the organisation (Figure 2.2)

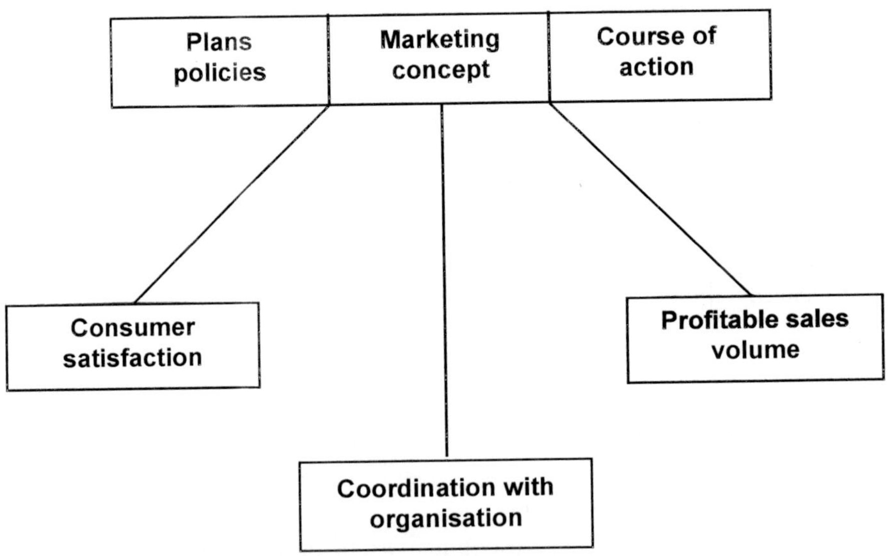

Figure 2.2. Elements of Marketing Management

Marketing is not the mere selling of goods and services. It may be considered as a process of planning, organisation and controlling resources, plans, policies, action programmes and activities of marketing to satisfy consumer needs and generate maximum profits.

Since the beginning of the industrial revolution, marketing management has evolved in the U.S.A. in various stages, namely, production, selling, marketing, and consumerism and relation management. Marketing is interpreted through traditional and modern concepts, the former is production-oriented. According to the traditional approach, production of goods and services gets priority over other distribution activities. Most of the resources of the organisation are deployed to increase production.

Marketing is treated as merely a selling activity. The scope of marketing begins only when goods are produced, there is no consideration of consumers' needs and wants. This concept is mainly followed by underdeveloped or developing nations having limited resources which are utilised to produce more. Whatever is produced is distributed among customers.

In the modern concept of marketing, the scope of marketing begins before production. Production of goods and services is carried out in accordance with the needs and wants of consumers; consumer preferences are ascertained by market surveys. This concept of marketing is basically consumer-oriented. Only those goods are produced and distributed which provide enhanced satisfaction to consumers and generate profitable sales volumes. It is popular in highly-developed economies where, due to rapid scientific and technological advancements and growing competition, the area of marketing is getting more importance as compared to production (Figure 2.3).

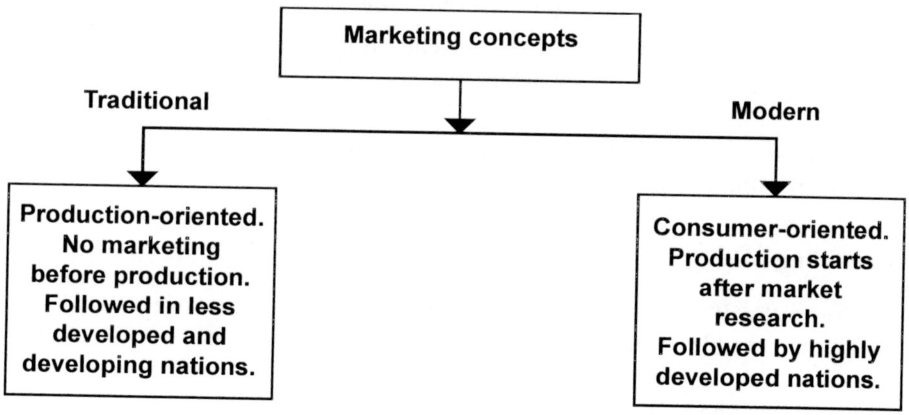

Figure 2.3. Elements of Modern Marketing approach

Objectives of Marketing Management

All marketing activities and operations, including buying, assembling, selling, advertising, storage and warehousing, insurance, banking, marketing research, etc., are managed to achieve the following primary objectives:

(i) To Create Demand

The basic objective of marketing management is to create demand of the product or service in the market. Profitable sales volume can be generated only by creating demand for which promotional activities including advertisement, personal selling and other activities are performed. The process of demand creation involves production of goods in conformity with the needs and wants of customers, familiarising them with the products and enticing them to buy them. Production of products of good quality and reasonable price may contribute to creation of demand.

(ii) To Create and Maintain Market Share

In a modern business marked by cut-throat competition, one of the major objectives of marketing management is to capture the market share and maintain it. Market share is an outcome of demand creation. As the demand for a product grows, the market share of the organisation may increase. The marketing manager, often adopts aggressive marketing policies and suitable strategies for this purpose.

(iii) Image Building

Marketing activities are managed to build the image of the products and the organisation in the minds of customers. Consumer satisfaction, fair dealing, maintenance of quality, regular supply of the product and a sense of social responsibility may help in earning a favourable image and reputation.

(iv) To Generate Profitable Sales Volume

Marketing management aims at generating an adequate sales volume to earn reasonable profit for which the distribution system has to be managed efficiently and cost-effectively. An optimal combination of the four Ps, known as the marketing mix, namely, product, price, promotion and physical distribution, is prepared to achieve the objective.

Marketing Mix

According to Philip Kotler, the marketing mix refers to the amount and kinds of marketing variables a firm is using at a particular time. It consists of wide-ranging variables such as product, price, promotion, physical distribution and external environment. The marketing mix is prepared in the context of a specific external environment, the main variables of which are within the control of the organisation, as under:

(i) Product Mix

This refers to those marketing activities and decisions which are directly related to the product or service being offered by the organisation such as product planning and development, introduction of new products, adding and dropping features of a product, branding, packaging, colour, positioning of the product, etc. The basic purpose of designing a suitable product mix is to make the product of the organisation more acceptable to buyers.

(ii) Price Mix

This refers to decisions made by the marketing manager with regard to determination of the price of the product . In this connection, the marketing manager determines the base price of the product taking into account numerous factors, including price charged by competitors, cost of the product, its life cycle, etc. In addition, the marketing manager has to formulate suitable pricing policies to deal with various situations arising out of the changing environment.

(iii) Promotion Mix

Promotion mix refers to those activities and decisions of the marketing manager which directly relate to popularising the product by informing prospective buyers and motivating them to buy it. It mainly consists of advertisement, personal selling and sales promotion through dealers, customers and sales force of the organisation. Since no one method of promotion is complete in itself, the marketing manager has to develop a combination of two or more methods depending on the nature of the product, allocation of budget, growth of demand and demographic characteristics of prospective buyers.

(iv) Physical Distribution Mix

All marketing activities are terminated at this point. It refers to those activities and decisions which relate to transfer of ownership and physical possession of goods from the seller to the buyer. It includes management of direct and indirect channels for efficient distribution of the product among customers (Figure 2.4).

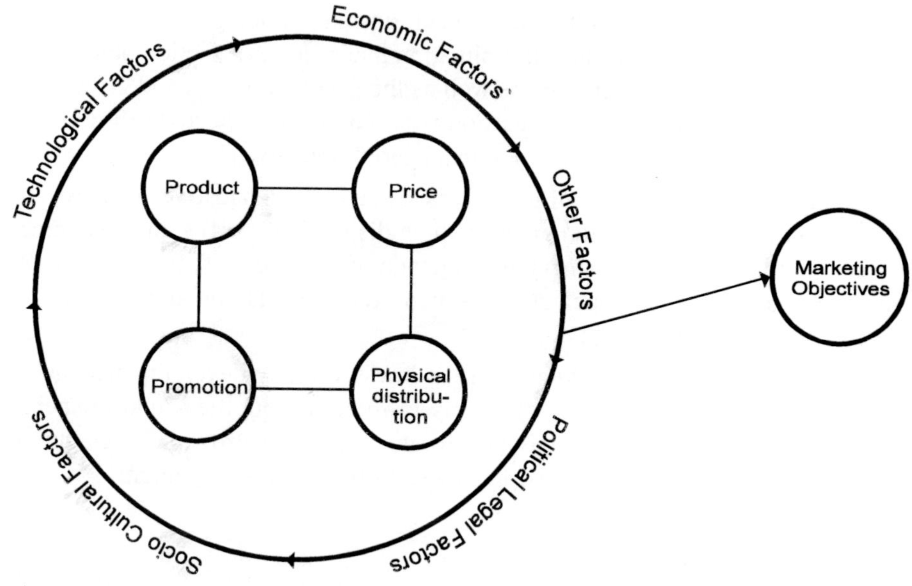

Figure 2.4. Marketing system

The main purpose of determining a suitable marketing mix is to provide maximum satisfaction to customers and maintain profitable sales volumes. The combination of the four 'P's in determining the marketing mix varies from situation to situation, depending on the needs of the customers, objectives of the organisation and environmental factors.

3. Financial Management

Finance is the life-giving element to business organisations. It may be considered as the foundation of all economic activities. An organisation cannot be founded without adequate finances. Finance is needed for conducting business activities, seeking its growth and development and for preserving and protecting its identity in a changing environment.

Generally, finance is referred to as the process of arranging timely procurement of required funds at a reasonable cost. It involves many problems, decision areas and operations and has emerged as one of the important functional areas of business management, attracting the attention of management scientists, scholars and practitioners.

In simple words, financial management may be defined as planning and controlling of financial activities of the organisation and refers to a process of efficient management of funds to achieve organisational goals. It involves an application of management principles and generalisations in the area of financial decision-making.

According to Phillippatus, "financial management is concerned with management decisions that result in the acquisition and financing of long and short term credits for the firm. It deals with a situation that requires selection of specific assets (or combination of liabilities) as well as the problem of size and growth of the enterprise. The analysis of the decision is based on the expected inflows and outflows of funds and their effects upon managerial objectives."

Although Phillippatus' definition seems to be very exhaustive, it does not include some important decision areas such as disposal of profits and financing of other activities. Broadly, financial management is a process of managing funds by making related decisions such as investment, requirement and arrangement of funds for overall organisational objectives.

The area of financial management has witnessed many developments and it is universally acknowledged that not merely profitability but the sound financial position of an organisation is a prerequisite for its success and growth. It is essential to study the traditional and modern approaches to financial management.

(i) Traditional Approach

This approach, popular during the early stages of development, restricted the scope of financial management to procurement of funds by corporate enterprises and meeting the capital requirements. It involved the following elements:

(a) Arranging of funds from financial institutions and organisation of the capital market.

(b) Arranging funds for the capital market through various financial instruments such as shares, debentures, bonds, etc.

(c) Managing legal and accounting relationships between the organisation and its sources of funds.

However, this approach to financial functions is considered inadequate in relation to problems faced by non-corporate industrial organisations. It is considered as an outsiders-looking-in-approach because finance functions are studied and analysed from the viewpoint of investors, bankers and other suppliers of funds and problems involved in internal decision-making are ignored. It mainly focuses on long-term financing and the problems involved in it. The area of working capital management which deals with short term-financing problems has been neglected.

It limits the areas of finance functions to procurement and administration of external long-term funds. The allocation of funds, leading to its utilisation, remains unattended.

(ii) Modern Approach

According to this approach, the finance function does not only cover arrangement and procurement of funds but includes allocation of procured funds for various uses. The modern approach may be viewed as a systematic and analytical way of studying the financial problems of an organisation and solving them. The main elements of the modern approach are:

(a) The total volume of funds an enterprise should commit.

(b) Specific assets an enterprise should acquire.

(c) How funds should be acquired and those at the disposal of the organisation be distributed?

These elements deal with decisions relating to fund requirements, financing, investment, and dividends. They are known as the functions of finance, a brief description of which is given below:

Investment Decision

To conduct the business of a company, certain assets are needed. The investment decision of the financial manager relates to the selection of various assets on which funds will be invested. Long-term investment decisions which are broadly based on relative benefit and returns associated with the project, cash outflows involved, risk and uncertainty, worth of project, etc., are known as capital budgeting. In addition, decisions for managing current assets are known as management of working capital.

Financing Decision

Financing decisions are mainly concerned with deciding about the capital structure or composition of capital or financing mix. A company has many sources of raising capital which have distinct implications on financing decisions. The financial manager must seek a proper balance between debt and equity capital while preparing the capital structure.

Dividend Policy Decision

An important area for the finance manager is to decide on the basic policy for distribution and disposal of profits. A part of net profit may be retained in business and reinvested profitably or shareholders may be given a higher divided. To formulate a suitable dividend policy, a set of factors affecting it should be taken into account (Figure 2.5).

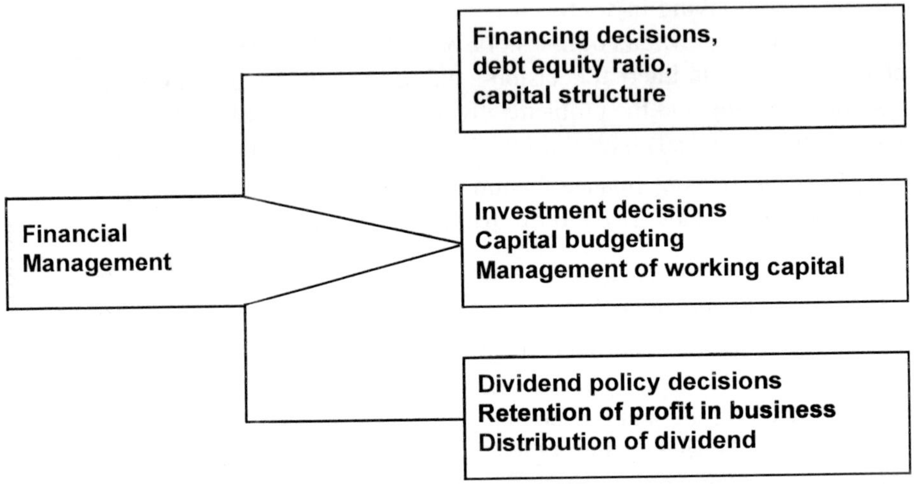

Figure 2.5. Decision areas of financial management

Objectives of Financial Management

For the efficient management of funds to achieve the organisation's objectives, there are criteria for decision-making, as outlined below.

(i) Profit Maximisation

All business organisations are profit-making entities. The financial manager should implement proposals and make decisions to increase profits. Broadly, in view of the objective of profit maximisation, all decisions, including financing, investment and dividend policy, should be oriented towards the maximisation of profits. Profit is a test of efficiency. The level of efficiency can be judged on the basis of the quantum of profits earned.

The criteria of profit maximisation for making decisions are, however, subject to the following limitations:

(a) The concept of profit maximisation seeks to be neither desirable nor practicable. It is quite vague and does not state what should be maximised, profit or profitability, short or long term profit, profit before tax or after tax.

(b) It ignores timings and the pattern of benefits accruing from a proposal. Two proposals giving similar benefits may have distinct patterns of benefits over a particular time-frame.

(c) It does not take into account the quality of benefits derived. Two proposals with similar benefits may differ in terms of the degree of certainty about expected profit.

(ii) Wealth Maximisation Objective

Wealth maximisation or value maximisation objectives is regarded as a more useful and rational criterion for making decisions. According to this objective, while selecting a proposal or asset, the value of an asset is considered in terms of the benefit it gives, minus the cost of implementing it. This criterion takes into account cash inflows generated by the proposal rather than profit earned over a given period of time. In addition, wealth maximisation objective facilitates the precise evaluation of quantity and quality dimensions of benefits and considers the time value of money, implying benefit received earlier would be valued more highly than benefit received later.

4. Personnel Management

To achieve organisational objectives, a large number of activities are performed and physical resources like land, building, capital, machines and raw material are utilised by the manpower employed in the organisation. Smooth functioning, efficient utilisation of resources and success, to a large extent, depend on the availability of a team of highly-talented, committed and motivated employees.

Personnel management assumes a significant role in the entire corporate sector. It is mainly concerned with managing the human aspect of the organisation. Rensis Likert stated: "Of all the tasks of management, managing the human component is the central and most important task, because all else depends on how well it is done."

The core of management lies in organising and guiding, directing and controlling the activities of employees working in an organisation. In simple terms, personnel management may be defined as the art of procuring, developing and maintaining a competent work force to realise the objectives of an organisation. A few important definitions of personnel management are:

> "Personnel management is the planning, directing and controlling of the procurement, development, compensation, integration, maintenance and separation of human resources to the end that individual, organisational and social objectives are accomplished." —*Edward Flippo*

> "Personnel management is the recruitment, selection, development, utilisation of and accommodation of human resources of an organisation. The human resources of an organisation consist of all individuals regardless of their role who are engaged in any of the organisation's activities." —*French*

> "Sound personnel administration means so organising and treating people at work that they will effectively utilise their maximum individual capabilities, thereby attaining maximum personnel and group satisfaction and rendering their maximum service to the enterprise of which they are part." —*Thomas G. Spates*

"Personnel management is that part of the management function which is primarily concerned with human relations within the organisation. Its objective is the maintenance of those relationships on a basis which, by consideration of the well-being of individuals, enables all those engaged in the undertaking to make their maximum personal contribution to the effective working of that undertaking."— *The Institute of Personnel Management, U.K.*

Broadly speaking, personnel management is a dynamic function which aims at optimising the effectiveness of human resources of an organisation by integrating individual goals with that of organisational goals, thereby providing more satisfaction to employees.

On the basis of a careful analysis of the above definitions, the following characteristics may be drawn:

(i) Personnel management implies managing humans in an organisation to achieve its objectives.

(ii) It consists of procurement, development and maintenance of the human force.

(iii) It is a dynamic and continuous process because the need for personnel functions arises time and again.

(iv) It integrates personal goals of the employees with that of the group as well as organisational goals.

(v) It facilitates maximum development of the human force for the benefit of individual employees as well as the organisation.

(vi) It helps in building a proper and congenial internal environment so that each employee can contribute the maximum to realise organisational goals.

(vii) Personnel functions are needed in every organisation, irrespective of its goal and nature.

(viii) Personnel management has emerged as one of the important functional areas of management. It is widely accepted as a line function.

Objectives of Personnel Management

Personnel management has emerged as one of the key areas of economic activity. It primarily aims at securing effective and efficient utilisation of the work force in the organisation to realise goals. The objectives of personnel management are as under:

(i) Effective and efficient use of the work force to achieve organisational goals.

(ii) Integrating individuals with informal groups and with the organisation.

(iii) Recognition and satisfaction of individual needs as well as group goals.

(iv) Maintaining good human relations in the organisation.

(v) Designing an appropriate and adequate organisation structure and creating desirable working relationships among members.

(vi) Enabling each employee to develop his maximum capacity and to contribute as effectively as possible.

(vii) Improvement of quality of work life of the human force.

(viii) Maintaining high morale among the employees of the organisation.

Functions of Personnel Management

To achieve its objectives, the personnel department performs wide-ranging functions which may be grouped into two broad categories, namely, managerial and operative.

(i) Managerial Functions

In the process of managing workers, a personnel manager has to perform certain managerial functions such as planning, organising, directing and controlling. Broadly, these managerial functions may be enumerated as follows:

(a) Manpower planning for the organisation.

(b) To design a suitable structure of the organisation for personnel staffing activities and establish a relationship of superior and subordinates among employees working in the personnel department.

(c) To formulate basic policies to deal with personnel matters such as promotion, selection, transfer, wage payment, employees welfare, etc.

(d) To coordinate with other functional departments of the organisation.

(e) To contribute significantly to designing an organisation structure and creating a conductive internal environment so that each employee may contribute the maximum to achieve organisational goals.

(f) To develop a suitable approach and techniques to motivate employees.

(ii) Operative Functions

To carry out basic policies on personnel matters, some lower level managerial functions have to be performed, known as operative functions for which standardised methods, procedures and techniques are laid down. These functions are as under:

(a) Recruitment, selection and placement of employees.

(b) Training and development of personnel.

(c) Job analysis.

(d) Performance appraisal.

(e) Transfer and promotion.

(f) Salary and wage administration.

(g) Maintenance of personnel records.

Every manager contributes significantly towards the achievement of organisational goals. Yet, the role of the personnel manager is crucial because he is directly concerned with procurement, development and maintenance of the human force. All decisions in an organisation are made by human beings and are implemented by them which shape success and growth.

SUMMARY

Management is a result-oriented process. In this process, managers perform certain functions. These are known as elements of the management process, such as planning, organising, staffing, directing and controlling. Planning, which aims at preparing a future course of action, is a starting point of the management process. It is followed by other management functions.

The process of management terminates at controlling which ensures the implementation of plans. These functions are also considered as sub-processes of management. Being sub-processes, they are closely related, interdependent and independent as well. These functions are performed to achieve goals.

To get better results, certain abilities are also used by managers. These are known as managerial skills such as conceptual skills, analytical skills, human relations skills, administrative and technical skills. Conceptual skills are more important for managers working at higher levels, while technical skills are more needed by supervisors working at lower levels of management. However, other skills are equally important for all managers at all levels.

A manager is a distinct personality enjoying status and authority and performing a difficult job. Every manager performs managerial functions in a different manner, which makes his style. This style may be entrepreneurial, conservative, methodical or quasi-professional.

Management is considered an important input in an organisation. It is only through management that all other inputs are used for the achievement of common goals. The role of the manager is identified in terms of his position and pattern of his behaviour towards his superiors, subordinates and peers. The various roles played by him are interpersonal, informational and decision-making.

The knowledge of management is applied on the various functional areas of an organisation such as production, marketing, finance and personnel with equal importance.

Production management deals with decision-making with regard to the production process as to produce required quantity and quality of goods within a given time schedule and cost. The main objective of production management is to ensure production of goods at a specific schedule at a reasonable cost and of a reasonable quality. Production management helps in achieving predetermined objectives of the production system.

The functional area of marketing is primarily concerned with the distribution system. The goods and services produced by the production department are made available to customers as efficiently as possible. Marketing management includes planning, organising, staffing, directing and controlling of various activities and operations, which are performed in the flow of goods from producers to consumers.

All marketing activities and operations aim at creating demand, maintaining market share, image building and generating profitable sales volume. For realising these objectives, an optimal combination of the four P's known as the marketing mix is required. They are Product, Price, Promotion and Physical Distribution.

Like production and marketing, finance is also a life-giving element to a business organisation. It is considered as the foundation of all economic activities. It primarily deals with the process of arranging and processing required funds in time and at a reasonable cost. In brief, financial management may be defined as planning and controlling of financial activities of the organisation and refers to the process of efficient management of funds to achieve organisational goals. It involves an application of management principles and generalisation in the area of financial decision-making. In the area of finance, various decisions are made such as investment decisions, financing decisions and dividend policy decisions. These are made to realise certain objectives of financial management such as profit maximisation and wealth maximisation. These two basic objectives provide the criteria for making various decisions in the area of financial management.

The functional area of personnel management primarily deals with procurement, maintenance development and utilisation of the human force in the organisation. It assumes an important place in the organisation. This is because all other material resources are used through human resources.

To achieve the objectives of the personnel department, a large number of managerial functions are performed. These are manpower planning, recruitment and selection, training and development, compensation management, performance appraisal, transfer and promotion, etc.

The personnel functions are performed to achieve certain objectives. These are efficient use of the work force, development of the human force, improvement of quality of life and maintaining high morale and motivation.

OBJECTIVE TYPE QUESTIONS

Which of the following statements are correct and which are not? Give reasons for your answers.

1. Management is a process that starts with planning and terminates with controlling.
2. Planning is a follow-up function of management.
3. Conceptual skills are equally important for managers at all levels.
4. Technical skills are more important for supervisors working at lower levels.
5. Behaviour skills are needed on the part of managers working at the top of the organisation.
6. Conservative style and methodical style are the same.
7. Management is a critical variable for the success of an organisation.
8. Profit maximisation and wealth maximisation are the same.
9. There is a difference between marketing and selling.
10. Personnel management is a management of the human force in an organisation.

TEST QUESTIONS

1. "Management functions are organically related to make the process of management". Comment.
2. Describe the various elements involved in the management process.
3. Define managerial skills. Why are they needed? Explain the various managerial skills.
4. Describe the various managerial styles. Which one best suits Indian conditions?
5. Explain the varius roles of the manager with the help of the Mintzberg model of managerial roles.
6. Explain the need and importance of the functional areas of management.
7. What do you mean by operations management? Describe its mechanism and objectives.
8. "Personnel management is more important than other functional areas." Comment.
9. How are the objectives of marketing management achieved by preparing a suitable marketing mix? Explain.

10. What is financial management? Discuss the traditional and modern approaches to it.
11. Write short notes on
    (a) Marketing mix.
    (b) Entrepreneurial style.
    (c) Conceptual skill.
    (d) Objectives of operations management.
    (e) Decisional roles of a manager.

REFERENCES

Drucker, P. F. *The Practice of Management*. New York, U.S.A.: Harper Row, 1954.

Ghosh, P. K. *Business Policy: Strategic Planning and Management*. Sultan Chand and Sons, 1997.

Glueek,W. F. *Business Policy and Strategy*. Hinsdale.

Kotler, P. *Marketing Management*. Englewood Cliffs, NJ., U.S.A.: Prentice-Hall, 1972.

Kreitner, Robert. *Management*. New Delhi, India: A.I.T.B.S. Publishers and Distributors, 1996.

Louis, K. Brandt. *Analysis for Financial Management*. New Jersey, U.S.A.: Prentice-Hall, 1972.

Mamoria, C. B. *Personnel Management*. Bombay, India: Himalaya Publishing House, 1980.

Solomon, Ezra. *The Theory of Financial Management*. New York, U.S.A.: Columbia University Press, 1963.

Steiner, George, A. *Top Management Planning*. New York, U.S.A.: McMillan, 1969.

Stoner, James A. F., Freeman, Edward R. and Gilbert, Daniel R. *Management*. New Delhi, India: Prentice- Hall of India.

INDIAN AND JAPANESE MANAGEMENT STYLES

Is there a distinctive Indian management style practised by all Indian organisations? Some scholars think so. In a recent study, Virmani and Guptan try to spell out what it is.

Virmani and Guptan examined work on past and present Indian management practices and also studied the management practices of four 'typical' Indian organisations—a multinational operating in India, a government department, a public sector undertaking and a traditional

Box continued

Box continued

family-owned organisation. Their conclusion was that Indian management is paternalistic and is characterised by the following:

- Patronage—giving of juicy titbits by the powerful to favourite subordinates in order to consolidate control.
- Familial feeling—a strong sense of belonging to the organisation as if the latter were an extended family or clan.
- Sense of security in the staff, by virtue of the feeling that they all belong to one big happy family.
- Obedience to authority—an organisational counterpart of obedience to elders in the family.
- Personality cult—dependence of the staff on the likes and dislikes, personality and competence of the top leaders. The climate and culture of the organisation is strongly, perhaps excessively, shaped by the personality of the top leader or leaders.
- Aversion of the staff to leaders who are 'outsiders'.
- Personality-based delegation—even when delegation policies are formally laid down, actual delegation hardly ever takes place and where delegation does take place, it comes about because of the trust that the manager has in his/her subordinate and because of formal decentralisation.
- Accent on short-rather than long-term planning.
- Gulf between personnel policies and practices—even when personnel practices are formally stated, there is usually a big difference between what is specified and what is practised vis-à-vis manpower planning, recruitment, training, appraisal, promotion, transfers, grievance handling, employee participation in management, etc. Much personnel management remains ad hoc.
- Restricted sharing of information—the tendency is to sharply limit the dissemination of operating information and withhold information so as to retain control.
- Top management interference in finance—there is much top management interference in the operation of the financial system.
- Low priority for technology upgradation—technology upgradation and the needed worker retraining generally have a low priority.
- Ad hoc expansion/diversification—considerations for expansion/ diversification are often political, extra-organisational, and so diversification and expansion often tend to be ad hoc rather than planned.
- Ad hoc marketing—marketing, too, tends to be ad hoc rather than as per plans and policies.

Box continued

Box continued

Although Japan is far more industrially advanced than India at present, the reported Japanese style of management does seem to have points in common with the reported Indian style. The chief characteristics of the Japanese style are reported to be:

- Treatment of staff as members of a big family and the nurturing of a sense of belonging.
- The leader as the father figure who has great powers, but also many restraints on their exercise.
- Permanent employment for core staff, seniority-oriented reward system, extensive provision of fringe benefits for core staff, moderated by extensive employment of temporary workers and widespread reliance on subcontractors.
- High premium on recruiting young managers directly from prestigious universities (which in turn have very rigorous entrance examinations). These managers are groomed to be generalists through a wide variety of assignments.
- Strong emphasis on self-discipline, teamwork and loyalty to the organisation.
- Strong emphasis on efficiency, quality and innovation through such management tools as quality circles, just-in-time system, total quality programme, etc.
- A cult of continuous training for employees to increase their versatility and to keep them updated and prepared for change.
- Collective decision-making.
- Close collaboration of the organisation with the government to further national goals—the ideology of Japan incorporated.

Both the Indian and Japanese management styles are seen to be essentially paternalistic. However, the Indian style is portrayed as a bad form of paternalism characterised by authoritarian ad hoc decision-making, nepotism and hypocrisy. The Japanese style is portrayed as a good form of paternalism with a strong emphasis on teamwork and collective decision-making, commitment to quality, efficiency, continuous learning and adaptation and patriotism. These portrayals, however, may mask enormous variation from them in practice in both the countries.

—oo(O)oo—

CHAPTER 3

ORGANISATION AND MANAGEMENT: HISTORICAL PERSPECTIVE

LEARNING OBJECTIVES

1. To get a general idea about the history of management knowledge.
2. To develop understanding regarding traditional, behavioural and modern management.
3. To try to get a precise idea about Taylor's approach of scientific management and bring out its principles, techniques and weak points.
4. To seek working knowledge of the basic principles of management developed by Henri Fayol.
5. To compare human relations approach with behavioural science approach so as to get an idea about both.
6. Remember the basic concept of system approach and its relevance to modern management.
7. Read out a contingency approach, remember its various stages and develop an understanding about its basic nature. Is it a commonsense approach or a well-researched one?

INTRODUCTION

The application of management knowledge in an organisation is as old as human civilisation. During the initial stages of its development there was a good deal of confusion regarding the contributions made by various management and social scientists to this field. It is because at that time management knowledge was not in an organised and systematic form. The existence and use of management knowledge during ancient times is clearly witnessed by the various projects which were implemented efficiently and successfully such as the Pyramids of Egypt, the Great Wall of China and many major irrigation projects. Though the practice of management relates back to thousands of years, the systematic study and analysis of this discipline is relatively new. It is only from the beginning of the 20th century that serious attempts were made to develop this field as a separate discipline. Now it has emerged as one of the important branches of the social sciences.

Before the 19th century, only three foreign universities, namely, Pennsylvania, Chicago and California, offered business management courses. Over the last ten-and-a-half decades management theory has developed in bits and pieces. In order to develop management theory, contributions of various scholars from different fields including psychology, sociology, anthropology, mathematics, economics and political science have been of great use. In addition, administrators and executives working in economic and non-economic organisations including government, business, health, education, army and churches have also contributed to the development of this field. Each group of scholars and practitioners has formulated its own theory of management. In order to get a proper and balanced perspective of the theory and practice of management all developments and changes taking place since the beginning of the 20th century till now may be placed under three main categories.

1. Classical management approach
2. Behavioural approach
3. Modern approach.

CLASSICAL MANAGEMENT APPROACH

The classical approach to management is one of the oldest and most popular approaches and is also known as the universal approach or traditional approach. This approach is based on the assumption that the objective of an organisation may vary from one another but the management of all organisations requires the same management process. This approach has its roots in the basic concept of division of labour and specialisation. It consists mainly of:

- Scientific management developed by F. W. Taylor.
- Administrative theory of management developed by Henri Fayol.
- Bureaucratic organisation by Max Weber (Figure 3.1).

SCIENTIFIC MANAGEMENT

The development of the approach of scientific management has been an outcome of a long movement in the field of management. It also incorporates the contributions made by various scholars and practitioners. But at the end, F. W. Taylor has given a concrete shape to these contributions. Therefore, he is known

Modern approach		
1. Quantitative approach	←	Operation research specialists of U.K. and U.S.A.
2. System approach	←	Organisation system theories Ludring & Kenneth, etc.
3. Contingency approach	←	Tomburns, Stalker, Paul Lawrence
4. Attributes of excellence	←	Thomas J. Peter, Robert Waterman

Behavioural approach	
1. Human relations approach	→ Elton Mayo and Associates
2. Behaviourial science approach	→ Douglas McGregor, Maslow, Barnard, Likert, Simon, etc.

Classical approach	
1. Scientific management	→ F. W. Taylor, Gantt, Gilbrith, Emerson, etc.
2. Administrative theory of management	→ Henri Fayol, Sheldon, Mooney, Follett, etc.
3. Bureaucratic organisation	→ Max Weber

Figure 3.1. Evolution of Management approaches

as the father of scientific management. He began his career as a machinist and went up to the position of chief engineer in the Bethlehem Steel Company, U.S.A. In view of many problems faced by the workers, such as rampant inefficiency and waste, restricted output, ill-equipped and inadequately trained workers and little cooperation between management and workers, F. W. Taylor committed himself to the development of the best way of doing things. His entire approach of scientific management aims at increasing operational efficiency of the workers. He was fully convinced that there was a scientific way of doing things in physical work situations at the shop floor level. His basic philosophy of scientific management is expressed in terms of the following principles:

PRINCIPLES OF SCIENTIFIC MANAGEMENT

- Science, not a rule of thumb
- Harmony, not discord
- Cooperation and not individualism
- Maximum output in place of restricted output
- Maximum development of each employee

1. Science, not Rule of Thumb

According to this principle, for solving problems and taking decisions, the manager should adopt a scientific attitude and use scientific thinking and methods. The approach of 'rule of thumb' or a hit-or-miss approach should be replaced and instead, the problem should be studied in all respects, the required data should be collected and analysed for solving it. So intuitive decisions should be substituted by decisions based on facts.

2. Harmony, not Discord

This indicates that all departments and workers are a part and parcel of an organisation working together to achieve common goals. Therefore, there should be complete harmony or coordination in their functioning and any kind of disagreement, clash or conflict should not be allowed to crop in, and if at all it arises, it should be reduced to a minimum.

3. Cooperation and not Individualism

According to this principle, instead of encouraging individualism, the importance of cooperative group efforts should be recognised. If the objectives of the organisation are accomplished successfully its credit should not be given to some individuals only. Rather, the contributions and cooperation of all the members should be equally acknowledged.

4. Maximum Output and not Restricted Output

This states that production of goods should be done at the maximum capacity available in a production unit. This is because as production increases, the overall cost of production is bound to decrease. So a policy of restricted output should be considered as an outdated one.

5. The Development of Each Man to his Greatest Efficiency and Prosperity

According to this principle, the efficiency level of the workers should be increased for the prosperity of individual workers and the organisation. This should be done by providing scientific training to them and developing their potential abilities to the maximum. It will benefit both employees and the organisation.

As a guide to the practice of management, Taylor developed a number of techniques of scientific management on the basis of his long experience at the shop floor level. They are as under:

Techniques of Scientific Management

- Scientific study and planning of work
- Scientific selection, placement and training
- Standardisation of raw material, machines and working conditions
- Division of responsibility between managers and workers
- Functional foremanship
- Mental revolution
- Wage incentives

1. Scientific Study and Planning of the Work

Taylor suggested that the work to be assigned to and performed by workers should be studied, analysed and planned so as to determine a day's fair work (standard of work) for each worker. He emphasised that several studies such as time study, speed study, fatigue study, work study and motion study should be conducted on various aspects of the work. This would give a precise idea to the worker as to what is to be done and how to do it efficiently.

2. Scientific Selection, Placement and Training

Taylor realised that to build up a team of efficient workers, their selection should be made by using scientific methods instead of intuition and the judgement of foremen. It implies the selection of workers for the job by tallying job requirements with their abilities and skills. Then they should be given placement in an organisation on the basis of respective capability as well as aptitude. Finally, scientific training should be imparted to them on a regular basis to develop their existing level of knowledge and potential abilities.

3. Standardisation

By studying metal cutting operations minutely, Taylor suggested that the scheme of standardisation should be adopted in respect of trade tools and equipment, raw material used by the workers and physical working conditions provided to them. It is because any difference in the quality of raw material and tools and equipment may directly affect the level of efficiency of the workers. Similarly, productivity is bound to differ when workers doing similar types of jobs are provided with a different set of physical working conditions.

4. Division of Responsibility Between Management and Workers

Taylor advocated that the two aspects of planning—thinking and doing—should be separated. Planning of work that involves thinking processes should be the responsibility of managers. They should develop work standards by conducting various studies, devise incentive schemes for workers, discipline them and assign work to them while the role of workers should be confined to the implementation of these plans. In this way, the benefits of the division of labour and specialisation may be secured.

5. Functional Foremanship

Taylor introduced and practised the concept of functional foremanship. According to this concept, instead of having one foreman as an in-charge for the entire production department, he suggested that at the lowest level of the department, all activities should be divided into two groups, namely, planning forum and workshop.

Each forum should have four supervisors to command the activities of workers. In doing so, dual command emerges, because each worker will get orders and instructions from eight supervisors dealing with different aspects of his job.

6. Mental Revolution

In order to get the desired results of scientific management, there should be a complete mental revolution on the part of workers as well as managers. Mental revolution is a process of bringing about drastic changes in the attitude, outlook and behavioural pattern of workers in respect of their duties towards work, towards their fellow workers and employers. A similar kind of change in the outlook of managers towards workers and their problems should be made. To bring out a change in the mental attitude of both, Taylor suggested a scheme of worker participation in management and sharing the surplus profit as bonus among workers.

7. Wage incentives

According to Taylor, "What the workmen want from their employers beyond anything else is high wages." In view of the assumption of 'economic man', Taylor suggested that incentives should be directly linked with productivity. The worker producing more should be given higher wages. For this purpose, he devised a 'differential piece rate plan' which implies different rates of wages for different levels of efficiency of workers.

CRITICISM

Although the valuable contributions made by Taylor and his associates, Frank Gilbreth, Henry Gantt, Emerson and Carl Barth to develop the approach of scientific management was accepted all over the world, this approach is not free from criticism. This approach is mainly criticised on the following counts:

1. Taylor and his associates have been criticised for their unrealistic assumption believing that a worker being a 'economic man' has only economic needs and therefore is interested only in more money. In fact, the economic needs of workers may be more pressing and influencing their working behaviour but the possibility of their other needs such as social, psychological, etc., affecting their behaviour cannot be ruled out completely.
2. Other critics fear that scientific management techniques have dehumanised workers by considering them only as a factor of production which is lifeless and unconscious. Workers are basically human beings and their behaviour is influenced by their needs, beliefs, values and perceptions and therefore they cannot be treated at par with other factors of production.
3. The approach of scientific management is also criticised on the ground that it advocates close supervision and control so as to get maximum contribution and a higher level of productivity on the part of workers. This practice has limited use and to get the whole-hearted cooperation from workers, self-regulating control and supportive supervision have proved more effective.

A systematic analysis of Taylor's contribution reveals that the entire philosophy of scientific management and its techniques and principles have considerable influence on modern management theory and practice. More so, the modern quantitative approach or 'management science approach' is largely based on Taylor's philosophy of scientific management. Many techniques and principles of scientific management have become an integral part of quantitative approach such as time study, motion study, work study, specialisation, standardisation, etc.

Administrative Theory of Management

Though the administrative theory of management is based on the contributions of many scholars and practitioners like Henri Fayol, Max Weber, Sheldon, Mooney, Allen, Urwick, etc., the most part of it relates to Fayol's work. Henri Fayol was a French mining engineer turned chief administrator in a large French mining and metallurgical company. He translated his rich and broad administrative experience into practical guidelines for successful managers and conceptualised it as an essence of management.

Fayol believed that a manager's job could be divided into five functions, namely, planning, organising, command, coordination and control and these functions have to be performed by every manager. He wrote a monograph tiled 'General and Industrial Managed' published in 1916. It is in four parts; the first part deals with the classification of business activities as technical activities (manufacturing or production), commercial activities (buying, selling and exchange), financial activities (raising and optimum use of capital), accounting activities (recording, costing and statistics), security activities (protection of persons and property) and managerial activities.

The second part of the monograph contained the basic functions of management performed by managers in all types of organisations. In this regard, Fayol's contention was that management is a continuing process beginning with planning and ending with controlling and in this process the following functions or elements are involved:

- Planning and forecasting
- Organising
- Commanding
- Coordinating
- Controlling

Fayol's Principles of Management

The third part consists of 14 principles of general management which are as under:

1. Division of Work

To divide work among various departments and employees according to the required abilities and skills so as to get the benefit of specialisation.

2. Authority and Responsibility

Authority should be commensurate with responsibility. More authority may result in mis-utilisation or under-utilisation.

3. Discipline

This implies compliance with organisational directives and rules, orders and instructions of superiors and co-operation with fellow workers.

4. Unity of Command

According to this principle, one subordinate should get all the orders and instructions regarding his work from only one superior. It helps in maintaining discipline among employees, controlling their activities, fixing responsibility and does not allow them to sidetrack responsibility.

5. Unity of Direction

All activities related towards common goals should be included in a single plan to be implemented by a particular manager.

6. Subordination of Individual's Interest to the Organisation

According to this, in every work setting, each employee should sacrifice and subordinate his personal interests and goals to accomplish the common goals of the organisation.

7. Remuneration

Employees should be paid fairly and reasonably in accordance with their contribution.

8. Centralisation

The relationship between centralisation and decentralisation of authority is a matter of basic philosophy of the organisation. But an optimum balance between these two should be maintained according to the needs of an organisation.

9. Scaler Chain

As a result of delegation of authority in an organisation, the line of authority and communication from the top to the lowest level is established. This is known as the scaler chain because all employees are attached to it in the relationship of superior and subordinate.

10. Order

In order to facilitate the smooth flow of work, efficient use of resources such as material, machine tools, equipment, as well as employees (human factor) should be placed and used in a prescribed manner.

11. Equity

The principle of equity suggests that similar treatment based on the principles of equity, fairness and impartiality should be assured to all employees working in an organisation particularly in respect to promotion, transfer, pay hike, etc.

12. Stability of Tenure of Personnel

Since people need time to learn their job, therefore they should not be allowed to move frequently from one position to another. Efforts should be made to retain them in the organisation for longer periods of time.

13. Initiative

According to this principle, employees should be provided an opportunity to develop and use their initiative to solve work-related problems. Due care should be taken specially for developing policies so as to regulate decision-making behaviour of managers on the one hand and on the other to provide them enough liberty to use their personal skills and judgement.

14. Esprit-de-corps

This implies the building of team spirit among the employees so that they work in a harmonious manner with proper mutual understanding to make their respective contributions more valuable to achieve goals.

Managerial Qualities and Skills

Besides these principles, the fourth part of the monograph deals with the managerial qualities and skills that should be possessed by managers. They are as under:

- physical qualities (health, vigour, personality)
- mental ability (ability to learn, to take decisions, creativity, etc.)
- moral education (loyalty, dignity, ethical values, etc.)
- general education
- special knowledge
- experience (knowledge arising out of practice).

The principles and functions of management developed by Henri Fayol got wide ranging applicability. In spite of reformulation and expansion of management knowledge, these are found in every text of management. Moreover, modern management theory to a large extent is based on these principles and functions.

He is, therefore, said to be the father of modern management. Many management scholars have expressed opinions regarding the contribution of Fayol and they have observed that "the classical functions of management still represent the most useful way of conceptualising the manager's job, especially for management education and perhaps this is why it is still the most favoured description of managerial work in current management textbooks.

"The classical functions provide a clear view of classifying thousands of different activities that managers carry out and the techniques they use in terms of the functions they perform for the achievement of organisational goals."

Fayol's main contribution to management theory was to show how the complex management process can be separated into interdependent areas of responsibility and functions. He had a strong conviction that a set of principles and the process of management were universally valid and applicable. Therefore, an administrative management approach is regarded as a functional approach, process approach and universal approach.

Bureaucratic Model of Organisation

One of the important components of the classical approach is the bureaucratic model of organisation. This model was developed by Max Weber, a German social scientist. According to Weber, it is a more efficient form of organisation because it aims at a high degree of precision, efficiency, objectivity and rationality. This particular form of organisation is well known and very popular in government and military organisations till today. In addition, every well-managed organisation, irrespective of its size and objective, possesses some characteristic of bureaucracy. The model of bureaucratic organisation suggested by Weber is based on the following characteristics:

1. Division of Labour

To get the benefits of specialisation, the principle of division of labour is followed in bureaucratic organisations. It implies the division and assignment of activities to various employees on the basis of their abilities, skills and aptitude. Repeated performance of the same job would lead to a higher degree of specialisation.

2. Hierarchy of Authority

All employees of bureaucratic organisations are attached to each other in the relationship of authority which lies on the position and not on the person.

3. Rigidity in Compliance with Procedures and Framework of Rules

To regulate and control the working behaviour of employees they have to observe prescribed procedures and rules strictly. No deviation, even on a minor scale, is allowed. But this kind of rigidity gives rise to red-tape and inordinate delay in decision making.

4. Impersonality

In a bureaucratic organisation there is no place for emotions, sentiments and personal attachment. The employees have a very formal and functional relationship among themselves.

5. Technical Competence

In this type of organisation people are hired and promoted on the basis of their technical competence, that is, what they know about the job. It is on the basis of job requirements that they are selected and placed in the organisation.

Weber has described this model to be the most rational and efficient form of organisation which is aimed at a high degree of precision, perfection and objectivity. It reduces subjective judgement, emotions, fear tactics and favouritism. It is because employees have impersonal and formal relationships and they have to comply with set rules and procedures for doing the job. Similarly, the hierarchy of authority also helps in maintaining discipline among the members and controlling their activities efficiently. Division of labour leads to specialisation and rationality makes decision-making effective. However, this model also has some negative points such as it is very slow, and insensitive to the needs of individuals. It encourages red-tape, inordinate delay in decision-making, goal displacement and lack of initiative and positive motivation ultimately results in inefficiency in such organisations.

Evaluation of Administrative Theory

In an administrative theory of management, the main emphasis is placed on those principles and concepts of management that are related to the structure of the organisation. A large number of these principles have been derived from military organisations.

Like in scientific management, administrative theory also ignores the human aspect involved in the management of the organisation. The principles of management which are regarded as building blocks of management theory are prescriptive in nature. These principles and functions do not provide any guarantee of success and often seem to be contradictory to each other. Similarly, experience proves that the organisation is not merely hierarchy of authority but much more than that. Thus, the bureaucratic model of organisation developed by Weber based on rationality perhaps finds very limited applicability in practice and often becomes the centre of inefficiency. In addition, closed system thinking about the organisation marked in administrative theory further reduces its validity, especially in the context of changing the business environment which is full of uncertainties and diversities.

Evaluation of Classical Approach with Respect to Work Organisation

1. Rational 'Economic Man' Model

Taylor and his associates worked on the 'economic man model'. They firmly believed that man is a rational animal and is interested in maximising his economic gains. They assumed that each individual working in an organisation is an isolated individual and not affected by his fellow workers and environment. Therefore, he can be treated in a standardised way just like a machine. They further indicated that the most important reason for his working is money. Pay more to him and he will produce more. But this assumption may be true only to some extent (relative fulfilment of basic needs). There may be many other reasons beyond that level which determine why an individual will or will not work.

2. Economic Needs

The above model assumes that money or economic incentives are the strongest to motivate the individual. It is because the individual has only one set of needs, that is, economic needs. The individual works to satisfy this need. But again, it does not hold good because the individual after satisfying his economic needs to a relative extent moves towards other higher order needs such as social needs, security needs and other psychological needs.

3. Organisation as Rational Legal System

Max Weber considered the organisation as a rational legal system based on the norms of impersonality and rationality. In this system, rules of law and prescribed procedures are followed by employees in performing jobs. Bureaucratic organisations placed too much emphasis on the chain of command from higher to lower level. Each employee works in the relationship of superior and subordinate which is impersonal and formal. But under this system individual differences were not recognised and the roles of motivation and personality were not given due weightage. Instead of giving more importance to workers, the job and job content were put on priority.

4. Higher Order Needs Neglected

The classical approach of management to work organisation has ignored the higher order needs and their satisfaction. Rather, advocates of this approach concentrated more on economic factors even to motivate the employees at work. It is, however, to be noted that man does not live by bread alone. He is a social animal and once he gets his need of bread satisfied, he develops other higher order needs mainly security needs and social needs. Similarly, the work of psychologists including Maslow, McGregor, Herzeberg, etc., proved that it is not only economic factors and social needs but psychological needs that are equally important in influencing the working behaviour of employees.

5. Organisation as a Closed System

Advocates of the classical theory strongly believe that an organisation is a closed system and does not interact with the external environment on a regular basis. They concentrated on internal environment to improve organisational functioning. But the latest researches on organisations have proved that factors of external environment also affect employee response and behaviour along with work environment. Thus, it is better to consider the organisation as an open adaptive system.

The traditional approach to management failed to bring about the desired increase in the level of efficiency of employees. By seeking too much specialisation, simplification and rationalisation of work it becomes monotonous and boring for employees. Consequently, they feel frustrated and alienated. Finally, this approach could not bring the needed improvement in the levels of motivation, performance and productivity.

2. BEHAVIOURAL APPROACH TO MANAGEMENT

This approach of management was developed gradually over many years. It is based on a strong conviction that efficient management depends on the manager's ability to understand work as well as people who have different backgrounds, needs, values, perceptions and personality. Thus, in this approach of management, the human factor remains the central focus and gets a high pedestal in the organisation. This approach can be studied in two phases:

1. Human relations movement, and
2. Behavioural science approach.

Human Relations Movement

The human relations movement was a remarkable attempt on the part of management practitioners to make managers more sensitive to the needs of employees. This movement is marked by threats of unionisation, findings of the Hawthorne studies and the philosophy of industrial humanism. Elton Mayo, Mary Parker Follet and Douglas McGregor have been the main contributors to this movement. The main features of the human relations movement are as under:

1. Human organisation was considered as a psycho-social system. The primary focus of psychologists was placed on the employees as an individual, while sociologists concentrated on the employee's interaction with others in a group which leads to the creation of inter-personal relations.
2. This movement took management theorists away from the simple model of economic man to a more humanistic view, the 'social man model.' They argued that apart from economic needs, employees have other social and psychological needs such as recognition, appreciation, self-respect, dignity, etc., and these are also to be taken care of.
3. Regarding human nature, optimistic assumptions were made such as they want to work, assume responsibility, are willing to cooperate and contribute to achieve a common goal provided they are given an opportunity. More so, it is the responsibility of the manager to seek their cooperation by establishing a congenial interpersonal relationship, adopting a sympathetic and friendly attitude towards them and recognising and providing for their social, psychological and other needs.
4. Advocates of the human relations approach strongly believed that there should be no conflicts or clashes in the organisation. And, if at all it arises, it must be removed completely because it is not desirable for healthy organisational functioning.
5. To secure maximum contribution, managers should get along with employees and workers. But reducing social distance, fair and frank communication would take place among them.

6. In order to motivate individual employees, his motivating desire should be ascertained in terms of his emotions, beliefs, attitudes, habits and needs.
7. A sense of belonging should be created among employees by giving them more importance and involving them in decision making and other affairs of the organisation.
8. A human relations approach basically aims at providing a high degree of satisfaction and motivation through improved working conditions, an effective style of supervision and by creating a sense of security among them.

In brief, early human relations theorists realised that satisfied employees would be less inclined to join a trade union movement. Therefore, managers should be forced to adopt morale-boosting human relations techniques. Apart from providing satisfaction to social, emotional and psychological needs, they should also recognise the importance of psychological and social factors in the working of an organisation.

The Hawthorne Studies

The Hawthorne Studies and its findings provided a concrete base to the human relation approach. It has a definitely significant impact on management thought. These studies began in 1924 in the Western Electric plant in the U.S.A. and were spread over a period of eight years. They were begun to envisage the relationship between light and productivity as a part of scientific management study. But at a later stage, a team of behavioural research scientists headed by Elton Mayo was called from Harvard to make more rigorous studies. The Hawthorne studies mainly consist of the following experiments:

Illumination Experiment

The main purpose of conducting this experiment was to assess the effect of illumination on the output of employees. It revealed that productivity can be raised only by improving physical workings conditions but the philosophy of human relations was needed to provide better treatment to them to raise their output.

Relay Assembly Test Room Experiment

This study was conducted with the purpose to remove the anomalies of previous experiments and confirm tentative conclusions brought about by it. In this experiment, some new variables were introduced such as friendly and informal supervision, shorter working hours and days, interaction among members of the group under study, improved physical working conditions, more wages, etc. On the basis of this experiment, it was concluded that the productivity and morale of the group increased and was maintained as such even after withdrawing improved physical conditions. These experiments finally summed up that the physical environment may or may not increase productivity but more important than these conditions are the attitude of management, morale of employees and other socio-psychological factors like importance, involvement of employees and informal relations among them.

Massive Interviewing Programme

This programme was aimed to find out the attitude of employees towards their job, working conditions and supervision styles. By interviewing thousands of workers it was further confirmed that informal relationships, social and psychological needs and the attitude of employees have a definite influence on their working behaviour.

Bank Wiring Observation Room Experiment

It was conducted to investigate the social pattern of behaviour of a group of 14 workers and their supervisors. Thus, the study confirmed that there existed informal group norms which were lower than officially prescribed standards and which regulated and affected their behaviour. This study further proved the importance of small informal social groups like cliques in an organisation.

Findings of the Hawthorne Studies

Contrary to the approach of scientific management, which is primarily focused on the study of tools and techniques, the human relations approach placed more emphasis on people. The findings or conclusions of the Hawthorne studies were indeed an eye opener in this direction. They were published in 1941 by Rowthlis, Berger and William Dickson in the form of a book titled 'Management and the Worker'. The major findings of the studies are as under:

Multiple Needs

The Hawthorne studies made it quite clear that the worker is not merely an 'economic man' motivated solely by financial incentives. Rather, his working behaviour is more influenced by his social and psychological needs. These studies reinforced the interest of management in the psychological and social factors of the work setting.

Interpersonal Relations and Work Situation

After extensive and rigorous studies it was also discovered that productivity of workers is less affected by change in the physical working conditions than by the relationship between members of a work group and between workers and their supervisors. The studies revealed that the worker responds to his total work setting of which social relations and interpersonal relations are parts of.

Informal Relations

The studies fully realised the importance of informal groups based on personal and social relations among workers and its impact on their working behaviour. It was demonstrated that effective communication, relaxed and friendly supervision, workers' attitude and informal leadership are important factors to productivity.

Historical Perspective

The Hawthorne studies also revealed that people were important to productivity and therefore an approach of human relations was needed to treat them in a better manner.

They create their own informal and powerful workplace culture and prescribe informal norms for members. It also came to light that personal and emotional factors were more important determinants of productivity than physical and logical factors.

The need was felt for a humanistic relation between management and workers. Mayo urged that managers provide work that would give personal and subjective satisfaction to workers and create a new social order so as to get their wholehearted cooperation.

The findings of the Hawthorne studies forced management scientists to turn away from from the 'economic man model' to a more humanistic approach of a 'social man model'. But these studies were criticised mainly for the type of methodology used and statistical innacuracies involved in it. It was argued that the findings of the Hawthorne studies are not based on scientific research and scientific techniques have not been used to derive the conclusions.

Regarding the findings, it was also alleged that they are influenced by preoccupied notions about him and behaviour in the minds of managers.

Further, the validity and applicability of these findings are was also questioned on the ground that since they were not drawn from the study and experiments on a small group of people, therefore they may enjoy a wide and general application in all kinds of work stations.

Evaluation of Contributions to Human Relations Movement

The human relations movement has provided a sound framework to develop a new philosophy of management based on socialisation and humanisation of the organisation. It is true that man-made organisations cannot function efficiently without giving due weightage to the human side of it. Efficiency of management largely depends on the ability of managers to understand work as well as people who have different backgrounds, needs, aspirations and personalities. But this approach is not free from inadequacies and demerits, some of which are as under:

(i) Productivity is Ignored

The human relations approach has ignored basic issues such as productivity, job satisfaction and efficient accomplishment of organisational goals. Too much emphasis on the human side of organisation does not guarantee a higher production on the part of workers. In order to get the desired results, managers have to be extraordinarily careful in establishing relationships between satisfaction and productivity of employees. It is because superficial satisfaction or mere happiness on the part of employees will not necessarily contribute to higher productivity.

(ii) Incomplete Package

The human relations approach cannot be treated as a complete package to deal with human beings effectively. It is because no attempt has been made by advocates of this approach to study and analyse human behaviour systematically and scientifically. Much more is needed to elaborate the concept of 'social man' so as to make it more acceptable and relevant.

(iii) Missing Link Between Humanisation and Productivity

The human relations approach aims at creating and maintaining cordial human relations among employees in the organisation. But in fact these relations are to be maintained and strengthened for efficient accomplishment of organisational goals. So the concept of humanisation and socialisation is to be made well connected and related to productivity levels of employees.

(iv) Keeping Employees Happy is not Enough

The entire approach of human relations aims at creating happiness and providing satisfaction to workers. But without translating these variables into high morale and motivation, the desired results can not be achieved. It is because if managers manipulate to keep their employees happy, they will not necessary produce more.

Behavioural Science Approach

In view of certain inadequacies and drawbacks associated with the human relations approach, serious efforts were made by many other social and behavioural scientists to study and analyse human behaviour systematically. The term 'behavioural science approach' may be defined as a systematic as well as a scientific analysis of human behaviour to determine the causes of the working behaviour of an individual. This approach is also known as 'organisational behaviour approach'. This is an interdisciplinary approach of studying human behaviour consisting of psychology, which deals with human behaviour, sociology (dealings of an individual in a group) and anthropology which is a study of physical, biological and cultural variables affecting the behaviour of individuals as members of a group.

The behavioural science approach has an significant impact on modern management theory because it helps in explaining why employees behave as they do. This approach is based on the following assumptions:

1. Socio-technical System

Advocates of the behavioural science approach strongly believe that the organisation is a socio-technical system which consists of individuals and their interpersonal and social relations with each other on the one hand and various techniques, methods and procedures used to perform several jobs assigned to them, on the other.

2. Integration of Individual and Organisational Goals

This approach highlights that individual goals and the interests of employees can be integrated with organisational goals so as to avoid conflict and clash among them.

3. Conflict and Cooperation

According to this approach, conflict and cooperation coexist in an organisation. To some extent, conflicts are inevitable and desirable. It is because an organisation is made up of many interest groups that are perhaps antagonistic and many individuals of different backgrounds, perceptions, personalities, aspirations and goals do work in an organisation.

This type of diversity is bound to create some conflicts. Similarly, it is in a conflicting situation that managers tend to behave carefully, cautiously and act efficiently.

4. Individual Difference

Behavioural scientists recognise individual differences in terms of their personality, goals, beliefs, values and perceptions. These differences matter a lot specially at the time of designing a motivation process.

5. People are the Key to Productivity

The behavioural approach assumes that people are the key to productivity. The technology, work standards and other physical factors do not guarantee higher performance. Instead it depends on wide-ranging variables such as satisfaction, morale, motivation of employees and sensitivity of managers to employees, needs, etc.

6. Contribution of Authors

Different aspects of this approach were developed by various behavioural scientists such as Douglas McGregor, Abraham Maslow, Chester Barnard, Resnis Likert, Herbert Simon, etc.

COMPARISON

The behavioural approach of management represents a significant advance over the human relations approach. It may be considered as a more refined and scientifically extended version of the human relations approach. It is because it fulfils some of the inadequacies left by human relations scientists and that too by retaining its focus on people in an organisation. These two approaches may be compared as under:

1. The human relations approach is solely confined to the concept of humanisation and socialisation of the organisation by recognising the human side of it. But the behavioural science approach aims at studying and analysing human behaviour systematically. This approach is broader and more inclusive in nature.

2. Advocates of the human relations approach strongly believe that an organisation is a 'socio-psychological' system emphasising the social and psychological needs of individuals working in an organisation. While the behavioural approach assumes that the organisation is a 'social-technical' system stressing on both the individual's interpersonal and social relationships and technique, methods and procedures are used by them to perform assigned jobs.
3. The human relations approach is mainly concerned with the human aspect involved in the organisation and considers all individuals as human beings. But the behavioural science approach recognises individual differences in terms of background, personality, values, goals and aspirations which helps in developing different motivational processes for them.
4. Human relations scientists believe that satisfaction provided to employees by giving economic incentives and improving their working conditions will force them to produce more. But behavioural scientists reject this assumption and believe that there are wide-ranging variables which affect the working behaviour of employees.
5. The human relations approach is based on the assumption that conflicts and clashes should be totally removed as they appear. But the behavioural science approach realises that conflicts are bound to crop up and to some extent they produce a constructive effect, especially on managers.
6. As compared to the behavioural science approach, the human relations approach seems to be more limited in scope and areas because it only deals with a set of economic, social and psychological needs and physical working conditions for raising the efficiency of employees. But behavioural scientists were more concerned about the technological aspect of job design, group dynamics, leadership, communication and motivation which provide a broad base to this approach.

Job Characteristics and Motivation

Focussing on the importance of job content and characteristics on the level of motivation, Turner and Lawrence developed in 1965 a set of characteristics which the job should possess. They found that these characteristics are closely related to the satisfaction and attendance of workers. These characteristics were:

1. Variety in work
2. Level of employee's autonomy in performing the work
3. Amount of interaction required in carrying out task activities
4. Number of opportunities for operational interaction
5. Level of knowledge and skill required
6. Amount of responsibility entrusted to the job holder.

On the basis of these characteristics Hackman and Lawler identified the following four characteristics in a study of telephone company jobs:

1. Variety
2. Task identity (doing the whole piece of work)
3. Autonomy
4. Job-based feedback.

They further concluded that if the jobs possess these characteristics a job holder would experience positive self-generated effective 'kick'. When they performed well it would lead to internal reinforcement and serve as an incentive for consistent good performance.

But on the whole, like the traditional approach, the human relations approach also suffered from many inadequacies and limitations. The advocates of this approach ignored the working of the 'technical system' in the organisation. They did not give due weightage to the importance of group relations and organisational environment.

3. MODERN APPROACH OF MANAGEMENT

The modern approach of management represents the latest development that took place after 1950. This approach can be studied and analysed in the following four phases, namely, quantitative approach, system approach, contingency approach and excellence approach.

Quantitative Approach

This approach is also well known as the management science approach. It was developed in 1950. It is based on the approach of scientific management. It offers a systematic and scientific analysis and solution to the problems faced by managers. The quantitative approach aims at achieving a high degree of precision, perfection and objectivity by encouraging the use of mathematical and statistical tools to solve complex problems. These quantitative decision-making tools are known as 'operation research' like linear programming, simulation, queuing theory, game theory, etc. It also implies the use of computer-aided technology in various fields like production, finance, costing, transportation, storage, etc. In simple terms, operation research may be regarded as the application of scientific methods to solve problems. These scientific methods consist of the following stages:

(a) Dividing a problem into small simple components.
(b) Gathering required information on each component.
(c) Analysis of data so collected.
(d) Finding out the solutions to the problem in hand.

The quantitative approach involves the use of knowledge and skills of several other disciplines such as statistics, engineering, electronics, accounting, etc. It has contributed significantly to management theory, electronic data processing systems and other sophisticated quantitative devices for making decisions. The consistent use of logic and reasoning to solve problems may help in reducing the personal bias and intuition of managers. But, on the whole, this approach has very limited application and that too only in respect of problem solving and decision making. Therefore, it is not considered as a full-fledged approach of management.

System Approach

The system approach of management represents new thinking and the latest developments that occurred in the field of organisations and management. It was developed after 1950, placing emphasis on interdependence and inter-relationship which exists among various activities and components of an organisation. Basically, this approach aims at identifying and analysing the nature of the relationship among various components or sub-systems of the organisation.

The term 'system' may be defined as a set of interrelated and interacting components assembled in a particular sequence so as to produce some results. These components may also be viewed as sub-systems of a larger system. It is only through these sub-systems that the larger system operates. Thus, the larger system can be viewed as a whole entity or in totality. The various sub-systems that are involved in the functioning of a larger one are closely related to each other and to a system as a whole. Similarly, these sub-systems interact with each other by getting influenced and influencing others.

Every system has a sub-system and every sub-system may be considered as a system because it may have sub-systems. Thus, in a system, there is a wheel within a wheel making and contributing to a larger system. Every system has certain boundaries, and within these there lies the internal environment which mainly consists of internal and controllable variables such as organisational culture, motivations systems, quality of leadership and communication network, nature of supervision, etc. Beyond these set boundaries there exists an external environment which is outside the control of the system. It includes a set of socio-cultural, economic, legal, political and technical factors affecting the functioning of an organisation. For instance, an individual firm is a sub-system of an industry which is a sub-system of business, which is further a sub-system of a larger economic system and which is again a part of a broader socio-economic system of the country which falls within an international system

The system approach defines an organisation as a complex whole consisting of mutually interdependent and interacting parts which are viewed as sub-systems. Therefore, this approach is said to be holistic in nature assuming that the whole is greater than the sum of its parts (Figure 3.2).

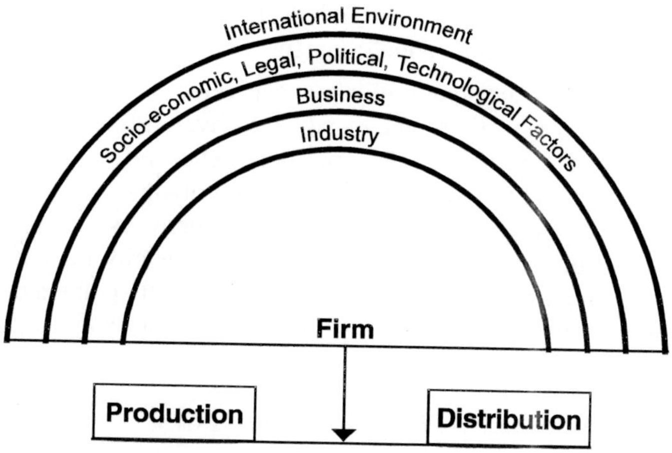

Figure 3.2. System with sub-systems inside

TYPES OF SYSTEMS

Systems may be broadly classified into four categories—physical, mechanical, biological and social. Physical systems are a part and parcel of nature or the sub-system of it. These are totally governed and regulated by mother nature, for example, the solar system, seasons, rivers, etc. Mechanical systems refer to those devices that are based on technology. These systems have been innovated by human beings for their betterment but are totally closed systems in nature. They do not interact with the external environment such as machines, motor cars, electric appliances, consumer durables, etc.

Biological systems are those systems that regulate and control the existence and survival of all living species. Humans and plants are good examples. Biological systems do operate in a particular life-cycle having several sequential stages such as conception, birth, growth, maturity, decay, death, etc. Lastly, social systems may be defined as a system which has been developed by human beings to facilitate cooperative working and to overcome the problem of isolation and desolation. All kinds of small and big, formal and informal and economic and non economic organisations are examples of social systems.

The system described above may be either an open system or a closed system or a partially open and partially closed one. Mostly, physical and mechanical systems are relatively closed systems. It is because they make the least interaction with the external environment. They are by and large self-sustained and do not depend much on other systems for the supply of inputs such as a battery powered digital watch. On the other hand, biological and social systems are relatively open systems. They interact with the external environment on a regular basis and depend on it for the supply of necessary inputs. In turn, after having processed these inputs they supply back these to the environment. The open and closed systems cannot be separated from each other. How much open or closed it is depends on the amount of interaction between the system and its external environment.

Being a social system, the organisation is a relatively open system. It is because it interacts with the external environment and its survival depends on its ability to cope with the changing environment. Organisations get power, strength and inputs from the environment and in turn strengthen and contribute to the functioning of the environment. But an organisation may not be considered as a completely open system. It is because to some extent it has to preserve its identity, maintain stability and protect autonomy. In this connection, Kreitner has rightly pointed out that just as no person is an island, similarly no organisation or organisational sub-system is an island.

The Organisation as an Input–Process–Output System

An organisation is basically an input-process-output system. It obtains various inputs, both physical and human such as land, capital, building, raw material, machines, technology, labour and management from society which is a larger system of it. These inputs are processed through conversion and some goods and services and produced which is considered as an output of the system. The output of the system is to be supplied back to society. Through the process of feedback, the organisation gets valuable information that helps in adjusting the system and making more responsible to the needs of society (Figure 3.3).

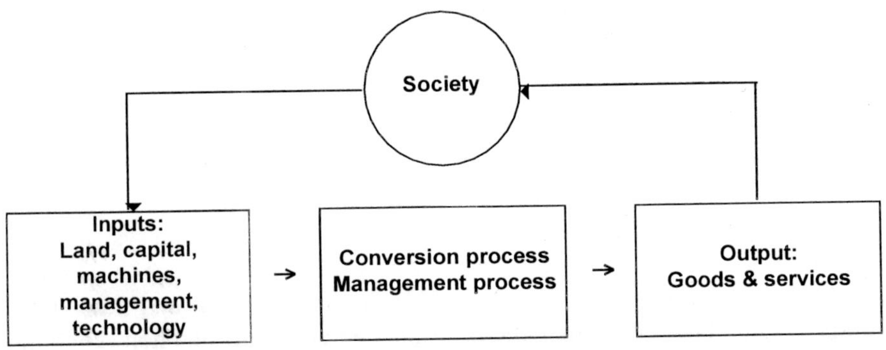

Figure 3.3. Input-process chart

To study an organisation as a system, various system approaches have been developed. Among these, the 'socio-technical theory' of organising the managing work is considered more relevant. According to this approach, while designing, managing and performing the work, the impact of both social and technical systems of organisation should be taken into account.

These two should be considered as a supportive sub-system of the organisation. This approach of designing work for employees in the organisation is based on the following principles.

1. Jobs and work groups in the organisation should be created on the basis of task requirements. The tasks that are small components of the job may be highly related to each other. Such tasks should be put in one group and should be performed by employees working in related roles.
2. Besides, wages, safety and security demands the job must also fulfil the psychological and social requirements of job holders. In order to make jobs more meaningful, the right to exercise control over it should be given to the job holders. The elements of mutual help, social support, decision making and planning should be introduced into the jobs and work groups.
3. The most important principle of the socio-technical theory is to consider the organisation as an open adaptive system. According to this principle, the organisation operates in an environment that has a direct impact on its functioning. Therefore, the organisation should develop enough capabilities to cope with the changing environment and balance its internal environment.

An organisation is an open adaptive system and has the following features:

1. Interaction

An organisation is an open system and interacts with its external environment on a regular basis. Its functioning is greatly influenced by the changes taking place in the environment. To some extent, the organisations in a collective form and autonomous organisations having huge resources at their disposal may also have some impact on external environment.

2. Input–Process–Output Model

The organisation is considered as an input–process–output system. It procures resources from society, which are known as inputs and these are processed and converted into output. The output is in the form of goods and services that are given back to society.

3. Integration of Sub-Systems

The organisation operates through may sub-systems. These sub-systems may be technical, social and power systems or production, distribution, finance, purchase, personnel, etc. These sub-systems are integrated and coordinated so as to facilitate the smooth function of the organisation. It is done through the process of communication, balance and decisions.

4. Multiplicity of Objectives

The organisation is a collective system. It involves the interest of many groups such as owners, customers, employers, financiers, government and society. To serve the interests of these groups, the organisation is bound to pursue two or more objectives at a time. It ultimately leads to multiplicity of objectives.

5. Sub-systems

The organisation is a sub-system of a larger system and has many sub-systems in it. The sub-systems of an organisation are closely related with each other. They interact with each other and supplement the functioning of each other so as to contribute to the overall functioning of the organisation. These sub-systems derive strength and power from the organisation and in turn make a contribution to the organisation.

Evaluation of System Approach

The system approach encourages meaningful analysis of an organisation and its various sub-systems or components and facilitates their management. It provides a sound basis for understanding organisations and their problems. System theorists strongly believe that the actions and decisions of managers influence and in turn are influenced by many organisational and environmental variables. Managers must take into account interdependencies, interactions and interrelationships among the various components of the system at the time of taking decisions.

They should also base decisions on the ground realities of both internal and external environment. Thus, the system approach facilitates the application of both the process of analysis and synthesis and differentiation and integration by relating the sub-systems of an organisation from the lowest to the highest level of the organisation. Another positive aspect of system approach is that it integrates various management approaches in a meaningful way. Although the classical and behavioural approaches place an emphasis on different aspects, these two are greatly influenced by the system approach.

In addition, some management scientists criticise the system approach as being purely theoretical, conceptual, vague and abstract. They argue that it has only an intellectual appeal and cannot be applied to practical situations. In the context of management of a modern organisation it is considered simply a way of thinking rather than one providing solutions to problems. The system approach neither offers any tool or technique for analysis and synthesis nor does it recognise the differences that exist between the various systems. Nevertheless, it represents a significant departure from the past and provides a new style of thinking to management knowledge.

Contingency Approach

The contingency approach is related to system approach, and represents a comparatively new line of thinking among management scientists. This approach basically discounts the concept of universal application of managerial principles and recommends that the application of these principles is subject to appropriateness of the situation.

It is a systematic attempt to determine the package of management techniques, approaches and practices that are appropriate to a specific given situation. Thus, according to the advocates of this approach, managers, instead of applying the principles in practices of management in an uniform manner to every situation, should study, analyse and diagnose the situation, understand situational requirements and then prepare a package of management principles and techniques to deal with it effectively.

So this approach makes it quite clear that instead of relying too much on preconceived assumptions and viewpoints, differences in the situations should be taken into account so as to design and implement a suitable management package. In the context of management, a contingency approach has become synonymous with situations and environmental management. According to one of its advocates, "the effectiveness of a given management pattern is contingent upon multitudinous factors and their interrelationship in a particular situation."

This means the application of various management techniques must be made appropriate to a particular situation. It is because each situation is made of different variables. This approach is also considered as pragmatic and open-mindeds it places more emphasis on situational variables and application of managerial tools and techniques is contingent upon that specific situation. The contingency approach offers the following guidelines for managers:

1. The contingency approach is situation-oriented urging managers to study, analyse and diagnose the situation. It is to be done in terms of component variables of the situation and external factors affecting the situation.
2. Subsequently, after the analysis of the situation, managers are expected to prepare inventories of management theory, principles, techniques and concepts.
3. In order to tackle the situation efficiently, the validity and applicability of management tools and techniques is to be examined. And finally, the package of these tools and techniques is prepared which is appropriate for that specific situation. This is because each situation differs and requires a different managerial response.

Nature of Contingency Approach

It is evident from the foregoing discussion that the contingency approach discounts the theme of universal application of management principles. It further upholds relevance and utility of situations as well as external factors for developing a suitable action programme. Outwardly, it appears that the contingency approach is merely based on commonsense because it has an intuitive appeal that there cannot be a single best way of doing things in every situation. It is merely a matter of commonsense that one particular solution cannot be universally applicable to all situations regardless of their individual characteristics and features.

Thus, managers should have flexibility and freedom to devise a suitable course of action for a given situation. It is because in real life the success of any management technique is largely conditioned by the situation.

It may also be considered as a commonsense approach because it widens the horizon of management from management theory, principles, techniques and concepts to situational variables and external environment. The manager has to apply innovativeness, creativity, analytical abilities and foresight to develop a suitable course of action contingent upon a specific situation.

In fact, the entire approach of contingency is much more than a mere application of commonsense. The application of this approach requires managers to have a thorough knowledge of the situation in terms of situational variables and external factors.

In addition to applying this approach, he must possess enough knowledge about management theory, principles, tools and techniques. It further calls for knowledge and analytical abilities on the part of managers about the contingencies under which a particular managerial response in the form of strategy or technique would work well.

The contingency approach suggests a comparative analysis of various organisations operative in different situations so as to get adequate knowledge about their functioning which may further help in formulating general guidelines to understand the behaviour of a situation.

Critical Evaluation of the Contingency Approach

The contingency approach seems to be a significant addition to the existing body of management knowledge. It is because it places more emphasis on the appropriateness of management tools and techniques for a specific situation. It offers practical direction to the system approach to choose a suitable form of departmentalisation for grouping activities, style of leadership and supervision, to determine the degree of centralisation and decentralisation and more appropriate motivational processes as per the demand of the situation.

Some management scientists believe that the contingency approach is a compromise between the system approach and a purely situational perspective. It is based on open system thinking, is pragmatic and encourages multivariable analysis.

It is clear from the above discussion that the contingency approach has wide-ranging applicability in organisation and management. This is because every manager is preoccupied with a responsibility to develop an alternative course of action suitable for a specific situation.

For instance, there exists many supervisory or leadership styles in management, but the successful manager has to develop and use a particular style which may prove more effective in a given situation. The contingency approach also helps managers to use research techniques of multivariable analysis to determine how a combination of variables leads to a particular outcome, for instance, the productivity which has been considered an effect of high morale only by traditional management scientists. But the multivariable analysis in the contingency approach has provided that many variables including the employee's personality, nature and content of job, motivation process, job satisfaction, etc., may collectively contribute to productivity (Figure 3.4).

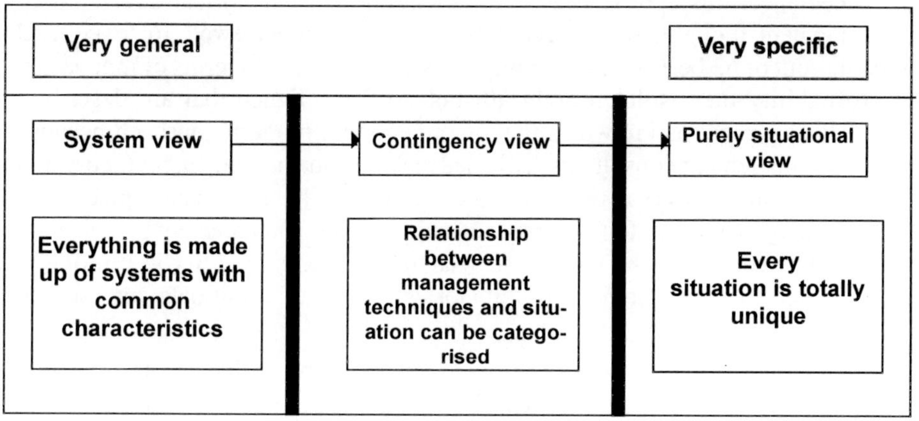

Figure 3.4. Contingency view

Nevertheless, the contingency approach is also criticised by many management scientists on the ground that it is totally a practical approach without being supported by the required theoretical and conceptual framework. Managers experience difficulty in analysing situations and discovering appropriate management techniques in the absence of necessary research devices and generalisations to understand the behaviour of a situation. However, the contingency approach may be regarded as a promising step towards the development of management theory and practice.

The contingency approach of management and organisation based on an analysis of situational variables was first proposed by Fred E. Fiedler. He advocated that to be more effective the manager must develop a specific response to a given specific situation. In brief, he has identified the following four main contingencies to be taken care of by managers:

1. The authority structure of an organisation must match the demand of its environment.
2. The authority structure of an organisation must coincide with the technical system (technology).
3. Individual sub-systems such as departments, workgroups and units must match their particular work environment and management authority must coincide with technological requirements of these sub-systems.
4. The leadership behaviour of managers in the organisation and its sub-systems must be appropriate to situational demands.

ATTRIBUTES OF EXCELLENCE: A MODERN UNCONVENTIONAL APPROACH

This approach has been developed by Thomas J. Peter and Robert H. Waterman, management consultants of the U.S.A. in 1982. They published a book popularly known as 'In Search of Excellence' which was considered a remedy to solve productivity-related problems faced by American companies. In view of its wide acceptance, this approach deserves mention in the historical development of management thought. After having surveyed and interviewed 36 'excellent' companies out of 62 best-managed companies of the U.S.A. in terms of innovation and profitability they isolated eight attributes of excellence that are described below. This approach is known as the unconventional modern approach because these two management consultants criticised conventional management theory and practice for being conservative, rationalistic and flexible. They also replaced the conventional management terminology such as planning, management by objective and control by certain catchy phrases such as 'do it', 'fix it', and 'try it'. Similarly, they presented their key points through stories instead of using data and facts to support their viewpoint.

The attributes of excellence approach seems to be really a commendable attempt on the part of Peter and Waterman to draw the attention of managers and their concentration on customers, employees and new ideas which they consider the basics of an organisation. In this, they noted that excellent companies were above all brilliant on the basic aspects. Tools did not substitute thinking. Intellect did not overpower wisdom. Analysis did not impede action. Rather, these companies worked hard to keep things simple in a complex world. Further, they insisted on top quality for their customers. They listened to their employees and treated them like adults. They allowed their innovative products and services 'champion' long letters. They allowed some chaos in return for quick action and regular experimentation.

The above findings amply make it clear that to achieve a target of excellence, an organisation and its management has to ponder over and act seriously on three important basics—customers, employees and research and development leading to innovation of new ideas and products.

The list of eight attributes and brief descriptions are summed up in Table 3.1.

The commendable piece of work done by Peter and Waterman has got wide recognition all over the world by most modern management thinkers. These eight attributes of excellence are based on practical experimentation of these two consultants. Though it would have been in the fitness of things if they had highlighted some of the major weak sides of 'excellent' companies, on the whole the approach may be used as an eye-opener for progressive managers.

SUMMARY

Although many past instances indicate that the use of management knowledge in one or another form has roots in human civilisation, the systematic study of this field began from the beginning of the 20th century. Over the past 100 years there have been drastic changes in this field and now it has emerged as one of the

TABLE 3.1: PETER AND WATERMAN'S EIGHT ATTRIBUTES OF EXCELLENCE

Attribute excellence	Key indicator
1. A bias for action	Small scale, easily managed experiments to build knowledge interest and commitment. Management stay visible and person ally involved in all areas through active informal communication and spontaneous management by wandering around (MBWA).
2. Close to the customer	Customer satisfaction is practically an obsession. Input from customers is sought throughout the design, production and marketing cycles.
3. Autonomy and entrepreneurship	Risk taking is encouraged; failure is tolerated. Innovators are encouraged to champion their pet projects to see them through competition. Flexible structure permits the formation of 'skunk works' (small teams of zealous innovators working on special projects). Lot of creative swings are encouraged to ensure some home runs (successful products).
4. Productivity through people	Individuals are treated with respect and dignity, enthusiasm, trust and family feeling are fostered. People are encouraged to have fun while getting something meaningful accomplished. Work units are kept small and humane.
5. Hands-on value drive	A clear company's philosophy is disseminated and followed. Personal values are discussed openly, not buried. The organisation's belief system is reinforced through frequently shared stories, myths and legends. Leaders are positive role models, not 'do as I say', not 'not as I do' authority figures.
6. Stick to the knitting	Management sticks to the business it knows best, emphasis is on internal growth, not merger.
7. Simple lean staff	Authority is decentralised as much as possible. Headquarters staff is kept small; talent is pushed out of field.
8. Simultaneous loose-tight properties	Tight overall strategic and financial control is counterbalanced by decentralised authority; autonomy and opportunities for creativity.

Source: Peter and Waterman's eight attributes of excellence from *In Search of Excellence.*

important branches of the social sciences. The changes in the nature and volume of management knowledge may be studied by dividing it into three phases:

1. Classical approach of management
2. Human relations approach
3. Modern approach including system and contingency approaches.

The classical approach includes scientific management, administrative theory of management and bureaucratic model of organisation. Many administrators, engineers and management authors have made valuable contributions to the development of this approach. Mainly, F. W. Taylor is considered as the father of scientific management. Henri Fayol and associates developed the process approach and administrative theory and Max Weber gets credit for developing the bureaucratic model of organisation. F. W. Taylor and his associates mainly focussed on work-related problems faced by workers. They believed that by simplifying and rationalising work and work methods, the operational efficiency of workers may be increased. Taylor introduced rationality for designing, organising and managing the work performed by lower level workers. He assumed that the individuals are basically economic beings and can easily be motivated to produce more by giving them financial incentives, payment of bonus and productivity-linked wage incentives. His associates also made many other interesting assumptions about human behaviour. They also proposed dual command and closed control system to be used in the organisation.

Although the approach of scientific management has great relevance in modern management, it has been criticised by many authors of management particularly in terms of its assumptions like close control and monotony on the part of workers.

Henri Fayol and his associates made a valuable attempt to develop the administrative theory of management based on certain principles. This theory has application even on the higher levels of management. Fayol attempted to describe management by using the process and functional approach. According to him, the managing process has many elements that are interrelated to each other and known as management functions.

These elements are to be carried out in a particular sequence to get results. The principles of management developed by him provide a base for modern management. These principles have a general applicability and are flexible in nature. Therefore, managers must be cautious about using them.

Max Weber developed the bureaucratic model of organisation. This model is based on the principles of division of labour, authority, relationship, total compliance with work procedures, impersonality and technical competence of the employees. This approach aims at securing a high degree of precision and perfection.

Although this model is subject to some criticism such as inordinate delay in decision making, more emphasis on authority relationship and lack of motivation and innovativeness, till today this form maintains its suitability in little modified forms.

The human relations approach which also consists of the behavioural science approach is considered as a significant move in the development of management knowledge. Human relations approach recognised the importance of the human element involved in the functioning of an organisation. It connects work with workers and by balancing these two higher productivity is sought. It also takes care of the higher order needs of employees such as security needs, social needs and psychological needs.

The findings of the Hawthorne studies are really an eye opener for managers. Along with it, the behavioural science approach attempts to study and analyse human behaviour to find out why they behave, what factors affect their behaviour and what else can be done to make their working behaviour more effective and desirable. Not only Elton Mayo but many other social scientists and psychologists such as McGregor, Maslow, Barnard, Likert, Simon, etc., have made valuable contributions to this field.

Modern management is primarily based on the system approach and contingency approach. System approach represents new thinking and latest development which took place in this field. According to the system approach, the organisation is considered an open adaptive goal-oriented system. It has many sub-systems such as social, technical and power systems and is also a sub-system of a large system. According to this approach inputs, which are also known as resources, are obtained from society, processed (conversion) and output (goods and services) is produced and given back to society. This approach also recognised that an organisation is part of a larger system and interacts with an environment on a regular basis. The changing environment may bring about new opportunities and may also create new problems for the organisation.

To survive and grow, an organisation has to cope with the changing environment effectively. This approach facilitates analysis and synthesis of organisation and its functioning which is helpful to make improvements.

The contingency approach really discounts universal application of management knowledge. It emphasises that effective and efficient use of management knowledge is contingent on given situations. Therefore, every manager should prepare management responses by making the required changes in the knowledge of management related to that situation. It is a systematic attempt to determine a management package, techniques, approaches and practices that are appropriate to a specific given situation. This approach is a significant addition to the existing body of management knowledge. Managers, to be effective, must study social, technical as well as situational variables. This approach is based on open system thinking, is practical in nature and encourages multivariable analysis.

The more recent development in the field of management is the 'attributes of excellence' approach developed by Peter and Waterman, management consultants in the U.S.A. This approach is widely accepted and many authors consider it as a part of modern management. This approach attracts the attention of managers on certain attributes of the organisation that are performing excellently and intelligently.

TEST QUESTIONS

1. The human relations approach weakens the role of management in achieving organisation goals. Comment.
2. The behavioural science approach represents a significant advance over the human relations approach. Comment.
3. Explain the basic philosophy of the human relations movement.
4. Comment on the major findings of the Hawthorne experiments.
5. What is the management science approach? What are its assumptions? How far is this approach a refinement of the scientific management approach?
6. Comment on "the contingency approach to management is a commonsense approach."
7. The behavioural science approach is more refined and an extended version of the human relations approach. Comment.
8. Evaluate the contribution of Taylor to the development of management thoughts.
9. What is the basic theme of the contingency approach to management? Explain the practical utility of adopting this approach.
10. Distinguish between the system approach and the contingency approach.
11. Write short notes on:
    (a) Organisation as an input–process–output system.
    (b) Contingency approach to management.
    (c) System approach of management.
    (d) Conclusions of the Hawthorne studies.

OBJECTIVE TYPE QUESTIONS

Which of the following statements are correct and which are incorrect? Give reasons to support your answers.

1. The human relations approach attempts to make every employee happy.
2. The administrative management theory is prescriptive in nature.
3. The contingency approach to management is a commonsense approach.
4. The system approach to management is holistic in nature.
5. The behavioural science approach attempts to remove the deficiencies of the human relations approach.
6. The management process approach is the same as the functional approach to management.

7. The quantitative school does not follow scientific methods in its approach.
8. The behavioural science approach concedes that business organisations are purely social systems.
9. The approach of scientific management aims at solving work related problems.
10. The human relations approach advocates that an organisation is a psycho-social system.
11. The behavioural science approach advocates that an organisation is a socio-technical system.
12. Modern business organisations are only relatively not absolutely open systems.
13. The contingency approach to management emphasises that there is no universal principle to be applied to all situations.

REFERENCES

Davis, Ralph C. *The Fundamentals of Top Management*. New York, U.S.A.: Harper and Brothers, 1951.

Fayol, Henri. *Industrial and General Administration*. Geneva, Switzerland: International Management Institute, 1930.

Gibson, Donnelly. *Management, Principles and Function*. New Delhi, India: A.I.T.B.S.S. Publishers and Distributors, 1994.

Koontz, Harold and Weihri, Heinz. *Essential of Management*. New Delhi, India: Tata McGraw-Hill Publishing Company, Ltd., 2001.

Louis, Allen. *Professional Management: New Concepts and Proven Practices*. Tokyo, Japan: McGraw-Hill, 1973.

Maslow, Abraham, H. *Motivation and Personality*. New York, U.S.A.: Harper and Row, 1964.

McGregor, Douglas. *The Human Side of Enterprise*. New York, U.S.A.: McGraw-Hill, 1960.

Moshal, B. S. *Management, Theory and Practice*. New Delhi, India: Galgotia Publishing Company, 2002.

Peterson, Peter B. 'The Evolution of the Gantt Chart and its Relevant Today'. *Journal of Management Issues,* 1991.

Stoner, Freeman and Gilbert. *Management*. New Delhi, India: Prentice Hall of India Pvt. Ltd., 2001.

Taylor, F. W. *Scientific Management*. New York, U.S.A.: Harper and Brothers, 1947.

Weber, Max. *The Theory of Social and Economic Organisation*. New York, U.S.A. Free Press, 1947.

CASE STUDY I

Nawal had just graduated from I.I.M., Bangalore and joined his father's small business, which employed 28 semi-skilled workers. After a week, his father, a retired government officer, called him and said, "Nawal, I have had a chance to observe your working with the men and women for the past few days. Although I hate to, I must say something. You are just too nice to people. I know they taught you human relations stuff at the I.I.M., but it just does not work here. I remember when the Hawthorne studies were first reported, everyone in the academic field got excited about them. But, believe me, there is more to managing people than just being nice to them."

Read the above case carefully and answer the questions below.

Questions

1. Do you think Nawal's father understood and interpreted the Hawthorne studies correctly?
2. If you were Nawal what would your reaction be to your father's comments?

—oo(O)oo—

CHAPTER 4

PLANNING FUNCTION OF MANAGEMENT

LEARNING OBJECTIVES

1. To understand planning, its nature and importance.
2. To know the planning process and stages involved in it.
3. To understand the principles of planning and features of a good plan.
4. To know about the relationship between planning and a changing environment.

Planning is the primary function of a manager. To get things done by others every manager has to plan. Planning is a basic requirement and important input of the management process. It helps to decide what is to be done, when, and by whom? Planning is the essence of the management process and has been attracting the attention of management thinkers since the early stages of development of management knowledge. Today, it is considered as a strategic area of management, especially in the context of the rapidly changing environment and globalisation of business operations.

DEFINITION

Simply, planning is regarded as a process of making decisions on what is to be done, when and how. Most management scholars and practitioners consider planning as a process of visualising or anticipating the future. It is not enough to have a vision of the future. It should be backed by ways of realising it. Broadly, planning is the process of determining objectives. Many stages are involved in the process of planning which have to be tackled in a logical sequence.

In the context of the globalisation of business operations, planning may be defined as a process of identifying the strengths and weaknesses of an organisation and matching them with environmental threats and opportunities by developing a suitable course of action. An exercise of this nature is known as strategic planning.

A few definitions of planning are given below:

> "Planning is the selecting and relating of facts and the making and using of assumptions regarding the future in the visualisation and formulation of proposed activities believed necessary to achieve desired results."—*Terry*
>
> "Planning is a process by which a manager looks to the future and discovers alternative courses of action open to him." —*Joseph Massie*
>
> "Plan is a trap laid to capture the future."—*Allen*
>
> "Planning is anticipating."—*Earl Strong*
>
> "Planning is deciding in advance what is to be done."—*Theo Haimann*
>
> "Planning is in essence the exercise of foresight."—*Hamilton Church*
>
> "Planning is deciding in advance what is to be done, that is, a plan is a projected course of action."—*Newman*
>
> "Planning is an intellectual process, the conscious determination of a course of action, the basing of decisions on purpose, facts and considered estimates."
> —*Koontz O'Donnel.*
>
> "Planning is a continuous process of making present entrepreneurial decisions (risk-taking) systematically and with best possible knowledge of their futurity, organising systematically the efforts needed to carry out these decisions and measuring the results of these decisions against the expectations through an organised systematic feedback."—*Peter Drucker*
>
> "Planning is the process of coping with uncertainty by formulating a future course of action to achieve specified results."—*Kreitner*

The key elements of planning are:

- Process of deciding in advance what is to be done, how, when and by whom.
- Logical thinking before doing.
- Process of visualising and anticipating the future by evaluating the past and assessing the present.
- Futurism and a sense of futurity is an integral part of planning.
- Process of determining objectives, discovering alternative courses of action and selecting suitable courses of action.

- Involves decision-making.
- Process of identifying strengths and weaknesses of the organisation and relating them to opportunities and threats arising out of the changing environment and discovering alternative courses of action.

The following features reflect the basic nature of planning:

(i) Planning is an Intellectual Activity

In every planning process, objectives are determined, future is visualised and forecasted, alternative courses of action are developed and finally a suitable course of action is selected for which managers require analytical abilities, imagination, judgement, creativity and innovativeness. Therefore, planning is considered an intellectual process.

(ii) Planning is a Primary Function of Management

The process of management starts with planning. It is only after planning various activities that the structure of the organisation is prepared. This is followed by staffing, directing and controlling. Without planning, there is little organising, staffing, directing and controlling.

(iii) Planning Involves Futurism

Plans are prepared to implement them in the future. The planning process calls for visualising the future with the help of analysis of past performance, and evaluation of the present position. Futurism has become an integral part of planning.

(iv) Planning Involves Decision-making

In the process of planning, after discovering various alternative courses of action, managers have to make a choice and select the best. For this purpose they have to take decisions.

(v) Planning is a Goal-oriented Process

At the very outset, managers determine objectives. It is to achieve these objectives that an action programme is formulated and implemented.

(vi) Planning is a Continuous Process

There is a continuity and regularity in the planning process. It is an on-going process having no definable end. A set of various plans made by managers have to be revised as per the changing environment. Managers keep a watch on the environment on a regular basis and revise plans in the light of changing situations.

(vii) Planning is All-pervasive

It is the prime mover of an organisation. By preparing and implementing various plans, different sets of activities and resources of an organisation are efficiently utilised to achieve predetermined objectives. Plans are made for various activities carried out by different departments. Planning is the basic function of every manager. A manager discharges his responsibility of directing and coordinating group efforts to seek objectives only by making sound plans and implementing them efficiently. Every manager, irrespective of his level and position, makes a plan.

However, the importance, nature and magnitude of planning depends on the level at which it is made. Corporate planning, at the top, is broad, fundamental and more strategic compared to departmental planning and plans made by first-line supervisors. The scope, extent and importance of planning tend to decrease as it descends downwards in the organisation.

The nature of the problem area and degree of delegation of authority also affects the coverage and scope of planning. For example, planning on vital matters affecting the survival and profitability of an organisation is usually done at a higher level.

Planning is also regarded as a critical variable for the survival, growth, development and diversification of organisational activities. It is found in practice that highly-developed and profitable organisations owe their success to sound planning and effectiveness in implementation.

The primacy and pervasiveness of planning may also be justified in terms of its crucial place in the hierarchy of management functions. All managerial functions like organising, staffing, directing and controlling are, by and large, follow-up functions.

Importance of Planning

The need and importance of planning can be judged on the basis of the following factors:

(i) Planning Determines the Future Destination of an Organisation

At the first stage of the planning process, the objectives of the organisation are determined. All the activities are directed and co-ordinated to accomplish objectives, thereby making the organisation a purposeful system with a predetermined destination.

(ii) Planning Makes the Activities of Employees Meaningful

A clear understanding of the objectives helps employees to know how their work is related to organisational goals and enables them to direct their efforts to make their contribution more valuable.

(iii) Planning Economises Operations

Activities are planned to reduce inefficiencies and wastage which leads to economy in operations. It improves the performance of other managerial functions like organising, staffing, directing and controlling by making the task of managing more effective.

(iv) Planning Helps in Reducing the Risk of Uncertainties

Uncertainties associated with the future are exposed by using the technique of forecasting which provides meaningful clues. Managers attempt to predict the future by identifying potential dangers and initiate action to reduce adverse effects.

(v) Planning Leads to the Discovery of New Ideas and Opportunities

Planning is an intellectual activity, involving the use of analytical, creative and innovative abilities which may throw up ideas and generate opportunities for profitable exploitation. The regular use of such abilities may inject dynamism into the management of the organisation (Figure 4.1).

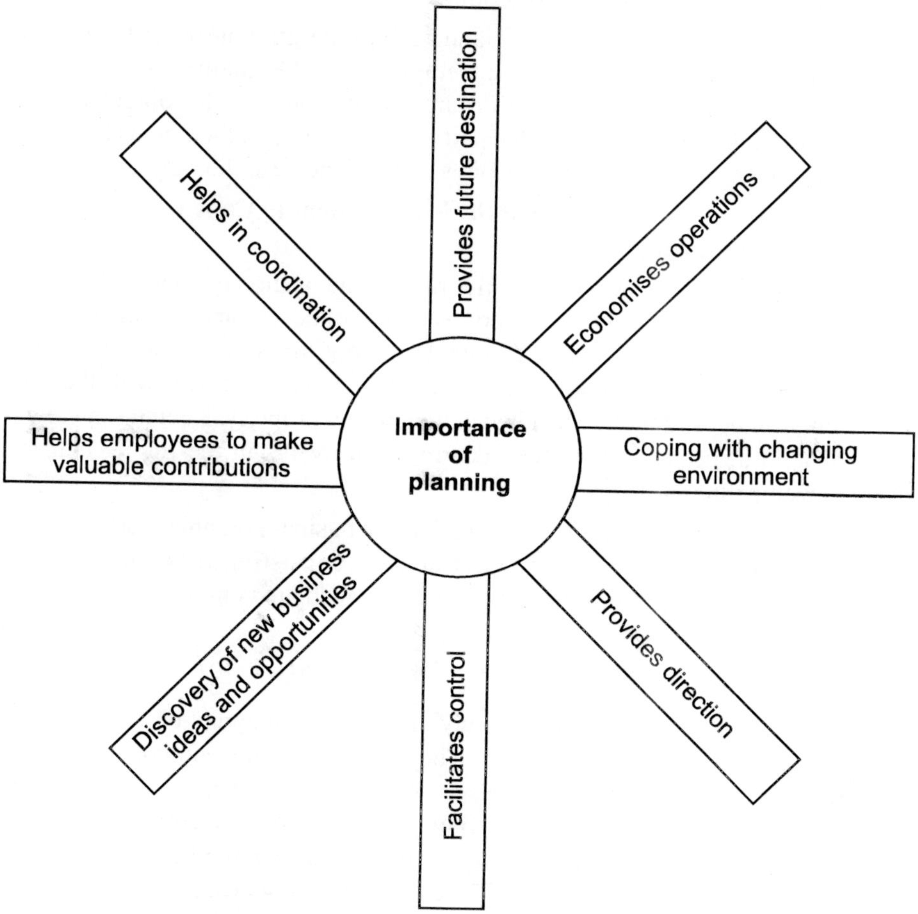

Figure 4.1. Importance of planning

(vi) Planning Facilitates Coordination

Plans are made by managers at different levels of the organisation which requires coordination. The corporate plan provides the guidelines and lays down the parameters for different departments. First-line supervisors plan within the departmental plan, thereby providing complete coordination of all activities from the lowest to the highest one.

(vii) Planning Facilitates Efficient Control

Control pre-supposes the existence of planning. Without planning, control has little meaning. The objectives serve as a base for control. Actual results are compared with objectives which also are a standard of performance. Deviations are sorted out and necessary remedial measures are taken to improve results.

(viii) Planning Provides Direction

The objectives laid down in planning become guiding posts for directing and mobilising the activities of employees. The qualities of leadership, motivation and communication are conditioned by the objectives. The knowledge of objectives on the part of employees and their contribution acts as a motivational force and inspires them to increase their efforts.

(ix) Planning is a Response of the Management to Cope with a Changing Environment

Planning enhances the capabilities of the organisation to cope with a rapidly changing environment. Managers keep track of developments which are likely to affect the future and take suitable, timely measures to deal with them. Without heroic planning efforts, the uncertainty associated with the future environment cannot be handled and managed properly. Keeping in view the degree of probability of the occurrence of events in the future, managers develop alternative plans.

The increased importance of planning for business organisations is a direct result of the fast-changing environment consisting of socio-economic, technological, political and legal factors which are complex and dynamic.

Relationship of Planning with other Management Functions

All managerial functions are closely inter-related and may be viewed as sub-systems or elements of management. They all account for and contribute to the achievement of organisational goals. In the process of management, five basic elements, planning, organising, staffing, directing and controlling are equally important. The primacy and pervasiveness of planning cannot be doubted because it helps to improve the efficiency of the entire managing process.

The process of management starts with planning, followed by organising, staffing, directing and controlling. Organising begins when planning determines objectives because, on the basis of these, organisational activities are enumerated and identified, divided and sub-divided, placed in different groups and finally, performance is sought.

The manner in which authority will be delegated, the degree of centralisation and decentralisation of authority, role and relationship among various departments and employees and design of the structure have to be meticulously planned.

In the event of changes in the business, strategies are altered and if required, the structure, roles and relationships within the organisation are re-defined to make it responsive. Planning makes this possible.

Staffing activities are carried out to contribute the maximum to the accomplishment of goals. The continuous review of the strength and quality of manpower in a changing environment is a part of the planning process. Sound plans are made, strategies formulated and programmes undertaken to acquire, develop and maintain human resources.

In the recent past, Indian organisations seeking foreign alliance experienced serious problems due to lack of proper planning of staffing functions.

The function of directing seems meaningless without planning. By familiarising employees with the objectives of the organisation, their activities and efforts are directed, guided, led and motivated to seek planned goals more efficiently.

Without planning, control is unthinkable. Planning provides the basic guidelines in the form of objectives, goals and targets, upon which the controlling mechanism is established. The process of controlling may be viewed as an extension of planning. Planning decides what is to be done, how, when and by whom it will be done while controlling ensures that each activity has been performed in a planned manner to achieve planned goals.

Plans are made not only for the activities and operations related to production and distribution but these are also prepared for managerial functions. Planning minimizes haphazard approaches, reduces duplication and overlapping, eliminates guesswork and makes activities purposeful and meaningful, helping the organisation to achieve the planned objectives.

Approaches to Planning

Managers adopt various approaches to planning based on the degree of participation, delegation of authority and required capabilities of lower level managers.

1. Top-down Approach

This is normally adopted in family-managed organisations or by traditional or conservative managers. In this approach, authority and responsibility for planning is centralised at the top. The top management formulates basic policies, determines corporate objectives, makes strategies and devises a course of action to achieve the objectives. On preparation, the plans are communicated to the managers at the lower level responsible for implementation. They have little say in planning but are involved only in implementation.

The organisation tends to be highly-centralised because managers at the higher level are more occupied with preparing plans and exercising final authority. Very little authority is delegated to lower level managers except for implementation of plans.

The top-down-approach is based on the assumption that managers working at higher levels are professionally qualified and well-experienced. However, it is found in practice that many organisations do adopt a modified and more refined form of this approach, either by involving lower level managers directly in the process or indirectly by seeking their suggestions and ideas. It is done to get the benefits of their involvement in execution.

2. Bottom-up Approach

This is based on the assumption that in planning, thinking and doing are closely related and both functions can be performed by the same managers. A higher degree of flexibility is maintained in planning in the bottom-up approach.

Accordingly, a rough draft or tentative proposal on various plans originate at the lower level and are communicated to higher level managers for review and final approval. However, it can be profitably used provided the managers, at the implementation level, have the requisite knowledge, awareness and creativity to undertake planning. The basic job of top executives is to unify and coordinate various sub-plans originating from lower levels. Considered as the 'participative approach' to planning, managers at lower levels are not confined to implementation only but are equally involved in initiating plans.

In the words of Alwin Brown, "it is impossible to separate all the planning from the duty of doing." Brown contended that planning is done most effectively by managers who have to carry it through.

3. Composite Approach

Combining the attributes of top-down and bottom-up approaches, the composite is more popular. Here, the top executives provide guidelines, parameters and limitations under which middle and lower level managers are expected to formulate tentative plans which are communicated upwards for review and approval. The authority for making plans rests with the top executives.

The composite approach offers the advantages of 'top down' and 'bottom up' approaches in as much as the managers at the action level are associated with the thinking process of planning and their involvement in thinking is regulated by prescribed guidelines and parameters.

4. Team Approach

It is always advisable to have as many managers as possible to participate in planning: the more active the managers are in planning, the more enthusiastic they will be in carrying out plans. In the team approach, the job of initiating plans is assigned to a team of managers from concerned areas. They do the spadework for preparing plans, initiate planning, identify the need and importance of plans, examine and analyse both internal as well as external environment, collect information and devise alternative courses of action. Finally, they formulate tentative proposals which are submitted to the chief executive under whose command they have been working. The team of managers works as a brain of the chief executive, suggesting and recommending proposals to him. However, the ultimate authority for approval lies with the chief executive.

The team approach has practical utility, especially when the task of preparing plans requires specialised knowledge of different areas.

In practice, organisations use a combination of approaches as per requirements. Nonetheless, it is evident that joint participation of subordinate managers in the planning process, in any form, is beneficial to the organisation.

ELEMENTS OF THE PLANNING PROCESS

Planning is an important sub-process of management and attracts the involvement of all managers. It has several elements, namely:

(i) To Identify the Need for Planning

Planning is a continuous process and all-pervasive in an organisation. Top managers have the responsibility of directing and mobilising resources as well as the efforts of employees to achieve planned goals. They are and should be sensitive to the need for planning. To make plans, an effective information and communication system is installed, authority is delegated to subordinate managers, decision-making centres are set up and connected with the information system and other actions are taken to seek the involvement of lower level managers.

(ii) Analysis of the Existing Internal Profile of the Organisation

Planning involves an assessment of the resource position, physical and human, of an organisation for realisation of objectives. Implementation of plans calls for utilisation of resources. But, if adequate resources are not available, the process of sound planning may be impaired. Consequently, the basic objective of analysing the current internal position of the organisation is to find the areas of strengths and weaknesses. Planning is undertaken to get the full advantage of the strengths of the organisation.

(iii) To Scan the External Environment

The external environment and its elements shape and condition the major plans of an organisation. Every organisation, to survive, succeed, grow and develop has to cope with the changing environment. To do so, necessary adjustments and modifications are made in relation to the existing set of managerial policies, procedures and goals. A changing environment may provide opportunities or pose new threats and challenges. By scanning the external environment, the required information is obtained for formulating the planning premises, known as 'informed assumptions.'

(iv) To Prepare a Statement of Objectives

The planning process is goal-oriented and plans are made and executed to achieve these goals. The objective may be defined as the future destination of the organisation or a desirable state of affairs which an organisation wants to achieve in the future.

This has been regarded as the first step in the planning process by Koontz O'Donnell, who has stated that it is only to achieve objectives that policies are formulated and procedures laid down, strategy is determined and a course of action is evolved. The objectives provide guidelines for vital decisions relating to resource allocation, schedule of work and nature of action. It is imperative that the objectives of planning are well-defined to avoid confusion and ambiguity.

(v) To Develop an Alternative Course of Action

There may be numerous courses of action to achieve an objective; some known to managers, others to be discovered. In the words of Koontz O'Donnell, "there is seldom a plan made for which reasonable alternatives do not exist." Before weighing alternatives and reaching a decision, it is wise to search for alternatives which may not be immediately apparent. Often, an alternative not immediately perceived may prove to be the most profitable way of undertaking a plan. Here, the experience of the manager and research and analysis undertaken by him may be useful.

(vi) To Evaluate Alternative Courses

It is more important to reduce the number of alternatives and choose the most promising one for the solution of a problem than finding new ones. This stage of planning virtually involves decision-making because managers have to decide upon a suitable course of action. The strong and weak points, associated with each course of action, are thoroughly examined. To make a decision, a course of action has to be evaluated in terms of cost involved, benefit to be derived, risk involved, availability of resources and long-term objectives of the organisation. In practice, these factors are mutually conflicting.

For instance, if the course of action is most profitable, it may involve maximum risk. Often, a course of action may be most profitable and less risky but the resources position may not allow it to operate. Therefore, due care must be exercised by planners to maintain a proper balance among these factors while selecting a suitable course of action.

(vii) Formulation of Derivatives Plan

Having decided upon a particular course of action, it is necessary to draw up detailed plans, including specific or operational plans, for each activity to be performed. Sometimes, a plan may be complex. It may have to be divided into sub-plans, known as derivative plans. With the help of these derivative plans, the main plan is implemented. For example, a plan of launching a new product in the market may be followed and implemented through various derivative plans such as sales promotion, physical distribution and advertising (Figure 4.2).

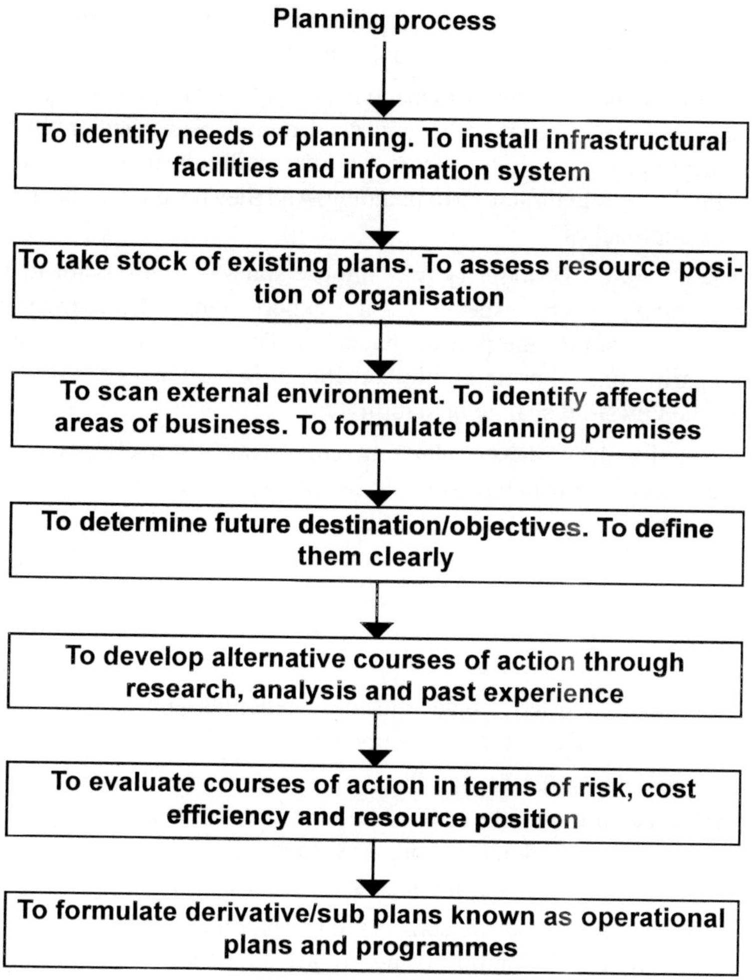

Figure 4.2. Showing Elements of Planning Process

Limitations of Planning

Managers encounter several barriers and difficulties in making and implementing plans despite the primacy of planning in the management process. While the difficulties may impede the planning process and reduce its usefulness, they cannot be taken as an excuse for not preparing adequate plans. Managers should develop awareness of these limitations. The major limitations faced by managers are described below:

(i) Planning involves futurism and the future is quite uncertain and complex and cannot be forecasted accurately. Managers must be aware that there is always a margin of error in forecasting.

(ii) Planning gives a false sense of security to managers vis-a-vis changes expected in the business environment.

(iii) Often, the philosophy of management may also impede the process of planning. Once managers become accustomed to a particular philosophy continued over a long period of time, it tends to impose internal inflexibility and limitation to planning. And they become hesitant to adopt new approaches.

(iv) The nature of the industry may impose some limitations for managers regarding planning, especially if it is experiencing rapid changes calling for dynamism on the part of managers. They may also find the job of preparing plans boring and less challenging particularly in an industry marked by slow change or stability.

(v) In practice, the process of planning remains no more useful, especially for those activities which require prompt attention, and any delay in making plans may complicate the situation.

(vi) The planning process encourages an element of inflexibility in the organisation because plans provide a ready framework within which managers have to function. Their initiative to develop new ones is discouraged.

(vii) The capital invested in plant and equipment puts a limit on the flexibility of planning. Once a huge investment is made, future planning is limited.

(viii) It stifles the initiative of subordinate managers because it is believed that if they are not allowed to take active part in planning and their role is confined to implementation, they do not get any opportunity to share experiences with senior managers.

(ix) Cost and time factors are considered as real limitations to planning. With regard to cost, it should not be, in any situation, more than the value of planning or benefits derived from it. Similarly, on some occasions, enough time may not be available to go through the entire planning process because planning is a time-consuming process. By the time a plan is made the situation may become more complicated.

(x) Plans have to operate in an external environment which keeps changing and is beyond the control of the organisation. In many situations, changes in the environment may render the plans inoperative and ineffective.

Features of Sound Planning

A sound plan must have the following characteristics:

(i) Plans are made and implemented to achieve objectives. The objectives must be well-defined, precisely interpreted and clearly followed by the employees and those involved in implementation. Lack of clarity may lead to chaos or disorder in the organisation.

(ii) Plans should be marked with a high degree of flexibility to enable modifications and refinements in accordance with the demands of the situation.

(iii) The plan should be reasonably economical because the cost involved in planning may limit its usefulness.

(iv) The plan should provide a sense of futurity to managers and attempt to anticipate the future.

(v) It should be pragmatic and practical.

(vi) It should attract wider participation of subordinate managers, especially those involved in implementation, to motivate them and seek their commitment on implementation.

(vii) Long- and short-term plans must be integrated in such a manner that the short range plan may contribute to long-range objectives.

Principles of Planning

Planning is a rational approach to the future. It is supported by a set of empirically-proved, inter-related principles. The following are some of the fundamental principles of planning:

(i) Principle of Contribution to Objectives

Managerial planning seeks to achieve pre-determined goals. The main purpose of preparing and implementing a plan is to facilitate the achievement of objectives. A plan should be prepared and put into operation to contribute the maximum to the accomplishment of objectives.

(ii) Principle of Primacy of Planning

In the process of management, planning precedes all other managerial functions like organising, staffing, directing and controlling which are, in fact, follow-up functions and performance of these depends on planning.

(iii) Principle of Planning Premises

Every plan is based on assumptions, known as planning premises, which relate to the anticipation of the future environment. In the words of Koontz O'Donnel, "the more the individuals charged with planning understand and agree to utilise consistent planning premises, the more coordinated enterprise planning will be."

(iv) Principle of Strategy and Policy Framework

If strategies and policies are understood, the more consistent and effective will be the framework of the entire plan. Clarity, in strategy and policy bring consistency and effectiveness to planning.

(v) Principle of Limiting Factor

At the time of choosing an appropriate course of action from among different alternatives, the limiting or critical factors must be recognised and taken into account. A limiting factor is one which makes accomplishment of objectives contingent to it, that is, without which goals cannot be met.

(vi) Principle of Commitment

Planning should cover a period of time which can be forecasted. The principle is used to determine the length of the planning period, taking into account the future risk and fulfilment of commitments.

(vii) Principle of Flexibility

Plans should be flexible to facilitate necessary modifications and changes in a situation of flux. The greater the flexibility in-built into plans, the lesser the danger of losses incurred through unexpected events. The cost of maintaining flexibility in plans should be weighed against its benefits.

(viii) Principle of Navigational Change

Managers should review events and expectations on a regular basis and redraw plans to maintain the course towards desired results. A navigational change can be brought about if plans have an in-built flexibility.

Planning and Environment

In a dynamic business environment, every organisation has to cope with the uncertainties of the external environment which are largely tackled through planning. Uncertainty may be defined as the unknown, unpredictable and random occurrence of an event and may be of three types. 'State uncertainty' implies that the environment or any of its elements may, or may not, change. 'Effect uncertainty' relates to the impact of an event on the functioning of an organisation. 'Response uncertainty' is the inability to predict the consequences of a particular decision, response or initiative.

Uncertainty in planning

Uncertainty has the following characteristics:

- The management experiences the problem of lack of required information and knowledge of making reliable estimates of the probable consequences of its decision and actions.
- The event occurs randomly without a set pattern and its happening cannot be predicted with accuracy.
- In the situation of multivariables, the relationship and interaction among them cannot be structured.
- The behaviour of the environment and its elements is beyond the comprehension of the management which cannot generate reliable and relevant information about it.
- The environment and its elements are conditioned by randomness, instability, complexity, diversity and turbulence.

The uncertainty experienced by managers in the process of planning may be classified as under:

(a) External uncertainty

(b) Internal uncertainty

(c) Uncertainty arising out of natural events and calamities.

(a) External Uncertainty

Related to external environment and its elements, beyond the control of the organisation. External uncertainty is mainly caused by the following factors:

(i) Political Factors

Political change occurring in environments such as change of ruling party, degree of political instability, ideology and attitude of a political party towards business, political morality and other factors.

(ii) Government Policies

The various policies and programmes of the government for regulating and controlling business activities and changes therein, may cause uncertainty. Examples are changes in fiscal, monetary, labour, import, export and other economic policies.

(iii) Economic Factors

The general economic condition to which an industry belongs and changes therein is also considered to be a cause of uncertainty.

(iv) Market Condition and Socio-cultural Factors

Demand dynamics, change in competition, customers' disposable income, habits and preference needs, changes in demand and supply position of goods and services and other resources such as labour, capital, raw materials, etc., fall in this category.

(v) Technological Changes

Changes in technological factors such as innovation in manufacturing process, development work and application of scientific and technological advancements may create uncertainty.

(b) Internal Uncertainty

Internal uncertainty arises from changes taking place in an internal environment of an organisation, either due to change in external environment or on account of some internal factors. The first kind of uncertainty is also known as derivative uncertainty because it arises out of changes in the external environment. Owing to these changes, the goals, policies, processes and strategies of the organisation may be affected. For example, the cost of operations may increase, utilisation of production capacity may be affected and availability of inputs, manpower, information, etc., may be disturbed.

The second type of uncertainty which is regarded as autonomous uncertainty may arise mainly due to breakdown in machinery, labour strike, power failure, incorrect decisions made by managers, ineffectiveness of managerial policies, etc.

(c) Natural Calamities

Calamities and events may affect the operations and overall functioning of an organisation. For example, due to droughts, floods, earthquakes and other natural phenomena, the supply of inputs and delivery of output may be affected adversely.

How to Cope with Uncertainty

A successful manager initiates action in response to uncertainties though these are beyond his control. A few general guidelines to cope with uncertainties are:

(i) By installing a management information system and using techniques of forecasting, relevant and reliable information can be generated on various elements of the external environment.

(ii) To check and regulate the occurrence of undesirable events and restrict its damage, both proactive and reactive measures may be initiated by adopting an adaptive philosophy of planning.

(iii) Decision making on various types of uncertainties faced by the organisation may be centralised with the top executive, who commands adequate resources and authority.

(iv) Sometimes, the satisfying philosophy based on conservatism, slow or no change, status quo and continuity may also be considered as one of the ways to face these uncertainties.

(v) Formulation of plans with a high degree of flexibility may be considered as one of the most effective devices or measures to cope with uncertainty and in reducing its adverse affects on the functioning of the organisation. Flexible plans should contain an alternative set of goals, strategies, and a course of action to be applied for a range of possible situations. As the situation changes, a new course of action may be followed in place of the old one which might have been rendered ineffective. One of the most important and desirable features of an organisational plan is flexibility.

In this regard, Koontz O'Donnell forwarded two important principles of planning, namely, flexibility and navigational principle. The principle of flexibility states that the more the flexibility inbuilt into plans, the less are the dangers of losses due to unexpected events.

However, the cost of flexibility should be weighed against the risk involved in future commitments. Flexible plans remain relevant in the event of a change in the environment. With the help of flexible plans, an organisation can change its direction without undue cost and friction. A flexible plan permits an organisation to move towards its future destination in the midst of environmental changes. However, a flexible plan involves cost. Inflexible plans are least costly.

Consequently, flexibility in planning should be restricted only to a critical variable or activity to reduce costs. For example, an alternative power system may be made available only to an operation theatre, casualty ward and intensive care unit of a hospital. As Koontz O'Donnell pointed out, flexibility is critical when the commitment is great and cannot be discharged in a short time. The cost of flexibility poses a limit to planning. Another limit to flexibility in planning is that options or alternatives incorporated in the plan cannot be kept open for a longer period of time.

For example, a student, who is an aspirant for a professional course of chartered accountancy, takes up a foundation course for company secretaryship as an alternative, in view of the growing competition for the former. The student can keep the option open only for a short time, that is, so long as he does not qualify for any course. The moment the student qualifies for one course, another option becomes invalid. Flexibility in planning tends to make a plan general in nature because of the inclusion of alternatives. Too much generality in a plan is neither desirable nor feasible, if the commitment is strong and specific. At the time of planning, the cost of flexibility should be weighed against the benefits.

Relevance of Planning in a Changing Environment

In view of the many limitations of planning and fast-changing environment, it is contended that planning has become a 'mere ritual.' This contention is based on the argument that plans are prepared to operate in a future environment which is full of uncertainties, diversities and complexities. Since behaviour and the nature of the environment cannot be forecast correctly, planning may be rendered a useless, empty and meaningless exercise.

A change in the environment may pose new challenges, difficulties and threats and the organisation may be left with no option but to drop the plan, a waste of precious resources. Usefulness of forecasting may be reduced due to lack of required resources and abilities on the part of managers to generate relevant and reliable information to formulate informed assumptions for planning. Plans are made in advance but, sometimes, there may be a big time-lag between formulation and implementation. Consequently, plans become outdated or inoperative when they reach the stage of execution, losing their value as a guideline for the future. It is inherent in the basic nature of planning that it consumes a lot of time. But in practice, many situations may be so complex and urgent that by the time the managers put them into a plan, the problem worsens. Such situations can be tackled by the manager more effectively on the basis of judgement and creativity rather than a rational process of planning.

Nevertheless, in the entire system of management, planning occupies primary place. A changing environment and uncertainties associated with it render planning useless. However, uncertainty has necessitated the concept of planning and its primacy and pervasiveness become more relevant in the event of uncertainty. Had there been no uncertainty, there would not be any need for planning. The basic philosophy of planning is based on the concept of faith in the future. Despite complexities and uncertainties involved in the future, planning provides some margin for managers so as to get the necessary clues regarding the future. It is the state of future uncertainty that forces the manager to act more carefully and take decisions with a sense of futurity so as to negotiate and compromise with it. Environmental uncertainties enable the manager to develop dynamism, creativity and innovativeness to make sound plans. In turn, planning provides a unifying basis for understanding the future behaviour of environmental factors and helps the manager to make projections, estimates and predictions. Thus, instead of getting scared and fearful of these uncertainties, managers should handle them efficiently by making flexible plans with proactive and reactive measures.

Role of Forecasting in Planning

Futurism has become an integral part of the planning process because plans are made to operate in the future. To get a systematic appraisal of the future environment, its behaviour and changes, managers must make relevant assumptions about it. These assumptions, known as planning premises, are based on forecasts of the future. Every decision made by managers involves some element of forecasting.

Forecasts may be defined as predictions, projections or estimates of future events or conditions in the environment in which plans operate. Since forecasting involves the use of sophisticated statistical analysis of the future, it provides an intellectual basis to formulate various plans. The techniques of forecasting aim at understanding various uncertainties and complexities associated with the environment. Forecasting does not render future conditions less complex and uncertain. It promotes a sense of confidence and competence among managers to make current decisions based on futurity as the techniques of forecasting are used for generating required, relevant and reliable information to formulate planning premises. Thus, forecasting always precedes the formulation of premises, known as 'informed assumptions' of planning.

According to Kreitner, forecasts may be of three types, that is, 'event outcome,' 'event timing' and 'time series' forecasts. Event outcome forecasts aim at predicting the outcome of events likely to occur in the future. Event timing forecasts seek to estimate the value of series of periodic data at a given period of time by making a trend analysis which is based on the assumption that past and present tendencies would continue in the future.

The techniques of forecasting may be used on the various elements and aspects of the general environment of business, for example, the future condition of the economy, prices, availability of various resources, changes in government policies towards business and socio-cultural variables. To prepare forecasts, various techniques of forecasting may be used such as judgement or intuitive forecasting, scenario analysis, survey, trend analysis and other statistical techniques.

Forecasting and Planning Premises

Since plans are implemented in a future uncertain environment, managers are required to formulate certain assumptions regarding those elements which may affect implementation. To generate necessary information required for formulating the premises, various techniques of forecasting are used. Every plan is based on these premises or assumptions which are formulated with the help of forecasting. Thus it makes forecasting an integral part of the planning process.

In other words, formulation of planning premises implies projecting and estimating future behaviour of those elements and variables which are likely to affect execution of the plan. These planning premises may be internal and external, tangible and intangible and controllable and uncontrollable. Internal premises include those variables that are within the organisation and related to the internal environment affecting implementation.

External premises are related to the external environment and its elements such as socio-cultural, economic, political, technological and legal factors. Some of the planning premises may be within the control of the organisation like internal environment, known as controllable premises, and others may be beyond the control of the organisation like government's policy, economic condition, changing socio-cultural pattern, etc. Tangible premises refer to factors, internal or external, that can be quantified in numerical terms. Intangible premises affect the implementation of the plan but are not quantifiable and visible such as motivation and morale of employers, consumer satisfaction, corporate image, etc. The basic nature, efficacy and implications of these premises can be understood with the help of the following example:

A company wants to launch a new product in the market after six months. The plan of launching a new product is based on certain assumptions or premises. These are mainly related to the internal and external environments. Quality, price, promotion and physical distribution are related to internal premises largely within the control of the organisation. But the government's policy regarding that product, competition, demand dynamics, changing pattern of consumption, etc., are related to the external environment, beyond the control of the organisation.

In the process of planning internal and controllable variables, assumptions regarding them are adjusted with external and uncontrollable variables to reduce the adverse affect to the minimum. For instance, the company cannot prevent other organisations from introducing a rival product but rivalry arising out of it can be faced by making necessary adjustments in internal premises to improve quality, reduce price or to spend more on sales promotion, etc.

It is evident that informed assumptions or premises provide a sound base for planning. It is advisable for managers to concentrate more on materially relevant and strategically significant premises to make planning more fruitful and economical.

SUMMARY

Planning is a basic function of management. Every manager has to plan to get things done by others. It is a process of determining objectives and finding the most efficient course of action to achieve them. It is a logical thinking before doing. It involves analysis, creativity, innovativeness and decision-making skills. It is an intellectual process involving futurism. Planning makes the activities of employees more meaningful, it economises business operations and reduces the risk of future uncertainties. It provides direction and facilitates; coordination and control. It also helps to cope with the changing environment.

All other managerial functions are closely related to planning. Without planning, there is little controlling, organising and direction. All these are largely dependent on planning.

Managers adopt various approaches to planning. They are top-down approach, bottom-up approach, composite approach and team approach. Top-down approach is popular in family-managed businesses wherein plans are prepared at a higher level and then communicated to lower levels for implementation. In the bottom-up approach, lower level managers participate in making plans. The composite approach is an attempt to get the benefits of both the above approaches.

The process of planning involves identifying the need for planning, analysing the internal profile of the organisation, scanning the external environment, preparing a statement of objectives, developing alternative courses of action, evaluating them and formulating derivative plans.

The process of planning is subject to certain limitations. They are that the future for which plans are prepared is uncertain, the process of planning is very lengthy, it involves some cost and time and the environment in which plans are implemented is ever changing and beyond the control of managers.

The concept of planning is based on certain principles. These are the principles of contribution, privacy, premises, policy framework, commitment, flexibility and navigational change. Plans are implemented in a future uncertain environment. These uncertainties may be external and internal as well. External uncertainties may include political factors, government policies, economic factors, market conditions and socio-cultural factors and technological factors.

To cope with these uncertainties MIS is installed, proactive and reactive measures are adopted, conservative philosophy is used and plans are made keeping in mind a higher degree of flexibility. The planning remains useful even in the event of future uncertainties. To adapt to the future, forecasting is done. It is a prediction, projection or estimates of future events in the environment in which plans will operate. Forecasting may be based on 'event outcome', 'event timing' and 'time series'.

Information plays a very important role in projecting the future environment. The manager uses variables, which are under his control to regulate external variables, which are beyond his control.

Internal variables include those variables that are internal to an organisation such as price, quality, finance available, management skill, etc. However, external variables include economic, political, socio-cultural, legal and technological factors.

In the process of planning, internal factors have to be adjusted with external factors to reduce an adverse effect. Thus, to compete in the market, which is an external factor, the quality, the price, the promotion and physical distribution have to be adjusted in such a way to generate profitable sales volume of that product.

OBJECTIVE TYPE QUESTIONS

Which of the following questions are correct and which are not? Give reasons for your answers.

1. Planning is a primary function of a manager.
2. Planning involves futurism.
3. Planning is a function of a higher-level manager.
4. Planning is a response of the management to cope with a changing environment.
5. Without planning, there is little controlling in the organisation.
6. A composite approach of planning is the best of all approaches.
7. Strategic planning is always made at the higher levels of an organisation.
8. Planning has become more of a ritual in the event of a rapidly changing environment.
9. The principle of navigational change implies recasting of planning in the light of new factors.
10. External variables are more important than internal variables in the event of implementation of plans.

TEST QUESTIONS

1. What is planning? Explain its importance in management.
2. Describe the philosophies of planning in detail.
3. Explain the various elements of the planning process.
4. Why is planning regarded as the pervasive function of managers?
5. Discuss the relationship of planning with other functions of management.

6. What purposes are served by planning? Outline the different approaches to planning.
7. Discuss the importance of forecasting as an element of planning.
8. Discuss the features of sound planning.
9. Describe the various principles of planning and explain the limitations of planning.
10. 'Planning is a mere ritual in fast-changing environment.' Comment.
11. Write short notes on:
    (a) Planning premises
    (b) Philosophies of planning
    (c) Planning is all-pervasive
    (d) Relevance of planning in a changing environment.

REFERENCES

Allen, L. A. *Management and Organisation*. Tokyo, Japan: McGraw-Hill, 1958.

Bhattacharya, S. *Corporate Planning*. India: Oxford and IBH Publishing Company, 1981.

Drucker, Peter F. *Managing for Results*. New York, U.S.A.: Harper & Row, 1964.

Granger, C. W. J. *Forecasting in Business and Economics*. New York, U.S.A.: Academic Press, 1980.

Haimann, Theo. *Professional Management*. New Delhi, India: Eurasia Publishing House, 1970.

Henkoff, Ronald. 'How to Plan for 1995'. *Fortune*, December 1990: 70.

Koontz, Harold and Heinz, Weihrich. *Essentials of Management*. India: Tata McGraw-Hill Publishing Company, 2001.

Kreitner, Robert. *Management*. Delhi, India: A.I.T.B.S. Publishers and Distributors, 1996.

Newman, William H. and Warren, E. K. *The Process of Management*. New Delhi, India: Prentice-Hall of India, 1988.

Steiner, G. A. and Miner, J. B. *Management Policy and Strategy*. New York, U.S.A.: McMillan, 1977.

Steiner, G. A. *Strategic Planning*. New York, U.S.A.: Free Press, 1979.

Taylor, Bernard. 'Corporate Planning for the 1990s: The New Frontiers'. *Long Range Planning,* 19 (December 1986), 13 to 18.

CASE STUDY I
Planning for a Miracle on 34th Street

"There's absolutely no reason for any reasonable person to worry about financial obligations". These were the confident words of R. H. Macy's CEO Edward S. Finkelstein in 1991. By April 1992, however, the $ 6.3 billion retailer had filed for Chapter 11 and Finkelstein was no longer CEO. Mounting debt, a lack of new equity and an antiquated operating system proved to be more imposing obstacles than initially expected.

Macy's, "The World Largest Store," was not yet ready to give in to defeat, however. Embracing a rather unorthodox idea, the directors placed the company's fate in the hands of two disparate co-CEOs: Myron 'Mike' Ullman III, a financial whiz and a relative newcomer to both Macy's and the retail industry, and Mark Handler, Finkelstein's protégé and a career-long Macy's merchandising executive. They were gambling on Ullman's ability to fix the numbers and Handler's skill in maintaining the company's image and revamping its product line.

Almost everything at Macy's was in need of repair: customer service, cost control, computer systems, even the type and price of its merchandise. Compounding the problem was the fact that almost all of Macy's competitors enjoyed substantial leads in all these areas. To make matters even worse, retailers everywhere were feeling the effects of penny-pinching consumers, and Macy's was no exception. A difficult road lay ahead for Ullman and Handler.

In November 1992, the duo released a five-year plan that would carry Macy's out of the red and back into the black. "We're not predicting 10 per cent sales growth and margins improving two points," said Ullman in his no-nonsense manner. "Our plan is realistic." In fact, the plan predicted slow sales for 1993 and did not project a return to previous cash flow levels until 1998. Macy's creditors were impressed by the down-to-earth plan and decided to lighten Macy's covenants and allow the company some breathing room.

Wasting no time, Ullman and Handler decided to shift the company's focus away from the high-priced, glitzy product line for which it had become famous to a new, more moderately priced line to appeal to the new wave of cost-conscious consumers. While some people claimed that such downscaling would cost Macy's its reputation as a fashion authority, the CEOs disagreed. "Moderate is a price point, not a fashion statement," Ullman asserted. "We can sell well-made stylish clothes that don't cost a fortune."

Case Study I continued

Case Study I continued

For example, Macy's began carrying Levi Strauss products again, after having dropped the brand in 1983 when Levi began to sell to competitors such as J. C. Penney's and Sears. At the time, Macy's had considered such retailers inferior and did not want to carry the same merchandise.

A change of heart came with the change in times. As Ullman explained, managers realised that "customers don't criticise us because they don't like the merchandise we carry". Rather, "We get criticised when we don't have what they want to buy when they come in to buy it." In order to remedy this problem, the CEO's implemented a new system referred to as the Buyer-Planner-Store, or BPS for short. "The buyer is the person who is going to shop the market and shop the competition," pointed out Jane Sanford, corporate senior vice president for BPS and MIS. "The buyer will get the best merchandise, the best price, and the best delivery. The planner will influence the quantities of the buys by the buyer and will track variations in customer response store by store. The store manager will pick up nuances in the store that we may miss—after all, this is the person walking the building." Such a system enables Macy's to plan for the customer.

While this represents a quantum leap from Macy's old system, the BPS is not a new idea. Specialty chains such as the Limited and the Gap have been using similar systems for years. Nevertheless, implementation of the system does demonstrate that Macy's finally waking up to the need for change. "When you had a buyer who was buying for eight or ten stores, back in the good old days," commented Handler, "he or she could make the distributions and still shop the market, and still do the advertising. But now we expect a buyer to deal with as many as 60 locations, the whole structure needs to be changed."

Attempting to improve customer service and store layout, Ullman and Handler installed a new satellite network to connect suppliers and salespeople, similar to the systems already in place in companies such as Home Depot and Dayton Hudson. Fashion designer Donna Karan, for instance, can inform people how best to coordinate her clothing and accessories for store display. Moreover, the satellite linkup permits Macy's executives to talk directly to their employees about issues or concerns.

In addition, Macy's has taken a step ahead of the competition in what may prove to be the most profitable and successful portion of the CEOs' plan: TV Macy's. Slated to begin in the fall of 1994, TV Macy's is a 24-hour cable channel selling Macy's own private-label apparel, housewares, and other items in addition to national brand products. While rivals such as Saks Fifth Avenue have experimented with one- or two-hour

Case Study I continued

Case Study I continued

spots on QVC or Home Shopping Network (BSN), TV Macy's will be the first channel devoted entirely to a single retailer. The channel, which will compete directly with HSN and QVC, hopes to tap into the rapidly expanding $ 2.25 billion home shopping market. In addition, it will serve to familiarise home viewers with Macy's products and provide access to those products to people not located near a Macy's store. Retail consultant Isaac Lagando estimates that the channel could generate upwards of $ 250 million in sales by its fourth year.

While Macy's is far from out of the woods, it appears that under the new direction of its co-CEOs, the 137-year-old retailing chain is at least on the right path. "This has been a very painful exercise," admits Ullman. "We've trailed the industry. But we're trying to return to a leadership position." Considering that Macy's headquarters store is on 34th Street in New York, anything is possible.

Case Questions

1. What steps have the CEOs taken to set realistic goals?
2. Analyse the CEOs' strategy according to the Porter framework.
3. What kind of planning and strategy techniques could Finkelstein have used to prevent the situation that the CEOs confronted when they took over?
4. What planning and strategic measures would you recommend?
5. How does TV Macy's fit into the company's overall strategy for survival?

CASE STUDY II

Environmental Forecasting at Holiday Inns, Inc.

Holiday Inns, Inc. uses several forecasting techniques to project changes in its remote and operating environments that are of major importance to the firm's future strategic position. The greatest emphasis, even at the corporate level, is on environmental forecasting for hospitality-related factors. The primary environmental variables emphasised include the following factors:

1. Customer
2. Social
3. Technological
4. Competition

Exhibit 1 summarises some of the forecasting techniques in terms of their focus relative to these key environmental factors.

Case Study II continued

Case Study II continued

EXHIBIT 4.1: ENVIRONMENTAL FORECASTING AT HOLIDAY INNS, INC.

Main environmental factors	Forecasting techniques		
	Trend analysis	Surveys scenarios	Judgement/
Customers	Changing demographic profile. Specific HI guest characteristics. Historical occupancy rate cycles	Changing consumer preferences. Perceptions and brand recognition of HI	Future travel patterns and destination areas
Social	Baby boom generation. Household composition. Women's changing role. Use of leisure time	(little use)	Worldwide status of the travel industry
Technology	Energy-saving technology especially in terms of automobile and hotel operation. Gas prices and impact on vacation travel.	(little use)	Future travel modes. Computer usage in property management. Communication, especially satellite developments.
Competition	Size and growth of competitors. Location emphasis (regions? type of location?) Key price/value available from competition.	Level of consumer name recognition. Consumer image and brand preference	When competitors represent key threat to aspects of HI operations.

To help understand forecasts and how they might be useful, a few items particularly relevant to the hotel business in Exhibit 1 are illustrated below.

In better managing properties on a weekly basis to ensure operating margins are maintained, projected occupancy cycles based on historical trends can be quite helpful from the corporate level (planning cash flows) to the individual hotel level (budgeting and scheduling).

Trend analysis, surveys and judgemental scenarios about changing customer profiles and social characteristics constitute the major forecasting emphasis at Holiday Inns. Using these techniques, the following forecasts have been made about customer and social characteristics:

Case Study II continued

Case Study II continued

- Fewer and later marriages mean that HI's customer base has broadened to include a greater concentration of single persons, couples, and business people with greater freedom to travel.
- The demographic characteristics of the typical hotel, restaurant and casino guests are virtually identical: age 24 to 49, income over $ 30,000, with a preference for reliable and quality service instead of the lowest price.
- In three out of four instances, HI guests were male, but the trend to more women travellers is steadily growing.
- The movement of the baby boom generation through the prime travelling age (25 to 45) over the next 15 years suggests unprecedented growth opportunity in the hospitality business.

—oo(O)oo—

CHAPTER 5

PLANS: TYPES AND TECHNIQUES

LEARNING OBJECTIVES

1. To learn about single-use and standing plan.
2. To understand the distinction between policies and strategies, policies and procedures and objective and strategy.
3. To know the various types of planning, particularly strategic and long term planning.
4. To have a thorough knowledge of M.B.O.

To provide guidance to managers to make decisions, take action and solve problems, various plans are drawn up. These plans help managers to manage day-to-day affairs, utilise resources of the organisation efficiently and to regulate the working behaviour of subordinates.

Some of the plans provide a unifying and consistent base for managerial decisions and action. These may be grouped as single use plans and standing plans.

SINGLE USE PLANS

Designed for achieving objectives in a specific situation, single use plans are basically developed for solving non-repetitive, novel and unique problems. They arc tailored to fit specific situations and once the objectives are achieved, the plans become useless and outdated. Single use plans include objectives, strategies, programmes and budgets (Figure 5.1).

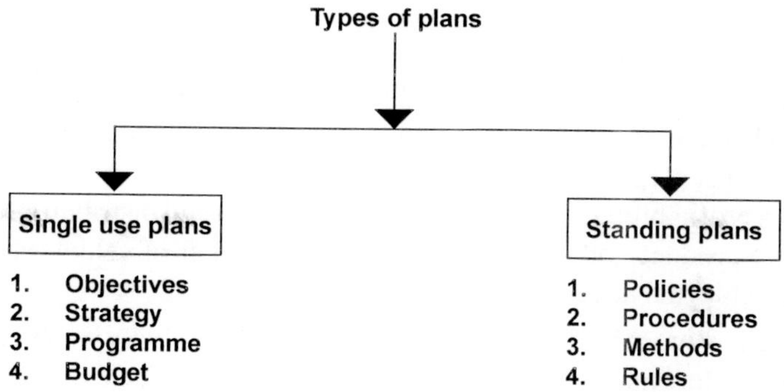

Figure 5.1. Type of Plans

TYPES OF PLANS

- Objective: Future destination or desirable state of affairs.
- Strategy: Course of action developed by relating strengths and weaknesses of an organisation with opportunities and threats arising out of the changing environment.
- Programme: Network of policies, procedures, rules and budgets designed to meet specific situations and all other needful actions required for implementing a given course of action.
- Budget: Numerical expression of plan in terms of expected revenue and expenditure over a period of time.
- Policies: General statement that guides decision-making.
- Procedure: Administrative action guide, setting chronological sequence for action.
- Method: Detailed manner in which specific activity will be performed.
- Rules: Directives for regulating and controlling the working behaviour of employees.

OBJECTIVES

Objectives or goals may be defined as a future destination or desired state of affairs that the organisation wants to attain. They represent not the end point of planning but future destinations towards which other functions of management such as organising, staffing, directing and controlling are directed. These objectives constitute the basic plan of the organisation, involving the planning process and represent future direction towards which the organisation has to move in. Without objectives, meaningful planning cannot be done. The objectives of an organisation are determined at the outset of planning. It is the basic responsibility of managers because the formulation of other plans like policy, strategy, rules, budgets, etc., to a large extent depends on objectives.

The objectives should be stated as clearly as possible so that each employee of the organisation can understand them. These objectives may be determined for the organisation as a whole, for an individual department or a division of it. But they should be coordinated in a manner that departmental goals may contribute to organisational or corporate goals. For example, if the corporate goal of an automobile company is profitability, so the goals of the production and distribution departments would be to produce and distribute the required number of vehicles over a period of time to achieve that objective of profitability.

In practice, organisations face the problem of multiplicity of objectives due to the inherent nature and philosophy of management. Nevertheless, they are made in a matrix of mutually supportive goals to reduce ambiguity and conflict.

In the words of Theo Haimann, "the real difficulty is not so much in determining the goals and the objectives; the real difficulty is in deciding how to balance the various objectives."

The organisational objectives are basic plans offering many advantages. They legitimise the very existence of the organisation, provide a sense of direction, a basis for unified planning, source of motivation for the employees, means of co-ordination and help in effective control.

STRATEGY

The term 'strategy' has been customarily used in respect of army organisations and games. But in view of growing competition and a rapidly changing environment, it has become equally relevant for business organisations. Strategy may be defined as a unified, comprehensive and integrated action plan designed to achieve specific objectives in the event of difficulty. It is concerned with the direction in which various resources of the organisation will be mobilised and utilised for maximising the chance of accomplishing specific objectives in a disturbed state of affairs.

According to Anthony, strategy results from "the process of deciding on objectives of the organisation, on changes in these objectives, on the resources used to attain these objectives, on the policies that are to govern the acquisition and use and disposition of these resources." This definition reveals that strategy like other plans flows from the objectives of an organisation and is related to acquisition, mobilisation and utilisation of resources to achieve changed objectives.

Strategy may be considered as an action plan, initiative or response of an organisation for seeking the achievement of the objectives in a changed specific situation. For example, Pepsi and Coca Cola are competitors in the soft drinks market. If Pepsi reduces the price of its products in the market, the counter-plan, that is, reaction, initiative or response of Coca-Cola to maintain its market share may be considered as strategy. Strategy is an organisational response in the form of deploying, mobilising and utilising its resources and strength, either to face problems or challenges arising out of the changing environment or to exploit opportunities provided by it. In other words, it is a set of moves and counter moves to be used by an organisation to get over a problematic situation by restricting rival organisations.

The following characteristics of strategy are evident:

(i) Strategy is a comprehensive and integrated action plan drawn to achieve objectives in a changed situation which is specific and novel in nature.

(ii) Strategies are basically formulated not only based on objectives to be pursued but based on careful situational analysis of the organisation and its environment.

(iii) Strategy aims at deploying, mobilising and utilising limited resources for maximising chances of achieving objectives in the event of difficulties.

(iv) Strategies are formulated to handle changes arising out of the environment. It ensures allocation of resources so as to exploit new opportunities profitably.

(v) Strategy is flexible and dynamic in nature because it is formulated to cope with the changing business environment and maintain the survival, profitability, growth and development of the organisation.

(vi) Strategies are usually drawn for a long period of time but it has short-term implications also.

(vii) Strategies, to a large extent, are imposed externally by the government, trade unions, competitors and trade associations in the form of regulations, agreements, informal understandings and many other conditions.

(viii) Strategy is regarded as 'interpretative planning' because it is formulated for the purpose of interpreting the meaning of other policies.

Strategies are formulated at the top level, known as corporate strategies, dealing with matters of vital importance for the survival, profitability, existence, growth and development of an organisation. However, middle and lower level managers are also associated in the process of formulating operational strategies at divisional and functional levels. The corporate strategies provide a broad framework to negotiate with the external environment, especially in the event of changes taking place in it.

Formulation of Strategy

Because of the statement of objectives, top managers formulate corporate strategy giving a general explanation as to how organisational objectives are to be achieved. These strategies are drawn from a careful and intelligent situational analysis of an organisation and its external environment.

Situational analysis, alternatively known as SWOT analysis, may be defined as a technique for matching organisational strengths and weaknesses with environmental opportunities and threats to determine the right course of action.

To discover opportunities and threats arising out of a changing environment, it is to be thoroughly scanned by using various techniques of forecasting. For this purpose, managers study shifts in the economy, recent innovations, market dynamics, growth of competition, availability of labour and other demographic shifts like education, disposable income, age, etc. Due care should be exercised by managers at the time of perceiving opportunities, potential threats and challenges because opportunities may turn out to be threats and vice versa.

After having scanned the external environment to identify opportunities and threats, the second phase of strategy formulation is to prepare a capability profile. This refers to a detailed analysis of the strengths and weaknesses of the organisation. Kreitner identified the following capability profile for today's organisations:

- Quick response to market trends
- Rapid product development
- Rapid production and delivery
- Continuous cost reduction
- Continuous improvement of process, human resources and products
- Greater flexibility of operation.

On the basis of matching organisational strengths and weaknesses with environmental opportunities and threats and designing various combinations or trade-offs, several strategic action plans may be developed. For example, after the entry of two giant multinationals, Pepsi and Coca Cola, the survival of other organisations engaged in the soft drinks market has been threatened. In order to maintain survival, they can develop many alternative strategies such as to seek alliances with any one of these multinationals, to make drastic changes in production and distribution processes so as to make them cost effective, to import required technology and lastly, to form a big organisation by integrating all small organisations engaged in the business.

The development of alternative strategies may pave the way for their evaluation in terms of the time factor, risk involved, cost and resource position of the organisation. By comparing alternative strategies, the most suitable one is selected and implemented. In order to evaluate the appropriateness of a particular alternative strategy, several factors may be taken into account by managers such as consistency with other plans matching with the environment, feasibility, practicability and degree of risk and appropriateness in terms of time and speed.

PROGRAMMES

A programme is a single-use plan, which refers to the outline of plans of work to be carried out in a proper sequence to achieve specific objectives. It may be considered a complex network of policies, procedures, methods, rules and budget designed to meet specific situations to achieve some objectives. In preparing a programme, task assignment is made, resources are allocated and requisite actions are initiated to carry out a given course of action. Programmes are usually supported by capital budgets. Once the pre-determined goal of a programme is achieved, it automatically comes to an end.

Programmes may be major or minor. Major programmes are usually in the form of a basic plan, initiated at the higher level of the organisation. Such programmes are prepared on vital matters concerning the survival and profitability of the organisation such as programme of extension, diversification, modernisation, etc. Minor programmes are developed on matters relating to day-to-day functioning of the organisation such as training, sales promotion and others, derived from major programmes.

The main features of programmes are that they are single-use; different programmes are to be prepared for different situations. Secondly, they aim at providing a detailed network of goals, policies, procedures and rules, supported by expenditure budgets. Thirdly, programmes are derived from corporate objectives. Lastly, it is an action plan, indicating a logical sequence in which various activities are performed for implementing it.

BUDGET

A budget is a single-use plan, which expresses anticipated results in numerical terms. A budget may be defined as an estimate of future needs arranged in an orderly basis, covering some or all activities of an enterprise for a definite period of time. It is a statement of expected results expressed in numerical terms over a specific period of time. Though a budget is commonly considered an important device of controlling, it is a type of a plan with a difference that it is expressed in quantitative terms, that is, rupees, person-hours, machine-hours, units of production, etc.

A budget may be prepared either for all activities undertaken and performed in an organisation or for specific operations and items such as expense budget, cash budget, sales budget, capital budget and production budget. Since the budget is a statement of expected results in numerical terms, often it is considered to be a part of control. However, it is to be noted that preparation of budget is a planning process because it is based on certain presumptions, like other plans, and has to be made for the future. In so far as its implementation is concerned, it is a controlling device.

In the words of Theo Haimann, "while budget-making is planning, budget-administration is controlling." A budget furnishes budgetary standards against which actual results are compared. In other words, it is a planning instrument used by managers to evaluate the success of a plan.

STANDING PLAN

Standing plans are usually made for a longer period of time and are applied repeatedly to various situations. They are formulated to handle similar types of problems and situations and are considered as a ready reference for solving problems. They provide a course of action, broad guidelines and a framework of parameters and constraints within which the manager takes decisions and initiates action. These plans may be used as a device for achieving coordination, to bring uniformity in action and maintain consistency with regard to the decision-making behaviour of managers.

Standing plans are prepared in advance and aim at handling repetitive and recurring problems faced by managers in day-to-day operations. They include policies, procedures, methods and rules. These plans are considered as a labour-saving device because whenever a problem of a recurring nature arises, managers solve it by applying a predetermined plan, without loss of time and effort. It also facilitates the delegation of authority to lower level managers, without loss of control.

Standing plans reduce the personal bias, likes and dislikes of managers because they have to solve the problem and tackle the situation by applying predetermined policies and procedures. In addition, standing plans provide criteria for evaluating the performance of managers in terms of their understanding, application and observance of these plans in the management of organisational affairs.

POLICIES

To manage the affairs of an organisation, managers have to make decisions on a regular basis. To control and regulate their decision-making, behavioural policies are formulated. Policies are general statements formulated by the organisation to guide managers in decision-making. Policies indicate the general attitude, intention and approach of the organisation in relation to certain specific matters concerning outsiders. The term 'policy' has been defined by Koontz O'Donnell, Beach and Allen in a similar manner. Koontz O'Donnell defines policy as a "general statement or understanding that guides thinking in decision-making." Beach describes it as "a pattern of direction for the guidance of those who carry responsibility for the management of activities of the enterprise." In the words of Allen: "Policies are standing decisions made to ensure uniform action in the handling of repetitive problems and questions that are significant to the organisation at large."

These definitions place emphasis on the basic nature of the plan, that is, policies are general statements and guidelines, which guide the thinking as well as action of managers. However, Davis has defined it in broader terms as "a business policy, essentially a principle or group of related principles with their consequent rules of action that conditions and governs the successful achievement of certain business objectives towards which they are directed." Here, the importance of policies, as a set of principles to be used for efficient accomplishment of objectives, has been highlighted.

The policies provide general guidelines and parameters within which managers have to make decisions consistent with objectives. The policies pre-decide issues, avoid confusion and provide a unified framework for other plans.

An organisation formulates policies in respect of various areas of operations such as production, distribution, finance, purchase, etc.

The policies of an organisation may be in writing or implied from conventions, practices, traditions, precedence behaviour of managers and philosophy of the organisation, reflected in documents like charter, memorandum, etc. However, normally, policies are written and communicated to managers to avoid confusion and provide a ready reference. But they do not provide ready-made decisions nor prescribe how managers will take decisions and implement them.

A guide to thinking and decision-making, policies should have an adequate degree of flexibility and allow discretion to managers. The idea is to regulate the decision-making behaviour of the managers as well as provide them an opportunity to use their skill, experience and talent.

Generally, policies are formulated at the top level on major and vital matters. These are known as corporate policies and are operationalised at the middle level; numerous minor policies are derived from it. On the basis of origin, policies may be of three types, namely, originated, imposed and appealed.

Originated policy is formulated by managers at the top, who visualise the need of formulating an overall policy. Within the framework of the overall policies, several minor ones are devised to deal with less important operations or activities at lower levels of management.

Sometimes, policies originate at lower levels, particularly at operating or supervisory level and travel upwards for final sanction and approval. In such cases, due weightage is given to the suggestions of the supervisory level managers.

Policies may also be imposed by the various elements of the external environment such as trade unions, government regulations and informal agreements of trade associations. They are known as imposed policies, for example, labour and taxation policies and agreements arising out of collective bargaining. To cope with some specific exceptional situations, wherein an existing set of policies is not adequate, a new policy may be formulated by managers at the higher level at the request of subordinate managers. Such policies are known as appealed policies and are normally formulated to solve current problems. They are revised to cope with the changing environment and matching corporate policies. Periodic reviews are undertaken to integrate various policies and remove contradictions arising out of practical use.

A number of factors influence the process of policy formulation such as objectives, philosophy and values of management, availability of resources, group pressure, environmental dynamics and legal issues.

A sound policy should be based on the following features:

- All major areas of functioning of an organisation should be represented by clear and definite policies.
- The policies of the organisation should be related to objectives and contribute to its accomplishment.
- The policies should be communicated to all managers of the organisation.
- Policies should be practical and easily understandable by the manager.
- An adequate degree of flexibility should be maintained in policies and, at the same time, they should remain stable over a period of time.

- Policies dealing with various areas of operations and activities should be in complete agreement and consistency.
- The policies to be efficacious should be socially sanctioned, ethically sound, and legally valid.
- Periodic reviews should be undertaken to make policies up-to-date and responsive to existing situations.
- The policies should be based on the principles of equity, fairness and reasonableness.
- It must specify broad limitations of its scope of action.

Objectives and Policies

The basic plans of an organisation are closely related to each other. Nonetheless, the following points of difference between objectives and policies are noteworthy:

(i) Objectives may be defined as the future destination or desired state of affairs which an organisation wants to achieve. Policies are means to achieve them. Policies contribute to objectives and maintain consistency with them.

(ii) Objectives may be general, justifying the scope of operations and activities. They are in the form of expectations and intentions. Policies are very specific and clear in nature dealing with an area of operation or smaller operations within that area. Policies give meaning and content to objectives and spell out their implications.

(iii) The organisation may have short and long-term objectives, but policies do not have a time dimension.

(iv) Objectives are meant to be achieved while policies are followed by managers as a guide to decision-making.

(v) Objectives are basic and critical for the existence of an organisation and to legitimise its existence. However, an organisation can exist without policies.

(vi) Objectives occupy a key position in the hierarchy of plans in an organisation. Policies have a lower place as a means to achieve objectives.

Strategies and Policies

The following are the differences between strategies and policies:

(i) Strategies are an intensive course of action, designed to tackle specific situations and achieve objectives but policies may be considered as a general statement for providing guidance to decision-makers.

(ii) Strategies relate organisational strengths and weaknesses with opportunities and threats arising out of the external environment. The idea is to tap opportunities in the areas of strengths. Policies exhibit the attitude and approach of an organisation on important matters and issues concerning organisational functioning.

(iii) Strategies are aimed at providing initiative, move or counter-move or response to the changing environment. Policies deal with areas of strategies, which require decisions and provide guidance and direction.

(iv) Strategies are single-use plans and designed to suit specific situations. Policies remain valid for situations or problems, which are repetitive in nature.

(v) The term 'strategy' has its origin in army organisations and games which require intelligent deployment of various resources to defeat the enemy or rival team. Policies deal with managerial decision-making and provide ready reference and guidance.

(vi) In the hierarchy of plans of an organisation, strategies are considered to be superior, broad and occupy a higher place as compared to policies which are supportive in nature.

PROCEDURES

To implement decisions, actions are initiated. Actions require guidelines that are provided by procedures. Procedures may be defined as an administrative action guide, prescribing a sequence in which various activities are to be performed.

Procedures determine the exact manner in which a certain activity must be performed. In the words of Koontz O'Donnell, "the essence of procedure is chronological sequence of required actions." Every manager has to follow prescribed procedures; top executives are no exception. Procedures are very rigid and do not leave scope for individual judgement.

Procedures are formulated on the basis of research and analysis of the various components of the work to be done. Related to action, they mostly originate at the lower level. Though procedures are a type of organisational plan, they have a significant role in the operational functioning of an organisation. In day-to-day functioning, they contribute in the following manner:

- Once a procedure is established for doing a particular activity, every manager follows it and ultimately, it ensures uniformity in performance and action.
- Procedures help in standardising and streamlining day-to-day activities to maintain smoothness in the functioning of the organisation.
- A set of procedures laid down for doing various activities facilitates implementation of decisions and policies of the organisation.
- They help in expediting and accelerating the performance of administrative action, contributing to the smooth functioning of the organisation.

- Procedures are prescribed for various activities to facilitate coordination.
- Procedures encourage delegation of authority to lower level managers because procedure-based activities can easily be delegated to the administrative staff to ensure they will perform the activities according to procedure and will take less time of superiors.

Policies and Procedures

Even though policies and procedures belong to the category of standing plans and have repeated applications, they can be differentiated on the following grounds:

(i) Policies are general statements providing guidance to managers in decision-making but procedures are regarded as detailed guidelines for performing various activities.

(ii) Compared to procedures, policies are flexible, leaving scope for managers for using experience, expertise and skill within prescribed limits. Procedures are more deterministic and rigid, leaving little scope for discretion to be used by managers.

(iii) Policies are related to the functional aspects of management dealing with decision-making, problem-solving and diffusing crises. Procedures deal with operational or administrative management relating to the implementation of decisions and performance of various activities.

(iv) Policies are, by and large, formulated by top management. Procedures are determined by managers at lower levels concerned with execution.

(v) Policies state relationships and fill the gap between the objectives and their accomplishment. Procedures are more concerned with activity and result or outcome.

(vi) In the hierarchy of organisational plans, policies occupy a higher position as compared to procedures.

(vii) The policies of an organisation are formulated on the basis of its objectives. Procedures are determined on the basis of study and analysis of work to be performed to implement decisions.

(viii) Policy documents encourage initiative on the part of managers by providing a higher degree of freedom to them. Procedures stifle innovativeness because they are very rigid and prescribe the manner in which an activity is to be performed.

METHODS

Methods provide details about a particular operation or activity. They prescribe the exact manner in which the operation will be performed, are more detailed and specific in dealing with a specific activity. Methods may be defined as a manual or mechanical means to perform a particular operation.

Methods may be viewed as specific, more detailed, and a rational means of simplifying and standardising work. The need and importance of determining the best method of doing things have been highlighted by Taylor in the approach to scientific management.

The use of scientific methods to perform various operations may lead to higher efficiency, more production and less fatigue on the part of workers. In brief, methods are based on research and analysis, require a high degree of standardisation and are more detailed but limited in scope as compared to procedures.

In a modern organisation, methods are determined for not only activities and operations to be performed by workers but are also considered desirable for clerical, administrative and managerial tasks and activities.

RULES

To regulate and control the working behaviour of employees and their performance, certain rules are framed by the organisation, defined as a specific statement or set of directives which employees are expected to comply with while performing an activity. They indicate acceptable limits or patterns of human behaviour in an organisation. They are made in writing to avoid confusion and are impersonal in nature.

While applying the rules, no personal bias or likes or dislikes or personal judgement is permitted. Rules are very precise, specific and clear, leaving no scope for confusion and controversy. They are determined in respect of behaviour and performance of employees as well as other functional and operational areas, including employment rules like leave, transfer, promotion, etc.

The essence of a rule is that it reflects a managerial decision, whether certain action is to be taken or not. The rules are very rigid and leave no scope for discretion and deviation. Non-compliance of rules attracts punishment. The rules are enforced for maintaining discipline among employees, and averting situations of disorder and chaos in an organisation. The observance of rules by employees leads to higher efficiency and smooth functioning. They create a sense of security and safety and reduce the need for close supervision.

However, rules are not free from drawbacks and pitfalls. In the presence of rules, every matter is to be treated according to the rules, leaving no scope for considering of individual needs and demands of the situation. Similarly, too much emphasis on the rules increases red tape and individual initiative, innovativeness and creativity get a lower priority. Proactive enforcement of rules may lead to tyranny or coercion, which has a negative impact on the behavioural pattern of employees.

TYPES OF PLANNING

Planning is all-pervasive. Yet, on the basis of importance, coverage, scope and time dimensions, it may be classified as under:

1. Corporate Planning

This term is used for planning undertaken by top managers for the whole organisation. It is a process of determining the overall objectives and discovering courses of actions for achieving them. It is broad and general in nature and scope. It lays down basic objectives, strategy, and policies to be pursued by managers for the whole organisation.

Corporate planning covers and integrates all those major and vital matters and issues that are directly concerned with the survival, profitability, growth and development of an organisation such as launching of a new product, switching to new technology, location decisions, designing a structure and making it in conformity with other plans of the organisation, diversification of organisational activities, etc.

Corporate planning is considered as a basic approach to the overall management of an organisation because it provides criteria for making managerial decisions regarding deployment and utilisation of resources and sets the necessary guidelines and frame of reference for middle and lower level managers.

2. Operational or Tactical Planning

Operational planning involves the conversion of corporate plans into detailed and specific ones, dealing with various activities. An individual activity generally does not take too long a time. An operational plan is prepared for a short period, less than a year, and is also known as a tactical or action plan because it divides corporate, strategic and long-term planning into various sub-plans and programmes.

Operational planning is done at the departmental, divisional and operative levels of an organisation that mainly deals with the performance of operations within the framework provided by broader plans. It directly helps in coordinating the various activities at the lower level with higher level activities and decisions.

Operational planning helps in allocating activities and resources to managers at lower levels, delegating authority to them and making them accountable for results. With the help of operational planning, specific and tangible goals for shorter periods of time are determined and accomplished which ultimately contribute to the achievement of overall objectives.

It is more structured and rational and is prepared for a short period of time that can be visualised and forecasted by the managers with confidence. It facilitates participation and involvement of lower level managers making them committed to the execution of plans.

Even so, the process of operational planning seems to be difficult because goals are determined and integrated at various lower levels. Inter-departmental conflicts have to be resolved and control devices developed to ensure effective implementation of plans.

Operational planning is pragmatic but requires flexibility because it involves actual commitment, mobilisation and utilisation of resources. For successful operational planning and its implementation, managers have to study and analyse every work-setting at which an operation is to be performed. Flexibility in operational plans helps in getting them adjusted with ground realities at the time of implementation.

3. Strategic Planning

Strategic planning has become relevant in a dynamic business environment. According to Anthony, "it is the process of deciding on the objectives of an organisation, on changes in these objectives, on the resources used to attain these objectives and on the policies that are to govern acquisition, use and disposition of these resources." This definition highlights the appropriateness of strategic planning in the event of changes in respect of objectives and policies to deal with acquisition and utilisation of resources.

In the words of Kreitner: "Strategic planning is the process of determining how to pursue organisational long-term goals with the resources expected to be available. A well-conceived strategic plan communicates much more than general intentions about profit and growth. It specifies how the organisation will achieve competitive advantage with profit and growth as necessary by-products."

Kreitner stressed on competitive advantages that can be obtained in addition to profit and growth by strategic planning. Some other authors have also defined strategic planning as the process of designing ways of achieving organisational goals of stability, growth, diversification, competitive standing, public image, developing integrated programme of action. etc.

More precisely, strategic planning is a process of developing an intensive course of action to achieve objectives in a changed situation. It basically aims at scanning environmental opportunities and threats by making situational analysis and studying their possible implications on the achievement of objectives. It also takes into account the strengths and weaknesses of organisations by preparing capability profiles. And, it devises ways in the form of an intensive course of action to relate strengths and weaknesses with opportunities and threats arising out of a changing environment.

The basic idea is to exploit opportunities for which the organisation is capable and has strength. In strategic planning, a course of action is devised in the form of response, initiative, move or counter-move to defeat competitors and surmount a situation to achieve objectives.

Strategic planning indicates the direction in which the organisation will move to seek its goal and structure and pattern of its response to changing situations. It calls for a high degree of innovativeness, creativity, farsightedness and other analytical abilities on the part of managers.

4. Long-range Planning

Long-term planning is a process of determining the long-term objectives of an organisation and preparing a broad framework useful for developing short-term action programmes. It is normally made for a period of five years or more depending on the needs of the organisation and the capabilities of managers to prepare forecasts, projections and estimates. It involves the tentative determination of the organisation's future destinations or broad objectives and basic strategies to be followed over that period of time.

Long-term planning is mainly related to long-term goals and goals to be achieved in specific situations arising out of the changing environment. It provides a broad framework within which short range action plans are developed.

In the context of the 'commitment principle', long-term planning is not really planning for future decisions; rather it is planning of future impact of today's decisions. This interpretation of long-term planning indicates a sense of futurity on the part of managers while making current decisions. Thus long-term planning aims at providing the required information on various elements of the future environment.

It helps in developing proactive measures to check the recurrence of an event in the future because long-term planning is based on certain relevant informed assumptions regarding future environment and its behaviour.

Often, some short-term decisions may actually impede the long-range planning process. Managers should exercise due care and judge the implications of the current decisions on the future environment.

Long-term planning has far-reaching implications on the practice of management as it forces managers to look into operations and activities in an analytical manner and calls for increased conceptual skills. It may encourage research and development activities, expansion and diversification and training and development programmes for managers to insure for the future at current expense.

MANAGEMENT BY OBJECTIVE (MBO)

Management by objective is a comprehensive system and technique applied in planning, motivating and controlling. The credit of developing this technique goes to Peter Drucker, who, in 1954, recommended it to promote managerial self-control. Since then, it has been in the focus of management authors and practitioners. It is also known as a technique of 'work planning and review, management by results' or accountability management.

Broadly, it is an integrative approach to planning and control. The concept has become important in modern management, especially due to the rapidly changing environment, emerging new techno-structure of business, need for result-oriented approaches, growing significance of individual personality in work setting, etc.

George Odiorne has described the system of management by objective as a process whereby superior and subordinate managers of an organisation jointly identify common goals, define each individual's major areas of responsibility in terms of results expected of him and use these measures as guides for the operating unit and assessing the contribution of each of its members.

The concept is based on measurable and participatively set objectives. It involves joint and participative goal-setting and the consultative and participative process of determining means of achieving them.

Dale D. McConkey defined it "as an approach to management planning and evaluation in which specific targets for a year or some other length of time are established for each manager on the basis of results which each must achieve, if the overall objectives of the company are to be realised. At the end of the period, the actual results achieved are measured against the original goals, that is, against the expected results which each manager knows he is responsible for achieving."

In this definition, the main emphasis has been placed on the basic concept, that is, planning and controlling. How the objectives and goals will be set has not been described.

MBO is considered as a system and philosophy of management rather than that of a simple technique. It is a goal-oriented approach that facilitates performance of all management functions in a logical and effective manner to achieve goals.

MBO CYCLE

The MBO approach combines planning and control. To complete the cycle of planning and control, one has to pass through the following sequential stages:

(i) To Define the Objectives of the Organisation

At the first stage of MBO, the objectives are determined; broad, general and strategic, involving the basic question: what rate of return should the organisation earn? And, what product is to be marketed. Determined by top managers and communicated to lower levels, these objectives form the basis of long-term planning and provide a sense of direction, harmony and unity to the efforts made by the employees.

(ii) To Formulate Sub-objectives or Goals

Short-term sub-objectives or goals are developed for every department, which are consistent and contributive to the overall objectives and provide performance targets for each department.

(iii) Determination of Individual Targets

Within the parameters and guidelines provided by organisational objectives, targets of performance are determined for every individual manager jointly by superiors and subordinates by mutual consent. Action plans are also devised. With a sufficient degree of operational autonomy, a lower level manager is made accountable for achievement of targets.

(iv) Periodic Review and Evaluation

As plans are put into operation, monitoring of performance of subordinates becomes essential. The MBO approach suggests holding of periodic face-to-face meetings between superiors and subordinates after a monthly, quarterly or half-yearly interval. On the basis of these periodic meetings, the validity of set objectives is judged against the occurrence of unexpected events and objectives are accordingly amended. If a subordinate has failed to make the expected contribution, the problems he has encountered have to be resolved.

(v) Performance Appraisal

At the end of the MBO cycle, generally one year after setting the original goals, a final performance appraisal is made by matching the performance of the subordinate with the goals agreed upon by him. The MBO approach is more concerned with results or performance rather than personalities or excuses. The control phase of the MBO cycle becomes complete after taking corrective measures to make further improvements.

The following observations may be made on the basis of the characteristics of MBO:

- Management by objective is not merely a tool and technique of management, it is an approach or system and philosophy of management.
- Although it deals mainly with planning and control, its increasing use as a motivational technique and coordination device has been established in practice.
- The MBO approach is goal-oriented. It places emphasis on clearly formulated goals and a fair and internally consistent hierarchy of these goals.
- It encourages joint participation of superiors and subordinates in the process of goal-setting for subordinates; joint goal-setting is critical to this approach.
- MBO is a continuous and systematic approach of goal-setting and devising an action plan, monitoring performance of subordinates and making an appraisal against the agreed set of objectives to initiate corrective action that completes the cycle and results in re-start of the planning process.
- Advocates of the MBO approach strongly believe that it can be applied to motivate employees by allowing participation in decision-making and goal-setting and recognising their achievements.

Advantages of MBO

The MBO approach offers the following advantages:

(i) It is a fine combination of planning and control because it suggests not only joint goal-setting but ensures efficient accomplishment of goals by exercising effective control.

(ii) It integrates individual targets and departmental goals with organisational overall objectives in such a way that goals and targets at lower levels contribute to the accomplishment of organisational goals.

(iii) It provides a definite direction to efforts as well as resources of the organisation by establishing specific, operational and measurable goals.

(iv) It is goal-oriented and directed towards results, performance and contribution of employees rather than their personalities and intentions.

(v) The active involvement and participation of subordinates in setting goals and making decisions makes them enthusiastic and committed to produce better results. It encourages self-management and personal commitment.

(vi) It encourages initiative, self-direction and self-control among employees. In the words of Peter Drucker: "The greatest advantage of MBO is that it makes it possible for a manager to give and retain control over his performance."

It is so because the manager gets a regular feedback on his performance and gets an opportunity to look at his short-comings and correct them.

(vii) The approach is highly objective and rational. The superior initiates the setting of goals for subordinates with the latter's involvement and participation. Appraisal of performance of subordinates is matched with clear, measurable objectives to avoid the personal bias of the superior.

(viii) It facilitates training and development of subordinate managers. They participate in goal-setting, devising action plans and decision-making with superiors through fair and frank interaction. This ultimately leads to automatic training and development of managerial skills.

(ix) The MBO approach provides clarification of the organisational role and structure by identifying the key result areas and translating them into various positions carrying responsibility and accountability to achieve predetermined objectives.

TABLE 5.1: ADVANTAGES AND LIMITATIONS

Advantages	Limitations
1. Joint goal-setting and effective accomplishment	1. It is not a complete approach of management
2. Individual targets and departmental goals are integrated with organisational goals	2. It emphasises quantitative objectives, ignoring intangible ones
3. It provides definite direction to resources and efforts	3. It is time consuming
4. It emphasises results and performance	4. No provision of training of subordinates before their participation
5. Involvement of subordinates makes them more committed to achieve assigned targets	5. It has limited application
6. It encourages self-direction and control	6. Lack of understanding and agreement between superiors and subordinates
7. It is a highly rational and objective approach	7. It requires numerous structural changes
8. It facilitates training and development	8. Self-control does not produce the desired effect
9. It identifies key result areas	9. More emphasis on goal-setting

Limitations of MBO

The application of this approach is subject to the following limitations and drawbacks:

(i) The approach of MBO is very often sold as a 'cure all'. But, in practice, managing various operations of the organisation on the basis of objectives does not provide a unified, comprehensive and total approach to management.

(ii) It places emphasis on measurable, quantifiable and specific objectives, thereby neglecting long-term, strategic and qualitative goals such as the image of the organisation and its products, morale of employees, their motivation, etc.

(iii) It takes too much time and effort and generates too much paper work.

(iv) It does not provide for scientific training and development of subordinates before they are involved in the process of decision-making and goal-setting.

(v) The MBO approach has limited application. It can be successfully applied only in those situations where subordinates are willing and capable of playing a meaningful role and superiors are interested to part with their authority and share it with subordinates.

(vi) The utility of this approach is also adversely affected by the fact that in practice superiors and subordinates find it very difficult to set goals on account of the lack of proper understanding, agreement and common interest.

(vii) Implementation of this approach calls for drastic structural changes in the existing structure of the organisation which seems to be difficult for a conservative and traditional organisation.

(viii) Although advocates of this approach strongly believe that self-control and direction is superior and more efficient, it alone does not produce desired results unless and until it is backed by well-designed controlling devices and necessary directives, guidance, help and leadership by superiors.

(ix) The MBO approach suggests a periodic review of performance so as to adjust goals according to the changed situation. By making such amendments in goals so frequently they may be rendered meaningless and create confusion among subordinates.

(x) In implementing this approach, the manager places too much emphasis on goal-setting as a result of which he may lose sight of other important managerial processes and activities. Thus, the approach fails in maintaining a proper balance between managing and goal-setting.

SUMMARY

In order to provide guidance to managers in decision-making and solving problems, various plans are drawn. These plans provide constancy in decision-making and action taking. These plans, which also regulate working behaviour of managers, may be 'single use plans' or 'standing plans'. Single-use plans are developed to solve non-repetitive and unique problems. These plans include objective, strategy, programme and budget, while standing plans are developed to solve repetitive problems which arise far and again in the working of an organisation. These are policies, procedures, methods and rules.

Objectives are the basic plans of an organisation. They provide the future destination towards which other managerial functions are performed. Without these objectives, no meaningful planning can be done. These objectives should be stated as clearly as possible. Multiplicity of objectives should be avoided and in case there is multiplicity, the objectives must be well integrated.

Strategy may also be defined as a unified, comprehensive and integrated action plan developed to achieve specific objectives. Strategic plans are primarily developed in the event of changing business environment as a response or initiative to that situation.

Strategies are generally formulated at the top level with regard to vital matters affecting survival, growth and development of the organisation. In these strategic plans, organisational strengths and weaknesses are matched with environmental threats and opportunities.

Programme is a single-use plan, which refers to the outline of a plan of work to be carried out in a proper sequence. It is a complex network of policies, procedures, methods, rules and budgets. Programmes are generally supported by capital budget. On the realisation of an objective, it automatically ends.

Budget is also a single-use plan, which expresses anticipated results in numerical terms. Budget may be defined as an estimate of future needs arranged in an orderly basis, covering some or all activities of an enterprise for a specific period. Although budget is considered more as a part of controlling, but making a budget is much a part of planning,

Policies are standing plans, which are used to solve problems arising again and again. Policies may be defined as a general statement formulated by the organisation to guide managers in decision-making. Thus, policies provide general guidelines and parameters within which managers have to make decisions contributing to objectives.

Procedure may be defined as administrative action guidelines prescribing a sequence in which various activities are to be performed. The essence of procedure is a chronological sequence of required actions. Procedures play an important role in the functioning of an organisation.

Methods provide details about particular operation or activities. They prescribe the exact manner in which an operation will be performed. Method may be defined as a manual or mechanical means to perform a particular operation. The use of scientific methods in an organisation to perform various operations may lead to higher efficiency, more production and less fatigue on the part of workers.

Rules are also a plan made to regulate and control the working behaviour of employees. These may be defined as a specific statement or set of directives which employees are expected to comply with while doing a job. Rules are very rigid and leave no scope for deviation and discretion.

On the basis of scope, significance and coverage, planning may be classified as 'corporate planning', 'operational planning', 'strategic planning' and 'long-range planning'. Corporate planning is considered as a basic approach to the overall management of an organisation. It covers all important matters that affect survival, growth, profitability and development.

Operational planning involves conversion of corporate plans into detailed and specific ones dealing with various activities. Strategic planning may be defined as a process of deciding objectives of an organisation on changes in these objectives, on the resources used to attain these objectives and on the policies that are to govern acquisition, use and disposition of these resources.

Lastly, long-term planning is a process of determining long-term objectives of an organisation and preparing a broad framework useful for developing short-term programmes.

Management of objectives is a comprehensive system and technique, which is applied to planning, motivating and controlling. Broadly, it is an integrative approach to planning and control. It is a process of defining objectives of an organisation, formulating sub-objectives or gaols, determining individual targets, reviewing and evaluating and making performance appraisal. It is a goal-oriented approach which encourages participation of superiors and subordinates and which motivates employees. It integrates individual targets and departmental goals with the basic objectives of an organisation.

OBJECTIVE TYPE QUESTIONS

Which of the following statements is correct and which is not? Support your answer with reasons.

1. Plan is an end result of the planning process.
2. Policy is a single-use plan.
3. Single-use plans are tailored to fit specific situations.
4. Objectives are basic plans of the organisation.
5. Strategy is formulated in the event of changing environment and growing competition.

6. Budget is a single-use plan having an aspect of controlling in it.
7. Policies are made and used to solve problems that arise occasionally and that are unique in nature.
8. Corporate planning is made at lower levels of the organisation.
9. Rules are impersonal, rigid and have no scope for deviation.
10. Management by objective is a technique of planning only.

TEST QUESTIONS

1. Explain the test you would apply to determine the suitability of a business strategy.
2. What is the desired relationship between objectives and strategies?
3. Explain the concept of operational planning and its relationship with strategic planning.
4. 'Strategic planning is the only option in a fast-changing environment.' Comment.
5. Define the term 'management by objectives' and explain its benefits and limitations.
6. Discuss the role of the network techniques of CPM and PERT in planning.
7. Distinguish between
   (a) Policy and procedure
   (b) Policy and objectives
   (c) Policy and strategy
   (d) Corporate and operational planning.
8. Write short notes on
   (a) Organisational objectives
   (b) Strategic planning
   (c) Evaluation of business strategy
   (d) Standing plans
   (e) Rules
   (f) Methods.

REFERENCES

Ansoff, H. Igor. *Corporate Strategy*. New York, U.S.A.: McGraw-Hill, 1965.

Barnard, Chester I. *Organisation and Management*. Cambridge, Mass., U.S.A.: Harvard University, 1958.

Drucker, Peter F. *The Practice of Management*. Bombay, India: Allied Publishers Pvt. Ltd., 1955.

Ghosh, P. K. *Business Policy: Strategic Planning and Management*. New Delhi, India: Sultan Chand and Sons, 1997.

Khandelwala, Pradip N. 'Some Top Management Styles: Their Content and Performance'. *Organisation and Administrative Sciences*. Vol. 7, N-4, Winter, 1976-1977.

Kreitner, Robert. *Management*. New Delhi, India: A.I.T.B.S. Publishers and Distributors, 1996.

Stoener, James A. F. and Wankel, Charles. *Management*. New Delhi, India: Prentice-Hall of India, 1986.

Thune, Stanley and House, Robert. 'Where Long-range Planning Pays Off'. *Business Horizons*. August, 1970.

CASE STUDY I

STRATEGY IN ACTION
Zale Corporation—Operating Philosophy

1. Marketing and customer service

(a) We require that the entire organisation be continuously customer oriented. Our future success is dependent on meeting the customers' needs better than our competition.

(b) We expect to maintain a marketing concept and distribution capability to identify changing trends and emerging markets and effectively promote our products.

(c) We strive to provide our customers with continuous offerings of quality merchandise, competitively priced—stressing value and service.

(d) We plan to constantly maintain our facilities as modern, attractive, clean and orderly stores that are pleasing and exciting places for customers to shop.

2. Management tasks

(a) We require profitable results from operations—activities do not necessarily equate with accomplishment—results must be measurable.

(b) We recognise there are always better ways to perform many functions. Continuous improvement in operating capability is a daily objective of the entire organisation.

Case Study I continued

Case Study I continued

(c) We expect all managers to demonstrate capabilities to plan objectives, delegate responsibilities, motivate people, control operations and achieve results measured against planned objectives.

(d) We must promote a spirit of teamwork. To succeed, complex businesses such as ours require good communication, clearly understood policies, effective controls and, above all, a dedication to "make it happen."

(e) We are highly competitive and dedicated to succeeding. However, as a human organisation we will make mistakes. We must openly acknowledge our mistakes, learn from them and take corrective action.

3. Human resources

(a) We must develop and maintain a competent, highly motivated, result-oriented organisation.

(b) We seek to attract, develop and motivate people who demonstrate professional competence, courage and integrity in performing their jobs.

(c) We strive to identify individuals who are outstanding performers, provide them with continuous challenges, and search for new effective ways to compensate them—utilising significant incentives.

(d) Promotion from within our goal. We must have the best talent available, and, from time to time, will have to reach outside to meet our ever improving standards. We heartily endorse and support development programmes to prepare individuals for increased responsibility. In a like wise manner, we must promptly advise those who are not geared to the pace, in order that they make the necessary adjustments without delay.

4. Finance and control

(a) We will maintain a sound financial plan that provides capital for growth of the business and provides optimum return for our stockholders.

(b) We must develop and maintain a system of controls that highlights potential significant failures early for positive corrective action.

CASE STUDY II

Managing by Objectives

"Managing by objectives is nothing new in our police department here", said Commissioner Aswini Kartik of the Metropolitan Police. "We have always established objectives towards which everyone in our department strives. Our job is varied and diverse but encompasses the maintenance of law and order, firmly but fairly; in addition, we have to protect human lives and property; and to be the conscience and spirit of the general welfare of the millions of people who inhabit our city and call it home. Every man is aware of these objectives in our department and knows he will have to strive towards it. Now, I am fully aware that, being a service operation, we cannot measure by the yardsticks of profits, costs, sales, or product output, as is done in manufacturing concerns. However, I reiterate very strongly that this does not mean we are not managing by objectives. Ask anyone in my department".

Commissioner Kartik was speaking to a management consultant who had come to discuss ways of improving the efficiency of the police force by introducing management by objectives in his department.

Questions

1. Do you think Commissioner Kartik is engaging in managing by objectives? What, if anything, is missing?
2. What would you suggest the Commissioner to do?

—oo(O)oo—

CHAPTER 6

BUSINESS POLICY AND STRATEGY FORMULATION

LEARNING OBJECTIVES

1. To develop conceptual clarity on business policy and its nature.
2. To identify various stages involved in policy formulation and relate it with some organisation.
3. To remember features of sound policy.
4. To learn the basic concept of strategy and its main features.
5. To go through the process of strategy formulation and bring out the main elements that are involved in it.
6. To develop an understanding regarding various strategy options.
7. To learn how strategy can be evaluated with a suitable example of any organisation.

BUSINESS POLICY DEFINED

Every organisation feels the necessity to make decisions to guide its future direction and destination. It has to make decisions regarding what business the organisation is in and what business it would like to be in the future. Will it continue with the same business or merge with another organisation? These decisions are basically strategic decisions because they involve not only the survival but also the future of the organisation. To take such vital decisions a framework is prepared which is known as business policy.

In other words, business policy refers to strategic decisions that are made within the broad guidelines and constraints about the future destination of the organisation. The term 'business policy' is used interchangeably with 'strategic management'. It is because business policy provides a broad framework within which the corporate plans are made. These are made in the context of a rapidly changing environment and growing competition in business. These plans that are strategic in nature aim at achieving a future destination. Business policy is formulated at the top of the organisation. Managers working at the top use their conceptual skills so as to identify opportunities, potential and possible threats arising out of a changing environment. The business policy also aims at developing a vision of the organisation for the future and seeks the mobilisation and utilisation of various resources to realise it.

In the words of Christensen, "Business policy is the study of functions and responsibility of top level managers, the crucial problems that affect success in the total enterprise and the decisions that determine direction of the organisation and shape its future." It involves making choice of purpose, moulding an identity and character of the organisation, defining what needs to be done and mobilising resources of organisation to achieve objectives in competitive and adverse situations.

Business policy deals with the process of determining long-term objectives of the organisation which may guide its destiny in the future. The concept of business policy originated in 1911, when an integrated course in management was introduced at Harvard Business School. Since then, it has been used with varying interpretations. Now it is considered as strategic management that includes the study of top management responsibilities of defining business mission and objectives and seek mobilisation of resources to achieve them.

Characteristics of Business Policy

Business policy has the following characteristics:

1. Business policy involves strategic decision making. Strategic decisions are those that affect the survival and future direction of the organisation. For example, launching a new product, diversifying existing business operations, getting merged with others, switching over to new technology, etc.
2. Business policy has long-term implications. It does not only deal with the survival of the organisation but equally takes care of the future destination of the organisation.
3. Business policy is generally formulated by top level managers. It is a document that defines responsibilities of top level managers to determine the future direction and objectives of the organisation.
4. Formulation of business policy is a continuous process. It is revised whenever there is a change in the capabilities, resources and environment of an organisation. As the environment changes, the organisation may also suitably change its vision, objectives, portfolio of business, markets and other strategies.
5. Business policy includes those sets of management techniques and measures that are used to ensure survival and success of the organisation particularly in a changing environment.

6. Formulation of business policy is considered as an entrepreneurial function that is related to the whole organisation. It also involves scanning of environmental elements to identify opportunities and problems and make an internal analysis to identify areas of strengths and weaknesses of the organisation.

CORPORATE POLICIES

Policy is a basic standing plan of the organisation. It is formulated to control the decision behaviour of managers. Corporate policies are general statements formulated by top management to guide management decision making. They may be defined as well established and with clear intentions and viewpoints of the organisation and its management on major and strategic issues that are involved in the functioning of the organisation. In other words, the corporate policies contain general attitude, intentions and approaches of the organisation on important matters that are related to outsiders who deal with the organisation. These may be considered as a general statement of guidelines prepared by top level managers to guide managerial decision making. It may be regarded as a basic framework within which managers have to take decisions. It also prescribes basic criteria, broad guidelines and constraints that are to be observed by managers while taking decisions.

According to Koontz O'Donnell, policy is a general statement of understanding that guides thinking in decision making. In the words of Brech, policy is a pattern of direction for the guidance of those who carry responsibility for the management of activities of the organisation.

The organisation formulates policies with respect to the various functional areas such as production, marketing, finance, purchase, personnel, etc. These policies are known as functional policies. Functional policies are more specific versions or an operationalised form of corporate policy. Although the responsibility of formulating corporate policies lies with top level managers, while developing functional or more operational policies, they take middle level managers into confidence. Similarly on the basis of origin, the policies may be of three types:

(a) Originated policies

(b) Imposed policies

(c) Appealed policies.

Originated policies are formulated by managers at the top of the organisation. By making use of conceptual skills they visualise the organisation as a single entity, form an image of it and develop a vision for the future. Within the framework of originated policy several other policies may be developed to deal with less important operations of the organisation. Most of the organisational policies owe their existence in originated ones. In originated policy, the basic philosophy of the organisation is reflected and described.

The policies may also be imposed by the changes taking place in the external environment elements. These are known as imposed policies. It is because of the change in the environment that the organisation may be forced to formulate a new set of policies to survive or use opportunities offered by the change. For example, the change in existing taxation laws or labour laws may compel the organisation to formulate new policies that are consistent with the new provisions of the law.

Sometimes, it may also happen that the existing set of policies may be inadequate to deal with some specific and exceptional situations. Subordinate managers dealing with such situations may request or appeal to higher level managers to formulate a new policy which may be known as an appealed policy. To keep pace with the changing environment and formulate matching policies, they have to be revised from time to time. Such periodic reviews of existing policies may be undertaken at the request of lower level managers.

POLICY FORMULATION

Generally, polices are formulated at the top level of the organisation. But with regard to functional and operational policies, the cooperation of lower level managers is also sought. Like the planning process, policy formulation also requires certain stages to be followed in a sequence. The following stages are involved in developing policies (Figure 6.1).

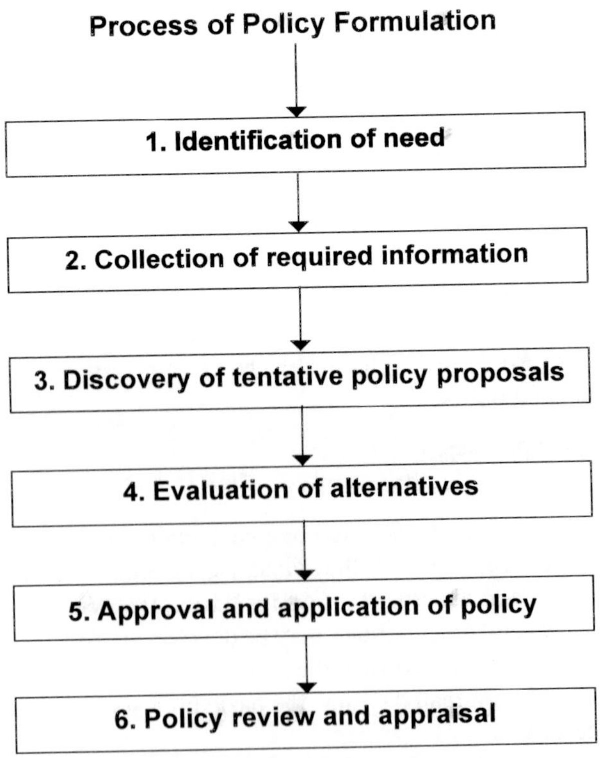

Figure 6.1. Showing Process of Policy Formulation

1. Identification of Need

At the very outset of the process of policy formulation, the top level manager must identify the need to prepare a new policy or revising the existing one. He should be sensitive to the need for policy formulation. This stage requires locating the area of operation where the organisation is lagging in this respect. At the stage of identifying, the needs and objectives of the organisation and the present state of its functioning should be taken into account. The need to make or revise policies may arise either in the functional areas of organisation or with regard to various management functions.

2. Collection of Required Information

The study and analysis of tentative policy situations arising in the organisation demands collection of relevant and required information about that area. It includes the collection of information on various elements of environment that are forcing the organisation to formulate a new policy or upgrade the existing one. Not only this, the information on the existing set of various plans has also to be compiled. This is done to get an idea about the present state of functioning of the organisation. An internal analysis may help in generating information on the resource position and constraints. Monitoring and predicting environmental changes as well as an analysis of the internal position of the organisation are important for formulating policies.

3. Discovery of Tentative Policy Proposal

Managers who have the responsibility of formulating policies may be acquainted with some policy alternatives. And they may discover others by using their experience, through research and analysis of possible opportunities and threats arising out of the changing environment and the strengths and weaknesses of the organisation. The use of conceptual skills, creativity and innovation on the part of the manager plays an important role in discovering alternative policy proposals.

4. Evaluation of an Alternative

Once various policy proposals to deal with a situation have been developed, managers attempt to narrow down their choices on more suitable proposals. With this decision, managers evaluate the contribution of each proposal for the accomplishment of objectives, the cost of the proposal, the resource position of the organisation, objectives, relevant provisions of the law, social implications, etc. Though these factors seem to be conflicting, for instance, the proposal that contributes the maximum towards the objective may be the costliest. But for making a final selection of the proposal the manager should strike a proper balance among them. In order to make the policy proposal more realistic, lower level managers should also be associated with it. It would also increase acceptability of the policy. It is, therefore, before selecting a particular policy, that drafts are usually circulated among the junior managers to get their suggestions.

5. Approval and Application of Policy

The ultimate authority of finally approving a policy lies with the top level managers. They can alone decide whether the policy adequately represents the objectives of the organisation or not. After deliberations, on all the relevant aspects of the policy proposal, it is finally approved by them. At this stage, it must be ensured that the policy is consistent with all the other plans and reflects the intention of the management in the best possible manner. Finally, the approved policy document is communicated and explained to those managers who are subject to its use. For this purpose, a well-prepared policy document is included in the policy manual for circulation and application.

6. Policy Review and Appraisal

Periodic reviews are conducted to update the policy and maintain its relevance. Such reviews are undertaken in the context of changing situations. The need to review policy arises mainly due to rapid changes in the environment. Its appraisal indicates how effective it is in its application. Necessary modifications may be made to maintain its effectiveness and usefulness.

Features of Sound Policy

An effective and sound policy should be based on the following features:

1. All major functional areas of the organisation should be represented by clear and definite policies.
2. The policies of the organisation should be consistent with the accomplishment of objectives.
3. The policy should be incorporated in the policy manual and should be circulated among all the managers.
4. The policy should be practical, realistic and easily understandable.
5. An adequate degree of flexibility should be maintained in the policies and at the same time they should remain stable over a period of time.
6. Policies that deal with different functional areas and operations should be in agreement and consistent.
7. Policies, to be more effective, should be socially sanctioned, ethically sound and legally valid.
8. Periodic review should be undertaken to update policies and made responsive to a given situation.
9. Policies of the organisation should be based on the principles of equity, fairness and reasonableness.
10. It should clearly specify the broad limitations of its scope of action or application.

STRATEGY DEFINED

The term 'strategy' is commonly used in respect of army organisations and games. But in the context of increasing competition and fast-changing environment, its use has become equally relevant for a business enterprise. Generally, strategy may be defined as a comprehensive and unified action plan designed to achieve specific objectives in a changed situation. It is concerned with the direction in which various resources of organisation would be deployed to maximise the change of accomplishing the specified objectives in a disturbed state of affairs. A few definitions of strategy are as follows:

> "Strategy results from the process of deciding on objective or organisation, on changes in these objectives, on the resources used to attain these objectives, on the policies that are to govern acquisition and use and disposition of these resources."—*Anthony*
>
> "Strategy can be defined as determination of basic long-term goals and objectives of an enterprise and the adoption of course of action and allocation of resources necessary for carrying out these goals."—*Chandler*
>
> "Strategy consists of four components, namely, product, market scope, growth, competitive advantage and synergy." —*Ansoff*
>
> "Strategy is a coherent set of actions aimed at gaining sustainable advantages over competition, improving position vis-à-vis customers or allocating resources."—*Waterman*
>
> "Strategy is a unified, comprehensive and integrated plan relating the strategic advantages of the firm to the challenges of the environment. It is designed to ensure that the basic objectives of enterprise are achieved."—*Glueck*

In brief, strategy may be considered as an action plan, initiative, response, move or counter-move to achieve organisational objectives in changed specific situations. For example, Pepsi and Coca Cola are competitors in the soft drink market. To increase sales volume and market share, Pepsi reduces the price. How will Coke respond? In short, strategy may be considered as an organisational response in the form of deploying resources to exploit an opportunity to face a threat arising out of a changing environment.

A careful analysis of the above definitions reveals the following characteristics of strategy:

1. Strategy is a single-use plan made to meet the challenge of a specific situation; when the situation changes, the strategy becomes outdated.
2. It is a comprehensive and unified action plan drawn to seek specific objectives in changed situations.
3. It is an organisational move, response or initiative which is well thought out and systematic to defend oneself or to defeat rivals.

4. Generally strategy is formulated for a long term but it may have short-term implications also.
5. Strategy, to a large extent, is imposed externally, either by the government, trade union, trade association or competitors and other conditions.
6. Strategies are basically formulated on the basis of corporate missions and objectives and situational analysis of the organisation and its environment.
7. It aims at deploying and utilising limited resources to maximise the changes of achieving the objective in the event of difficulties.
8. Strategy is also regarded as an 'interpretative plan' because it is formulated to interpret other plans.

Importance of Strategy

As stated earlier, strategy is a basic plan which occupies a higher position in the hierarchy of organisational plans. Generally it draws the attention of the chief executive to be alert and cautious regarding an environment in which an organisation operates. The long-term success of an organisation to a great extent depends on successful formulation and implementation of strategies. Its significance can be understood on the basis of the following factors:

1. Strategy Relates the Organisation with its External Environment

Organisations are formed and they operate within a socio-economic and political environment. As stated earlier, all the components or elements of an external environment are ever changing. Any change in an environment greatly influences the process of setting objectives and the overall functioning of the organisation.

It is with the help of suitable strategies that an organisation attempts to cope with the changing environment because strategies are made in changing situations to face challenges and exploit opportunities. The whole process of strategy formulation aims at matching the strengths and weaknesses of an organisation with opportunities and threats arising out of changing situations.

2. Strategies Provide Future Direction to an Organisation

The grand strategy formulated by top management provides direction in which the resources of an organisation are deployed and used to achieve corporate objectives. Strategy includes all those action plans that an organisation intends to take to reach the position it wants to be in. It also implies a long-term vision of what an organisation seeks to do and what kind of organisation it intends to become.

3. Strategy Formulation is a Significant Area of Management Decision

Strategic decisions are generally made by top level managers and such decisions are related to interface between an organisation and its external environment. Such decisions have long-term implications and determine the long-term success of an organisation.

4. Strategy Increases Competitive Strength of an Organisation

Strategy is a unified course of action which is prepared to meet competitive situations more efficiently. Strategy is formulated keeping in view the policies of rival organisations. It is used as a response, initiative or countermove to defend the organisation.

5. Strategy is More Effective and has a Rational Approach

Strategy is formulated on the basis of objectives of the organisation. And while formulating it, the environmental factor, objectives of the organisation and internal profile of strengths and weaknesses are taken into account. In this way, when compared to other plans, it is a more rational and effective approach to achieve objectives.

6. Strategy Calls for an Efficient Deployment and use of Resources

SWOT analysis which is conducted for the formulation of strategy helps the organisation to adopt a suitable course of action to exploit opportunities and combat threats. It will also help to drop those businesses that do not meet objectives and to mobilise resources from there to those areas which are more profitable.

7. Strategy also Helps in Maintaining Coordination

In an organisation, the 'grand strategy' is formulated and strategic decisions taken by top level managers. To implement it successfully, the grand strategy is translated into sub-business units (SBU) strategy which is further converted into various functional strategies. In doing so, the activities and plans at the functional level are coordinated with SBU plans and these are coordinated with the grand strategy or top-level plans.

PROCESS OF STRATEGY FORMULATION

Strategy formulation is an intellectual process that calls for use of analytical abilities, imagination and creativity on the part of managers. It involves the following steps:

1. Determining Mission and Objectives of the Organisation

The organisational mission and objectives serve as the basis to develop a suitable strategy. The statement of mission or purpose of the organisation tells what the organisation is and why it exists and functions. In other words, the mission defines the social purpose and scope of the organisation. It is determined by top level managers and is generally incorporated in the memorandum of association. They include intentionally wide-ranging activities.

For example, the mission statement of the Oil and Natural Gas Commission of India is to "stimulate, continue and accelerate efforts to develop and maximise the contribution of the energy sector to the economy of the country." Similarly, Voltas Ltd. has defined its mission or purpose as "profit, growth and excellence."

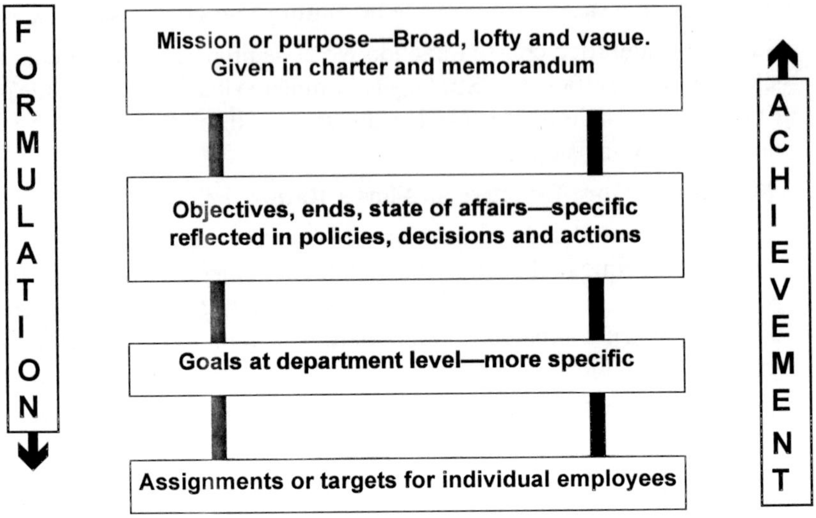

Figure 6.2. Organisation missions, objectives, goals and targets

To translate organisational missions into results, they are spelt out in a specific form known as objectives. The objectives are the ends towards which all activities of the organisation are directed. They are the basis of functioning of an organisation and legitimise its existence. These objectives are further broken up into sub-objectives or goals (departments) and individual assignments or targets (Figure 6.2).

2. SWOT Analysis

SWOT is an acronym for strengths, weaknesses, opportunities and threats. It begins with scanning the external environment to identify opportunities and threats and analysing the internal position of the organisation to discover its strengths and weaknesses.

(a) Environmental Analysis

Organisational missions and objectives are determined by analysing various factors of the environment. These factors affect the formulation of strategy and identification of objectives. Changes in the environment may bring opportunities or may pose threats and challenges. According to Kotler, environmental threat is a challenge posed by an unfavourable trend or development in the environment that would lead, in the absence of purposeful action, to the erosion of a company's position. "Environmental opportunity is an attractive area for company's action in which the particular company would enjoy a competitive advantage."

A clear message that emerges is that threats and opportunities are functions of the managerial viewpoint and action. For example, the economic liberalisation in India has opened up many new opportunities for some organisations. For others, it has posed challenges and threats. To a large extent, it is purely a matter of managerial action and handling of these situations in favour of the organisation.

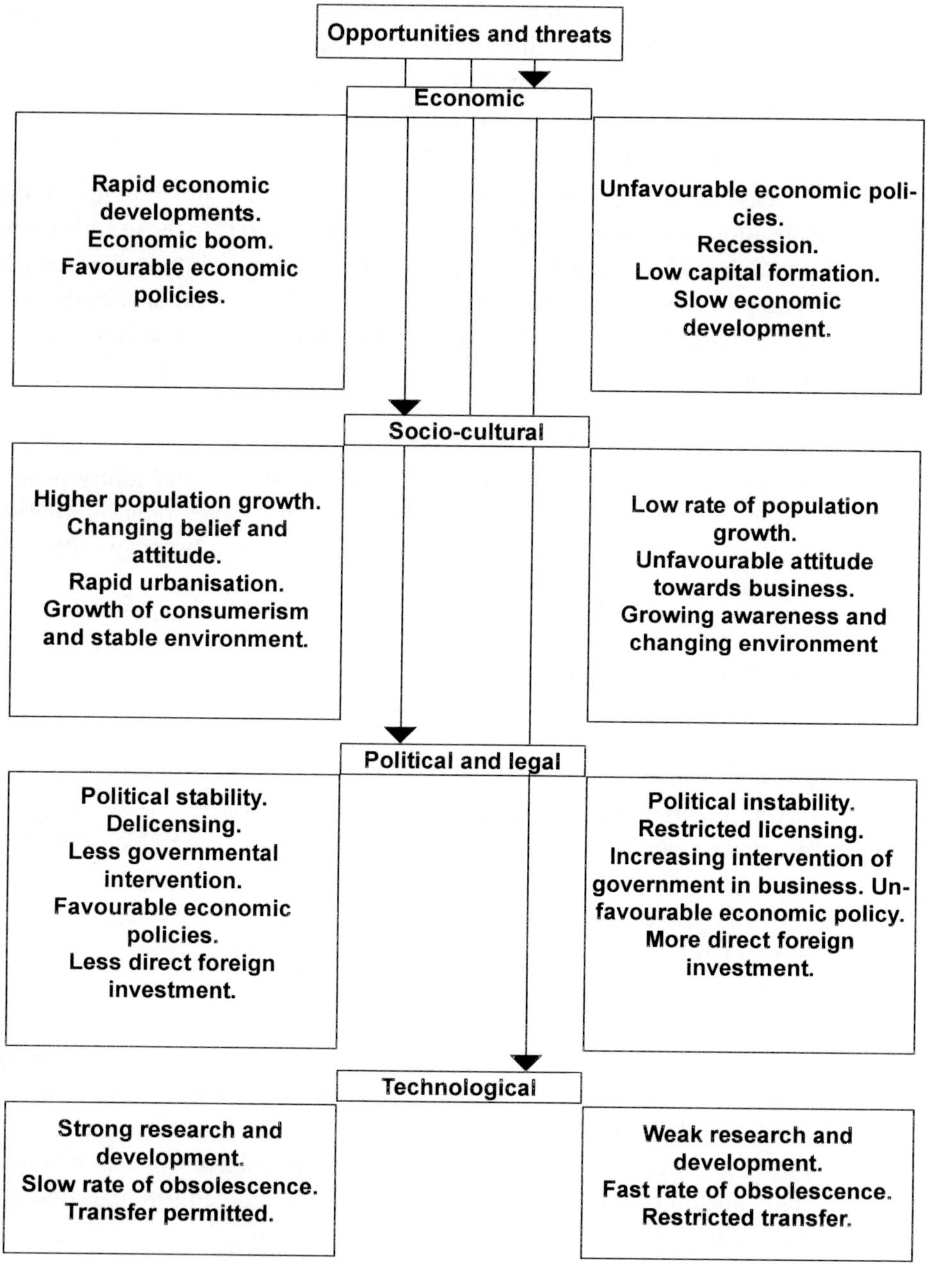

Figure 6.3. Chart of opportunities and threats

(b) Capability Profile

After scanning the external environment to identify opportunities and threats, the manager attempts to discover the strengths and weaknesses of the organisation. The exercise may be regarded as an 'internal corporate analysis' or 'capability profile.' Strengths are internal competencies of a particular organisation over its competitors. It refers to competitive advantage and other competencies such as the company's image, brand image, synergies, etc. These strengths mainly lie in the various functional areas of the organisation such as marketing, production, finance, personnel and management.

Weaknesses are those factors that reduce the competencies of the organisation in comparison with its competitors. It refers to those constraints or obstacles which check the organisation from moving in the desired direction such as poor quality of the product, obsolete technology, inadequate infrastructure, inefficient management, unsatisfactory financial position, etc. (Figure 6.3).

(c) Developing Strategic Alternatives

After having analysed the external environment and the capability profile of an organisation, the manager proceeds towards developing alternative strategies, matching opportunities and threats with strengths and weaknesses on the basis of the following:

(a) High opportunity and high strength

(b) High opportunity and low strength

(c) High threat and high strength

(d) High threat and low strength.

At times, the strong strength position of an organisation may be nullified by major weaknesses that are critical for success. To achieve a given objective, there may be many strategic options. For example, to achieve the objective of growth in sales, the organisation may launch new products, extend the existing market or discover new markets (Figure 6.4).

(d) Evaluation and Choice of Suitable Strategy

Alternative strategies are developed and evaluated to choose the most appropriate one. Strategic alternatives can be evaluated in terms of suitability, feasibility and acceptability. As far as the suitability factor is concerned, it implies that strategy should match the corporate philosophy; it should help in achieving objectives, it should facilitate the use of organisational strengths of exploiting opportunities.

In judging feasibility, the manager should ensure that the required inputs are available for implementing the strategy and required volumes of sales are generated to support extra investment and expenditure. Similarly, to ascertain the degree of acceptability, the effect of strategy on cash flow and profitability, capital structure, corporate image and internal environment should be evaluated thoroughly.

Strengths		Weaknesses
	Management	
Professional management. Dynamic leadership of top management. Integrated management approach. Administrative expertise at lower level		Family management. Lack of conceptual skills among top managers. Lack of coordination in efficient management. Lack of future direction and required managerial skills.
	Production	
Sophisticated modern technology. Strong research and development. Prompt availability of required inputs at reasonable cost.		Outdated technology. Non-availability and high cost of inputs. Lower capacity utilisation. No maintenance management.
	Marketing	
Company image. Brand image. Effective distribution system. Optimal product mix. Efficient relations management.		Less customer satisfaction. Unfamiliarity with market conditions. Lack of trained sales force. Lack of marketing research.
	Finance	
Adequate reserves and surplus. Favourable debt equity ratio. Satisfactory financial position. High credit rating. Market standing.		Unsatisfactory financial position. Poor credit rating. Utilisation of funds. Rigid capital structure.
	Personnel	
Highly motivated and committed employees. Increased labour productivity. Healthy industrial relations. Availability of technical and skilled human force.		Lack of appraisal and motivation of employees. Overstaffed organisation. Low productivity. More industrial disputes. Poor industrial relations.

Figure 6.4. Chart of strengths and weaknesses

(e) Implementation

After narrowing down the choice on an appropriate strategy, the necessary administrative arrangements are made. These are delegation of authority, allocation of resources, creating accountability centres, formulating necessary policies and generating the required information. To seek an effective implementation of strategy, it is to be translated into functional and operational strategies for the various departments or operative units.

(f) Evaluation and Control

To achieve the given objective by implementing the selected strategy, it is necessary to monitor the environment on a continuous basis so that corrective action can be taken for efficient implementation.

Levels of Strategy

In order to understand the basic nature, coverage and orientation of strategy it is necessary to put them into three levels.

1. Corporate level strategy
2. Business unit strategy
3. Functional strategy.

Corporate Strategy

Corporate strategy is a long-term comprehensive plan that covers the whole organisation and all sub-units or sub-systems. It is formulated by top level managers such as board of directors and chief executive officer. It aims at determining what is the purpose of an organisation. What business it wants to be in? What are the objectives of the various sub-units? How resources of the organisation are allocated to achieve the various objectives of the organisation? It also decides the type and nature of business to be conducted.

Business Unit Strategy

This is also known as 'line of business strategy' which is mainly concerned with the activities and operations of a particular line of business being conducted by the organisation. It is formulated and implemented to succeed in that line of business. It deals with decisions that are made regarding product mix, market segments and competitive advantages of a particular line of business and allocation of resources among various sub-units of that line.

Functional Strategy

This is made and implemented to carry out corporate level and business unit strategies. These strategies may be considered a more operationalised form of corporate level strategies. Functional strategies represent such functional areas of the organisation such as production, distribution, purchase, personnel and research and development. These strategies deal with various activities and operations that are being performed in these functional departments. While formulating functional strategies functional heads of respective departments are also taken into confidence (Figure 6.5).

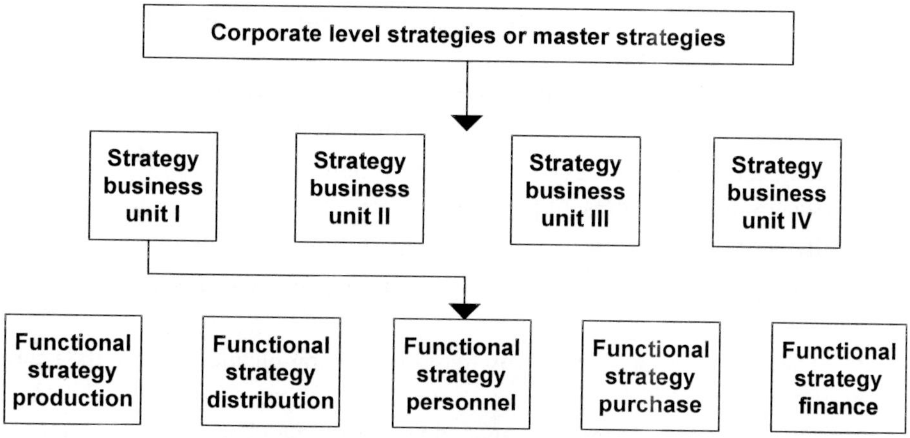

Figure 6.5. Levels of strategies

TYPES/OPTIONS OF CORPORATE LEVEL STRATEGY

Corporate level strategy deals with the overall functioning of the organisation towards achievement of corporate objectives. At the corporate level, the top-level management may have the following strategy options:

1. Stability strategy
2. Growth strategy
3. Diversification strategy
4. Retrenchment strategy
5. Defensive strategy
6. Combination strategy.

Stability Strategy

In the existing line of business, if the organisation is functioning fairly well and there is hardly any scope for future growth the top level managers would prefer to use stability strategy. It involves the optimum utilisation of existing resources to maximise the level of performance. It aims at improving the functional performance of an organisation and maintain the present level of achievement. Stability strategy is considered to be a cautious and conservative move on the part of management. But it should not be regarded as a 'do nothing strategy' because it involves making an upward revision in the existing level of performance of the organisation. In other words, stability strategy calls for doing the same thing in a better manner to optimise the results in the short term as well as in the long term. Stability strategy involves the use of innovativeness, creativity and better quality of research. It has the following features:

1. Stability strategy is based on a conservative philosophy of management which is marked by a slow change and continuity and maintaining the status quo.

2. It aims at restructuring and improving business in terms of existing products and markets.
3. It involves the maximisation of the existing level of performance of the organisation only with respect to this present business.
4. It necessitates the development of a competitive strategy to remain successful in the present position.

Stability strategy is generally adopted for the following reasons:

1. The organisation is doing fairly well in the existing business on a sustained basis.
2. There is no scope for the growth of the existing business line in the near future.
3. The organisation may be managed by family members of the owner and they may be unwilling to dilute the base of ownership.
4. They strongly believe in a conservative philosophy and do not go for change.
5. The organisation may not have the required capabilities of research for further growth.
6. The organisation may not have enough resources for expansion and development.
7. There is a fair margin of doing better in the present line of business.
8. The organisation has developed special competence to increase the margin of profit on a regular basis in the present business line.

Growth Strategy

If the business that is being conducted by the organisation has already reached saturation point, it requires to adopt a strategy of growth for further development. The growth strategy involves the expansion or extension of the existing line of business or entering into new business lines. In growth strategy, the business is re-defined by raising the existing level of objectives and setting them at a higher level that it has achieved in the recent past. It also includes the addition of new products and discovery of a new market to increase market share. Growth strategy may also be defined as one that an enterprise pursues when it increases its level of objectives upwards in a significant increment much higher than its part achievement level. The most frequent increase which indicates growth strategy is to raise the market share and sales objectives upwards significantly. It has the following features:

1. It involves entering into a new line of business by adding new products.
2. It also includes raising the existing market share and sales volume significantly by extending and discovering new markets.
3. The growth strategy aims at attaining growth which is more than the normal rate of growth and which can be secured under stability conditions.

Growth strategy is adopted for the following reasons:

1. The existing line of business has already reached saturation point.
2. Growth is often necessitated due to changes taking place in the external environment. It may either use new opportunities or face new problems arising out of it.
3. The resources and strengths of an organisation can not be fully utilised by remaining in the existing line of business.
4. Growth strategy may be adopted to secure economies of large-scale operation which is possible by adding a new line or product.
5. It may also be warranted by strong managerial motivation because the growth may provide new opportunities of career development for managers.
6. On account of a natural urge to grow on the part of the organisation, growth strategy may be pursued.
7. The performance reward for the organisation may also attract it to grow in size and experience.

DIVERSIFICATION STRATEGY

This is one of the important variants of growth strategy. Under the strategy, the organisation enters an altogether new line of business that is different from the existing ones. It involves the use of different skills, technology and knowledge to manage the new line of business. It may be defined as a portfolio change to achieve the target of the business. Diversification strategy may also be considered as strategy in which the growth objective is sought to be achieved by undertaking a new line of business. It may be adopted for the following reasons:

1. If the existing line of business is already on the decline and it may be necessary to add a new line to it.
2. Diversification provides an altogether new opportunity for the growth of the organisation.
3. It may also be used to disperse the risk involved in the various lines of the business.
4. It may be adopted to make efficient use of the existing resources and new sophisticated technology.
5. Diversification strategy may also be used to get a competitive edge over a rival organisation.

RETRENCHMENT STRATEGY

This may be defined as a reduction in the existing line of business by dropping some unprofitable product or service. It may aim at setting a level of objectives below past achievement. It may be adopted to maintain survival in the event of economic recession. Besides, poor performance in competition, financial difficulties, hostile business environment, etc., may also force an organisation to go for retrenchment strategy. It involves the cutting down of operations and activities and dropping of those products that are not economically viable and affect the overall performance of the organisation in an adverse manner. Sometimes it may be regarded as a defensive strategy which calls for the contraction of the existing level of business operations. Retrenchment strategy is used for the following reasons:

1. Because of poor economic viability and negligible contribution of some products or units, the organisation may close them to recover itself from a bad situation.
2. Hostile changes taking place in the business environment may also force the organisation to close some of its affected divisions.
3. If the deployment of resources in other available alternative proposals provides a higher return, the organisation may go for retrenchment strategy to get the benefit of this situation.
4. Decline in the performance level on a regular basis which is not within the control of the organisation may compel the organisation to downsize it by using retrenchment strategy.
5. Highly scattered and diversified business operations which may not be feasible from the management point of view may be trimmed to economise the overall functioning of the organisation.
6 To provide additional funds for more profitable operations, financial restructuring may be necessary. This may also be done through retrenchment strategy.

External Growth Strategy

In order to achieve the objectives of growth, external growth strategy may be adopted. It mainly includes merger, acquisition and joint ventures. This strategy has become very popular and a regular feature of corporate strategic planning.

In the context of the Indian situation, globalisation of economic operations has encouraged the application of this strategy to obtain the benefit of complementary competencies of the various organisations. In a merger, two or more organisations come together, get merged by losing their identities and form a new one. In acquisition, one organisation undertakes the business of the other organisation. Similarly, in a joint venture, two or more organisations collaborate by sharing equity. In all these instances, the main objective is get the benefit of large-scale operations and to safeguard mutual interests by using complementary collaboration by each organisation. This strategy is normally adopted for the following reasons:

1. The organisations might be interested in using each other's competencies for their mutual benefit.

2. It may be used to reduce unhealthy competition among rival organisations.
3. It may also be used by those organisations that fail to generate strength to bear the load of environmental changes.
4. Sometimes cost benefit analysis may also attract the organisation for using this strategy. For example, the acquisition of an ongoing business may be a cost effective proposal rather than setting a new business.
5. To achieve the overall growth target which may not be possible by using other strategies, external growth strategy may be followed.

Combination Strategy

In order to get the relative benefits of two or more of the above options of corporate strategy, the combination form may be used. By using this strategy, the organisation may maintain stability in respect to some operations and at the same time achieve a higher growth rate. Growth strategy may be use used in other areas of operation. Sometimes the use of such a strategy becomes necessary for the organisation so as to use new opportunities and to overcome new challenges arising out of a changing environment. The process of redefining the existing business lines may also force the organisation to go in for such a strategy. The organisation may use the following combinations of two strategies:

1. Stability and growth strategies
2. Growth and retrenchment strategies
3. Stability and retrenchment strategies
4. Growth, retrenchment and stability strategies.

Combination strategy may be pursued by the organisation for the following reasons:

1. If the organisation has multi-product lines and these products are in different stages of their life cycle, combination strategy is used to deal with the situation.
2. It may also be used to get the relative advantages of two or more strategies at a time to increase the growth rate.
3. The nature and size of the business operation may also force the organisation to use combination strategy.
4. To optimise the performance of the organisation in some of the areas of operation, it may need growth strategy and another area may demand retrenchment strategy.
5. Environmental changes may force the organisation to use combination strategy to cash in on opportunities and to counter new threats and challenges.

Evaluation of Strategy

Like all other plans, this strategy also needs periodic review and evaluation. This is done to ensure that it is implemented as effectively as possible. Many times even carefully drawn strategies may not remain effective due to environmental changes or changes in the situation. Therefore they should be reviewed and evaluated from time to time to maintain their effectiveness by updating them.

As far as the criteria for evaluating strategy is concerned, there is diversity among management authors. In this regard, the study made by Steiner has suggested a list of factors that are considered critical and important for the successful implementation of strategy. These factors are as follows:

1. Quality of top management
2. Development of future managers
3. Managerial interaction and drive to earn profits for the firm
4. Managerial needs and opportunities for products on the basis of environmental analysis specially with regard to marketing
5. Improved system of long-range planning
6. Better judgement, creativity and imagination at top-level management
7. Improvement in services to customers
8. Assuring competitive financial return to investors
9. Maximise the value of shareholder's investment
10. Developing willingness to take risks which commensurate returns and growth objectives

Taking into account the primary objectives of the organisation which are to be achieved by using a specific strategy, Steiner further suggested two sets of factors against which implementation of strategy can be evaluated.

1. Quantitative factors
2. Qualitative factors.

The strategy can be evaluated in terms of the following quantitative factors:

1. Net profit
2. Market price of shares
3. Dividend rates
4. Earnings on capital employed
5. Return on equity
6. Market share
7. Growth in sales volume
8. Production cost and efficiency
9. Distribution cost and efficiency
10. Employee turnover, absenteeism and satisfaction indices.

To evaluate strategy that is being pursued to achieve qualitative objectives, Titles has suggested a set of the following factors:

1. Internal Consistency

To achieve the objectives of an organisation a number of plans are formulated and implemented such as policies, procedures, rules, methods, budgets, etc. Strategy is also one of them which is known as a single use plan. It is designed to achieve objectives in a changed situation. It is a part of the whole planning system of the organisation. Therefore, it is expected to be consistent and contributive to other plans, so that it may fit into an integrated pattern of planning. Strategy may also be evaluated in terms of its relationship with other plans of the organisation. It is however to be noted that in no case the organisation can afford to have a disagreement or clash among them.

2. Consistency with Environment

Strategy is primarily designed and pursued to relate the organisation with its external environment. At the time of its formulation, due care should be taken to identify new opportunities and problems and to discover the strengths and weaknesses of the organisation. It is done to establish a match between these two in such a way so that the strengths may be used to exploit opportunities. It is therefore desirable that strategy must be made in conformity with the changing business environment. It is only then that the objectives may be achieved successfully even in a changed situation.

3. Appropriateness of Strategy in the Light of Available Resources

Strategy is basically a plan that involves commitment and utilisation of resources for its implementation. Thus, it may also be evaluated in terms of resources that are available in the organisation. According to the resource position of the organisation, necessary modifications may be made in strategy. Thus, while formulating strategy, its appropriateness to the resource position of the organisation must be assessed carefully. It should be evaluated in terms of financial resources, skill profile of the organisation particularly in the field of production and distribution, research and development, location of physical facilities, etc.

4. Acceptable Degree of Risk Involved in Strategy

Strategy is made and pursued to achieve objectives in a changed situation. The element of uncertainty that is associated with the environment makes strategy proposals risky. It is because if the change beyond the prediction takes place, it may render implementation of strategy ineffective. Therefore, strategy should also be evaluated in terms of the degree of risk involved in its implementation. Generally, a higher risk may yield a higher gain. But it is advisable for managers to pursue these strategies that carry an acceptable amount of risk. The degree of risk involved in the strategy depends on the following factors:

(a) Changing Resource Position

Uncertainty regarding the availability of resources that are required to implement strategy may affect the degree of risk involved in it. It is because, over a period of time when strategy is to be implemented, the resource position and skill profile of the organisation may change which may adversely affect its implementation.

(b) Time Gap

There is generally a gap of time between the formulation and implementation of strategy. During this gap, environmental elements may change and bring new threats and challenges. This may also affect the degree of risk associated with strategy.

(c) Quantity of Resources

The amount and value of resources to be used to implement the strategy may affect the quantity of risk involved in effective implementation. Generally, if the volume is larger, the outcomes of implementation cannot be predicted precisely and the degree of risk will increase.

5. Appropriateness of Time Horizons of Strategy

Although strategy is generally formulated for a longer period of time, the span of time involved must be within the reach of managers so that they can forecast and prepare assumptions of strategy with a greater degree of confidence and accuracy. The time element may have a considerable impact on the effective implementation of the strategy. Even a well-designed strategy may prove ineffective if it is not undertaken at an opportune time. Therefore, while making an evaluation of strategy options, the time element associated with it must be given due consideration.

6. Workability of Strategy

Strategy options may also be evaluated in terms of their workability, feasibility and practicability. Sometimes, the strategy option may appear less risky and more effective but it may be far from reality and practicability. Thus, strategy should be capable of being implemented within the available resource position, time frame and given managerial capabilities. The workability of strategy can not alone be evaluated on the basis of its results. Some other indicators should also be taken care of. For example, consensus among the managers regarding corporate goals and policies, time available for judging the effectiveness of other options should also be given serious thought. In brief, the workability of strategy depends on:

1. Can required resources be obtained?
2. Is the technology needed appropriate?
3. Can necessary input such as power, raw material, etc., be arranged?
4. Can estimated sales be generated and profit position attained?

SUMMARY

Every organisation needs a future vision or destination towards which resources are mobilised and utilised. The visionary statement is prepared by top-ranging managers. They also formulate basic policy that provides a framework within which strategic decisions are made. In other words, business policy may be defined as a basic framework within which the managers operate to decide the future destination and take decisions to shape the future of the organisation.

Business policy also facilitates an effective and efficient mobilisation and utilisation of resources to achieve the business mission and objective. It is strategic decision making which has long-term implications and involves entrepreneurial functions of scanning the external environment and making a situational analysis.

But corporate policy is different from business policy. It may be defined as a general statement which guides and regulates the decision making behaviour of managers. The corporate policies are formulated with respect to various functional areas such as production, marketing, finance, purchase, personnel, etc. Generally corporate policies are formulated by top managers but functional heads are taken into confidence. These policies may be either originated at the top or may be imposed by environmental factors or may be formulated on the basis of appeal made by lower level managers.

Policy formulation is a difficult task. Managers have to go through a process which involves many stages. They are identification of needs, collection of data and development of tentative policy proposals. These proposals are evaluated and a suitable one is selected. Approval of high-level managers is sought and periodic review is conducted to update the existing policy.

A sound policy is really an asset for the whole organisation. It must contribute to the accomplishment of objectives. It should be practical, socially sanctioned and legally valid. Like corporate policy, strategy is also one of the important plans of an organisation. It may be defined as an action plan that is formulated to achieve objectives in a changed situation. It is a response, move or counter-move of the organisation to cope with the changing environment and growing competition. It is a single-use plan designed and used in a specific situation. It relates the organisation with an external environment and provides future direction to the organisation. It also aims at deploying the organisation's resources efficiently to achieve objectives in the event of change.

Strategy formulation is an intellectual process. It begins with determining the mission and objectives of the organisation. The environmental analysis and analysis of capability profile of an organisation are two major steps that are involved in strategic formulation. By conducting an environmental analysis, managers identify opportunities and problems. An analysis of the capability profile will indicate the strengths and weaknesses of the organisation which lie upon various functional areas of the organisation.

On the basis of these two analyses, strategy options are developed and evaluated so as to arrive at a suitable one. Strategy may be formulated either at the level of the organisation of its business line or at the level of the functional areas of the organisation. Corporate strategy covers the entire organisation. Business strategy deals with various lines of business operations and functional strategies are made and implemented to carry out corporate and business strategies.

The organisation has many strategy options to deal with the changing environment and the new situations arising out of it. Stability strategy is considered to be the most important option. It is a comprehensive action plan to be implemented to optimise the existing level of performance of the organisation. It is adopted generally by conservative managers to improve business in terms of the existing product and market. It aims at doing the same thing in a different manner. Contrary to it, there is another type of strategy that is based on the concept of growth. It is formulated and implemented to facilitate growth and expansion. New objectives are set at a higher level with new products and new markets. Diversification strategy is a variant of growth strategy. It is an action plan that is made to expand the operations of the organisation in a new line of business which needs different skills, technology and knowledge. Retrenchment strategy aims at coping with a hostile business environment. It may be defined as an action plan that is designed to drop some unprofitable products and operations so as to cut operational costs to redeploy and redistribute the available resources among more profitable areas of operation.

External growth strategy may be described as an action plan that facilitates the growth of an organisation through external means such as merger, acquisition, joint venture, etc. This kind of strategy seems to be appropriate in the event of globalisation of business operations that require a combination of complementary competencies of two or more organisations.

Similarly, combination strategy provides a suitable action plan based on two or more strategies. It is used to obtain the benefits of more than one strategic plan.

Strategic plans are drawn specially to cope with a changing environment. Regular changes in the environment may render an existing strategic plan less effective. Therefore strategic plans should be evaluated from time to time to discover their effectiveness and update them as per requirement. To evaluate effectiveness, factors may include profit, market share, cost of production, earnings, growth of sales and income and changes in the net worth of the organisation. Similarly, evaluation of strategy can be made in terms of its consistency with both internal as well as external environments, suitability in terms of resources, degrees of risk, etc.

TEST QUESTIONS

1. Define the term 'business policy' and explain its characteristics.
2. Explain various elements that are involved in the process of formulation of policy.
3. What is strategy? Describe its main features.
4. Discuss the importance of strategy in a rapidly changing business environment and growing competition.
5. Describe the various major elements of the process of strategy formulation.
6. Define stability strategy, its characteristics and enumerate the reasons for which it is adopted.
7. Define growth strategy. Explain its main features. Why is it adopted?
8. Describe those factors against which strategy is evaluated.
9. Write short notes on the following:
   (a) Corporate policy
   (b) Types of policies
   (c) SWOT analysis
   (d) Environmental analysis
   (e) Capability profile of organisation
   (f) Evaluation of strategy
   (g) Combination strategy
   (h) Retrenchment strategy

OBJECTIVE TYPE QUESTIONS

Which of the following statements are correct and which are incorrect? Give reasons for your answers.

1. Business policy is formulated at a lower level of management.
2. Policies are formulated at a lower level of management.
3. Strategy is a comprehensive response to a changing environment.
4. Strategy relates organisation with external environment.
5. SWOT analysis aims at discovering strengths, weaknesses, opportunities and threats.
6. Stability strategy means 'do nothing'.
7. Combination strategy is adopted for accelerating growth rate.
8. Retrenchment strategy is followed for retrenching employees in the organisation.

REFERENCES

Ansof, H. J. *The New Corporate Strategy*. New York, U.S.A.: John Wiley and Sons, 1988.

Cherunilan, Francis. *Strategic Management*. Delhi, India: Himalaya Publishing House, 1998.

David, Fred R. *Fundamentals of Strategic Management*. Columbus, Ohio, U.S.A.: Merrill Publishing Company, 1986.

Drucker, Peter F. *Management*. Mumbai, India. Allied Publishers Pvt. Ltd., 1975.

Gluck, William F. *Business Policy and Strategic Management*. Auckland, Australia: McGraw-Hill International Book Company, 1972.

Hamel, Gary and Prahalad, C. K. *Competing for the Future*. Boston, U.S.A.: Harvard Business School Press, 1996.

Hamel, Gary. 'Strategy as Revolution'. *Harvard Business Review*, July–Aug, 1996.

Holland, Leslie and Holland, Phyllis G. *Strategic Management*. New York, U.S.A.: McGraw-Hill Book Company, 1989.

Jauch, Lawrence R and Gluck, William E. *Strategic Management and Business Policy*. New York, U.S.A.: Free Press, 1979.

Koontz, Harold and Weihrich, Heinz. *Essentials of Management*. New Delhi, India: Tata McGraw-Hill Publishing Company Ltd., 1998.

Larange, Peter; Scott Morton; Michael F and Ghoshal, Sumantra. *Strategic Control*. St. Paul, U.S.A.: West Publishing Company, 1986.

Ohami, Kenichi. *The Mind of the Strategist*. New York, U.S.A.: Penguin Books Ltd., 1982.

Pearce, John A. and Robinson, Richard B., Jr. *Strategic Management: Strategy Formulation and Implementation*. Delhi, India: A.I.T.B.S. Publishers and Distributors (Regd.), 1997.

Pearce, John A. II and Robinson, Richard B. Jr. *Strategic Management*. New Delhi, India: All India Traveller Book Seller, 1998.

Porter, Michel E. 'What is Strategy'. *Harvard Business Review,* Nov–Dec, 1996.

Rue, Leslie W. and Holland, Phyllis G. *Strategic Management*. New York, U.S.A., McGraw-Hill Book Company, 1989.

Schendel, Dan E. and Hoffer, Charles W. *Strategic Management. A New View of Business Policy and Planning*. Boston, U.S.A.: Little Brown, 1978.

Steiner, George. *Strategic Planning. What Every Manager Must Know*. New York, U.S.A.: The Free Press, 1979.

Stoner, Freeman and Gilbert, Jr. *Management*. New Delhi, India: Prentice-Hall of India Pvt. Ltd., 2001.

White, E. 'Manage Beyond Portfolio Analysis'. *Harvard Business Review*, Jan–Feb, 1984.

EXPERIENCE I

Suzuki Hikes Maruti Export Prices Before IPO

- In a bid to shore up its net worth before its forthcoming Rs. 830-crore Maruti IPO, parent Suzuki has increased the export process of its frontrunner, the Alto. The hike, estimated around 1–2 per cent will increase overseas earnings and offset the losing revenue caused by rupee appreciation.
- Senior Maruti officials said the price hike was marginal and is being implemented to cash in on the high demand that Maruti Alto enjoys in Europe. "The effects of rupee appreciation and hike in other input costs would be offset by the price hike. It will lead to greater export earnings."

However, market watchers termed this as a strategy to shore up revenues before the IPO. "Just before the IPN, the firm has announced a record growth in profits and then announced a dividend. And export prices are hiked amid cut-throat competition that is forcing car makers to offer better prices. These may be ways to tell the investor about Maruti's strengths and ensure its success," said a Mumbai-based analyst.

But the officials pointed out: "We can afford a price hike because the car is in great demand."

Suzuki Motor CEO Osamu Suzuki has already stated that Maruti is looking at exports to drive revenue growth in the current financial year.

It expects shipments to Europe to rise 21 per cent this year and Suzuki will use its 250-dealer European network to export Maruti's small cars to the Continent.

Besides, Maruti has been allowed to independently cater to the southeast Asian markets. Maruti currently exports its Alto to the Netherlands, Germany, Italy, the U.K. and Switzerland, while the M-800 is shipped to Bangladesh, Nepal, Sri Lanka, Chile and Egypt.

Its export sales in 2002–03 stood at Rs. 670.80 crore, which is almost 7.4 per cent of its total sales revenue.

EXPERIENCE II
Why Good Executives Back Bad Strategy

Hidden Flaws in Strategy

The world of business is full of examples of bad strategy. One reason for this, say behavioural economists, is that the human being is not a purely rational economic decision maker. That is because the human brain, has, over the millennia of its evolution, developed shortcuts, biases and basic bad habits.

The Sunk-cost Effect

A familiar problem with investments is called the sunk-cost effect, otherwise known as "throwing good money after bad." When large projects overrun their schedules and budgets, the original economic case no longer holds; however companies still keep investing to complete them.

Financial institutions often face this dilemma over large-scale IT projects. There are numerous examples most of which remain private. One of the more public cases was the London Stock Exchange's automated-settlement system, Taurus. It took the intervention of the Bank of England to force a cancellation, write off the expenses and take control of building a replacement.

Executives making strategic-investment decisions can also fall into the sunk cost trap. Certain European banks spend fortunes building up large equities businesses to compete with the global investment banking firms. It then proved extraordinarily hard for some of these banks to face up to the strategic reality that they had no prospect of ever competing successfully against the likes of Goldman Sachs, Merrill Lynch and Morgan Stanley in the equities business. Some banks in the United Kingdom took the agonising decision to write of their investments; other European institutions are still caught in the trap.

Why is it so hard to avoid? One explanation is based on loss aversion: we would rather spend an additional $ 10 million completing an uneconomic $ 110 million project than write off $ 100 million. Another explanation relies on anchoring: once the brain has been anchored at $ 100 million, an addition $ 10 million does not seem so bad. What should strategies do to avoid the trap?

1. Apply the full rigour of investment analysis to incremental investments, looking only at incremental prospective costs and revenues. This is the textbook response to the sunk-cost fallacy and it is right.

Experience II continued

Experience II continued

2. Be prepared to kill strategic experiments early. In an increasingly uncertain world, companies will often pursue several strategic options. Successfully managing a portfolio of them entails jettisoning the losers. The more quickly you get out, the lower the sunk costs and the easier the exit.
3. Uses 'gated funding' for all strategic investment, much as pharmaceutical companies do for drug development: release follow-on funding only once strategic experiments have met previously agreed targets.

The Herd Instinct

The banking industry, like many others, shows a strong herd instinct. It tends to lend too much money to the same kinds of borrowers at the same time—to U.K. property developers in the 1970s, less-developed countries in the 1980s, and technology, media and telecommunications companies more recently. And banks tend to pursue the same strategies, be it creating internet banks with strange-sounding names during the dotcom boom or building integrated investment banks during the 'big bang', when the London stock market was liberalised.

This desire to conform to the behaviour and opinions of others is a fundamental human trait and an accepted principle of psychology. Warren Buffett put his finger on this flaw when he wrote: "Failing conventionally is the route to go; as a group lemmings have a rotten image, but no individual lemming has ever received a bad press." For most CEOs, only one thing is worse than a huge strategic mistake: being the only person in the industry to make it.

We all felt the tug of the heart during the dotcom era. It was lonely being a Luddite, arguing the case against setting up as a stand-alone internet bank or an online brokerage. At times of mass enthusiasm for a strategic trend, pressure to follow the herd rather than rely on one's own information and analysis is almost irresistible. Yet the best strategies break away from the trend. Some action may be necessary to match the competition—imagine a bank without ATMs or a good online banking offer. But these are not unique sources of strategic advantage, and finding such sources is what strategy is all about. 'Me-too' strategies are often simply bad ones. Seeking out the new and the unusual should therefore be the strategy's aim. Rather than copying what your most established competitors are doing, look at the periphery for innovative ideas and look outside your own industry.

Experience II continued

Experience II continued

Initially, an innovative strategy may draw scepticism from industry experts. They may be right, but as long as you kill a failing strategy early, your losses will be limited; when they are wrong, the rewards will be great.

Mis-estimating Future Hedonic States

What does it mean, in plain English, to mis-estimate future hedonic states? Simply that people are bad at estimating how much pleasure or pain they will feel if their circumstances change dramatically. Social scientists have shown that when people undergo major changes in circumstances, their lives typically are neither as bad nor as good as they had expected—another case of how bad we are at estimating people adjust surprisingly quickly, and their level of pleasure (hedonic state) ends up, broadly, where it was before.

This research strikes a chord with anyone who has studied compensation trends in the investment-banking industry. Ever-higher compensation during the 1990s led only to ever-higher expectations—not to a marked change in the general level of happiness on the street. According to Tom Wolfe's Sherman McCoy in *Bonfire of the Vanities*, it was hard to make ends meet in New York on $ 1 million a year in 1987. Back then, that was shocking hubris from a (fictional) top bond salesman. By 2000, even adjusted for inflation, it would have seemed a perfectly reasonable lament from a relatively junior managing director.

Another illustration of our poor ability to judge future hedonic states in the business world is the way we deal with a loss of independence. More often than not, takeovers are seen as the corporate equivalent of death, to be avoided at all costs. Yet sometimes they are the right move. Two once-great British banks—Midland and National Westminster—both struggled to maintain their independence. Midland gave in to HSBC's advances in 1992; NatWest was taken over by the Royal Bank of Scotland in 2000. At both institutions, the consequences were positive for customers, shareholders and most employees on any test of the 'greatest good of the greatest number.' The employees ended up being part of a better-managed and stronger, more respected institutions. Morale at NatWest has gone up. Midland had achieved what was, for an independent bank, an unrealistic goal: to become part of a great global bank.

Often, top management is blamed for resisting any loss of independence. Certainly, part of the problem is the desire of management and boards to hang on to the status quo. That said, frontline staff members often resist a takeover or merger however much they are frustrated with the existing top management. Some deeper psychological factor appears

Experience II continued

Experience II continued

to be at work. We do seem very bad at estimating how we would feel if our circumstances changed dramatically—changes in corporate control, like changes in our personal health or wealth.

How can the strategist avoid this pitfall?

1. In takeovers, adopt a dispassionate and unemotional view. Easier said than done—especially for a management team with years of committed service to an institution and a personal stake in the status quo. Non-executives, however should find it easier to maintain a detached view.
2. Keep things in perspective. Do not over-react to apparently deadly strategic threats or get too excited to good news. During the high and low points of the crisis of Lloyd's of London in the mid-1990s, the chairman used to quote Field Marshal Slim: "In battle, nothing is ever as good or as bad as the first reports of excited men would have it." This is a good guide for every strategist trying to navigate a crisis, with the inevitable swings in emotion and morale.

False Consensus

People tend to overestimate the extent to which others share their views, beliefs and experiences—the false-consensus effect. Research shows many causes for that, including:

- Confirmation bias, the tendency to seek out opinions and facts that support our own beliefs and hypotheses.
- Selective recall, the habit of remembering only facts and experiences that reinforce our assumptions.
- Biased evaluation, the quick acceptance of evidence that supports our hypotheses, while contradictory evidence is subjected to rigorous evaluation and almost certain rejection; we also often impute hostile motives to critics or question their competence.
- Groupthink, the pressure to agree with others in team-based cultures. Consider how many times you may have heard a CEO say something like, "The executive team is 100 per cent behind the new strategy" (groupthink). "The chairman and the board are fully supportive and they all agree with our strategy" (false consensus). "I've heard only good things from dealers and customers about our new product range" (selective recall). "OK, so some analysts are still negative, but those 'teenage scribblers' don't understand our business—their latest reports were superficial and full of errors" (biased evaluation). The role of any strategic adviser should be to provide a counter-balance to this tendency towards false consensus. CEOs should welcome the challenge.

Experience II continued

Experience II continued

False consensus, which ranks among the brain's most pernicious flaws, can led strategists to miss important threats to their companies and to persist with doomed strategies But it can be extremely difficult to uncover—especially if those proposing a strategy are strong role models. We are easily influenced by dominant individuals and seek to emulate them. This can be a force for good if the role models are positive. But negative ones can prove an irresistible source of strategic error.

Many of the worst financial services strategies can be attributed to over-dominant individuals. The failure of several Lloyd's syndicates in the 1980s and the 1990s was due to powerful underwriters who controlled their own agencies. Over-dominant individuals are associated with several more recent insurance failures. In banking, one European institution struggled to impose effective risk disciplines because its seemingly most successful employees were, in the eyes of junior staff, cavalier in their approach to compliance. Their behaviour set the tone and created a culture of non-compliance.

The dangers of false consensus can be minimised in several ways:

1. **Create a Culture of Challenge**

   As part of the strategic debate, management teams should value open and constructive criticism. Criticising a fellow director's strategy should be seen as a helpful, not a hostile act. CEOs and strategic advisers should understand criticism, seek contrary views on industry tends and, if in doubt, take steps to assure themselves that opposing views have been well researched. They should not automatically ascribe to critics bad intentions or lack of understanding.

2. **Ensure that Strong Checks and Balances Control the Dominant Role Models**

   A CEO should be particularly wary of dominant individuals who dismiss challenges to their own strategic proposals. The CEO should insist that these proposals undergo an independent review by respected experts. The board should be equally wary of a domineering CEO.

3. **Do not Lead the Witness**

   Instead of asking for a validation of your strategy, ask for a detailed refutation. When setting up hypotheses at the beginning of a strategic analysis, impose contrary hypotheses or require the team to set up equal and opposite hypotheses for each key analysis. Establish a

Experience II continued

Experience II continued

'challenger team' to identify the flaws in the strategy being proposed by the strategy team.

An awareness of the brain's flaws can help strategists steer around them. All strategists should understand the insights of behavioural economics just as much as they understand those of other fields of the dismal science.

This will not put an end to bad strategy: greed, arrogance and sloppy analysis will continue to provide plenty of textbook cases of it. Understanding some of the flaws built into our thinking processes, however, many help reduce the chances of good executives backing bad strategies.

VIDEO CASE STUDY I

Trying to Swallow a Whale when You're a Minnow

Although in 1991 Pan Am was forced to sell its assets to other airlines, in May 1989 it made an unusual bid for the parent company of Northwest Airlines, NA Corporation. What made the deal surprising was not that the size and prestige of the firms are in stark contrast, but that the relative health of the two airlines in recent years would have made one think the deal would have been working in the opposite direction.

Since 1981, Pan Am had totalled over $ 1.7 billion in losses while Northwest had managed to build up over half a billion in profits. To analysts, it appeared that the deregulation of the airline industry in 1970 had sent Pan Am into a tailspin—one that it was still struggling to get out of. Other airlines had the means and resources to establish domestic networks and root systems, while Pan Am lagged behind and had slowly diminished into a 'cash-poor minnow'. Despite its poor performance, though, evidence suggested that Pan Am had solidified its base and may have been on more solid ground.

Northwest, by contrast, was a promising firm with a sound root system and a solid cash base—a 'cash whale'. The main negative in Northwest's situation was its relationship with its pilots; contract negotiations had been going on for more than two years with little success.

Pan Am was not the only bidder for Northwest. Others included that of oil man Marvin Davis, who had little experience with the airline industry and would have had to borrow most of the money. Another offer came from Alfred Checchi and Gary Wilson who seem interested in buying

Video Case Study I continued

Video Case Study I continued

Northwest to break it up and sell it. Fortsman, Little & Company was also interested in buying Northwest to improve it and then sell it for a higher price.

Northwest, of course, would prefer to see the airline remain intact, but it was also in getting the most it can. Also, one of the major obstacles in any negotiations was the pilots' strong desire to keep the airline intact.

Questions

1. How would you evaluate Pan Am's strategy? What are the major impediments to implementing its strategy?
2. What can Pan Am do to make their bid more attractive to Northwest?
3. What are the biggest problems that Pan Am will face in integrating Northwest's systems, pilots, routes, planes and so on, into Pan Am's operations?

—oo(O)oo—

CHAPTER 7

DECISION MAKING IN AN ORGANISATION

LEARNING OBJECTIVES

1. To develop understanding about decision making as an important managerial action.
2. To remember various types of decisions and distinguish between programmed and non-programmed, strategic and operational, individual and group decisions.
3. To bring out elements of the decision making process and relate them with the process of making decisions.
4. To understand the role of information in decision making.
5. To develop conceptual clarity with regard to various techniques of decision making.
6. To analyse the role of creativity in decision making.
7. To distinguish between the normative and behavioural models of decision making.
8. To get a clear idea of bounded rationality.
9. To suggest improvements for effectiveness of decision making.

INTRODUCTION AND MEANING

Decision making is the essence of the managing process. In the managerial hierarchy, all managers take decisions, although the nature and significance of decisions made by them may vary from manager to manager and situation to situation. But without taking decisions they cannot manage. Decisions are made by them to solve problems, tackling the situation, handling crises and resolving conflicts that are inevitable in the functioning of an organisation.

Decision making is at the core of planning. This is because in the process of planning, managers have to take decisions to select a suitable course of action to be adopted to achieve objectives. It is a managerial process or activity of choosing an appropriate course of action from several alternative courses. The decision making process takes place only when managers have two or more options or alternatives.

The term 'decision making' has been defined by various management authors. Decision making is a process of judging various available options and narrowing down choices to a suitable one. According to Allen, management decision making is "the work a manager performs to arrive at conclusion and judgement." This definition reveals that all is inclusive in decision making, which the manager does to arrive at a conclusion and to make a judgement. Shull, Delberg and Cummings have defined decision making as "a conscious and human process involving both individual and social phenomena based on factual and value premises which concludes with a choice of one behavioural activity from among one or more alternatives with the intention of moving towards a desired state of affairs."

This definition seems to be broad and comprehensive, because it covers many basic issues involved in decision making. It also reveals the importance of human and social values in decision making and that it has been considered as behavioural activity based on certain facts and value premises. Further, according to Kreitner, decision making is a process of identifying and choosing an alternative course of action in a manner appropriate to the demand of the situation. The act of choosing implies that an alternative course of action must be weighed and weeded out. He has emphasised that judgement and discretion are fundamental to decision making.

Broadly, decision making involves much of managerial activity. It directs the organisation along a specific course of action and entails commitment of resources in a particular manner. It is only by making decisions and getting them implemented that the resources of an organisation are mobilised and utilised to achieve its objectives. To identify the basic nature of decision making, George Terry regards managerial life as a perpetual decision making challenge.

Similarly, Peter Drucker said that whatever a manager does he does through decision making. In other words, at every stage of managing, the manager faces the challenge of making correct, qualitative and effective decisions to get the best out of a situation. In the context of organisation functioning, managers take decisions regarding organisational goals, policies, strategies and other plans, selecting lines of business, range of products and product line, profitability, market share, and growth and diversification of organisational activities. In addition, decisions are also made on various aspects related to functional areas like production, distribution, finance, purchase, personnel, research and development.

Managerial decisions are formally directed towards making the organisation a functional entity preserving its identity and maintaining continuity in its working life.

On the basis of various definitions and discussions made above regarding several aspects of decision making, the following characteristics may be derived:

1. Decision making as in integral part of planning. Every planner has to choose an appropriate solution or alternative among the available options.
2. It aims at choosing a suitable course of action by weighing and weeding out several available alternatives.
3. It involves the judgement and discretion of the decision maker. It is not an entirely rational process because decisions are bound to be affected and coloured by the personal likes, dislikes and whims of the manager who makes them.
4. Decisions made by managers involve the commitment of the organisation to adopt a specific course of action and utilise resources in a particular manner.
5. Decision making like managing is a human and social process implying the interference of an individual as well as social factors. An intelligent manager will always take into account the social and human implications of a decision before making a final choice.
6. Decision making is a purpose activity because it is directed towards the achievement of a goal and objectives.
7. Decisions are made by managers to solve problems, resolve crises and conflicts and tackle the situation.
8. Decisions made by managers may sometimes have a negative effect for a short period of time. For example, decisions on retrenchment, demotion, dismissal of employees, reduction in the scale of operation, introduction of change, closing down of some units, withdrawing a product from the market, etc.
9. Decision making requires enough liberty to be given to managers so that they can also make use of their experience, skill and judgement. This is the reason that policies that guide decision making are made flexible enough.
10. Pervasiveness of decision making: Decision making is not only at the core of planning, but is also an important managerial activity. The manager manages by making decisions and getting them implemented. The effectiveness of decision making and the quality of the decisions made by a manager, to a large extent, depends upon his skill, judgement, competence and abilities. Every manager has to make a decision to solve problems, tackle and handle situations while dealing with his subordinates. The efficiency of managers, among other factors, is also measured in terms of the quality of decisions made by him.

In the managerial hierarchy of an organisation, the required structural and administrative arrangements are made to delegate authority to lower level managers so as to authorise them to make decisions. The top executives take decisions only on basic and major issues and matters that are directly concerned with the survival, profitability and growth of the organisation. For handling the matters arising out of day-to-day operations, lower level managers are granted authority to decide upon them. Besides delegation of authority, other administrative arrangements are also made including installation of an information system, formulation of basic policies, training of subordinate managers to develop the required abilities and create a proper conducive internal environment in the organisation which facilitates decentralised decision making.

As stated earlier, decisions are made not only regarding the various elements of management and matters involved therein such as determination of organisational goals and other plans, designing the structure of an organisation, devising controlling techniques, providing effective leadership, scheduling a network of communication and designing motivations systems. But managers have also to decide upon various issues related to functional areas like, production, distribution, finance, personnel, purchase, etc. Thus, it runs through the entire process of management and all sub-systems of the organisation.

In an organisation, resources can be mobilised and utilised in the direction of achieving the desired goals only by taking decisions and getting them implemented. In the light of the primacy and pervasiveness of decision making activity in organisational functioning and its management, it seems to be desirable for the manager to take quality decisions timely as the situation demands. Apart from maintaining a proper balance between timeliness and quality of decision, the human needs and social implications of the decisions should also be taken into account at the time of taking decisions.

TYPES OF DECISIONS

Although every manager takes decision, the significance and nature of them differ. Some decisions are made by them to solve repetitive problems. Others they make only once in a while to solve non-repetitive problems. Similarly, sometimes the managers make decisions at the individual level exercising their authority and in some situations they take decisions in a group. These decisions may be classified as under:

1. Programmed and Non-programmed Decisions

Programmed decisions are routine and repetitive in nature. They are made by managers on a regular basis. They refer to decisions made by managers to solve those problems or tackle those situations that require the application of a predetermined set of procedures, techniques and rules. As the problem arises, the prescribed procedure is applied and a decision is made, for example, hiring of employees, purchase of raw material, payment of bills, etc. Programmed decisions are made with regard to routine and recurring problems. These require structured solutions that can be arrived at with the help of operating procedures and processes determined in advance. In connection with programmed decisions, the 'decision rules' are very important. It is a statement that identifies the situation in which a decision is required. It also specifies how the decision will be made. The 'decision rules' permit busy managers to make routine decisions quickly without going through a comprehensive problem-solving procedure.

Carefully and intelligently formulated and conceived decision rules may also encourage lower level managers to share responsibility for programmed decisions. It allows higher level managers to concentrate more on important non-programmed decisions. The process of decision making in respect of programmed decisions is simplified by decision rules. No judgement or discretion is needed to find solutions to such problems. It is simply a matter of identifying the problem and applying decision rules to get it solved. The programmed decisions remain consistent for a relatively longer period of time and over many situations. It is, however, to be noted that programmed decisions are not always made to solve simple problems, because decision making may be programmed for even more complex problems.

Non-programmed decisions are made with respect to problems that are unique, non-repetitive and about which the required information is not available. Such decisions are made under new and unfamiliar circumstances, much less frequently as compared to programmed decisions, since non-programmed decisions are made with regard to a new situation arising for the first time. It renders standard and predetermined procedure and decision rules ineffective and irrelevant. And it demands experience, creativity, innovativeness, farsightedness and use of judgement by managers to make such decisions.

Non-programmed decisions are usually made to solve unstructured problems that keep changing in character from time to time. These problems are marked by a high degree of uncertainty. To make such decisions, managers have to redefine and reformulate the problem by applying managerial skill, judgement and creativity. Examples of non-programmed decisions include deciding whether to merge with other organisations, to diversify, open a new branch in a foreign country, appoint of a chief executive, introduction of a new product or service, etc. One of the decision theorists has put non-programmed decisions as follows: "There is no short cut and direct method for handling the problem, because it has not arisen before, or because its precise nature and structure are elusive and complex or because it is so important that it deserves a custom-tailored treatment." This interpretation reveals that non-programmed decisions are made on complex, novel and non-routine problems. It requires creative decision-making.

2. Strategic and Operational Decisions

Strategic decisions are usually made by top-level managers on problems and matters that are important and critical for the survival, success and profitability of the organisation. These decisions have a great influence on the functioning and direction of the organisation. The strategic decisions normally do have long-range implications because they are tenable for a longer period of time. They define and establish a relationship of the organisation with its external environment. Such decisions require more resources, judgement and skill and therefore responsibility for such decisions is assumed by top management. The main characteristics of strategic decision is that once they are taken, it is neither desirable nor feasible to withdraw them, for example, the selection of a product, locational decisions, switching to new technology, taking over other organisations, etc. Strategic decisions, to some extent, resemble non-programmed decisions. They possess some of the characteristics of non-programmed decisions. These decisions are made under the conditions of 'risk', that is, managers may have partial knowledge and may not be sure about the outcome of decisions.

To implement strategic decisions, some other decisions known as tactical or operations decisions, are made by managers. A single strategic decision may involve a number of tactical decisions or the full package of them. These decisions are concerned with routine and repetitive matters arising again and again in the functioning of the organisation. They do not require much managerial judgement and skill on the part of managers because they are related to the implementation of strategic decisions. This is the reason why the authority for making tactical decisions is vested in lower level managers. The tactical decisions are more specific, functional and have short-term implications. Since they are of a routine nature, certain established guidelines, procedures and rules may be followed to make such decisions. The difference between strategic and operational decisions can be understood with the help of the following example.

In a manufacturing organisation, strategic decisions of selecting products and processes, making capacity planning and selecting the location of a plant are made by higher level managers. Now these strategic decisions have to be implemented by making many other operational or tactical decisions such as production planning, quality control, cost control, inventory control, etc. These operational decisions are made by departmental managers by using set procedures, rules and techniques.

3. Individual and Group Decisions

Decision making is an integral part of the manager's job. Every manager has to make a variety of decisions to deal with a situation effectively, to resolve conflicts amicably and solve problems efficiently. To take a decision, the manager is delegated with enough authority and within the extent and scope of it he makes decisions, both on more important as well as less important matters. Such decisions that are made by individual managers by using managerial skill and judgement on the one hand and set procedures, techniques and rules on the other, are known as individual decisions. To make such decisions, they are supplied with the required and relevant information and other inputs and they also get help from their subordinate managers. But the ultimate responsibility and authority for making decisions lies on them. Individual decisions are made by all managers right from top executives to first-line supervisors.

Group decisions are those that are made by two or more managers jointly. In order to make such decisions, managers working at the same or different levels come together, and deliberate over the problem. They express their viewpoints on different aspects of the problem and finally, by using their collective wisdom, they solve it. Such types of decision-making seems to be very common with regard to problems that involve an interest in many functional divisions or departments. For example, the decision of product selection may be arrived at by joint efforts of the production manager, marketing manager and manager of the research and development department.

In a joint stock company, the board of directors, known as the chief organ of the company's management makes group decisions. Whatever power and authority they have, they can exercise it only through meetings. They make decisions unanimously or by majority votes. The board of directors is also known as a plural executive body. Apart from the board of directors various committees may also be formed for the purpose of deciding the various matters at the lower level of the organisation. These committees may be known as task forces or teams or managing committees constituted for a specific purpose. On the same lines, sometimes the superior may involve his subordinates to get their cooperation and their involvement in decision regarding matters that may be of more concern to them. For example, while taking decisions regarding sales promotion or price or quality of a product, the marketing manager may in an informal manner invite some sales managers having the required knowledge on a particular matter to help him take a right decision.

The nature of the involvement of the members of the committee formed to decide some specific matter may differ. Their involvement may be restricted only to the level of doing the necessary spade work such as collecting data, expressing their viewpoint, making suggestions and recommendations and helping the chief executive officer in all respects. But the final choice is to be made by the chief executive officer himself. This kind of involvement on the part of members or subordinates is known as 'group participation in the decision making.' However, in some other situations, the members or subordinates may share the authority of decision making with the chief executive. This type of involvement is known precisely as 'group decision making'. In a group decision, the final authority to take decisions is vested in the group itself rather than in an individual. On the whole, the group decision-making in any form whether simple participation or full-fledged decision making certainly helps in implementation and seeking more cooperation and acceptance from subordinates.

ADVANTAGES AND DISADVANTAGES OF GROUP DECISIONS

As compared to individual decisions, group decisions offer certain advantages:

1. Group decisions are based on collective knowledge and judgement pooled together.
2. Group decisions are considered to be more balanced in every respect. This is because they are made after considering the different viewpoints expressed by the group members.
3. The group decision making process provides a positive contribution to the training of the executives and their development. This is because subordinates get an opportunity to get an insight into the problem by discussing it with superiors.
4. The participation of subordinates or other members in decision making serves as a motivation for them because they get involved in the problem. If it is solved, the need for their self-fulfilment is satisfied.
5. Group decision making seems to be more desirable to solve complex interdepartmental problems. This is because the group of managers representing their respective departments may handle such a situation more efficiently.
6. Group decision making represents the cooperative nature of management. It is considered more important to create team spirit among the group members and define their role and get maximum contribution from them.

At the same time, group decision making is also beset with certain problems and limitations. First, it encourages indecisiveness and compromise on the problem. It happens because sometimes the least competent member may impede the efforts of the most competent ones. Second, divided responsibility in group decisions also affects the quality of decisions adversely. Because of this, members do not take an active and serious interest to solve problems and do not exhibit a sense of responsibility. Third, inordinate delay in decision making is also marked in a group decision because of long discussions, procedural technicalities and the diverse opinions of members. It ultimately reduces the effectiveness of the decision making process (Figure 7.1).

ELEMENTS OF DECISION-MAKING PROCESS
1. Identification of problem
2. Definition of problem
3. Specification of objectives
4. Collection of data
5. Developing alternative courses of action
6. Evaluation of alternative courses of action
7. Selection of appropriate alternative
8. Implementation of decisions

Figure 7.1. The decision making process

ELEMENTS OF THE DECISION MAKING PROCESS

In practice, different decision making procedures are used in different situations depending on the nature of the problem in hand, environment—both internal and external, time and cost factors. Although decision making is a systematic and rational process that describes how decisions are made by managers, it does not point out how they actually make decisions in practice. It is found that managers do not follow a rational process step by step. Nevertheless, theoretically, each decision making process involves the following steps that are known as the elements of decision making:

1. Identification of a Problem Situation

The process of decision making begins with the unfolding of or discovering the problem. To discover it in full, all the relevant internal as well as external situations are to be scanned. Identification of the problem situation represents the need to take a decision and locate the problem on which a decision is to be taken. The problem may relate to any area of the operation of the organisation, the management process or it may concern the external environment and the changes taking place in it. Along with the location of the problem, its basic nature has also to be ascertained so as to know whether it is strategic or operational, major or minor and a long-term or short-term problem. According to Chester Barnard, the occasions for decisions originate in three distinct fields:

1. from authoritative communication from a superior
2. from cases referred for decisions by subordinates
3. from cases originating in the initiative of the manager concerned.

2. Definition of the Problem Situation

Once the problem is clearly perceived by the manager and the need to solve it well felt by him, he proceeds to analyse it thoroughly as the next stage. In this regard, the manager attempts to define the problem as clearly as possible. It is generally believed that a well defined problem is halfway solved. The efficiency of the decision making process and quality of the decision to a large extent depends on a clear definition of the problem. To define a problem in most cases is a difficult task. It is because the real problem may be quite different from the problem appearing before the managers. Thus, the problem situation has to be defined and described in terms of its origin, scope, symptoms, causes, importance, gravity, intensity and ramifications. In case of a major and complex problem it seems desirable to break it into simple components and to study them thoroughly. As defining a problem is a time-consuming job, managers prefer to define only the strategic and critical aspects of it to save time.

3. Specification of Objectives

The decision making process does not work in a vacuum. Rather it has certain objectives. And it is directed towards the achievement of those objectives that are likely to be achieved by solving that problem, for example, if the company is facing a problem of cut-throat competition in the market regarding some of its products which seems to be strategic in nature. By tackling and solving the problem carefully and wisely, the objective of maintaining survival or increasing demand and enhancing market share may be achieved. These objectives may be both quantitative as well as qualitative in nature. They serve as a yardstick for measuring and evaluating the efficiency and effectiveness of various alternative courses of action, particularly of that one which is chosen to solve the problem.

4. Collection of Data

Relevant and reliable information has a very important role in decision making. Information is required not for uncovering and defining the problem but it is equally useful for the other stages involved in the process. Thus, the needed information is gathered in both forms from internal as well as external sources to provide a factual framework to managers to solve the problem. The use of information in the decision making process facilitates the definition of the problem and the making of factual decisions. It is the availability, reliability and surety with which the needed information can be obtained that determines decision making for managers.

5. Developing Alternative Courses of Action

The next step for managers, after having defined the problem and collecting the required information, is to develop alternative solutions. The quality of the decisions made by managers is going to be affected by it. Therefore, he should leave no stone unturned to develop all the possible solutions. In fact, the process of decision making becomes relevant, meaningful and a challenging exercise for managers if there are many alternatives to be examined to make a final decision. Alternative solutions may not be obvious and apparent. It is the duty of managers to search for them. Some alternatives may be developed by managers quickly with reference to their past experience and expertise. And others may be generated through research and analysis, creative thinking and innovativeness on the part of managers.

6. Evaluation of Alternative Course of Action

The objective of decision making is to choose from alternatives the one that will provide the greatest amount of wanted consequences and the smallest amount of unwanted consequences. For this purpose, each alternative is to be valued to the extent that its consequences of alternatives can be estimated through forecasting and other devices. Each alternative should be thoroughly evaluated in detail in terms of the risk involved, time consumed, efficiency of alternative and resource position of the organisation to implement a course or action or decision. However, it should be noted that to evaluate alternative courses of action, qualitative factors should also be taken into account such as ethical and moral values, social implication, image of the organisation, etc.

7. Selection of Appropriate Alternative

This stage calls for making the final choice by selecting a suitable alternative solution. This is done by screening and conducting a critical evaluation so as to eliminate a large number of alternatives and narrowing down the choice to a few. In making a final choice, managers have to rely on past experience, managerial skill and judgement. Side by side, feasibility, acceptability, practicability and simplicity of alternative solutions should also be considered. Not only this, various organisational plans, policies, rules, basic philosophy of management, other human factors, etc., should also be given due weightage while making the final choice. It would help in ensuring that decisions are consistent with these plans.

8. Implementation of Decision

Decisions are always made for the purpose of getting them implemented. Implementation of a decision implies a series of actions and involves the utilisation of resources. To implement decisions, necessary structural, administrative and logical arrangements are made such as delegation of authority, allocation of resources, assignment of activities, installation of controlling mechanism, etc. As discussed earlier, to secure maximum cooperation, commitment and acceptance to implement decisions the lower level managers are taken into confidence by getting them involved in the process of decision making.

DECISION MAKING ENVIRONMENT

Managers make decisions in different situations which are known as the environment of decision making. The effectiveness of the decision-making process and quality of decisions to a large extent depends on the type of decision making situation and its components. These decision making situations may range from certainty to highly impracticable uncertain situations.

Certainty

The situation of certainty encourages factual decision making. In other words, in such a situation the required relevant and reliable information may be available to managers on several aspects of the problems regarding its tentative solutions. In such situations, since managers have full knowledge of the problem, they can predict future outcomes of alternative solutions with more confidence and accuracy. It may help in choosing the most appropriate alternative. The concept of certainty is relative rather than absolute. This is because even in a situation marked by a high degree of certainty there will be some element of uncertainty. Therefore, managers sometimes confine themselves to those factors or variables that are well known to them and avoid other factors by making simple assumptions that are least related to them.

Risk

The situation of risk is said to exist when managers take decisions on the basis of incomplete and less reliable information. Although on the basis of partial and less reliable information he may be able to develop some alternative course of action, he may not be that much sure and deterministic about the outcomes of alternatives. At the most, he can probably estimate the outcomes of alternatives by using such information. Similarly, by assigning probabilities to the likelihood of occurrence of an event having a bearing on the decision, he may predict its future behaviour. Decision making based on probabilities has become very common and popular in all areas of management. For instance, a company may introduce a new product by determining the probability of its acceptance by prospective buyers through test marketing, consumer panels, etc.

Uncertainty

The state of uncertainty is marked by non-availability and unreliability of relevant information on the problem. The situational variables may be so random and unstructured that their future behaviour cannot be predicted. In a situation of uncertainty, managers may not have an idea about the outcome of an alternative course of action or their probabilities. Due to lack of the required and relevant information, managers are forced to rely on subjective probabilities that can be estimated and assigned on the basis of past experience and judgement. In brief, the uncertainty may arise either out of a fast-changing external environment and lack of relevant and reliable information on the problem.

In a practical solution, a manager may experience some elements of certainty, risk and some elements of uncertainty. Therefore, he makes decisions by applying his judgement, creativity and experience to the extent to which it is uncertain and he uses data base procedures to the extent to which it is certain. Kreitner has rightly pointed out the relationship between the degree of confidence with which the manager can make decisions and the degree of uncertainty being forced on him.

Relationship between uncertainty and confidence shown in Figure 7.2

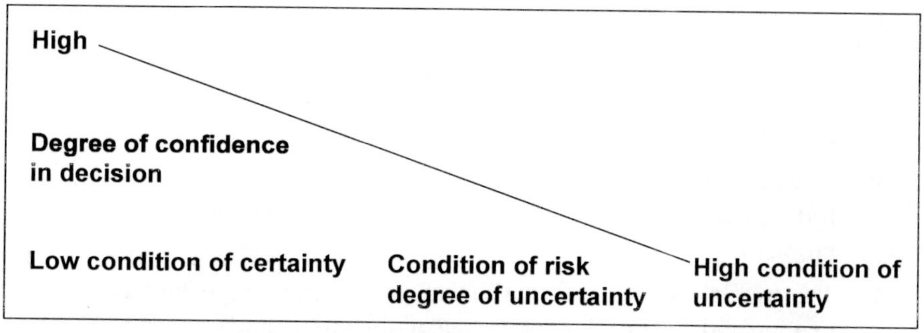

Figure 7.2. Relationship between uncertainty and confidence

Figure 7.2 reveals that as the degree of uncertainty increases, the confidence in a decision decreases and vice-versa. The more uncertain a manager is about the key or principal factor in a decision, the less confidence he or she will have about the successful outcome of the decision.

ROLE OF INFORMATION IN DECISION MAKING

In real-life situations, managers make two types of decisions, that is, intuitive and factual decisions. Intuitive decisions are those decisions that are made by managers on the basis of their personal experience, skill, judgement and intuition. These decisions are based on the assumption that whatever they feel and believe is best, they choose it. On the one hand, factual decisions are based on the analysis of required and relevant information regarding the problem. Since such decisions are backed by facts and data, they carry a higher probability of being correct. Although the supply of information to managers both in the process of planning and controlling is of special importance, its role in decision making is not less significant.

Information is considered as a basic requirement for decision making. This is because not only the quality of the decision but the effectiveness also of the entire decision making process to a large extent depends on the availability of the required, relevant and reliable information. In the process of decision making, information is also regarded as an important input and its profitable at every stage of the decision making process makes it more effective. This is because managers require information on the various aspects of the problem right from the stage of identifying and defining the problem. It is only with the help of information that the problem can be defined in its right perspective which in a long way would help a manager to solve the problem more effectively. Information regarding the problem has a contributory role in providing a proper and better view of the decision situation and in reducing the degree of uncertainty and complexity involved in it. Similarly, a manager needs information even to develop alternative courses of action and then selecting the most appropriate one. In brief, the role of information in decision making may be outlined as under:

- Information plays a significant role in identifying and defining the problem situation.

- ❖ It also helps in developing tentative solutions and selecting a suitable one to solve the problem.
- ❖ The availability of required information encourages managers to use quantitative techniques in decision making.
- ❖ Adequate and relevant information on the problem situation may be of further help in reducing uncertainty and complexity associated with the problem.
- ❖ The availability of information may also encourage factual decision making and ensure a higher degree of objectivity and precision in making decisions.

In order to ensure timely availability of the required quantity and quality of information to managers at different levels of the organisation for the purpose of decision making, a management information system is installed. This helps in organising and maintaining a flow of information through its network in the organisation. In a management information system, information is generated systematically both from inside and outside the organisation. It is compiled, stored, processed and then supplied to managers working at different levels in the organisation. Different levels of management are identified as decision making centres and are thereby connected with the MIS in such a way so that the needed information in usable form may be supplied to managers without loss of time and value.

In modern organisations, computer-aided information systems are being used to facilitate the collection, storage and rapid transmission of the needed information. Nevertheless, it cannot substitute the decision making process and role of the manager. At the most, it can help managers in the process of decision making by providing a support system.

TECHNIQUES OF DECISION MAKING

Decision making is an integral part of a managerial job. Not only the efficiency of the manager, but also the success, growth and development of the organisation to a great extent depends on the quality of decisions taken by managers. To help them in the process of decision making, meaningful efforts have been made to develop techniques for it.

The use of these techniques improves the efficiency of decision making as well as the quality of the decisions made by the manager. These techniques of decision making may be grouped into two groups, that is, traditional techniques and modern techniques. Traditional techniques may further be classified into two groups: techniques for programmed decisions and modern techniques for non-programmed decisions.

TRADITIONAL TECHNIQUES OF DECISION MAKING FOR PROGRAMMED DECISIONS

1. Habits

It is a very common technique of decision making used to solve repetitive and routine problems. In this technique, less or no efforts are to be made to make decisions. As the problem arises, it is solved without much deliberation or thinking about it. Gradually, the habit is formed in respect of such repetitive problems which is used as a technique of decision making. For example, we make many decisions in our daily life to solve simple, minor and routine problems in an inherited manner by using the force of habit.

2. Standard Procedures and Rules

In every organisation, certain procedures and rules are formulated to solve simple and repetitive problems. So when the problem arises, managers apply these procedures and rules and solve it. These procedures and rules are basically in the form of standing plans such as policies, procedures, rules, etc. These operating procedures and rules have twin objectives. On the one hand, they help and guide managers to make decisions and solve problems. On the other hand, they also help to maintain coordination as well as consistency in respect of managerial actions and decisions. It is because the same procedure and decision are followed by every manager.

3. Organisational Structure

The relationship of superior and subordinate arising out of assignment of work and delegation of authority in an organisation also serves as a systematic and continuous means of decision making. As stated earlier, managers need to have enough authority to solve problems and make decisions. So authority is delegated from the top to the lower levels. It includes, among other rights, the right to make decisions. The authority for making decisions is also supported by a proper information network. All managers or decision making centres at which they work are attached with an information system so that the required information to make decisions may be supplied to them.

DECISION-MAKING TECHNIQUES FOR NON-PROGRAMMED DECISIONS

The quantitative and scientific techniques of decision making are included in this group. These techniques have a greater application to solve complex and novel problems. In order to make non-programmed decisions, managers do not totally rely on their personal abilities like judgement, skill, creativity, etc. They also use these abilities through some scientific method and prepare an optimal blend of the two.

The main objective of developing and introducing these quantitative techniques is to ensure a high degree of precision and accuracy in decision making. These techniques are also known as techniques of 'operation research', which are very often used to solve complex problems regarding inventory control, capacity planning, product mix, sales forecasting, production planning and control, capital budgeting, etc. Some of these techniques are described as under:

1. Linear Programming

This technique is used to determine the optimal combination of limited resources to achieve a given purpose at a minimum cost. It is based on the assumption that there exists a linear relationship between the variables. For example, in the production department these variables may be identified as units of output per machine in a given time, direct labour/material cost per unit of output, number of operations per unit, etc. These variables have a linear relationship that the greater use of resources will increase production in the same proportion but within certain limits. Thus, by developing liner equation optimum combination of cost, time and utilisation of machines can be prepared. The objective function of this technique is either to maximise benefit or to minimise cost.

2. Queuing Theory

This is also known as the 'waiting line theory' to be applied to maintain a balance between the cost of the waiting line and the cost of preventing a waiting line in respect of personnel, equipment and services. It is based on the assumption that although delays are costly, eliminating them may be even more costly. This technique may be used in service organisations like transportation, hospitals, banks, etc.

3. Games Theory

Games theory is used to make decisions specially in competitive and conflicting situations. The competitor or conflicting party is also involved in the game and its role is assigned to another member in the game. Moves and counter-moves are made by each member considering the other as a rival. In the games theory, one member chooses a particular course of action which will frustrate and defeat a rival's action and help in winning the game.

4. Probability Theory

This statistical device is based on the assumption that certain things are likely to happen in future in a pattern which can be predicted to some extent by assigning various probabilities. The decision making based on probabilities is common in all areas of management and the organisation such as production, distribution, finance, etc. In this technique, pay-off matrices and decision trees are constructed to represent variables. Pay-off matrices help in choosing an appropriate strategy which most likely would make the maximum contribution to achieve the objectives.

A decision tree is an extension of payoff matrices helping managers to assign financial results to various available courses of action, modifying these results with probabilities and finally making a comparison to select an appropriate course of action.

5. Simulation

According to the simulation technique, instead of studying and analysing the behaviour of a particular system under several alternative conditions in a real situation, a model of it is prepared in an artificial setting. All the features and variables of the actual system are structured in the model and by making changes in the variables, their consequences are studied and a suitable course of action is developed to tackle the situation in a real system.

For example, instead of studying and analysing the transportation system of Delhi in a real setting, its model can be prepared and various properties of the real situation can be simulated in it. By making changes in respect of several variables of the model, the results can be evaluated and the likely behaviour of events can be observed in the model. On the basis of it, the necessary modifications can be made in the transportation systems and solve the problems related to it.

6. Network Techniques

Network techniques of project evaluation and review technique (PERT) and critical path method (CPM) are used for planning, monitoring and implementing time-bound projects. These techniques help managers to decide the logical sequence in which various activities will be performed. By applying these techniques large and complex projects can be executed successfully within the given time schedule and structure of cost.

MODERN TECHNIQUES OF DECISION MAKING

On account of drastic changes taking place in the field of management, the process of decision making has also become complicated and complex. In the context of a fast-changing environment and growing competition it has attracted the attention of management scholars. Consequently, new techniques of decision making and problem solving have been developed some of which are:

1. Heuristic techniques

This technique is based on the assumption that the process of decision making with regard to complex and strategic problems cannot be fully rational and scientific. In an environment of uncertainty and diversity, which is further marked by conflicting interest, the information gap and subjective human behaviour, norms of rationality cannot be followed.

Thus, it is necessary for the decision maker to take a fragmented view of the problem breaking it into small components. Decomposition of the complex problem into small parts and study and analysis of each part may lead to an appropriate solution by developing heuristics. These can be developed on the basis of the trial-and-error technique or rule of thumb by managers for various components at different stages. These heuristics may be used with the help of a computer in a more efficient manner to solve highly complex and strategic problems.

This technique is a more refined way of the trial-and-error method. It is because with the help of the trial-and-error method, heuristics are developed which are further used to apply an analytical approach and creativity to solve problems.

2. Participative decision making

In order to encourage industrial democracy and to make the role of employees more meaningful and contributive, the need of the participation of workers in management and decision making has become more pressing. Normally, decisions are made at a higher level of management and imposed on lower level managers for implementation. But to secure the maximum cooperation and commitment from the lower level managers, they have to be involved and associated in the process of decision making. By associating lower level managers or subordinates in decision making, balanced and timely decisions are made. It also helps to boost morale and motivate subordinates and provide training and development opportunities to them.

Creativity

Creativity is a human faculty which helps managers to solve complex and non-repetitive problems. Bu applying creativity, managers generate new, novel, improved ideas and approaches to solve problems. Creativity may be defined as the ability to think originally and come out with some novel idea. It is a part of the genuine human thinking process by which a particular individual comes up with an idea that may not occur to others. Nevertheless, it is neither a superhuman ability nor a divine gift. It can be developed through proper training and hard work. Creative ideas may be generated at individual as well as group levels. Interaction among the members of the group is considered a more important source of creativity. In every situation, creative persons go beyond the conventional and beaten track and come up with offbeat ideas and new ways of doing things. The process of creativity consists of the following stages:

Preparation Stage

Creative ideas need some preparation. They do not arise in a vacuum, rather a creative thinker has to play with vague and wild imagination for quite some time. It mainly involves turning and twisting the problem, looking at it from different angles and relating it with similar problems.

Incubation Stage

If a creative person draws a blank during the preparation stage, he forgets the problem and goes to other problems or activity. After some time, he may experience a sudden reflection of that which he had relegated to the background. So he forms a new idea about it by default.

Illumination Stage

This stage implies a sudden flash of an idea which was being hatched by a creative person. Once the idea is illuminated, the creative person experiences profound relief and satisfaction.

Elaboration Stage

The illuminated idea conceived by a creative person is to be set in the right perspective. It has to be verified, revised, modified and accommodated to suit the problem or decision situation.

The creative approach to problem solving and decision making is marked by the following features:

1. The creative approach discards habitual and conventional ways of doing things and the creative thinker normally deviates from them.
2. Application of the creative approach calls for looking into the problem situation from diverse angles which have not been tried so far.
3. The creative person does not take things for granted; rather he challenges them. He redefines and restructures the problem situation afresh in a new way.
4. A creative approach allows deviation from rationality and systematic approach.
5. The application of a creative approach may begin with wild, impracticable and speculative ideas. But to make them more acceptable and accommodating they have to be revised and modified.

TECHNIQUES OF GROUP DECISION MAKING

In order to increase the effectiveness of the decision making process and increasing the quality of decisions made, certain techniques are used. These techniques are as under:

1. Brainstorming

This is one of the important techniques of group decision making. In this technique, a small group of managers ranging between five and 10 is formed. Generally one of them is given the role of leader of the group. He throws light on the various aspects of the problems and explains its nature to the members.

He also keeps them informed about the decision rule to be followed in the process. All the members sit together and begin discussing the problem and seek its solution as members of free association. They concentrate mainly on the generation of ideas about the problem and its solution. All ideas generated by the members are put on a blackboard to make every member familiar with the ideas generated. They are also given an opportunity to make improvements upon them.

The following rules are generally followed by the members in the process of brainstorming:

1. The members of the group are asked to generate ideas about the problem and its solution and they are not allowed to criticise and evaluate the ideas of other members.
2. All ideas generated by the members are taken care of; even if the idea is wild or crude it is included in the list. Sometimes such ideas may prove to be a real solution to the problem.
3. The entire process of brainstorming is focused on generating as many ideas as possible. It is done so that the best solution may not be overlooked.
4. Every member is allowed to give suggestions on the various ideas so generated. This is done to improve upon these ideas.
5. In the subsequent session, ideas so generated are reviewed and alternatives are evaluated.

The technique of brainstorming is to produce new ideas and solutions by stimulating creativity among the group members. They are given an opportunity to do so by working on the contributions of others. This technique does not offer a readymade solution to the problem. Rather, it aims at generating possible alternative solutions and leads to evaluation of those for selecting a suitable one.

2. Delphi Technique

This technique is a more refined and modified version of the brainstorming technique. In this, a small group of specialised experts is formed and they are asked to express their opinion on the problem or situation and its solution. The opinions expressed by individual experts are not made known to the others because anonymity is desired. The Delphi technique is a method of collecting the various judgements of experts to solve the problem. These opinions are consolidated and summarised by the leader of the group and are sent back to the experts for further analysis. The Delphi technique involves the following steps:

1. A questionnaire is prepared on the various aspects of the problem.
2. The questionnaire is sent to experts to seek their responses on the various questions. The experts respond independently and send their responses to the leader of the group.

3. The leader of the group compiles and analyses the responses received by him and a second questionnaire is prepared on the basis of it.
4. The second questionnaire is sent to the members and they are asked to respond to the new set of questions.
5. On analysis of the second set of questions, if any area remains untouched or not touched adequately, a third questionnaire may be designed and sent.
6. The leader attempts to develop unanimity on each aspect of the problem and may come to know a new and more refined version. It may help to develop a possible solution to the problem.

In the Delphi technique, anonymity is maintained and the members keep responding to the responses of others. There is no direct interaction among them. Every expert gives his independent opinion. He does not know on whose response what new question has been framed.

3. Nominal Group Technique

This is also one of the important techniques that is used to improve the effectiveness of group decision-making. It resembles the brainstorming technique but is considered more effective. This is because all the members of the group are physically present but do not interact with each other. This technique is specially used to identify a problem and select criteria to be used to evaluate various alternatives. Under this technique, a group of individuals is formed to address a particular problem. The problem is experienced by them and they are asked to write all the possible ideas that come to their mind about it. Discussion among the group members is not allowed. Rather, they report their ideas to the leader who puts them on a flip chart. The members are further asked to add new ideas to the list on the basis of the ideas of others. Once all possible ideas have surfaced and been recorded, the members may be allowed to suggest a possible solution and comment on the ideas. After discussing all the ideas, their relative merits and demerits are ascertained. After this, the members of the group privately vote on an idea and assign a particular rank to it on the basis of priority of the alternative solutions. The idea getting the highest ranking is selected as a solution to the problem. The group members further discuss the result and continue to generate and discuss ideas. The technique of a nominal group like other techniques encourages creativity among the members. It also helps to overcome the negative effect of authority and status among the members. It is used not only to generate

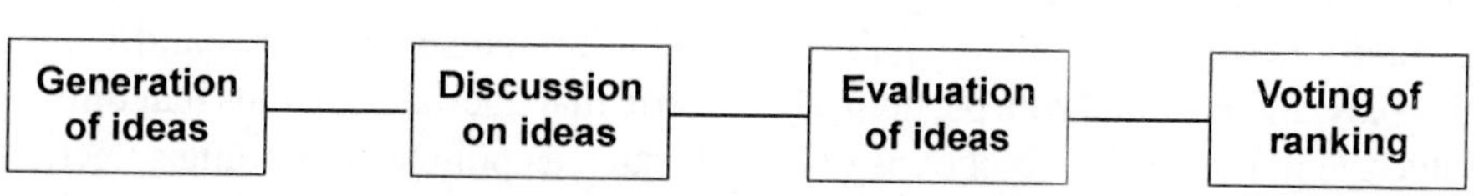

Figure 7.3. Nominal group process

ideas but it follows the sequence of generation, discussion and vote on the ideas of members. Since it is a high structured technique, it may possibly limit creativity to some extent.

4. Fish Bowl Technique

This is an extension of the brainstorming technique. It is more structured and direct in nature. In this technique a group of experts is formed. They sit around the table and the central place is occupied by the leader of the group. In the first instance, the member who occupies the central place expresses his opinion on the problem and suggests some solution for it. The other members are allowed to ask questions and clarification of the problem put forward by the group leader.

Once his viewpoint has been discussed fully and understood, he gives up his chair to another member who now becomes the leader. Again, the second member gives his viewpoint in the light of the views expressed by the first leader. The members can ask questions based on the new ideas which must stem from the first round of discussion. This cycle of discussion continues till all the members have done their turn as group leader.

The exchange of ideas and discussion takes place only between members of the group and the group leader. The members are not allowed to interact with each other. In this technique, the members of the group have opportunities to express their viewpoints as members as well as leaders. At the end, all the viewpoints and ideas are taken stock of and further discussed collectively to arrive at a suitable solution.

ETHICS OF DECISION MAKING

Managers who take decisions in the organisation are known as captains of industry. They take decisions to solve problems faced by them. Many decisions made by them may not directly affect the interest of society and its culture. This is because being at the realm of using resources of the organisation they are expected to take decisions that maximise the gains of the organisation. But in practice modern managers are under great ethical pressure while taking decisions. It is not only the economic implications of decision made by them. their social value and ethical dimensions have become equally important. Therefore a discussion of decision making seems to be incomplete without considering its social and ethical implications. In many organisations, ethical considerations and values have become a part of decision making criteria.

Briefly speaking, the ethical behaviour of a manager may be defined as a pattern of behaviour that conforms to established and accepted social norms and values. Ethics play an important role particularly in those managerial decisions that directly involve the interests and objectives of society such as policies regarding selection, recruitment, dismissal, salary and wages, etc. For example, a decision to close one of the unprofitable units of the organisation involves the ethical issue of reducing employment opportunities. Similarly, a decision to switch over to a new technology should be made by taking into account not only economic considerations but ethical ones as well as social implications.

Managers should carefully understand and consider the ethical values and implications of their decisions. It requires a high degree of honesty and integrity on the part of managers.

FACTORS AFFECTING ETHICAL BEHAVIOUR

Why do managers make ethical decisions that benefit them most and the interests of others are affected adversely? There are many factors which affect ethical decision making behaviour among managers. These factors may be classified into two groups:

1. Individual personality
2. Organisational environment.

An individual's personality traits and their development have a definite impact on his ethical behaviour. Generally, an individual whose morale has been fully developed and who is capable of judging what is morally right would behave ethically. The level of ethical behaviour would also depend on the value system of his or her family and other social institutions affecting the growth of his personality. It is in the light of this that many business schools are making efforts to inculcate moral values in the personalities of prospective managers. This is done to make them readily acceptable by the organisations at the time of selection.

Similarly, the internal environment of an organisation and its culture also affects one's ethical behaviour. Many organisations support and reward ethical behaviour of employees. Rather, it becomes a well-established norm for employees to be ethical while working in the organisation. By being morally and ethically sound, they meet the expectations of the organisation and get many benefits like promotion, pay hike, higher status, etc. But business ethics is a very complicated matter. Some ethics experts have rightly pointed out that "just being a good person, in your own way, having sound personal ethics, may not be sufficient to handle the ethical issues that arise in a business organisation. Many people who have limited business experience suddenly find themselves making decisions about product quality, advertising, pricing, hiring practices and pollution control. The values they learned from family, church and school may not provide specified guidelines for these complex business decisions. Years of experience in a particular industry may be required to know what is acceptable."

The above lines indicate that it is not only a matter of learning ethical and moral values on the part of employees but also long experience in an organisation may help managers to address ethical issues efficiently.

DECISION CRITERIA FOR ETHICAL DECISIONS

Modern managers face many situations that require ethical decisions. They can use three criteria to make such decisions:

1. Utility
2. Right
3. Justice

According to utilitarian criterion, managers take hard decisions by taking into account all possible consequences or outcomes of the decision. In other words, they evaluate the decisions and actions on the basis of their consequences. While taking a decision they ensure that it should produce the greatest good for the greatest number of people. This mode of taking decisions is very popular in business.

The second ethical criterion for decision making mainly focuses on 'rights'. It holds that all people have basic rights. According to this criterion, the decisions and actions of managers in a business must be consistent with these rights. These fundamental rights may include the right to property, freedom of expression, knowledge, privacy, etc. The decisions made by managers should respect and protect these rights.

Another criterion to be used to make ethical decisions is 'justice'. According to this criterion, decisions made by managers must ensure equitable distribution of cost and benefit among the various parties entitled to it. It urges upon managers to be fair, impartial and equitable, while making decisions and taking action. This criterion if followed by managers would ensure the protection of the less powerful and unrepresented group of people.

While using the above criteria one should look into both the positive as well as the negative aspects. For example, in profit-making organisations, managers tend to feel safe and comfortable while using criterion based on utility. But a growing awareness among customers, employees and other parties about their rights may force managers to adopt criterion based on rights.

Similarly, in a society that consists of weaker sections, managers may adopt a third criterion of justice to make decisions. In is, therefore, the top management of the organisation that generally attempts to build an environment that encourages ethical decision making. James Weber has suggested the following guidelines to add an ethical dimension to decision making:

1. By formulating and implementing an appropriate policy and 'code of ethics'.
2. By using a formal committee to ensure that a code of ethics is followed by the employees of an organisation.
3. By including techniques of ethical and moral values in training and development programmes of the organisation.

In order to encourage the use of ethical values in decision making, Saul Gellerman has suggested the following guidelines:

1. Provide clear guidelines for ethical behaviour.
2. Teach ethical guidelines and their importance.
3. In grey areas where there are questions about the ethics of an action, refrain from it.
4. Set up an auditing agency that checks on illegal and unethical deeds.
5. Conduct frequent and unpredictable audits.
6. Punish trespassers in a meaningful way and make it public so that it may deter others.
7. Emphasise regularly that loyalty to the organisation does not excuse improper behaviour or actions.

LEARNING TO BE MORE CREATIVE

All persons are creative but the degree of creativity differs. In order to become more creative the following mental locks suggested by Roger Von seem to be relevant because these mental locks tend to stifle our creativity:

1. Looking for the Right Answer

The given problem may have several right answers depending on one's perspectives.

2. Always Trying to be Logical

Logic does not always prevail; given human emotions and inconsistencies of the organisation, ambiguity and contradiction may dominate the situation.

3. Strictly Following the Rules

If things are to be improved, arbitrary limits on thinking and behaviour need to be questioned.

4. Insisting on being Practical

Impractical answers to 'what if' questions can become stepping stones to creative insight.

5. Avoiding Ambiguity

Creativity can be developed by objectivity and specificity.

6. Fearing and Avoiding Failure

Fear of failure can polarise us into not acting on our good ideas. This is unfortunate because we learn many valuable and lasting lessons from our mistakes.

7. Forgetting how to Play

The playful experimentation of childhood too often disappears by adulthood.

8. Becoming too Specialised

Cross fertilisation of specialised areas helps in defining problems and generating solutions.

9. Not Wanting to Look Foolish

Humour can release tension and unlock our creative energies. Seemingly foolish questions can enhance understanding.

10. Saying 'I am not Creative'

By nurturing small and apparently insignificant ideas, we can convince ourselves that we are indeed creative.

If the above-mentioned mental locks are conquered and unlocked, the creative problem solving process can be used to its full advantage.

ROLE OF CREATIVITY IN DECISION MAKING

The process of management is dynamic in nature. It requires an innovative and creative approach on the part of managers. Its role in decision making is more significant. While managing the affairs of organisations, managers very often face problems that are open-ended and unstructured. These problems perhaps cannot be solved by applying predetermined procedures and rules and other scientific and rational approaches. To solve these problems, managers redefine and reformulate them in their own way and discover solutions by applying a creative approach.

For example, problems of growth and development, industrial discipline, sales promotion, development and introduction of a new product, motivation and morale, productivity and resolution of conflicts, etc., can be solved by adopting this approach. The creative approach of problem solving and decision making does not help the manager in only discovering and generating alternative courses of action but also provides new ground to make a proper diagnosis of the problem and defining it precisely. By applying a creative approach, the manager may get an insight into the problem and can throw sharp light on it from different angles.

It stimulates the unconscious mind of the manager and forces him to come up with new ideas, which otherwise would never have been discovered. Thus, whether in the definition stage, or search for alternatives or the final selection of an appropriate alternative, the creative approach may prove more useful for the manager in all these stages.

In the context of problem-solving and decision-making, the significant role of creativity has been described by one management consultant as "Creativity is a function of knowledge, imagination and evaluation. The greater our knowledge, more ideas, patterns or combinations we can achieve. Merely having the knowledge does not guarantee the formation of new patterns; the units and places must be shaken and inter-related in new ways. The embryonic ideas must be evaluated and developed into usable ideas."

These lines clearly reveal that a creative approach requires not only knowledge but also involves the use of imagination and abilities to analyse and synthesise the problem in new ways. Similarly, in the beginning, ideas or solutions so discovered may not be that much practical and acceptable. They are to be revised, modified and properly accommodated within the problem situation.

DECISION MAKING BEHAVIOUR MODELS

When a manager is confronted with some problems, how he perceives it, how he reacts to it, and finally, how he moves to solve it, all amount to his decision-making behaviour. There are two basic approaches or models of decision-making behaviour among managers.

1. Normative Model or Rational Model or Economic Man Model

This model is idealistic, rational and prescriptive in nature because it prescribes how managers should behave in the process of decision making. It is idealistic in the sense that it cannot be fully applied to a practical solution and rational in the sense that while using this approach the manager tries to become as much rational as is possible.

This approach implies the use of scientific and logical methods. It is marked by the following features:

1. The approach of decision making followed by managers is systematic, logical and full of reasoning.
2. The use of scientific and systematic methods call for a scientific attitude on the part of managers backed by empirical verification.
3. In this model, the manager is expected to be objective on his part. He should not allow his bias, emotions and likes and dislikes to interfere with decision making.
4. The manager using this model should have an access to required, relevant and reliable information on the problem situation.
5. The manager must attempt to reach some goals that require positive action on his part. These goals must be definite and clear.
6. The manager must have a clear understanding of action by which goals can be achieved under the existing environment.
7. The manager who uses this approach must have an ability to analyse and evaluate alternatives in the context of the goal to be pursued and must have a desire to optimise benefits by selecting the best course of action.

The model of rational decision making is preferably applied to problems that are routine and repetitive in nature and can be programmed. As the problem arises, the manager studies and analyses it. He applies predetermined procedures and rules without allowing his personal bias to interfere and finally solves it. The decision making environment seems to be certain because the decision maker has full knowledge regarding the problem faced by him. Rational decision making occurs relatively in a close setting intentionally created by the decision maker.

He takes into account only those variables that can be quantified. And he avoids the complexities of the external environment by making very simple assumptions regarding it. Also, a model of rational decision making facilitates the application of quantitative techniques for decision making to make it more precise and accurate. This approach, to some extent, is related to the 'economic man model'. This is because economic man is always in search of an optimal solution or the best way of doing things to maximise his benefits. He is also solely governed by economic considerations and uses mathematical and statistical devices to solve problems. By and large, he behaves like a rational decision maker.

2. Behavioural Model or Bounded Rationality or 'Administration Man Model'

In real life situations, the decision maker cannot be fully rational in his approach to solve all types of problems. This is because absolute rationality is a superhuman phenomenon and cannot be attained. On the basis of this assumption, the behavioural approach has been developed.

Contrary to the normative approach of decision making, it highlights how decisions are actually made by managers in practice. This approach of decision making is more pragmatic.

The manager who is basically a human being cannot be fully rational. He may be confronted with many personal and organisational constraints, problems and limitations, for example, lack of resources, information, his capabilities, and complexities and uncertainties involved in a decision making environment.

After having taken into account several factors that affect real-life decision making, Herbert Simon has proposed the theory of 'bounded rationality' This theory states that the real-life decision maker must reconcile with inadequate information about the nature of the problems and their solution, lack of time or money to compile more complete information, distorted perception, an inability to remember a large amount of information and the limits of his own intelligence. In other words, the norm of rationality is bounded by these limitations and therefore this concept is known as 'bounded rationality.' The major limitations and inadequacies that bound the rationality of a manager are as follows:

1. Lack of Information

This is one of the most important limitations to rationality. In some cases, managers may not have access to the required and relevant information on the problem. Therefore, they are bound to deviate from the norms of rationality to solve it.

2. Time Constraint

In order to comply with the norm of rationality, managers are required to study and analyse the problem to discover alternative courses of action, to evaluate them and then to select an appropriate one. This is a time-consuming job and does suit every type of problem. This is because some of the problems may require the prompt attention of managers and by the time they complete the formalities, there may be further complications.

3. Environmental Uncertainties

Decisions are made by managers and are got implemented later. But the future environment is full of complexities and uncertainties. They cannot be predicted with a high degree of accuracy. These environmental complexities and uncertainties may force managers to accommodate their choice accordingly. Sometimes, they are totally dominated and guided by these forces.

4. Conflicting Objectives

Many decision situations may involve the formulation of multiple objectives that may be conflicting to each other. In these situations the process of compromise and adjustment becomes more relevant and effective rather than rationality. This is because to reduce conflict the formula of 'give and take' has to be adopted which is less rational and more situational.

5. Nature of the Problem

The concept of rationality is also bounded by the nature of the problem. Sometimes, the problem may be very complex, unstructured and cannot be defined by using the norms of rationality. To solve such problems, managers have to use their own intuition and experience to restructure and reformulate them.

6. Organisational Constraints

The rationality involved in the process of decision-making is also affected by several organisational variables. These are the philosophy of the organisation, power structure, multiplicity of goals, existence of informal groups and set of organisational plans. To deal with the situation, the manager has to be firm and flexible, cautious and bold. And he may be bound to make those decisions which are more practicable and feasible even by defying the norms of rationality. This is because he is more concerned and guided by these organisational variables.

Thus, in real-life situations, decision making on the part of the manager is sub-rational, fragmented and pragmatic activity. This is because the rationality used by the manager is subject to the ground realities of decision situations. According to Herbert Simon, the norms of satisfying represents and describes the actual decision making behaviour of the manager in the organisation. The norms of satisfying imply picking a course of action that is satisfactory or good enough under the circumstances. It is true that many managerial decisions are made with a desire to be as safe as possible. It is also believed that most managers do attempt to make the best decisions within the limits of rationality and in the light of the size and nature of risk involved in uncertainty. One who makes decisions within the limits of rationality is considered as an administrative man as against an economic man who represents rational decision making. The administrative man makes satisfying decisions by playing safe. Such decisions are easy to understand, more acceptable and practical.

HOW TO IMPROVE THE EFFECTIVENESS OF DECISION MAKING AND PROBLEM SOLVING

Decision making is an integral part of a managerial job. The efficiency of a manager largely depends on how he has been making decisions to solve problems and tackle situations. Decision making, in fact, is a tough task because excellent decisions may turn out poorly on account of an unforeseen event. Even if a decision works well as per prediction, a manager cannot be completely sure about the effectiveness and outcome of another decision. In this connection, Norman Mailer has suggested two criteria by which the potential and effectiveness of decisions can be estimated. The first is the objective quality of the decision that is determined by how well the formal decision making process is carried out. The second is an acceptance of the decision by those who would execute it, which is to be determined by its nature and by who makes it.

In addition to using the process of rational decision making and making effective decisions there are certain guidelines that may be followed by managers:

1. In day-to-day functioning, managers are preoccupied with many problems. Some of them may be more urgent and others may allow managers to defer them for some time. To be effective at his job, he must set a priority order of these problems and get them solved accordingly.
2. The availability of required, relevant and authenticated information is a basic requirement of effective decision making. This is because it facilitates factual decisions that are more qualitative as compared with intuitive ones.
3. Though there are many processes and models of rational decision making, they will be of use only when managers know how and when to use them. To ensure effectiveness one has to be more methodical and careful, keeping in mind common mistakes.

4. The rule-of-thumb approach or heuristics may have both positive as well as negative aspects. Managers need to understand how these can lead to bias or overconfidence. Once managers of aware of them, they can make deliberate efforts to avoid and check them.
5. To ensure effective decision making, enough authority has to be delegated from higher levels to lower levels of management so that every manager is made capable of taking decisions without loss of time.
6. Effective decision-making in an organisation calls for well-coordinated decision making centres to maintain consistency and cooperation because the decisions made at a higher level may be used as input by managers at a lower level.
7. To simplify the decision-making process, a required set of procedures, rules, policies and methods should be formulated in a clear manner and should be communicated to all concerned managers in the organisation.
8. Participative decision-making should be encouraged to get maximum contribution, cooperation and commitment of subordinates to implement decisions.
9. To make the decision-making process more effective and to ensure quality of decisions, a proper combination of rationality with reality should be prepared as per the requirements of the situation.
10. To decide upon complex, diverse and novel situations, creativity, effectiveness and dynamism are required on the part of managers. To develop these qualities, systematic training should be imparted and a development programme should be conducted for them.

CHALLENGES FOR DECISION MAKERS

The foregoing discussion on decision making reveals that it is really a tough job for the manager to decide accurately and precisely on each and every problem faced by him. Not only the survival of the organisation but also his own existence in it to a large extent depends on his capabilities and talent for making qualitative decisions. To keep pace with the changing environment, the entire process of decision making has to be accelerated and toned up so that he can cope with new challenges and added dimensions of the problem. New elements are to be introduced through training to force the manager to become more capable and confident to deal with complex and diverse situations. The proper knowledge of the following factors can help him to understand the complexities of decisions and to cope with them effectively:

1. Multiple Criteria

In a modern organisation, decisions must satisfy multiple conflicting criteria representing the interests of different groups.

2. Intangibles

While evaluating and selecting an appropriate course of action, intangible factors such as customer satisfaction, image of the organisation, morale of employees etc., should also be taken into account.

3. Risk and Uncertainty

These two factors are mainly related to the decision making environment. More risk and a high degree of uncertainty may force the manager to go for that course of action that is being dictated by the environment.

4. Long-term Implications

While making decisions, the manager should also consider the long-term implications of it.

5. Interdisciplinary Input

The decisions made by a manager may affect several interest groups. Therefore, their advice may be sought and considered.

6. Pooled Decision Making

In view of the possible advantages of participative decision making, the manager, instead of taking decisions on his own, should prefer to consult and involve his subordinates in the decision making process.

7. Value Judgement

Decisions are made by managers who are of different backgrounds, perceptions, aspirations and values. They may generate controversy of what is good or bad or ethical or unethical.

In order to make qualitative decisions, managers must be aware of the rapid changes taking place in the external environment. They are expected to tone up the whole process of decision making and make it more responsive to the situation.

SUMMARY

Decision making is an important managerial activity. Every manager has to take decisions to solve problems and handle situations so that he can get things done by others. Decision making is not only a part of planning but is an integral part of the managing process. It may be defined as a process of choosing a suitable option from available alternative options. The decision-making process is a social process that involves the use of ethical and moral values also. It is goal-oriented and an all-pervasive activity that permits the manager to use his discretion along with decision rules. In an organisation, the decisions made by a manager ensure an efficient utilisation of resources to achieve 'objectives'. Not only the survival and prosperity of the organisation, the existence of the manager also depends on the quality of decisions made by him.

In order to solve routine and repetitive problems, the manager makes a programmed decision. They are made by using the prescribed decision rules and techniques. Whenever the problem arises, he applies those rules and gets them solved. On the other hand, sometimes the manager faces a problem that has not arisen in the past and is unique in nature. To solve such a problem he has to make a non-programmed decision. To much such a decision, no set rules or technique can be applied. Rather, the manager solves such problems by using his managerial experience and creativity.

Strategic decisions are those that are made on vital issues by top-level managers having long-term implications and that affect many functional areas. To implement strategic decisions, certain other decisions are also made by the manager. These decisions are known as operational decisions. Such decisions are made by lower-level managers who are mainly involved in the implementation of strategic decisions. Decisions are also made either by the manager at his individual level by using the authority delegated to him. Such decisions are known as individual decisions. As against this, sometimes decisions are made by two or more managers who may be working in similar positions or may be in the relationship of superior and subordinate. These decisions are known as group decisions that are considered to be more qualitative and superior.

The process of decision making involves many stages including identification and definition of the problem, specification of objectives, collection of data, developing alternatives, evaluating them and finally selecting a suitable one.

Managers make decisions in a different environment. Sometimes they may face complete uncertainty and do not know the nature of the problem. But sometimes, they may have full knowledge of the problem and they may also predict the outcome of a decision. Such situations are considered as certainty. Between these two they may face a situation known as environment of risk.

Information is one of the important inputs to be used by managers in decision making. Information does not only help in defining the problem but an effectiveness of the entire decision making process depends on the availability of relevant and reliable information on the problem. It helps the manager at every stage of the decision making process.

In order to make programmed decisions, three important techniques are used. These are known as traditional techniques that include habit, organisational plans and procedures and organisational structure. In addition to these, many techniques are used to make non-programmed decisions such as linear programming, queuing theory, game theory, probability theory, simulation and network techniques. Apart from these, modern managers also use the heuristic technique, participative technique and the creative technique. Among these, creativity has a very important role in decision making particularly to solve unstructured and complex problems. It is mental ability that can be developed by rigorous training and practice. The creative individual thinks of a situation or problem in an altogether new manner and finds out new and novel ideas about it. He does not follow a beaten path, rather he is regularly in search of new ones which deviate conventional ones. By using creativity, the manager makes an insight into the problem and comes to know about new aspects or dimensions of the problem. Creativity in fact stimulates the unconscious mind of the person and forces him to develop new ideas.

In order to understand the decision making behaviour of the manager, two important models may be used: rational model and behavioural model. These two models indicate how the manager behaves while making decisions. According to the rational model, the manager acts systematically, logically, uses scientific methods and remains very knowledgeable about the problem. He remains objective on his part and does not allow his biases to interfere. But in practice, many environmental, organisational and personal constraints limit his rationality. These factors include lack of information, environmental uncertainties, conflicting objectives, nature of the problem and other factors. Due to these, the manager is bound to reconcile with the ground realities while making decisions. This type of model is known as the model of bounded rationality or 'behavioural model'. In practice, a combination of these two is followed by the manager.

In modern organisations, the practice of using techniques of group decision making has been well established. These techniques are very helpful in making the entire process of decision making more effective and encouraging the use of creativity in it. The techniques of group decision making include brainstorming, Delphi technique, nominal group technique and fish bowl technique. Brainstorming is mainly focused on generating new ideas by acting upon the ideas of others. It stimulates the sub-conscious mind of the people to develop new ideas. Later, these ideas which seem to be wild and crude may be further refined and made useable.

The Delphi technique is a more extended version of brainstorming. It aims at generating and evaluating ideas through repetitive use of questionnaires. In the nominal group technique, which is similar to brainstorming, the members of the group generate, discuss, evaluate and vote for each idea. First of all, the members without interacting with each other are asked to write all the possible ideas about the problem that come to their mind and report them to the leader of the group. The leader puts them on a flip chart and the members continue to develop new ideas on the basis of those given in the chart. Similarly, in the fish bowl technique, which is more structured and direct, each member is given an opportunity to express his opinion on the problem as a leader of the group as well as a member of the group. All ideas so generated are further discussed at the end collectively and a final solution to the problem is chosen.

Modern management has added a new dimension of ethics to the decision-making behaviour of managers. While making decisions, they are also expected to consider the ethical aspect. The ethical behaviour of the manager may be considered as a pattern of behaviour consistent with accepted social norms and values. Ethical behaviour is greatly influenced by personality factors and the internal environment of the organisation. It requires a higher degree of honesty and integrity on the part of managers. And such behaviour must be encouraged by implementing suitable policies. While making decisions, managers generally adopt the criteria of utility, right and justice. For promoting ethical behaviour in decision making, a 'code of conduct' is framed and efforts are made to ensure that it is followed by managers.

TEST QUESTIONS

1. Decision making involves choosing from among alternative solutions. Comment.
2. Discuss the elements involved in the decision-making process.
3. Managers cannot be rational decision-makers in real-life situations. Discuss.
4. Explain the various modern techniques of decision making for programmed decisions.
5. Compare and contrast the decisions made under conditions of certainty, risk and uncertainty.
6. Explain the role of creativity in decision making.
7. What are programmed decisions? Briefly discuss the various traditional and modern techniques of taking such decisions.
8. Define the term 'bounded rationality'. Explain the practical limitations to decision making situations.
9. Define the role of information systems in decision making.
10. Give suggestions to improve the effectiveness of decision making.
11. Write short notes on
    (a) Strategic and tactical decisions.
    (b) Programmed and non-programmed decisions.
    (c) Creativity in decision making.
    (d) Pervasiveness of decision making.

OBJECTIVE TYPE QUESTIONS

Which of the following statements are correct and which are incorrect? Give reasons to support your answers.

1. Creative decision-making rejects all past decisions.
2. A management information system is designed to transmit information from one manager to another.
3. Brainstorming permits group members to openly criticise each other.
4. Tactical decisions are made to implement strategic decisions.

5. A real-life decision-maker who makes decisions within bounded rationality is known as an 'administrative man.'
6. Managerial decision-making is a sub-rational and pragmatic activity.
7. A rational decision maker operates in a 'closed system.'
8. A rational approach of decision-making is generally applicable to non-routine and new problems.
9. A rational approach of decision-making is normative, idealistic and prescriptive.
10. Programmed decisions involves more use of intelligence, skill, judgement and experience of managers.
11. Non-programmed decisions implies more use of predetermined procedures and rules.
12. Strategic decisions are similar to non-programmed decisions.
13. Non-programmed decisions demand a low amount of subjective judgement from managers.

REFERENCES

Alter, Steven. *Decision Support System: Current Practice and Continuing Challenges.* Reading, Mass., U.S.A.: Addison Wesley Publishing Company, 1980.

Barnard, Chester I. *The Functions of Executive.* Cambridge, U.S.A.: Harvard University Press, 1938.

Drucker, Peter F. *The New Realities.* London, U.K.: Mandarin, 1990.

Drucker, Peter. *The Practice of Management.* Allied Publishers, Mumbai, India: 1955.

Ercher. 'How to Make a Business Decision—An Analysis of Theory and Practice'. *Management Review.* February, 1980.

Freeman, Stoner and Gilbert, Jr. *Management.* New Delhi, India: Prentice Hall of India Pvt. Ltd, 2001.

Haiman, Theo. *Professional Management.* New Delhi, India: Eurasia Publishing House, 1970.

Kallman, Ernest A and Reinhart, Leon. *Information System for Planning and Decision Making.* New York, U.S.A.: Van Nostrand and Reinhold, 1984.

Keen, Peter G. W. and Scott Morton, Michael, S. *Decision Support System—an Organisational Perspective.* Reading, Mass., U.S.A.: Addison Wesley Publishing Company, 1978.

Koontz, Harold and Weihrich, Heinz. *Essentials of Management.* New Delhi, India: Tata McGraw-Hill Publishing Company Ltd., 2001.

Kreitner, Robert. *Management*. Delhi, India: A.I.T.B.S. Publishers and Distributors (Regd), 1966.

March, James G. and Simon, Herbert A. *Organisation*. New York, U.S.A.: John Wiley and Sons, 1988 and 1966.

Meyer, Alan D. 'Mingling Decision Making Metaphors'. *Academy of Management Review*, January 1984.

Moshal, B. S. *Management Theory and Practice*. New Delhi, India: Galgotia Publishing Company, 2001.

Newman, William H. and Warren, E. K. *The Process of Management*. New Delhi, India: Prentice-Hall of India, 1988.

Schendel, Dan E. and Hoffer, Charles W. *Strategic Management—A New View of Business Policy and Planning*. Boston, U.S.A.: Little Brown, 1978.

Shrivastava, R. M. *Corporate Strategy and Planning*. New Delhi, India: Tata McGraw-Hill Publishing Co., 1989.

Simon, Herbert A. *The New Science Management Decision*. Englewood Cliffs, NJ., U.S.A.: Prentice-Hall, 1977.

Weber, Max *The Theory of Social and Economic Organisation*. New York, U.S.A.: Free Press, 1957.

CASE STUDY I

Why the Ford Mustang Wasn't Put Out to Pasture

It's a miracle the car is still around. The ageing coupe was scheduled to die by now because of the costs of keeping up with safety, pollution and fuel economy regulations. Yearly sales slipped from 500,000 in the Mustang's mid-60s heyday to fewer than 100,000 in the 90s.

"The Mustang was literally resurrected within the company", development engineer Kurt Achenbach says.

What kept the Mustang alive was the dedication of a small group of Ford engineers, themselves Mustang buffs, who couldn't imagine Ford without Mustang. Known as the Gang of Eight, they secretly culled the debris of earlier, unsuccessful plans to continue the Mustang. Most of those were radical, expensive redesigns that changed the character of the car. Or they were cheap-to-build cars not better enough than the current Mustang to justify the expense.

The reprieve came through extraordinary means. In the process, Ford learned more about cutting costs and development than it probably could have learned any other way. Some of these lessons already have been

Case Study I continued

Case Study I continued

rolled into development of the next-generation Taurus family car and a truck due in 1996, engineers say.

The Gang of Eight concentrated on keeping some key hardware engine, transmission and parts of the chassis, or platform to retain the Mustang's identity and keep it cheap and quick to develop. At the same time, they identified ways to eliminate quality and handling problems that had plagued the car.

They pitched the notion to top management and after tough questions from CEO Harold 'Red' Poling got a thumbs-up. "This was not an easy project. Some very important people, who shall remain nameless, said we could never do it", project boss Will Boddie recalls. "We basically signed a contract with (Poling) saying we agree to deliver this car at this budget by this time."

The team promised a 37-month turnaround three months sooner than Ford's previous fastest, the 40-month development of the 1990 Lincoln Town Car. Mustang's team, by slashing red tape and bureaucracy delivered in 35 months. The budget was to be $ 565 million, but was expanded, by consensus, to $ 700 million. That was after managers decided to re-equip the ageing Mustang Factory at Dearborn, Michigan, to build 175,000 a year, instead of 140,000.

It helped that Ford President Alex Trotman, then running the company's North American operations (later promoted to CEO) was also a Mustang buff. "He was our guardian angel on the project", Mustang business manager Johan Coletti says. Other key executives of sales and marketing boss Robert Rewey and vice-chairman Allan Gillmouru also were early backers.

Once the pact was made, the Gang of Eight moved more people and equipment into an old Montgomery Ward warehouse in Alien Park, the Detroit suburb adjacent to Dearborn. At maximum, the team numbered 450. Today it is a skeleton crew of 60. Says Coletti: "It was very un-Ford. Usually guys won't move in until the carpet's down and everything's done. We had guys in there doing design before there was even running water. We were using porta-johns. We didn't shake hands much in the early days."

Although Ford dislikes the comparison, the Mustang group operated much like Chrysler's platform team that brought out the successful line of family cars collectively known as LH. The keys: group members focus on one car, instead of splitting time among several projects; and everybody is under the same roof.

"We made decisions in minutes around the coffee pot that would normally take three months," Boddie says.

Case Study I continued

Case Study I continued

And there was a vision, mainly shaped by the seemingly endless consumer clinics Ford conducted with both Mustang enthusiasts and ordinary buyers. "Cheap, beautiful and powerful. Those were the goals. Any decision you made along the way that didn't accomplish those goals, you were making the wrong decision," Boddie says.

Thus the Mustang team nixed using the Ford Thunderbird's sophisticated good-handling rear suspension. Too costly. "About $ 300 per car," Boddie says.

And it spurned the company's world-class overhead-camshaft Romeo V-8 engine. "Remember cheap speed," says engine and transmission engineer John Bicanich.

"The Mustang buyer is not the $ 100,000-a year guy trying to decide how much to spend. It's the guy in love with the car, has to have it and is scraping together every cent he can afford," Boddie explains.

Just like at Chrysler, Ford executives helped by steering clear. "The big boost we got from our management was freedom. We didn't have to check every time we wanted to do something," Boddie says. "I didn't expect that level of trust."

Questions

1. What evidence of the seven sources of decision complexity can you detect in this case?
2. Which source of decision complexity was probably the most difficult for the Mustang team? Explain your reasoning.
3. Why was the team approach appropriate for the Mustang project?
4. What was the key (or keys) to Ford's successful development of the new Mustang?
5. How well did Ford adhere to the principles of total quality management (TQM) when developing the new Mustang? Explain.

CASE STUDY II

In a large state electricity board, the maintenance of records and decision-making in the personnel department was a gigantic task. While the individual service records of senior engineers were maintained at the central office, those of junior engineers and operating staff were scattered all over the state. All decisions concerning senior engineers were taken at the central office. Some decisions concerning creation of posts, promotions and inter-regional transfers of junior engineers were also taken at the central office.

Case Study II continued

Case Study II continued

Moreover, requests for posts from field officers were also finally approved at the central office. In the case of senior engineers, an attempt was made to put individual records on the Cardex System. However, this experiment could not succeed for a variety of reasons. Consequently, files had been developed for their promotions and transfers.

The General Manager, Personnel, felt that to keep track of a vast number of personnel and to enmesh the organisational needs with those of individuals, it was very necessary to obtain all the relevant data with respect to each individual and to process all personal data with the help of modern digital computers. He felt that a computerised information system would result in the following advantages:

1. More objective assessment of manpower requirements and availability of skill in the organisation.
2. More speedy and efficient handling of personnel issues such as appraisal, training, promotions and transfers.
3. Availability of more accurate information regarding increments, efficiency bars, retirement dates and benefits.

The General Manager, Personnel, was aware of the fact that within the organisation operational data on power generation and distribution thereof was being analysed with the help of computers by a group of specially trained staff. He, therefore, requested this group to help him prepare a proposal on a computerised manpower information system.

The salient features of the proposal were as follows:

1. A beginning may be made with computerised data for all engineering staff.
2. Two data files may be developed. The master file may contain all the basic data, while the secondary file may contain data which requires updating at quarterly intervals.
3. For several purposes, the programme could be relatively simple, while special programmes would have to be prepared for certain purposes. In some cases, the computer may have to just scan its memory and print the outputs.
4. The cost of the project would include the initial cost of the hardware and necessary accessories. Development of software, creation of a data bank, periodical updating of data and the systems development for special reports requested by the Personnel Department. The cost would also include salaries and benefits for staff associated with this activity.

Case Study II continued

Case Study II continued

Questions

1. Is the computerised system in line with the existing culture of decision making in the organisation?
2. In what way could a computerised system affect decision-making in the Personnel Department?
3. What would be the possible unfavourable reaction of engineering staff to the new proposal?
4. Should cost-benefit analysis be undertaken before implementation of the proposal?

—oo(O)oo—

CHAPTER 8

ORGANISATIONAL DESIGN AND PROCESS

LEARNING OBJECTIVES

1. To develop understanding about meaning, process and structure of an organisation.
2. To bring about the main contents of an organisational chart and understand its uses and limitations.
3. To enumerate all the principles of organising and understanding their role in the design structure of an organisation.
4. To learn about the span of management and the various factors affecting it.
5. To identify the effects of the narrow and wide spans of management on the functioning of an organisation.

INTRODUCTION AND MEANING

The efforts of members and their activities should be organised properly to achieve the common goals of an organisation. For this purpose, some kind of relationship has to be established among them. In simple words, organising is a process of establishing a working relationship among the members of an organisation. This working relationship which is also known as 'relationship of superior and subordinate' arises out of assignment of work and delegation of authority. It is because the employee who delegates part of his authority is known as *superior* and to whom he delegates is known as *subordinate*. The term *organising* refers to a process of integrating, unifying, balancing and coordinating the activities being performed by members to accomplish a predetermined objective. It may also be defined as a process of making an orderly determination and arrangement of various activities, functions, roles and relationship for some purpose.

Organising also implies a pattern or way in which a large number of people engaged in group efforts relate themselves to each other in a conscious and systematic manner for the accomplishment of a mutually agreed purpose.

Oliver Sheldon has defined the term 'organisation' as a process of combining the work that individuals or a group have to perform with the facilities necessary for its execution, that the duties so performed provide the best channels for the efficient, systematic, positive and coordinated application of the available efforts.

In this definition, the author has pointed out that the process of organising various activities performed by its members has to be integrated and coordinated in an efficient, systematic and positive manner to achieve objectives.

Thus, organising is the process of designing a well coordinated system of authority relationship and task responsibilities that involves the enumeration and identification of activities, dividing them among various members or departments and establishing a relationship of authority among them (Figure 8.1)

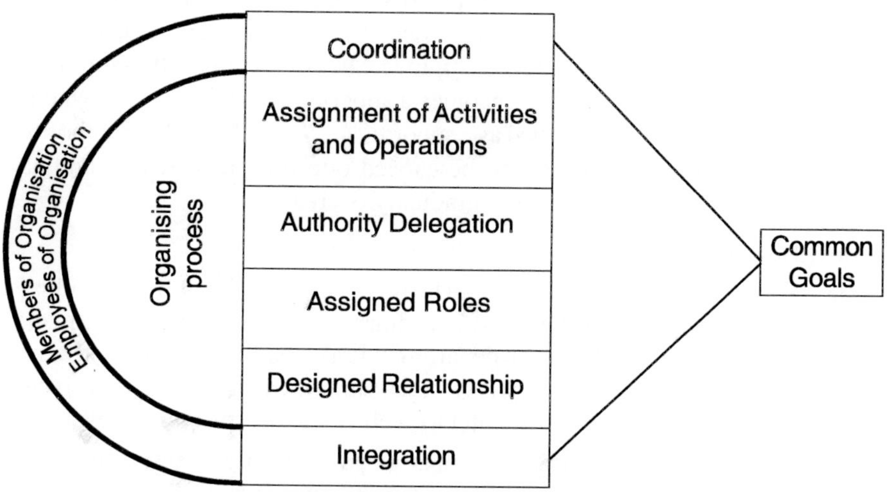

Figure 8.1. Organising process

Organising as a process involves the following:

1. Enumeration and Identification of Activities

In organising, the manager must identify and determine the work and activities that are essential to accomplish objectives. Thus, organisational objectives and goals do provide criteria to determine and identify the nature of work and activities.

2. Division of Work

Total work and activities are determined and further divided and sub-divided into small jobs and tasks that can be performed by single individuals.

3. Grouping of Jobs

After having divided the work into small jobs, they are grouped into different groups, divisions or departments. While grouping of jobs, their relationship and homogeneity are taken into account. For example, jobs related to a particular product, process, customer and territory may be put in a specific group accordingly.

4. Assignment of Groups of Jobs

To perform different groups of jobs and activities, various departments or divisions are created and developed and these groups are assigned to them accordingly. In the process of assignment, a proper relationship of a particular job is established with the department.

5. Creation of Managerial Hierarchy

After having assigned groups of jobs, authority is delegated to the various departments or divisions. It is further distributed among the employees working in those departments. In this way, an authority structure is created that gives a definite position to each employee. In this hierarchy, the employee delegating part of his authority becomes a superior and the person to whom authority is delegated is identified as a subordinate. The delegation of authority from the top to lower levels is to be carried out in a planned way and as authority travels down, its content gradually decreases.

6. Integration and Unification of Jobs and Groups of Jobs

The various jobs that are being performed by employees in individual departments are to be unified and coordinated at the departmental level. Similarly, the functioning of each department is also harmonised to contribute to the smooth functioning of the whole organisation. The basic idea is to create a team spirit both at the departmental as well as the organisational level.

In brief, the organising process consists of two sub-processes, namely—*process of differentiation* and *process of integration*. In order to pool group efforts effectively there must be a division of the total work and activities, so that every member of the group performs a meaningful and purposeful job and contributes to the accomplishment of objectives.

This process, which is known as differentiation, involves the division and sub-division of activities into small tasks and jobs. It facilitates the assignment of work among various departments and employees. In the process of integration, the first jobs assigned to various employees within a department are unified and then the work that is being performed by various departments or units has to be coordinated in such a way so as to make the organisation a whole system.

ORGANISATION AS A STRUCTURE

Once the above-mentioned stages in the organising process are completed, it results in the creation of a formal structure of organisation. The term 'organisational structure' may be defined as a system to job positions, the role assigned to them and the authority relationship among the various positions. It is known as 'formal structure' because it is being created intentionally in a planned manner. It may be described further as a network of assigned jobs and work, well defined roles and designed relationship among the employees working therein to seek common goals. The structure of an organisation provides a basis or framework within which managers and non-managerial employees perform the jobs assigned to them. In other words, an organisational structure may be considered as a core element around which various functions are performed and several processes operate. The structure of an organisation seems to be a pyramid with less positions on the higher side and positions at the bottom.

Although the structure of an organisation is deliberately designed and consciously planned, certain factors have a direct bearing on the design of the structure of the organisation. These factors are as under:

1. Objectives and Goals

An organisation is a powerful system. It is designed and operates to achieve certain predetermined objectives. The objectives and goals provide proper direction to organisational activities. Enumeration and identification of activities to a large extent depends on these objectives. The objectives and goals have a direct bearing on the pattern and structure of an organisation. Since the objectives and goals justify the very existence of an organisation, its structure should be designed in such a way as to contribute the maximum for the accomplishment of objectives.

2. Technology

An organisation may also be considered as a socio-technical system. The technological aspect refers to the way or manner in which various activities will be performed. It is an important part of the organisational structure as the activities are related to objectives and they are also related to technology. It is because every activity to be performed requires some kind of technology. The type of technology being used in an organisation to perform different activities would also affect the structure of an organisation directly and indirectly. For example, the use of sophisticated technology leading to more specialisation may complicate the pattern of relationship among the employees. The technological aspect is more significant in relation to the overall functioning of an organisation. The span of management and the number of non-managerial employees and flow of work which are related to the structure are greatly influenced by technology.

3. Environment

An organisation is a system and it operates within certain boundaries. Beyond these boundaries there exists an external environment that affects not only the formation and functioning of the organisation but also its structure. To cope with the changing environment among other things, organisational process, goals and structure are changed and made in line with changes. The environment is a larger system of which the organisation is a sub-system. It includes all those economic, social, cultural, political, legal and technological factors that directly or indirectly affect the functioning of an organisation. Therefore, the structure of an organisation has to be designed in view of the changes that are likely to take place in the environment. Added to this, an organisation, being a sub-system, interacts with the environment on a regular basis. It gets resources and strength from the external environment and contributes to its functioning. So the structure of the organisation is bound to be affected by the environment. If the organisation operates in a fast-changing uncertain environment, its structure tends to be more adaptive, dynamic and flexible. On the other hand, if the environmental changes have a slow pace and are less complex in nature, the structure of the organisation will be marked by a high degree of stability and a lesser degree of flexibility. However, it is to be noted that rapid, diverse and more complex changes in the environment tend to make traditional structures ineffective.

4. People

Organisations are formed by and operated through people. A large number of people are hired for both managerial and non-managerial jobs. Various activities are assigned to them and finally they are put in a relationship of authority. These people carry some goals, values, perceptions, beliefs and attitudes that have a direct reflection on the structure of an organisation. Therefore, these factors must be taken care of at the time of designing the organisational structure. Indeed, the tasks, activities, goals and technology will gain more meaning if they are built around the people and their needs. In addition, an organisation operates through the people and its efficiency, to a large extent, depends on the level of efficiency of its employees. The efficiency of its employees is affected by many provisions already made or to be made in the structure of an organisation, such as supportive supervision, participative decision making and problem solving, existence of an informal group, democratic leadership, operational authority granted to lower level managers, etc. These factors have a direct impact on the structure of an organisation (Figure 8.2).

NEED AND IMPORTANCE OF ORGANISING

Organising is basically a process of creating a formal organisational structure of role relationship, position and authority. A sound organisational structure contributes greatly not only to the survival and success of the enterprise but also to its continuity and stability. The organisation may also be viewed as a mechanism,

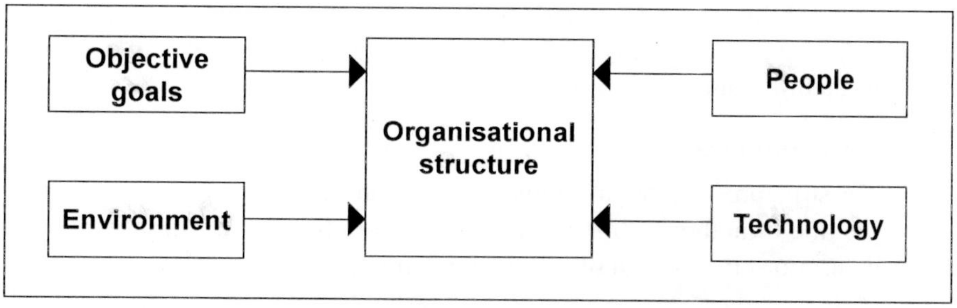

Figure 8.2. Organisational structure

device or indispensable means to achieve objectives. The need and importance of organising an organisational structure can be understood precisely on the basis of the following points:

1. Effective Management

A sound organisational structure facilitates effective management. It is a mechanism through which managers direct, coordinate and control the activities of enterprises. If the structure of an organisation is ill-designed, the entire management process is bound to ineffective.

2. Coordination

The whole process of organising helps in coordination of various jobs in the department or division and by relating them to departmental work. It further integrates and unifies the functioning of various departments in such a way as to contribute to the overall functioning of the organisation.

3. Clarity of Job

A logical and clear-cut division of work and delegation of authority among the various members leads to many benefits. Every member knows it very well what exactly he is expected to contribute and to what extent is his authority to operate.

4. Efficiency

Both the sub-processes of 'differentiation' and 'integration' may directly affect the operating results of an enterprise. If these processes are conducted in a proper manner, the overall organisational efficiency tends to increase.

5. Decentralisation

The creation of an organisational structure also necessitates the delegation of authority among various managerial positions. A decentralised organisational structure encourages prompt decision-making and efficient control.

6. Coping with Change

The organisational structure also provides the basis and framework to the manager which enables him to cope with the changing environment. Elements of flexibility, dynamism and adaptability in the structure of an organisation help him to face the diverse and complex uncertainties without undermining its stability and continuity.

7. Communication

The structure of an organisation also facilitates formal communication through the line of authority that is established from the top to lower levels. It also determines the pattern of interaction among various employees.

8. Broader Span of Control

The creation of staff units in the activity structure of an organisation broadens the span of control of the manager and helps him to discharge his responsibility in a more efficient manner.

9. Discipline

Organising virtually means order and discipline both in respect to the working behaviour of the employees and their role and relationship.

10. Management Development

A highly decentralised structure of organisation may have a strong influence on the development of managers. This is because the delegation of authority to lower level managers provides an opportunity to them to make decisions and exercise administrative authority.

ORGANISATIONAL CHART

An organisational chart is a diagram of the formal position of organisation and the formal line of authority. It is a visual display of organisational structure. In other words, an organisational chart is a graphic and systematic description and presentation of a formal structure of an organisation. It is also regarded as a useful tool to help in visualising the entire organisation and pattern of authority relationship involved. It also helps to prepare an organisational blueprint for deploying human resources. It is a two-dimensional graphic presentation of authority structure and the activity structure.

Organisational charts usually provide necessary information on how the process of differentiation and integration have been conducted to build the structure of organisation and which scheme of departmentalisation has been adopted (product, process, geographical or customer-wise, functional, etc.). It also reflects the flow and pattern of distribution and delegation of authority among the various positions created in an organisation that makes it clear who reports to whom. On the one hand, an organisation chart depicts line, staff and functional relationship and the communication line between managerial positions. It also gives information on various authority positions and the status associated with them

It is to be noted that an organisational chart shows the relationship of functions and flows of authority and responsibility. It also clearly brings out the relationship that exists between various functional departments and divisions. In brief, these charts may be considered as devices to show vertical hierarchy that establishes a chain of command and horizontal specialisation that establishes a division of labour.

Dale has considered the organisational chart "as a diagram of formal authority structure". But the definition given by him has virtually ignored the horizontal dimension of the organisation. A more suitable definition of an organisational chart has been forwarded by Terry.

In his words, "Organisational chart is diagrammatical form which shows important aspects of organisation including the major functions and their respective relationship and the relative authority of each employee in charge of each respective function."

The structure of organisation can be graphically presented in the following manner:

Vertical Chart

This is the conventional way of preparing an organisational chart. It indicates the position of the chief executive on the top of which successive managerial positions are attached. As the chain of command travels down at every successive stage, the content of authority tends to decrease. Vertical charts take the shape of a pyramid with lesser managerial positions on the higher side and more positions on the lower side.

Horizontal Chart

There is not much difference between vertical and horizontal charts except that the pyramid line remains in a horizontal position instead of a vertical position. The line of authority will sum from the left to the right in a horizontal manner.

The position of the chief executive lies on the extreme left and as it moves to the right, it represents a lower level of managerial hierarchy. Since horizontal charts do not serve any additional purpose except complicating the diagram, they are less common in practice.

Circular Chart

Circular charts or concentric charts indicate the highest managerial position at the centre and other middle and lower managerial positions rotate from the centre in concentric circles. As against the top position, the lowest managerial position lies on the outermost circle.

Circular charts clearly show the scope of each manager's responsibility and authority and eliminate status implications which are inherent from the top to lower levels. It takes less space to present different managerial positions. But its main weakness is that it is difficult to draw and often creates a lost of confusion regarding managerial positions

CONTENTS OF ORGANISATIONAL CHART

Organisational charts are aimed at providing the required information both on vertical and horizontal dimensions of the organisation. But more precisely, the exact contents of a chart to a large extent depends on the purpose of preparing it and requirements of an organisation. However, in general, an organisation chart may reflect information on the following aspects:

1. Basic organisational structure and flow of authority
2. Responsibility assigned to individuals and departments
3. Line and staff and functional relationships
4. Position and incumbents holding the position
5. Management development requirements
6. Communication channels to connect various positions
7. Basis of departmentalisation such as product, process, territory, etc.
8. Chain of command or line of authority in an organisation
9. Present and proposed structure
10. Interplay of functions, roles and relationships.

To reduce complications and complexities in an organisation chart, reasonable care should be exercised at the time of designing it so that it includes only needed information on various aspects of organisation that need to be presented. Accuracy, clarity and simplicity are considered the main features of a sound organisational chart.

USES OF AN ORGANISATIONAL CHART

Organisational charts are considered as useful devices or tools of management to show the entire organisation at a glance. The usefulness of these charts can be well understood on the basis of the following points:

1. Organisational charts provide a complete picture of the entire organisation in a simple and understandable manner. They also give a clear-cut overview of the total texture and shape of the organisation.
2. By studying and analysing the organisational chart, one can get an insight of the organisation in terms of its structure, processes, both differential and integration, delegation and distribution of authority, line of staff relations, etc.
3. Organisational charts can also be used as useful devices to deploy the resources of the organisation.
4. The preparation of organisational charts may also remove many drawback and inadequacies associated with an organisation such as dual command, overspecialisation, overlapping of activities and other inconsistencies.

5. Organisational charts can be of great use in the sphere of human resources management, especially in respect of providing training and development facilities to employees, determining their promotional avenues, etc.
6. These charts may also be used profitably for SWOT analysis to evaluate the strengths and weaknesses of an organisation.
7. They also provide a sound basis to management to help them cope with the changing environment and to plan organisational changes.
8. Organisational charts may also be used as partial evidence of discipline order and purposefulness of the system because they avoid haphazard hodgepodge of people and activities involved in the organisation.
9. On the basis of information provided by an organisational chart, outsiders dealing with the organisation can get a sharp view of the component departments of the organisation and their orderly arrangement on the horizontal line.
10. Preparation of organisational charts also facilitates the smooth functioning of the entire organisation. This is because it reveals all the possible hindrances or roadblocks obstructing the flow of work in the organisation.

LIMITATIONS OF AN ORGANISATIONAL CHART

Besides the above-mentioned uses of these charts, they are also riddled with certain drawbacks and limitations. Some of them are:

1. Most organisational charts are merely a 'snap-shot' of the existing organisation. They present it in a mechanistic and engineering fashion thereby ignoring dynamism and an open system of approach to the organisation.
2. They bring forth excessive bureaucratic rigidity in the relationship between the managers at the higher and lower levels as a result of which the organisation tends to become bureaucratic.
3. To cope with the changing environment, frequent changes are initiated in respect of the structure, processes and design of the organisation which ultimately render these charts ineffective and less useful.
4. One of the serious drawbacks associated with organisational charts is that they do not contain and reflect any information on informal relationships among the employees which greatly influence their working behaviour.
5. Poorly constructed organisational charts may create a misleading effect. This is because they tend to show what should be the organisational chart and how it should be constructed and ignores how exactly it is prepared in practice.

   Thus, an organisational chart represents a normative model of organisation and its contents. The real quality and contents such as organisational climate, efficiency, effectiveness and morale of employees do not find any place in the charts. And they show only the superficial and cosmetic aspects of the organisational structure.

6. Organisational charts often fail to depict what the exact contents of authority are, and also what is the extent of responsibility assumed by employees. In spite of the above drawbacks, organisational charts still remain very useful for managers, especially to make analyses of the organisation and highlight inadequacies and inconsistencies in the existing structure of the organisation.

PRINCIPLES OF ORGANISING

The principles of organisation refer to those well-established and accepted general statements and guidelines that are to be used in the process of organisation so as to prepare a sound organisational structure. These principles serve as general guidelines to the managers to evolve a sound and more effective pattern of relationship in designing an organisation. Most of these principles have a classical flavour. This is because they have been developed by early management writers including F. W. Taylor, Henri Fayol, Urwick and others. With the passage of time, these principles have been further refined and modified by many modern management scientists so as to make them more efficacious and relevant in the modern context. Some of these principles are discussed below:

1. Principle of Division of Labour

This is the basic principle of organising which represents division of work and activities into small tasks and jobs that are to be performed to achieve set objectives. This is to be done in such a way that each job may be assigned to and carried out by individual employees. An individual employee performing a specific job repeatedly for a longer period of time, gets specialised knowledge about it. Subsequently, he would be able to perform it with less effort and time which may lead to higher efficiency. Thus, the principle of division of labour encourages job specialisation, increases the efficiency of employees and facilitates the smooth flow of work in an organisation. The application of this principle should be confined to the work to be performed by the non-managerial employees but it should be equally applied to managerial jobs. But too much emphasis on the division of labour may also lead to oversimplification of the job which makes it monotonous and boring. Similarly, it may also lead to overspecialisation (as witnessed in functional foremanship) which proves to be counter-productive after some time.

2. Principle of Functional Definition

In order to discharge assumed responsibility by completing the job assigned to an employee, he has to perform many functions. According to this principle, the functions to be performed by an individual employee or by a department must be well defined. This principle also suggests that the job, activities, role, relationship and expected results should be specifically spelt out in terms of functions. It involves defining the job clearly, laying down an amount of authority given to job holders, describing this relationship with others and establishing the desired level of performance for him. This is to be done to make the job holder more responsible and efficient to achieve the objectives of the organisation.

3. Principle of Scalar Chain

This principle is also known as the scalar chain or line of authority or chain of command. It states that there exists an unbroken line of authority or scalar chain from the top to the lowest level of the organisation. This scalar chain is established on account of assignment of work and delegation of authority from the higher to lower levels. Every employee is attached to the scalar chain in the relationship of superior and subordinate. The content of authority tends to decrease as one moves down the chain.

The principle of the scalar chain also suggests that a well-defined and uninterrupted chain of authority should be established from the top to all levels of management down the line. Such a scalar chain promotes smooth communication between the superior and subordinates. It also facilitates effective decision making in the organisation because it gives a sense of confidence to managers to make decisions within the extents of authority.

4. Principle of Span of Control

This principle refers to the number of subordinates to be placed under the command of a manager whose work he can manage efficiently. It recognises that there is a limit in each managerial position of the number of subordinates an individual manager can manage effectively. Detailed discussion on this principle is made ahead.

5. Principle of Unity of Command

The principle of unity of command implies oneness of command, and a single source of authority over a subordinate. According to this principle, at the time of designing a structure of an organisation, the rule of one subordinate and one superior should be followed, so that the subordinate gets all the orders and instructions regarding the work only from one superior or only one superior commands his activities.

It also suggests that to create a greater feeling of personal responsibility for results, an individual must have a reporting relationship to a single superior. The principle of unity of command offers many advantages. It reduces conflict of instructions because they are being given by only one boss. Discipline can be maintained among subordinates, efficient control can be exercised over them and responsibility can be fixed on a particular superior. Employees do not get an opportunity to sidetrack their responsibility.

6. Principle of Objective

This principle refers to the functioning of an organisation and its components and that they should be directed towards the accomplishment of predetermined objectives. This is because an organisational structure is designed and a process is conducted to achieve objectives. The principle also suggests that the objectives of an organisation should be spelt out in the clearest possible terms and all employees should be made familiar with them. It also recommends that personal goals and interests of employees should be integrated and balanced with that of the organisation in such as way so as to contribute later. Thus, the organisational structure should be in conformity and consistency with objectives for the achievement of which it is designed.

7. Principles of Balance

According to this principle, all techniques and principles being applied to a particular structure of organisation must be balanced properly in the light of the overall effectiveness of the organisation. While maintaining balance, reasonable care should be taken to ensure that one principle does not contradict another or the benefits of one are not outnumbered by the benefits of another. For example, the advantages of unity of command should be balanced with the possible advantages of specialisation which calls for dual command and the same is applicable to the line-and-staff relationship, centralisation and decentralisation, vertical and horizontal dimensions, etc.

8. Principle of Flexibility

The principle of flexibility states that adequate provisions of flexibility should be made in respect of organisational structure. It further suggests that the structure of an organisation should be designed in such a way so as to permit growth and diversification in the future. Not only this, in the event of changes in the environment adequate flexibility in the structure would permit the management to make necessary changes in respect of the process and goals to cope with it.

9. Principle of Absoluteness of Responsibility

According to this principle, responsibility once assumed by a manager cannot be shifted to subordinates. It is often asserted that what is delegated to a subordinate is part of the authority of the manager, not his responsibility or obligation. Although by delegating authority to subordinates, he can assign part of his job to them, if subordinates fail to perform in a satisfactory manner, the ultimate responsibility lies on the superior. In other words, responsibility is indivisible and it cannot be transferred to a subordinate and the superior remains responsible and accountable to his boss.

10. Principle of Delegation by Result Expected

Delegation of authority is a basic principle of organising. It aims at enabling managers to achieve results expected of them. To create the structure of an organisation, authority should be delegated in such a way so as to clarify performance expectations in terms of cost, volume, time, effort, etc. It further recommends that only that much authority should be delegated to the manager that is enough to meet expected performance, targets and results.

11. Principle of Parity of Authority and Responsibility

According to this principle, the authority vested in a manager should be equal to the responsibility assumed by him. This principle further suggests that there should be a compete balance or parity between authority and responsibility and only that much authority should be delegated which is needed to carry out an assigned job. If the amount of authority is less that that the employee may not be able to perform his job in a satisfactory manner. On the other hand, if it is more than the assumed responsibility, it may result in either mis-utilisation or under-utilisation and both are undesirable situations. However, in practice, this principle is often violated. Some conservative managers may still have the tendency to retain more and more authority and assign more and more work to subordinates. Similarly, some subordinates may also be interested to get more authority without commensurate responsibility.

12. Principle of Efficiency

According to this principle, the organisational structure should be designed in such a way so as to facilitate efficient accomplishment of objectives. It further states that the structure should permit optimum utilisation of resources. Since an organisation is an 'input-process-output' system, it should be designed and directed in such a manner so that maximum output is created with minimum input.

13. Principle of Continuity

The principle of continuity states that while designing a structure of organisation, due care should be taken to maintain continuity in respect of its existence and functioning. It may function continuously only when it is capable of coping with the changing environment and maintaining its survival.

14. Principle of Cooperation

This principle of organisation is more concerned with the functional aspect of an organisation rather than its design. According to this principle, an organisation is considered as a team aimed at achieving objectives. Therefore, all the members of the organisation should perform their assigned works in cooperation with each other. Any kind of disagreement, class or conflicting situation may lead to inefficiency and poor performance.

SPAN OF MANAGEMENT

The basic responsibility of every manager is to get things done by others. To do this, he has to communicate and give orders and instructions to his subordinates, plan their activities, direct and control them to establish interpersonal relations and interact with them frequently. The entire process of getting things done by others consumes a lot of time on the part of the manager. Since he is basically a human being bounded by certain natural limitations in terms of effort, time, energy, etc., he cannot manage an unlimited number of subordinates under his command at a time. The concept of span of management also known as 'span of control' or 'span of supervision' refers to that number of subordinates whose work can be managed at a time by a superior efficiently.

The span of management can also be defined as the 'number of subordinates who report directly to the manager'. The concept of span of management has great relevance in creating a number of managerial positions, levels, dividing managerial work and formation of a compact work group under the command of managers.

The classical principle of span of management has been developed in the context of human and organisational constraints that prevent a manager from managing and controlling the activities of an unlimited number of subordinates under his control. Therefore, these constraints and limitations create a need of thinking over a size of a group consisting of a specific number of employees that can be placed the command of a manager. If the group consists of a small number of employees, the span of management is said to be narrow and on the other hand if the work group consists of a large number of employees, the span of management is said to be broad.

Management practitioners and scientists have devoted a lot and energy throughout the decades to determine the ideal span of management. In this connection, early management theorists have specified exactly how many individuals should be in a manager's span of management. In the words of one of the authors, "no superior can supervise directly the work of more than five or at the most six subordinates whose work interlocks." But modern managers do not endorse the classical version of span of management; rather they strongly believe that though the manager cannot manage the work of an unlimited number of employees, the exact span of management may differ from one situation to another depending on the wide range of variables. Hence, there is no one optimal span of management for all managers in all situations. The modern management approach, especially contingency and system approaches are more realistic in determining an appropriate span of management. This is because in choosing an appropriate span of management, the capability of both the superior and the subordinate and the environment in which they work are taken into account. Some of the factors that affect the span of management are as under:

1. Quantity and Quality of Delegation of Authority

In an organisation, well-defined, clear and more delegation of authority by a manager to his subordinates tend to widen the span of management. This is because on the one hand, subordinates know clearly what is expected from them, what to do and what is the extent of authority, and on the other, by exercising the given authority, they would be solving all work-related problems on their own. In doing so, they will take less time of the superior and subsequently he may be able to manage a larger number of subordinates at a time because the subordinate's dependence on the superior is reduced largely.

2. Formulation of Organisational Plans

A well-designed set of organisational plans such as policies, rules, procedures and methods facilitates the smooth flow of work in an organisation. This is because these plans do serve as a guide to decisions and action by a manager. Every manager makes use of these plans to solve problems and tackle situations. It gives him more time to concentrate on planning and control and consequently his span of management is bound to be wide.

3. Availability of Staff Assistance

Induction of staff specialists in an organisation to help and guide line managers affects their span of management. The availability of staff services to line managers widens their span making them capable of getting things done by a larger number of subordinates. Lack of these services may narrow down the span of management.

4. Nature of Work Performed by Subordinates

If subordinates perform highly complex activities they require more attention of their superior and take more of his time. Hence, it would narrow down his span of management. On the other hand, if they are performing simple, routine and standardised jobs, their dependence on their superior is bound to be less and it widens his span of management.

5. Communication Network

Well-connected superiors and subordinates through the network of communication may also affect the span of management. Direct, fast and free flow of communication between a superior and his subordinates makes the former capable of managing a greater number of subordinates and vice-versa.

6. Abilities, Skills and Training of Superior and Subordinates

Highly qualified and professional managers are usually well equipped in respect of leadership and other administrative qualities that help them in managing a larger group of subordinates at a time efficiently. Similarly, if the subordinates are skilful and well trained in performing their jobs they can be managed in large numbers by a superior.

7. Dispersion of Subordinates

Widely scattered subordinates under the command of a superior will narrow down his span of management. On the other hand, if they belong and work in the same work of the manager, he will be able to manage and control a larger group of subordinates.

Kreitner has pointed out certain determinants of the span of management as given in Table 8.1.

TABLE 8.1: SITUATIONAL DETERMINANTS OF SPAN OF CONTROL

	Wide span of control appropriate to 10 or more	Narrow span of control appropriate to 2 to 4
1. Similarity of work performed by subordinates	1. (Identical)	Distinctly different
2. Dispersion of subordinates	2. (Same work area)	Geographically dispersed
3. Complexities of work performed by subordinates	3. (Simple and repetitive)	Highly complex and varied
4. Direction and control required by subordinates	4. (Little and/or frequent)	Intensive and/or constant
5. Time spent on coordinating with other managers	5. (Little)	A great deal
6. Time required for planning	6. (Little)	A great deal

This table of situational determinants of the span of control reveals that in a wide span of control the manager needs less time for planning, coordinating and directing the simple, repetitive, identical activities performed by subordinates at the same work place. A narrow span of control is marked by more time taken by the manager for planning, directing and coordinating subordinates' activities which are highly complex and varied in nature and the subordinates are geographically dispersed.

A discussion of the span of management seems to be incomplete without giving attention to Gracuna's theory of subordinate-superior relationship. French management consultant V. A. Gracuna analysed the subordinate-superior relationship and developed a mathematical formula based on the geometric increase in the complexities of relationships of managing as the number of subordinates increases. Gracuna has identified three types of relationships between a superior and subordinates.

1. Direct single relationship
2. Direct group relationship
3. Cross relationships.

For example if A has three subordinates B, C and D, there will be three direct relationships

A–B, A–C and A-D

There will be nine (9) group relationships

With	With	With	With	With	With	
A to B-C	B-D	C-B,	C-D,	D-B,	D-C,	B with C
C with	B and D,	D with C	and B			

There will be six (6) cross relationships

B to C, B to D, C to B, C to D.

The total number of relationships can be determined with the help of the following formula given by him:

$$n = \left[\frac{2^n}{2} + n - 1\right] \quad n = \text{Number of subordinates}$$

On the basis of the above formula, possible relationships for a different number of subordinates will be as given in Table 8.2 This table of relationships indicates that in case of arithmetical increase in the number of subordinates, the geometrical increases takes place in the number of relationships.

TABLE 8.2: ARITHMETICAL INCREASE IN THE NUMBER OF SUBORDINATES AND GEOMETRICAL INCREASE IN THE RELATIONSHIP

Number of subordinates	Number of relationships
1.	1
2.	6
3.	18
4.	44
5.	100
6.	222
7.	490
8.	1,080
9.	2,376
10.	5,210
11.	11,374
12.	24,708
18.	2,359,602

WIDE VERSUS NARROW SPAN OF MANAGEMENT

The wide and narrow span of management has a direct impact on the structure of an organisation as well as on the efficiency level of managers. A wide span which implies a larger number of subordinates being managed and controlled by a superior may force him to overlook and condone serious errors on the part of subordinates.

Similarly, a narrow span may indicate that the capabilities and skills of managers are not being utilised fully.

So far as the structure of the organisation is concerned, if the span of management is wide, the structure tends to be flat because the organisation needs a lesser number of managerial positions. If it is narrow, the organisational structure tends to become taller in size, because there exist more managerial positions in the organisation, of course, in a vertical direction. This can be understood well with the help of Figure 8.3.

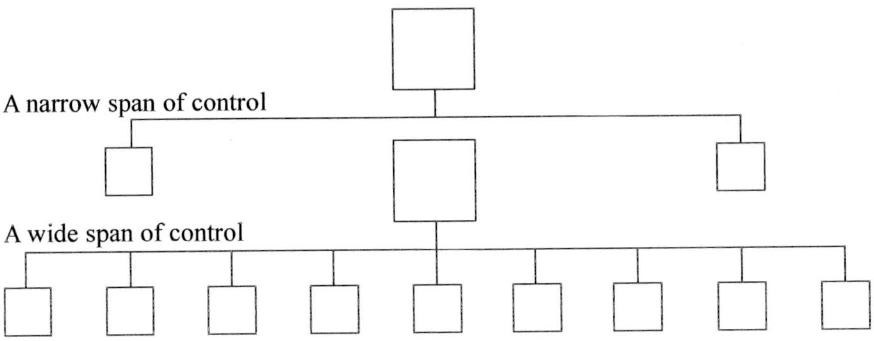

Figure 8.3. Narrow and wide span of control

SUMMARY

Organising is one of the important elements of the managing process which is mainly concerned with creating working relationships among the members of an organisation. This is considered as a process of integrating, unifying and coordinating efforts and activities of the employees to achieve predetermined objectives.

The term 'organising' has two interpretations:

(a) organising as a process and

(b) as a structure.

As a process, it includes the determination of activities necessary to achieve objectives, dividing, sub-dividing and regrouping them, assigning them, granting authority and coordinating their performance towards accomplishment of organisational goals.

As a structure, organising represents a network of authority relationship, job positions and various roles to be played by employees. The organisational structure comes into being when various activities involved in organising are performed. It is greatly influenced by objectives, technology, environment and people working therein. If the environment is less changing it tends to be mechanistic in nature and in a rapidly changing environment it becomes an open adaptive system. Similarly, value system, perception, attitude, needs and wants of the people working in the organisation and the type of technology being used to perform a variety of activities would also affect the structure as well as the functioning of an organisation.

Organising helps in creating managerial hierarchy and performing management functions. It facilitates coordination, management development, prompt decision making and decentralisation, effective communication, discipline, growth and development.

In order to describe formal official positions in the organisation some charts and manuals are used. The organisational chart is a graphic representation of both authority structure as well as activity structure of an organisation. The use of an organisational chart facilitates the smooth functioning of an organisation, clarity of role and relationship, human resource management, and help in identifying inadequacies of the existing structure of an organisation.

While designing the structure of an organisation many principles are used to make it sound and effective. These principles include the division of labour, functional definition, scalar chain, unity of command, principle of objectivity, balance, flexibility, absoluteness of responsibility, delegation by result expected, authority responsibility, continuity, efficiency cooperation and span of management.

The principle of span of management refers to a number of subordinates whose work can be managed efficiently by a manager at a time. According to the contingency approach of management, the span of management cannot be prescribed. Rather, it varies from manager to manager depending on several factors. These factors include quantity and quality of delegation, organisational plans and policies, availability of staff assistance, nature of work performed by subordinates, communication network, abilities and training of superior and subordinates, and dispersion of subordinates.

If a manager can manage a large number of subordinates his span would be wide and if he is capable of managing a small number of subordinates his span tends to be narrow. The span of management has implications not only on the structure but on the functioning of the organisation as well. If the span is narrow, there would be many levels of management and the operational cost may tend to be high. On the other hand, if it is wide, the operational cost will be less because there will be only a few levels of management.

In this connection, Gracuna's theory on the relationship between a superior and his subordinates is very interesting. He has mentioned that three types of relationships exist between a superior and his subordinate. These relationships are direct single relationships, direct group relationships and cross relationships. According to this theory, if there is an arithmetical increase in the number of subordinates, the number of relationships will witness a geometrical increase. Although the principles of organising are conventional in nature, they are equally important today and relevant such as the principle of unity of command, scalar chain, parity between authority and responsibility, etc. It is widely acknowledged that if these principles are taken into account and used in the correct perspective, the structure of organisation would be sound, effective and dynamic.

TEST QUESTIONS

1. Define the process of organising. How does it differ from an organisational chart?
2. What are organisational charts? Discuss the uses and limitations.
3. Define the term 'span of management'. Discuss the merits of a wide span of management.
4. What is an organisational structure? Discuss the major determining factors of an organisational structure.
5. An organisational structure provides the framework to undertake managerial functions. Discuss.
6. Explain the steps involved in an organising process. As a prospective chartered accountant how would you apply them to set up a chartered accountant's office?
7. Discuss the various principles of an organisation in detail.
8. Write short notes on the following:
   (a) Gracuna's theory of span of management
   (b) Organisational structure
   (c) Organisational chart
   (d) Span of management.

OBJECTIVE TYPE QUESTIONS

Which of the following statements are correct and which are incorrect? Give reasons for your answers.

1. An organisational structure refers to the network of managerial functions.
2. The authority level principle suggests that managers should undertake managerial jobs within their jurisdiction.
3. A narrow span of management results in a flat organisational structure.
4. A narrow span of management is more expensive than a wide span of management.
5. The organising process consists of two sub-processes.
6. The span of management will be the same in all organisations of the same size.
7. An organisational chart is only a normative model of organisational structure.
8. Unity of command means that a manager must issue the same instructions to all his subordinates.

9. Formal organisations are hierarchical.
10. A formal organisation has two dimensions.
11. Horizontal dimension is represented by activity structure.
12. Activity structure and authority structure are the same.
13. An organic organisational structure relies on stable rules, procedures and regulations.

REFERENCES

Etzioni, Amitai. *Modern Organisation*. New Delhi, India: Prentice-Hall of India, 1964.

Balu, P. M. and Scott, W. R. *Formal Organisation: A Comparative Analysis*. San Francisco, U.S.A.: Chander Publishing Company, 1962.

Ernest, Dale. *Planning and Developing the Company Organisation Structure*. New York, U.S.A.: A.M.A., 1952.

Tosi, Henri I. *Theories of Organisation*. Chicago, U.S.A.: Clair Press, 1975.

Mitzberg, Henry. *The Structuring of Organisation*. Englewood Cliffs, N.J., U.S.A.: Prentice Hall, 1979.

Urwick, Layndall, F. 'The Manager's Span of Control'. *Harvard Business Review*. May–June, 1956.

Moorhead, Gregory. 'Organisational Analysis: An Integration of Macro and Micro Approaches'. *Journal of Management Studies,* April, 1981.

Child, Johy. *A Guide to Problems and Practices*. New York, U.S.A.: Harper and Row, 1984.

Hall, Richard H. *Organisation, Structure and Process*. Englewood Cliffs, N.J., U.S.A.: Prentice Hall, 1982.

Dalton, Dan R., Todor, William; Gordon, Michael J. and Layman Porter. 'Organisation on Structure and Performance: A Critical Review'. *Academy of Management Review,* January, 1980.

Pearce, John A., II and David, Fred R. 'A Social Network Approach to Network Design Performance'. *Academy of Management Review*, July, 1983.

INDIAN CONQUEST OF THE GLOBOCORP

Know yourself and you will win a thousand battles. Even as India Inc. struggles to acquire a global competitive advantage, Indians have already succeeded in acquiring a global managerial edge. So much so, tomorrow is being perceived as the era of the international Indian CEO.

Box continued

Box continued

The latest to join the top rank is 53-year-old Arun Netravali, a multimedia communications expert, who has become the president of Bell Labs. Just what are the ingredients of the great Indian success? Answers Ravi Virmani, CEO, Nobel & Hewitt India: "Indian managers can handle diversity, ambiguity, multiple tasking better. It comes natural to them. After all, they have been exposed to a competitive environment right from the start, at school and college."

Agrees Preety Kumar, managing director, Amrop International: "The value system in which Indians are brought up make them put in that extra bit, walk that extra mile."

True. But all this boils down to a mix of Emotional Maturity (determination, a flexible mindset and self-awareness) and Entrepreneurial Zeal (the ability to take risks)—the EE factor—say management experts. While the first is the product of cultural upbringing, the second flows from the genes.

Besides technical expertise, what global CEOs need is the ability to think and react differently. In a world where business models are constantly changing and globalisation has become an engine of growth, managers who think unconventionally fit the global bill.

It was entrepreneurial zeal that tempted Shailesh Mehta, who is now the CEO of Providian Financial, to join a start-up in the middle of his careers, sacrificing a secure future. And it was emotional maturity that drove Rana Talwar, group chief executive, Standard Chartered Bank, from investment banking to consumer banking in 1982—a critical career move that brought him closer to the customer.

Indians are present in diverse fields—from financial services (Hartford's Ramani Ayer), banking (HSBC's Aman Mehta), airlines (United Airlines Rono Dutta and US Airways Rakesh Gangwal), consultancy (McKinsey and Co's Rajat Gupta and Arthur Andersen's Jamshed 'Jim' Wadia), infotech (Computer Associates' Sanjay Kumar) to communications (Bell Labs' Netravali).

Although educational background has a role to play in India's rise to the top, the environment also breeds success. Explains Professor Sadagopan, director, Indian Institute of Information Technology, Bangalore: "Successful software entrepreneurs in the US have a good educational background—often they are IIT products. Traditionally, things in India are so difficult; but when they work in the US, they realise that its possible to achieve a lot."

Box continued

Box continued

Indeed, there's still more to be achieved. Indians are just attaining critical mass as CEOs. Much of today's top-notch Indian talent entered the global corporate world in the 1980s. With factor advantages like entrepreneurism and the ability to manage diversity, Indians are perhaps well-suited to manage tomorrow's megacorps as they battle fleet-footed smaller firms.

WIPRO—ORGANISING WITH A DIFFERENCE

Premji hired Wipro's first quality assurance manager, who reported directly to the CEO. "The quality assurance manager could overrule the factory manager." That commitment hasn't changed. Five months ago, Wipro hired GE's Six Sigma head corporate vice president to determine Wipro's quality standards. Predictably, he reports to Premji.

Former Wipro-ites also believe that Wipro is respected because it is among the few organisations that really nurture independent thinking. A manager, who as part of Wipro Infotech, was involved only in domestic hardware and software maintenance.

He had been repeatedly pitching for Premji's permission to export embedded software which Premji repeatedly denied. In one meeting, the manager stood his ground. Premji finally relented. Today, embedded software is one of Wipro's greatest strengths.

At Wipro, the space for dissent and independent thinking is unbelievable. It's usually difficult to listen to thousands of views. So it's a culture shock to me to see how much dissent exists and is listened to.

The organisation has encouraged entrepreneurship by cross-fertilisation of talent and fostering diversity.

Source: Business World.

ORGANISATION AT GODREJ

Godrej Consumer Products chairman started an exercise to split the erstwhile Godrej Soaps into two companies, Godrej Consumer Products and Godrej Industries. "We realised that the demerger was an opportunity to create a board-driven culture," says Godrej.

After the demerger, he and his management were happy with the company's progress. They were confident that the restructuring had sorted

Box continued

Box continued

out most problems. The toilet soaps business (Rs. 268 crore or 52.5 per cent of sales) was growing at a healthy 8 per cent. The hair colour business (Rs. 1.75 crore or 2.9 per cent of sales) was doing much better with a growth of 17 per cent. From the management's point of view, everything was just fine.

But a few months ago, the four independent directors of Godrej met to take stock of the company. Their diagnosis took the Godrej team by surprise. The hair colour business (it was growing twice as fast as soaps) was being under-leveraged, they argued, as Godrej was organised on functional lines (the same marketing team was handling both soaps and hair colour). Recommendation: 'Atomise' and reorganise the company along product lines. This would increase focus on hair colour and let it grow at full potential. Godrej agreed and is now implementing the change. Without this crucial bit of detached, independent perspective, the hair colour business would have suffered unnoticed.

Source: Business World.

CASE STUDY I

Boeing Becomes a New Company

Since 1994, Boeing began the process of remaking the company for the next round of aircraft purchases. Every part of the company is involved, from engineering to manufacturing. The focus of the change is that Boeing is a manufacturing company rather than an engineering and technology company. Due to changes in the air travel business, the major commercial airlines are demanding lower airplane prices and significantly lower operating costs. Airbus continues to be a fierce competitor, so Boeing must meet the competition early and on every front. (Boeing bought McDonnell Douglas in 1997).

It is not as if the company is in financial trouble. Its new model, the 777, is generating lots of orders, plants are in the works for a new supersonic and another jumbo jet for commercial sales, and several new project possibilities exist for the defence division. The new 777 was designed completely on the computer so that designs went straight from the designers' computers to the machine tools for manufacturing. It can carry as many as 400 passengers, 50 more than the comparable Airbus 33T. It

Case Study I continued

Case Study I continued

is 15 per cent more fuel efficient, and can fly over 8,000 miles non-stop. Orders are coming in faster than for any other new plane, although its price is pretty steep: $ 12–$ 15 million depending on the interior layout.

Boeing's new CEO, Philip Condit, must continue the reductions in cycle time and cost cutting started by his predecessor, Frank Shrontz, because airlines are making their purchase decisions differently than in the past, even choosing in some cases to refurbish older planes rather than buy expensive new ones. The changes started with Condit and his team of presidents of divisions of commercial planes, defence and space, and computer services. This group differs notably from its predecessors in that they have met together for several years to discuss the good and bad things about each other's divisions and the future of the company. They all embrace the new togetherness theme as the primary means through which the company will be able to reduce cycle times, improve delivery times, cut product development time, and reduce total costs.

In the former structure, the design and manufacturing groups were separate. Design and engineering groups would design the planes and then give the plans to manufacturing to build. When problems existed in the design, they would be sent through hierarchy back to engineering for correction. Under the new structure, comprehensive design-and-build teams include members of all groups involved. Therefore, planes are originally designed to meet customers' needs, are easier to build, and corrections are made faster. For example, previously when tool builder Tony Russell had a problem with an engineering design or specification, he would have to go to his supervisor and the problem would be shuffled through to engineering. Now he goes directly to the engineering and design group, gets the problem solved and gets back to work with the correct design. This type of revision in the process has helped reduce the product delivery time from 18 to 10 months. The team approach and working-together ideas were used extensively on the 777. Some teams included tool makers, designers, manufacturing workers, suppliers and even customer representatives. Contrary to past procedures, workers on the line were allowed to change how planes were built, which has significantly decreased costs. Condit has instituted 36-degree performance review in which they are evaluated by their subordinates, their peers, and their own supervisors to improve understanding of how they are doing from all perspectives. Employee empowerment is increasing at all levels. Condit and his team are having quite an impact throughout the company.

Case Study I continued

Case Study I continued

Questions

1. The new way of organising at Boeing most resembles which of the classical types of organisation?
2. How have responsibility and authority been altered under Condit's new approach?
3. Describe the new ways of organising at Boeing in terms of the configurational and operational aspects of structure. Draw an organisation chart for Boeing.

Source: Kelly Holland, 'New Hands on Boeing's Controls', *Business Week,* March 11, 1996, p. 4; Michael J. Parks, 'How Boeing Hatched its High-Tech Bird', *Business Week,* January 22, 1996, pp. 18–19; Seth Lubove, 'Destroying the Old Hierarchies', *Forbes*, June 3, 1996, pp. 62–71; Alex Taylor, 'Boeing: Sleepy in Seattle'. *Fortune*, August 7, 1995, pp. 92–98; Dori Jones Yang, 'When the Going Gets Tough, Boeing Gets Touchy Freely', *Business Week*. January 17, 1994, pp. 65–67.

—oo(O)oo—

CHAPTER 9

HORIZONTAL DIMENSION: DEPARTMENTALISATION

LEARNING OBJECTIVES

1. To develop understanding about the horizontal dimension of an organisation and how it is created.
2. To learn the meaning and importance of various patterns of departmentalisation.
3. To bring out the main features and relative merits and demerits of functional, product and geographical departmentalisation.
4. To identify the various factors and their role in selecting a suitable pattern of departmentalisation.
5. To get conceptual clarity about the hybrid form or composite form of departmentalisation and know the reasons for adopting it.

INTRODUCTION AND MEANING

Departmentalisation is the process of dividing and sub-dividing activities into small components and regrouping them into various units or divisions.

It is one of the important processes through which the formal structure of an organisation is brought into existence. It is only through departmentalisation that the other two sub-processes involved in organising, that is, differentiation and integration are conducted. In other words, departmentalisation is a process of dividing and sub-dividing the activities of an organisation into smaller jobs and tasks and further integrating, combining and grouping them into convenient, administrative and easily identifiable units.

It ultimately involves the grouping of activities and employees into different departments or divisions. Departmentalisation is also considered to be a process of making an activity structure of the organisation. Different departments so created are placed in a horizontal line. It is also considered as an integrating process. This is because it is through the process of departmentalisation that related jobs, activities or processes are grouped into major organisational sub-units and finally placed in a horizontal or lateral relationship. For example, all jobs involving staffing activities like manpower planning, recruitment, selection, training, etc., are often grouped into personnel or human resources department and the department is placed in horizontal relation with other functional departments like production, marketing, purchase, finance, etc.

The process of departmentalisation is required to be conducted at every level of an organisation. It may be noted that the chief executive makes out and divides the groups of activities into major departments and departmental heads further group them into sub-departments or units and again the manager heading the unit may repeat the process. On the basis of the level of organisation at which the grouping of activities is done, departmentalisation may be of three types, namely, primary departmentalisation that involves the grouping of basic activities of the organisation, intermediate departmentalisation that involves the creation of departments at the middle level and ultimate departmentalisation that represents the grouping of activities at the lower level of an organisation.

NEED AND SIGNIFICANCE OF DEPARTMENTALISATION

The process of departmentalisation has an important role not only in designing the structure of an organisation but also in maintaining its smooth functioning. Its need and importance can be described on the basis of the following points:

1. Growth of the Organisation

As long as an organisation remains small in size and its activities can be managed and controlled by a single individual, it hardly requires any format of organisation and grouping of activities. But as it grows, may activities come within its fold that are to be performed to accomplish objectives. The process of organising starts with departmentalisation which facilitates the creation of different departments on the basis of grouping of various activities. In this connection, it is, however, to be noted that the span of management restricts the size of an organisation but the process of departmentalisation facilitates the growth and extension of an organisation to a reasonable degree.

2. Decentralisation of Authority

In many respects, the process of departmentalisation may be considered as a primary vehicle or means for decentralisation of authority because once the activities have been successfully grouped, the required authority to make decisions is to be delegated to managers heading these groups of activities at all levels of the organisation.

3. Classification of Activities

The process of departmentalisation is primarily concerned with the activity structure of the organisation. To design this kind of a structure one has to study, analyse, divide and group the various activities into different groups and then integrate and combine them into a horizontal relationship. While doing so, activities that are known as the building blocks of an organisation have to be identified in terms of critical activities or key activities and other activities.

The critical or key activities are more important to achieve objectives and deserve the highest priority and be placed at the core of the organisational structure. Around these key activities, other supportive and secondary activities are positioned in such a way so as to contribute to the performance of key activities.

4. Coordination

Departmentalisation is also helpful in seeking coordination in respect of the functioning of various departments. In the words of James D. Thomspon, grouping of activities through departmentalisation permits coordination to be handled in the least costly manner. A degree of coordination is achieved through departmentalisation because the members of the department work on related tasks and jobs, follow the same departmental rules and report to the same departmental head. In other words, all the activities of an organisation may be coordinated right from the top level to the lower level through primary, intermediate and ultimate departmentalisation.

5. Smooth Functioning

Departmentalisation also facilitates the smooth flow of work in an organisation. This is because through this process that clear-cut divisions or units of various activities may be formed, overlapped and duplication is reduced to a minimum. They are integrated and unified to eliminate disagreement and discord. Departments so formed operate independently but in a related manner so as to contribute to the smooth functioning of the entire organisation.

6. Training and Development

The process of departmentalisation also encourages training and development of the managers at various levels of the organisation. This is because every department or unit or division is made operationally autonomous by delegating enough authority to their heads. The managers leading these departments make decisions to solve work-related problems and frequently interact with other related departmental heads as well as managers at higher levels.

This contributes to their growth and development, achievement and satisfaction. Besides, proper departmentalisation of activities of an organisation would ultimately contribute to its overall effectiveness and efficiency.

PATTERNS OF DEPARTMENTALISATION

There are many alternatives for departmentalising organisational activities. The most common patterns are grouping of activities by functions, products, processes, territories and customers.

FUNCTIONAL DEPARTMENTALISATION

The functional departmentalisation has become quite popular because of the growing complexities and new dimensions of management. Since all organisations are engaged in the creation of utility, they undertake and perform various activities and functions to achieve objectives. If the jobs and tasks of an organisation are grouped into different groups or departments strictly on the basis of various functions that are to be performed in respect of these jobs and tasks, such a pattern of departmentalisation is known as functional. This pattern is to be used by profit as well as non-profit organisations. In a typical profit organisation, activities are grouped into various departments on the basis of functions such as production, purchase, finance, personnel, public relations, accounting, etc. These departments are known as functional departments. In this pattern, related and required skills, processes, abilities and expertise to perform a similar type of specialised functions are built up around that functional department. Departmentalisation of activities can be made either on the basis of major functions or minor or other derivative functions depending on the need of organisation and its level at which departmentalisation is being conducted (Figure 9.1).

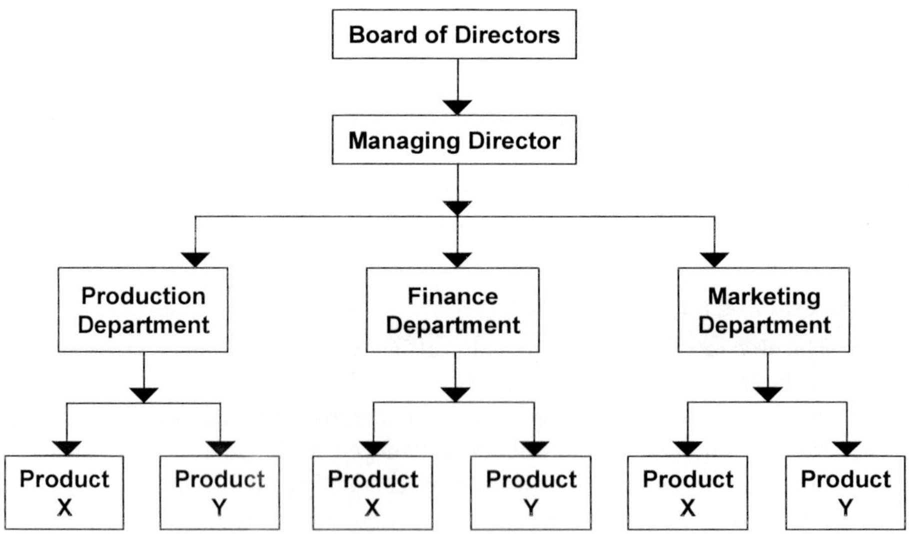

Figure 9.1. Functional departmentalisation

A number of advantages are claimed for functional departmentalisation, some of which are as under:

1. It is one of the simplest patterns of grouping of activities in an organisation and is therefore commonly used for both economic as well as non-economic organisations.
2. It is also considered a natural and logical way of arranging the various activities of an organisation.
3. Functional departmentalisation takes advantage of occupational specialisation because it involves grouping of those functions together which belong to and are performed by the same specialists using similar equipment and facilities. Since each manager is concerned only with one type of function, thus all his energy will be focused on it. This will lead to optimal utilisation of equipment and facilities and economies in the performance of functions.
4. It also facilitates the hiring, training and career development of managers who are qualified and experienced in their respective fields of specialisation.
5. It encourages coordination at every level of organisation because all product or project departments get expertise and specialised services on a particular matter only from one functional department. For example, if an organisation produces three different products, each product department will get necessary orders and instructions regarding production from one production department.
6. The pattern of departmentalisation seems to be most suitable for small and medium-sized organisations that handle a limited number of products.
7. Another advantage of functional departmentalisation is that it makes the specialised services of one individual or one department available to the entire organisation. This is because under the pattern the necessary expertise and other facilities are built around that department or individual (Figure 9.1).

A negative aspect of functional departmentalisation involves the following limitations:

1. Sometimes, organisational harmony and the process of unification may be affected adversely because of the functional grouping of activities. This is because members of a particular functional department tend to develop a functional bias. And they do not cooperate with other functional departments.
2. However, it is also noted that various economies brought about in the organisational functioning through functional departmentalisation may be outweighed by additional managerial and staff salaries and other overhead costs.
3. The pattern of functional departmentalisation is also criticised for

encouraging differentiation and division at the expense of integration and unification of various functions and activities.

Product or Service Departmentalisation

Product grouping is considered to be a more integrating and unifying pattern of departmentalisation as compared to functional departmentalisation. This pattern is common with large multi-product organisations that have various product lines or several products. In this pattern, organisational activities are grouped around product lines or products. The organisation identifies important functions that are necessary to be performed with regard to products such as engineering, marketing and financing and other functions. These functions are attached to various product departments.

Unlike a functional department, a product department is considered more independent and autonomous like a separate business unit. This is because the product head Paces primary emphasis on the operations of his product department. He is accountable for profit or loss and may even compete with other product departments of the same organisation. However, it is to be noted that a product department does not act as a full-fledged independent unit and its head has to report to the chief executive to whom heads of other departments also report. In this sense, it is very much a part and parcel of the entire organisation.

In product departmentalisation, each department of a product operates as a multifunctional unit. This is because all the necessary functions such as production, marketing, personnel, finance, etc., are performed in every product department. In a pure product departmentalisation, the head of every product department is given enough authority to perform various functions. The chief executive is mainly concerned with the overall planning, control and coordination of various product departments. But in a mixed form, product managers share authority with the chief executive regarding these functions. The organisation involved in the production and distribution of services which are intangible may also find it advantageous to group various activities and functions around the various categories of services being rendered (Figure 9.2).

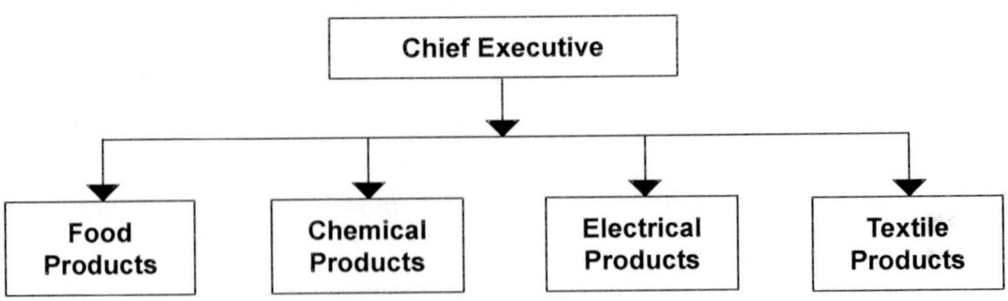

Figure 9.2. Product departmentalisation

It offers the following advantages:

1. Product departmentalisation facilitates coordination in respect of the performance of various functions. This is because functions, skills and expertise that are required to produce and distribute a particular product are put into one group and under one head. Thus, the whole job can be easily coordinated and a high degree of efficiency with regard to work performance may be maintained.
2. Product departmentalisation also helps in integrating and unifying various activities and functions performed in one department and the functioning of these departments with the entire organisation.
3. It encourages decentralisation of authority in a more systematic and logical manner. This is because the authority to deal with a concerned function is given to a product head and authority to prepare a corporate plan to exercise efficient control over departments and to coordinate their functioning is exercised by the chief executive.
4. This pattern of grouping also facilitates the training and development of managers of various product departments. This is because every product manager gets operational authority to perform a variety of functions and with the passage of time, they may become well-versed and trained in respect of all the functions to be performed in their product departments.
5. Product departmentalisation also reduces the burden of work of the top executive and the chief executive can concentrate more on key functions of management. The most important advantage of product departmentalisation is that it helps to fix and make accountability quite clear to product heads. This is because the performance of each product department can be measured in terms of profit/loss over a particular period of time. Moreover, a produce head cannot shift his accountability to others.

The major disadvantages with this form are as under:

1. Product departmentalisation is considered to be very costly because duplication of functions and activities in various product departments tend to increase overall operational costs.
2. The grouping of activities in terms of products may also lead to difficulty in coordination because successive managers of a product department will try to seek more power and authority to manage the unit. In view of this situation finances and other important tasks such as policy formulation and training tend to be centralised with the top executive.
3. As a result of more operational autonomy granted to product departments and fixation of accountability on them, they are bound to place more emphasis on their departmental goals and performance. This may lead to displacement of organisational goals. Apart from this, the product heads may concentrate more on short-term goals at the expense of the long-term objective of profitability.

GEOGRAPHICAL DEPARTMENTALISATION

In an organisation that conducts widely scattered business operations with nationwide or global markets, geographical departmentalisation becomes a more pressing need of the organisation. In geographical departmentalisation, all the activities in a given area are grouped together and placed under the control of one manager. For example, in our country, Indian Railways, Life Insurance Corporation of India, Air India, Indian Posts and Telegraph Department, State Bank of India, etc., have departmentalised their activities in terms of geographical locations. They have developed various zonal, regional and divisional departments. Similarly, many multinationals like Ford Motors, Phillips, etc., have adopted this pattern to produce and distribute their products all over the world by dividing the entire world market into various continents like Asia, Europe, Africa and Australia, America and dividing continent-wide markets into countrywide markets.

This pattern of departmentalisation is considered secondary in nature as it can be used in respect of some activities or functions to be performed area wise. Thus, first of all, necessary functions and activities are grouped into several groups and these are further departmentalised area-wise (Figure 9.3).

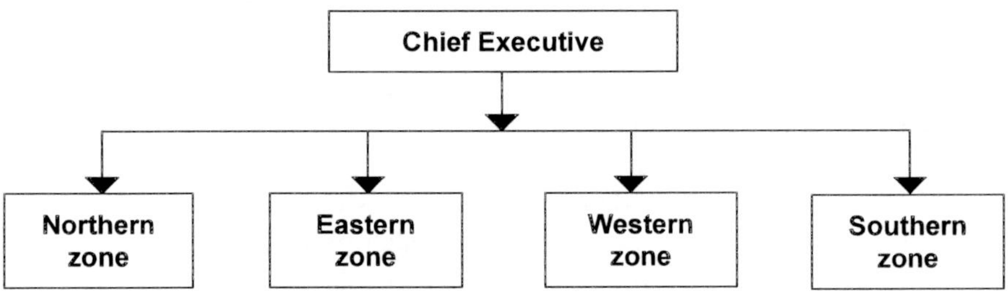

Figure 9.3. Geographical departmentalisation

Geographical departmentalisation has the following advantages:

1. This pattern of departmentalisation serves customers', needs and interests in an efficient way. This is because the department operating in a particular area will be quite familiar with the needs and wants of the local customers of that area. Production as well as the distribution system can be made more meaningful and responsive to local requirements.
2. Geographical grouping also encourages training and development programmes for versatile managerial personnel. This is because managers working in a particular territory will have an opportunity to gain experience in all major functions and develop themselves in all respects.
3. It also facilitates zone-wise and region-wise integration, unification and coordination of activities and functions performed therein.
4. Departmentalisation of activities on the basis of territories may also help in securing various economies of localised operations because goods are produced and distributed locally instead of producing them at distant

places. Therefore, saving in transportation cost both in respect of raw material as well as finished products becomes a point of attraction.

5. In view of the growing competition, this pattern of grouping of activities seems to be more desirable to get a competitive edge. This is because in this pattern, departments operating in a particular region may fully concentrate on the needs and wants of local customers and better quality of service can be provided to them. Use of locally available resources may also help in economising the operations. Phillips India Ltd. produces and distributes electrical goods locally, according to the needs of customers.

Geographical departmentalisation has the following limitations:

1. By creating various departments in various areas, delegating them adequate authority and making them operationally autonomous, control of top management in their activities is diluted. Not only this, operational autonomy may also complicate the task of coordination. This is because the managers heading departments in different areas may adopt different styles of functioning which suits local needs and requirements.
2. In geographical departmentalisation, though certain economies may be obtained due to localised operation, at the same time repetition and duplication of activities and functions in every territory may outnumber those economies.
3. It has a limited use as it can be profitably applied to multinational companies and other big organisations whose operations are widely scattered. Moreover, it is used only as a secondary pattern for departmentalisation.

Process/Equipment Pattern of Departmentalisation

In addition to the patterns of departmentalisation given above, the activities of an organisation can also be grouped according to the process or equipment used in the entire production system. This pattern of grouping activities is often used by a manufacturing organisation which have assembly line production or a production system consisting of various processes to be conducted in a logical sequence. The output of a particular process becomes the input for the next succeeding process and the same is repeated till the production of the finished product. For example, in a cotton textile manufacturing organisation, the entire production system is marked by various processes such as ginning, spinning, weaving, dyeing, colouring and finishing. In such an organisation, activities or functions that are needed to be performed with respect to a particular process of equipment are grouped in one group and made around that particular process. Like process departmentalisation, sometimes various processes are performed through some equipment, hence it is also possible to departmentalise activities on the basis of equipment being used in the process. In the case of sophisticated technology in production, this pattern seems to be useful (Figure 9.4).

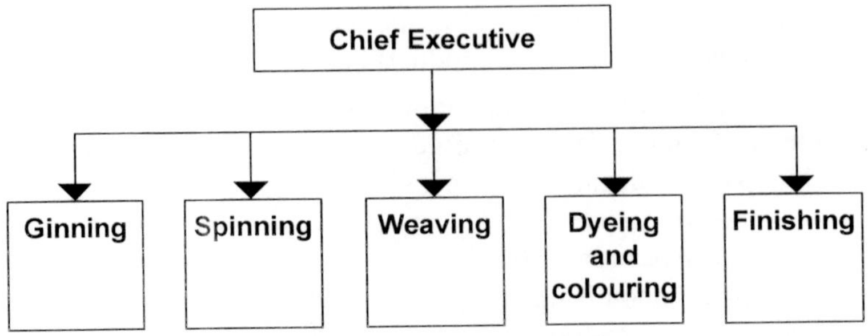

Figure 9.4. Process departmentalisation

Although by using this pattern of departmentalisation, an organisation can seek effective and maximum utilisation of various equipment and machines, the problem of planning and coordination becomes more difficult. If a particular process is not conducted properly in time as planned, the entire production system comes to a halt and heavy cost is incurred. Similarly, employees using particular equipment in a process are confined only to that process. They do not develop any expertise and skill relating to other processes. Besides, this pattern can be used profitably in those manufacturing organisations that have several processes and enough workload for each process.

Customer's Market Pattern of Departmentalisation

This pattern of departmentalisation is often used by organisations that are engaged in producing and distributing goods and services for various groups of customers. In this pattern, the activities of an organisation are grouped according to the types of customers to be served. The rationale behind this pattern of departmentalisation is to serve the different needs of various sets of customers in an efficient manner. For example, an automobile company may group its activities on the basis of various types of customers to be served such as heavy vehicle servicing, light vehicle servicing and scooter servicing departments (Figure 9.5).

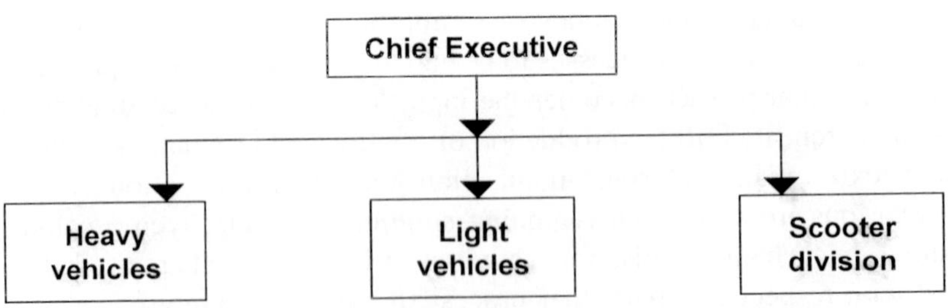

Figure 9.5. Departmentalisation by customers

The main advantage of customer departmentalisation is that it focuses on the needs and wants of a particular group of customers and they can be served better. Greater satisfaction on the part of customers may further enhance the image of an organisation.

On the other hand, the difficulty in coordinating various customer departments and duplication of activities and underutilisation of services and facilities of customer departments are some of the limitations of this pattern. On the same lines, sometimes, the activities of an organisation may also be grouped on the basis of various markets to be served by an organisation. This pattern facilitates the formulation and implementation of suitable policies to deal with different markets, for example, if the organisation produces goods both for domestic consumption and export. So the requirements of the local market may be different from that of the export market and activities to deal with each market may be grouped into different groups.

Composite Departmentalisation

There is no hard and fast rule that organisations should adopt a particular pattern of departmentalisation to group their activities. Each of the preceding patterns of departmentalisation has been presented in its pure form. But in actual practice, a hybrid of two or more patterns is developed according to the needs of the organisation. It is found that some organisations combine the product form with the functional form while others develop a combination of the functional and geographical departmentalisation according to their needs (Figure 9.6).

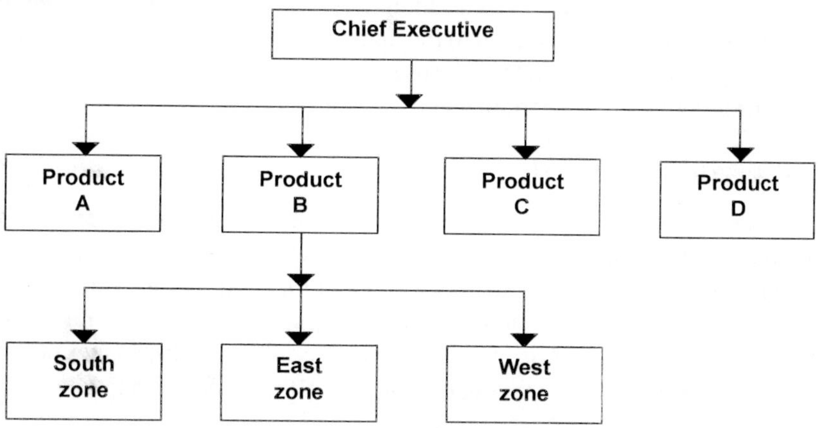

Figure 9.6. Composite departmentalisation—Product and geographical form

The main objective of using a composite pattern of departmentalisation is to seek relative advantages of two or more patterns. But a hybrid of patterns finally depends on the requirements of the organisation to adapt to situational needs.

CHOOSING A PATTERN OF DEPARTMENTALISATION

The process of departmentalisation is aimed at seeking a sound and effective structure of the organisation. It differentiates and integrates the various activities performed in the organisation to achieve objectives. It is obvious that if it is not conducted properly, it may prove an expensive, ineffective and wasteful exercise. Hence, the process of departmentalisation should be looked upon as major surgery and the required attention should be given to it. Otherwise, it may create more problems than it solves. To choose an appropriate pattern of departmentalisation the following factors should be taken into account.

Decentralisation

In many respects, the process of departmentalisation is looked upon as a vehicle for decentralisation of authority. This is because to perform various groups of activities, managers heading them are to be given adequate authority. To make decentralisation more meaningful and successful in an organisation, authority for strategic planning, managerial control and coordination should remain with the top executive. On the other hand, managers heading departments should not fee handicapped by inadequate operational authority to run their respective departments.

Specialisation

The state of specialisation in the performance of business operations fetches many economies. Hence, while selecting the pattern of departmentalisation it should be taken into consideration. However, it should be noted that activities should be departmentalised in such a way so as to maintain a balance between specialisation and operational autonomy granted to the manager to perform a variety of functions. Too much specialisation as in the case of functional departmentalisation may prove counter-productive after a certain stage.

Management Development

The decision of departmentalisation of activities may also affect training and development of managers in an organisation. Functional grouping may restrict their development and training only in respect of major functions because they concentrate only on one function. Thus, management development may be encouraged by using a product or territory pattern of departmentalisation as each product department operates as a small business unit by itself and the manager heading it gets an opportunity to develop in every respect.

Coordination

Although the process of departmentalisation facilitates coordination, it is complicated further when some of the patterns are used. For example, in product or territory-wise departmentalisation, every department has its own operating objectives varying from one to another. This makes the task of seeking effective coordination more difficult but the functional type of grouping tends to bring coordination easily. Functional heads in respect of performance of departmental activities operate independently and it is only at the level of the chief executive that their activities are coordinated which is not a very difficult task.

Control of Operations and Performance

While selecting a pattern of departmentalisation, managerial control and its efficiency with regard to measuring results, discovering deviation and initiating remedial measures should be taken care of. In spite of granting operational autonomy to various departments, managerial control should be exercised by the chief executive. This is because self-sustained and operationally-autonomous departments can be created within an organisation only to the extent to which the chief executive makes provisions to measure and evaluate the operating results of those departments.

Human Considerations

Human factors should also be given due weightage to develop an appropriate pattern of grouping of organisational activities. This is because these factors directly affect working behaviour and performance of the employees in an organisation, such as information relations, cultural pattern, value system, supporting leadership, etc.

Economical Operations

The major objectives of departmentalisation are to facilitate coordination, training and development, efficient control, etc. This also helps to maintain the smooth functioning of organisation and economise its operations thereby enhancing the overall efficiency of organisation. Duplication and repetition of various activities in several departments may add to the cost of operations. Too much centralisation may also prove counter-productive. Hence, some of the key functions are centralised with top executives and others are to be performed through various departments so as to secure various economies with regard to performance of those operations.

It is evident from the above discussion that no pattern of departmentalisation is complete and perfect in itself in all respects. Each pattern offers certain advantages along with certain inherent limitations. It seems to be desirable that while developing and selecting a pattern or combination of patterns of departmentalisation flexibility, requirements of the organisation and situational demands should also be taken into account.

SUMMARY

The process of departmentalisation is carried out to build the activity structure of an organisation. It consists of division and integration of activities and their components. This is a process of dividing and sub-dividing the activities of an organisation into small components and then regrouping them into several small units or divisions.

The process of departmentalisation has an impact on the structure as well as the functioning of an organisation. It encourages decentralisation of authority, facilitates growth and development, coordination, helps in analysing and classifying activities, training and development and ensures the smooth functioning of the organisation.

In order to departmentalise the activities of an organisation, various patterns may be followed. The selection of a pattern, to a large extent, depends on the requirement of the organisation. Some important patterns are functional, product, geographical, process and customer or market-based patterns. Many organisations use a combined form of two or more patterns so as to get multiple benefits. Functional departmentalisation is a process of dividing and sub-dividing activities into small jobs and tasks and regrouping them on the basis of functions that are to be performed in respect of those groups. It is considered to be very simple, logical and economical. It encourages coordination, training and development. In a product departmentalisation, the activities of the organisation are divided into small components and grouped into different groups on the basis of products. In other words, activity divisions are made around the product. It suits the organisations that are engaged in the production and distribution of many products. Each product department operates as a multifunctional unit because all the functions related to that product are performed in that department. This facilitates coordination, decentralisation of authority, training and development of managers and reduces the burden of work of top level managers.

Geographical departmentalisation is a process of dividing activities and regrouping into various groups on the basis of geographical areas of operation. In other words, activities to be performed in a particular area are grouped in one group and the same criterion is followed for other areas. This pattern is suitable for an organisation which has business scattered widely throughout the country or continent or global. It focuses on local needs of the customers, provides wide-ranging exposure to managers and helps in securing economies of local operations. But dilution in the control of top managers and duplication of functions may limit its advantageous use.

Process departmentalisation may be defined as the process of dividing and grouping activities on the basis of and around various sub-processes that are involved in the system as a whole. Each grouping is made around the machines or equipment. It leads to optimum utilisation of machines and equipment.

In many organisations, the market of the products may be segmented and consumers in each segment may possess varying demographic and psychographic features. The groups of activities are made around those segments. Thus the customer/market departmentalisation is a process of dividing and grouping various activities on the basis of requirements of specific consumer groups or markets.

In a composite departmentalisation, two or more patterns are used in combination to secure benefits of both and meet the requirements of the organisation.

The process of departmentalisation which includes differentiation and integration of various activities of the organisation plays a key role in shaping its activity structure. On the one hand, it encourages specialisation, decentralisation of authority, management development, coordination and effective control of various operations. On the other, it economises performance of activities and operations and takes care of human factors such as informal relations, work culture, value systems, supportive leadership, etc.

TEST QUESTIONS

1. Define the term 'departmentalisation'. Explain its need and importance.
2. What is functional departmentalisation? Explain its advantages and limitations.
3. What do you understand by departmentalisation? Discuss the factors that are to be taken into account for this process.
4. Define product departmentalisation and explain its benefits.
5. Write short notes on
   (a) Product departmentalisation
   (b) Geographical departmentalisation
   (c) Composite departmentalisation
6. What is departmentalisation? Discuss the role of activity analysis in the process of departmentalisation.
7. Explain the need and importance of departmentalisation and the various bases of departmentalisation in brief.

OBJECTIVE TYPE QUESTIONS

Which of the following statements are correct and which are incorrect? Give reasons to support your answers

1. Composite departmentalisation is an amalgam of two or more forms of departmentalisation.
2. Departmentalisation creates a horizontal structure.
3. The concept of departmentalisation is classical in origin.
4. The customer form of departmentalisation is applicable for segmenting marketing activities of an organisation.
5. Functional departmentalisation appears to be more appropriate for small and medium-sized enterprises.
6. Complete departmentalisation combines many departments for collective functioning.

REFERENCES

Dale, Ernest. *Organisation.* New York, U.S.A.: American Management Association, 1967.

Davis, K. *Human Behaviour at Work.* New Delhi, India: Tata McGraw-Hill, 1975.

Freeman, R. Edward, Stoner, A. F. and Gilbert, Daniel, R. *Management*. New Delhi, India: Prentice Hall of India Private Limited, 2001.

Hickson, D. J., Kimmings, C. R., Lee, C. A. and Schneck, R. E. 'Strategic Contingency Theory of Intra Organisational Power'. *Administrative Science* (Quarterly journal), 1971.

Koontz, Harold and Weihrich. *Essentials of Management*. New Delhi, India: Tata Mc Graw-Hill Publishing Company Limited, 2001.

McClelland, David C. and Burnham, David. 'Power is the Great Motivator'. *Harvard Business Review*. March–April, 1976.

Newman, William H. *Administrative Action*. Englewood Cliffs, U.S.A.: Prentice Hall Inc., 1951.

Robbins, S. P. *Organisation Theory*. Englewood Cliffs, N.J., U.S.A.: Prentice Hall, 1983.

Robbins, Stefen P. *Organisation Behaviour: Concepts and Controversies*. Englewood Cliffs, U.S.A.: Prentice Hall, 1979.

Rogers, R. E: *The Political Process in Modern Organisation*. New York, U.S.A.: Exposition Press, 1971.

Simon, H. A. *Administrative Behaviour*. New York, U.S.A.: McMillan Inc., 1976.

CASE STUDY I

The New Controller

Statewide Electrical Supply Inc. is a wholesale distributor of electrical supplies serving a population area of three million persons. Business has expanded gradually and during the last eight years the number of accounting clerks has grown from one to 12. The first clerk employed was a middle-aged woman who had completed two years of college and taken two accounting courses. She proved to be a loyal and capable clerk. So when the department expanded to three persons, she was promoted as chief accounting clerk with supervisory duties over the two other clerks. She reported to the firm's general manager and depended on him to handle accounting decisions that were more than routine.

As the business grew larger, the existing accounting arrangement became inadequate so the general manager decided to employ a controller to handle all the financial and accounting functions of the firm. The chief clerk recognised that she was not qualified to handle the accounting and financial affairs of this magnitude, and she did not seek promotion to this job. She did, however, welcome the idea of a controller, because she was overloaded with work and felt that the new controller might help relieve her of some of her more difficult responsibilities.

Case Study I continued

Case Study I continued

An additional factor in the firm's decision to establish the position of controller was that there were many complaints about the chief clerk's supervisory ability. She appeared to be effective with the first two or three clerks when the department was small and duties less complex, but she was unable to handle the larger department and the more complex duties. Her problems seem to be confined mostly to internal supervision in her department. Other departments in the firm reported that she worked effectively with them, and they expressed some fear that the new controller might upset this favourable working relationship.

The general manager is not sure how to handle the problem of integrating the new controller into the organisation. He wants to retain the chief clerk because she is a valuable employee but he is concerned that if he demotes her from supervisory duties at the time the controller is employed, she may resign.

Questions

1. How do you recommend that the new controller's department should be organised?
2. What can be done to improve the behavioural environment in this situation?

—oo(O)oo—

CHAPTER 10

VERTICAL DIMENSION: AUTHORITY AND ITS DELEGATION

LEARNING OBJECTIVES

1. To understand the meaning, concept and various sources of authority.
2. To remember the limits of authority on the part of the person who uses it.
3. To develop conceptual clarity regarding delegation of authority, its elements and importance.
4. To bring out the barriers to effective delegation and suggest how to make it more effective.
5. To follow the basis concepts of centralisation and decentralisation of authority and remember the relative advantages and disadvantages of these two situations.
6. Establish proper balance between centralisation and decentralisation.
7. To establish a proper balance between delegation and decentralisation of authority.

Vertical dimension is an important aspect of organisational structure. It is also known as authority structure of an organisation. After having built activity structure and creating several positions in an organisation, the authority structure is built around those positions. In order to do so, authority is delegated to different departments and employees working therein so as to enable them to perform an assigned group of activities and tasks. So authority and its delegation is a central part of the vertical dimension of an organisation.

AUTHORITY DEFINED

An authority is a central part of vertical dimension of an organisation and it is vested in the positions created therein. It is regarded as a positional right rather than a personnel right. Once a person vacates a position, he ceases to have authority. Generally, authority refers to a relationship which exists between two employees, that is, superior and subordinate. It may be considered as a power or right of a superior to take decisions and to guide the actions of subordinates. The concept of authority is basic to organisational theory and practice. It has been described and analysed by various authors. According to Henri Fayol, authority is the "right to give orders and power to exact obedience". Thus, he has defined authority as a power to exact others and to take action that is considered appropriate to the achievement of predetermined objectives.

According to Koontz O'Donnell, "authority is the power to command others, to act or not to act in a manner deemed by the possessor of the authority to further enterprise or departmental purpose." Both Terry and Koontz have pointed out the area of application of authority. According to them, authority is a power to be exercised for directing the activities of subordinates for the accomplishment of objectives of an organisation. All these definitions are based on the concept of 'formal authority theory'. According to this theory, authority originates from the top and travels down the line through the process of delegation.

In the context of management, authority includes the following rights:

1. Right to take decisions on the problems, situations and issues that are related to activities assigned to employees.
2. Right to use resources to perform assigned activities in a satisfactory manner.
3. Right to give orders and instructions to subordinates regarding the work being performed by them and to seek compliance to given orders.

SOURCES OF AUTHORITY

Although there has been controversy regarding the sources of authority, the basic sources can be identified as under. According to Max Weber, a German social scientist, there are three bases of authority, namely,

1. charismatic authority,
2. traditional authority, and
3. rational legal authority.

Charismatic authority refers to those rights and powers that a person acquires through his personality and its traits. The magnetic force associated with his personality attracts people to follow him. This type of authority is without position and without institution and simply flows from the charming personality of an individual. History speaks a lot about such personalities like Mahatma Gandhi, Nelson Mandela, Napoleon, Abraham Lincoln and others. In fact, individuals having a charismatic authority create history because they are highly respected and blindly followed by the public.

Traditional authority comprises those rights and powers that are sanctioned and granted by the traditions and customs prevailing in society such as guardians, teachers, religious heads, parents, etc., who belong to social institutions and enjoy traditional authority. As a matter of customary practice they are respected and followed. For example, in many societies it is customary that the eldest son of the king succeeds him regardless of his merit and abilities.

Rational legal authority refers to the formal rights and powers that have been vested in the organisation by the state. In fact, the ultimate source of legal rational authority is society. Society sanctions it to the state, and the state to the organisations which finally grant it to the various positions created therein. Rational legal authority is institutionalised rights, because these rights are vested in the institutions and organisations, both economic as well as non-economic such as military organisations, educational organisations, hospitals and other governmental organisations. The authority is rational in the sense that it is be exercised rationally to make optimum utilisation of resources to seek predetermined objectives or to maximise benefits. It is legal in the sense that it is legally and formally sanctioned by society having a legitimate base and in the form of laws of the state.

It is only by exercising rational legal authority do managers perform the basic job of mobilising and utilising resources to reach their goals. However, managers are required to exercise their authority in a specific, definite and well-defined manner without allowing personal likes and dislikes to interfere with it. In other words, they are expected to exercise it in an impartial and objective manner free from personal prejudices and favouritism.

Acceptance Theory of Authority

The basic concept of formal authority that has been developed by Henri Fayol and his associates was not fully endorsed by behavioural scientists. They argued that the formal authority vested in the position of the manager is just a nominal authority and it becomes real authority only when it is accepted by subordinates whose activities are to be commanded by exercising authority. According to advocates of the acceptance theory, an authority seems to be meaningful and real only when it is used effectively. For example, if the manager having formal authority gives orders and instructions to his subordinates, and they do not comply with them due to any reason, it renders the whole exercise of authority ineffective.

Hence, the concept of the acceptance theory originates out of failure of a formal authority. It recognises only that part of authority which subordinates are really accepting. Barnard has put it as "the decision as to whether an order has authority or not, lies with the person or persons to whom it is addressed and does not rest in the person of authority and can be judged in terms of its acceptance by the person to whom it is addressed rather than who issues the orders." According to the acceptance theory, presence of authority in any particular law is solely determined by the receiver and not by the issuer of the order. The area of acceptance of such orders depends on the following factors. A person can and will accept communication authoritative containing orders and instructions if

1. He can and does understand the communication.
2. At the time of his decision he believes that he is not inconsistent with the purpose of the organisation.
3. At the time of his decision he believes it to be compatible with his personal interest as a whole.
4. He is able mentally and physically to comply with it.

Thus, in order to make an authority acceptable to subordinates, it should fall within the area of application.

There are many critics of this concept of authority especially Theo Haimann and Koontz O'Donnell who believed that it is unrealistic and unethical on the part of subordinates not to comply with orders and instructions given to them by a superior. Had there been this kind of situation all around the organisation, it would have been reduced to chaotic conditions. In fact, formal authority is accepted and complied with by subordinates to maintain order and discipline and to secure smooth functioning of the organisation. All the more, formal authority is accepted by members of an organisation because insubordination and chaos are not norms of organised activities.

Competence Theory of Authority

In addition to formal authority and the acceptance theory of authority, some management scientists and practitioners advocate that authority also flows from personal competence of the person. The competence theory states that personal competence in terms of abilities, knowledge, skill and other qualities of personality may also help the manager to influence the working behaviour of his subordinations and decisions of his superior. According to Urwick, formal authority is conferred by an organisation, technical authority as being implicit in a special skill and knowledge, and personal knowledge is conferred by seniority and popularity.

Thus, a person may get his orders and advice accepted not only because he is having any formal authority but also because of his personal qualities and influence. The competence theory is related to the acceptance theory of authority. In practice, it is often found that the words of a few individuals carry more weight and are easily accepted by others in an organisation irrespective of their position in the hierarchy of management. The advocates of this theory firmly believe that the real source of authority lies in the competence of individuals. They are accepted as authoritative not only because they possess formal authority but also because they have more knowledge and technical competence to guide subordinates in the right direction.

Nevertheless, the competence theory of authority represents a partial view of authority. This is because in the absence of formal authority, the former two may become irrelevant and ineffective. In a real sense, acceptant and competence authority supplement the formal authority of the manager and make it more effective and meaningful.

LIMITS OF AUTHORITY

Managers do not enjoy absolute and unlimited authority. Rather, authority is subject to certain limits by internal as well as external environment. Apart from the authorities described above which may reduce the formal authority of managers, there are some other factors which also restrict it. Some of them are:

Organisational Constraints

In an organisation, authority is vested in the position of the manager which is identified in terms of jobs and tasks, functions and activities assigned to him as well as his role and relationship with others. Only that quantum of authority is granted to him which is required for performing the assigned work. In addition, his authority is also subject to organisational plans, policies, methods and procedures.

Legal Constraints

The authority vested in the position of the manager and its use is governed and regulated by the relevant provisions of the laws, for example, the personnel manager will have to exercise his authority only within the legal framework of various laws such as the Trade Union Act, the Industrial Disputes Act, the Payment of Bonus Act, etc.

Personal Constraints

How effectively a manager exercises his authority over his subordinates is also determined by his personality traits, abilities, skill and knowledge. The absence of these may render his authority less effective.

Social Limitations

In an organisation, employees work as members of a group and their working behaviour is largely determined by social factors. This is because their behaviour is more dominated by group norms, values and beliefs. Any order and instruction given by a superior inconsistent to these norms may not be properly followed by them.

Other Environmental Factors

Managers are expected to exercise authority rationally to optimise the gains of the organisation. But in many situations due to the pressure of environmental factors they may be forced to take hard decisions and instead of being rational, they may also go by their intuition and judgement. Such decisions are made by managers to cope with the changing environment and to protect and promote the identity of the organisation. Due to the pressure of environmental factors, managers may be forced to exercise authority with great restraint as the situation demands.

DELEGATION OF AUTHORITY

Managers require enough authority to perform various managerial functions and to get things done by others. Similarly, authority is to be delegated to design a structure of the organisation. This is the core of the organising process because organising will have little meaning without delegation of authority.

Delegation Defined

Delegation is a process of assigning various degrees of decision-making authority to subordinates. There are at least five different degrees of delegation. This is a process by which the manager assigns some of the tasks to his subordinates on a selective basis and allows them to exercise authority on his behalf to perform assigned tasks. According to McFarland, "delegation is the primary formal mechanism by which network of authority relationship is established." In this definition more emphasis has been placed on the relationship of a superior and his subordinate. The person who delegates part of his authority is known as a superior and to whom it is delegated is known as a subordinate. Terry has defined it in a different manner. According to him, delegation means "conferring authority from one executive or organisational unit to another to accomplish a particular assignment."

This definition indicates that delegation of authority takes place between two executives or two units to perform assigned work. Broadly, delegation of authority is that managerial activity in which the employee transfers a part of his authority to another or allows others to share authority with him to perform assigned tasks (Figure 10.1).

Since no superior can perform all the activities or tasks assigned to him he assigns a part of his activity to his subordinates. Every managerial position in an organisation is marked by authority, role, responsibility, relationship and obligation. Through the process of delegation part of these is given to subordinates so that they can help the superior in discharging his responsibility (Figure 10.1).

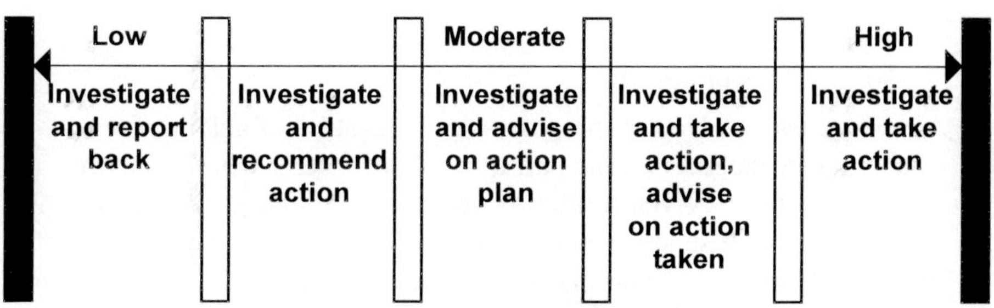

Figure 10.1. Degree of delegation

Delegation of authority does not only mean granting some rights to subordinates but is much more than that and involves assignment of work as well as the creation of accountability on the part of subordinates. A careful analysis of the act of delegation indicates that it consists of many stages or steps that are to be conducted in a particular sequence to affect the process of delegation. These stages are:

1. To Size up the Work Load

At the very outset of the delegation process, the superior sizes up his work load in terms of activities and tasks assigned to him and the result or performance expected of him. This is because his managerial position consists of role, relationship, responsibility, authority, contributions and results expected. So the manager divides the total activities into two sets, one he handles alone and another he decides to assign to his subordinates.

2. Assignment of Work

After deciding which part of his activities is to be assigned to a subordinate, the manager must be very clear in his mind regarding his expectations from subordinates. While assigning work, the superior should take into account the abilities and potential of his subordinates. It seems to be desirable to assign only those tasks which the subordinate can perform in a satisfactory manner. This is because the ultimate responsibility regarding those parts rests with the superior. In practice, it is considered desirable to assign only operative parts of the activities to subordinates.

3. Granting Authority

Assignment of work is to be followed by granting the necessary authority to subordinates so that he can perform the assigned work efficiently. While granting part of the authority to subordinates, the principle of parity between authority and responsibility should be followed. Only those rights should be granted to subordinates that are essential to perform the assigned work and which enable the subordinate to function effectively. The exact degree and contents of rights which a superior grants to a subordinate depends on wide-ranging variables.

4. Creation of Accountability

All the stages involved in the process of delegation of authority results in creating accountability on the part of a subordinate. When the subordinate exercises authority given to him to perform an assigned job, he becomes accountable to the superior. Accountability is an obligation on the part of a subordinate that he performs his duties to the best of his abilities by exercising authority in a proper manner.

RESPONSIBILITY, AUTHORITY AND ACCOUNTABILITY

In order to understand the basic concept of delegation of authority and its various implications, it is desirable to have a conceptual clarity of three terms involved in it, that is, responsibility, authority and accountability. Generally, responsibility refers to those obligations which a person is expected to perform to the best of his abilities in a given direction. Theo Haimann has defined responsibly as "an obligation of a subordinate to perform the duty as required by his superior." McFarland defines responsibility "as the duties and activities assigned to a position or to an executive."

On the basis of these definitions it is clear that responsibility has two interpretations. According to some management authors, it is considered as a set of tasks and duties that have been assigned to the manager. However, it should be noted that mere assignment or allotment of work to the manager does not make him responsible. He becomes responsible only when he accepts the assigned work. In another sense, responsibility is considered as a corollary of authority and is the obligation of a person to whom authority is delegated to act in response to orders and instructions given by the superior. The subordinate to whom the work is assigned and authority is delegated owes an obligation to the superior. According to Peterson and Plowman, responsibility involves three main elements of conduct. They are:

1. Compliance
2. Obedience
3. Dependability.

These elements provide the basis on which the relationship of a superior and a subordinate is established.

Responsibility is generally marked by the following features:

1. The essence of responsibility is an obligation to perform the assigned work in a satisfactory manner.
2. It arises from division and assignment of work. The person becomes responsible when he accepts the assigned work.
3. It is a corollary of authority which implies that the subordinate has to obey the orders and instructions of his superior who has given a part of his authority to him.
4. Responsibility cannot be transferred. By assigning a part of the work to a subordinate, the superior gets his help in discharging his responsibility. But if the subordinate fails to perform the assigned work in a satisfactory manner, the ultimate responsibility lies with the superior.
5. In an organisation, the employee who assumes responsibility also becomes accountable to his superior.
6. Responsibility flows from the lower to higher levels of management. Every subordinate is responsible for his work to his immediate superior.

'Authority' has been defined as a set of formal rights which are vested in the position to be occupied by employees. In brief, these formal rights include the right to make decisions, right to use resources and right to command over others. In an organisation, every manager gets authority through the process of delegation from the top to lower levels.

'Accountability' is also an obligation of the subordinate and it arises out of exercise of authority by a subordinate given to him by his superior. In other words, when the subordinate exercises authority to perform an assigned work he becomes accountable to his superior.

Accountability is an obligation to keep superiors informed about the progress of work on a regular basis. If the subordinate fails to perform his assigned work in a satisfactory manner, he has to give an explanation to his superior, whose part of authority he has used. Thus, accountability arises out of exercise of authority.

In brief, *authority* is delegated, responsibility is assumed and accountability is imposed. Responsibility arises out of division and assignment of work. Authority arises out of responsibility and accountability arises out of use of authority.

Need and Importance of Delegation of Authority

Delegation of authority is a key activity to design the structure of an organisation. It has a significant role not only in creating an organisational structure but also helps in efficient functioning of an organisation. In detail, its need and importance can be judged on the basis of the following factors:

1. Creation of Managerial Hierarchy

Delegation of authority is crucial to create managerial hierarchy in the organisation. This is because through the process of delegation, every manager delegates part of his authority to the other and it continues till the lowest level of organisation. Every employee is attached to this hierarchy in the relationship of superior and subordinate. The managerial hierarchy provides a unified basis to perform managerial functions. Every superior plans, organises, directs and controls the activities of subordinates working under his control. Managerial positions will have no meaning without delegation of authority.

2. Enhancement of Efficiency of a Manager

Delegation of authority in a planned manner permits managers to concentrate on key activities which require their prompt attention. These activities include decision making, planning, coordinating and controlling. On the other hand, another group of activities that is related to the operative part is to be assigned to subordinates. In doing so, managers can manage a larger number of subordinates at a time efficiently and their span of management broadens. In fact, effective delegation multiplies the efficiency and effectiveness of managers. By sharing their tasks with subordinates and getting it done through them, managers can accomplish much more that what they can do individually. Delegation is a means of pooling together distinct efforts, skills and knowledge to perform difficult and complicated activities.

3. Prompt Decision Making

Delegation of authority also facilitates prompt decision-making. This is because valuable time is lost when the subordinate visits a superior before making decisions. Delay in decision-making is reduced when subordinates are authorised to make necessary decisions on the spot. By delegating authority, subordinates are granted enough rights to handle and solve work related then and there.

4. Training of Subordinates

In addition, delegation causes subordinates to accept accountability and exercise judgement to solve problems. This not only helps in training them but also improves their self-confidence and willingness to take decisions. It also activates interaction between the manager and his subordinates and promotes better understanding between them which goes a long way in seeking more cooperation from subordinates.

5. Motivation of Subordinates

Delegation of authority is based on the principle of division of work. No manager can perform his assigned work in an efficient manner on his own. He gets a part of it performed by his subordinates. This is because through delegation, part of the work is assigned to subordinates, enough rights are given to them and accountability is imposed on them. The fear of accountability forces subordinates to complete the given work efficiently. The importance of delegation also stems from the fact that it satisfies the needs of employees and thereby motivates them to work efficiently. This is because granting rights to them creates a sense of self-importance, confidence and recognition among them. It also provides an opportunity to exercise authority.

In brief, delegation of authority offers the following advantages:

1. It reduces the work load of superiors and permits them to concentrate on key areas and functions that are more important.
2. It provides an opportunity to subordinates to grow and develop.
3. It also helps in exercising effective control over the activities of subordinates.
4. It provides satisfaction to subordinates in terms of recognition, opportunity to use authority and interact with superiors.
5. It also satisfies the egoistic need and need of self-actualisation of employees.
6. Accountability imposed on them forces subordinates to behave and act in a more meaningful and responsible manner.
7. It encourages prompt decision making.
8. It facilitates decentralisation of authority in an organisation, thereby granting operational autonomy to lower levels.

Barriers to Delegation (Non-delegation of Authority) of Authority

There are several reasons why managers generally do not delegate as much as is required by the situation.

1. Some managers believe in the fallacy that if you want it done right, do it yourself and, therefore, they do not realise the importance of delegation.
2. Sometimes, managers may fail to size up their work load and to divide it into functional and operations parts. Consequently, they remain indecisive regarding assignment of work to subordinates.
3. Managers lacking the required confidence and trust in subordinates may not be interested in delegating more authority to them.
4. Fear of competition from subordinates may also hinder the process of proper delegation.
5. Low self-confidence and over-confidence among managers about their performance may also create bottlenecks in the process of delegation.
6. Subordinates may not be well-trained, cooperative and capable of contributing more. It also forces superiors not to delegate more.
7. Some managers, particularly conservative ones, may be very fond of authority and fear that if they delegate part of it to subordinates they may lose status and position.
8. Managers believe that they cannot transfer their responsibility to subordinates and therefore there is no point in delegating authority to them.
9. Some managers may be quite sensitive about their weaknesses and inadequacies. They do not delegate to subordinates fearing that they may be exposed by them.
10. A poor example is set by superiors who do not delegate and this may discourage managers to delegate to subordinates.

In practice, progressive managers can improve the quality of delegation of authority to recognising and correcting those tendencies both among superiors and subordinates.

Effective Delegation

Delegation of authority is one of the most important managerial activities which is aimed at improving the overall effectiveness of organisational functioning. Apart from handling the above barriers, the following guidelines may also be adopted to make delegation more effective.

1. To Establish Objectives

In order to make delegation more effective, its goal or objectives must be established clearly. Subordinates do not simply perform the work because they have been assigned it. They want to know what objectives it is going to achieve. They need to know that their work is both necessary and important. For example, the crews of a public transportation system do not drive the buses simply because they have been asked to do so, but they also want to know the importance and necessity of the entire transport system.

2. To Evaluate Competence

At the time of assigning part of the work to subordinates, the superior must look to the capability, knowledge and skill of subordinates. Further, he must ensure that only those tasks and jobs have been assigned to them which they can perform comfortably.

3. To Define Responsibility and Authority Clearly

To make delegation more effective, there is need to define the job and task assigned to subordinates. At the same time the content and extent of authority granted to them should be defined clearly without any ambiguity and confusion.

4. To Motivate Subordinates

The superior, to be effective on his part while making delegation, must motivate subordinates to work within the given range of authority to perform assigned works. Assignment of work and granting of rights to subordinates is not enough and will not produce the desired results without inspiring and motivating them. Motivation is considered as the moving force in delegation and delegation may become effective only if subordinates perform assigned work enthusiastically and willingly.

5. To Establish Communication Channels

To make delegation effective, there should be well-established channels of communication between a superior and his subordinates because it is only through improved and effective channels that necessary information in the form of directives, orders and instructions can be passed on to subordinates. Similarly, subordinates can also address their objections, problems and suggestions to their superior.

6. To Impart Proper Training

Proper training should be imparted to both superiors and subordinates regarding delegation of authority. As a result of it, a superior may learn the art of delegation, and on the other hand, subordinates may be well trained to perform assigned jobs. Training in delegation, according to Louis A. Alien, should follow three well-defined steps:

1. Appraisal of current performance in delegation.
2. Counselling for improvement.
3. Coaching on the job.

Suitable modifications of these steps can be made so as to permit training and development of managers in all aspects of delegation to make it effective.

7. To Provide Supportive Supervision

To get the best out of subordinates, the superior needs to adopt a supportive type of supervision. In this approach of supervision, he establishes cordial, warm and friendly relations with subordinates, guides them, helps them in all respects so as to make them bold and responsible to perform given tasks.

8. To Set Standards of Performance

To ensure more efficiency on the part of subordinates to perform their assigned activities, superiors require to establish clear-cut standards of performance for subordinates. It is only against these standards can their actual performance be compared and further improvements can be made by taking corrective measures.

9. To Follow Unity of Command

To avoid confusion, each subordinate should be made accountable to just one superior and he should get each order and instruction only from that superior. Although this helps in making delegation more advantageous, in a fast-changing environment the use of more sophisticated and complicated forms of organisation such as functional, matrix, etc., call for modifying this principle.

10. To Establish Feedback System

A system of feedback needs to be established to remain well informed about the progress of work being performed by subordinates and to initiate follow-up action. It aims at providing the required information to managers and enables them to place some checks on subordinates.

CENTRALISATION AND DECENTRALISATION OF AUTHORITY

Authority is one of the most activating forces of an organisation. It serves a dual purpose. On the one hand, by delegating authority, managerial hierarchy is created and on the other hand, by making effective and adequate delegation operational autonomy is granted to the departments and subordinates. Delegation of authority does not only affect organisational structure, it also has a direct impact on the overall functioning of an organisation. As a result of delegation of authority in an organisation, two situations of centralisation and decentralisation arise. The concepts of centralisation and decentralisation are closely related to distribution of authority and its delegation. These two concepts refer to a pattern of location and distribution of managerial authority within the organisation. The degrees of centralisation and decentralisation have certain implications not only to the managerial hierarchy but also on the functioning of an organisation. Thus, to have conceptual clarity of these two, it is necessary to describe them in detail.

Centralisation of Authority

The term 'centralisation' can be defined as a systematic and relative retention of management authority in key managerial positions at the top level. In a centralised organisation, almost all decision-making authority is retained by top management and a little part of authority may be pushed down towards the lower levels of the organisation. In other words, an organisation is said to be centralised to the extent to which authority is concentrated at the top of the organisation. According to Alien, "centralisation is the systematic and consistent reservation of authority at central points within an organisation."

But Henri Fayol has defined it in a slightly different manner. In his words "everything that goes to increase the importance of a subordinate's role is decentralisation, everything which goes to reduce it is centralisation." This definition reveals that in a centralised organisation, the role of a subordinate is reduced and top management assumes full responsibility for running the organisation and accomplishing its objectives. The top management takes responsibility to prepare plans, organise, direct and control all the aspects of organisational functioning. They also apply close supervision and control over each and every activity. Ultimately, managers working at lower levels have little role in decision-making and they are more occupied with the responsibility of executing plans and decisions taken at higher levels. A centralised organisation binds its components or sub-systems together into a more compact manner (Figure 10.2).

Advantages and disadvantages of centralisation

Advantages

1. **Unified direction**
2. **Simplified organisational structure**
3. **Powerful top management**
4. **Economies in operations**
5. **Integration of operations**
6. **Effective leadership**

Disadvantages

1. **Decreased/efficiency of top management**
2. **Under-utilisation and misuse of authority**
3. **Imbalance in organisational structure**
4. **Less effective role of midde and lower level managers**
5. **Closed supervision and control**
6. **Lack of coordination**
7. **Inadequacies in organisation**
8. **Bureaucratisation in organisation**

Figure 10.2. Figure showing advantages and disadvantages of centralisation

The state of centralisation of authority in an organisation offers the following advantages:

1. Unified Direction

Centralisation of authority facilitates a unified and single-minded direction for the activities to be performed by employees. The reasons behind this are that all important decisions are made, moves are initiated, policies are formulated and plans are prepared by the top management itself. By doing so, a high degree of uniformity and consistency is maintained in respect of organisational functioning.

2. Simplified Organisational Structure

In a highly centralised organisation, the structure of organisation tends to be simple and clear. Since there exist mainly two levels of managerial ranking, top level management is engaged in performing the functional part and the lower levels implement and execute it.

3. Powerful Top Management

Since centralisation of authority encourages concentration of authority with the top management, it becomes more powerful and resource to take bold decisions, take initiatives, face crises and provide a dynamic leadership in a compact manner to the entire organisation.

4. Economics in Operation

A high degree of centralisation may result in several economies in the operations of an organisation. This is because the many levels and positions of management are reduced which may result in reducing overhead costs. It also permits the effective utilisation of highly qualified and technically sound personnel in an organisation.

5. Integration of Operations

Centralisation of authority in an organisation may also help in integrating the total operations because in this situation close supervision and control is exercised over the activities of the employees.

6. Effective Leadership

Effective leadership by top management may be encouraged by centralisation of authority. This is because more authority lies with the top managers who are supposed to be mature and professionally qualified. They may provide dynamic leadership and guide the activities of the employees in the proper direction.

Besides the above advantages, the centralisation of authority particularly when its degree is exceptionally high, may also lead to some advantageous positions which are as under:

1. Decreased Efficiency of Top Management

In a highly centralised organisation, the top management is loaded with full responsibility and authority to manage each and every aspect of the organisation. Consequently, it cannot devote sufficient time and resources for more crucial and vital matters. Due to a heavy workload, their efficiency is bound to decrease.

2. Under-utilisation and Misuse of Authority

Excessive centralisation of authority at the top level with a few managerial functions may also result in abuse or underutilisation of power and authority. This is because top managers may exercise their authority in a more discretionary manner. If they do not have matching qualifications and abilities, it may lead to underutilisation of authority.

3. Imbalance in Organisational Structure

A high degree of centralisation of authority may also cause imbalances in the structure of an organisation. This is because top heavy positions and empty lower positions indicate an improper distribution of authority which leads to reduced participation of lower level and middle level managers in the functioning of the organisation.

4. Less Effective Role of Middle and Lower Level Managers

Middle level and lower level managers feel many inadequacies and limitations while performing assigned work. This is because they do not possess the required authority to deal with the situation effectively. The situation of excessive centralisation does not provide an opportunity to lower level managers to develop their potential and maximise their contribution to the accomplishment of objectives.

5. Close Supervision and Control

Close supervision and control applied in a highly centralised organisation may also create some problems regarding the motivation and morale of employees. They feel suffocated and are unable to contribute in a meaningful manner because of imposed and tough control. However, in a modern organisation, self-discipline and self-regulatory control is considered more effective and contributive.

6. Lack of Coordination

The overall functioning of an organisation is bound to be affected adversely because of a wide gap between the top level where decisions are made and the lower levels at which they are implemented. This is because a low degree of no participation of lower level managers in decision-making reduces their morale, enthusiasm and degree of commitment for effective implementation.

7. Inadequacies in an Organisation

Inordinate delay in decision making, distortions in communications and lack of cordial friendly interpersonal relations are also marked in a highly centralised organisation. This makes the organisation inadequate and ineffective.

8. Bureaucratisation of Organisation

Over-centralisation and concentration of authority at the top may also make the organisational structure more rigid and bureaucratic in nature. It may erode dynamism, initiative, motivation, commitment and cooperation on the part of employees at the lower levels.

Centralisation and decentralisation are relative terms, particularly when they are used in the context of modern and large-sized organisations. However, absolute or excessive centralisation of authority may be possible in owner-managed small organisations in which the total authority to manage the business is centred around the owner only. Other employees who have little or no authority just help him. Even if the organisation has grown in size, volume and status, it may sometimes be marked by excessive centralisation. For instance, Ranbaxy Ltd., an Indian pharmaceutical giant, claims to be multinational in status but its management control and direction remained a one-man show till recently. In such a type of highly centralised organisation, the top management having no required capability is normally backed by a team of professionals but in an informal way. Several levels of management remain only on paper and their managerial style and approach is totally conditioned by the bias, whims, likes and dislikes of the owner. This practice of excessive retention of authority at the top level is common with other organisations that are still considered as 'family managed affairs'. In such organisations, managers working at middle and lower levels may be professionally competent but are usually not allowed to do things in their own way. Rather they remain at the mercy of the dictates of the owner or top level managers.

Decentralisation of Authority

The term 'decentralisation of authority' may be defined as a partial and systematic dispersal and devolution of managerial authority from the top level management to the middle and lower levels. Although the term 'decentralisation of authority' is well conceived in connection with decision-making and functioning of an organisation, at some time it is confused with delegation of authority.

Some practitioners of management consider it as a geographical dispersion of organisational activities or as a format of organisation. But in more precise and clear terms decentralisation of authority refers to delegation of authority by the top management to lower level managers who constitute operative levels so as to make them self-sustained and possessive.

In a highly decentralised organisation, authority is partially pushed down through the line of authority up to the supervisory level. In doing so, managers working at different levels are given enough authority commensurate with the task and responsibility assumed by them.

It has been rightly pointed out by Keith Davis that "decentralisation takes place when some higher central source of responsibility and authority assigns certain functions and duties to subordinate individuals and groups for performance." But the definition still seems to be incomplete because it does not make any mention of dispersal of authority. Simple assignment of functions and duties to lower level managers may not result in decentralisation unless it is accompanied by delegation of enough authority to these levels. Broadly, decentralisation implies delegation of power and authority from higher to lower levels of the organisation, often accomplished by the creation of small self-contained organisational units or divisions.

Characteristics

Decentralisation is in contrast to centralisation of authority. The main feature is that decision-making also takes place at the lower levels of the organisation. These levels become autonomous in their functioning. While discussing the basic nature of decentralisation, Earnest Dale has pointed out that the degree of decentralisation of authority in a company is greater when

1. The number of decisions made lower down the hierarchy is greater.
2. The important decisions are made low or down the management hierarchy. For example, the greater the sum of capital expenditure that can be approved by the plant manager without consulting anyone else, the greater the degree of decentralisation in this field.
3. More functions are affected by decisions made at the lower level. Thus companies that permit only operational decisions to be made at separate branches or plants are less decentralised than those that also permit financial and personnel decisions at branches or plants.
4. There is less checking required on the decisions. Decentralisation is greater when no check is made at all. It is less when superiors have to be informed of the decisions after they have been made. It is still less if superiors have to be consulted before a decision is made. The fewer people to be consulted and the lower they are on the managerial hierarchy the greater the degree of decentralisation.

Earnest Dale has further pointed out the following characteristics of decentralisation in a large corporation:

1. The administrative unit that usually covers the company as a whole as well as its plants are broken down into smaller administrative units either on a geographical or a product basis.
2. Provision is made for the effective utilisation of centralised staff or specialists to aid decentralised operations.
3. A series of general staff may be provided for the chief executive.
4. Centralised controls are designed to ensure that the chief executive can find out how well the delegated authority and responsibility are exercised.

On the basis of the above discussion, it is evident that while there could be absolute or almost absolute centralisation of authority, there could not be absolute or total decentralisation of authority. This is because even in a highly decentralised organisation, top management retains adequate authority to make strategic planning, direct and control. Such authority could not be delegated to the lower levels. In other words, decentralised organisation contains some amount of centralisation and without such centralisation, decentralisation will lose its meaning and importance. Thus, for all practical purposes, decentralisation in its true sense implies centralised planning and control with decentralised operations and performance.

Need for Decentralisation

In view of the demerits of a highly centralised organisation, most organisations prefer optimal balance of these two situations and place more emphasis on decentralisation of authority for the following reasons:

1. The growth and development of an organisation both in terms of volume and size of business necessitates decentralisation of authority. This is because an increased number of activities can be performed only by having a decentralised organisational structure.
2. To cope with uncertainty, complexity and diversity of a rapidly changing environment due to economic, political and technological changes, top management requires to concentrate more on important functions such as formulating strategies, policies and action plans. This can be made possible by decentralising operative authority to various concerned departments at lower levels to perform supportive functions.
3. Diversification of organisational activities is more complex and specialised sets also call for decentralisation. This is because every set of such activities requires to have a separate division with operational autonomy thereby paving a way for decentralisation.
4. Physical dispersion of activities also compels top management to decentralise more managerial authority to divisions or departments

working in different areas or countries. For example, a multinational company having widely scattered operations throughout the globe is bound by a high degree of decentralisation. Each subsidiary of it working in a different country enjoys full operational autonomy in respect of authority as well as resources (Figure 10.3).

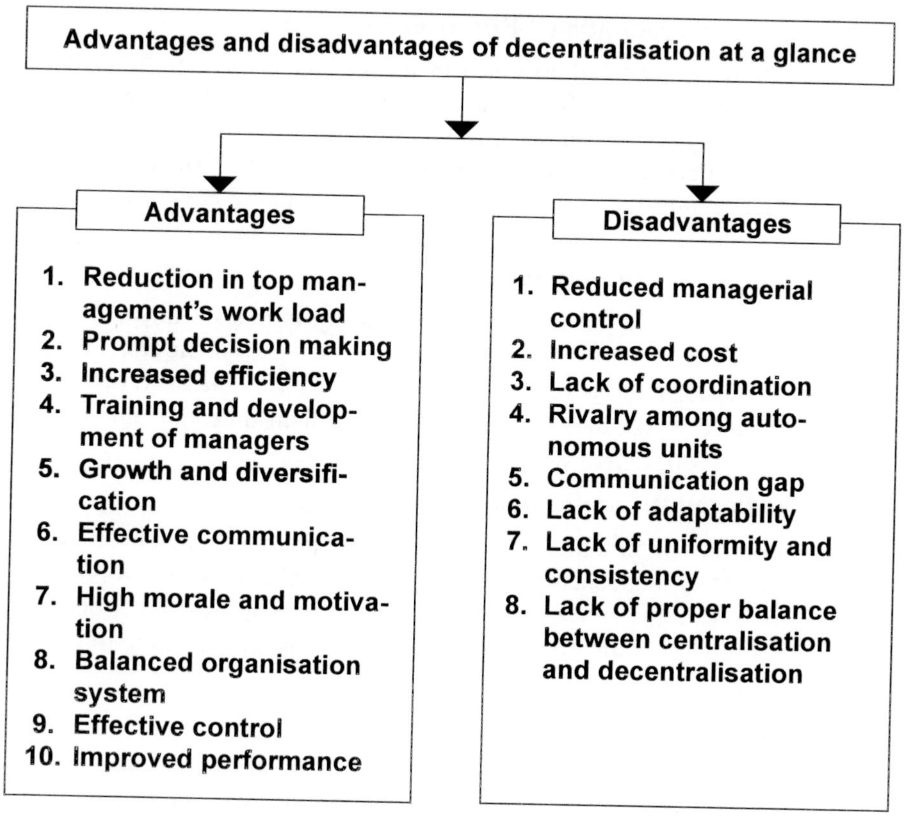

Figure 10.3. Caption showing Advantages and disadvantages of decentralisation at a glance

Advantages of Decentralisation

Decentralisation of authority does not take place only because of the above-mentioned reasons. It can also be done to secure the following advantages:

1. Reduction in Top Management Work Load

In a decentralised organisation, more emphasis is placed on delegation of authority as a result of which top management is made free from routine and time-consuming tasks and its work load is drastically reduced. In doing so, the chief executive of an organisation finds enough time to deal with strategic matters effectively.

2. Prompt Decisions and Actions

Decentralisation of authority facilitates prompt decision-making to solve problems faced by lower level managers. This is because they enjoy operational autonomy and have enough authority to deal with work-related problems.

3. Increased Organisational Effectiveness

Decentralisation of authority is a means of increasing the effectiveness of large organisations that have many products, widely scattered operations and diverse, complex as well as specialised activities. This is because through systematic decentralisation they are all integrated and brought together into compact sets in such a way so as to contribute to the effective functioning of the organisation.

4. Development and Training of Managers

In a decentralised set up operative authority is pushed down the line of authority. Lower level managers get enough rights to handle work situations, make decisions and take necessary action. With the passage of time their initiative develops, they become trained and their potential can be realised fully to achieve organisational goals.

5. Growth and Diversification Strategies

A decentralised structure in an organisation provides suitable strategies to implement various schemes of growth and diversification of the organisation. It is only with the help of decentralisation that many additional operational units or divisions may be created at the lower level according to the needs of the organisation.

6. Effective Communication

Decentralisation encourages the development of an effective communication system. In a highly decentralised organisation, every unit or department operates independently and communicates with top management on a selective basis. Thus, each unit needs to be well connected with the top level.

7. High Morale and Motivation

Since a lot of managerial authority is delegated to middle and lower level managers, they are made self-possessive. It ultimately enhances their morale and they feel highly motivated because of their recognition, self-fulfilment and self-achievement.

8. Balanced Organisational Structure

Truly speaking, decentralisation refers to centralisation of planning and control and decentralisation of operations and results. This kind of distribution of authority makes the organisational structure more balanced and sound. In such an organisation, things move in a systematic way towards betterment.

9. Effective Control

Self-regulating control and discipline may be encouraged by decentralisation. This is because through the process of decentralisation, managers working at lower levels of the organisation are made accountable and more responsible for their decisions and actions. Moreover, authority to exercise strategic and managerial control is centralised with top management which they use to seek balanced, well-coordinated and efficiently controlled functioning of various operating units or departments.

10. Improved Performance

The state of decentralisation may also help in improving the performance of an organisation. In a highly decentralised situation, various autonomous units are created at lower levels which compete with each other to optimise the level of productivity.

Along the advantages given above, decentralisation is also riddled with certain limitations that restrict its usefulness to specific situations. These limitations are

1. Reduced Managerial Control

In a highly decentralised organisation, a lot of managerial authority is delegated to the middle and lower levels. Operational autonomy is granted to individual divisions or departments. In doing so, the role of top management to control the affairs of these departments becomes less effective. Sometime, the situation of 'power centres within power centres' may arise, particularly when autonomous units exceed the degree of authority granted to them. Ultimately, top management becomes less powerful and redundant.

2. Increased Cost

Too much decentralisation may also result in increased operational cost. This is because on the one hand some specialists are retained at the top for strategic planning, control and direction of the organisation and on the other hand, every autonomous unit has to have its own team of various experts and specialised staff. This kind of duplication prevents the organisation from securing economies of specialisation and it increases the cost of maintaining the autonomous units of the organisation.

3. Lack of Coordination

The decentralised structure of an organisation may also complicate the problem of coordination. This is because every unit is so possessive that it operates on its own not taking into account the common interest of the organisation. In this way, it is really a difficult task to coordinate the various units operating in a different manner but as part of a single organisation.

4. Rivalry Among Autonomous Units

In a highly decentralised organisation, autonomous units are created and they operate as independent units of the organisation. These units make all attempts to optimise their performance even at the cost of other units of the organisation. To have more say in top management these units may also adopt unfair practices and create a situation of contradiction and conflict in the organisation.

5. Communication Gap

It has been found that in a highly decentralised organisation, there exists a problem of communication gap and mutual understanding between the top management and operative units, especially in respect of corporate objectives, policies and strategies.

6. Lack of Adaptability

In a decentralised organisational structure it becomes difficult to cope with the changing environment. This is because managers working at the lower levels tend to develop a narrow outlook and concentrate entirely on their respective units. On the other hand, operational autonomy granted to individual units makes top management very weak and ineffective to develop suitable strategies and moves to cope with a changing environment.

7. Lack of Consistency and Uniformity

All autonomous units of an organisation operate independently to achieve their goals in their units irrespective of some common policies, procedures and decision-making rules. There remains no uniformity in their functioning and consistency cannot be maintained in the atmosphere of diversity.

8. Lack of Proper Balance Between Centralisation and Decentralisation

Since in every decentralised organisation, some degree of centralisation of authority exists, in practice it is difficult for top management to decide how such managerial authority should be delegated to create an operating unit and how much should be retained to exercise control over their activities. More operational autonomy may reduce effective control of the top management but on the other hand inadequate delegation may hamper the independent functioning of operating units. It is only after careful analysis of the situation that the extent of centralisation and decentralisation can be determined.

Creating a Workable Balance Between Centralisation and Decentralisation

A proper balance should be struck between organisational structure and its functioning to increase effectiveness. These two relative situations have their own advantages and limitations. In order to get the benefit of most of the advantages and lessen limitations, these two opposite ends are brought together. On the one hand, centralisation of authority offers the advantages of uniformity of policy and action, utilisation of centralised and specialised staff and closer control and supervision, prompt decision making, etc. On the other hand, decentralisation encourages initiative, boosts the morale and motivation of employees working in operating units and further enhances the level of participation in management.

In order to determine the degree of centralisation and decentralisation, various relevant factors are taken into account. These two situations have a direct bearing on the functioning of an organisation. According to Earnest Dale, "basically the economic issue between centralisation and decentralisation is between total administrative cost and more effective performance." Thus, decentralisation should not be considered as a panacea for all sorts of organisational inadequacies and illnesses. Some of the organisations following the concept of decentralisation blindly have experienced serious problems in respect of control and cost.

However, to implement schemes of growth and diversification and allow geographical dispersal of operations, organisations are generally left with no option but to go for higher and higher degrees of decentralisation. It has been pointed out earlier that multinational companies having subsidiaries all over the world have been facing a problem of reduced managerial authority at the top level. Thus, to a large extent, it is a matter of basic philosophy of management and the requirements of the organisation to determine the degree of decentralisation. There are many examples of Indian organisations having acquired multinational dimensions but still the top level management is occupied by family members who have a great say and control over the activities of autonomous units created within the organisation either as a division or department or as a subsidiary. They have not been granted operational autonomy.

It is desirable that when organisations grow in size and volume, the limits of centralisation and decentralisation have to be further adjusted as per the demand of the situation because they are mutually dependent processes. If the degree of centralisation increases, it will result in less decentralisation and vice versa. For a large growing organisation, the degree of decentralisation is to be increased by delegating more authority to operative levels. In this case, top management wishes to confine itself to strategic matters related to planning, control and direction of the organisation. However, it should not be forgotten that to get the benefits of decentralisation there should be a strong and dynamic central management and its power and authority should not be allowed to erode. While determining the degree of decentralisation, it should also be borne in mind that enough authority has been delegated to operative levels to make them self-sustained, more contributive and flexible in their working.

According to Kreitner, a set of factors given in Table 10.1 affects the relative degree of centralisation and decentralisation. The table reveals that in establishing a workable balance between these to relative situations, the number of decisions, their importance, relationship with major functions like production, distribution finance, personnel, etc., and degree of control exercised by top management should be taken into consideration. It however, falls short of many other variables that are also to be considered at the time of setting a balance between these two situations. These variables are as given in the box.

Other variables for setting a balance between centralisation and decentralisation

1. Administrative cost of centralised and decentralised functioning.
2. Development and training of managers in the organisation.
3. Degree of specialisation and its possible benefits.
4. Growth of diversification or organisational benefits.
5. Philosophy of top management.
6. Degree and pace of changing environment.
7. Size and volume of operation of the organisation.
8. Geographical dispersion of activities of the organisation.
9. Degree of managerial control on the part of top management.

However, it is to be noted that decentralisation can be made effective if it is balanced by an appropriate degree of centralisation. The central management authority must decide on planning, organising, motivating, coordinating and controlling. Decentralised operating units should work with uniformity and coordination towards the accomplishment of the common goals of the organisation.

TABLE 10.1: FACTORS IN RELATIVE CENTRALISATION AND DECENTRALISATION

Factors	Highly centralised organisation	Highly decentralised organisation
How many decisions are made at lower levels of the hierarchy?	Very few, if any	Many or most
How important are the decisions that are made at lower levels, that is, do they impact organisational success and dollar values?	Not very	Very important
How many different functions (production, marketing, finance, personnel) rely on lower level decision making?	Very few, if any	All or most
How much does top management monitor or check up on lower level decision making?	A great deal	Very little, or none

DISTINCTION BETWEEN DELEGATION OF AUTHORITY AND DECENTRALISATION

The concepts of centralisation and decentralisation are closely related to the delegation of authority. There are many points of difference between delegation and decentralisation which can be understood on the basis of the following points:

1. Scope

Delegation of authority is that managerial activity that helps in creating a relationship of superior and subordinates and facilitates assignment of part of the work of a superior to subordinates. However, decentralisation is a strategic decision of granting operational autonomy to various units of the organisation working at lower levels and finally to cope with the changing environment.

2. Nature

Delegation of authority is a means of getting things done by subordinates by assigning work to them, granting rights and making them accountable. However, decentralisation is a more basic and strategic activity which is undertaken at a higher level of organisation to create a self-sustained and possessive operating unit.

3. Necessity

Delegation of authority is almost essential to create a structure of an organisation and managerial hierarchy but decentralisation seems to be optional for the organisation. This is because an organisation may have the choice whether to decentralise its operations and to what extent it should do so.

4. Concept

Delegation of authority is a managerial activity or process but decentralisation is a situation or state of affairs arising out of delegation as its consequence.

5. Importance

Decentralisation is to be sought through delegation of authority but effective delegation of authority does not require decentralisation.

6. Degree of Operational Authority

Delegation of authority simply concerns assigning some work, granting some rights and making subordinates accountable. It does not necessarily grant operational autonomy to subordinates as the concept of decentralisation implies creation of self-possessive and autonomous units in an organisation.

7. Reversal

Authority which has been delegated to subordinates can be withdrawn by a superior at any time. But for change in the degree of decentralisation, the decision is made at the top level because it has wider implications all around the organisation.

Although decentralisation is affected by delegation of authority from the top to various lower levels, it is only a partial indicator of decentralisation. The real test of decentralisation is the degree of operational authority granted to operating units working at the lower levels of an organisation.

Forms of Decentralisation

The following patterns may be adopted to decentralise authority. These patterns are based on the same footing as the patterns of departmentalisation.

1. Geographical Decentralisation

In this pattern, dispersal of authority is made on the basis of geographic locations of different units or divisions. These units which are formed on the basis of location are treated as operating units and enough authority is delegated to them to make decisions on routine matters.

2. Functional Decentralisation

The activities of the entire organisation are divided into various functional groups like production, finance, marketing, personnel, etc., and authority is delegated to each functional department which is considered as an operating unit.

3. Product-based Decentralisation

Operational authority is granted to each product department. Product departments operate as independent units performing almost all the functions that are required to achieve their goals.

4. Profit Decentralisation

Each operating unit created either on the basis of geographical location or functions or products may also be considered as 'profit centres' and adequate authority is granted to the head of each profit centre. He is made liable for generating a specific percentage of profit on the capital invested in the centre. The head of the profit centre is given enough authority to exercise full control over those items or matters that affect the profitability of that centre. These items may be revenue items and items of expenditure. It is only on the basis of exercising control over them that he may be able to generate the given rate of return on capital employed. This pattern of decentralisation is considered more desirable in the case of product-based or geographical-based departmentalisation of an organisation.

SUMMARY

Management is a system of authority and without adequate authority the manager cannot perform his managerial functions. The term 'authority' may be defined as a set of formal rights to make decisions, to utilise resources and to command over the activities of subordinates. Max Weber has pointed out three important bases of authority. Charismatic authority flows from the traits and quality of one's personality which attracts others and makes them follow. Traditional authority flows from customs and traditions of society. Legal rational authority is a legal and formal right vested in the position of the organisation.

The acceptance theory of authority states that the real authority is a part of the formal authority that is accepted by subordinates. Subordinates generally accept authority provided it is properly communicated, is consistent with the purpose of the organisation and is compatible with personal interests. The competence theory of authority recognises personal competence, knowledge and personality of the individual as a source of authority. The words of a few individuals carry more weight and are easily accepted by others in the organisation irrespective of their position.

In practice, managers do not enjoy absolute and unlimited authority. Rather, it is limited by organisational, legal, personal, social and environmental constraints.

Delegation of authority is a process of transferring some rights to subordinates so as to make them capable of performing assigned works and making them accountable. It involves responsibility, authority and accountability. Responsibility is an obligation to perform assigned jobs in a satisfactory manner. Authority is a set of formal rights. Accountability is also an obligation of keeping superiors informed about the progress of work and to explain if he fails to performed assigned jobs.

Delegation of authority is an important managerial activity which creates managerial hierarchy, encourages prompt decision making, training of subordinates, increases the efficiency of managers and helps to motivate subordinates. But in practice many managers, particularly conservative ones, delegate very little or no part of their authority. They believe in doing things on their own as they lack confidence in their subordinates and may not like to expose their own inadequacies. Besides, subordinates may not be well trained.

To make delegation more effective its purpose must be made clear. Assignment of work should be made by taking the capability of subordinates into account and the authority granted to them should be made clear. They should be motivated, training should be given to them, communication channels should be established, necessary support should be provided, standards of work should be set for them and periodic feedback should be obtained.

Centralisation and decentralisation are two important outcomes of the delegation process. Centralisation of authority is a systematic retention of authority at the top of the organisation.

The organisation is said to be highly centralised if little or no authority is given to lower level managerial personnel. In such cases the role of a subordinate is reduced and top level managers assume full responsibility for achieving organisational objectives. The centralisation of authority facilitates unified direction, powerful top management, simple organisational structure, effective leadership and integration of operations. It also helps in securing economies in performing various operations.

But in a highly centralised organisation top level managers remain overburdened, their level of efficiency falls and they fail to devote more time to vital issues and matters. Such organisations tend to become bureaucratic ones, many inadequacies arise, lower level managers do not cooperate and contribute in a significant way. Top level managers may misuse authority or may fail to utilise it properly.

Decentralisation of authority is a partial dispersal of managerial authority from a higher level to lower levels. In a highly decentralised organisation the middle and lower level managers become more powerful and contribute in a significant way. Every manager gets enough authority commensurate with the task and responsibility assumed by him. The main feature of a decentralised organisation is that a greater number of decisions and more important decisions are made at the middle and lower levels. Centralised control systems are designed and implemented to maintain uniformity, to bring coordination and to guide middle and lower level managers.

In a highly decentralised organisation, the work load of top level managers is reduced and they concentrate more on basic problems and issues. A lively environment is built around the organisation and every manager contributes his maximum to achieve organisational goals.

But in many cases it has been found that high decentralised organisations have many managerial levels which may result in increased operational cost, lack of coordination communication gap and lack of consistency and uniformity.

Considering the merits and demerits of both situations, it seems desirable to strike a proper balance between them. While determining the extent of centralisation and decentralisation many factors are taken into account. Among them, the basic requirements of the organisations and the philosophy of its management are important. Besides, administrative cost, degree of specialisation, changing environment, size and volume of business operations and development and training of managerial personnel are also given due consideration.

Delegation and decentralisation of authority are two related but distinct terms. Distinction can be made on the basis of many factors such as scope, nature, necessity, basic concept, importance and others.

Decentralisation of authority can be made on the basis of function, geographical dispersal of operations, product and profit. To make profit decentralisation, each operating unit created at a lower level of the organisation is considered a profit centre. The heads of such units are given authority on important items of revenue and expenditure so that they can generate the required amount of profit on the capital invested.

TEST QUESTIONS

1. Define authority and discuss its nature.
2. How can delegation be made effective to improve managerial effectiveness?
3. What is delegation of authority? Why is it necessary? Discuss the various elements involved in the delegation process.
4. Explain the term 'decentralisation of authority'. Discuss briefly the various barriers to its effective use in an organisation.
5. State the difference between authority and power. Why do organisation members accept their superior's authority?
6. What is delegation of authority? What are the requirements of effective delegation?
7. How will you strike a workable balance between centralisation and decentralisation?
8. Distinguish between
   (a) Delegation and decentralisation of authority.
   (b) Profit decentralisation and profit-based decentralisation.

OBJECTIVE TYPE QUESTIONS

Which of the following statements are correct and which are incorrect? Give reasons in support of your answers.

1. Authority is imposed, responsibility is delegated and accountability is assumed.
2. The notion of functional authority implies violation of the principle of unity of command.
3. Delegation of authority is only a partial indicator of decentralisation.
4. Profit decentralisation and federal decentralisation are the same.
5. Rational legal authority is the same as positional authority.
6. Authority in bureaucratic organisations lies in the formal position rather than in people who occupy those positions.
7. Functional authority is a part of formal authority.
8. The real test of decentralisation lies in the operational autonomy granted to the work unit.
9. Absolute or excessive centralisation is generally found in small owner-managed businesses.
10. Delegation multiplies the effectiveness of the manager who delegates.
11. Rational legal authority is an institutionalised right.
12. Charismatic authority rests in those who have a magnetic personality.

REFERENCES

Dale, Ernest. *Organisation*. New York, U.S.A.: American Management Association, 1967.

Davis, K. *Human Behaviour at Work*. New Delhi, India: Tata McGraw-Hill, 1975.

Freeman, R. Edward, Stoner, James A. F. and Gilbert, Daniel R. *Management*. New Delhi, India: Prentice Hall of India Private Limited, 2001.

Hickson, D. J., Kimmings, C. R., Lee, C. A., and Schneck, R. E. 'Strategic Contingency Theory of Intra Organisational Power'. *Administrative Science* (Quarterly Journal), 1971.

Koontz, Harold and Weihrich, Heinz. *Essentials of Management*. New Delhi, India: Tata McGraw-Hill Publishing Company Limited, 2001.

McClelland, David C. and Burnham, David. 'Power is the Great Motivator'. *Harvard Business Review*, March–April, 1976.

Newman, William H. *Administrative Action*. Englewood Cliffs, U.S.A.: Prentice Hall Inc., 1951.

Robbins, S. P. *Organisational Theory*. Englewood Cliffs, N.J., U.S.A.: Prentice Hall, 1983.

Robbins, Stefen P. *Organisational Behaviour: Concepts and Controversies*. Englewood Cliffs, U.S.A.: Prentice Hall, 1979.

Rogers, R. E. *The Political Process in Modern Organisation*. New York, U.S.A.: Exposition Press, 1971.

Simon, H. A. *Administrative Behaviour*. New York, U.S.A.: McMillan Inc., 1976.

EXPERIENCE I

Authority—Centralised at the Top

In the Birla group of companies, various cells have been created. Each operating division of the company is represented on the cell and they come together to work towards standardising all procedures—financial reporting MIS— to get efficiency. For instance, work is done towards centralising procuring components from various sources for group companies, or centralising production and MIS. The technology cell discusses all the yield, productivity, rejections and plant utilisation of all divisions. Each of these cells writes a report which is placed in the corporate tracking cell headed by Birla. These are then analysed with the CEOs of all companies. "Implementation is either by skill, recognising the work, or capital infusion. But it motivates people to perform. It gives a spirit of competitiveness and respect in the organisation."

Monthly review meetings are held with the CEO where the minutes of each cell are discussed, targets are set and financial performance of the whole group is reviewed. Here not only the CEO, but also the marketing, accounts, production and R&D chiefs meet with Birla and review the targets, what has been achieved, what has been projected, what improvements have been made and what has been done wrong.

"It has been working quite well because everyone gets a chance to interact, brainstorm certain problems which we are not able to get out of, so it is thrown to the members to see if they have any way of coming out of it." There is greater interaction amongst people and this helps the company to grow. For the Delhi-based companies, Birla travels there for the meetings, at last once in two months.

EXPERIENCE II

Delegation at Bharti Enterprises

What has made people stay on at Bharti is the amount of freedom that is given to them in their work. So much so that according to Sunil Mittal, he has stopped signing cheques some 16 years ago, a discipline that was brought in when Bharti was still a small company. According to Rakesh Mittal, why people like staying is, one, they have a visionary in Sunil. Because a person who comes into an organisation has expectations of career growth and when you have a visionary sitting at the top you have all-round growth. Two, the work culture. "We give a lot of independence. We delegate authority, we let them do whatever they want to after the budgets have been finalised, they can go ahead and meet the targets month after month."

EXPERIENCE III

Decentralisation at UTI

Welcome to the new world of UTI, where all decisions have decentralised. Empowerment, accountability and incentives are the buzzwords wafting across this 40-year-old institution. This Rs. 42,000-crore financial behemoth, which will soon become history after being bifurcated into two—UTI-I and UTI-2 by an act of Parliament—is entering the new phase that apparently seems more challenging.

Radical structural changes have been brought in. From an organisation that was standing on a single pillar (chairman-centric), he made it a multiple-pillar organisation which can withstand severe tremors. "It's a tripod model—empowerment, accountability, and incentivisation", explains Damodaran. "If you empower people, and if you incentivise performance, then people will take decisions that make commercial sense. Today, all decision-making is decentralised, albeit with checks and balances. The biggest change I have seen in the last decade is empowerment, which has led to high morale. There is a sense of freedom. There is an excitement in the job." He and his 16-member team, all of whom are double graduates and recruited from campuses, provide advisory services to the fund manager.

In a path-breaking move, the whole front office system has been computerised since October 2002. the earlier practice of a fund manager writing a buy/sell order on a piece of paper which travelled up to the chairman for approval has been dispensed with. Besides, somebody could misuse the information. Instead, fund managers and dealers have been empowered to buy/sell. For this, new software has been installed with safeguards and protocols defined.

Source: *Business India.*

CASE STUDY I

Hiren Dasgupta, Sales Manager of Fashion Fabrics, Eastern Region, did not find the performance of Harish Mastana, one of his sales representatives, upto the mark. On six separate occasions, Hiren personally discussed with Harish about his various problems, suggesting ways and means so that he might improve his sales performance. During the last conference, Hiren said, "Harish, I'm going to have to let you go if your sales are not up to quota this month."

Harish failed to meet his quota. Hiren could not bear with the situation and decided to go for further action. He wrote him a letter informing him of his dismissal. Three days later, Hiren received a call from Mr. K.T. Parekh, General Sales Manager, "Hiren, I want you to put Harish Mastana back on the payroll immediately. You know he is the nephew of Mill Mazdoor Union President." "O.K.", sighed Hiren, "I'll see that it's done."

Questions

Read and analyse the above carefully and answer the following questions:

(a) What are the authority-power-responsibility-accountability relationships in this case?

(b) What can be the possible impact of these relationships on the functioning of the company?

(c) Advise Hiren Dasgupta about the action to be taken.

—oo(O)oo—

CHAPTER 11

ORGANISATIONAL STRUCTURES

LEARNING OBJECTIVES

1. To develop conceptual clarity regarding various traditional forms of organisation.
2. To bring out the main features, relative merits and demerits of line, line and staff and functional organisations.
3. To remember the possible causes of mutual conflict between line managers and staff specialists.
4. To give suggestions to resolve such conflicts.
5. To evaluate the need and importance of staff specialists in an organisation.
6. To remember the meaning, features and advantages and disadvantages of project and matrix organisation.
7. To make out a strong case against traditional forms of organisation.
8. To bring out the essential features of a free form of organisation.

After having discussed the patterns of departmentalisation of various organisations and assignment of these activities to various departments it is also necessary to know what type of authority is allocated to these departments, and what will be the nature of the authority relationship among them. It is true that without making a proper distribution of authority to various departmental heads, the smooth functioning of an organisation cannot be maintained. Activities performed by these departments cannot be properly coordinated to achieve organisational goals. Classical management theorists have identified three types of organisational structures based on three types of authority relationship. These structures are known as traditional organisational structures as listed below:

1. Line structure
2. Line and staff structure
3. Functional structure.

Historically, these forms belong to the classical and traditional approach of management. But till today, their popularity and relevance has not only remained intact but has increased. These are considered as time tested structures and are used without hesitation.

LINE ORGANISATION

This is one of the oldest forms of organisational structure and all other forms are modifications of it and directly or indirectly based on it. Line structure is basic and indispensable to all kinds of organised efforts that are made to achieve common goals. It is still considered as the backbone of group efforts. In this organisation, authority flows from the top levels to lower levels through all managerial positions. These positions are created around basic or core activities that are essential to achieve organisational objectives. In the line of authority, each manager is attached with the relationship of superior and subordinate. There is a direct vertical relationship among them. In the line structure, there are no separate services or supportive units and these activities are also included in line departments. The line of authority therefore consists of those executives who are directly responsible for accomplishing organisational goals.

The line structure of an organisation may take two forms, pure and departmental. In each pure line organisation activities at every level of organisation are the same with each employee performing the same type of work and departments are created only to facilitate control and direction. For example, if three sales managers work under the command of a marketing manager dealing with sales activities of the same product in different areas, it is known as 'pure line structure'. On the other hand, in a 'departmental line structure' work performed in different departments is of a different nature. For example, if grouping of activities is made on the basis of functions such as sales, production, finance, personnel, etc., these departments are placed under the command of a general manager (Figure 11.1).

CHARACTERISTICS

A line organisation has the following characteristics:

1. In line structure, authority flows from the top level to lower levels through various managerial positions.
2. The flow of responsibility starts from the lower level and flows towards the higher ones. Every subordinate is responsible to his immediate superior to perform work assigned to him.

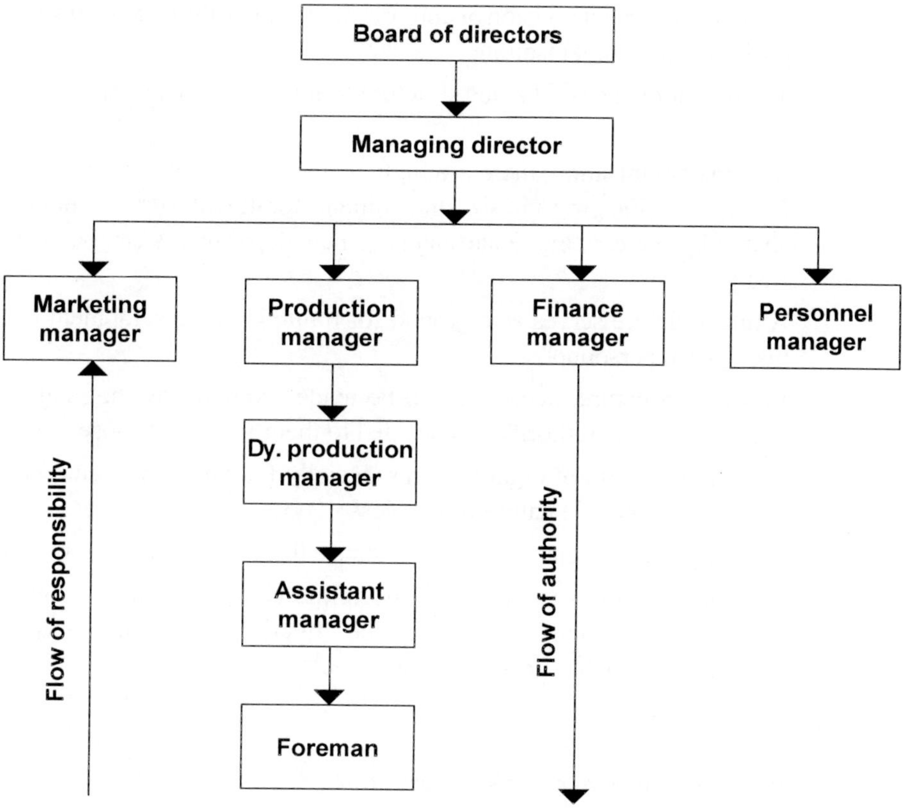

Figure 11.1. Line structure of organisation

3. There is a direct reporting relationship between a superior and his subordinate.
4. All managers work in a line of authority in the relationship of superior and subordinate and are known as line managers.
5. A line manager has line authority and performs line activities and functions and is directly responsible for the achievement of the objectives of the organisation.
6. Line activities are those activities that are core and essential to achieve organisational goals.
7. The principle of unity of command is followed for designing a line structure.

Advantages

1. A line structure is quite simple to understand and implement and no complications are involved in it.

2. There is a clear-cut division of authority and responsibility among various positions in an organisation.
3. The operational cost of a line structure is minimum as compared to other forms.
4. In a line organisation, there is a high degree of flexibility because when the organisation grows in size and volume, additional work can either be shared by the existing departments or new departments can be created easily.
5. A line structure serves as a ground for training and development of all managerial personnel.
6. In a line structure, decisions can be made promptly by the managers because enough authority is delegated to them for this purpose.
7. It is an ideal form of organisation especially for small-sized enterprises engaged in a simple nature of business.
8. It facilitates communication by providing a line of command as a channel.
9. Because of unity of command, discipline can be maintained among employees and their activities can be effectively controlled and they cannot sidetrack their responsibility.

LIMITATIONS

The major limitations of a line structure are

1. Line managers are preoccupied with a heavy work load. This is because they have to perform all kinds of activities, not only key activities but supportive activities also. Consequently, they do not get enough time to devote to basic managerial functions.
2. Due to a heavy work load, their working efficiency is also bound to decrease.
3. Line managers normally do not possess the required knowledge to perform each and every activity assigned to them. Due to changes in the nature of the business, many new dimensions are added to the existing set of activities. These activities demand specialised knowledge on the part of the manager. It is not possible for line managers to acquire all sorts of knowledge. Even then, they have to carry out these activities. This results in lack of specialisation.
4. In the event of growth and development of the organisation, further differentiation of activities is needed which does not seem to be feasible in the case of a line organisation.
5. Line organisations do not encourage and permit the use of specialised services from outside and attempts are made to introduce specialised supportive service departments in an organisational structure.

6. Duplication of similar types of activities being performed in every department may enhance the operating cost of an organisation and it remains no more economical.
7. One of the major drawbacks of a line organisation is that it tilts towards a bureaucratic form and ignores human needs and values affecting the working behaviour of employees in an organisation.

LINE AND STAFF ORGANISATIONS

On account of inadequacies and drawbacks associated with the line form of organisation and the growing complexities of modern business, certain modifications may be introduced in the line form to make it effective. Another new form is developed which is known as line and staff organisation. This may be considered to be a more refined and extended form of a line organisation. In a line and staff organisation, a distinction is made between line positions—those in a formal line of authority and staff positions and those serving in an advisory capacity outside the formal line of authority. Line managers have the authority to make decisions and give orders to subordinates in the chain of command. But those who occupy staff positions merely advise, help and support line managers. They do not have any relationship of authority.

The rationale behind the development of this form is to separate line activities which are basic and core in nature from other supportive or auxiliary activities which are to be performed by specialised staff. Hence, in line and staff organisations, both line activity units as well as staff activity units co-exist. Staff units render various types of services to line activity units so as to facilitate the performance of line activities in a satisfactory manner. However, the role of specialised staff is purely advisory in nature (Figure 11.2).

CHARACTERISTICS

Line and staff organisations are marked by the following characteristics:

1. In a line and staff organisation, there are two types of relationships, that is, line and staff.
2. Line managers work in the line of authority, give orders to subordinates and are directly responsible for achieving organisational objectives.
3. Staff specialists possess specialised knowledge of their respective areas, perform supportive and auxiliary activities and guide, help and advise line managers.
4. Line managers and staff specialists are not in the relationship of superior and subordinate because staff specialists are appointed beyond the line of authority and they work independently.
5. Like in a line organisation, this structure is also marked by unity of command.

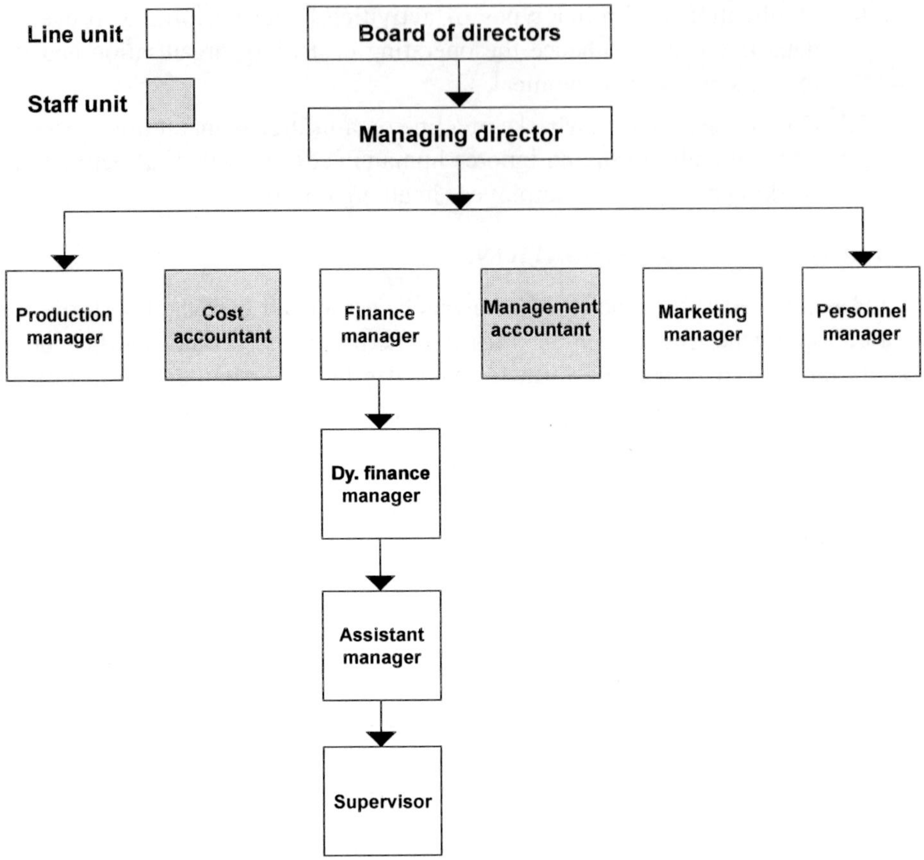

Figure 11.2. Line and staff organisation

ADVANTAGES

The following advantages are associated with this organisational structure:

1. Line managers are relieved of routine, supportive and auxiliary activities; their work load is reduced and they find enough time to concentrate on key and basic activities that are directly related to achievement of organisational goals.
2. The organisation gets the benefit of specialisation. This is because to handle various activities requiring specialised knowledge, staff specialists are appointed. They provide ready help and guidance to line managers on these activities.
3. The strength and efficiency of line managers is bound to increase because their working is supported by specialised staff and their span of management becomes wide. This promotes executive effectiveness.

4. With the help of staff specialists belonging to various areas of operation, research and development work is encouraged and creativity and innovativeness is developed.
5. The existence of staff specialists in an organisation provides ground for training to line managers in respect of specialised activity. This is because line managers very often interact with staff on a regular basis regarding those activities.
6. In a line and staff organisation, the quality of decisions made by line managers improves. This is because by mutual exchange of ideas and viewpoints and seeking the advice of experts, they can make proper and balanced decisions.

LIMITATIONS

A line and staff organisation is not free from inadequacies and deficiencies. It has the following limitations:

1. By introducing a staff relationship in the line structure, the overall organisational structure becomes more complicated and complex.
2. A line and staff structure also suffers from the drawback of poor coordination because of the dual relationship in the organisation.
3. A line and staff structure may also result in high operating cost especially if the services of staff specialists are not properly used in a desirable manner.
4. The position of staff specialists in an organisation seems to be very weak because they do not have any authority to assert on line managers and do not assume any responsibility.
5. In this type of organisational structure, difference of perceptions and orientation of line and staff managers does create serious problems with respect to the smooth functioning of the organisation.
6. Due to many reasons, clashes and conflicts occur between line managers and staff specialists.

WHY DOES AN ORGANISATION NEED STAFF SPECIALISTS?

1. Classification of Activities into More Important and Supportive Ones

The origin of staff units in an organisation is closely related to inadequacies and limitations of line structure because it is suitable only for small businesses and that too of a simple nature. In a real sense, the need and necessity of creating separate staff units and incorporating them into the structure of an organisation has risen due to the growth and development of the organisation.

So long as the size of the organisation remains small, all activities can be performed by line managers and there seems to be no need of staff units. But once the activities of a business grow in size, nature and number, it goes beyond the capacity of line managers to perform them in a satisfactory manner. Not only this, at this stage it also seems desirable to make a distinction between more important and less important activities as basic activities and auxiliary activities. Hence, there arises a need to place these activities in different groups and therefore creation of staff units is inevitable.

2. Complexities of Management Functions and Activities

The growing complexities of top management functions have also produced valid reasons for introducing the concept of staff specialists in an organisation. This is because many new dimensions have been added to the existing nature of business activity which requires specialised knowledge on the part of the manager dealing with it. It is only through staff specialists that the position of line managers can be made stronger, effective and more meaningful.

These specialists will provide the required help, guidance and advice to line managers on those difficult aspects of activity. For example, in modern business the finance function has become so complex and vast that a financial manager cannot possess the required knowledge on all aspects of it. Therefore, it is in the fitness of the situation to introduce specialists such as management accountants and cost accountants to help the finance manager in discharging his responsibility in a satisfactory manner.

3. Professional Outlook of Staff Specialists

Similarly, staff specialists are professionals having command in that area of activity. They do no have an authority relation with line managers. It encourages them to work with a high degree of objectivity, impartiality and integrity. They tend to look into the problem without any burden of authority and responsibility. They usually perceive it in the broader perspectives in a detached manner by using a scientific approach and analytical abilities. To get the benefit of their approach, style of functioning and possible contribution to strengthen the position of line managers, it becomes almost necessary to induct them in the formal structure of the organisation.

4. Supportive Role of Staff Specialists

In the words of Mooney and Railey, the basic purpose of staff specialists is "to facilitate organised planning and procedure." Staff specialists provide the necessary information that enables line managers to make balanced and correct decisions. However, in modern business, the effective use of specialists is of great importance because line managers are exposed to increasing pressure caused by the pace and effects of technological changes, increased competition, complexities of human relations and other environmental changes. The line manager can easily succumb to these forces if he has no support from staff specialists. They help him in analysing, interpreting, assessing the problem and recommending a suitable course of action

Types of Staff Specialists

As discussed earlier, staff specialists refer to those elements of an organisation that provide help, advice, service and guidance to line managers so that organisational goals can be accomplished effectively. In this regard, it seems to be desirable to distinguish between various types of staff units which may possibly be inducted into the organisation. Generally, there are three types of staff units in an organisation, namely personal, general and specialised staff.

1. Personal Staff

Personal staff is introduced to relieve the line manager of much of his work load. They help, advise and provide service to individual line managers. Personal staff is appointed specially to share that part of the work of line managers that they cannot delegate to others. For instance, a chief executive is provided personal staff as personal assistant or private secretary or special assistant. Personal staff can be considered as an extension of the manager's strengths because they help him in handling the tasks assigned to managers. They may be used to collect information, solve problems, write speeches, etc.

2. General Staff

General staff is commonly used in military organisations. This refers to a group of officers or units that undertakes planning and coordinating the functions on behalf of the chief of the army. In business too, general staff is introduced in an organisation to help and advise the chief executive in respect of various functional areas such as production, finance, personnel, etc. They help the chief executive in overall management of the organisation by preparing various reports, making recommendations and developing alternative proposals on major organisational activities which may be related to different departments.

3. Specialised Staff

Specialised staff is appointed to help, advise, assist and serve all line units at various levels of the organisation. They provide help in specialised fields to all line managers working in the organisation. The assistance and guidance provided by specialised staff to line managers at various levels really helps them in performing the basic functions of management. Specialised staff may be considered as the fountain of specialised knowledge, special skill and advice which can be used in the entire organisation. In view of the growing complexities the use of specialised staff has become inevitable.

DIVISION OF LINE AND STAFF IS SUPERFICIAL

Line and staff relations are not new to business organisations especilly in a situation, when the work that is to be performed to achieve objectives becomes so technical and complicated that one individual finds it difficult to deal with all its aspects. The need arises to get other persons who have specialised knowledge for doing that work. The division of line and staff employees seems to be theoretical especially in the context of modern business. If we consider an organisation as an open adaptive system these two become part and parcel of it.

But a careful analysis of growth and development of an organisation, changes in the basic nature of business activity and the philosophy of modern management indicates that a division between line and staff functions and their relation seems to be inevitable so as to provide specialised functional assistance to line managers. It is necessary to ensure a proper control and to maintain accountability to achieve objectives. However, the division between these two seems to be obsolete and artificial due to the following reasons:

1. To achieve organisational goals, a large number of activities are performed. Regardless of the basic nature of these activities, they have a collective contribution to organisational goals. Therefore, taking into account the relationship of one activity with another and their collective contribution, it does not find any ground to divide them into line and staff activities. This is because activity is to be performed in an efficient manner even if it is less important or supportive in nature.
2. The importance, role and contribution of a particular activity may differ from one organisation to another, even if it cannot be generalised as to which particular activity should be considered as a line activity and which one is supportive to it. It also renders the division between these two insignificant.
3. Due to the fast-changing business environment, traditional structures of organisation have become less effective and responsible because as per the demand of the situation more emphasis is to be placed on the functional type of division of authority and responsibility. In doing so, instead of distribution of authority, the coordination and performance become more significant for the organisation.
4. It is found that in many organisations all members associated with achievement of common goals work together as members of a team. Therefore, instead of making any division between line and staff and their role, the informal relationship among members should be given more weightage. This is because it affects the working behaviour of the members in a significant way rather than as a formal relationship.
5. On many occasions, it becomes difficult for top management to identify and decide what is line, what is staff, and what relationship should exist between them.
6. Instead of making a distinction between line and staff relationships, they should be considered as supplementary to each other. This is because a pure line organisation is rarely found in business. Rather, a proper combination of these two is quite popular. Similarly, staff units in organisations will have no meaning and purpose if there is no line organisation.

7. Since staff specialists are appointed in organisations to help, guide and advise line managers on technical as well as specialised matters, therefore, instead of making a division between line and staff, both of them should be made jointly accountable to perform that particular activity or project. However, division between line and staff is necessary to establish and fix accountability, particularly when a large number of people are working together to accomplish common objectives.

LINE AND STAFF CONFLICT

Although the role of line and staff is supplementary to each, and in the event of growth and development of an organisation, introduction of the staff element becomes almost necessary. Both of them are expected to cooperate with each other and work as members of a team to accomplish given objectives. In practice, instead of mutual cooperation and collaboration, staff becomes a source of conflict. It impedes the smooth functioning of an organisation. Some of the major reasons for such a conflict are :

1. Loss of Line Function

At the introduction of the staff element in an organisation the line managers feel deprived of some of their functions. Instead of making a constructive attempt to seek their cooperation they are viewed as unwanted elements. It also creates a feeling of inadequacy and suspicion among line managers. This is because the line manager suspects that the staff element has been introduced on account of his incompetence and inability to handle a given task. As a result, they turn hostile to staff specialists.

2. Superiority Complex

Line managers and staff specialists suffer from superiority complexes. Line managers feel that they are more important, powerful and directly responsible for achieving the objectives of the organisation, while staff specialists possess the feeling that they have the specialised knowledge and skill that line managers do not possess. This kind of attitude on the part of both brings them into conflict.

3. Status of Staff

Staff specialists, having specialised knowledge and academic superiority, enjoy a better status in terms of salary, perks and recognition as compared to line managers. This is because staff managers are very close to the chief executive and they command more influence on the top management. Thus, to counter this influence, the advice, guidance and help offered by them is rather opposed by line managers.

4. Weaker Positions of Staff

Staff managers do not possess any authority over line managers. Rather, their role is purely advisory in nature. They cannot force line managers to follow their advice and it depends on the discretion of the line manager. Due to weak position, staff specialists feel envious of line managers which results in natural conflicts.

5. Difference in Perception

Staff specialists are more radical and believe in change for the better functioning of the organisation. But line managers are conservative in their approach and prefer to maintain the existing position and resist change.

6. Nature of Staff Expert's Advice

Staff expert are generally qualified professionals. They are highly educated and make a close analysis of the organisational problems but in a detached manner. Their recommendations and reports reflect an intellectual and academic flavour which is from practice and sometimes not backed by required information. Consequently, due to this, line managers develop reservations regarding such reports and do not implement them. Staff experts feel ignored by line managers.

7. Interdependent Role

The successful discharge of responsibility by line managers to some extent depends on the help and advice of staff experts. Similarly, the very existence and survival of staff experts depends on whether their advice and recommendations are being used by line managers. Such interdependency also gives rise to conflicts.

8. Lack of Clarity of Role

Line and staff conflicts arise on account of ambiguous and confused role and relationship between line managers and staff experts. Because of lack of clarity about roles, line managers complain that staff experts encroach on their duties, responsibilities and prerogatives. In a similar way sometimes, line managers also overstep their authority to counter the popularity of staff experts in the organisation.

HOW TO RESOLVE LINE AND STAFF CONFLICT

In a traditional structure of organisation, line and staff elements are considered to be two important parts. To maintain smooth functioning of the overall organisation, they are expected to cooperate and collaborate with each other. Both line and staff elements must become well acquainted with the role that each element is expected to play.

Instead of going by the formal relationship of line and staff they should work for the betterment of the organisation as a member of the team. The following guidelines may help in making the role and relationship between line and staff more successful and effective.

1. Full Cooperation of Staff

It is obvious that staff experts are inducted into an organisation to help and guide line managers especially in respect of those activities or proposals or projects which require specialised knowledge. Line managers may seek the help of staff provided it is characterised by reality, pragmatism and feasibility. Line managers would sometimes willingly put the ideas and advice given by staff to operation if the staff gives time and makes an effort to discuss and explain them to the line managers.

2. Supply of Necessary Information

Regarding the advice and recommendations made by staff experts, it is alleged that they are prepared in isolation or in a detached manner and not backed by the required information. Hence, to increase the degree of acceptability of these recommendations, staff experts may be called up to supply necessary information and background material. These recommendations should be complete in all respects.

3. Team Spirit

The growing complexities of business operations, fast changing environment and growth and diversification of an organisation have forced line managers and staff specialists to work in cooperation with each other. Both of them should not insist much on their formal role and relationship but should fully realise and accept that they are part and parcel of the same organisation. Therefore, they should work as members of a team to achieve objectives.

4. Mutual Trust and Cooperation

The effectiveness of the role and contribution of both line and staff to some extent depends on the internal environment of the organisation. It should be marked by a sense of mutual trust and confidence and line and staff should accept each other's role in a positive way. The line manager should attempt to utilise the valuable services of staff when and where required and similarly staff specialists should cooperate with line managers in all respects taking the larger interests of the organisation into account. Staff specialists should establish their own credibility as dependable guides to line managers. Likewise, line managers should shed their prejudices against staff specialists and should take them into confidence at the time of implementing their recommendations.

5. Clarity of Role and Responsibility

It often happens that conflict exists between line managers and staff specialists because of confused and ambiguous role of staff specialists. Hence, before inducting them, proper planning should be done with regard to their role and relationship. In many organisations, because of lack of clarity in their roles, there is a clash between them which ultimately affects the functioning of the organisation in an adverse manner. The role of staff experts can be made more meaningful and effective by making them jointly accountable with line managers in respect of implementation of recommendations made by staff experts. On the other hand, managers should be educated and encouraged to make use of staff experts.

FUNCTIONAL ORGANISATION

The functional structure of an organisation is based on the concept of functional foremanship developed by F. W. Taylor. This may be considered as an improved and effective form of line and staff organisation. This is because this particular structure has been developed to counter inadequacies and drawbacks associated with line and staff organisation particularly in respect to role, relationship and position of experts in an organisation.

In a functional structure, the activities of an organisation are grouped into various units on the basis of functions that are to be performed with regard to that group of activities. Each functional head is given full authority over those functions irrespective of the level at which they are performed. In a functional organisation, authority does not flow from the top to the bottom of the line. Instead, each activity is divided according to functions. The manager having a specialised knowledge of that function is made in charge of that group of activities and to be given the necessary authority to perform them.

Characteristics

1. In a functional organisation, the activities are grouped in different departments or divisions on the basis of functions that are required to be performed for that group.
2. Each functional department is to be headed by a manager who has specialised knowledge of that function.
3. The functional head will exercise final authority over that function irrespective of the level at which it is being performed.
4. In this kind of structure unity of command is broken because one subordinate has to seek orders and instructions from two or more functional managers. The functional authority of the manager extends to similar activities of several work units (Figure 11.3).

Advantages

A functional organisation offers the following advantages:

1. It enables the organisation to make full use of expert and specialised knowledge to perform various functions.

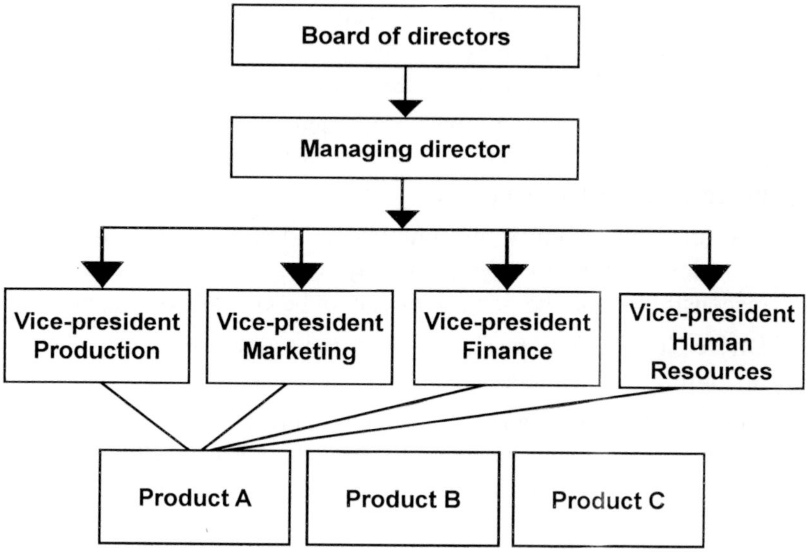

Figure 11.3. Functional organisation

2. It facilitates prompt decision making because the required authority with regard to a particular group of activity is delegated to the departmental head.
3. Consistency and uniformity can be maintained with regard to the functioning of various work units operating under the command of functional heads.
4. This kind of organisational structure permits a maximum degree of specialisation and various economies can be secured.
5. Research and development work is encouraged in such structures because the services of various specialists are made available to the organisation.
6. The functional structure is a combination of staff and functional authority. This is because a departmental head who has specialised knowledge of that area is also delegated the needed authority to make his position more effective and contribute significantly to achieve the objectives of the organisation.

Limitations

The functional structure of an organisation is beset with the following major drawbacks:

1. Due to multiplicity of command in the organisation, its structure becomes very complicated and complex.

2. It becomes very difficult to coordinate the functioning of several work units under the command of functional managers. This is because each work unit is subject to many more functional commands.
3. It is also found that in a functional structure specialisation exceeds the desired limit and beyond which its advantages may be outnumbered by the cost incurred to achieve it.
4. The principle of unity of command is violated as a result of which indiscipline crops in among employees. They tend to sidetrack their responsibility and their activities cannot be controlled efficiently.
5. Divided loyalty of the head of the work units may also result in the creation of conflicting situations.

The functional structure of an organisation is subject to scathing criticism both from management scholars and business executives. They plead that one person cannot serve many bosses at a time to perform his job efficiently. Besides, each functional head considers his departmental goals more important and concentrates on them. Consequently, the overall organisational goals are neglected. Not only this, many management authors including Peter Drucker do not consider the functional structure as a full-fledged organisational structure because of the many inadequacies involved in it.

MODERN ORGANISATIONAL STRUCTURES

Modern management authors and practitioners consider all traditional structures inadequate to fulfil the requirements of modern business. They strongly believe that traditional forms of organisation can operate properly only if the business environment is relatively stable. Such a structure operates in a closed setting and does not interact with the external environment. Traditional structures are found inadequate on the following grounds:

1. High Degree of Specialisation

All traditional structures are marked by a high degree of division of labour and specialisation of jobs, tasks and role and relationship. It ultimately leads to oversimplification of jobs. They become monotonous, repetitive and simple in nature. Employees performing such jobs do not feel thrilled and are bound to lose interest and meaning in the job. It ultimately results in decreased productivity.

2. Rigidity of Role and Relationship

There seems to be a rigidity of role and relationship in a traditional structure. Instead of developing team spirit among the employees, they work in a fragmented way giving more weightage to their formal relations. This kind of attitude on the part of employees makes the organisation more bureaucratic and authoritative.

3. Too Much Division and Integration

Too much division and differentiation of activities may also create a problem of coordination. Due to lack of a proper balance between differentiation and integration, group efforts cannot be successfully mobilised to achieve organisational goals.

4. Hierarchy or Authority

Traditional structures are also marked by rigid hierarchy of authority, narrow span of management, centralisation of authority, rule-ridden systems, one way communication and emphasis on predetermined rules, procedures and methods. These features of traditional form do not allow employees to make all-round development of their personality and to contribute their maximum to achieve organisational goals.

Although advocates of the classical approach of management emphasised the rigid organisational structure and rationality in management, it is to achieve a high degree of effectiveness and efficiency. Environmental complexity and uncertainty have upset them. The increasing complexity of markets, variety of products, changes in science and technology, changing patterns of demand, etc., have forced them to realise the significance of these variables in the functioning of an organisation. The net result of these challenges was a desire to look at an organisation in some new ways as system structure, project form, matrix form, free form, etc. These new structures are, of course, a more refined and modified version of traditional structures and are designed to bring more flexibility and adaptability in an organisation to enable it to cope with a changing environment. The more important and popular structures of modern organisation are as follows:

PROJECT ORGANISATION

The project structure basically consists of a number of horizontal organisational units that are designed to complete various projects (Figure 11.4). The term 'project' may be defined as a complex set of activities which are diverse, specialised and technical to be performed within a given time frame and cost structure.

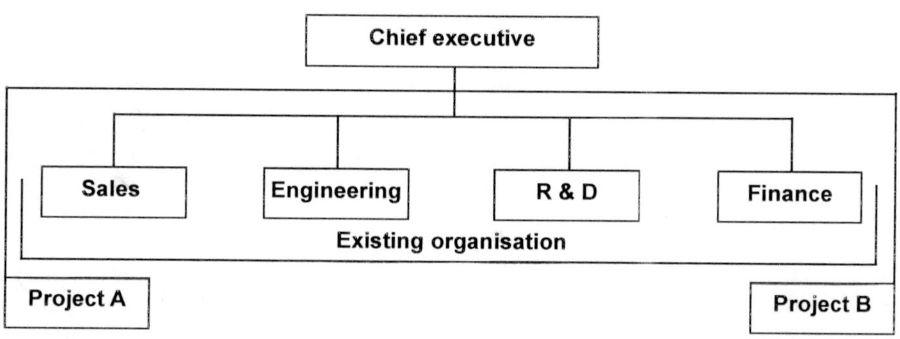

Figure 11.4. Project structure

The project structure is designed to handle a set of activities related to projects within an existing organisational structure. It is a temporary structure which is designed under the following situations:

- There is a unique and peculiar problem for which no precedent exists.
- There is a high stake in the successful completion of the project in time. Any delay may attract punishment.
- It is a one-time task with a definite objective.
- It is larger in size and scope.

Some of the projects may be the setting up of a thermal power plant, building a hospital, constructing roads, bridge building, launching new products, conducting three-month training programmes, computerising the purchase and inventory control system, etc.

Project organisation permits an existing organisation to continue on its regular business. Project management concentrates on a special assignment to complete the project in time within the scheduled cost structure. Since the project manager is wholly responsible for the project results, he places more emphasis on efficient control and better customer relations. He uses his initiative and dynamism for the successful completion of the project. To build the project team personnel are drawn from various departments of the organisation and from outside.

On the completion of the project they will be sent back to their respective parent departments or may be shifted to another new project. This is because projects are time bound and have to be completed within that time. For various projects, there may be several project managers for coordination and each of them gets the required resources and personnel from the organisation to complete the project in time. In project organisation, the role of the project manager is very important.

There could be three possible alternative arrangements to determine the relationship of the project manager with his team members. They are:

1. Staff Specialist

In the first alternative, the project manager acts as a staff specialist to the chief executive. And as staff advisor he may coordinate the activities of different project team members. He cannot exercise direct control over the members because they are subject to the command of functional heads. Only by using his personality and power can he coordinate and guide the activities of members to complete the project.

2. Full-fledged Line Manager

In the second arrangement, functional heads who have line authority give up part of it in favour of the project managers which enables him to exercise a unified command and control over the activities of project team members. Members working in a project are under the command of the project manager.

3. Functional Head

In this arrangement, the project manager acts as a functional head. As a result, team members are subject to dual command. For some of their activities they are accountable to the project manager and for others they are at the command of their parental heads.

ADVANTAGES

The project structure offers the following advantages:

1. The project form of organisation is more suitable to handle complex projects which are to be executed within a given schedule of time as well as cost.
2. Though the project structure is a temporary arrangement, it provides a greater degree of flexibility. This is because the organisation can undertake project work without disturbing regular business.
3. It also facilitates the optimum utilisation of manpower available in the organisation because the members are mostly drawn from it to make up the project team and join it on promotion. The remaining manpower is acquired for a specific period of time from outside the organisation.
4. The project form of organisation has a built-in arrangement to cope with the changing environment. This is because prompt adjustments can be made in an organisation according to the situation. Implementation of changes may be carried out through project operations. Similarly, increased competition may also force an organisation to seek higher productivity to maintain high morale and motivation, to exercise control, etc. These changes may possibly be brought about through project organisation.

LIMITATIONS

Although project structure is a refined way to cope with the changing environment without disturbing the normal functioning of the existing organisation, it develops certain limitations and dysfunctional aspects if not handled properly.

1. There exists a considerable degree of uncertainty and insecurity of job for those who work in a project team. This is because project work is temporary in nature and is undertaken for a specific period of time. On completion, members drawn internally have to be further absorbed in the functional departments and members drawn from outside are bound to be dismissed.
2. In a project form, lack of proper communication, clarity of role and relationship, prescribed processes and set standards to measure performance adversely affect the smooth functioning of the project team.
3. The project manager cannot contribute more effectively and in a meaningful way because he has limited authority to command over the activities of team members.

4. The existence of dual command in the project form makes it more complicated and less effective since the members working in the project have to report to two bosses, the project manager and the functional head of the department to which they belong.
5. Shifting of personnel from one project to another also creates a problem for the members. This is because they may not get a similar type of work on each project and specialised knowledge and expertise cannot be developed on their part.

Matrix Organisation

When multiple projects of short duration are undertaken by an organisation, the matrix organisation structure is used to execute them efficiently. In such a structure, project representatives of each project represent different functional areas. The essential feature of a matrix organisation is the superimposition of the project structure over the functional structure of the organisation. To design a matrix organisation, the activities of the organisation are first grouped into functional groups on the basis of functions that the group requires.

For example, all production activities are put in the production department and all purchase activities in the purchase department. Similarly, separate functional groups are made for finance, marketing and personnel activities. These departments of activities will be headed by managers having specialised knowledge of these functions. These functional departments are not only specialised in a particular function but are common and centralised. They provide services to the different product or project departments. In other words, in a matrix organisation, personnel are drawn to constitute a project team from various functional departments as per the requirements of a particular project or product.

In a matrix organisation, each functional manager holds the resources. Each project manager coordinates the use of these resources through the project representative drawn from that functional department. Thus, functional services and resources are drawn from central common pools through s the project representative and they are coordinated and mobilised by the project manager for the successful completion of the project.

For example, if an organisation deals with the production and distribution of five products, the head of each product division gets all the necessary resources and services from the various functional departments and his main responsibility is to coordinate these resources and services to achieve the goals of his product division (Figure 11.5). The matrix organisation is regarded as a hybrid form of functional structure and product or project structure.

The functional part of a matrix organisation is relatively permanent in nature. But so far as the project part is concerned it remains temporary because when a specific project is completed, representative members of the functional departments will switch over to other projects or go back to their parental functional departments.

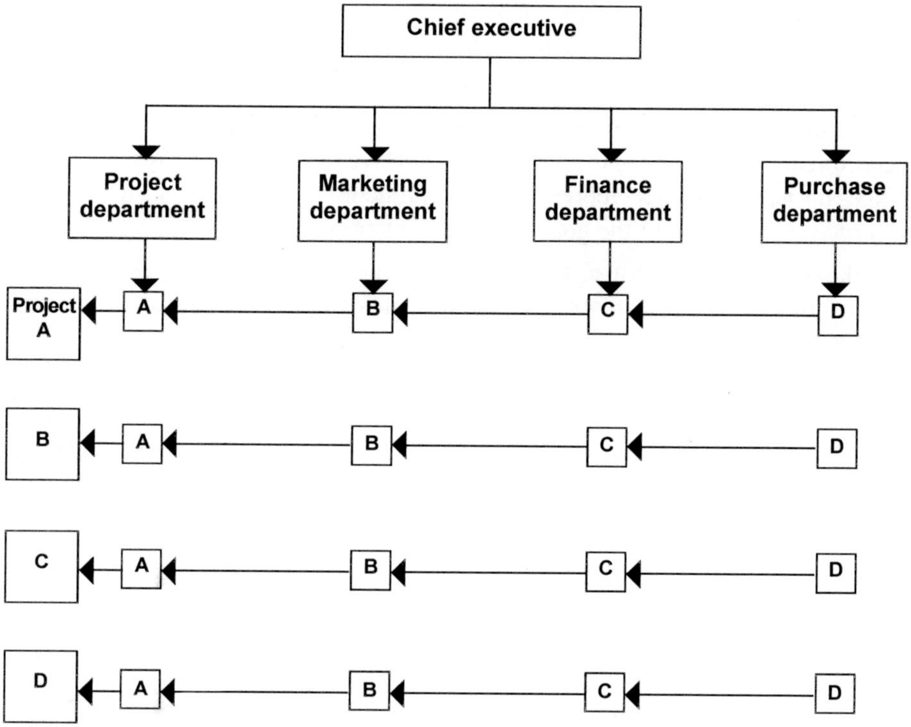

Figure 11.5. Matrix organisation

These functional departments create a vertical chain of command which connect the various positions in the functional department. But project departments constitute a horizontal dimension because each project division may consist of representatives from these functional departments.

Consequently, project representatives drawn from functional departments have to serve two bosses, the project manager as well as their functional head. The matrix form of organisation was first developed in the aerospace industry in the U.S.A. Now its use in business has received tremendous response particularly in the context of globalisation of business activity. Organisations having global operations prefer the use of the matrix structure.

The functioning of a matrix organisation is different from traditional structures. It depends on the role of project managers and functional manager, distribution of authority from the higher level to lower levels of the organisation, the role and relationship of the matrix boss and matrix subordinates. In a matrix organisation, the top management consists of a chief executive who is responsible for formulating basic plans, strategies and controlling devices and also resolves the dispute arising from dual command in the organisational structure. The term 'matrix boss' refers to the functional head who has specialised knowledge and expertise in respect of a specific function. He is considered the boss because a large number of subordinates, known as matrix subordinates, work under his command. Matrix subordinates are considered as project representatives of functional departments.

In a matrix organisation, the project manager is the focal point. He operates as coordinator, facilitator and integrator. He derives the necessary resources and services through the project representatives of functional departments. He is mainly concerned with achieving the goals of his production unit.

Like a project structure, the matrix form also de-emphasises authority relationship giving more importance to informal relations among the members working in a project.

Advantages

The matrix organisation is a combination of both functional and product departmentalisation and therefore derives the advantages of both these forms. Some major advantages are:

1. Better Use of Resources

In a matrix organisation, each functional manager holds resources in terms of specialised knowledge, expertise and services. Each project manager coordinates and mobilises the use of assigned resources through the project representatives draws from functional departments. It ultimately facilitates the better use of resources to achieve overall organisational objectives.

2. Suitable for Changing Environment

The matrix structure of organisation is considered a more useful form to cope with the fast-changing environment. This is because in this form one can undertake as many projects as possibly subject to availability of resources in various functional departments.

3. Coordination

There is a clear and workable device in a matrix organisation to coordinate the work performed through various project units because it permits coordination across functional departments.

4. Specialisation

It encourages specialisation and the organisation gets benefits arising out of it. Specialised central pools are created in the form of functional departments that provide specialised services and resources to project units.

5. Effective Communication

The matrix organisation also helps to improve the flow of communication around the organisation. Information can be communicated both vertically and horizontally.

6. Flexibility

The matrix form of organisation is marked by a high degree of flexibility and adaptability as compared to other traditional forms. This is because without disturbing the existing structure new projects may be undertaken and on the completion of a project, personnel drawn are sent back to their respective functional departments.

7. Responsive to Situations

In this structure, the project manager is solely responsible for achieving the goals of his project unit. He concentrates fully on project needs and requirements and can make the project structure more responsive to the situation.

8. Motivation

The involvement of both functional managers as well as project managers in decision making further improves the motivation and commitment on their part.

LIMITATIONS

The matrix organisation has the following limitations and drawbacks:

1. Dual Command

The major disadvantage of a matrix organisation is that it violates the principle of unity of command. This is because the project representatives drawn from functional departments have to face the situation of two bosses, the project manager and the functional manager. As a result, he may sidetrack his responsibility easily. If the project unit fails to achieve its goals it is difficult to fix responsibility on a particular functional department.

2. Difficulty in Coordination

In a matrix organisation, the problem of coordination becomes more complicated because neither the functional head has authority over the project unit in a direct manager and nor does the project manager have full authority over the project activities. He works as a coordinator and facilitator but without the required authority.

3. Higher Operating Cost

The operating cost of a matrix organisation seems to be on the higher side, because it is not only the functional departments and their heads but for every project a separate project manager is appointed and excessive overheads are incurred in respect of each project unit.

4. Indiscipline Among Employees

Dual reporting relationship in a matrix organisation also contributes to indiscipline, ambiguity and role conflict. This is because the project representatives who are subject to dual command cannot satisfy the priorities of both the bosses.

5. Clash Among Project Divisions

In a matrix organisation, each project unit is mainly concerned with the accomplishment of the goals of its unit. This creates rivalry among various project units to get a larger share of resources and services from the functional departments which may possibly bring them into a conflicting situation.

6. Less Formal Authority of Project Manager

One more serious disadvantage associated with the matrix structure is the gap of authority being faced by the project manager. He has to complete the project within the assigned schedule of cost and time in spite of lack of formal line authority. He makes use of negotiation, persuasive tactics and technical competence to compensate for lack of authority.

7. Complex Network

Apart from the above demerits, the matrix organisation has turned out to be a very complex and complicated structure which may pose many problems of coordination, line relationship, distribution of authority, etc.

In spite of the limitations mentioned above, the matrix organisation still remains one of the most popular forms of organisation. It may be either due to the growing complexity and uncertainty of the global environment or an extension of the business operations throughout the globe. In the recent past, one study reveals that about 89 per cent of 387 U.S. and Canadian companies use this structure of organisation.

FREE FORM STRUCTURE OF ORGANISATION

Similar to the project and matrix forms of organisation, there is one more structure known as the free form of organisation. This may be considered to be a rational combination of both formal as well as informal relations that exist among employees in a work setting. On the one hand, this structure de-emphasises authority relationships among employees and on the other it recognises the growing significance of the changing attitude of people towards their job, content, authority, performance and control. This structure of organisation is also highly adaptive, ad hoc, naturalist and organic. It is ad hoc in the sense that it is built around a specific problem or task by that group of employees with a diverse professional skill. Once the problem is solved, the group tends to be dissolved. However, in some cases, it may be used as a relatively permanent structure as a part of the main organisation. For example, multinational companies adopt this form as per the requirement of the situation prevailing in different countries. In the words of Bennis, the free form of organisation is a rapidly changing, adaptive, temporary system organised around the problems to be solved by a group of strangers with diverse professional skills. In this definition, he has pointed out some of the basic features of the free form of organisation such as adaptability, ad hocism and the use of professional skill involved in it. The free form of organisation is marked by the following main characteristics:

1. In this structure, the role and relationship among employees is not well defined. There is a minimum of predetermined tasks to be performed by employees. They themselves decide what task is to be performed by whom and how and when.
2. The authority structure in this form is also reduced to a minimum. This is because all employees working in a particular work setting assume responsibility and exercise authority collectively. There is no such chain of command in the structure and hence no relationship of superior and subordinate.
3. In this form, employees interact with each other in an informal, spontaneous and natural manner as in a formal organisation.
4. The free form of organisation is highly flexible and adaptive. This is because as the situation changes it gives rise to new problems and the existing structure can be restructured without any serious problem.
5. It is a combination of both traditional principles and the changing attitudes of employees towards their role, relationship and job assigned to them. For example, in this kind of structure, there is no chain of command but the concept of authority and responsibility exists in collective form.

Advantages

The free form of organisation offers the following advantages:

1. It reduces emphasis on formal positions, departments, and hierarchy of authority. All employees work in a particular work setting sharing collective responsibility. Such an organisation operates as a cohesive group and every individual tends to make full contribution.
2. It has the maximum flexibility, and adaptability as compared to other forms and therefore it is a more suitable and feasible form to cope with the changing environment.
3. In this form of organisation, the value of innovation, freedom, team spirit, self-discipline and collective contribution are given more importance.
4. It liberates the structure from rigid traditional principles and rules and makes it a part of 'auto-management'.

Apart from the above advantages, this form of organisation suffers from certain drawbacks. The major one in this form is that employees working in it do not realise collective responsibility and do not believe in collective contribution and the organisation may turn out to be chaotic. This is because there is no predetermined structure and role and relationship. Thus, instead of totally ignoring traditional principles and rules, they should be modified to face the present situation.

Similarly, free movement of employees from one job to another deprives them of gaining specialised knowledge and the organisation does not get the benefit of it. It also brings employees into a state of uncertainty and insecurity because they do not know what exactly they may be asked to perform. So unpreparedness on their part may affect their productivity in an adverse manner

SUMMARY

In order to organise activities to be performed by employees to two types of structures may be used. These are traditional structures which include, line, line staff and functional organisations and product structures including project, matrix and free form of organisation.

The line organisation is one of the oldest forms and is still considered as a basic structure. In this organisation, all employees are attached to the line of authority flowing from the top to the lowest level. They work in the relationship of superior and subordinates. They have a direct vertical reporting relationship among them. In this form, the authority flows from the top to lower levels. Every superior commands the activities of subordinates and in turn the subordinates report to him and are responsible for performing their assigned tasks.

This form is very simple, encourages prompt decision making, training and development of all managers and has less operating cost. But line managers are over-burdened and cannot devote more time to important matters.

The line and staff form is considered as an extension of the line structure. In this form, employees have two types of relationships, for example, line and staff speciality. Line managers work in the line of authority they possess, play a more important role and are directly responsible for achieving the objectives of the organisation. Staff specialists are appointed beyond the line of authority, possess specialised knowledge of their respective fields and help, guide and advise line managers.

By introducing staff specialists, the work load of line managers is reduced. They become more efficient and concentrate more on important areas. By using the services of staff specialists, research and development work is encouraged and the organisation gets the benefits of specialisation.

On the other hand, its makes the structure of the organisation more complicated. It becomes difficult to maintain coordination and verticality and very often a clash or conflict develops between line managers and staff specialists.

The main reasons for such conflicts are that line managers feel inadequate and insecure after the induction of staff specialists. Staff specialists enjoy a better status, higher perks, etc. They maintain proximity with the CEO and at the same time their position is weak in terms of authority.

In spite of these reasons, the organisation always strives to maintain a balance between these elements and to some extent crisis situations are resolved. This is done by creating a sense of goodwill, mutual respect and team spirit among both types of employees. The role and responsibility of staff specialists is made clear. They are urged to make feasible and practical recommendations to line managers.

The staff services and assistance may be made available in three important forms such as personal staff, general staff and specialised staff.

The functional form of organisation is based on the principle of dual command. In this form various activities of the organisation are grouped into different groups on the basis of the functions that are to be performed by that group. The manager who has specialised knowledge of those functions gets full authority over that group of activities. Thus it combines specialised knowledge with adequate authority.

But dual command, which appears in functional organisations creates many problems such as indiscipline and lack of responsibility among employees. Besides, specialisation goes to such an extent that it starts becoming counter-productive.

As far as the inadequacies of the traditional forms are concerned, these forms tend to be more rigid giving too much emphasis on authority relationships and division of work. These factors turn to be disadvantaged particularly in a rapidly changing business environment.

Modern forms of organisation are the project form, matrix form and the free form.

Project organisation is an extended form of the existing organisation. With an addition and change within the existing structure various project divisions are created. They are created by drawing employees from the various departments of the organisation and from outside for a specific project. This project is worked on and when completed, the employees of the organisation who have been working on it will go back to their parental departments. The project division may be headed by a project manager. His role is very important in coordinating and utilising the resources to complete the project within the given period of time.

The project manager may be given any one of the three roles in managing and controlling the project. He may be asked to work as a staff or chief executive officer of the organisation or he may work only as a functional head having authority only for a specific function. The third role may be that all departmental managers of the organisation may give up the required authority in favour of the project manager and he enjoys the status of a line manager but only to complete the assigned project.

But if the projects are many in number there is another short-term form known as the matrix organisation. This form is a combination of functional and project organisation. The main difference between a project and matrix form is that in a matrix organisation, project divisions or units are made within the functional structure. This is the only form in which the project team is drawn from the resources and manpower of functional departments.

The matrix form leads to specialisation, better use of resources, effective communication and motivation. This form is more suitable in a rapidly changing environment.

But in a matrix form, the structure becomes complex and operational cost goes up. The position of the project manager is less effective and many other drawbacks crop up due to dual command.

On many occasions, to achieve objectives in the short term or in a particular venture the free form of organisation is used. This form deemphasises the line of authority and both formal as well as informal relations are used in the functioning of the organisation. It is a network of both formal and informal relations with a collective authority and responsibility designed to suit a given situation. The free form of organisation is ad hoc in nature, because it is built around a specific situation.

This form of organisation is more adaptive and flexible which suits the changing environment. It encourages innovation, the use of creativity to solve a given problem. But since there is no predetermined structure, role and relationship, there is always the danger of a chaotic situation arising.

TEST QUESTIONS

1. Define line structure and explain its merits and demerits.
2. Distinguish between line and line and staff structures and explain why line and staff structure is superior.
3. "Line and staff dichotomy is obsolete and artificial". Explain.
4. Explain the cause of conflict between line and staff members.
5. What do you understand by functional organisation and explain its merits and demerits.
6. What is a matrix organisation? How is it different from a project organisation? Briefly explain the advantages of a matrix organisation.
7. Write short notes on
   (a) Matrix organisation
   (b) Project organisation
   (c) Free form organisation.

OBJECTIVE TYPE QUESTIONS

Which of the following statements are correct and which are incorrect? Give reasons to support your answers.

1. The matrix organisation structure contains the features of two or more forms of departmentalisation.

2. The matrix organisation is a superimposition of the project structure over the functional structure.
3. In a free form organisation the role and relationships are determined before -hand.
4. The free form organisation is not suitable for a modern business organisation.
5. A project structure of organisation is a permanent structure.
6. Modern structures of organisation are more organic, flexible and suitable for the organisation operating in a fast-changing environment.
7. A traditional structure is characterised by the division of labour and specialisation.
8. The functional structure is a modification of the line and staff organisation.

REFERENCES

Bartlett, Christopher A. and Ghoshal, Sumantra. 'Matrix Management: Not Structure a Frame of Mind'. *Harvard Business Review*, July–August, 1990.

Bryne, John A. 'The Horizontal Organisation'. *Business Week,* December 20,1993.

Burns, Tom and Stalker, G. M. *The Management of Innovation*. London, U.K.: Tavistock, 1961.

Koontz, Harold and Weihrich, Heinz. *Essentials of Management*. New Delhi, India: Tata McGraw-Hill Publishing Company Limited, 2001.

Lawrence, Paular and Lorsch, J. W. *Organisation and Environment: Managing Differentiation and Integration*. Homewood, U.S.A.: Irwin, 1967.

Peter, Tom and Waterman, R. H. Jr. *In Search of Excellence*. New York, U.S.A.: Harper and Row, 1982.

Quinn, J. B. *Intelligent Enterprise: A Knowledge and Service-based Paradigm for Industry*. New York, U.S.A.: Free Press, 1992.

Singh, Y. P. and Pradeep Kumar. *Organisational Behaviour*. New Delhi, India: Cyber Tech Publications, 2005.

Weber, Max. *Economy and Society: An Outline of Interpretation Sociology*. New York, U.S.A.: Bedminster Press, 1968.

Woodward, Joan. *Industrial Organisation*. London, U.K.: Oxford University Press, 1965.

CASE STUDY I

ABB: A Huge Global Matrix

If lean and mean could be personified, Percy Barnevik would walk through the door. A thin, bearded Swede, Barnevik is Europe's leading hatchet man. He is also the creator of what is fast becoming the most successful cross-border merger since Royal Dutch Petroleum linked up with Britain's Shell in 1907.

In four years, Barnevik, 51, has welded ASEA, a Swedish engineering group, to Brown Boveri, a Swiss competitor, bolted on seven more companies in Europe and the U.S.A. and created ABB, a global electrical equipment giant that is bigger than Westinghouse and head to head with GE. It is a world leader in high-speed trains, robotics and environmental control.

To make this monster dance, Barnevik cut more than one in five jobs, closed dozens of factories and decimated headquarters staffs around Europe and the U.S.A. Whole businesses were shifted from one country to another. He created a corps of just 25 global managers to lead 21,000 employees. IBM has talked with Barnevik and his team about how to pare down its own overstafed bureaucracy. Du Pont recently put Barnevik on its board. Says a senior executive at Mitsubishi Heavy Industries: "They're as aggressive as we are. I mean this as a compliment. They are a sort of super Japanese."

ABB is not Japanese, nor is it Swiss or Swedish. It is a multinational without a national identity, though its mailing address is in Zurich. The company's top 13 managers hold frequent meetings in different countries. Since they share no common first language, they speak only English, a foreign tongue to all but one. Like their boss, senior ABB managers are short on sentiment and long on commitment. An oil portrait of a 19th century founder of Brown Boveri hangs in ABB's headquarters, but few are sure what his name is. (It's Charles Brown). Ask for a fax number, though and you're likely to get two, office and home.

To Barnevik, today's competitive market economy is a 'cruel world'. Not making it any kinder, he has launched a personal war on what he sees as excess capacity— 2 per cent to 3 per cent in the electrical equipment industry in Europe alone. Educated in Sweden and the U.S.A. (he studied business administration and computer science at Stanford in the mid-1960s), Barnevik thinks European industry must be restructured massively to become competitive in world markets. He foresees billions of dollars and mergers and acquisitions in the next three to five years. Europe's best strategy against the Americans and Japanese, he believes, is to break free of protected national markets.

Case Study I continued

Case Study I continued

Before the merger, Brown Boveri had four people in Baden, Switzerland and ASEA had as many as 2 in Vasteras, Sweden. The combined company now employs just 15 in a modest six-storey building across a train station in west Zurich. Where did everybody go? Many were fired. The rest were sent to subsidiaries or offered jobs in new companies set up or assume many headquarters functions. (ABB Marketing Services, for example, creates and runs campaigns for ABB, but also takes on a few other clients). And Barnevik expects to make money). It's not just cost cutting Barnevik is after, though that is obviously important. Says he: "Ideally you should have a minimum of staff to disturb the operating people and prevent them from doing their more important jobs."

Barnevik's master matrix gives all employees a country manager and a business sector manager. The country managers run traditional, national companies with local boards of directors, including eminent outsiders. ABB has about two such managers, most of them citizens of the country in which they work. Of more exalted rank, are 65 global managers who are organised into eight segments: transportation, process automation and engineering environmental devices, financial services, electrical equipment (mainly motors and robots) and three electric power businesses: generation, transmission and distribution.

Barnevik is well aware that the once popular management by matrix is in disfavour in the U.S. business schools and has been abandoned by most multinational companies. But he says he uses a loose, decentralised version of it—the two bosses are not always equal—that is particularly suited to an organisation composed of many nationalities.

The matrix system makes it easier for managers like Gerhard Schulmeyer, a German who heads ABB's U.S. businesses as well as the automation segment, to make use of technology from other countries. Because of the matrix, Schulmeyer has a better idea of what is available where. He says that the techniques developed by ABB in Switzerland that he uses to service U.S. steam turbines are more reliable and efficient than those of General Electric and Westinghouse, his main American competitors. Schulmeyer also relied on European technology to convert a Midland, Michigan, nuclear reactor into a natural gas-fired plant.

ABB executives say the value of the company's matrix system extends beyond the swapping of technology and products. For example, the power transformer business segment consists of 31 factories in 16 countries. Barnevik wants each of these businesses to be run locally with intense global coordination. So every month the business segment headquarters

Case Study I continued

Case Study I continued

in Mannheim, Germany, tells all the factories how all the others are doing according to dozens of measurements. If one factory is lagging, solutions to common problems can be discussed and worked out across borders.

Questions

1. How is ABB achieving integration (coordination) of its global operations? Hint: Use Figure 11.1 as a guide).
2. Which of the four basic departmentalisation formats do you detect in ABB's structure of eight segments? Explain.
3. Has Barnevik created an effective balance between centralisation and decentralisation? How can you tell?
4. Relative to the advantages and disadvantages, is ABB's matrix structure appropriate to its situation?
5. How does ABB apparently avoid unity-of-command problems with its matrix structure?

CASE STUDY II

There have been periods in which a product has got into difficulty because of loss of favour with the public, bad management or even neglect. Attention of the Sales Vice President to the problems of some products has caused him, at times, to fail to recognise difficulties in others even though the product manager of such products has recognised them and had brought them to his attention. The burden on the present officers is becoming too heavy to ensure proper attention to all their responsibilities. Employment of assistants apparently causes loss of the close touch of the top group that is necessary to ensure success.

Opportunities for increasing the line of products and expanding the business are being lost because of lack of time among the executives to study them or manage new products. In any business where specialities sold under trademark brands are the major business of a company, it is necessary for that company to continually bring out new products and to study old ones to determine, in their case, the point of no return with regard to promotion and advertising expenses.

Once the top executive group has approved the idea of a new product, it is put under the responsibility of one of the Vice-Presidents. He develops an organisation and brings it along; at first, the advertising appropriate for the product, accounting and public relations.

Top executive conclude that Modern Corporation has a problem of organisation.

Case Study II continued

Case Study II continued

Questions

1. How have changed conditions in this company affected the appropriateness of its organisation structure?
2. What changes do you recommend to be made in the company's organisation structure? Indicate.
   (a) how can the desired product responsibility be achieved
   (b) any changes in line authority
   (c) the use, if any, of staff functional authority or committee.

—oo(O)oo—

CHAPTER 12

MOTIVATING PEOPLE AT WORK

LEARNING OBJECTIVES

1.

1. To develop conceptual clarity about the process of motivation.
2. To remember several views such as traditional, human relations and systems views on motivation.
3. To relate motivation with morale, job satisfaction and ability.
4. To bring out Maslow's need for hierarchy and Herzberg's two-factor theory of motivation.
5. To learn about equity theory, expectancy theory and ERG theory of motivation with suitable examples.
6. To distinguish between McGregor's theory of X and Y.
7. To evaluate the significance of monetary and non-monetary rewards in motivating employees.
8. To bring out the main features of job enlargement and job enrichment and relate them to motivation.
9. To analyse the significance of quality circles, supportive supervision and workers' participation in motivation.

INTRODUCTION AND MEANING

The basic responsibility of a manager is to get things done by others. To discharge such a responsibility he has to perform various managerial functions and develop cordial interpersonal relations with subordinates by exercising human skills.

In this regard, it is necessary for the manager to find out what makes people do things and to discover the source of energy that causes individuals to behave as they do since the use of individual skill, knowledge and abilities and their collective contribution is critical for the smooth functioning of the organisation and the achievement of its objectives. Thus, the manager has to understand how individuals behave in a particular work setting. Why do they behave as they do? And finally, what else is to be done so that they produce the desirable working behaviour?

Generally speaking, motivation refers to that set of wishes, desires, needs and drives that stimulate or activate individuals to behave or do the things they do. The term 'motivation' has been derived from the word 'movement' and in the context of management it is used in the sense of seeking desirable and effective 'movements' among the employees with regard to their performance and working behaviour. A man is said to be motivated when his latent or concealed energy is directed towards the accomplishment of certain goals. Broadly, motivation may be regarded as the driving force or power to carry out the plans of the organisation through the enthusiastic efforts of its members.

The term 'motivation' has been defined by many authors. According to Stanley Vence, motivation implies "an emotion or desire which so conditions one's will that the individual is propelled into action." In this definition, motivation has been described with the help of these emotions and desires which frame or create a willingness among individuals to act in a particular manner. Robert Dubin defines it as "the complex of forces starting and keeping a person at work in an organisation." According to this definition, motivation is a force that compels a person to join an organisation and keep on working therein. The *Encyclopaedia of Management* has described motivation thus: "Motivation refers to the degree of readiness of an organisation to pursue some designated goals and implies the determination of the nature and locus of force inducing a degree of readiness." It reveals that motivation is a force that makes an individual ready to move towards some predetermined goal.

According to Brech, motivation is an inspirational process which gets members of the team to pull their weight effectively, to give their loyalty to the group, to carry out their accepted jobs properly and generally to plan an effective part in the job that the group has undertaken (Figure 12.1).

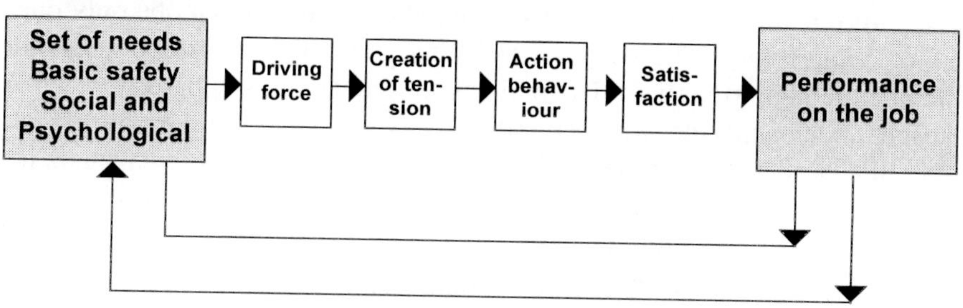

Figure 12.1. Motivation process

On the basis of the discussions above, the following observations can be made regarding motivation:

1. Motivation is an inner psychological force that activates and compels a person to behave in a particular manner.
2. The motivation process is partly influenced by perceptions, learning abilities, personality traits and competence of the individuals.
3. Highly motivated employees work more efficiently, their level of performance tends to be higher than others.
4. Motivation is also based on individual needs and wants. It is for the fulfilment of needs that he behaves in a specific manner.
5. Motivation is a process of stimulating an individual to direct his energies to achieve some goals.
6. Studies on motivation have also verified that motivation plays a crucial role in determining the level of performance. In the case of an average employee, if the level of capabilities and skills is enough to perform a job in a satisfactory manner, the presence or absence of motivation will make a lot of difference in the level of performance.
7. Motivating force or stimulation differs from one to another individual depending on needs, level of capability, attitude, etc.
8. The motivation process not only helps the manager to understand human behaviour it also facilitates ways to discover how an individual can be induced to produce the desired behaviour.

EARLY VIEWS OF MOTIVATION

Like all other approaches and principles of management, motivation also has its origin in the traditional theory of management. With the passage of time, the necessary modifications were made in the traditional model of motivation and a human relations model was developed. Similarly, after developing a system approach of management, the motivation process has also been made the system perspective.

The traditional model of motivation is mainly associated with Taylor's approach of scientific management. Taylor has pointed out that there can be only one best way of doing things. The workers, by being given a wage incentive, should be motivated to adopt that way. The main assumption of this approach was that the manager understands the work better than the workers. The workers are essentially lazy and can be motivated only with money. Under this model, managers have a responsibility to exercise close supervision and control and to simplify operations so as to make workers produce work of the standard required.

However, advocates of the human relations model strongly felt that apart from financial incentives social contact of the workers with their supervisors and fellow workers may also help in creating and sustaining motivation. Workers can be motivated by acknowledging their social needs and recognising their importance and usefulness in the system. The human relations model of motivation further suggests that the manager should give his subordinates some freedom to take decisions regarding the work assigned to them. Finally, under this model, employees were expected to accept the authority of management because the manager treats them as human beings and allows them some degree of freedom to exercise self-direction and control to perform routine jobs.

SYSTEM VIEW OF MOTIVATION

The system model of motivation is a complex behavioural phenomenon and can be understood precisely by applying the system approach. In the words of Lyman Porter and Raymond Miles, the system perspective towards motivation is very useful for managers. This is because the behaviour and motivation process can be understood with the help of system of forces operating on the employees. Porter and Miles believe that a motivation system consists of three sets of variables affecting motivation as an individual in the organisation. These may be considered as sub-systems of motivation.

1. Individual characteristics
2. Job characteristics
3. Work situation characteristics.

1. Individual Characteristics

Each individual employee, when he joins an organisation, carries with him skills, abilities, interest, needs, attitude and other personality traits. He differs from others in terms of these characteristics. The motivation system to be designed for them will also differ. These factors are considered more important in the process of motivation because the behaviour of the individual is greatly influenced and moulded by these factors. Brief descriptions of these are given below:

(a) Needs

This is one of the important factors that is taken into account to understand human behaviour because such behaviour is need based. The need of an individual may be defined as a state of deprivation or deficiency felt by him which creates some pressure, stress and disequilibrium. It ultimately gives rise to a drive which forces him to do some thing to satisfy that need.

(b) Ability and Competence

This includes mental and physical energies and abilities that the employee uses to perform assigned jobs. The level of ability and competence will affect the level of performance of the employee.

(c) Personality Traits

A number of traits associated with the personality of an individual also affects his working behaviour in an organisation. These traits such as trust, openness, self-reliance, control of emotions, social sensitiveness, assertiveness, etc., reflect the tendencies of an individual to behave in a particular manner.

(d) Motives

The behaviour of an individual consists of some needs, desires, urges and instincts. These needs and urges create disequilibrium in the mind of a person and ultimately gives rise to some drives and motives. These drives or motives are inner psychological factors that activate, compel and direct the individual to behave in the direction of achievement of goals.

(e) Perception

An employee who interacts with the variables of environment starts attaching meaning to objectives, events and other variables of environment and forms some impression about them. The process of forming opinions or impressions is known as 'perception'. The process of perception is subjective because it depends on the individual's personality, beliefs, attitude and other factors.

2. Characteristics of the Job

The characteristics of a job and its elements is a second set of variables that affect the motivation of employees in an organisation. These characteristics are within the control of the manager. By making suitable changes or redesigning a job, it can be made more meaningful for the employees. It has also been established by researchers that a particular job may affect the desire of an individual to perform that job. For example, an assembly line type routine job reduces the employee's motivation and produces dissatisfaction. The relationship of job-contents and motivation which has been discussed as a two-factor theory by Herzberg is quite relevant in this regard. The job characteristics mainly include a degree of operational autonomy of tasks, job content, types of intrinsic rewards, etc.

3. Characteristics of Work Situation and Environment

The work situation characteristics include those factors of the work environment that also affect the motivation of the employees in the organisation. The work situation involves the following factors:

(a) Organisational Policies, Reward System and Culture

Though organisational policies on various matters do not directly affect job motivation, they influence the desire of employees to remain with or leave the organisation. A reward system has the greatest influence on the motivation and performance of individuals. Provision should be made to reward extra effort and improved performance. Similarly, organisational culture, norms, values and beliefs of employees can also help in shaping their working behaviour and affect their performance.

(b) Immediate Work Environment

This includes the attitude and actions of peers and supervisors and the atmosphere they create in the work setting. It has been concluded in a number of studies that peer groups at work have a definite impact on the performance of an individual. Norms and values pursued by peer groups, attitude of peers, degree of help, guidance and support provided by a supervisor have a direct bearing on the performance and motivation of employees working in a work setting.

In an organisation, the process of motivation is closely related to many other concepts like morale, job satisfaction and ability of the employees. A brief discussion on these is made here.

MOTIVATION AND MORALE

Morale is closely connected with the concept of motivation. This is a crucial factor in the functioning of any group activity. It refers to the attitude and behaviour of individuals towards their work environment. Many authors of management believe that morale is the esprit-de-corps or the attitudes of a collective body. Therefore, morale is a synthesis of how employees think and feel about their jobs, working conditions, peers, supervisors, superiors, organisation and its goals, etc. It could also be the individual factor, because it also represents the feeling of an employee towards his work, in terms of job satisfaction, fulfilment of his needs and his interaction with fellow-workers, superiors and subordinates. Thus, it is a state of mind and emotions that have a direct reflection on the attitude of a person or persons.

More often, morale is described as being high or low because it is a dynamic and relative concept. Generally, high morale exists when the employee's attitude is favourable towards his job, organisation, fellow workers, working conditions and to the total situation of the group. Low morale exists when doubts and suspicion are common, when individuals are discouraged and depressed, there is a lot of mental tension and willing cooperation is withheld. It is marked by apathy, bickering, jealousy, pessimism, reduced output, absenteeism, resignation, formation of resistance groups, etc.

Though motivation and morale are cognitive concepts, high morale and motivation generally lead to a higher level of performance. There is a difference between these concepts which can be understood on the following basis:

1. Motivation is an inner-psychological drive of an individual which activates and compels him to behave in a particular manner. But morale is more of a group situation. It is a socio-emotional association and attitude of the members of a group towards each other, towards group goals and towards the organisation and its goals.

2. In every work setting, the performance and behaviour of individual members is governed by wide-ranging variables and motivation is one of them. It explains why members perform or behave in a specific way. On the other hand, morale is the result of all interacting variables present in the entire work situation. The morale of the members will be high when they carry a favourable attitude towards these variables.
3. A high degree of motivation generally contributes to high morale among employees but if the morale of employees is high they may or may not be motivated. Thus, high morale does not guarantee high motivation because to have a favourable attitude towards all factors of a work situation may not necessarily compel employees to work more efficiently. However, on the other hand, if employees are highly motivated it may contribute to high morale.
4. Motivation has both positive as well as negative aspects. In some cases, in order to force employees to perform as per the required standard and behave in the desired manner authority is exercised, punishment is given and other coercive measures are adopted.

   The concept of morale involves only positive aspects and negative measures may further lower the degree of morale. The attitude of employees can be made favourable only through positive measures, so as to improve working conditions, to redesign the job, to provide supportive supervision, to integrate personal interest with organisational goals, etc.
5. Keeping in view the direct relationship between motivation and productivity, the organisation concentrates more on those factors that directly contribute to motivation. Morale is regarded as a secondary phenomenon, because high morale may not necessarily contribute to higher productivity.

   Because of this, the field of motivation seems to be more explored and backed by many theories on the various aspects of motivation which have been developed by psychologists, sociologists and management scientists. Even in a modern organisation, motivation assumes top priority as compared to morale.
6. Morale is generally considered as a group concept whereas motivation is largely an individual concept. Therefore, to raise the morale of employees, those factors that affect a group situation or the entire work setting are taken care of. But a motivation system is designed in the organisation after taking into account individual differences among employees.

MOTIVATION AND JOB-SATISFACTION

Every individual who joins an organisation is given some work or job to perform. Performance of the job requires the use of necessary skill, knowledge, experience and other capabilities. Not only these, but the aptitude and interest of the employee for a specific job is also taken into account to make his placement in the organisation. This is done to provide more job satisfaction. The term 'job satisfaction' may be defined as a psychological satisfaction which the employee derives by performing a job. Performance of the job by the employee also requires that his expectations and aspirations in terms of rewards, consideration, fulfilment of his needs, etc., have been met. If these are fulfilled properly, he will be satisfied with the outcome of job performance and greater job satisfaction would generally motivate employees to perform their jobs more efficiently. Stability of tenure is also ensured by job satisfaction. This is because in view of recognition, achievement and advance being provided to the employee, he decides to stay and continue in the organisation for a longer period of time.

Job satisfaction and motivation reinforce and promote each other. If an employee is satisfied on the front of job performance he tends to be motivated and a highly motivated employee performs better on the job and derives more satisfaction out of it. Apart from this, motivation and job satisfaction are both psychological forces what create tension of pressure for behaving or doing things in a particular manner.

It is because of the close association between motivation and job satisfaction that job characteristics have been considered as part of the motivation system. However, the effect of motivation on productivity and behaviour of the employee is well established. It implies that if the employee is not motivated his level of performance is bound to be on the lower side.

On the other hand, job satisfaction has wider implications on many other factors regarding the performance of the job. For example, turnover and absenteeism are also related to job satisfaction. Those employees who have low job satisfaction are more likely to leave their employer and the same rule applies for absenteeism also. If they have low job satisfaction, they are likely to be absent from their jobs very often. Similarly, with regard to employees and characteristics, there seems to be a positive relationship between age and job satisfaction. As workers become older, they tend to be more satisfied with their jobs. This is because on the basis of his experience, the employee gets adapted to the job and older employees have less expectations of promotion and further growth.

MOTIVATION AND ABILITY

Candidates are selected for various jobs on the basis of job requirements. It implies presence of some degree of various physical and mental abilities which are required to perform the job. Further, to develop the level of ability and potential, training is provided and development programmes conducted. Thus, ability is a combination of many physical as well as mental factors such as physical strength, stamina, knowledge, experience, skill and competence. Motivation is an inner-psychological factor that activates the individual to use his abilities to achieve given goals. When people join an organisation, they bring with them certain needs, goals and interest along with a certain level of ability and competence.

They use their abilities to perform assigned jobs through which they tend to move towards the achievement of personal goals and interest. If the organisation provides for the satisfaction of their needs, they are motivated and perform assigned jobs more efficiently. From this point of view ability assumes a more important place because, first it is to be developed then it is followed by motivation to realise it fully to achieve organisational goals. On the other hand, if employees are capable of doing things having enough ability and competence, if they are not motivated, the level of performance is bound to be low.

Motivation is a psychological force which is related with the working behaviour of employees. They can be motivated by providing necessary stimuli by moulding their pattern of behaviour, modifying their perceptions and values and inspiring them, whereas ability can be acquired by formal education and training. It is not behavioural in nature, rather it is more related to physical and mental competence. Ability can be further developed by providing the necessary training, by conducting development programmes, by providing a proper environment of learning and by giving supportive facilities to employees.

So motivation involves both positive as well as negative variables whereas ability always moves in a positive direction through positive measures. To some extent, motivation and ability reinforce each other as the ability of an employee can be realised fully only by motivating him. If motivational factors are not present in a work setting, the level of performance tends to be low in spite of an able and capable work force. It has been found in practice that a high degree of ability and competence may also create a feeling of self motivation among individuals. This is because they perform an assigned job more efficiently even if motivational factors are not present to the desired extent. Besides, a highly motivated employee can also produce the desired results in spite of a lesser degree of ability and competence. This is because he may do it to get over his inadequacies and deficiency.

THEORIES OF MOTIVATION

No organisation can succeed without a highly motivated and committed team of employees. It is only through them that all other physical resources like land, building, capital, machines, etc., are used to achieve predetermined goals. Because of the enormous effect of motivational factors on the working behaviour and level of performance of the employee, a lot of research work has been done and consequently many theories of motivation have been developed. Some of the theories are discussed here.

Need Theories of Motivation

Human behaviour is basically a need-based phenomenon. It is greatly influenced by needs. Need theories of motivation are based on the assumption that an individual behaves in a particular manner to satisfy his needs. These theories are also known as 'content theories' and focus on inner needs that motivate an individual to behave.

So, provisions to reduce or satisfy their needs would force them to behave in a particular way. Some of the important need theories are:

Maslow's Need Hierarchy

This theory of motivation has received more attention from managers than any other theory of motivation. Abraham Maslow, an eminent U.S. psychologist has classified human needs in a logical and convenient way (Figure 12.2)

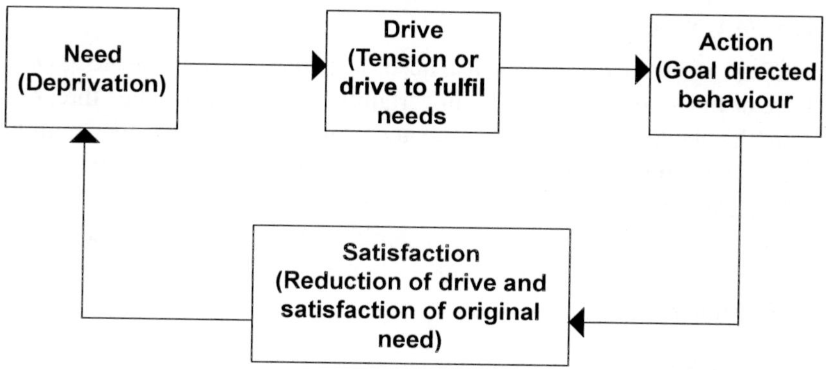

Figure 12.2. Need theory of motivation

This has important implications for managers. In this theory, he has pointed out and explained the needs that influence human behaviour. Maslow has attempted to describe human behaviour with the help of an hierarchy of five needs ranging from most basic physiological needs to the highest needs for self-actualisation (Figure 12.3).

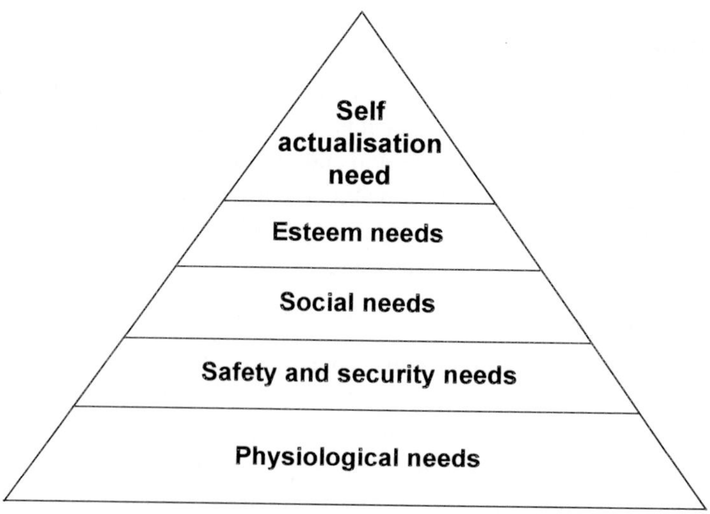

Figure 12.3. Maslow's need hierarchy

1. Physiological Needs

These are the most basic needs that include food, shelter and clothing. These needs are very powerful motivators because individuals cannot survive without them. Physiological needs must be satisfied to some level or these should be partially satisfied before the individual moves to satisfy other higher category needs. Maslow observed "that man lives by bread alone, when there is no bread."

2. Safety Needs

After the satisfaction of physical needs to a relative extent, one feels concerned about his safety from future uncertainty, enemies and other threats. These are the needs of self-preservation and protection. At this stage, an individual begins to think for the future and makes efforts to provide for rainy days. It is concluded by Maslow that employees need sufficient wages to feed, shelter and protect him and his family satisfactorily. He also attempts to secure a safe working environment before attempting to satisfy other needs of a higher order.

3. Social Needs

After having secured satisfaction of physical and safety needs one focuses on satisfying the needs of love and affection which are known as social needs. These include the need to love and be loved and the need to belong and be identified with a group. Though these needs are strongly felt by an individual in respect of his family, it also affects his work environment and his working behaviour. Along with the first two levels of needs, relative satisfaction of social needs gives rise to the next higher level need.

4. Esteem Needs

Employees in an organisation who perceive themselves as worthwhile are said to have esteem needs. Self-respect is the key to such needs. Much of our self-respect comes from being accepted and respected by others. But esteem need will emerge only when other lower category needs are satisfied to a relative extent. Esteem needs include the need for self-respect and appreciation from others, status, prestige in society, etc.

5. Self-actualisation Needs

At the top of Maslow's hierarchy of needs lies the need for self-actualisation. This is an open-ended need because it is related to the need to become more and more of what one is to become everything that one is capable of becoming. It includes the need for realisation of one's full potential of development, maturity and autonomy. On the relative satisfaction of this need, an individual becomes growth-oriented, self-directed, detached and creative. But in an organisation he hardly achieves self-realisation and actualisation. However, creativity of an individual in producing new and practical ideas in bringing about innovation, increasing productivity and reducing cost might satisfy some of the needs of self-actualisation.

Regarding the need theory of Maslow, the following observations may be made:

1. Hierarchy of needs has been prepared in a logical sequence. Needs have been put into different levels according to their effect and dominance on human behaviour and performance.
2. Individuals generally attempt to satisfy their basic needs the first of which is on the lower side of hierarchy.
3. Maslow made it clear that the need or deprivation of some things affects and dominates one's behaviour.
4. Lower category needs require prior attention as compared to the higher order needs and lower level needs are more powerful and pressing.
5. Relative satisfaction of one category need gives rise to another level need and continues till the last level.
6. If the need is satisfied, it remains no more a motivator and it is only unfulfilled needs that affect human behaviour and performance.

Behavioural scientists who have attempted to test Maslow's theory of needs hierarchy in practice have found many deficiencies in it. They argue that it does not explain the complexities involved in human behaviour. Behavioural scientist Edward Lawler has observed that the higher order needs come into play after the lower ones are satisfied and the order in which they come into play cannot be predicted. However, it provides a great lesson to managers that fulfilled needs do not motivate individuals. An efficient manager anticipates each employee's need profile and provides an opportunity to fulfil emerging needs so as to motivate them.

Herzberg's Two-Factor Theory

Herzberg, a U.S. behavioural scientist, has developed a theory of employee motivation which is based on satisfaction. His theory explains that a satisfied employee is motivated from within to work harder and a dissatisfied employee is not self-motivated. Since Herzberg has discovered two sets of factors associated with satisfaction and dissatisfaction of the employee, therefore it is known as Herzberg's 'two-factor theory'. The first set of factors known as 'satisfiers' or 'motivators' are responsible for self-motivation of employees. These factors include the job, its importance, opportunities for advancement, achievement, recognition, sense of responsibility, etc. These factors are known as 'job content factors' and are the real motivators because they are capable of providing satisfaction to employees. They are also known as 'intrinsic factors'.

The second set of factors called 'hygiene factors' or 'maintenance factors' or 'dissatisfiers' include working conditions, job security, salary, quality of supervision, organisational policies, interpersonal relationships and other factors in the immediate work environment. They are job context and extrinsic to the job. Any deficiency or absence of these factors would simply create dissatisfaction, demotivation and low performance but their presence does not motivate employees. These have been considered as hygiene factors or maintenance factors because their role is supportive just to maintain a healthy and congenial atmosphere in a work setting.

By identifying and differentiating various factors as dissatisfiers and motivators, Herzberg encouraged managers to think carefully about what actually motivates employees. According to Herzberg, the opposite of job satisfaction is not job dissatisfaction, but rather no job satisfaction, and similarly the opposite of job dissatisfaction is not satisfaction but no dissatisfaction. Like Maslow's theory, this theory of motivation has also been criticised on account of lack of empirical validation. In spite of criticism, Herzberg's contribution to the motivation theory remains very useful. This is because he has made it quite clear that money is a weak motivational tool, at best it can only eliminate or reduce dissatisfaction. Moreover, this theory has placed emphasis on motivating potential which can be profitably used to enrich the job.

Achievement Motivation Theory

This theory has particular reference to industrial organisation. The motive of achievement and its fulfilment for employees determines the success or failure of these organisations. David McClelland and his associates like John Atkinson and others in Harvard University have developed this theory of motivation. The main elements of this theory is the need for achievement, power and affiliation. This theory assumes that some people are much more achievement-oriented than others. Therefore, they get job satisfaction and derive a special kind of pleasure in achieving their objective successfully or performing challenging jobs, rather than receiving monetary and other rewards.

Atkinson's model of motivation relates behaviour and performance of the employees to three basic drives such as the need for achievement, the need for power and the need for affiliation or close association with others. The balance between these drives varies from individual to individual. For example, one individual might have a strong need of affiliation while another might have a strong need for achievement. The need for achievement is a need to excel or succeed in a competitive situation. This is related to how well individuals are motivated to perform their jobs. People with a high need of achievement would like to take responsibility to solve problems. They tend to set moderately difficult targets for themselves and take calculated risks to meet those targets.

Thus, those with high achievement needs tend to be highly motivated by challenging and competitive work situations. Achievement-oriented individuals seek satisfaction in doing things better and in assuming personal responsibility to solve problems. But people with low achievement needs tend to perform either poorly or average in the same situation. There seems to be a relationship between high achievement need and high performance. This is because the people who succeed in competitive situations are well above average in achievement and highly motivated. High achievement needs can also be strengthened by an individual's fear of failure. Managers may be strongly motivated to take suitable action with a fear of possible embarrassment if they fail.

Like the need for achievement, the need for control or domination of people and events is also considered one of the important motivational factors. Such individuals, if given a position marked by higher authority and power, tend to perform better as compared to other positions having less power. Similarly, other individuals may derive satisfaction from better friendly interpersonal relations in a work setting. They can be motivated by providing an atmosphere of support and friendship and social affiliation. This need is more likely a social need which has been described earlier.

ERG Theory of Motivation

This theory was developed by Claynton Alderfer on the same lines as Maslow's theory of hierarchy. It is considered as a reformulation or refinement of Maslow's need theory. This theory states that people attempt to meet a need of existence, relatedness and growth needs. If the efforts to seek one level of needs are defeated, individuals would regress to lower levels of needs.

Alderfer classified needs into three categories. Existence needs include basic needs and some other factors such as fringe benefits in the work place. Relatedness needs by and large resemble social needs and mainly include the need for interpersonal relations. Growth needs reflect many aspects of the need of achievement and self-actualisation including the need for personal creativity and influence.

Although the ERG theory is also based on need hierarchy, it differs from Maslow's need hierarchy on two grounds. Alderfer stated that needs at more than one level may arise at a time as against Maslow's assumption that at a time only one category need arises. Secondly, in a more significant way, Alderfer stressed that when a higher category of needs are not fulfilled, the lower level needs will return even though they are already satisfied to a reasonable extent. In addition, Alderfer strongly felt that people move up and down in the hierarchy of needs from situation to situation. Both these theories of needs do provide an useful insight into human needs which greatly influence his working behaviour. The conclusions derived from these theories may be used by managers while thinking over and selecting incentives or stimuli to motivate employees. They may also help in understanding human behaviour.

OTHER THEORIES OF MOTIVATION

Advocates of need theories believe that it is only the need that influences human behaviour. Therefore, adequate provisions to satisfy these needs will motivate employees to behave or act in a particular manner. The process approach to motivation implies that need is just one element in the process. The behaviour of an individual is influenced more by his abilities, role and perception. What kind of behaviour he needs to display to achieve a high performance and his expectations depends on the results of specific behaviour.

Expectancy Theory

This is also considered as the 'expectancy/valence' approach which attempts at overcoming criticism of other motivational approaches. The expectancy approach aims at differentiating individuals and situations. It deviates from the assumption that all employees are alike or all situations are alike. Therefore, there is only one way of motivating them. The expectancy approach advocates that the behaviour of an individual is influenced by their expectations, perceptions and calculations regarding the relationship between performance and rewards. It specifies that the efforts to achieve a high performance can be achieved and will be rewarded if achieved and that the reward will be worth the efforts made. This approach has three basic elements:

1. Performance Outcome Expectancy

An individual who is expecting some consequences of his behaviour would in turn affect his decision to behave in a particular manner. For example, the sales executive who is thinking about exceeding his sales target may expect praise, a bonus or no reaction.

2. Valence

The outcome of a particular behaviour has a specific valence that is the power to motivate which varies from individual to individual. For example, promotion to a higher position may have a somewhat different valence for the manager who gives too much importance to money as compared to another manager who attaches more significance to status, development and growth.

3. Efforts Performance Expectancy

The expectation of an individual about how difficult it will be to perform successfully will also affect his decision about behaviour. For example, if choices are given, an individual will select that level of performance that has the highest possibility of achieving an outcome that they value.

Although this approach has been developed by Victor Vroom, it was further refined by Lyman Porter and Edward Lawler who made it more useful and practical. They based the expectancy model of motivation on the following assumptions:

(a) The behaviour of an individual is determined by a combination of factors such as characteristics of individuals and characteristics of the work environment.

(b) Individuals make decisions consciously and deliberately regarding their behaviour in an organisation.

(c) Individuals have different needs, goals and devices to fulfil.

(d) Individuals decide from alternative behaviour on the basis of their expectations that a given behaviour will lead to the desired outcome.

The elements mentioned above may be viewed in the form of the following three questions:

1. "If I do this what will be the outcome?"
2. "Is the outcome worth the efforts put in by me?"
3. "What are my chances of achieving an outcome that will be worthwhile to me?"

This model has highlighted that people can differ greatly in how they size up their chances for success in different jobs. Therefore to motivate people it is just not enough to offer them some rewards. They must also feel convinced that they have the ability to get the reward.

Equity Theory

This theory has been developed by J. S. Adam. The essence of this theory is that employees generally make a comparison of their efforts and rewards with those of others in a similar position and a similar work situation. This approach is based on the basic assumption that employees working in an organisation should be treated equally in terms of justice, balance and fairness. When they join an organisation they carry some qualifications, skill and knowledge with them to perform assigned jobs that involves the use of these abilities and qualities which are known as 'inputs'. In return for these inputs, whatever they get from the organisation such as compensation, recognition, position, status, etc., is known as 'output'.

In practice, they have a natural tendency to compare the ratio of input and output with that of other employees working in the same position. It should, however, be remembered that comparison is purely subjective in nature depending on personal feeling, value system and perception of an individual. If there exists a balance in the ratio, an individual gets a positive feeling of fairness and equity. But if the ratio is significantly less than that of others, he feels not rewarded and paid according to his inputs and ultimately starts creating doubts regarding the fairness and equality of the organisation's system and policies.

Contrary to this, if the ratio is higher than that of another, an individual feels over-rewarded which may create a sense of guilt in his mind. But in both cases, the individual feels some tension and uncomfortableness and finally he is motivated to reduce the inequity or difference by way of making necessary adjustments with regard to input and output. Since individuals differ, their method of evaluating and reducing inequity would also differ. For example, some of them may rationalise their value system and perception and others may try to make fellow-workers change their behaviour.

The equity approach of motivation seems to be useful for managers in determining the appropriate level or reward for employees. This is because it emphasises the role played by an individual's belief in the equity and fairness of reward and punishment in determining his performance and satisfaction.

Reinforcement Theory

This has been developed by B. F. Skinner and his associates. It is based on the 'law of effect' that behaviour with positive consequences tends to be repeated but with negative consequences tends not to be repeated. They have mainly emphasised on the fact that the consequence of past behaviour affects future actions in a cyclical learning process in the manner shown in Figure 12.4.

Figure 12.4. Reinforcement of behaviour

The behaviour of an individual which is voluntary in the form of a response to a situation or event or stimulus is the cause of specific consequences. If these consequences are positive, the individual will behave in a similar manner in the future. But if these consequences are unpleasant or negative, the individual will modify or change his behaviour.

Similarly, employees attempt to seek goals in a work situation because they have learned that they stand a good chance of being rewarded. This theory is also known as the learning or conditioning theory. This is because through the process of learning in the past, it conditions the future behaviour and action of an individual. For example, if an efficient employee has been suitably rewarded in the past, he would like to repeat his behaviour on the basis of his past learning.

There are four methods to be used by managers to modify the behaviour of employees:

1. Positive Reinforcement

Desirable behaviour is encouraged or reinforced by positive consequences, that is, rewards.

2. Avoidance Learning

Employees change their behaviour to avoid unpleasant consequences such as criticism, poor evaluation, etc.

3. Extinction

Absence of reinforcements.

4. Punishment

Application of negative consequences.

Amongst all these, positive reinforcement seems to be a more powerful and useful method to make it more desirable for the future.

OTHER APPROACHES

Besides the theories on motivation discussed above, the following two approaches deserve mention here.

Carrot-and-Stick Policy

It is necessary that a conducive work environment be built for the smooth functioning and successful accomplishment of organisational goals. Among other factors, it should be accompanied by an appropriate system of reward and punishment. All individuals who join an organisation carry some goals, interest and expectations along with their ability, competence, knowledge and skill. To make them committed and involved in a work setting it is necessary that those who are working efficiently be rewarded and those who are not working efficiently be punished. For treating employees in this way, the policy of carrot-and-stick is followed. This is based on commonsense, simplistic in assumptions and conservative in nature. This is because it recognises reward and punishment as the only means to motivate employees. This is based on the assumption that individuals can be motivated by the hope of getting a reward or fear of being punished; employees may be motivated to produce as per standard of performance. He behaves in a desirable manner because poor performance and undesirable behaviour may be punished.

Similarly, rewards are also made conditional and contingent on effective performance. This approach generally succeeds in motivating people as long as their physiological and safety needs remain unsatisfied. In this regard, McGregor has rightly pointed out that the carrot-and-stick approach does not work at all once an individual has reached an adequate subsistence level and is motivated primarily by higher needs. While make using of this approach, managers should concentrate more on the positive aspect. The stick should be used only when it is unavoidable or necessary for setting the erring employee right in terms of performance and desirable behaviour. For example, casual absence of the employee from work does not require the use of the stick unless and until he starts forming a habit on his part to remain absent. Thus, the use of punishment should be aimed to reform or modify the behaviour of an erring employee and should not come in the way of establishing cordial interpersonal relations.

McGregor's Theory X and Theory Y

Douglas McGregor, a U.S. behavioural scientist, developed an approach to manage and motivate on the basis of various assumptions relating to human behaviour. It has been formulated as Theory X and Theory Y. Both these theories are based on certain assumptions regarding human behaviour. Though he was a great critic of the classical approach of management, his Theory X is related to the philosophy of traditional management. Theory Y is based on humanistic assumptions about employees and describes the approaches of management and motivation.

Theory X describes that

1. The average employee in an organisation is lazy, dull, self-centred, resists change and does not want to share responsibility.
2. He has a limited number of needs, mostly physical, and to some extent security needs.
3. The average employee lacks responsibility and has little ambition.
4. The responsibility of getting things done to achieve organisational goals lies on managers who must use coercive measures to control workers. They must be threatened and punished so as to get them to work.
5. To get things done by employees, McGregor suggested rigid, bureaucratic and a rules-based organisation.
6. A narrow span of management, one-way communication, close supervision, more concentration on monetary incentives and centralisation of managerial authority should be followed.
7. It was also thought necessary to guide, direct and control employees in a strict manner and the carrot-and-stick approach should be used to motivate them.

Theory Y is based on and describes the following:

1. Work is as natural as play or rest for workers.
2. The average employee or worker likes work he is capable of assuming responsibilities for and accepting challenges.
3. He is ambitious, achievement-oriented and capable of exercising self-control.
4. He has a wide range of needs, both economic and non-economic.
5. He has the potential; he can learn to accept and seek responsibility. He has large imagination and creativity that can be applied to work.
6. In view of these assumptions, the role of management is to develop his potential and help employees to achieve common objectives.
7. The organisational structure should be marked by open communication, flexibility, informal relations and decentralisation of authority.
8. The approach of management should include participative management, supportive supervisory style, self-direction and control. It should also be marked by opportunity for developing and using creativity and innovativeness and a package of both monetary and non-monetary incentives.

ROLE AND IMPORTANCE OF REWARDS AND PUNISHMENT IN MOTIVATION

All individuals who join an organisation devote their time, energies and efforts to perform assigned jobs. In return, they expect to be rewarded for their contributions.

Broadly, reward may be defined as material and psychological payoffs to perform tasks in a work situation. In other words, it may be considered as an incentive, both monetary and non-monetary, which is given to employees for their performance at a particular level. It may also be regarded as cause and effect of performance. This is because incentives induce the employee to perform better and if he performs better he gets it. As stated earlier, reward is a consideration given to the employee as a carrot for his better performance and higher efficiency. It is found that job performance and satisfaction can be improved by a properly designed and administered rewards system in the organisation. Rewards may be classified as:

1. Extrinsic and intrinsic rewards
2. Monetary and non-monetary rewards.

Extrinsic and Intrinsic Rewards

Extrinsic rewards are those that are offered to the employee either by his employer, supervisor, colleagues or subordinates. These rewards are, of course, external to the job and job performance. Extrinsic rewards are payoffs granted to the individual by other people. Such rewards may include money, employee benefit, promotion, recognition, praise, status and others.

Intrinsic rewards are those that the individual gives to himself. These rewards are internal and related to job and job performance because they directly arise out of them. These may be considered as self-granted and internally experience payoffs that are earned by the employee. These rewards include job satisfaction, sense of achievement, sense of accomplishment, self-esteem, self-actualisation, self-development, etc. Usually, extrinsic as well as intrinsic rewards are intermingled on the job. For example, if an employee completes a big and challenging project he experiences psychological satisfaction, his need of achievement is fulfilled. On the other hand, he may also get some additional monetary benefit from the organisation.

Monetary and Non-monetary Rewards

Right from the initial stages of development of management knowledge till today, monetary rewards assume a significant role in motivating employees. Money is considered to be the most powerful motivator because by spending money, the employee satisfies his physiological and security needs. Monetary rewards which are also known as pecuniary rewards are those that are associated directly or indirectly with money. Wage and salary are the most important monetary rewards.

Other monetary rewards are bonus, profit-sharing, retirement benefits, vacation pay, free medical service, health insurance, etc. Monetary rewards play an important role as the mainspring of motivation. This is because money does not only satisfy lower level needs such as physical and security needs, but also needs of a social status and power are to be satisfied by it. Therefore, money is considered as a basic incentive for the individual and it motivates him to a large extent provided such rewards are linked to performance.

In an economy like ours, it is safe to assume that all employees, regardless of their rank, perceive money as an important reward. The majority of employees, even those working at a higher level, recognise the significant role of a monetary reward. It is perhaps due to inadequate payments made to the employees by an organisation. Many multinational companies in India have been successfully attracting the best brains in the country in various fields by offering them higher monetary rewards. But in other highly developed economies like the U.S.A., Japan, the U.K., Germany, etc., the situation regarding monetary rewards is different. Due to a higher level of per capita income and handsome payments made to employees by organisations, they tend to be motivated more by non-monetary rewards such as appreciation, recognition, self-achievement, self-fulfilment, etc. However, they still have an attraction for monetary rewards.

Nevertheless, the conclusions derived from many researches that have been conducted in this regard reveal that monetary rewards have an appeal to employees but it does not remain a strong motivation for everyone. The role of monetary rewards may be followed on the basis of the following factors:

1. As stated earlier, in developing and underdeveloped countries, the per capita income remains on the lower side and people have low buying capacity. In this situation, monetary rewards that help in satisfying many lower order needs have a greater motivation force as compared to developed nations.
2. To make monetary rewards more effective, it is necessary that there is a clear link between reward and performance of the employees, because it is only with one desire to get a reward that he may be inclined to perform his job satisfactorily.
3. The economic man model of traditional approach gives undue weightage to economic gains which the employee wants to achieve by performing a job. The model states that the employee has only economic needs and to satisfy them he attempts to maximise his monetary rewards. Advocates of this model believe that monetary rewards are enough to motivate the employee.
4. While administering monetary rewards, the principle of equity should be followed. If an employee feels that others who are performing at his level are being given proportionately more rewards, he may feel dissatisfied and may adjust his output with the reward.
5. In order to design an effective motivational system, it should however be noted that along with monetary rewards, non-monetary rewards should also be used equally. This is because loyalty, sincerity and a sense of belonging cannot be purchased by giving monetary rewards only. Rather, it requires a sound organisational environment.
6. Although monetary rewards have value for everyone, how they value it differs from individual to individual. Some individuals may give too

much importance to it and another may attach less significance to it. It is a matter of one's perception and value system. It is clear that they will be motivated by it to the extent they value it.

7. Although monetary rewards have a greater value to satisfy the basic needs of food, clothing, shelter and security, they can also influence and contribute to the satisfaction of higher order needs. For example, they can be directly used to get into friendships and other social affiliations and can also be used as a status symbol to buy more. It may also help an individual to get a higher status in society and make him more powerful.

Non-Monetary Rewards

Rewards or incentives that are not measurable in terms of money are known as non-monetary rewards. They are intangible and designed to meet the higher order needs of employees. Individuals, particularly working at a higher level of the organisation, attach greater importance to social and psychological needs. These needs cannot be satisfied by money alone. Non-monetary rewards thus aim at satisfying higher order needs such as ego needs and the need for self-actualisation. Non-monetary rewards mainly include meaningful and interesting jobs, career advancement opportunities, supportive supervision, participation in management, quality circles, etc. Some of these are discussed in detail below:

ROLE OF JOB DESIGN IN MOTIVATION

Every individual who joins an organisation is given some job to perform. The nature of the job, its content and its design have a great impact on the working behaviour and level of performance of the individual. It has been the practice in the past that jobs to be performed at the lower level are usually designed in such a way so that the employee performs them easily. These jobs are marked by certain characteristics as given below:

(a) Employees require little training to perform them.

(b) Supervision and control become easier.

(c) They work with higher efficiency.

But such design of the job may create some problems for employees in the long run. This is because with the passage of time such jobs become routine and repetitive in nature and create monotony or boredom in the individual performing them. In such cases, employees start losing interest in the job and jobs also lose their meaning and significance for the employee. Therefore, such jobs are to be restructured and redesigned so as to make them more meaningful, interesting, thrilling and motivating. Jobs are simply a set of tasks that provide various stimuli to job holders. By redesigning them, new stimuli can be offered to job holders to motivate them. Jobs can be redesigned in the following two ways:

1. Job enlargement
2. Job enrichment.

1. Job Enlargement

If jobs become too specialised they are bound to create monotony and boredom for the job holders. They feel alienated and this results in a high level of absenteeism, turnover and tardiness. Under such situations, jobs have to be enlarged. An enlarged job would offer a greater variety of operations to job holders. As a result of job enlargement, they get the following opportunities:

(a) Use a variety of skills to perform a variety of jobs.

(b) Exercise control over how and when the work is to be completed.

(c) Be responsible for the entire piece of work.

(d) Get feedback of information.

As a result of job enlargement, the job cycle becomes lengthier and the frequency of repetition of jobs is reduced. In simple terms, job enlargement implies adding more variety of operations to the existing job and enabling job holders to utilise their range of abilities. Though, by enlarging jobs, the number of operations performed increases, the worker gets more satisfaction out of it and his motivational level goes up. In fact, job enlargement is a procedure of redesigning jobs or modifying work so that employees can feel more involved and responsible for what they do.

There is always scope for enlarging various types of jobs such as clerical, administrative and technical. The need for job enlargement becomes more pressing specially for jobs that are very simple, routine and too specialised such as assembly line jobs. For example, a typist in the office may be given some other operations such as drafting letters, putting them on the notice board, filing them and forwarding them to superiors. This will reduce repetitiveness and too much specialisation of typing which must have been monotonous.

2. Job Enrichment

This is a process of designing a job to increase its motivational potential. This is done by incorporating several inducements and attractions in the job so as to make it more meaningful and interesting. In job enrichment, the job holder is allowed to exercise more influence over several aspects of the job. Regarding job-related problems, he is granted enough operational autonomy so that he can solve problems as they arise. Job enrichment makes a job more meaningful and interesting. It introduces planning and decision-making responsibilities into it. Some jobs are enriched in such a manner that job holders get an opportunity to use and develop their skills in a more meaningful and satisfying manner. They also develop initiative and innovativeness for career development. A successfully enriched job would satisfy the need of achievement and self-fulfilment. Such job enrichment offers an opportunity of self-direction and control. Herzberg described job enrichment as job content or motivator which may give workers more of a challenge, more of a complete task, more responsibility, more opportunity for growth.

Jobs can be enriched by upgrading the following aspects:

(a) Skill Variety

This provides an opportunity to job holders to perform a variety of operations to use a variety of equipment and procedures.

(b) Task Identity

This allows job holders to perform the entire piece of work so that they can identify the results of their efforts clearly.

(c) Task Significance

This makes job holders feel that jobs performed by them have a substantial impact on the lives of other people both inside and outside the organisation.

(d) Autonomy

This provides substantial freedom, independence and discretion to job holders to schedule their work and select equipment and procedure to be used in their work.

(e) Feedback

Job holders must receive useful and reliable information regarding their job performance. Feedback of such information may come from the job itself, or from supervisors or other persons.

How to Enrich Jobs

Job enrichment in an organisation is to be undertaken by managers with the help of some management consultants and behavioural scientists. Generally, this is done by analysing the existing content of jobs. Jobs are then redesigned and restructured in such a way so as to reduce monotony and boredom and make them more interesting, meaningful and paying. There are many ways in which a job can be enriched. The following techniques may be used:

1. Rotation of the task, giving more responsibility and reducing supervision and broadening the qualifications and skills of the job holders.
2. Giving job holders more scope to change the method, sequence and pace of their work.
3. Allow new and more difficult tasks not handled by job holders earlier.
4. Supplying necessary information to job holders which they need to monitor their performance.
5. Assigning job holders more specific projects that give them more responsibility and help them increase their expertise.

For example, the job of conductors (crewmen) in DTC can be enriched by less given them more operational freedom to decide their work schedule for a day as whole, to handle daily cash, to check passengers without tickets and to attend to the complaints of commuters. By doing this, supervision exercised by ATIs is reduced. The conductors will determine standards of performance on their own, have more responsibility and more opportunities are provided to them to increase their expertise.

MERITS AND DEMERITS OF JOB REDESIGN

Job enlargement and enrichment offer the following advantages:

1. Job becomes more interesting, meaningful and paying for job holders.
2. They are motivated to work more efficiently because boredom and monotony are reduced by redesigning the job.
3. Job holders can get opportunities to develop and increase their expertise which may help them in getting promoted to higher positions.
4. Operational cost of job performance is reduced because the cost involved in supervision and control is saved.
5. Job redesign also helps in satisfying various higher order needs such as ego needs, need for self-actualisation, etc.
6. It increases commitment, contribution and motivation of job holders.

But job redesign has the following limitations:

1. Job redesign has limited application, because usually only those jobs can be redesigned that have become too specialised, too simple and too boring for job holders.
2. In order to redesign a job, many administrative and organisational changes are to be made, such as the relationship between superior and subordinate is to be redefined and the degree of centralisation and decentralisation of authority is to be changed. These changes may further limit the usefulness of job redesign.
3. Redesigning of job may also strongly be resisted by the concerned employees. This is because it may call upon to develop new skills, expertise and additional responsibility without getting additional benefits.
4. Job enrichment and enlargement may also create conflicts between superiors and subordinates because of their changing roles, freedom and responsibility.

ROLE OF MANAGEMENT BY OBJECTIVES

The technique of MBO has a motivational aspect. It helps in motivating employees working in an organisation. Under this technique for setting targets or standards of performance for employees, the participative approach is followed. According to this approach, both superiors and subordinates jointly determine standards. Subordinates are helped by their superiors in determining a course of action to achieve their allotted targets. Sufficient freedom and independence is granted to them to solve work-related problems.

EMPLOYEES' PARTICIPATION IN MANAGEMENT

In the context of modern organisations, it is widely accepted that participation of workers in the management of an organisation leads to motivation, increased commitment and higher productivity. Though this concept has its origin in the behavioural approach of management, in the recent past due to social, cultural, economic and political changes around the world, this concept is gaining ground in almost every country. Generally speaking, the employees' participation in management implies the association or involvement of non-managerial employees in the process of management. There are authors who feel that employee participation is an important tool to solve labour management related problems. They consider it as a part of industrial democracy. Others believe that participation is confined to specific procedures such as consultative machinery in the organisation, negotiation and profit sharing by workers. Broadly, employees' participation in management is a process whereby those who work at lower levels and are particularly concerned with the implementation or execution are involved in the process of management (which includes planning, organising, staffing, directing and controlling).

The basic logic to seek participation of non-managerial employees is that if they are involved in the process of decision making, which is an integral part of the management process, they will offer more cooperation, contribution and commitment to implement those decisions. It is merely through participation that a sense is created among them that decisions are not imposed, rather they are also a part of such decisions. In other words, employee participation can be defined as a method or mechanism through which workers are allowed to express their views collectively on the functioning of the organisation. The following are some of the characteristics of employee participation in management:

1. Participation implies those methods and practices that increase the influence and say of non-managerial employees in decision making.
2. Participation can be offered to employees at several managerial levels of organisation.
3. Participation presupposes willingness among employees to accept responsibility.
4. The ultimate goal of employee participation is to make management as 'auto-management' by transferring managerial functions and more authority to employees.
5. It is a management initiated process to get the maximum cooperation and commitment of employees to achieve organisational goals.
6. Participation may be given by employees through various mechanisms and practices which seek the association of workers' representatives in decision-making bodies.

In this connection it is important to know on which matters employees should be allowed to participate and what should be the form of participation. There are certain matters or issues that are directly related to the interest of employees, for example, service conditions, physical working conditions, job design, work schedule, compensation system, incentives, safety, health, welfare schemes, fixation of standard performance and other related operational problems. This is considered desirable to associate employees while deciding over these matters. On the other hand, they may also be given participation on other important organisational matters that are of a general and common interest such as determination of organisational goals and other plans, structure of the organisation, employment policy, management system, etc. The basic reason for extending their participation to these matters is that they are part and parcel of organisation and they contribute to the accomplishment of organisational objectives. Thus, they must be well informed with regard to organisation functioning and its various aspects. This can possibly be done by associating them in the managing process.

So far as the forms of participation are concerned, they can be classified into the following four groups:

1. Informative Participation

Under this form, employees of the organisation share information on important matters which are directly or indirectly related to them. On the basis of such information they can get an idea of what is going on in the organisation. Information can be supplied to them on profit position, financial condition, production, sales growth and development, diversification and on other decisions taken by managers.

2. Consultative Participation

In this form of participation, employees are consulted on various issues that are directly related to them such as welfare measures, safety schemes, method of work, etc. Before making final decisions, employees or their representatives are given an opportunity to express their opinions and to give ideas and suggestions.

3. Associative Participation

Under this form, the role of employees in participation becomes more effective. They do not simply express their viewpoints as in the case of consultative participation. But the management comes under the moral obligation to accept their valuable suggestions, to accommodate their viewpoints and implement decisions taken jointly.

4. Decisive Participation

In this form, employees share decision making authority with managers. They are considered as part of managing and decision making process on related matters. Employees or their representatives may be associated with many decision-making committees at various levels such as at the plant level, departmental level and at the level of the board of directors. This leads to complete involvement of employees in management.

Importance of Employee Participation

It is being widely accepted that in spite of favourable market conditions, sophisticated technology, huge capital and a strong base of research and development, the importance of the human factor for the success of an organisation cannot be discounted. This is because a well-informed and committed work force is an asset of the organisation. Not only the success of an organisation, the pace of industrial development to a large extent is governed by industrial harmony and productivity of labour. In more detail, the importance of participation can be understood on the basis of the following factors:

1. Employee participation in management helps in reducing the psychological and social distance between managers and non-managerial employees. Non-managerial employees get an opportunity to interact fairly and frankly with senior managers. In this way, the management of the organisation becomes broad based because of the large number of employees participating in it.

2. It encourages industrial democracy which is a prerequisite for the industrial development of the country. Since the employees are also stakeholders in an organisation, therefore, they should have some say and influence in the process of decision-making at least on matters that are directly concerned with them.

3. Employee participation also improves industrial relations. This is because decisions are not imposed on them for implementation but they are involved in making them. Their views are heard, opinions are taken note of and suggestions accepted. By doing so, they are made co-owners of the organisation. A sense of belonging is created among them and they are firmly committed for the achievement of organisational goals.
4. Employee participation may foster a cooperative attitude among employees and managers. It may help in raising efficiency by improving teamwork and reducing inefficiency arising out of conflict and disputes.
5. Participation of employees may also help in satisfying various higher order needs of employees. In the process of participation, they share information with managers, interact with them, and exchange views.
6. In also enables employees to grow and develop their potential. This is because by participation they get more knowledge about the functioning of the organisation. They understand the problems faced by it and help managers to solve them. In this way, their knowledge and skills are bound to increase.
7. Employees working at operative levels may have new ideas and valuable suggestions because they are directly involved in implementing plans. Through the process of participation they can forward them to managers who can utilise such information at the time of making plans.

In the words of Dr. V. V. Giri: "Such an association of labour and management at all levels would lead to promotion of increased productivity for the general benefit of the enterprise, the employees and the community. Given employees better understanding of their role in the working of the industry and in the process of production, the satisfaction of the urge of self-impression, thus, would lead to industrial peace. Better relations and increased cooperation will enable employees to win confidence and cooperation of the employees."

Despite the benefits of participation of employees in management mentioned above, it could not succeed much because of the following limitations and problems:

1. Generally, it is found that employees or their representatives do not possess the required knowledge and skill to participate in management, specially at higher levels. Thus, to make it more effective, necessary education and training is to be provided to them.
2. The indifferent attitude of employees and managers towards each other creates another hurdle in the participation process. This is because conservative managers do not believe in reducing social distance with subordinates. They feel encroachment in their authority if they share it with subordinate employees.
3. Workers organise themselves into trade unions to protect and promote their common interests. They do not get much from these trade unions if they are involved in the process of participation in management. Such alienation of the workers from trade unions also limits their usefulness and effectiveness in participation.
4. Mere consultation with employees by the management will not create much enthusiasm among them unless they can influence the management in the formulation of policies on matters that directly affect them.
5. Multiple unions and inter-union rivalry also pose problems for employee participation. It is because of these factors that it becomes difficult to determine the real representatives of the employees who can act as their spokesmen in the various committees formed for the purpose of participation.
6. Lack of clarity of objectives of participation also creates hindrance in the process of participation. In the context of Indian industries, it has been found that both the parties do not have the required understanding of the objectives to be pursued through participation.

QUALITY CONTROL CIRCLES

The concept of quality circles was developed in Japan in early 1960 and widely used in the U.S.A. during the 1970s and early 1980s. Quality control circles commonly known as 'quality circle' is a group of five to ten employees formed on a voluntary basis to solve work-related problems from the same work area. These members meet regularly to discuss quality improvements and ways to reduce costs.

In other words, it is a small group of employees belonging to the same work unit that meets frequently with their supervisor who is known as the 'quality circle leader' to identify, discuss and solve work-related problems of their work unit. There may be a number of quality circles in an organisation depending on its size and nature of activities. Each circle may consist of a leader and up to 10 employees as members. The quality circle leader is supposed to be more knowledgeable because he has to lead the discussion and record the suggestions given by the members of the circle.

The members are also given an exposure to a new set of experiences regarding problems. It also offers an opportunity to them to think over the problem, express their opinions and offer suggestions to solve it. In order to coordinate the work being performed by various quality circles, a coordinator or facilitator is selected. Similarly, at the apex level, a steering committee is formed with a senior manager picked from various departments. The main function of this committee is to provide guidance to quality circles. It provides direction and formulates policies, programmes and procedures to be used by these circles. The committee also helps in implementing the suggestions of circles and rewarding excellence of work performed by the circles.

Generally, members of quality circles hold meetings with their leader once a week or month to discuss work-related problems such as breakdown of machinery, problems regarding raw material, safety measures, etc. In the first stage, a case study is prepared and methods for its prevention are tested. In the second phase, every member expresses his ideas and opinions on several aspects of the problem. In the third stage, relevant data are collected. The fourth stage is devoted to taking a final decision and making the necessary arrangements for its implementation.

Quality circles are considered as a means of motivating employees. These circles provide a chance to them to develop their potential and offer satisfaction to their higher order needs. They have the freedom of expression, authority over their work, involvement in discussing the problem and finding a solution. It is a participative process which improves the quality of the working life of employees. Quality circles cannot be formed in every organisation. But they lead to many benefits such as cost savings, improved worker-management relations, greater individual commitment and participative problem solving.

SUPPORTIVE SUPERVISION

Supportive supervision is one of the important means to improve interpersonal relations with workers. It also plays an important role in motivating employees. In the process of supervision, the supervisor or manager gives necessary orders and instructions to employees regarding work. He guides them, helps them and inspires them to work in conformity with the standards set for them and to comply with the rules and procedures of the organisation.

The supervisor may do it in different styles; he may be autocratic on his part doing every thing on his own and simply asking workers to follow his orders and instructions.

He may choose another style based on mutual help, cooperation, team spirit and a supportive attitude. In practice, it is found that the latter style which may be termed as 'supportive supervision' is more effective specially in motivating employees and getting the best out of them. In supportive supervision, the employees are given timely support and help in terms of proper guidance and directives to boost the confidence of employees to perform their job.

It also aims at reducing the social and psychological distance with the employees. This is done by making frequent interactions with them, understanding their problems and maintaining friendly and warm interpersonal relations with them.

FEATURES OF A SOUND MOTIVATION SYSTEM

On the basis of the discussion above on motivation, it can be safely inferred that the motivation system in the organisation should have the following features:

1. As far as possible, a positive and reward-based approach should be followed to motivate employees in an organisation. The 'stick' policy should be used to mould and reform the behavioural pattern of erring employees.
2. The carrot-and-stick approach should be followed in a balanced manner so as to motivate both efficient and inefficient employees.
3. Good performance should be rewarded adequately at the earliest and should also be given due publicity.
4. A constructive and objective system of performance appraisal and merit rating of the employees should be adopted with the aim to improve them and not to punish them.
5. While designing a motivational system, individual differences should be recognised and given due consideration.
6. Difficulties and grievances faced by employees should be handled promptly so that employees get the feeling that they will be heard and justice done to them.
7. The participative and consultative style of management and supportive supervision should be adopted.
8. Self-motivation of the top, middle and lower level managers is necessary to motivate employees working under their command.
9. Jobs should be redesigned and restructured as per the need of the situation and feasibility.
10. A clear-cut statement of objectives of the motivational system should be prepared. The need and importance of motivation should be identified clearly.
11. The motivational system should carry both monetary as well as non-monetary rewards aimed at satisfying the higher order needs of employees.

12. There must be a proper relationship between monetary reward and performance of employees. Monetary rewards should be adequate and preference should be given to lower level employees because they may be hard-pressed to satisfy their lower level needs.

WHAT INDICATES MOTIVATION AND DEMOTIVATION

An employee is considered motivated if:

1. He wants to come to work and works willingly.
2. When at work he gives his best.
3. He has a sense of belonging and pride in the organisation.

INDICATORS OF DEMOTIVATION

1. Increasing absenteeism among employees, excessive labour turnover.
2. Low output and productivity.
3. Increasing rate of accidents and wastage of raw material.
4. Rank indiscipline and insubordination.
5. Frustration and unrest in the work force.
6. Defiant and violent behaviour of workers.
7. Non-cooperation, strikes, gheraos, violent demonstrations, etc.

SUMMARY

Management is a result-oriented process. To get better results, employees are motivated to work efficiently. To motivate subordinates, managers need to understand what makes people to work, and how they can be inspired to work hard. Motivation is an inner psychological drive that compels people to work efficiently. It is a force that makes the people ready to move towards achievement of predetermined goals. Motivation has a direct relationship with the level of performance. If other conditions remain the same, highly motivated employees would produce more.

In traditional management, monetary incentives occupy central place while the human relations approach recognises the fulfilment of other higher order needs provides motivation. But modern views on motivation indicated that the motivation system consists of individual characteristics, job characteristics and characteristics of the work environment.

Motivation and morale are related to each other. Morale is defined as a state of mind and emotions, which affects the attitude of the person. High motivation contributes to high morale and more production. But high morale alone does not result in higher performance.

Motivation and job performance reinforce each other. Job satisfaction is defined as a psychological satisfaction that the employees gets by performing a job. Job satisfaction contributes high motivation and highly motivated employees derive more satisfaction by performing jobs. Therefore job content and job characteristics are considered a part of the motivation system.

Similarly, motivation is also related to the use of abilities by employees. In fact, high performance = Ability × Motivation. Ability refers to the physical, mental and intellectual qualities of a person that he uses to perform assigned jobs. The ability of a person can be realised fully by motivating him. It is found that highly capable and less capable persons are self-motivated. It is only a moderately capable person who requires motivation to work hard.

Motivation is directly related to human behaviour which is need-based. Expecting satisfaction is one of the needs that motivate a person to move towards specific goals. Many theories of motivation are based on the needs of the person such as the Maslow need hierarchy, Herzberg's two-factor theory, achievement motivation theory and ERG theory of Motivation.

Maslow studied and analysed human behaviour in terms of five needs that arise in a particular sequence. He concluded that it is unfulfilled needs that motivate a person. Herzberg discovered two sets of factors that are associated with satisfaction and dissatisfaction of the employee in a job. In the achievement theory, David and his associates classified human needs as the need of achievement, power and affiliation. To seek satisfaction of these he moves towards the achievement of his goal.

The expectancy theory of motivation recognises individual differences and further states that behaviour of an individual is influenced by his expectations. This is based on performance outcome expectancy, valence and effort performance expectancy.

The equity theory recognises the relationship between knowledge, skill and education (input) and reward and return (output) to motivate employees. In the case of any single employee if these two are not balanced as compared to others, he may feel demotivated.

The reinforcement theory is based on the law of effect that states that behaviour with positive consequences would be repeated. In other words, if some one does well and has been rewarded for it, he would repeat his performance. Therefore to encourage desirable behaviour one must be given positive consequences.

According to the carrot-and-stick policy, efficiency must be rewarded and inefficiency must be punished. If this is done, the efficiency of more efficient employees is bound to increase. It is based on commonsense, simple in assumptions and conservative in nature. In this policy rewards are made contingent upon performance and given to those who outperform on the job.

McGregor's Theory X and Theory Y is based on two sets of assumptions about human behaviour. Theory X states that employees are lazy, have limited needs, are self-centred, lack responsibility, need close supervision and deserve to be rewarded and punished according to the carrot-and-stick policy.

Theory Y states that they like work, take responsibility, are ambitious and have higher order needs. Therefore, non-monetary incentives should also be made part of the motivation system.

Rewards should be given to employees to motivate them. These rewards may be of two types—monetary rewards or incentives and non-monetary rewards. Monetary rewards are considered more powerful incentives which include wage and salary and other allowances such as D.A., bonus, medical benefits, etc. In developing countries, this has a special role. To get the desired results, it should be linked with performance, must be adequate and based on the principle of equity.

Non-monetary rewards are equally important to motivate employees. High order needs of employees are satisfied by these rewards. They may include job design, management by objective, employee participation in management, supporting supervision, quality circles, etc.

Job content is designed around employees to motivate them and provide more job satisfaction to them. This is done by enlarging and enriching existing jobs. A job is said to be enlarged if certain new operations are added to it on a horizontal level.

Similarly, it can be enriched by granting more autonomy, responsibility and authority to job holders in a vertical line. By doing so, jobs are made more interesting and meaningful.

In management by objective, subordinates are given a say while determining the standard of work for them. Superiors and subordinates jointly do this job and the superior keeps making periodical reviews of performance and provides all kinds of help to subordinates to meet the given targets.

In modern management it is widely accepted that employee participation in management has a definite motivational aspect. By associating non-managerial employees in the process of management, their full cooperation, commitment and contribution is sought. They feel part of plan making and decision making. They can be given participation by sharing information, by consulting them, associating them and sharing authority with them.

Supportive supervision is also considered one of the important ways of improving interpersonal relations and the level of motivation. In supportive supervision, the supervisor shares his experience with workers, listens to them, looks into their needs and gives them a helpful hand to perform their assigned jobs.

Quality control circles are also catching the attention of managers to motivate employees. In this approach, small teams of workers from the same workplace are formed to discuss and solve work-related problems by sharing the experiences of each other.

TEST QUESTIONS

1. Define 'motivation' and explain the motivation process.
2. Would you suggest the same method for motivating managers and non-managers? Give reasons for your answer.
3. Briefly explain the equity theory of motivation. What are its uses and shortcomings?
4. Why is it important to understand individual needs to motivate employees? Is it necessary that a quality satisfied person will have a high performance?
5. Compare morale and job satisfaction. Discuss the factors that contribute to these in an organisation.
6. What do you mean by 'employee participation in management'? Explain the merits associated with it.
7. 'Job enlargement and job enrichment are important means of motivating job holders to achieve higher productivity and derive job satisfaction'. Comment.
8. Discuss the various assumptions underlying Theory X and Theory Y that were developed by McGregor.
9. Describe the role and importance of reward and punishment in motivation.
10. Write short notes on
    (a) Job enrichment
    (b) Quality circles
    (c) Need hierarchy theory
    (d) Need for achievement
    (e) Two-factor theory of motivation
    (f) Achievement motivation theory

OBJECTIVE TYPE QUESTIONS

Which of the following statements are correct and which are incorrect? Give reasons to support your answers.

1. Intrinsic rewards are that which the individual gives himself.
2. Indirect punishment to one person teaches a lesson to another.
3. When management is consultative in nature, motivational devices are threats and punishment.
4. Self-actualisation needs are realised through self-development.
5. Under an unfreezing state of behavioural change, individuals experience a need to learn new behaviour.

6. Job enrichment is intended to make workers richer.
7. Douglas McGregor propounded the need hierarchy theory of motivation.
8. The manifest need theory also means that there is a hierarchy of needs.
9. According to Frederic Herzberg, job enrichment is a way of internalising motivators in the job itself.
10. Job enlargement makes the work cycle lengthier.

REFERENCES

Alderfer, C. *Existence, Relatedness and Growth: Human Needs in Organisational Setting*. New York, U.S.A.: Free Press, 1972.

Conner, P. F. 'Decision Making Participation Patterns: The Role of Organisational Context'. *Academy of Management Journal*. March, 1992.

Davis, Keith. *Human Behaviour at Work: Organisation Behaviour*. New York, U.S.A.: McGraw-Hill, 1981.

Drucker, P. F. *The Practice of Management*. New York, U.S.A.: Harper and Row, 1954.

Gellerman, W. *Motivation and Productivity*. New York, U. S. A.: American Management Association, 1963.

Gray, J. L. and Starke, F. A. *Organisational Behaviour*. Ohio, U.S.A.: Charles E. Merrill Coy, 1977.

Griffin, Ricky W. 'Effect of Work Redesign on Employees' Perception, Attitude and Behaviour: A Long Term Investigation'. *Academy of Management Journal*, June, 1991.

Hampton, D. R. *Contemporary Management*. New York, U.S.A.: McGraw-Hill, 1981.

Herzberg, Frederick; Mausner, Bernard and Bloch, Barbara. *The Motivation to Work*. New York, U.S.A.: Wiley, 1959.

Homans, G. C. *Social Behaviour in Elementary Form*. New York, U.S.A.: Harcourt Brace Jovanovich, 1961.

Karroll, S. J. and Tosi, H. L. *Management by Objectives: Application and Research*. New York, U.S.A.: McMillan, 1973.

Katergerg, R. and Blau, G. J. 'An Examination of Level and Direction of Efforts and Job Performance'. *Academy of Management Journal*, June, 1983.

Kreitner, Robert. *Management*. Delhi, India: A.I.T.B.S. Publishers and Distributors (Regd), 1996.

Latham, G. F. and Yukl, G. A. 'A Review of Research on the Application of Goal Setting in an Organisation'. *Academy of Management Journal,* December, 1975.

Locke, A. and Whiting, Roman, J. 'Source of Satisfaction and Dissatisfaction among Solid Waste Management Employees'. *Journal of Applied Psychology*. April, 1974.

Luthanas, Fred and Kreitner, Robert. *Organisational Behaviour Modification and Beyond: An Operant and Social Learning Approach.* Glenview, IL, U.S.A.: Scott Foresman and Coy, 1984.

Maslow, A. *Motivation and Personality.* New York, U.S.A.: Harper and Row, 1954.

Miller, Katherine I. and Monge, Peter, R. 'Participation, Satisfaction and Productivity: A Meta-analytic Review'. *Academy of Management Journal.* 29, December 1986.

Minter, J. B. *Theories of Organisational Behaviour.* Hinsdale, IL., U.S.A.: Dryden Press, 1980.

Moshal, B. S. *Management Theory and Practice.* New Delhi, India: Galgotia Publishing Company, 2001.

Ouchi, William. G. '*Theory Z: How American Business can Meet the Japanese Challenges.* Reading, Mass., U.S.A., Addison Wesley, 1981.

Popp, G. E., Davis, H. J. and Herbert, T. T. 'An International Study of Intrinsic Motivation Composition'. *Management International Review.* January, 1986.

Robbins, Stephen P. *Organisational Behaviour, Concepts, Controversies and Application.* New Delhi, India: Prentice-Hall of India Private Limited, 1997.

Rosen, C. M. and Quarrey, M. 'How Well is Employee Ownership Working'. *Harvard Business Review,* September–October, 1987.

Steers, R. M. and Porter, L.W. *Motivation and Work Behaviour.* New York, U.S.A.: McGraw-Hill, 1991.

Steers, Richard M. and Porter, W. Lyman. *Motivation and Work Behaviour.* New York, U.S.A.: McGraw-Hill, 1991.

Stoner, James A. F. and Freeman, Edward. *Management.* New Delhi, India: Prentice-Hall of India Private Limited, 1995.

Vroon, Victor, H. *Work and Motivation.* New York, U.S.A.: Wiley, 1964.

EXPERIENCE I

How to Enrich Jobs

Usually, job enrichment is undertaken at the management initiative, often with the assistance of behavioural scientists as consultants to analyse the content of the job and design a new job structure. The management's initiative is aroused by its perception of the workers' apathy and indifferent performance, high rate of absenteeism and other symptoms which indicate that workers do not like the jobs they are doing.

There is no one way of enriching a job. The technology and the circumstances dictate which techniques or combination of techniques

Experience I continued

Experience I continued

could be appropriate. According to Tripathi, some of the important techniques followed are:

1. Rotation of tasks, broadening of qualifications of skills and responsibilities, enhancement of the intrinsic interest of the job and removing or lessening supervision.
2. Increasing responsibilities of individuals for their own work.
3. Giving employees more scope to vary the methods, sequence and pace of their work.
4. Giving a person or a work group a complete natural unit of work, that is, reducing task specialisation.
5. Removing some control from above while ensuring that individuals or groups are clearly accountable for achieving targets and standards.
6. Allowing more say or influence in setting targets and standards of performance.
7. Giving employees the control information that they need to monitor their own performance.
8. Encouraging the participation of employees in planning work, innovating new techniques and reviewing results.
9. Introducing new and more difficult tasks not previously handled.
10. Assigning individuals or group specific projects that give them more responsibility and help them to increase their expertise.
11. Making crisis decisions in problem situations rather than relying on the boss.

As observed by Edwin B. Flippo, the most critical core dimension of job enrichment is that of job autonomy. It is certainly the critical difference between job enrichment and job enlargement. The autonomy is created through a process of 'vertical loading', that is, the worker is given self-management rights in multiple areas. In various programmes, such additional responsibilities include the setting of one's own work schedule and work break, in establishing work methods, making one's own quality checks, varying the work place, changing duties with others, setting priorities as to work performed, making crisis decisions in problem situations rather than relying on the boss and training less experienced workers.

Flippo outlines the theory of job enrichment in the model prepared by J. Richard Hackman and Greg R. Oldham. (Figure 12A.5)

Experience I continued

Experience I continued

Model of Job Enrichment		
Core job Dimensions Skill variety Task identity Task significance	Critical Psychological states Experienced meaning- fulness of work	Personal and work Outcomes High interest Work performance
Autonomy	Experienced Responsibility for outcomes of the work	High quality Work performance
Feedback	Knowledge of the actual work activities	High motivation with the work
	Employee growth needs strength	Low absenteeism and turnover

Figure 12A.5

EXPERIENCE II

Impact of Motives on Employee Behaviour

Motive	Meaning	Behaviour indicators of the motive
Achievement	A concern for excellence, a desire on the part of the person to do things to meet a particular standard of excellence	Persons dominated by this motive are generally active. They work hard, set high goals, take challenging tasks, derive pleasure from doing difficult things and look for quality. They may have a standard in mind with which they keep comparing themselves. They dream about accomplishing tasks.
Affiliation	A concern for establishing or maintaining warm and affectionate relations with others	Persons with dominance of this motive want to have close relationships with people and establish emotional relationships with others. They join groups, invite people, develop attachments, feel depressed when

Experience II continued

Experience II continued

Motive	Meaning	Behaviour indicators of the motive
		separated from dear ones. Club membership, frequent social parties and organised friendship circles are indicators of this
Power	A desire to influence others and gain control over others or to be superior to others	People with high levels of this need like to be in positions where they can lead, influence or control others. They seek opportunities for leadership. Argumentativeness, always wanting to be first, enjoying giving directions to others, etc., are indicators of this need
Extension	A desire to be helpful to others, or to provide one's services to the organisation, nation or any external agent	People dominated by this motive are good social workers. They enjoy helping others and they look for opportunities where they can be of help. They join social service organisations and probably maintain good interpersonal relations
Aggression	A need to dominate others and to demonstrate one's own strength, at times even physically	People having this need are argumentative, talk loudly, may get into physical fights and always want to win or show their strength
Dependence	A need to consult others before making any decision. This may arise out of feelings of insecurity	People dominated by this need will always look for direction from others, cannot take any independent decisions, want to be protected by someone, and lack initiative
Independence	Opposite of dependence, a desire to do things individually and to be one's own self	People dominated by this need like to make decisions on their own without seeking any one's approval. They

Experience II continued

Experience II continued

Motive	Meaning	Behaviour indicators of the motive
		prefer to have freedom and dislike interference from outsiders including superiors. They may consult others, but do not seek approval
Security	A need to be secure about one's own living and to be sure one continues to have it	People dominated by this need generally express it by their frustration at lack of job security, economic security, etc. This is a very important need and if many employees have this as a high need, the organisational policies may be worth looking at
Status	A desire to be respected and treated with deference especially by others in the social environment	People high on this need would not violate social norms or would do so only when they get recognition positively. They run for office, like to show their authoritarian tendencies when they work with others. They may be categorising people into status groups and interacting with them selectively and differently
Recognition	A need to be recognised for one's accomplishments	People with this need work hard to lose their motivation completely if their work is not recognised immediately. They try to make their presence felt and strive to get attention. This is another basic need in all of us
Activity	A desire to be constantly doing things	This kind of person is always active, a hard worker and is constantly engaged in some activity. The opposite of this is passivity, which is also a need to relax and not be disturbed

CASE STUDY I

Passion—The Missing Link

Sandeep's company Market Movers has people, projects and potential, but not passion. How can he inspire his people?

For over a year now, Sandeep, the CEO of the consulting firm, Market Movers (MM) had been trying to inculcate a deep involvement with customers as a way of life at MM. The involvement of the staff seemed to only skim the surface. Of course, the teams worked very diligently, but Sandeep always felt that there was something missing in their approach. He had tried many models and methods but after a grand start full of enthusiasm and effectiveness, somehow the momentum would be lost.

The incidents kept coming to his mind as if to remind him to find the elusive 'something'. What had triggered his thinking today was an angry exchange between him and Vinay Chabra the previous evening over what Sandeep felt was the inability to look beyond the nose. "A little loss of decorum is good," Sandeep had said later. "It allows you to go beyond the ordinary. And I don't want the ordinary! We are working with minds and the mind is such that it can create just as well as it can destroy as it can go into a state of inactivity. But because the mind controls when you are not in control, I admonish to demand commitment to their innate creativity. It's a reminder of what they truly are—passionate people who must control the mind's meanderings from the focus."

Sandeep was aware of the potential creativity of his team. But what nullified his efforts was the between ideas and execution. Whey they brainstormed, bright ideas emerged. But after that, there was a virtual paralysis: the ideas did not lead to performance. Rather the passion in the performance did not match the passion in the ideas, so there was a breach opening up between inspiration and motivation. At MM, there was no performance bonus. Sandeep's view was: "Perform we will; that's what we are here for. If I give you rewards for performing, you will only perform. But we will reward creative observation."

Sandeep did not believe in motivation. It led to performance—doing an act that had to be done—but not to creativity. This then was the substance of his appeal for passion. Motivation presumed the existence of knowledge that had to be turned into action, execution and application. So he said: "Knowledge + motivation = activity or event." But the event itself was a tried and tested one. Therefore, motivation was only a means to deliver the desired results. But the business they were in could not operate from known past outcomes any more. Today's business demanded all-new,

Case Study I continued

Case Study I continued

outstanding outcomes. That originality and uniqueness was possible only if there was passion to go beyond known 'knowledge' and trained abilities, what he called passion for creativity, not mere productivity. "Anyone can produce based on another's template and ideas. But to be the template generator, that's originality."

Keya said: "This radical approach is not conducive for our kind of timeframes!" Sandeep said: "In consulting, the cutting edge is innovation. The tried and tested consulting model of doing process reviews and model-building wither away because the faith in models is dying. Innovation can happen only if the people involved have a passion for it. The key differentiator between businesses that succeed and those that fall is passion. The moment there is a mismatch between personal passion and the product line, it fails to work."

Questions

1. Does motivation help in raising performance only, or does it also inspire creativity and innovativeness among employees?
2. Why is Sandeep's approach of motivation not suitable?
3. Does an organisation need a team of highly motivated employees to succeed? Give reasons.

CASE STUDY II

The Piano Builder

Mr. Waverly Bird builds pianos from scratch. His occupation is a piano consultant to a piano manufacturer. He is on call and works about one week a month, including some travel to solve problems of customers. He also rebuilds about a dozen grand pianos every year for special customers, but, according to Bird, the most satisfying part of his life is his hobby of building pianos from the beginning. "It's the part that keeps a man alive," he says. The challenge of the work is what lures Bird onwards. He derives satisfaction from precision and quality, and he comments, "Details make the difference. When you cut a little corner here and a little corner there, you've cut a big hole. A piano is like a human body; all the parts are important."

Bird has a substantial challenge in making a whole piano. His work requires skills in cabinet making, metalworking and engineering with knowledge of acoustics and a keen ear for music. It requires great precision, because a tiny misalignment would ruin a piano's tune. It also requires versatility, ranging from a keyboard that is balanced to respond

Case Study II continued

Case Study I continued

to the touch of a finger all the way to the pin block that must withstand up to 20 tons of pressure. Bird had to make many of his own piano construction tools.

Bird has built 40 pianos in his 34-year career. Though construction takes nearly a year, he sells the pianos at the modest price of a commercial piano. He is seeking not money but the challenge and satisfaction. He says: "The whole business is a series of closed doors. You learn one thing, and there's another closed door waiting to be opened." Bird says his big dream is to build a grand piano. "It's the one thing I haven't done yet and want to do."

Questions

1. Discuss the nature of Bird's motivation in building pianos. Discuss whether an organisation could build the same motivation in most of its employees.
2. Will Bird succeed in making a grand piano?
3. Explain this with the help of the achievement theory of motivation.

—oo(O)oo—

CHAPTER 13

LEADERSHIP IN AN ORGANISATION

LEARNING OBJECTIVES

1. To define leadership and analyse its main features.
2. To identify the position of a leader with the help of various functions performed by him.
3. To analyse the relationship between management and leadership.
4. To describe the Greatman theory and trait theory of leadership in the modern context.
5. To distinguish between employee-oriented and task-oriented behaviour of a leader.
6. To remember the leadership grid and the relevance of the five positions in it.
7. To identify and discuss Likert's management systems.
8. To bring out the main theories of leadership.
9. To suggest measures to develop leadership in an organisation.

LEADERSHIP DEFINED

Every manager is a leader because he has to mobilise the efforts of people in the direction of achieving common goals. By exercising leadership qualities and human skills he establishes cordial interpersonal relations with the individuals working under him. In every organisation, be it a social, educational, political or business organisation, the success or failure to a large extent depends on the quality of its leadership. Peter Drucker has rightly pointed out that managers or business leaders and the basic and quite scarce resources of any business enterprise and most of the failures of the business establishment have been attributed to ineffective leadership. This is merely because no organisation can function effectively without leadership and all organisational activities are directed at the behest of the leader for achieving objectives. It is the leader who creates enthusiasm among members and inspires them to move towards appointed destinations.

Terry has defined leadership as "the ability of influencing people to strive willingly for mutual objectives." More precisely in the context of business organisations, McFarland has defined leadership "as a process of interpersonal influence by which executive or manager influences the activities of others in choosing and attaining given goals."

Leadership may also be defined as the art of inducing subordinates to accomplish their assignments with zeal and confidence. It is a position of power occupied by the individual in a group whereby he exercises interpersonal influence on the members of the group to direct their activities towards the realisation of goals. His position in an informal organisation of power is backed by the acceptance of the members and his personality traits and qualities. But in a formal organisation it is backed by authority which is vested in his position. In both cases, he is at the centre of the group, keeps members of the group together, infuses life into it and activates it to achieve goals. Although the leader is a part of the group, he maintains his own identity to lead, to guide, conduct, direct and precede others.

Ralph M. Stogdill has defined managerial leadership "as a process of directing and influencing the task related activities of group members." This definition has been further analysed in the light of the following implications.

1. People

Leadership involves other people, that is, subordinates or followers who are willing to accept his direction. Group members give acceptance to the position of the leader and make the leadership process possible. Leadership without a group has little or no meaning.

2. Position

The position of the leader represents power which is backed by formal authority, his personality, traits and group acceptance.

3. Process

Leadership is the process of influencing the behaviour of group members; the leader influences the member to move in a given direction by making use of his power position.

According to Hersey Blanchard, leadership is a function of the leader, his followers and other situational variables. Among these, more importance is attached to situational variables because effectiveness of leadership may vary from situation to situation depending on the make up of the situation, its nature and intensity of factors involved in it.

On the basis of the above discussion on leadership, the following features may be derived.

1. Influence Process

Leadership is an influence process whereby the leader shapes, regulates, modifies, controls and directs the behaviour of the members in the direction of achieving predetermined objectives. The effectiveness of leadership largely depends on how much influence the leader can exercise on the followers or members of the group. Through the influence process, a sense of commitment, devotion and loyalty can be created among the members.

2. Presence of Followers

The existence of a leader is justified in terms of his followers, that is, the members of the group whose efforts are being directed by him. It is difficult to imagine leadership without followers. It is only over followers that a leader can assert his authority. Almost in every group of people there are some who are interested to be led and others interested in leading them.

3. Reciprocal Relationship

A reciprocal relationship exists between a leader and his followers. This relationship arises out of regular interaction between them. According to Mary Parker, reciprocal relationship between leaders and followers is one of the main characteristics of leadership. A leader is one who dominates over others and is also influenced by others.

4. Common Goal

The main responsibility of a leader is to lead, guide, inspire and motivate the members to make efforts to seek common goals. These common goals are expressed very clearly and explained to the members.

5. Leadership is Highly Situational

The effectiveness of leadership is, to a large extent, governed by situational variables. These variables include the whole work environment which consists of the nature of the job, interpersonal relations, group relations among the members and policies and procedures of the organisation. The leader performs various functions in a given situation and to be more effective he has to modify his approach and style of functioning as per the demand of the situation.

6. Leadership is Power Based

In every situation, the leader has a power which he exercises to influence the behaviour and performance of the members. There are mainly five bases of power enjoyed by the leader:

(i) Knowledge, experience, skill and competence of the leader.

(ii) Resources for rewarding, punishing and giving favours to members.

(iii) Charismatic qualities and traits which attract members towards him.

(iv) Formal authority that one gets by virtue of holding a position in the organisation.

(v) Personality traits such as the will to lead, resourcefulness, rapport with higher-ups, pleasing personality, etc.

7. Need Satisfaction of Members

One of the more important characteristics of leadership is that people tend to follow those who are capable of satisfying their personal needs, interests and goals. Generally, it is found that the more a manager understands what motivates his subordinates and how the motivation operates, the more effective as a leader he is likely to be. Thus, to be effective in a group every leader should develop that capability and competence which he may use to integrate personal goals of the members with common goals.

FUNCTIONS OF A LEADER

To understand the basic nature of leadership, which is considered a part of the directing function, one should look into the role played by the leader in a group. The role of a leader can be defined in terms of various functions performed by him. The leader performs these functions in every situation. He takes the initiative to form a group by bringing members together, infuses life into it and makes it operational to achieve common goals. He also establishes interpersonal relations with members, inspires them, guides them and helps them to march in the given direction. He takes care of the members by making adequate provision to satisfy their personal needs and interests so that they stay in the group for a long period. Broadly, it is a leader who makes a group move towards the achievement of objectives. He seeks better performance and maintains high morale among the members of the group led by him.

In this regard, Krech and Crutchfield have pointed out that all leaders must perform the following functions at least to some degree:

1. As an executive
2. As a planner
3. As a policy maker
4. As an expert
5. As a group representative
6. As an arbitrator
7. As a model of behaviour

Some other authors mention that the essential functions of a leader are to work towards unity and cohesiveness in the organisation and to see that the membership of the group is a pleasant and satisfying experience. According to Killian's study brought out by the American Management Association, the following are the five functions of leadership:

1. Leadership renders a service (by multiplying the contribution of every individual who is its beneficiary).
2. Leadership makes decisions (not a reckless shooting from the hip but a calculated searching and weighing of facts).
3. Leadership elicits a response (leading others to sufficient understanding to motivate the response necessary to accomplish the task at hand).
4. Leadership achieves results (by guiding human energy in a definite direction for a specific purpose).
5. Leadership is a willingness to be different (a discipline and standard of performance higher than that followed by a non-leader).

On the basis of the above regarding the role and functions of leadership, the more common functions may be enumerated as under:

1. Forming Group

The main task of a leader is to form a group and inspire people to become its member. He also determines common goals that are to be achieved by group efforts:

2. Motivating Members

The basic job of a leader is to inspire and motivate members of the group to achieve common goals.

3. Morale Boosting

By reshaping, modifying, regulating and controlling the behaviour of members, the leader boosts the morale of the members.

4. Support Function

By establishing friendly interpersonal relations with members, he helps them, guides them and activates them to perform better.

5. Satisfying Needs of Members

To maintain a group intact, the leader has to make adequate provisions to satisfy personal needs and aspirations of the members.

6. Accomplishing Common Goals

In fact, leaders to seek common goals. For this purpose, the leader has to exercise his influence over the members and motivate them to work in the direction of achieving common goals.

7. Representing Members

A leader is basically a representative of the members. He is supposed to protect and promote the interest of members against any outside challenge and threats.

8. Creating Confidence

The leader is also expected to build confidence among the members of the group. He does so by providing ready help, advice, guidance and support to them. He looks into their problems and difficulties and solves them.

9. Implementing Changes

The leadership process provides a proper mechanism for bringing about and implementing changes in the group. A leader uses his skill, innovativeness and creativity to discover changes and takes the members into confidence to implement them.

10. Resolving Conflicts

Leaders play an important role in resolving the conflict arising in the group by explaining common goals to the members and integrating them with individual goals of the members.

RELATIONSHIP BETWEEN MANAGEMENT AND LEADERSHIP

The manager gets things done by other people. Therefore, he will be more effective if he is also a leader. The terms 'management' and 'leadership' are very often used interchangeably. But these two are not the same concepts. It is understandable that a manager can do a reasonably good job of managing without being a leader.

The relationship between leadership and management can be understood on the basis of the following points. Similarly the concept of leadership may also be viewed differently from that of managing people.

1. Scope

The term 'management' is basically concerned with people, things and ideas. It involves the mobilisation and utilisation of both physical as well as human resources to achieve predetermined objectives. But the concept of leadership is mainly confined in the direction of human resources, that is, people or followers. And to direct their activities the leader has to create interpersonal relations with the followers. Thus, the concepts of leadership is highly related to management but it is certainly narrower than management.

2. Power Base

The position of the manager in an organisation is marked by formal authority which he derives from his position by virtue of occupying the position. By exercising his authority, he influences the working behaviour of subordinates and gets things done by them. But leadership is a position held by the leader of the group which is backed by acceptance, knowledge and charismatic personality of the leader. He derives power from these to influence followers.

3. Knowledge

To become an effective manager, one has to acquire knowledge of management through formal education and training. He uses this knowledge in a practical situation along with his other skills. Unfortunately in India, the base of theoretical knowledge is almost non-existent in the case of leadership. There are no institutes like that of management institutes imparting knowledge on the various aspects of leadership. Thus, one becomes a leader because he has a desire to do so and he is accepted to be so by the members.

4. Relationship

To get things done by others, managers place more emphasis on the formal authority of superior and subordinate. It is considered as the backbone of the organisation. However, leaders place more emphasis on personal and social relationship with followers. Members of the group follow the leader because they accept and respect him. Moreover, the leader has reciprocal relations with members which are based on mutual trust, satisfaction and support.

5. Mode of Selection

Managers are selected to fill positions which are identified in terms of authority, responsibility, functions and activities. They are selected in a highly rational, objective and formal manner. This is because the organisation has expectations from them to contribute as effectively as possible to achieve objectives. But leadership occurs in a situation in which the members of a group give their acceptance to a particular individual to act as a leader. Thus, leaders are generally elected by members in a highly subjective and informal manner.

6. Nature of Environment

Knowledge of management is applied on the work-setting and organisation. It is marked by predetermined policies, procedures, rules and methods which are to be followed by members of the organisation. However, the leadership situation is highly flexible, unstructured and not backed by predetermined procedures and rules. Although both management and the leadership situation have to operate in an uncertain environment, it seems to be more complex and dynamic in the case of leadership as compared to management.

7. Interdependence

More interestingly, these two concepts of management and leadership are highly related to each other, but are different from each other. Managers can manage without having the qualities of leadership, and leaders can lead others without being good managers. Contrary to this, to become more efficient, a manager has to have leadership qualities and similarly a leader can become more effective if he manages like a manager.

LEADERSHIP THEORIES

Like the study of management knowledge, the leadership concept has also been supported by various theories. These theories of leadership have been developed through several stages of evolution, ranging from the Greatman approach to the transformation theory of leadership, some of which are discussed below:

PERSONALITY THEORIES OF LEADERSHIP

Much has been said and written about leadership since ancient times when the main emphasis was placed on the personality of a leader. For many years, it was recognised that leadership is the ability of a person apart from his official position. Personality theories can be classified as 'the Greatman Theory' and the 'Trait Theory' of leadership.

Greatman Theory

This theory represents the initiation stages of evolution of leadership. During the initial stages, it was held that certain people were born to be leaders having inherited a set of characteristics from their ancestors. It was also believed that these characteristics cannot be acquired in any other way and are inborn in nature. According to this theory, leaders are born and not made and the various qualities which a leader is supposed to have cannot be cultivated or developed because they are present and carried in the genes. It was further supported by the fact that leadership emerged frequently within the same prominent families. Leaders such as Alexander the Great, Napoleon, George Washington, Mahatma Gandhi, Nelson Mandela and others were said to have been blessed with an inborn ability to lead the masses. These leaders in fact have created history with their charismatic and commanding personality. The courage, boldness, determination, sense of sacrifice and other qualities associated with the personality of a person cannot be formally taught. Rather, they must have been inherited from their ancestors. According to this theory, leaders are born in some prominent families, race, creed and religion. Advocates of this theory also forward the following arguments in favour of it.

1. They believe that leaders are God's gift to mankind and that they have come to earth to seek the welfare of mankind by using their gifted qualities.
2. Every one cannot become a great leader because these qualities of leadership cannot be acquired through formal education and training.
3. They strongly believe that it is only a personality and inborn qualities associated with it that go to make a great leader. Other elements of leadership like situational variables, needs of followers and environment do not have an impact on the leadership process.
4. The Greatman theory also assumes that the set of qualities that the leader uses to influence others are entirely his personal possession which he must have received from his family and cannot transfer to others.
5. It was also believed that it is only that set of qualities which a leader posseses that are necessary for effective leadership and not other qualities.

But the Greatman theory is subject to the following criticism:

1. This theory of leadership has no scientific basis and has not been supported by empirical studies. It was just a matter of chance that some people happened to be great leaders who belong to a particular family, caste or creed.
2. Further, this theory of leadership ignores the effect of situational variables like the need and aspiration of the followers, environment and other related factors.

3. Theorists did not forward any concrete proof that only a particular set of qualities make a person a leader.
4. The theory does not state why, how and when leadership occurs.
5. Advocates of this theory could make it clear that an inborn leader had such a set of qualities which perhaps cannot be learned by training and education.
6. While developing this concept, it was also not considered whether some class and caste barriers had prevented other people outside certain families from becoming leaders, as has happened in India.

The Greatman theory of leadership and its criticism paved the way for the development of another theory of leadership which is also based on personality and acquired traits. Therefore, this theory is known as the traits theory.

TRAITS THEORY OF LEADERSHIP

This theory advocates that leadership qualities and traits are not inborn but can be acquired by an individual through education, training and other forms of learning. Advocates of this theory of leadership are Tead, Schell and others. Tead holds that there are 10 less qualities that are essential for effective leadership, namely, physical and nervous energy, a sense of purpose and direction, enthusiasm, friendliness and affection, integrity, technical mastery, decisiveness, intelligence, teaching skill and faith. It was thought that a successful leader is one who has specific leadership traits that can be acquired. At the development of the traits theory, it was accepted that leadership traits are completely inborn, but can also be acquired through learning and experience.

> Showing an interest in the traits theory in the U.S.A., James M. Kouzes and Barry Z. Possner surveyed over 7,500 managers during 1980 to determine the traits that made them superior and effective leaders. In this connection, honesty was selected by 87 per cent of the respondents, outstanding competency by 74 per cent, forward looking by 67 per cent, inspiring by 61 per cent and intelligence by 46 per cent.

Similarly, in the words of Ralph Stogdill, the leader to be effective should have qualities like drive for responsibility, task orientation, vigour and persistence in pursuit of goals, venturesomeness, originality, problem-solving skills, drive to exercise initiative in a social situation, self-confidence, ability to influence other persons, etc.

But in all these cases, it has not been pointed out what are the essential qualities or traits of a leader and how he can prove to be an effective leader. It is criticised mainly on the following grounds:

1. Traits theory also lacks a scientific basis. It does not offer any explanation as to why leadership occurs.

2. It does not state which set of qualities are more important for a leader and which are least important.
3. It does not take into account situational variables, the needs of followers and the environment which determines the effectiveness of leadership.
4. The traits theory does not establish a relationship between a particular trait performance and effectiveness.
5. The traits theory has also failed to discover any trait which clearly and consistently distinguishes leaders from followers.
6. In practice, it is also possible that an individual becomes more assertive, self-confident and acquires other traits of leadership when he occupies a leadership position. So traits of leadership which have been identified earlier become the result or outcome rather than the cause of leadership.
7. The traits theory of relationship also suffers from a cultural bias. For example, tallness has been associated with American leaders. Does this mean that the height of a person also is a leadership trait?
8. It has also not been possible for advocates of the traits theory to isolate and identify those traits that are common to all leaders.

BEHAVIOURAL APPROACH TO LEADERSHIP

Since the personality theories of leadership mainly focused on the traits and qualities of leadership which are related to the personality of an individual, it could not discover and identify which set of traits and qualities are required to become an effective leader. Thus, researchers further tried to isolate the behavioural characteristics of effective leaders. In other words, instead of finding out what effective leaders were, researchers attempted to determine what effective leaders did, how they assigned tasks, how they communicated, how they motivated subordinates, how they carried out their job, etc. Unlike the traits and qualities of leadership, behaviour can be learned. So it followed that individuals trained in appropriate leadership behaviour would be able to lead more effectively. In this approach, the focus shifted from traits to the behaviour of the leader.

Intensive research studies in the behaviour of leaders in the U.S.A. at the Ohio State University and the University of Michigan revealed that there are two broad dimensions of leadership behaviour, namely, 'initiating structure' and 'consideration'. Initiating structure, which is also known as task-oriented behaviour, implies setting goals by the leaders, defining and organising the tasks to be performed by his followers, determining a working relationship and controlling their behaviour and performance.

In other words, a task-oriented leader closely supervises subordinates to ensure that the task is performed in a satisfactory manner. On the other hand, consideration, which is also known as 'employee-oriented' behaviour, refers to friendship, trust and support of the leader towards the members of the group. Such leaders believe in motivating subordinates rather than controlling them. They allow subordinates to participate in decision making that affects them.

Among the several theories of leadership, these two aspects of a leader's behaviour occupy an important place.

HIGH-INITIATING STRUCTURE OR TASK-ORIENTED OR JOB-ORIENTED LEADERSHIP BEHAVIOUR

Such a leader places too much important on organisational goals. He works whole-heartedly to achieve these goals and firmly believes that what is good for the organisation is always good for members. He exercises close supervision and control over the activities performed by them. He determines and assigns work to them and forces them to comply with set norms and standards. He does not allow his subordinates to use their judgement to perform assigned jobs. Such a leader focuses more on authority relationship of superior and subordinate.

He seeks a high degree of conformity on the part of subordinates for organisational rules and norms. He punishes the inefficiency of subordinates and does not allow any insubordination or indiscipline. He goes by the targets of high performance and productivity. He expects subordinates to sacrifice their personal goals to accomplish organisational goals. His style and approach of functioning is very similar to an autocratic leader.

HIGH CONSIDERATION OF EMPLOYEE-ORIENTED BEHAVIOUR

Employee-oriented leaders encourage subordinates to participate in goal-setting and other decisions. He helps, inspires, trusts and respects his subordinates by establishing and maintaining cordial and friendly interpersonal relations with them. On the basis of such relations, he seeks high performance. As against a task-oriented leader, he focuses more on the well-being and happiness of his subordinates. He allows them to express their opinions, listens to them and offers a helping hand to solve problems. He believes in granting more operational autonomy to subordinates and seeks their participation in decision making. Such a leader believes that what is good for the group is good for the entire organisation. He makes adequate provision to serve the personal interests of members by integrating them with the interest of the organisation.

To get maximum cooperation from subordinates, he attempts to promote their satisfaction. He is very liberal, humanistic and informal in his outlook. He is more like a democratic leader in his style and approach. It is also found that such leaders have a supportive leadership with subordinates. They depend on group rather than on individual decision making and regularly encourage subordinates to achieve high performance.

By making a matrix of these two distinct dimensions of leadership behaviour, the Ohio State researchers identified four styles of leadership (Figure 13.1).

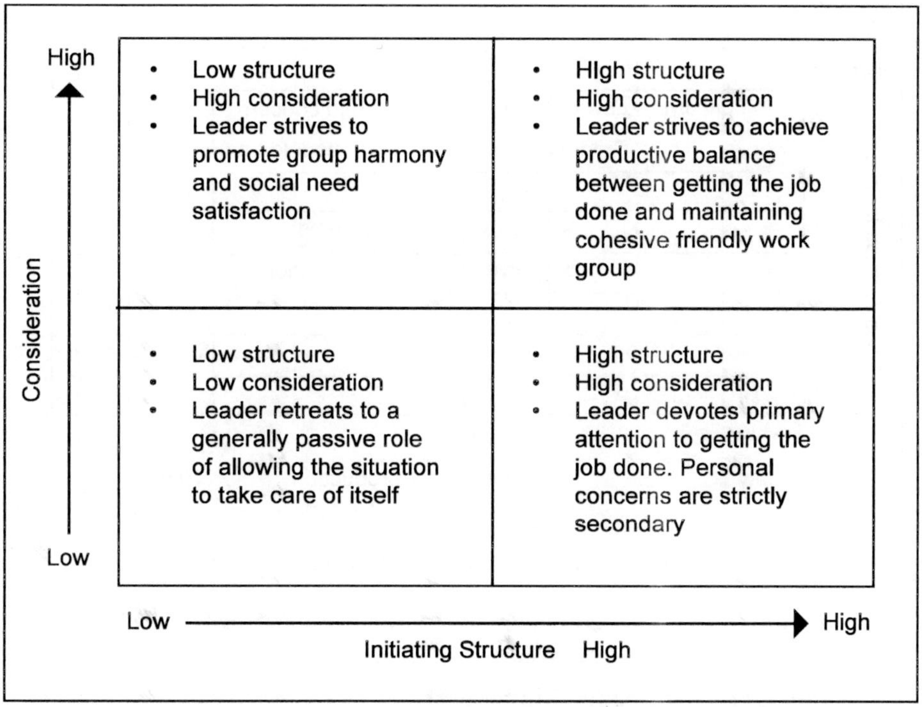

Figure 13.1. Basic leadership style from Ohio State University

Leadership theorists started a search for the most suitable style of leadership. The combination of high structure and high consideration style is generally considered as the best style of leadership. This is because it includes the best of both behavioural dimensions.

On the basis of conclusions from the Ohio State and Michigan University studies, the following theories have been developed:

1. MANAGEMENT GRID OF LEADERSHIP GRID

The conclusions of the studies mentioned above on the behavioural pattern of leaders make it clear that the leadership style is multidimensional. Both task-orientation and employee-orientation may be important for better performance. The management grid which has been developed by Robert Blake and Jane Mouton reflects the multidimensional nature of leadership. It helps in measuring the relative concerns of the manager for people and tasks. The management grid identifies various alternative combinations of both styles of 'concern for people' and 'concern for production'. These combinations are put in horizontal and vertical dimensions of the grid having a scale of 1 to 9 (Figure 13.2).

In this grid, concern for production has been shown on a horizontal axis and concern for people on a vertical axis

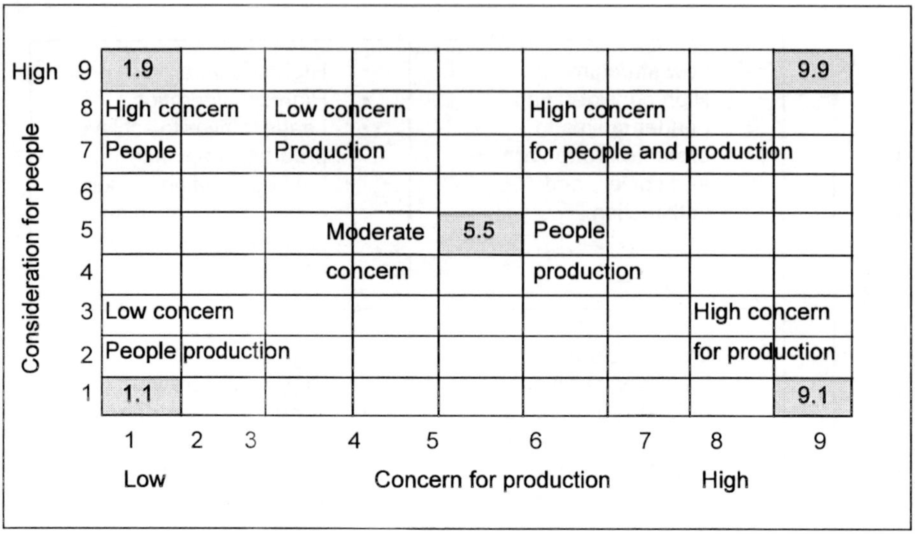

Figure 13.2. Management leadership grid

From the 81 possible combinations, they have identified five combinations (1,1), (1,9), (5,5), (9,1), (9,9) as shown in Figure 13.2.

1. Impoverished Leadership Style (1.1)

The first combination at the lower left hand corner of the grid represents impoverished management. This style refers to minimum concern on the part of the leader for both production as well as people. The role of a leader is passive and he allows the situation to take care of itself. This style is sometimes called 'laissez faire' management, because the leader abdicates his leadership role and leaves everything to the situation. He believes that use of minimum efforts is required to get work done and to sustain morale of the members.

2. Team Leadership (9.9) or Democratic Management

This refers to a high concern for production and people. It is considered as an effective management style. It is because this style of leadership may result in higher performance, low absenteeism, low turnover and higher satisfaction among employees.

Such leaders are successful in creating a highly encouraging organisational climate of commitment and cooperation. They also build interpersonal relations based on mutual trust and respect. In a recent study made by Blake and Mouton, experienced managers overwhelmingly preferred the 9,9 style regardless of the variation in the situations.

3. Middle of the Road Leadership (5.5)

This refers to a style that gives equal concern for production and people. Such leaders believe that an adequate level of organisational performance is possible to balancing the necessity to get the work done and by maintaining the morale of the people at a satisfactory level. It is a safe style seeking a balance between the requirements of production and the needs of the people.

4. Task Leadership (9.1)

This represents a high concern for production and a low concern for people. The leader places more emphasis on production, targets and productivity. Other factors like people's needs and satisfaction become secondary for him. The leader seeks a high degree of authority compliance. He arranges conditions of work in such a way that the human element has the least interference in a work situation. This style is similar to authoritative management with a high concern for production and efficiency but a low concern for people and their needs.

5. Country Club Leadership (1.9)

This refers to a low concern for production but a high concern for people. This style is the antithesis of task leadership. Such leaders believe in creating a friendly interpersonal relation with people at work. They create enthusiasm among followers and motivate them to work efficiently. Thoughtful attention to the needs of people and adequate concern to satisfy them may lead to a comfortable and friendly organisational atmosphere and work tempo.

Such leaders give little importance to production targets and other matters like work requirements. They are overly human-relations oriented with a primary concern for people and their needs and satisfaction.

2. LIKERT'S MANAGEMENT SYSTEMS

Rensis Likert and his associates at the University of Michigan, U.S.A., conducted studies on the various patterns and styles of leadership and management followed by managers. On the basis of their conclusions, they developed some concepts and approaches which seem to be important to understand the behaviour of leaders. Likert developed four models of management known as 'systems of management'. These were developed on the basis of seven important variables closely related to and involved in the management process. These variables are leadership, motivation, communication, interaction, influence, decision making, goal setting and control. According to Likert, most managers adopt one or the other system of management developed by him to get things done by others. These systems are:

System 1: Exploitative or Authoritative

Under this system, a manager is high autocratic while dealing with subordinates. Organisational goals, performance inputs and standards and means of achieving them are determined by the manager on his own. He issues orders and instructions to subordinates regarding the job to be performed and seeks total compliance. He takes decisions unilaterally and does not seek the participation of his subordinates. Communication is formal in nature down the line of authority, full of directives and orders. Managers maintain unfriendly relations with subordinates which are marked by distrust and ill-will. He exercises close and rigid supervision and control which involves the use of threats and punishment.

System 2: Benevolent Authoritative

In this system, the manager deviates a little from the first one. Although he is autocratic in his approach but not exploitative, a little improvement in the relationship with subordinates is made. The relationship is made more likely as between a master and servant. He adopts a patronising and paternalistic approach towards subordinates. He also allows some degree of freedom to subordinates to perform the job within prescribed limits. The authority for setting goals and making decisions is centralised at the top of the organisation and subordinates are supposed to implement them faithfully. To motivate subordinates, the carrot-and-stick policy is followed and efficient employees are rewarded and the inefficient punished. Communication is again one way down the line of authority. The organisational climate is marked with suspicion and fear. Close supervision and control is exercised to regulate the working behaviour of subordinates.

System 3: Consultative

In this system, goal-setting and decision making is consultative, because subordinates are allowed to express their opinions and give suggestions. Authority is delegated only to decide routine matters. Communication is maintained between the superior and his subordinates from both sides. To motivate subordinates, more emphasis is placed on the 'carrot policy' rather than the 'stick policy'. The control system tends to become a little flexible and goal-oriented. Interpersonal relations between a superior and his subordinates are marked by mutual trust and confidence. On the whole, this system of management to some extent recognises the importantce of the human factor involved in the functioning of the organisation.

System 4: Participative-Democratic

In this system, the management approach of getting things done by others becomes humanistic in nature. Managers maintain cordial and friendly relations with subordinates. They actively participate in the process of goal setting and decision making. The manager adopts supportive supervision and the leadership style to help and guide subordinates in respect of job performance. The structure of the organisation is marked by a high degree of decentralisation of authority, greater and wider participation of lower level mangers in decision making and open and effective channels of communication. The control system is relaxed and changed into self-regulatory control. Subordinates are motivated to assume responsibility to achieve organisational goals and a higher level of performance. This helps in satisfying the need for self-achievement and fulfilment.

After having analysed their four systems of management in terms of productivity, absenteeism and turnover, quality control, resource wastage and scrap losses, Likert concluded that system 1 scores very poorly. And system 4 is an ideal one which the organisation should adopt. He regarded it as one of the best ways to develop and utilise the human aspect of organisation. He suggested leadership training at all levels of management so as to make managers move to system 4. He found that participative and democratic leadership develops supportive relations among subordinates which ultimately leads to higher productivity and greater satisfaction to them.

SITUATIONAL/CONTINGENCY APPROACH TO LEADERSHIP

Both personality and behavioural theorists of leadership have completely ignored the effect of situational variables in the process of leadership. Personality theorists believed that one can become a successful leader if he possesses some traits and qualities. Similarly, behaviourists assumed that a leader becomes effective and successful if he behaves in a particular manner. But with the passage of time, many researches conducted on leadership revealed that apart from leadership traits and behaviour, the effectiveness of it, to a large extent, depends on situational variables.

Although a number of situational theories of leadership have been developed so far, they share one fundamental assumption that successful leadership occurs when the leader's style matches the situation. They emphasise the need for greater flexibility in leadership and reject the notion of a universally applicable style. The situational factors or variables which dominate effectiveness of leadership may be described as under:

1. Leadership Factors

Leadership factors mainly include all those that are related to the personality of the leader, his orientation and skills that he uses to influence others.

2. Group Factors

They include all those factors and forces that operate in a group and affect the leadership process. For example, interaction and relations among group members, attitude of the members towards the leader, task and organisational goals, size of the group, group norms, values and goals, group structure and processes, etc.

3. Other Factors

In addition, there are a number of other factors that also have a significant effect on leadership from outside such as authority structure of an organisation, organisational plans, values and goals, motivation, communication and control system of the organisation and other economic, political, socio-cultural, legal and technological factors. Various situational theories of leadership are discussed below:

LEADERSHIP CONTINUUM

Though this theory of leadership was developed in 1958 by Robert Tannenbaum and Warren Schmidt, its more refined version came into being in 1973. In this theory they have described various leadership styles and placed leadership behaviour on a continuum having two extremes and many styles between them. At one end of the continuum behaviour of the leader is authoritative which is marked by exercise of power and influence over subordinates. At the other end, the authority, power and influence structure moves towards subordinates and get a lot of freedom and participation in management (Figure 13.3).

Tannenbaum and Schmidt strongly believed that situational variables play an important role in determining the effectiveness and appropriateness of leadership style in various situations. Thus, in the light of situational variables they have identified seven styles of leadership which seem appropriate in different situations. They also advocated that there cannot be one best style of leadership which is effective and appropriate in all situations. Therefore, a leader must be sensitive enough to choose and modify his style as per the need of the situation. He must take into account his strengths and weaknesses and match them with the situational variable so as to select the style.

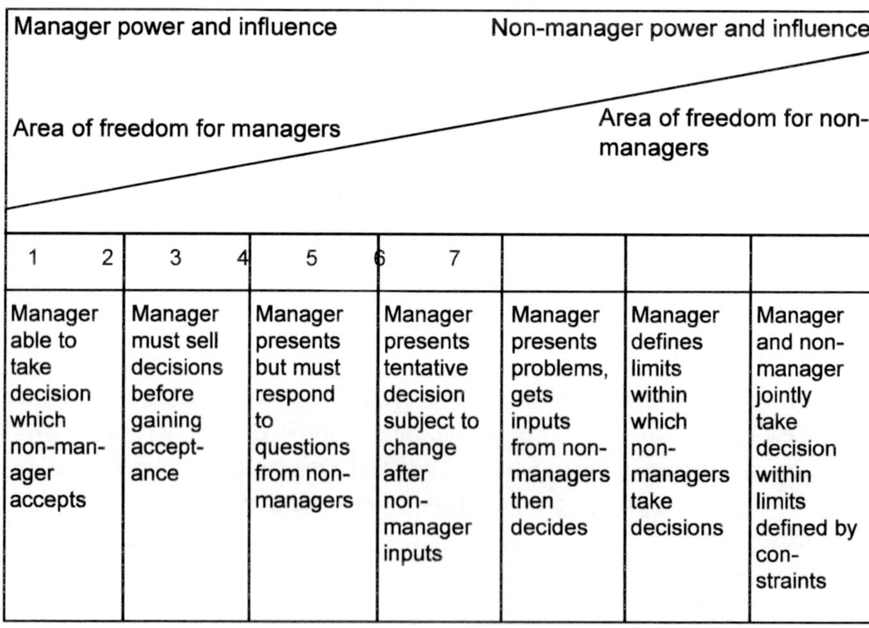

Figure 13.3. Continuum behaviour of leadership

CONTINGENCY THEORY

The contingency approach of leadership states that the management and leadership style that best contributes to the achievement of organisational goals might vary in different types of situations or circumstances. Fred Fiedler developed the theory of leadership after having conducted extensive research on leadership for 30 years. This theory is known as the contingency theory of leadership based on the following assumptions. The performance of a leader depends on two inter-related factors (Figure 13.3).

(1) The degree to which a situation gives a leader control and influence, that is, the likelihood that the leader can successfully accomplish the job, and

(2) The leader's basic motivation, that is, whether a leader's self-esteem depends primarily on accomplishing the task or having close supporting relations with others.

Fiedler identified three leadership situations which help to determine which leader's style will be effective. They are:

(1) Leader-member structure;

(2) Task structure; and

(3) Leader's position of power.

Leader-member relations has a significant influence on the manager's authority and effectiveness. If he gets along well with group members and they also respect him for his personality and character then the manager may not have to rely on formal authority and position. But if he is disliked and distrusted by group members, he may not be able to lead them. He has to rely on his authority to get assigned jobs performed.

In a structured task, for which prescribed procedures and instructions are available, members of the group have a clear idea of what they are expected to do and managers in such a situation enjoy high power. In unstructured tasks like committee meetings and group meetings, the power of the manager is reduced because group members can more easily disagree with his instructions.

The power held by a manager may be great or small depending on a specific position. For example, the position of president carries a great deal of power while as chairman of a fund-raising drive he has little power over the activities of volunteers.

More interestingly, Fiedler pointed out that effectiveness of leadership depends on the interaction between leadership qualities and the type of situation. He firmly believed that instead of switching from one style to another, unfavourable situations can be made more comfortable and favourable by restricting and redefining the task and by strengthening the leader's position of power.

PATH GOAL THEORY

Like other contingency theories of leadership, path goal theory also helps in understanding and determining the effectiveness of leadership in different situations. This theory has been developed by Martin G. Evans and Robert J. House. It is derived from the expectancy theory of motivation and based on the assumption that the effective leader can increase a subordinate's motivation by

(a) Clarifying the subordinate's perception about the goals of work;

(b) Explaining how goals and desired rewards can be achieved; and

(c) Linking meaningful rewards with goal attainment.

In other words, the leader should motivate his followers by providing clear-cut goals and meaningful incentives to achieve them. The path goal theory advocates that motivation is an essence of effective leadership. Although there are a number of ways to influence subordinates, according to Evans, the most important is the ability of the manager to provide rewards and to specify what subordinates must do to earn them.

Thus, managers determine the availability of rewards or incentives and the path that will earn them. For example, employee-centred managers will offer not only pay and promotion but also provide security, encouragement and respect.

They will also take into account individual differences to determine rewards for them. But task-oriented managers will offer a less individualised set of rewards and will relate subordinates' performance to reward in a better way.

Path goal theorists have also identified two sets of variables which help in determining an effective leadership style, namely, personal characteristics of subordinates and environmental pressures and demand. Advocates of the path goal theory believe that managers need to rely contingently on the following leadership styles:

1. Directive Style

In this style, the manager tells his subordinates what is expected of them and sets goals and task responsibility for them. He provides specific guidance, schedules, rules, regulations and standards and monitors their performance regularly.

2. Supportive Style

According to this style, the leader treats his subordinates as equals in a friendly manner. He establishes friendly interpersonal relations with them, shares their feelings and viewpoints and attempts to improve their well-being.

3. Participative Style

Such a leader seeks the participation of his subordinates. He consults them to get their suggestions and considers them seriously at the time of making decisions. He also keeps them informed on various task and goal situations.

4. Achievement-Oriented Style

The leader sets challenging goals. He places emphasis on developing skill, talent and excellence among his subordinates and seeks continuous improvements. He makes their job more interesting and meaningful and finally provides enough freedom to them. He carries a high degree of confidence that subordinates will meet difficult challenges in a responsible manner.

LEADERSHIP STYLES

In order to lead the efforts of group managers, the leader has to communicate, interact and guide them. He becomes a role model for the followers and adopts a particular type of behaviour pattern. In general, his style of leadership exhibits his pattern of behaviour that he follows in a given situation. The style of a leader to a large extent is a result of his personality and experience, situational variables and type of followers to be led by him. It is found in practice that most people want to be led and not to lead. An exception to this, in rare circumstances, people prefer to lead rather than be led. Such a factor will greatly contribute to the style of the leader. Some of the well-established styles of leadership are described below:

1. Autocratic leadership
2. Participative leadership
3. Free rein leadership.

Autocratic or Authoritarian Leader

Autocratic leaders assume full responsibility and authority to lead members of the group towards the accomplishment of common goals. They give orders and seek full compliance of them by members. They believe in the philosophy that whatever the members are told, they must do it. Thus, autocratic leaders take decisions and ask members to just implement them. Such leaders expect that members should follow given orders and instructions blindly and show full loyalty to the leader.

This style of leadership is marked by a high degree of centralisation of authority and close supervision and control. Members are not given any say in decision making. Rather their role is confined to implementation. Autocratic leaders believe in one way communication and that too from the higher level to the lower level.

Such leaders assign well-defined tasks to members and seek performance without any deviation. Under a highly autocratic leadership style, members remain uninformed, feel insecure and do not get any opportunity to develop.

Autocratic leaders can make prompt decisions, provide unified direction control and maintain order and discipline among members. But this style of leadership can be criticised on the following grounds:

(1) It does not encourage the development of initiative among members, rather it kills it.

(2) Due to negative motivation such as punishment and use of coercive measures, stress and fear is created among members.

(3) Such leaders adopt exploitative tactics to influence the behaviour of members.

(4) Unilateral decision making on the part of the leader comes in the way of securing full cooperation from members.

Democratic or Participative Leader

A democratic leader delegates greater amount of authority to his followers. He seeks their participation in decision making. While leading and guiding group activities he goes by the consent of members and makes little use of his authority. Such kind of leadership style is marked by decentralisation of authority, participating decision making and two-way communication between the leader and members. By involving members in decision-making, he seeks their maximum cooperation to implement decisions. Such leaders follow democratic principles of majority rule in deciding matters. Democratic leaders provide opportunities to members to express their opinions and give suggestions. They enjoy the confidence and loyalty of group members. Such type of leadership is considered a key to productive and happy employees. This is because leaders listen to members, look into their problems and share experiences with them. Such type of leadership is considered more effective due to the following reasons:

(1) Resistance to change among members is reduced.

(2) It increases the level of motivation among members and encourages a favourable attitude.

(3) The relationship between employer and employees is improved.

(4) It provides an opportunity to develop.

(5) It enhances the level of cooperation and commitment among members.

But this style of leadership is criticised for the following reasons:

(1) It ignores the aspect of productivity and emphasises more involvement and participation of members in decision-making.

(2) It is more time-consuming, because the members take their own time to express their viewpoint and give suggestions.

(3) Many members do not want to lead.

Free Rein Leader (Laissez Faire)

Such a leader assigns responsibility and delegates authority to members being represented by him. The members are told to decide things themselves and do their best. Free rein leaders leave everything to the members believing that they are fully competent and capable of doing everything. He preaches self-discipline and self-regulatory control to them. He simply coordinates the functioning of group members and that too on the basis of his personal influence. In other words, such a leader abdicates his position of leader by making the members of the group fully responsible to achieve group goals.

Such a style of leadership is almost contrary to the autocratic style. This is because a free rein leader allows his followers to determine goals and find suitable means to achieve them. It is marked by a high degree of decentralisation of authority and horizontal communication among fellow members.

Such leaders permit members to begin work on their own at a time they think is good and do not interfere in their working. It may be considered as a part of 'auto management'. Without exercising formal authority and control over the activities of group members they direct them.

However, in a modern organisational setting, such type of leadership may not contribute effectively because of the following reasons:

(1) Such a leadership style may yield desired results only in those situations in which members are competent and fully conscious of their responsibility.

(2) Under such a leadership style, the leader does not contribute much because he transfers his role to the group members who manage the group activities collectively.

(3) In the absence of the leader's role, the performance level of the members is also bound to be affected adversely.

Table 13.1 reveals the path goal theory that allows a leader to change his style as per the demand of the situation. It indicates that the directive style of leadership will provide more satisfaction to subordinates and meet their expectations if they perform ambiguous tasks. This is because in such situations they need directives, rules, procedures and standards to perform the job. But if the job is of a routine type and repetitive in nature they hardly require directives and even if they are given it will lead to dissatisfaction.

TABLE 13.1: EFFECTIVENESS OF VARIOUS STYLES OF LEADERSHIP ON CONTINGENCY RELATIONSHIP IN PATH GOAL LEADERSHIP MODEL

Leadership styles	Effect in various situations
1. Directive	1. Positively affects satisfaction and expectancies of subordinates working on ambiguous tasks Negatively affects satisfaction and expectations of subordinates working on clearly defined tasks
2. Supportive	2. Positively affects satisfaction of subordinates working on dissatisfying, stressful or frustrating tasks
3. Participative	3. Positively affects satisfaction of subordinates who are involved in non-repetitive tasks
4. Achievement-oriented	4. Positively affects confidence that effort will lead to effective performance of subordinates working on ambiguous and non-repetitive tasks

Similarly, if subordinates are working in a stressful and frustrating situation they need the support of the leader and thus, the supportive style will contribute to more satisfaction for subordinates. The participative style seems to be effective and promotes satisfaction if adopted with respect to non-repetitive tasks involving the ego of subordinates. This is because by giving them participation in decision-making their egos will be satisfied. The achievement-oriented style seems to be more appropriate in a work-setting that consists of ambiguous and non-repetitive tasks because it may create a challenging situation for subordinates.

HOW TO DEVELOP LEADERSHIP

The discussion above on the various theories of leadership indicates that to manage effectively, managers should possess the qualities of leadership. Many organisations owe their success to dynamic and effective leadership. The leadership qualities of managers would help in discharging their responsibility and achieving the organisational goals successfully. These qualities of leadership can be developed among managers and they can be made more effective and efficient in their functioning. But in spite of the growing importance of leadership in the managing process, till today a formal way of developing leadership qualities has not emerged. It is only through rigorous training and other kinds of measures used by individual organisations that some leadership traits can be cultivated in the personality of the manager. To develop leadership, the following guidelines may be adopted:

(1) Training and Development

Training programmes may be conducted by the organisation on a regular basis to achieve various objectives. Such programmes aim at making the necessary changes in the working behaviour of the employees. In a similar way, specific training programmes may be formulated and implemented in the organisation to develop leadership qualities. Through these programmes, a target group of managers is trained and encouraged to acquire certain traits and abilities in leadership.

(2) Organisational Culture

The internal environment of an organisation may also help managers to get exposed to a variety of situations and to tackle them efficiently. It may also lead to development of some required skills on their part which makes them good leaders. To provide such exposure, groups of subordinates may be created and committes formed. Through interaction among them, the target manager may be acquainted with various group dynamics such as group problem solving, decision making, group leadership, group unity, cohesiveness, etc.

(3) Coaching and Guidance

Managers who are interested in cultivating leadership qualities in their personality may also be given required coaching and guidance. This may be provided by some senior managers or consultants from outside the organisation. The mentor or coach must identify potential areas of leadership which can be developed in a particular individual. The grooming of leaders is done by the coach as per the requirement of the organisation and personality of the prospective leader.

(4) Outside Exposure

Leadership does not occur alone in a business organisation. It may be developed among managers by providing them an opportunity to work in the community, clubs and other informal groups. This is because the prospective leader learns qualities of leadership by doing things on his own. Thus, the social environment outside the organisation may also be considered as an important device to groom leaders,

(5) Job Design and Rotation

Learning occurs both on and off the job. On the job learning may also help individual managers to develop them into good leaders. For this purpose, due care is taken to design the job to be assigned to prospective leaders. By adding a variety of operations to a managerial job, it may be made useful to develop leadership. Similarly, prospective leaders may be asked to perform various types of jobs through job rotation. In doing so, they may get exposed to several dynamics of job-performance.

(6) Interaction with Superiors and Subordinates

Leadership also needs the application of behavioural skills. This is because the leader has to develop cordial interpersonal relations with his followers. To develop such qualities he may be given an opportunity to interact both with superiors as well as subordinates. By doing so, he may learn how to tackle subordinates and how to deal with superiors. For proper interaction, he needs or may be forced to develop communication ability, sense of empathy, understanding about members' needs, problems and their attitudes.

WHAT MAKES LEADERSHIP EFFECTIVE

The concept of leadership assumes an important role in management. This is because to get better results, increased efficiency and more cooperation from subordinates, the manager has to be effective and successful. The qualities of leadership would definitely help to discharge his responsibility of getting things done by others efficiently. Moreover, success and failure of the organisation to some extent depends on the effectiveness of the leadership on the part of its managers.

It is only through dynamic and effective leadership can one take the entire organisation to great heights. We have many examples of Indian industry in which the leadership qualities of the owner-manager could help them build big industrial empires. In view of its growing importance in the field of organisation and management, a lot of research work has been done. Many theories and approaches have been developed ranging from the personality theory to transformational or charismatic leadership. But different approaches to leadership have generated controversy regarding what makes a leader effective.

Advocates of the personality theory strongly believe that it is a set of inborn as well as acquired qualities and traits that must be possessed by a leader to become an effective one. But this version of leadership effectiveness seems to be inadequate because it does not take into account other factors that are involved in the process of leadership and may help in determining its effectiveness.

In this connection, the contributions of behavioural theorists hold good. They have strongly argued that instead of concentrating on traits and qualities of a leader, equal attention should be given to how they behave. This is because the pattern of behaviour may help in determining the effectiveness of leadership. For a number of years, researchers and managers hailed democratic leadership as a key to productivity and satisfaction of employees.. But at a later stage, experience has shown that the democratic style of leadership does not always produce a better performance because some employees prefer to be told what to do rather than participate in decision-making.

Therefore, on the basis of conclusions drawn from various studies conducted at the Ohio State University and Michigan University in the U.S.A., two important dimensions which determine the effectiveness of leadership were developed, namely, employee-oriented and work-oriented dimensions. After having considered that no single best style of leadership exists, management scientists developed new thinking which is known as the situational or contingency approach of leadership. This is based on the assumption that successful and effective leadership occurs when the style of the leader matches the situation and its variables.

In the recent past, there has been the development of the concept of transformational or charismatic leadership which envisages that leaders have a major impact on the functioning of an organisation through their personal vision and energy, and the ability to inspire workers. Thus, apart from traits, behaviour and situations, the charismatic qualities of a leader should also be taken into account to determine the effectiveness of the leader. This combines both the behavioural style and situational approaches and seems to be more appropriate when the situation is rapidly changing.

Today, many business organisations deploy 'self-managed work groups' having responsibility for the whole task, methods of work schedules, assignment of tasks among members, feedback about performance, etc. From such a work setting, a new leadership style known as 'self-leadership' has emerged. This refers to the ability of workers to motivate themselves to perform both kinds of tasks that are appealing and rewarding to them and those that do not appeal but are necessary to perform. This approach advocates that an individual's attitude and value system should be given due weightage, while getting their involvement to achieve organisational goals. In brief, effective leadership depends on an integrated approach formulated on the basis of the following elements:

(1) Personality traits and qualities to be possessed by the leader.

(2) Leadership style based on his behaviour.

(3) Situational variables.

(4) Charismatic qualities and energy of the leader.

(5) Basic philosophy of management and self-leadership.

SUMMARY

Managing is a result-oriented process. To get better results the manager should be a good leader. It is only by exercising the qualities of leadership can he get things done by subordinates as efficiently as possible.

Leadership may be defined as a process of influencing others in the direction of achieving goals. This involves the people who are influenced. The use of position of power may be formal or sanctioned by the people. It determines the process which the leader uses to influence the direct workers towards given goals.

The leader maintains reciprocal relation with his followers and leads their activities towards the achievement of common goals. This is highly functional and power based.

Although leadership is a part of direction function, the role of leaders depends more on the functions performed by them. He forms groups, infuses life into it and makes it operational to achieve common goals. He maintains interpersonal relations with followers, guides and motivates their working behaviour and makes adequate efforts to satisfy their needs to win their confidence.

Leadership and managing seems to be related with each other but these two can be distinguished in terms of scope, nature of power, knowledge, relationship, mode of selection, nature of environment in which managers work and interdependence of these two.

Being an important part of management, a lot of research work has been done to develop various theories of leadership. The first set of theories based on personality may be grouped into two, the Greatman theory and Traits theory.

According to the Greatman theory, leaders are born. They are great leaders because they inherit qualities of leadership in their personality from their ancestors. The traits theory of leadership states that the qualities of leadership can be acquired by individuals through education, training and other forms of learning. The personality theories were found inadequate and failed to isolate those qualities that are essential to become a good leader.

In view of this the behavioural approach to leadership was developed which mainly focuses on the pattern of behaviour of the leader. It consists of task-oriented and people-oriented patterns of leadership behaviour. On the basis of the behavioural pattern, several combinations of these two were developed by Robert Blake and

Mountion which is known as the Leadership Grid. In this grid, there are 81 possible combinations out of which they have identified five which include impoverished leadership, team leadership, middle-of-the-road leadership, task leadership and country club leadership.

Similarly, Renis Likert and his associates conducted several studies on the various styles and patterns of behaviour followed by managers. They developed four main systems of management followed by managers to get things done by others. These are Exploitative, Benevolent, Authoritative, Consultative and participative and democratic. Analysis of these four management systems reveals that the fourth one was considered ideal in terms of productivity, absenteeism and turnover of subordinates.

The above-mentioned two sets of leadership theories have ignored the effect of situational variables in the process of leadership. A third set was developed which is known as the situational or contingency approach of leadership. It states that apart from leadership traits and patterns of behaviour, the effectiveness of leadership largely depends on situational variables including leadership, group and a set of other factors. This approach includes leadership continuum, contingency theory and path goal theory.

According to the continuum theory on the basis of the use of power and influence by the leader, many alternative combinations may be developed between two extremes—maximum use of power and maximum freedom granted to subordinates or followers.

The contingency theory states that management and leadership styles which contribute the maximum to achieve goals may vary from situation to situation. It established relationships among style or pattern, goals and situation.

The path goal theory states than an effective leader can enhance the level of motivation of followers through goals to be achieved by them. He improves the perception of subordinates about the goals explained to them and establishes a link between goal achievement and suitable rewards.

Developing leadership is a difficult task. It includes the grooming of prospective managers as effective leaders. This is done by inculcating possible qualities of leadership among them. Leadership can be developed through training and development, by providing a suitable organisational culture, coaching and guidance, outside exposure, job design and interaction with superiors and subordinates.

Organisations owe their success to dynamic and effective leadership on the part of management. An effective leader makes the difference in the level of performance and the efficiency of subordinates. To be more effective, a leader has to adopt an integrated approach formulated on the basis of personality traits, pattern of behaviour, situational variables, basic philosophy of management and both internal as well as external environments. Many modern organisations use self-managed work groups which may give rise to the concept of self-leadership.

TEST QUESTIONS

1. Define leadership and explain its importance in management.
2. Describe the various functions of a leader.
3. Leadership is an influence process. Comment.
4. Explain the Greatman theory of leadership.
5. Discuss the relationship of management with leadership.
6. Discuss the Likert systems 1 to 4 approach to leadership. Which of these systems is considered the most effective and why?
7. What makes leadership effective? Discuss.
8. Explain the qualities of a good leader.
9. Effective leadership is that which goes well with a given situation. Comment.
10. Leadership abilities of the manager are not totally inborn, they can be acquired or learnt also. Comment.
11. A good leader is one who understands his subordinates, their need and their source of satisfaction.
12. Write short notes on
    (a) Leadership continuum
    (b) Path goal theory of leadership
    (c) Grid (managerial grid)
    (d) Situation leadership.

OBJECTIVE TYPE QUESTIONS

Which of the following statements are correct and which are incorrect? Give reasons in support of your answers.

1. Management styles are the same as leadership styles.
2. The path goal theory of leadership suggests that an effective leader provides subordinates with a path to a valued goal.
3. Initiating structure is the same as 'employee-centred leader behaviour'.
4. Manager-leaders who are autocratic in their behaviour are invariably able to build high morale among employees.
5. A leader who shows high consideration brings higher satisfaction to group members but low productivity in a group.
6. Leaders are born not made.
7. A democratic leader leaves nothing to chance.

8. Middle-of-the-road leadership maintains a balance between the requirements of the people and production.
9. Likert's system 4 approach ignores situational factors and their influence on the effectiveness of leadership.
10. Achievement-orientation leadership aims at developing and utilising the skill and talent of group members.
11. A leader's effectiveness is contingent on his abilities to follow the dynamics of a situation and the attitude of people in a correct perspective.
12. Leadership is nothing but to exercise influence over followers.

REFERENCES

Bass, Bernard M. *Bass and Stogdill's Handbook of Leadership*. Riverside, N.J., U.S.A.: Free Press, 1990.

Cummings, Thomas. 'Self-regulated Work Groups: A Socio-technical Synthesis'. *Academy of Management Review*, 3, 1978.

Desslre, Gary. *Organisation and Management: A Contingency Approach*. Englewood Cliffs, N.J., U.S.A.: Prentice-Hall Inc., 1976.

Farris, George F. and Lim, Francis G. 'Effect of Performance on Leadership, Cohesiveness, Satisfaction and Subsequent Performance'. *Journal of Applied Psychology,* 53, December 1969.

Fiedler, Fred E. *A Theory of Leadership Effectiveness*. New York, U.S.A.: McGraw-Hill, 1967.

Ghiselli, Edwin E. *Exploration in Managerial Talent*. Palisades, Calif., U.S.A.: Goodyear, 1971.

Gray, Jerry L. and Stards, Frederick A. *Organisational Behaviour*. London, U.K.: Charles Merrill Publishing Company, 1980.

Hersey, Paul and Blanchard, Kenneth H. *Management and Organisational Behaviour: Utilising Human Resources*. Englewood Cliffs, N.J., U.S.A.: Prentice Hall, 1977.

Karmel, B. 'Leadership: A Challenge to Traditional Research Methods and Assumption'. *Academy of Management Review*, July, 1978.

Katz, Theodore and Herbert. *Dimensions of Organisational Behaviour*. Macmillan Publishing Company, 1981.

Kenny, David A. and Zaccaro, Stephen J. 'An Estimate of Variation due to Trait in Leadership'. *Journal of Applied Psychology*. November, 1983.

Koazes, J. M. and Posner, B. Z. 'Credibility: How Leaders Gain and Lose it and why People Demand it'. San Francisco, U.S.A.: Jossey Bass, 1993.

Koontz, Harold and Wihrich, Heinz. *Essentials of Management*. New Delhi, India: Tata

McGraw-Hill Publishing Company Limited, 1998.

Kreitner, Robert. *Management.* Delhi, India: A.I.T.B.S. Publishers and Distributors (Regd), 1996.

Manz, Charles C. 'Self-leadership: Towards an Expanded Theory of Self-influence Processes in Organisation'. *Academy of Management Review*, 11, 1986.

Mitchell, Terence R. 'Motivation and Participation: An Integration'. *Academy of Management Journal,* 1973.

Moorhead and Griffin. *Organisational Behaviour: Managing People and Organisation.* Delhi, India: A.I.T.B.S. Publishers and Distributors, 1999.

Peters, Thomas J. and Waterman, Robert H. Jr. *In Search of Excellence.* New York, U.S.A.: Harper and Row, 1982.

Ross, Murray G. and Hendry, Charles E. *New Understanding of Leadership.* New York, U.S.A.: Association Press, 1957.

Selznick, C. F. Philip. *The Organisational Weapon.* New York, U.S.A.: McGraw-Hill, 1952.

Stoner, James A. F. and Freeman, Edward R. *Management.* New Delhi, India: Prentice Hall of India Private Limited, 1995.

Tannenbaum, Robert and Schmidt, Warren H. 'How to Choose Leadership Pattern'. *Harvard Business Review.* April, 1984.

Vroom, Victor, H. *Leadership: Handbook of Industrial and Organisational Psychology.* New York, U.S.A.: Wiley, 1983.

William, J. Clifton. *Human Behaviour in Organisation.* Cincinnati, U.S.A.: South Western Publishing Company, 1978.

Wofford, J. C. and Liska, Laurie Z. 'Path Goal Theories of Leadership: A Meta-analysis'. *Journal of Management*, vol. 19, 1993.

Yuki, Gary A. *Leadership in Organisation.* Englewood Cliffs, N. J., U.S.A.: Prentice Hall, 1994.

EXPERIENCE I

Leadership: At the Level of Organisation and Individual—Building Global Leaders in India

Over the last decade, a few Indian companies have been quite successful at delivering consistently superior business performance. Companies such as ICICI, Ranbaxy, Dr. Reddy's Labs, Infosys, Reliance and Wipro have not just become leaders in their respective industries but have also earned the respect of the global community.

Experience I continued

Experience continued

However, Indian companies have not yet emerged as true global leaders. There are still no Hondas, Nestles and Sonys in India. Even the best Indian companies still have some way to go before they can be counted among global leaders.

What differentiates global leaders from successful Indian companies is their larger size (in terms of market capitalisation, revenues and global presence), their ability to deliver consistently superior returns to global shareholders over long periods of time, their ability to grow despite economic cycles, and a well-established global brand. As great Indian companies think about sustaining their growth rates, going global has not become critical and imperative. There are three reasons for this belief.

Firstly, India constitutes a very small proportion of the global market. The big opportunity for growth lies in markets outside India. The U.S.A. constitutes around 26 per cent of the world's gross domestic product. Europe accounts for another 30 per cent.

Being able to carve out even a small piece of this large market can deliver enormous returns as companies like Ranbaxy and Infosys have demonstrated. Also, for companies that have achieved leadership in the Indian market, opportunities to grow further will diminish and they will have to expand into new geographies if they are to continue to grow at explosive rates.

Secondly, if these companies want to compete with the current global leaders, they need to start globalising now. High-performing Indian companies are more profitable and have better cash flow than players in other markets. It makes sense for them to expand in today's soft economic environment which has made assets cheaper. Wipro seems to be following this route and has snapped up AMS Utility Consultancy and the Nerve Wire financial services consultancy in the last few months.

And finally, there is no escaping global competition. In the integrating global economy, as barriers to trade are systematically dismantled, local players will face fierce competition from global leaders. For example, Citigroup will probably be among the leading financial institutions in each important market. The only way to survive and succeed today is to be globally competitive.

Becoming a global leader is a long and arduous journey. McKinsey's research on globalisations shows that organisations have achieved global leadership only after striving to do so for eight to 15 years.

Experience I continued

Experience continued

HSBC, until the late 1980s, was primarily a Hong Kong-based bank with revenues of approximately $ 5 billion. Today, it is the world's third-largest financial services institution by market cap with revenues of $ 28 billion. It took HSBC a decade to grow and expand to reach the position it is in now. Similarly, Samsung, the leading electronics company, took eight years to reach the top.

The exception to this rule is demonstrated by only a handful of companies, the notable examples being SAP, Dell and Nokia. These are essentially innovation-driven companies which significantly changed the nature of their industry and the basis of competition.

Companies wanting to become global leaders need to expand their capabilities in multiple areas to achieve such a leadership position. Obviously, they need to get their strategy right, and undertake smart moves in terms of selecting the right markets, customer segments and building distinctive value propositions. What is not so obvious is the need to build a global executive cadre, sustained financial commitment and an organisational design that balances a global coordination with local independence.

The value of a cadre of global leaders that can manage global businesses cannot be over-emphasised. HSBC, for example, has a handpicked group of global executives who have been sufficiently trained to successfully lead HSBC country operations in many different types of countries. Global executives are paid globally competitive salaries. Indian companies will have to pay their global executives at those rates as well.

In addition, Indian companies need to realise that this path requires significant commitment in terms of both human as well as financial capital. They will need to make large financial investments and sustain these investments over a long period of time. These financial risks will have to be carefully managed.

Finally, it should be recognised that commitment to excellence does not end even when the company has achieved global leadership. Global leadership is not a destination, it is a journey. Indian companies must start on their journey to global leadership now. It is a long and difficult path but there simply is no choice.

Relationship Management

A few years back, the media was full of headlines relating to the 'talent market' and the changing nature of work. The 'battle for talent'

Experience I continued

Experience I continued

has been a rallying call for many companies as they have watched, or been involved with the dot-com phenomenon that proved a challenge to attracting talent—if you were not able to offer shares and the chance to become a millionaire through an IPO then you were not a company worth considering. And job seekers were drawn by the pull of working in a 'cool' company where their demands were taken seriously. So what are the lessons to be learned from the dot-com era? Mainly that people with talent have greater expectations than ever before. And due to the practical reality of the demographics, the talent pool is not expanding in line with the demand. In many countries where competition is fierce, companies have been taking wider regional and global approaches to their recruitment strategies to try and win the talent they need. The most critical challenge, however, is keeping the talent you already have.

ENTREPRENEURSHIP AND THE NEW LEADER

The key to talent acquisition and retention is leadership—these leaders being men and women who can create the right environment in which people are encouraged to perform well and enjoy what they do. The hallmark of a talented leader is someone with genuine passion, a desire to make an impact, an understanding of when to lead and when to step back and empower a team to deliver. True leaders are easily approachable. They have mastered the art of relationship. They understand the power of networks. It goes without saying that companies which recognise leaders who understand the difference between management and leadership—and that people are their best with strong leadership—already have a head start. Another vital asset in the 'leadership profile' is diversity. Companies have awakened to the need for diversity in their leadership whether diversity of age, gender or ethnicity. Real talent knows no age barriers and so career development opportunities and progression must be based not on tenure but on capability—"If I am good and I demonstrate that I can deliver, I want it now!" A corollary to the above suggests that the right environment is non-bureaucratic, supports risk takers, provides constant intellectual challenges, is fun and fast. Entrepreneurial environments give individuals the chance to get involved in many aspects of the business. In today's world, slow is riskier than wrong—great leaders turn mistakes into opportunities.

Finally, while good leadership and the right environment are fundamental, so are 'the basics'—setting realistic expectations, giving timely feedback, having meaningful career discussions, delivering against the promises of learning opportunities and new experiences. A little real attention may mean more than a hundred hours of process. The basics are about helping talented individuals to set their goals and develop, to

Experience I continued

Experience I continued

enable them to build their network, to connect with others, to learn, to coach and to stretch themselves at the same time.

MAKING WORK/LIFE CHOICES EASY

Having identified certain criteria for the new, enlightened leadership, how do these qualities impact on a company's day-to-day operations? First of all, the traditional 9–5 Monday to Friday work week is rarely applicable any more: technology and globalisation have changed us into a 365/24/7 world in which people can be accessible anywhere, anytime. This requires re-assessing the changes in our working lives and adopting new approaches, not by gimmicks and trendy offerings, but by the fundamental realisation that human beings have expectations and desires both from their work and their private lives—not one at the expense of the other, not one to the exclusion of the other.

Leaders who understand the work/life balance argument need to move beyond an intellectual grasp or paying lip service to the issue. They need to understand what it really means. Most importantly, they need to lead by example. The issue is not about dividing time between work and private life; it is more about empowering people to choose between what really needs to be created and the ability for individuals to navigate around the conflicting priorities and demands on their time.

It is about being flexible with one's own life, thereby giving others flexibility with theirs. What this means for sensitive leaders and their teams is that it's all right to put a personal priority above work. Again, the issue is about changing the relationship, changing the climate, creating a different, looser, more flexible alliance, one based on trust. Young people today watch their parents struggling with the work/life balance and are determined not to travel the same route. This does not mean they do not want to work hard. On the contrary, they welcome a challenge. But they want to be in the driver's seat as to when and how they work. If they are allowed to choose how to spend their time, and if they have clear objectives as to what they need to deliver, and by when, then it is best to just let them get on with it. The company's responsibility is to help them by supporting them, by using technology to provide flexibility; by making moves within the company easier; culturally by leadership actions, setting objectives and providing the freedom to deliver against those objectives. The older worker is another issue that many companies are overlooking; how to use the older worker who still has much to give, who wants more personal time but who also wants to continue to be involved and stimulated? Creating the environment in this knowledge economy for these seasoned

Experience I continued

Experience I continued

and experienced workers to coach and mentor younger colleagues can bring many benefits.

People Relationship Management

All of these concerns have resulted in what is hinted at in the title of this article: namely the shift from human resources management as we know it to the more inclusive mission of people relationship management (PRM). The CEO can set the strategic vision of a company, but it is the leaders in that company who deliver the vision, who create the culture for attracting and retaining talent. The PRM community has the chance to drive the changes needed. How? By communicating both internally and externally. By being a conduit to the market place. People Relationship Managers need to work hand-in-hand with the teams responsible for brand management, for getting the messages right. They help the company's leadership to understand new trends and how to take advantage of them. And, most importantly, they need to break down preconceived ideas, old ways and open up management's mind to what it really takes to retain talent. This requires strong leadership development programmes; a culture will not tolerate bad people management; as strategy that will dismiss managers who have delivered their numbers but have not delivered on their people promise. If we agree that the environment in which we operate as employers has changed dramatically, can we say the same about human nature? The war being waged for talent is happening. The demographic changes, they're happening, too. But are we suffering from a lack of leadership to meet these issues head on? Are we burdened with managers so driven by the bottom line that they have become emotionally disabled and fail to understand the link between talent retention and that very bottom line retention that drives them? The battle, if not the entire war, will ultimately be won by those leaders who wake up to the personal impact they have on the people they were hired to lead.

CASE STUDY I

Mr. Soni had recently joined as the managing director of a car manufacturing company which at present is incurring heavy losses. Mr. Soni has been entrusted with the formidable task of rejuvenating the company. He faces many challenges to achieve this task, such as controlling costs and expenses, increasing the productivity and boosting the morale of the employees so that they unhesitatingly cooperate to achieve the set standards of output.

Case Study I continued

Case Study I continued

Mr. Soni, in his previous company, also a car manufacturing company, as the deputy managing director have proved to be a proficient manager and a talented leader who had successfully inspired his employees to increase productivity. He was commended for this maximum concern by both the workers and production and also for bringing an integration and harmony between the needs of employees and of their production.

In the new company also, Mr. Soni continued his policies of participative management and his high concern for production and people. To revive the company back to health, he effected some major changes. First of all, he decentralised the organisation so that subordinates could exercise their discretion and initiative in decision-making and their imagination and creativity in performing other managerial functions. Furthermore, he empowered junior managers to sanction expenditure up to an approved limit without seeking prior approval of higher management. The communication system was also improved to facilitate free flow of upward and downward communication.

Mr. Soni also adopted several measures to cut costs and wasteful expenditure. He banned donations to charitable institutions but increased the amount being spent on the welfare activities of employees.

Will Mr. Soni's leadership style prove effective in ensuring a bright future of the company? Some employees are of the view that things are being done but they might not be effective in the long run. Others disagreed with them and said: "O.K., we'll give it a try."

Questions

Read and analyse the above case and answer the following questions.

1. Is Mr Soni a Theory X or a Theory Y manager? Give reasons for your answer. Will you advise Mr. Soni to change his presumptions about the nature of the people at work? Give reasons.
2. In terms of the 'management grid' developed by Blake and Mouton, how would you describe Mr. Soni's leadership style? Is it the best style in the managerial grid? Give reasons.

—oo(O)oo—

CHAPTER 14

COMMUNICATION NETWORK IN AN ORGANISATION

LEARNING OBJECTIVES

1. To study the meaning, concept and features of communication.
2. To discuss various elements involved in the communication process and give suitable examples.
3. To describe the role of communication and job performance.
4. To analyse the role of communication and job performance.
5. To identify and learn the main features of upward, downward and horizontal communication.
6. To analyse the importance of informal communication or grapevine with suitable examples.
7. To learn about communication barriers and suggest ways to overcome them.
8. To bring out the main features of oral and written communications.

Communication is considered a part of the directing function of management. But the performance of all other functions of management also requires communication. Without a proper network of communication, neither directing function can become operative nor other functions of management can be performed successfully. It is in this light that communication may be regarded as a 'link function' of management just like decision making.

MEANING AND CHARACTERISTICS

Generally communication means an exchange of ideas, facts, opinions, information and understanding between two or more persons. In the context of an organisation, it may be defined as the transmission and receipt of information on various organisational matters either between two employees of an organisation or between two or more work units or departments. It may also occur between an organisation and outside parties dealing with the organisation. The word 'communication' is derived from the Latin word 'communis' which means common. "When you communicate," says Wilbur Schramm, "we are trying to establish a commonness with someone," that is, we are trying to share information, an idea or an attitude.

According to the Oxford English Dictionary 'communication' means "the imparting, conveying or exchange of ideas, knowledge, etc., whether by speech, writing or signs." In the words of Keith Davis, "Communication is a process of passing information and understanding from one person to another," the act of communication thus includes transmitting and receiving information from one person to another to create mutual understanding. Louse A. Allen defined it thus: "Communication is a sum of all the things one person does when he wants to create understanding in the mind of another. It is a bridge of meaning. It involves a systematic and continuous process of telling, listening and understanding." In the words of McFarland, "Communication may be broadly defined as the process of meaningful interaction among human beings. More specifically, it is a process by which meanings are perceived and understanding is reached among human beings."

On the basis of the above definitions of communication, the following characteristics may be derived:

(1) Communication is a social process because it involves two or more persons and they exchange ideas, information and knowledge.

(2) It is a two-way process in which a sender sends information to the receiver who receives it, understands it and starts acting upon it and gives a feedback to the sender.

(3) Communication is an all pervasive function, because information, knowledge, facts and opinions are exchanged between two or more employees at every level of the organisation as well as between organisations and outside parties.

(4) It is a continuous and ongoing process because every superior has to be in regular touch with his subordinates to know about the progress of work in conformity with standards.

(5) The communication process aims at creating understanding or commonness or unity of mind on a particular matter between the sender and receiver of information.

(6) Communication is a multidimensional and multidirectional process because it may be formal or informal or it may be upward, downward and horizontal. It may also take place between two employees of the organisation or between an organisation and outsiders dealing with the organisation.

COMMUNICATION PROCESS

Communication is regarded as a system that consists of many interrelated and interdependent elements. John Kotter has defined communication as "a process consisting of a sender transmitting message through media to a receiver who responds." This indicates that there are three essential elements of communication and if one of them is missing no communication can take place. By analysing the communication process, one discovers that it is a whole system made up of various identifiable elements including sender, encoding, medium, decoding, receiver and feedback (Figure 14.1). These may also be considered as sub-processes of communication:

Figure 14.1. Figure showing communication process

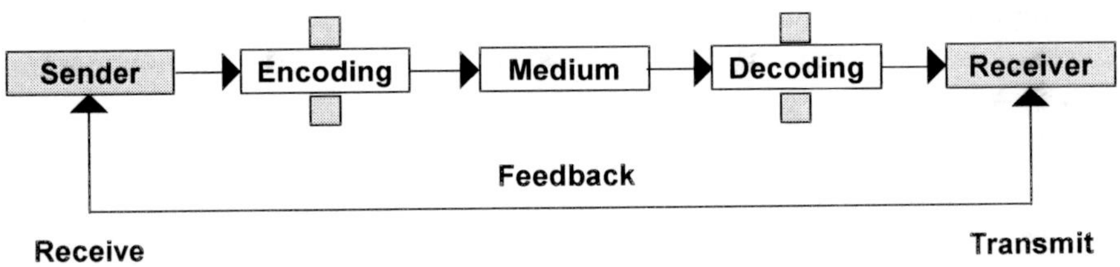

Figure 14.2. Communication process

1. Sender (source)

The sender of a message is at the starting point of the communication system. It is he who initiates the communication. The sender is a person who is willing to communicate. He has a need to do so, or he is under an obligation to pass information to another. For example, the deputy production manager wants to inform the production manager regarding the progress of work or the production manager gives orders and instructions to the deputy production manager.

2. Encoding

The purpose of encoding is to translate an internal thought of the sender into a language or code so that the receiver of the message will probably understand it. Through the process of encoding, the sender attempts to establish 'mutuality' of meaning of the message with the receiver by choosing a symbol, usually in the form of words and gestures that the sender believes to have the same meaning for the receiver. The choice of a symbol or gesture to a large extent depends on the nature of the message being communicated and the purpose of the communication.

3. Message

This is the physical form into which the sender encodes information. It can be in any form which may be understood by the receiver. For example, written words may be read, and gestures may be seen. The message may be regarded as the subject matter of the communication. It is usually made in the form of verbal or non-verbal language. In practice, non-verbal messages are regarded more important because they are often more effective or meaningful than oral or written messages.

4. Channel (medium)

The channel is the method or path in which the message is transmitted from one person to another. The sender may have a variety of channels available to him such as face-to-face conversation, telephone calls, letters, bulletins and publications of the organisation. Each channel has its own advantages and disadvantages. It should, however, be noted that the efficiency and effectiveness of a communication to a large extent depends on the appropriateness of the channel selected for communicating the message. While selecting a channel of communication, the need and requirements of the receiver must be taken into account.

5. Receiver

The receiver is a person who receives or perceives the message of the sender. The communication does not serve any purpose unless it is properly understood. Therefore, after receiving the message, the receiver must study and comprehend it. Briefly, communication does not take place if it is not received by the receiver and it does not serve any purpose if it has reached the receiver but he does not understand it.

6. Decoding

It is a process whereby the receiver interprets a message into meaningful information. This process has two steps, first to receive the message, and then to interpret it. The effectiveness of a communication depends on how much the receiver's decoding matches the sender's message. The receiver's willingness to receive the message is a basic prerequisite for successful decoding. To increase the chance of success of decoding, it is necessary that the receiver knows the language and terminology used in the message. Knowledge about the sender's background and his purpose is also important for the receiver. In addition, effective listening also helps him to receive and interpret the message.

7. Feedback

To complete the communication process, some verbal or non-verbal feedback from the receiver to the sender is required. Feedback is a reversal of the communication process in which the receiver expresses his reaction to the sender regarding the message. The feedback may be in a variety of forms such as direct or indirect. In organisational communication, the higher the frequency of the feedback, the more effective the communication process is likely to be. This is because without feedback the sender has no means of knowing whether his message has been understood by the receiver. For example, if the manager communicates some orders and instructions to his subordinates, it is only through the process of feedback that he comes to know that instructions were correctly received and carried out by subordinates.

NEED AND IMPORTANCE OF COMMUNICATION IN MANAGEMENT

The importance of communication in management can be hardly overemphasised. Management functions cannot be performed efficiently without an effective network of communication in the organisation. It is only through the process of communication that the manager establishes an interpersonal relationship with subordinates so as to get things done by them. Not only this, the overall functioning of an organisation is supported by an effective communication network. The importance of communication in management may be explained as follows:

(1) Communication Facilitates Sound Planning

The entire planning process to be conducted effectively requires communication. Through it, the manager gets the required and relevant information to formulate planning premises. He also seeks the participation of subordinates in the process of planning by interacting with them and listening to their valuable suggestions. In addition, a sound plan cannot be formulated without getting the much required information on the strengths and weaknesses of the organisation and on the various environmental factors in which such a plan is likely to operate. Thus, it is only through a proper communication process system that all the relevant pieces of information may be made available to the manager at the time of making plans.

(2) It also Encourages Factual Decision Making

Modern managers usually take decisions by applying scientific methods and adopting a scientific attitude. They prefer to base decisions on facts rather than on intuition. They consider information as one of the important inputs of the decision-making process. Without required information managers cannot evaluate various alternatives at their disposal and cannot arrive at quality decisions. In this sense, communication helps in improving the quality of decisions and the decision-making process becomes more effective.

(3) It Creates Interpersonal Relations

Management is a social process and to get things done by others, managers have to establish interpersonal relations with them. These relations can be created by exchanging ideas, opinions, information, directives, suggestions and instructions. To provide an opportunity to them to express their opinions, viewpoints and suggestions, listening to them will contribute to establishing interpersonal relations.

(4) It is a Means of Achieving Coordination

In every organisation various activities are to be divided, sub-divided and assigned among several departments and employees. All of them have to work in a well-coordinated manner to achieve the common goals of the organisation. Coordination can be maintained among various related departments by exchanging information on a regular basis. For example, the production and marketing departments can achieve coordination by exchanging and sharing related information on various products. Thus, communication is really an aid to coordination.

(5) It Boosts the Morale of Employees

Communication is helpful in boosting morale and motivation of the employees which largely depend on the effectiveness of the communication network in an organisation. Sharing of information, experiences and viewpoints with superiors provides satisfaction to subordinates particularly on concerned matters. Similarly, prompt redress of subordinates' grievances by higher level managers also signifies the recognition of their importance in the organisation. This ultimately creates a sense of belonging among them and they are motivated to work more efficiently.

(6) It Helps to Create Better Human Relations

Effective communication also helps in creating better human relationships in an organisation especially between management and employees. Through various means of communication, necessary information can be supplied to employees and all sorts of misunderstandings are removed. It goes a long way to create a congenial environment and improving human relations. This is because through communication, a feeling is created among employees that they are also a part and parcel of the organisation and therefore they should bear with it.

(7) It Improves Public Relations

Public relations is also built and improved through proper communication. Many outside parties like customers, community, financiers, suppliers and government agencies who deal with the organisation and have a stake in its functioning are to be supplied the required information on various matters that are related to them. By furnishing information on profitability, financial position, problems faced by the organisation and its contribution towards social development, a good public image of the organisation is built.

(8) It Helps in Reconciling with the Environment

Communication also helps the organisation to cope with a rapidly changing business environment. By generating and compiling information on various aspects of the environment, and timely supply of such information to managers, it helps them significantly to develop suitable strategies to cope with the changing environment.

(9) It is Important for Global Operations

Globalisation of business operations has increased the need and importance of communication. For a successful executive, it has become necessary to be aware of communication procedures and conventions the get the required knowledge of different cultures that prevail in various countries. For example, Americans are comparatively direct in their communication style compared to the Japanese who use ceremonial details to communicate. Besides, modern techniques of communication have reduced the entire globe into a small global village (Figure 14.3).

Purpose	Mechanisms
Downward communication	
1. Diffusion of routine information	Circulars, bulletin boards, wall magazines
2. Diffusion of procedural information	Circulars, handbooks, manuals
3. Socialisation	Special publications, lectures, meetings
4. Providing job-related information	Special publications, lectures, meetings
5. Feedback	Conversations, memos
6. Employee development	Conversations, group meetings
Upward communication.	
1. Control	Periodical information, special reports
2. Problem solving	Periodical meetings, grievance procedures
3. Ideas for improvement	Suggestion box, exit interviews
4. Group building	Review meetings (Mecom)
Horizontal communication	
1. Experience sharing	Joining forum
2. Problem solving	Task force, problem clinics
3. Coordination	Periodical meetings
External communication	
1. Image building	Annual reports, balance sheets, brochures, advertisements
2. Credibility building	Balance sheets, correspondence
3. Influencing	Conferences, dialogues

Source: Y. P. Singh, *Studies in Agricultural Communication in India.*

Figure 14.3. Purpose and mechanisms of different directions of communication

ROLE OF COMMUNICATION IN IMPROVING INTERPERSONAL RELATIONS, JOB SATISFACTION AND JOB PERFORMANCE

In order to get things done by subordinates, the manager has to have cordial interpersonal relations with them. In establishing and improving interpersonal relations, communication plays a vital role. The manager needs to have communication skill to describe, clarify, interpret and interact on various matters with subordinates. It is not enough to give orders and instructions regarding the work allotted to them. Through effective communication, these instructions and orders are made and through follow-up action they are inspired to comply with them effectively. The role of communication and its overall performance and job satisfaction may be explained as under:

(1) Interpersonal relations are created by making regular interaction with subordinates and by giving them orders and instructions regarding the work and explaining these to them.

(2) These relations can be further strengthened and promoted through an effective communication system. This is done by sharing feelings, experiences and exchanging information with subordinates.

(3) The confidence of employees can be won and more cooperation can be sought from them by providing necessary information to them on various aspects of organisational functioning, keeping them informed regarding problems faced by the organisation and the progress made by it on several fronts.

(4) A sense of commitment and responsibility can be created among employees by involving them in the process of management. They can be consulted, their viewpoints can be heard and they can be made party to various decisions through open channels of communication.

(5) Through various means of communication, higher level managers can get an idea about the needs of employees and the degree to which such needs are satisfied. On the basis of such information, measures can be initiated to provide more safety and security to them which leads to more satisfaction and higher productivity.

(6) By sharing and exchanging information about the job and job content with employees, the complexities involved in them can be reduced to a minimum and they may perform their jobs in a relaxed manner.

(7) An effective communication system promotes socialisation among employees of the organisation. By facilitative informal communication among them, personal and social relations are created and a feeling of isolation is reduced to a minimum.

(8) Communication also helps in reducing and eliminating conflicting situations arising out of varying perceptions, roles and multiplicity of objectives. An atmosphere of goodwill can be created in organisations. Misunderstandings are removed and ignorance and confusion are averted by transferring the necessary information to employees.

(9) Job performance of lower level employees can be improved. More cooperation and commitments may be sought from them to solve their job-related problems promptly and creating confidence among them which is possible through communication.

(10) Performance of higher level managers can be improved with the help of an effective communication system in the organisation. This is because through various channels of communication they are kept informed regarding various trends likely to be witnessed in the environment. On the basis of such advance information, they may initiate adequate measures to bring the situation under control and formulate suitable strategy.

(11) Surprisingly enough, modern managers spend more than 75 per cent of total time available in communicating with subordinates, superiors, peers, customers, suppliers and other parties. With an efficient means of communication, they can spare time for other managerial functions.

(12) Communication improves organisational effectiveness as well as performance of its members. This is because in a modern organisation more emphasis is placed on communication skills to get things done by others as against the direct use of authority which is less effective. Presentation and negotiation may help in winning their confidence.

COMMUNICATION CHANNELS

Communication channels may be classified as under:

1. Formal channels
2. Informal channels

Formal Channels

Formal channels are those channels that are officially designed by management to facilitate decision-making, planning, coordination, controlling and other higher level management functions. The basic purpose of designing such channels is to link various sub-systems of the organisation. Through these channels, official matters such as orders, instructions and other organisational information is communicated to employees at different levels. These channels are a part of the organisational structure which is based on the authority relationship between employees. A formal structure of organisation provides these channels to communicate messages in all three directions. These channels are a part and contribute to the functioning of formal organisations. According to the directions these channels may further be classified into three categories—upward, downward and horizontal and diagonal channels.

Upward Channels

All employees in an organisation work in the relationship of superiors and subordinates. They communicate with each other through the line of authority.

Upward channels are those channels that are used by subordinates to transmit information, ideas and requests to their superiors. Such information may be related to the job, role, responsibility and other problems faced by them. The organisation should encourage the free flow of upward communications. This is because it is through upward communication that higher level managers ensure that the communicated message has been properly followed by lower level employees. Upward channels carry the message which is partly task-related and partly interpersonal.

Task-related matters like performance report, replies to queries, information for planning and decision making are transmitted upward. Similarly, suggestions, difficulties, grievances are also communicated through these channels from subordinates to superiors. In addition, every subordinate is accountable to his immediate superior to keep him informed about the progress of work. He discharges this accountability by using these upward channels. The upward communication is invariable non-directive, as no orders and instructions are communicated upwardly from lower to higher levels. The lack of an effective upward communication in an organisation may thwart the natural desire of people to communicate and will also lead to frustration among employees working at lower levels.

Downward Channels

Downward channels refer to the communication that takes place from the upward level down to the operative levels. These channels are employed by superiors at various levels of the organisation to transmit information, orders and instructions to their subordinates. Downward channels of communication also carry information on plans, policies, managerial decisions and programmes from higher levels to lower levels.

These channels are both directive as well as non-directive because not only orders and instructions travel down from higher to lower levels but superiors also use them to guide, help, advise and motivate subordinates in the day-to-day functioning of the organisation. Interestingly enough, the major part of the manager's time is consumed by these channels to transmit messages to the lower levels of the organisation. In an organisation, the process of delegation is itself a downward channel of communication. Downward channels help in tying up various levels of the organisation together and are instrumental in seeking the effective use of authority

Horizontal and Diagonal Channels

Horizontal channels of communication are employed to facilitate the exchange of information between managers working at the same position or at the same level. It may also be used by various departments working at the same level. For example, communication between the production manager and the marketing manager about a product to be produced and to be marketed will be made through horizontal channels. In other words, horizontal channels cut across hierarchical channels based on superior subordinate relations. Horizontal channels of communication facilitate the smooth functioning of an organisation. It also helps in maintaining and encouraging coordination and participative problem solving. Horizontal channels also enable managers to establish cordial relationships with their peers. These relationships offer satisfaction to them. Information, ideas and facts are exchanged through these channels with the knowledge and approval of superiors who understand that these channels often relieve their communication burden.

Similarly, through diagonal channels, two or more managers working at different levels having no reporting relationship of authority may also make communication which cuts across the line of authority. Such channels are needed when line managers delegate functional authority to line or staff units. For example, if the finance manager delegates functional authority to some chartered accountant working with the assistant finance manager, he needs to have a diagonal channel to communicate with him.

The need for horizontal and diagonal channels arises in an organisation especially when the organisation grows in size. Besides, modern organisations which de-emphasise hierarchical communications prefer to have horizontal and diagonal channels which tend to be shorter and more effective.

Informal Channels

Informal channels are based on personal and social relations. These relations develop among employees while working in an organisation. These channels do arise out of interaction that takes place through formal channels. Such channels exist beyond the line of official or formal communication and work independently.

Actually, the need to establish informal channels arises among members or employees of an organisation to satisfy their social needs. Through these channels they get socialised and interact socially with each other. Through these informal channels they exchange ideas, feelings, share experiences both on personal matters as well as organisational matters related to them.

The network of informal communication which is not officially sanctioned but operates in the formal organisation is known as the 'grapevine'. It overlaps and intersects at several points, because some well-informed individuals may belong to two or more informal groups. It de-emphasises and disregards authority ranking for communication purposes and may combine members of an organisation in any direction—vertical, horizontal and diagonal.

In the words of Keith Davis, the grapevine "flows around the water-cooler, down hallways, through lunch rooms and wherever people get together in a group." Though the grapevine, mostly oral and unofficial information is circulated among members. These channels are very flexible and dynamic. Although it is difficult for managers to control the functioning of the grapevine, it is much faster than formal communication channels. Managers may use it to distribute information by saying "it is just between you and me."

The grapevine or informal communication networks operating in an organisation offers the following advantages:

(1) It offers social satisfaction to employees especially working under conditions of rigid control. They socialise with each other and feel more homely in a work-setting.

(2) It helps individuals to communicate on matters that they cannot do through official channels.

(3) It provides a means of communication among employees who are otherwise not linked through the official line of authority. This is because informal channels operate in any direction through personal and social relations among employees.

(4) It supplements formal communication channels because it fills the gap, if any, in the formal communication channels and reaches wherever the latter is inadequate or ineffective or does not reach.

(5) Informal communication channels are faster than formal ones.

(6) Employees' attitudes and reactions towards plans and policies of the organisation can be ascertained accurately on the basis of information obtained through informal channels.

(7) Informal channels are considered more effective and powerful in reducing stress of work among employees and provide psychological and moral support to them.

(8) In an emergency situation or during a crisis in the organisation, the formal network of communication fails to operate and in such a situation greater reliability may be placed on the informal network.

Though the relevance of an informal network of communication in the overall functioning of an organisation is widely accepted, it is beset with certain limitations which are as under:

(1) Communication messages flowing through informal channels tend to be distorted. This is because messages are mostly oral and have to pass through several people having different perceptions.

(2) It is found that 'gossip' is half truth and sensational news finds top priority to be communicated through an informal network.

(3) An informal network is unsystematic, unreliable and full of uncertainties as such channels can stop functioning any time when personal ties are snapped.

(4) Such a network does not find suitability for communicating confidential messages because the possibility of the messages getting leaked is very high.

Thus, an informal network can prove helpful and more effective but with some negative force associated with it. To use it as supplementary to formal channels, managers must monitor the grapevine and correct it officially as it reduces its damaging effect in the functioning of the organisation.

For example, by controlling the rumour-spreading tendency of informal communication channels, they can be used to communicate information as fast as possible.

Oral and Written Communications

On the basis of the form of message to be communicated, the communication may be of two types, oral and written.

Oral Communication

This refers to messages that are to be expressed, sent and received verbally. The sender and receiver exchange information by word of mouth. Generally, oral communication may be in the form of face-to-face interaction or communicated through a mechanical or electronic device such as telephone, loudspeaker, etc. In an oral communication the role of talking and listening seems to be very important. It is because the effectiveness of communication depends on the art of talking and listening on the part of the sender and receiver of the message. Managers spend much of their time in making verbal communications by giving verbal orders and instructions to subordinates, discussing the progress of work and problems faced by them and explaining how to perform better. It has the following advantages:

(1) Oral communication is more suitable and useful where detailed explanation of a message is required and doubts need to be clarified, for example, discussion on some problems or matters.

(2) Oral communication takes time and travels faster than the written form of communication.

(3) It is believed to be more appropriate for communicating messages at the operative level where employees find it difficult to make it in writing and to interpret it.

(4) Oral communication is also considered to be more lively, informal and humane in nature as compared to written communications. For example, if a superior greets a late-coming subordinate and says 'good morning' by raising his eyebrows, it may have more than the desired effect on the subordinate.

(5) Oral communication is more flexible and can be combined with gestures and other expressions.

However, oral communication has the following drawbacks:

(1) The oral form of communication seems to be loose and ineffective. It may reduce the effectiveness of the communication and seriousness of the receiver.

(2) There no record of such communications.

(3) Some form of oral communication such as meetings, conferences and discussions are time-consuming.

(4) Implementation of directives given verbally may create a problem for both the sender and the receiver because orders given orally may be denied easily.

Written Communication

Written communication refers to messages conveyed in writing and includes letters, notes, circulars, memoranda, etc. It provides a record and ready reference of the message communicated. It is more structured and formal in nature because such communication can be made after giving due thought. Moreover, written communications are taken more seriously and cannot be denied. It offers the following relative advantages:

(1) A written communication is more credible and authentic than an oral communication.

(2) It offers an opportunity to verify it because a record of the communication is maintained.

(3) It is taken more seriously and is binding on the parties involved.

(4) It has wider coverage and therefore is suitable for a situation that involves a large audience.

It has the following limitations:

(1) A written communication is costlier in terms of time and resources.

(2) Response of such communications is not available instantly.

(3) It is more impersonal and formal in nature.

(4) It is unsuitable for those who cannot write and read well.

(5) It is less flexible as compared to oral communication because once a written message is sent, it becomes difficult to amend.

(6) It may create confusion in the mind of the receiver if it has not been carefully designed and has no clarity of expression and interpretation.

COMMUNICATION BARRIERS

The communication process is very complex. It is a human process that involves the sender and receiver. Its effectiveness is affected by many factors such as language difference, noise, individual perceptions, emotions and inconsistencies between verbal and non-verbal communication and distrust. These are known as barriers of communication. Some of them are explained below.

(1) Differing Perceptions

This is one of the most common barriers of communication. People differ in terms of background, knowledge and experience. More often than not, due to these differences they perceive the same thing in a different perspective. These individual differences not only distort the message but vitiate the entire process. The way a communication is perceived is influenced by the circumstances in which it occurs.

For example, disagreement between two managers during a planning session may be considered healthy or acceptable but a similar kind of disagreement in the address of a chairman may be regarded differently.

(2) Lack of Mutuality between Sender and Receiver

This is one of the common causes of misunderstanding or failure of communication. It occurs when gestures or symbols used by the sender to code a message may not be understood in the same way and given the same interpretation by the receiver. In other words, both of them do not have identity of minds in respect to the gestures used, interpretations given and symbols followed.

(3) Language Differences

Language differences are closely related to perception differences. For a message to be properly communicated, the words used must convey the same meaning to the sender and the receiver. Lack of clarity, use of jargon, lack of coherence, omission and commission in the process of constructing sentences and other deficiencies may possibly result in language differences. Language problems which affect the communication process in an adverse manner are known as semantic barriers.

(4) Noise

Communication does not occur in a noise-free environment. Noise, though of varying degrees, disturbs, confuses or interferes with communication. Due to a high level of noise in telephone connections, sometimes irrelevant information may be screened out and sometimes relevant information may be left out.

(5) Organisational Barriers

Traditional organisational structures that are based upon authority relationship restrict free and frequent communication. Subordinates develop a tendency to communicate only those matters which please their superiors or superiors maintain a distance by not communicating those things that may have a direct reflection on their efficiency.

(6) Barriers due to Resistance to Change

Resistance to change for preserving the status quo may cause another communication barrier. Although resistance to change is not considered healthy, it is a natural inclination on the part of the person who does not want to leave the existing environment in which he feels comfortable and well adjusted. Thus, when the communication message is to convey new ideas, it may not be properly received by the receiver because new ideas may result in conflict with what he already believes in.

(7) Physical Layout

In a modern organisation, it is also found that the physical layout of the workplace influences the communication pattern. Thus, the layout should be designed in such a way so as to facilitate frequent interaction and to maintain privacy that both contribute to effective communication.

(8) Distrust

The receiver's trust or distrust of a communication message also affects its effectiveness. It is based on the credibility of the sender in the mind of the receiver which is a factor of the integrity, honesty and reliability of the sender of the message.

(9) Other Barriers

Apart from the above-mentioned barriers, there are many more which arise due to emotional reactions, deep-rooted feelings and prejudices, physical conditions, distance, etc. All of these constitute serious barriers to effective communication. Unless they are known to the sender he cannot overcome them effectively.

OVERCOMING BARRIERS TO EFFECTIVE COMMUNICATION

Since effective communication is vital to manage people effectively, it is equally important for the smooth and coordinated functioning of an organisation to seek its objectives. Thus, managers ought to be familiar with several methods, techniques and guidelines, which are helpful in maximising their communication abilities and effectiveness. It order to make the communication process more effective and responsive, the above-mentioned barriers are to be handled effectively:

(1) To reduce and remove the perception barrier, the sender of a message should attempt to know the background knowledge of those with whom he is communicating. When the subject is not clear, asking questions becomes critical for effective communication.

(2) Language differences can be handled by explaining the meaning of unconventional or technical terms in simple language. As far as possible, use of ambiguous words or words having dual meaning or multiple interpretations should be avoided.

(3) Emotional reactions can be tackled by accepting them as a part of the communication process. These should be analysed properly when they create problems. If subordinates are talking aggressively, it is necessary for the manager to understand their reaction; only then he may be able to improve the situation. The manager should also think about his own moods and must know how they influence others.

(4) Organisational structure, its rigidity and line of command also create a problem that can be solved by de-emphasising authority relations and making more use of informal relations for communicating messages.

(5) In a modern organisation, to become a good communicator, the manager has to learn three important skills, namely, skills of listening, talking, writing and conducting a meeting.

(6) An atmosphere of mutual trust and goodwill is to be created in an organisation to make the communication process more effective.

(7) The channels of communication should be direct, short and straightforward to reduce delay and distortion in communication.

(8) The communication system of an organisation should consist of both formal as well as informal networks.

(9) There should be two-way communication channels to provide the necessary feedback essential for its effectiveness.

SUMMARY

Communication is an important aspect of directing a function. Without communicating with subordinates, the manager cannot direct their activities towards the accomplishment of organisational goals.

It may also be considered as a link function of management. This is because performance of managerial functions demands communication on the part of the manager. Communication may be defined as a process of exchanging information between two or more persons to establish mutual understanding between them.

The communication process basically consists of many elements including the sender, receiver, channel, message and feedback. The starting point of this process which is also known as the source is the sender of the message. He uses some channel or path to transmit a message to the receiver. Once the message is received, he acknowledges it through the process of feedback.

The effectiveness of the managing process and the overall organisational functioning depend on the network of communications around the organisation. On the one hand, a manager needs to communicate with his subordinates to establish interpersonal relations with them. On the other, it supplements the smooth functioning of the organisation. The manager gets the required and relevant information to make sound plans, take factual decisions, maintain coordination through the communication network, communicate with subordinates, boost their morale, remove misunderstanding and create better human relations. It also helps in improving the public image and in reconciling with a changing business environment.

Managers also need communication skills to improve interpersonal relations, job satisfaction and performance of subordinates. Therefore, managers spend a considerable part of their time on communication.

In a communication network, two channels are mainly used—informal and formal. Informal channels are based on personal and social relations which normally develop among employees working in an organisation. Such communication satisfies the social needs of employees, fills the gap of formal channels and helps reduce work stress. Through such channels, they can share unofficial and official information without putting any cost on the organisation.

At the same time, through these informal channels, rumours and half-truths spread quickly. Such channels are unreliable and full of uncertainties and do not find suitability to communicate confidential information.

Besides these channels, some other channels are known as formal channels. These include upward, downward, horizontal and diagonal channels.

Through upward channels, messages are communicated from lower to higher levels in the form of progress reports, difficulties and suggestions.

Downward channels are meant to send messages from higher to lower levels in the form of orders and instructions, directives and plans and decisions to be implemented.

Horizontal channels are used to exchange information between or among managers working at similar positions. Such communications may help in maintaining coordination, solving problems and maintaining cordial relations.

Diagonal channels cut across the line of authority for sending messages. For example, the production manager directly communicates with the works manager or the finance manager with his staff management accountant.

In addition to the above channels, two important modes are used to send information, for example, oral and written communications. Both of them have their relative merits and limitations which are taken into account by managers. They use these modes separately or in combination as per the requirement of the situation, for example, to make oral communications less time is required but it may be distorted easily.

The entire process of communication is very complex. Its effectiveness may be limited by many factors that are related either to the persons involved or the channel used or the design of the message or lack of proper feedback. These barriers may arise due to differing perceptions, lack of mutuality, language differences, noise, organisational constraints, distrust and tendency to resist change.

To make communication more effective, the above-mentioned barriers must be looked into and taken care of by the communicator. Effective communication implies that the message has been well received, understood and properly acted upon.

In view of the growing importance of communication, many business schools and other professional institutes make adequate provisions to develop communications skills among prospective managers and professionals.

REVIEW QUESTIONS

1. Why is effective communication important for managers?
2. Explain the role of communication in job performance and job satisfaction.
3. Briefly discuss the various elements of the communication process.
4. Communication is to create commonness and understanding. Comment.

5. Informal channels are more human and homely. Discuss.
6. Describe the various communication barriers and how to overcome them.
7. What do you mean by 'grapevine'? Why is it considered more important and effective in a modern organisation?
8. Explain the factors that contribute to the effectiveness of communication.
9. How can a manager become a good communicator? Explain.
10. Write short notes on
    (a) grapevine
    (b) communication process
    (c) oral and written communications
    (d) horizontal and diagonal communications
    (e) communication skills
    (f) role of communication in creating and improving interpersonal relations.

OBJECTIVE TYPE QUESTIONS

Which of the following statements are correct and which are incorrect? Give reasons for your answers.

1. Communication improves job performance and provides satisfaction to employees.
2. Informal channels are more human and homely.
3. Downward channels carry messages which are only directive in nature.
4. Downward channels convey both directive and well as non-directive messages.
5. Upward communication carry task-related as well as impersonal matters.
6. Horizontal and diagonal channels are the same.
7. Horizontal communication takes place between managers working at different levels of the organisation.
8. Horizontal communication aims at problem-solving and coordination.
9. Diagonal communication takes place between line managers and staff specialists.
10. Informal channels carry gossip, half-truths and sensational news only.
11. Downward communication is always made only through a line of authority.

REFERENCES

Berlo, D. K. *The Process of Communication*. New York, U.S.A.: Holt Rinehart and Winston, 1960.

Cupach, W. R. and Spitzberg, B. H. (Eds.). *The Dark Side of Interpersonal Communication*. Hillsdale, N.J., U.S.A.: Erlbaum, 1994.

Davis, Keith. 'Management Communication and the Grapevine'. In: *Organisational Behaviour*. New York, U.S.A.: McGraw-Hill, 1981.

Gibson, James L., Ivancevich, John M. and Donnelly, James H. *Organisation Behaviour, Structure Processes*. Dallas, U.S.A.: Business Publications, 1985.

Golen, S. 'A Factor Analysis of Effective Listening'. *The Journal of Business Communication*. Winter, 1990.

Kalbfleisch, P. J. *Interpersonal Communication*. Hillsdale, N.J., U.S.A.: Erlbaum, 1993.

Kreitner, Robert. *Management*. Delhi, India: A.I.T.B.S. Publishers and Distributors (Regd), 1996.

Lesikar, Raymond V. *Business Communication: Theory and Application*. Homewood, Ill., U.S.A.: Irwin, 1984.

Luthans, Fred and Larsen, Janet K. 'How Managers Really Communicate' *Human Relations* (journal), 39, 1986.

Rowan, Roy. 'Where did the Rumour Come From?' *Fortune*, August, 1979.

Scott, W. G. and Mitchell, T. R. *Organisation Theory: A Structural and Behavioural Analysis*. Homewood, Ill., U.S.A.: Richard D. Irwin, 1976.

Smeltzer, Larry R. and Waltman, John L. *Managerial Communication: A Strategic Approach*. New York, U.S.A.: Wiley, 1984.

Victor, D. A. *International Business Communication*. New York, U.S.A.: Harper Collins, 1992.

Zaremba, Alan. 'Working with Organisational Grapevine'. *Personnel Journal*. 67, July 1988.

EXPERIENCE I

Role of Information in Changing Environment

INFORMATION REPLACED AUTHORITY

The new age executives are also required to work in situations lacking traditional hierarchies. They have to work with people who are not their employees. This is the outcome of their downsizing strategy. They are increasingly outsourcing whenever possible. The outsourcing is largely guided by quality considerations rather than economising. If this trend

Experience I continued

Experience I continued

of outsourcing continues in the 21st century, they will outsource all work below the level of senior management. The authority of the executives will be placed in such situations by information. Take the example of a company treasurer. He is likely to have only two assistants and a receptionist. He may use information technology to perform his task. His decisions are very crucial for the survival and growth of the company. If he makes effectives decisions on foreign exchange, the company can make plenty of money in a single day. On the other hand, if his decisions are wrong, the company is bound to lose profusely.

Synthesis Rather than Analysis—A Need for Communicating Competence

In today's information-based organisations, most of the management layers are becoming redundant globally. They are only information relays with enhanced information responsibility. Accordingly, the executives act as synthesisers. They bring resources together and sell opportunities and timings. They are required to have more perceptiveness than analytical skills. They have to recognise what is there rather than provide an analysis of what is expected. In addition, they must understand the meaning and significance of respect for their people.

Again they have to ensure that the contributions are accepted and properly understood by others in the organisation. They must tell about their performance and contributions to people who will otherwise guess inaccurately. If there is a lack of communication about their strengths and weaknesses, they may be forced to work on tasks which are least suited to their qualifications. The executives are required to understand not only their own competence and communicate it to people around them but also that of others in the corporation.

Information Responsibility

The new age necessitates that executives expand on their idea of information responsibility. They are needed to assimilate it into their task of managing today's corporations. They have to operate with both internal and external information. They must evolve innovative ways to use this vital device for corporate excellence. They are required to understand what information is needed to effectively satisfy their customers. While performing their information responsibility, they can attempt to organise their work by initiating action with specific jobs. Then, they can move to the information input. Finally, they have to focus on human relationships

Experience I continued

Experience I continued

required to get their job done. In this context, they can resort to re-engineering in converting the organisation from the flow of 'things' to flow of 'information'.

INFORMATION VS. KNOWLEDGE—A NEED FOR EXPOSURE

Information can be differentiated from knowledge. In the preceding machine age, knowledge was power and people used to keep it secret. In today's information age, power stems from transmission of information rather than hiding it. This is the new way of making it productive. Accordingly, knowledge workers are required to ensure that they are properly understood by every one around them. They must establish a balance between specialisation and exposure for effective performance of their tasks. By using the exposure technique they can manage specialists in their organisation. Take the American example. There may be specialists (say, meteorologists) as members in a team of weather forecasting.

They may lack expertise in mathematics. They are rotated to provide an extensive exposure of mathematics; they are put to work on the new mathematical model of hurricanes for a specified period. Such exposures and translations into action are highly relevant for outstanding performance. This technique has enabled Americans to be three times more accurate than Europeans in weather forecasting. This example demonstrates how an executive can use his team to effectively manage knowledge. Japanese executives have taken the lead in this context. In Japanese corporations, executives take knowledge and make it more productive. The productivity of knowledge involves both qualitative and quantitative aspects. This necessitates that executives must be both specialists and synthesisers of knowledge from varied fields of work.

EXECUTIVE VS. MANAGER

It would be more appropriate to use the term 'executive' than 'manager' in the new age. While the latter implies subordinates, the former embraces responsibility for an area not necessarily over people. The term 'boss' (coined during the first World War) implies a mentor's role (who can back you up on a decision). The new age demands a mixture of sponsor and mentor relations rather than senior-junior polarities. It no longer requires a blend of rank and power. The performance of the emerging organisation in the new age is an optimal combination of mutual understanding and responsibility.

Experience I continued

Experience I continued

Knowledge as a Resource

Last, but not the least, the new age is marked by flux. In this age, success can be accomplished only through deliberate, construction action. There is an urgent need for adequately understanding, measuring and managing knowledge. Only well-informed executives who are competitive enough can survive in this turbulent environment. The reason is obvious. Things are changing very fast in every business. Accordingly, they have to learn more and more about how the world works. Their knowledge is the only meaningful resource in their possession.

CASE STUDY I

Mr. Gautam Ghosh founded a small radio manufacturing plant in western India in the late Sixties. From this small beginning came one of the country's largest radio, television and allied products companies. By 1996, it had recorded annual sales of Rs. 800 million with 25,000 employees and eight manufacturing locations. Throughout its growth, the founder remained active, imaginative and the driving force behind his company. In earlier days, every manager and worker knew him, and he was able to call most of them by their first names; even after the company became fairly large, people felt they knew the founder and chief executive and their strong feeling of personal loyalty had much to do with the fact that the company's workers never formed a union.

However, as the company prospered and grew, Mr. Ghosh thought that it was losing its 'small company' spirit. He also felt that communications were suffering, that his objectives and philosophy were not being understood in the company, that much wasteful duplication was occurring through poor knowledge of what others in the company were doing, and that new product development and marketing were suffering as a result Likewise, he was concerned that he had lost touch with the people. To solve the communication problem, he hired a director of communications reporting directly to him. The issues were discussed in detail between the two. They then put into effect every communication device they found in other large companies, namely,

(a) bulletin boards in every office and plant throughout the country.

(b) a revitalised company newsletter carrying detailed company and personal news affecting all locations.

(c) 'Company Facts Book' for every employee, giving significant information about the company.

(d) Regular profit-sharing letters.

—oo(O)oo—

CHAPTER 15

CONTROLLING PROCESS IN AN ORGANISATION

LEARNING OBJECTIVES

1. To understand the basic concept, meaning and characteristics of controlling.
2. To analyse the significance of control in business with suitable examples.
3. To remember the relationship between planning and controlling.
4. To identify various elements involved in the control cycle.
5. To describe various stages of the controlling process.
6. To develop conceptual clarity on various dimensions of control.
7. To understand the types of control with suitable examples.
8. To learn the concept of management and operational control and relate them with some practical solutions.
9. To evaluate the effect of control on behaviour with job performance of employees.
10. To highlight the main features of a good control system.

CONTROLLING DEFINED

Controlling is often regarded as a core of the management process. This is because the process of management begins with planning, followed by organising, staffing and directing and comes to an end with controlling. As a management function, control is a process of taking the necessary preventive and corrective actions to ensure that organisational objectives are achieved as effectively as possible. It may also be considered as a process of ensuring that actual activities conform to planned activities and have been performed in a planned manner. From this, one might infer that control simply picks up where planning leaves off. But control is a more comprehensive and pervasive concept.

It helps the manager to monitor the effectiveness of planning, organising, staffing and directing functions. It is only through controlling that managers ensure execution of plans and achievement of objectives. In its absence, planned activities may not be carried out according to predetermined procedures and methods. Lack of effective control may also create delay in performing the work which leads to more wastage of effort and resources and the desired results may not be achieved.

Thus, controlling also implies to make things happen, to obtain desired results and to take corrective action to command the situation. Control also means order and discipline. This is because it not only affects events to occur but also regulates and checks undesirable tendencies in the working behaviour of employees. It forces them to fall in line with predetermined standards of performance and behaviour.

Control thus consists of knowing the extent to which actions are in conformity with plans and issuing necessary instructions so that errors and deviation are promptly reported, analysed and suitable corrective measures taken. A number of remedial actions are taken and adjustments are made as a part of control. But the purpose of the control function is always the same, that is, to 'get the job done despite environmental, organisational and behavioural obstacles and uncertainties.'

NATURE OF CONTROL

The nature of control may be understood on the basis of the following points:

(1) Control is a Basic Function of Management

Efficient control is required to be exercised in the process of management to get better results and to achieve organisational objectives.

(2) Control Depends on and Contributes to other Functions of Management

By setting standards of performance and behaviour for each employee and comparing their actual performance with it, their efforts are made more meaningful to achieve the objectives of the organisation. It is not related only to planning but organising, staffing and directing also require efficient control to get the desired results.

(3) Control Relates to People, Things and Actions

It is only by taking controlling measures that employees are forced to behave in a desired manner. Control is also required to maintain discipline and order and to comply with predetermined norms, rules and values. Similarly, by watching, monitoring and steering a situation it may be brought under control. Not only this, controlling also ensures that each action on the part of employees is checked and made in conformity with predetermined standards and procedures.

(4) Control is all Pervasive

Every manager working in an organisation, irrespective of his position has to control and command the activities of subordinates to produce the desired results. Not only managers, but every organisation needs to exercise efficient control to secure optimum effective utilisation of all resources to accomplish objectives.

(5) Control is a Continuous Process

Like planning, controlling is also a continuous process having no definable end. It involves constant and regular monitoring of events and performance, analysis of standards, procedures and policies. It also suggests remedial measures to control the situation or to improve the performance.

(6) The Controlling Process Aims at Taking Corrective Measures

In the controlling process, the actual performance is measured and compared with the standard of performance to discover deviations. Once they are brought to the surface, suitable corrective actions are suggested by the manager so as to check their recurrence in the future.

NEED AND IMPORTANCE OF CONTROL

The working of human organisations is subject to imperfection and dysfunction. It is because these organisations are managed by individuals who carry a natural tendency to distort the functioning of the system and make it as per their own convenience and comfort. In practice, if such imperfections and distortions are allowed to crop into the functioning of an organisation, disorder, indiscipline and chaotic conditions may be created. Such a situation may lead to more wastage, spoilage and inefficiency in the utilisation of resources. Thus organisational functioning needs have a built-in system of controlling so as to gear it up in the right direction to achieve objectives. It is only through the efficient controlling mechanism performance of the employees that it is regularly monitored, regulated, evaluated, analysed and corrected. It is made more productive to achieve organisational goals.

Control facilitates effective and optimum utilisation of resources of the organisation. It helps in achieving goals by reducing spoilage, wastage and inefficiency. Controlling ensures the performance of activities in accordance with predetermined standards, procedures and norms.

Although the determination of goals and selecting an appropriate course of action to achieve them are indispensable to efficient management of an organisation, it also generates the need of control. This is because control ensures that plans are implemented in a predetermined manner, required progress is made towards goals and policies and procedures are followed.

The efficient utilisation of resources is also encouraged by control. This is because in the controlling process managers are expected to keep a close watch over the utilisation of both physical and human resources. They have to prevent misuse and wastage of resources and ensure their proper utilisation. In this regard, controlling is the only means by which the manager can ensure that the work is done as intended in terms of quantity, quality, time and cost which ultimately leads to the effective use of resources.

Controlling helps in boosting the morale of employees working in an organisation. This is because controlling creates order and discipline in the organisation. Every employee knows very well what he is expected to do and what are the standards of performance against which his performance is to be compared. It induces them to comply with the set standards in performing their jobs efficiently. Such a healthy attitude on the part of employees towards work helps in maintaining the morale of the employees at a higher level.

The basic purpose of management control is the accomplishment of both short-term as well as long-term objectives in a most effective and efficient manner. By exercising effective control, the behaviour of events and people at work can be influenced and made desirable and more contributive. It also helps in reducing conflicts arising out of different perceptions and values observed by managers. In brief, the controlling function remains basic and more significant due to the following reasons. Controlling

(1) helps plans to be implemented effectively;

(2) facilitates coordination in organisational functioning by reducing diversity;

(3) encourages high morale on the part of employees;

(4) ensures order, discipline and obedience on the part of subordinates;

(5) helps the organisation to preserve and promote its distinct identity against environmental changes;

(6) ensures the efficient use of physical and human resources to achieve organisational goals;

(7) enables the organisation to keep a watch on the external environment and to command it; and

(8) promotes integration between short-term and long-term objectives, corporate goals and departmental goals and between and enterprise and the environment.

RELATIONSHIP BETWEEN PLANNING AND CONTROL

The process of management begins with planning and comes to an end with controlling. Thus, these two basic functions of management may be considered the two sides of a coin because they cannot be separated. In the absence of planning, control cannot be exercised. Similarly, it is the controlling process that ensures effective implementation of plans. In other words, planning has little meaning without control and control totally depends on it.

Once a plan becomes operational, control is necessary to monitor its progress, measure it, discover deviations and initiate corrective action. In some cases, control may also result in setting new goals, formulating new action plans, changing the structure of the organisation and making improvement in staffing and techniques of directing and leading. Thus, the purpose of control is to ensure that the event conforms to the plan. It keeps the plan on the right track by attacking the forces of disruption and distortion. It also gives feedback to the manager to modify and redefine plans in the changed situation. On the other hand, objectives, determined in the process of planning, forms a basis of the controlling mechanism. This is because these objectives are translated into standards of performance and the actual performance compared for conducting the control process. The relationship between planning and controlling can be described on the basis of the following points:

(1) Planning is an intellectual process that involves the use of thinking, articulation and analysis, paving the way to discover and select an appropriate course of action to achieve objectives. Matters that are included in control are result-oriented, practical and administrative in nature. The controlling process translates decisions into action to achieve organisational goals. Thus, control simply picks up where planning leaves off.

(2) Planning implies scientific and rational decision-making on various problems faced by the organisation. It enhances the capability of the organisation to cope with the changing environment and gain control over environmental factors. Controlling is more concerned with attacking and removing disruptive forces to preserve and promote integrity and identity of the organisation. It helps in reducing inefficiency, spoilage and wastage with regard to the use of resources of the organisation.

(3) Planning and control may be considered as inseparable twins of management. Both help to mobilise and utilise scarce resources of the organisation in the most efficient manner to achieve goals. It also enables the organisation to survive, grow and develop in a state of complexity, diversity and uncertainty arising out of the fast-changing external environment.

(4) Planning is considered a forward-looking approach. This is because in planning, the future destination of the organisation is decided, a course of action selected and decisions are made with a full sense of security. Hence, plans are made for the future. But controlling is regarded as a backward looking activity. This is because in controlling whatever remedial measures are taken, it is based on measurement and comparison of performance in the past. Controlling is based on the philosophy that whatever has happened cannot be controlled but on the basis of that control can be exercised to check the recurrence of that event in the future.

(5) Planning and controlling are closely related, interacting and complementary to each other. Being a part of the management process, they are organically or functionally related to each other. Similarly,

effective implementation of a plan is influenced by controlling and vice versa. In addition, these two are complementary to each other. As controlling makes planning more meaningful and relevant and planning makes controlling more effective and purposeful, both these functions produce integral action to realise the goals of the organisation.

CONTROL CYCLE

Application of the system approach implies that management is a system or process consisting of many sub-systems like planning, organising, staffing, directing and controlling. Controlling as a sub-system of management has the following features which may also be regarded as its elements or sub-systems:

1. Objectives or Goals

A controlling system aims at achieving some goals or objectives. These goals are formulated and coordinated with organisational goals in such a way so that the former contributes to the achievement of the latter. In the context of control, goals are formulated with respect to quantity, cost of output and the required time within which they are to be produced. These goals are an operational form of organisational goals. This is because they are derived from organisational goals and are made in terms of standards of performance, specifications of quality, cost of output and time frame.

2. Action Plans

Once the objectives of a controlling system are determined, necessary action plans and programmes are developed to achieve them. These action plans mainly include a controlling device or mechanism to be installed in the organisation to maintain efficient control.

3. Resource Allocation

Implementation of action plans calls for allocation, commitment and utilisation of various physical as well as human resources. Allocation of resources is made on the basis of requirement of workload which is involved in each work unit.

4. Authority Delegation

To operate a controlling mechanism or device which is installed in an organisation, the manager needs adequate authority. This is to take action, monitor performance and get his orders and instructions followed by subordinates.

5. Performance Comparison

In a controlling system, the performance of employees is compared with operational goals, which may be stated in the form of standards of performance. This is done to ascertain and ensure that everyone performs according to those standards.

6. Performance Evaluation

Any division or difference in the performance level of the employees is to be evaluated and analysed thoroughly. This would help the manager to take necessary action to ensure conformity with standards.

7. Feedback

A controlling system remains incomplete without a feedback mechanism. It is required to make the desired changes and adjustments in the controlling system so as to make it more effective and responsive. It is only by feeding corrective and adaptive information that the entire controlling system may be set right. All the elements mentioned above may be put together in a logical sequence to make a control cycle (Figure 15.1).

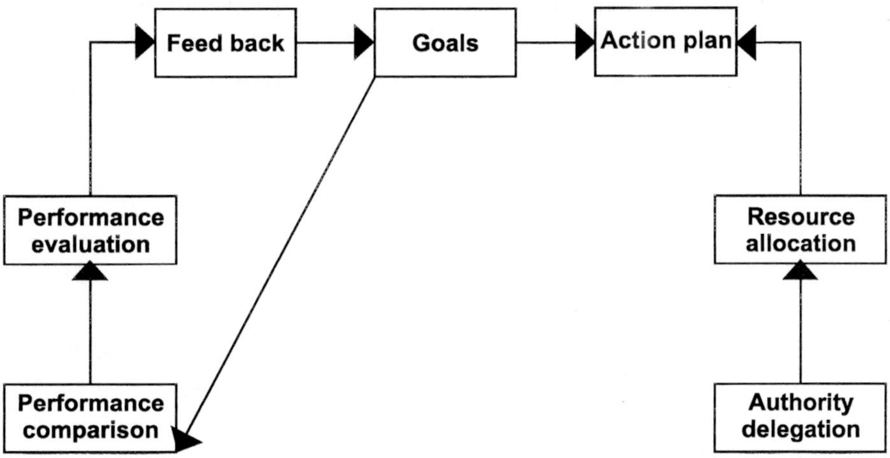

Figure 15.1. Control cycle

In this figure, it is indicated that to achieve goals of the controlling system, an action plan is prepared on the basis of allocation of resources and delegation of authority.

The action plan is implemented and actual performance is measured and compared with the desired goals. Deviations are evaluated and analysed. Finally, corrective action is taken to make the desired change in the system.

ELEMENTS OF A CONTROLLING PROCESS

Management control is a systematic process that involves the following elements:

(1). Setting of Standards of Performance

The goals and objectives determined in a planning process may be considered as desired results or a particular future destination which the organisation wants to achieve. These overall objectives of the organisation are known as corporate goals. They are further broken down into various departmental goals. These are further narrowed down to operational goals such as standards for quality, quantity, cost, time, sales quota, schedule, budget, etc. These operational goals are indeed the standards of performance that the individual employee or department is expected to achieve. The standard of performance may be defined as the specific quantity of work that an average employee can perform in a normal situation and within a given period of time. In other words, standards are efforts against which actual performance of the employees is compared.

At this stage of the controlling process, a link or relationship is established between planning and control. This is because objectives and goals formulated in the planning process provide a base to set standards of performance to exercise control. Thus, standards may also be interpreted as objective criteria or norms towards which the performance of the employee is directed.

Normally, standards are set and expressed in quantitative terms such as quantity of output, man-hours, sales, revenue, cost, expenses, etc. On the basis of the above discussion, the following observations can be made on standards of performance:

(1) Standards are a more operationalised form of corporate objectives and goals.

(2) These standards of performance establish a relationship between planning and control.

(3) The standard of performance should be set in physical and monetary terms such as cost, revenue and expenses in rupees, volume of production, sales in units, etc.

(4) Standards of performance are generally determined keeping in view the capability and competence of the employee concerned.

(5) These standards should be defined clearly, must be understandable, attainable and realistic in nature.

(6) Standards of performance should be set in all key and strategic areas of a business organisation, such as productivity, quality, profitability, development of personnel, motivation and morale of the employees, customer satisfaction, market standing, research and development, etc.

2. Monitoring and Measuring Performance

Once the standards of performance have been developed and allotted to the various employees, managers keep a regular watch on the actual performance. They exercise control over the activities of subordinates by observing their work and motivating them to follow predetermined norms, rules, procedures and methods of performing the job. The main objective of doing this is to direct the activities of employees to meet the standards of performance.

Monitoring of the performance involves motivation. This is because at this stage the employees are motivated to produce desirable behaviour according to set norms and standards. To motivate and direct them, the manager provides effective leadership and guidance. The effectiveness of the entire controlling process depends on how promptly and efficiently a manager guides, directs, helps and motivates subordinates to behave and act in conformity with standards of performance. A continuous watch and alertness on the part of the manager would enable him to bring the situation under control immediately as subordinates deviate from given direction and standards.

Monitoring is to be followed by measurement of actual performance. This implies the evaluation of work actually performed and the results achieved by subordinates. The measurement of actual performance is to be made in the same unit in which the standards have been set. Performance with regard to sales and production activities can be measured in terms of number of units produced and sold or cost incurred, revenue generated, etc. Measurement of performance of the service department and of higher level managers may be very difficult. This is because the performance of managerial activities and service departments are qualitative in nature.

Thus, measurement of actual performance may be direct or indirect or may be undertaken through observation or through regular, oral or written reports. Generally, measurement and reporting of performance takes place at periodic intervals—weekly, monthly, quarterly or yearly. With regard to monitoring and measuring performance, the following guidelines should be taken into account:

(1) Monitoring and measurement of performance should be undertaken only with regard to key and critical activities. By being selective, the efforts and resources may be saved and concentration may be placed on these important activities.

(2) The system of reporting should be restricted to only those cases in which deviations are of a serious nature and have gone beyond permissible limits. In other words, if the employee performs well, there is no need of reporting it to the higher level. It would unnecessarily lead to wastage of time and effort.

(3) In order to measure the actual performance objectively, scientific methods should be used to reduce the personal bias of the manager.

(4) Control reports indicating the measurement and evaluation of actual performance should be sent to those managers who are directly responsible for ensuring conformity of standards with actual performance and have the authority to initiate remedial measures.

3. Comparing Performance Standards

In the controlling process, the actual performance is compared with the standards to discover deviations. These deviations are studied and analysed to identify possible causes. If performance matches the standard, the manager feels that everything is under control. And if it happens to be more or less than the standard, it amounts to deviation, positive in the case of the former and negative in the case of the latter. Generally, minor deviations within permissible limits do not get the attention of the manager. To save time and efforts, he concentrates only on major deviations beyond permissible limits.

4. Analysing Causes of Deviations

Once deviations have been discovered by making a comparison between standards and actual results, the manager becomes conscious of those situations in which the deviations are major and serious in nature. He identifies and investigates these deviations to find out the possible causes responsible for the situation. Deviations may have multiple causes for their origin such as deficiency and inadequacy of resources, defective process, structural drawback, lack of proper monitoring, measurement and organisational constraints and other environmental factors, many of which are beyond the control of the employees. Therefore it is necessary to identify and separate the exact cause or causes of the deviation. Sometimes, when deviations are found to be positive the standards of performance may be defective and may be the capabilities and competence of the employees have been underestimated.

5. Taking Corrective Action

The purpose of controlling is not only to discover deviations but also to take corrective measures to check their recurrence. Corrective actions are initiated on the basis of careful analysis of possible causes of deviations. All controlling activities terminate at this point. Corrective measures may also involve changes in the standards originally established. If managers do not see the controlling process in terms of corrective action and logical conclusions they may be confining themselves only to monitoring of performance rather than exercising control. In the light of the cause of deviation mentioned above, corrective or remedial measures may include changes in methods, machine and process, improving physical conditions, providing suitable incentives to employees, improving the nature of supervision, etc. Thus, control is not only a fact-finding process but its existence lies in taking suitable corrective action to improve performance.

DIMENSIONS OF CONTROL

The word 'control' suggests activities of checking, testing, regulating, verifying and making necessary adjustments. As a managerial function, it also involves taking preventive and corrective action to ensure that organisational objectives are achieved as efficiently as possible. Thus, managers have to decide in advance the area of operation and set of activities that are more important, key or critical, and require the special attention of managers so that they can concentrate on these areas to make control more effective. In this regard, he has to look into the following two dimensions of control, namely 'critical point control' and 'control by exception'.

Critical Point Control

If the operating system in an organisation is very simple and involves a less number of activities, the manager can easily exercise effective control over each and every activity. However, operating systems may be very complex and involve a large number of activities and a lot of resources. In such a situation, it is not possible for managers to control each and every activity involved in the system. Therefore, he becomes selective. He has to identify and isolate those activities of the system which are critical, strategic, key and more important for the system so that he can concentrate more on those activities.

In this way, by controlling key and critical activities he can control the entire operating system. The critical point control calls for careful analysis of all activities involved in the system to identify critical ones. Critical activity may be defined as an activity which assumes a key role in the functioning of the entire system and if something goes wrong, the entire system comes to a halt. Once the critical activities or points are identified, suitable standards of performance can be evolved to control them. Key areas of activities of any organisation depend on the nature of its operations. For example, activities directly related to profitability, growth, development, innovation, and diversification may be considered as key activities. Similarly, for the marketing department, customer satisfaction, motivation of sales force, creation of demand, etc., may be identified as the set of key activities. More suitable examples of critical point control are an ABC analysis which is used to control inventories. In this control system, more emphasis is focussed on 'A' category inventory items, which are small in number but large in value.

Control by Exception

In controlling the activities of subordinates, the superior may find that many of the activities have been performed as per standards. He can easily pass over these activities and concentrate more on those activities that have been subject to major deviations. This principle, which has been developed by F. W. Taylor, suggests that the manager should give more and prompt attention to unusual or exceptional matters. In other words, while controlling the activities of subordinates, he should measure, evaluate and report only those activities in which major deviations have occurred. On the other hand, if some activities have been performed well, he need not report them to the higher level. The concept of control by exception is based on the assumption that 'no news is good news' for the manager. If there is nothing to report, it may be assumed that the system is functioning well. In 'control by exception' the manager might even request the subordinate not to send any report on those activities that are within predetermined standards and report only those items that have not been performed in conformity with standards.

To make 'control by exception' more effective and successful, it is necessary to have enough mutual trust and confidence between superiors and subordinates. Superiors must know that subordinates will not hesitate to report deviations honestly. The exception principle is different from strategic point control. In the latter, the manager concentrates on selected strategic or key activities but according to the former, he is mainly concerned with major deviations regardless of the fact where they occurred.

TYPES OF CONTROL

The organisation, like other man-made systems, does not have automatic controls. Instead, they require constant monitoring and adjustment to control deviations. For this purpose, on the basis of analysis of possible causes, the manager takes corrective action. According to the time when corrective actions are taken, there could be three types of control; post, current and pre-control (Figure 15.2).

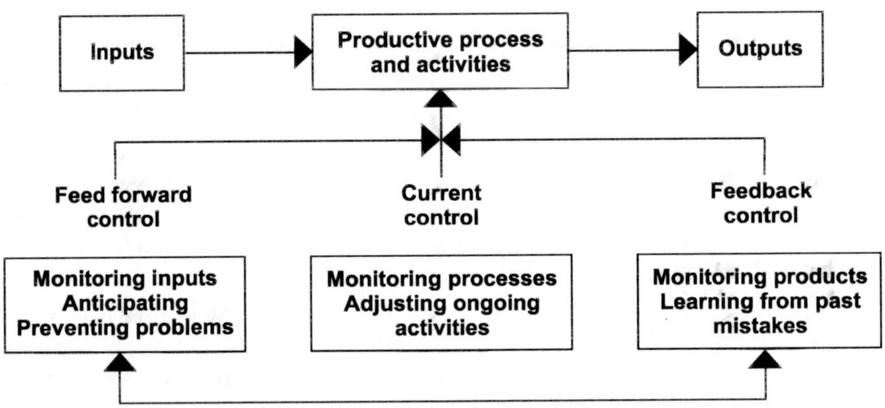

Figure 15.2. Three types of control

1. Post Control

Most of the organisations do have this type of control. This is also known as 'feedback control' or 'after the event control.' Post-control includes the collection of information about the completed activity, the evaluation of information and the taking of corrective action to improve performance.

In other words, it permits the manager to use information on past performance to bring future performance in line with planned objectives and standards. For example, by monitoring the complaints of CA students who appeared in an examination, the chairman of the CA institute learns that the evaluation division requires attention. Post-control involves a time gap between the occurrence of an event and taking corrective measures. It is based on the assumption that the manager has control only on the event that is to take place in the future and not on events that have already taken place. But it is on the basis of careful analysis of past results and experience that some lessons are drawn about what is to be done in the future to maintain conformity with standards. To make post-control more meaningful and effective, analysis of past-performance is required to be made as quickly as possible. And control reports should be submitted to the manager concerned without loss of time so that remedial measures are taken immediately.

Post-control helps in testing the validity and appropriateness of standards. If they prove impossible to be attained, they should be made more reasonable. And if they prove too easy, they need to be raised.

For example, a bank loan officer learns that potentially profitable business has been reduced because of strict credit criteria used to grant loans. By exercising post-control or feedback control, the credit standards may be relaxed to make lending operations of the bank more profitable. However, post control is criticised on the ground that it is useless to close the gates after the horse is gone. This is because corrective actions are taken only when deviations occur. But it should not be forgotten that the right lesson learnt from the past may help managers to prevent the occurrence of similar types of mistakes in the future.

2. Current Control

This type of control is also known as 'real time control' because it is more concerned with the present rather than the future or the past. In a current control to keep the system or process on track, attempts are made to evaluate and analyse performance as quickly as possible and initiate prompt corrective action. As the process starts operating, the activities are continuously monitored to ensure that they are being performed as per standards. If it is not so, necessary instructions in the form of corrective action are fed into the process so that the required adjustments are made automatically. In other words, current control is monitoring and adjusting of on-going activities so as to ensure conformity of actual results with predetermined standards. The manager keeps a vigilant watch on the process, monitors it and if he finds that it is moving off track, he immediately puts it back. For example, first line supervisors are usually involved in current control. They help operators and mechanics performing difficult tasks in the production process.

The main feature of this type of control is that there is a little time gap between deviations and correction action. Moreover, by exercising this type of control the situation can be prevented from going worse by taking timely action. This is the reason that current control is exercised by many organisations in respect of inventory control, production control, quality control, etc. It is also known as 'steering control' because control is designed to detect deviations from standards and allow corrective action to be taken before a particular sequence of activities is completed. For example, leakage of a question paper in an examination may prompt the authorities to cancel or postpone the examination.

'Internal control system' installed in the organisation to control the use of financial resources is also an example of current control.

3. Pre-control or Feed Forward Control

This is also known as 'pro-active' or 'preventive control' or 'feed forward control'. This is because in this type of control, the main emphasis is placed on preventing the performance of the system to be deviated from standards. For this purpose, the functioning of the system is watched closely with constant alertness to discover likely problems or disturbances so that advance action can be taken to avert them. In feed forward control, a lot of forecasting is involved. This is made to anticipate the behaviour of the functioning of the system and its environment. An early signal of possible disorders may be obtained and rapid response action taken to bring the situation under control.

Feed forward control implies active anticipation and prevention of problems and disturbances rather than passive reaction. It is considered more effective and superior compared to post and current control. It does not allow deviations to occur and averts the disorder or disturbance by taking suitable action in advance. In brief, feed forward control calls for close monitoring and analysis of inputs and processes so as to make necessary adjustments before output is produced.

Preventive control, like current control, is very expensive and difficult to operate. It addresses the issue of 'what can we do ahead of time to help our plans being implemented?' It aims at protecting the system from environmental pressures and disturbances and allows it to function in a planned manner. For example, if the purchase manager of a home appliance manufacturing company warns production and marketing managers of a delay in receiving an important sub-component, corrective action can be taken to avoid a costly delay. The production manager can reschedule the workload and the marketing manager can negotiate a delivery date for the final product. In the absence of preventive control, the situation is bound to go from bad to worse.

On the basis of the above discussion, it can be safely inferred that successful managers must exercise all three types of controls to meet the requirements of a modern complex organisation. Feed forward control helps managers to avoid mistakes in the first place, current control enables them to catch mistakes as soon as they are made, and finally feedback control keeps them away from repeating past mistakes. Thus, it seems to be desirable to maintain a workable balance among these three types of control. It is done to prepare an optimal contribution of these to exercise efficient control.

ROLE AND SIGNIFICANCE OF COMMUNICATION IN CONTROL

All management functions like planning, organising, directing and controlling are necessary for the smooth functioning of an organisation. To support these functions, especially planning and controlling, communication systems are of special importance to managers. Only with accurate and timely information can a manager monitor progress towards predetermined goals and turn a plan into reality. The manager cannot anticipate potential corrections in the absence of availability of relevant, required and reliable information.

A communication network and the free flow of information play a significant role in every type of control. This is because in order to exercise efficient control communication of information becomes a prerequisite at several stages involved in the controlling process. After translating corporate objectives into departmental goals and operational goals, they are required to be communicated by the top management to the lower level managers. It is only through a proper communication network available in the organisation that these goals are converted into standards of performance which are communicated to employees working at different levels of the organisation.

The next phase of the controlling process represents constant monitoring of performance. This requires that the needed information should be communicated on a regular basis to keep the manager informed of the progress of work being performed by subordinates. Thus, like setting standards of performance, monitoring and evaluation of actual results also requires communication between the manager and his subordinates. Communication is also needed at other stages of the controlling process. This is because one actual performance has been measured and compared with a standard to discover deviations, remedial action will be taken by the manager. These actions would also need to be communicated to the employee concerned. Communication of information assumes a more significant role especially in real time or current control and feed forward control. This is because in these types of control, even minor deviations are communicated rapidly to the manager so that he can take immediate remedial action.

Besides, in the process of controlling, feedback of information is an important aspect without which the process is not complete. Feedback may be defined as communication of results and their positive and negative aspects. Feedback of information is necessary to enable the working unit to know the result of its activities and to know how actually they have been performed, and if there has been any deficiency, what action has been taken to set it right.

Feedback of information is generally considered as a 'loop' or 'circuit'. There may be two types of loops, namely, closed feedback loops and open loops. In the closed feedback loops, direction on corrective action is quite definite and certain to ensure the functioning of the system in a deterministic manner. They are maintained and incorporated in the control system itself. In other words, these are built in within a system for automatic regulation and adjustment. No outside intervention is allowed to correct deviations. But in open loops, adequate margin is maintained for outside intervention to correct and adjust the functioning of the system. Such feedback loops are open and flexible because they allow the manager to apply his mind in a discretionary manner to correct deviations. Both these types of feedback circuits have their own utility in the system.

CHARACTERISTICS OF AN EFFECTIVE CONTROL SYSTEM

The basic requirements of an effective and workable control system are listed below:

(1) It Must be Understandable

The first requirement of a workable control system is that it must be well understood by both superiors and subordinates. The superior, while exercising control, must ensure what is to be controlled, who is to be controlled and what is sought through the control system. Similarly, subordinates must know what superiors are seeking and they are expected to contribute in this regard.

(2) Control Must be Flexible

An important consideration with regard to an effective control system is that it must be flexible to permit change as required. In the absence of required flexibility, unforeseen circumstances and happenings could possibly play havoc with the successful implementation of plans.

(3) Control Must be Economical

The cost of setting up and implementing a control system should not exceed the benefits which may possibly be derived from it. Therefore, it must be worth the expenses involved. Generally, small organisations cannot afford an elaborate control system that involves a huge financial outlay. To make the control system economical, the principle of exception and strategic point control should be followed strictly.

(4) Control System Must Point out Corrective Action

The essence of a control system is corrective action. Therefore, it must suggest remedial action. It is not enough for a control to discover deviations. It must be followed up with appropriate remedial measures to prevent the recurrence of the event and improve the existing level of performance.

(5) Appropriateness of a Control System

The control system must be appropriate to suit the requirements of the organisation. It must follow the pattern of the organisation. The control system in large organisations may be more elaborate and comprehensive as compared with that of a small organisation. Similarly, different types of controls are needed in marketing, finance, production and other departments.

(6) Objective

Every control system is designed and installed to accomplish some objectives. These objectives should be made clear and should be coordinated with the higher level objectives in such a way as to contribute to them. For example, the objective of inventory control may be to reduce the cost of the inventory used in production. These objectives should be coordinated with the objective of the production department such as continuity of the production process and reducing the total cost of production.

(7) Concentration on Exceptions

In this regard, there is a general rule that if the manager attempts to control every thing, he ends up controlling nothing. Therefore, the control system should concentrate on serious and major deviations. It must focus attention only on those factors that are critical for the performance of the functioning of the system. Generally, the more a manager concentrates his energies on important major deviations, the more effective will be the process of control.

(8) Objectives and Quantitative Yardstick

A workable and effective control system should possess a high degree of objectivity, fairness and rationality. An attempt should be made to use quantitative standards and scientific methods to reduce personal bias of the manager.

(9) Other Variables

The control system should give due allowance to factors and variables that cannot be controlled, but at the same time affect the performance of employees. It should be given careful thought at the time of developing standards of performance and their evaluation.

(10) Control Should be Forward Looking

Although instant control is considered more effective, it should also focus on providing early information regarding the changes that are likely to occur in the environment. The manager would definitely prefer a forecast of what may probably happen next week or next month or next year. Accordingly, he may prepare a package of remedial measures to avert undesirable situations.

(11) Interactive Nature of Control

In order to devise a control system for an organisation, care should be taken that all types of controls have been included in the system. This is because various types of controls are complementary to each other.

OPERATIONAL AND MANAGEMENT CONTROLS

The controlling device may be applied to an organisation as a whole or to any sub-system of the organisation. It may be applied to a particular operation or activity. On the basis of the area of application and scope, the controls may be divided into two categories such as 'operational control' and 'management control'.

Operational Control

Generally, when control is applied to a specific operation, it is known as operational control. According to Robert Anthony, "operational control is a process of ensuring that specific tasks are carried out effectively and efficiently. The thrust of operational control is on the individual task or transaction as against total or more aggregative management functions."

Operational control is based on the simple assumption that plans are made for various activities or departments of the organisation as a whole. Similarly, control can also be exercised in respect of a specific activity or group of activities or for the entire organisation. But the process of control will have the same stages for both operational and management control. The only point of difference is that the scope of operational control is limited to a specific activity. The standard of performance will be determined only for that activity to ensure that it is being performed in an efficient manner. However, in the area of operational control, there is a well-defined, measurable and proportionate relationship between input and output. Operational controls are generally programmed before. They do not require application of managerial knowledge on the part of managers handling such control. The following are examples of operational control:

(1) Stock control: Maintaining stock between the upper and lower limits.

(2) Budgetary control: Keeping performance in conformity with budget standards.

(3) Quality control: Maintaining product quality between set standards.

In order to enforce operational control, the procedures, rules and processes are formulated in respect of various operations. These are applied in a routine manner to perform those operations and controlling them. Thus, operational controls are self-regulatory rather than adaptive. They are hardly influenced by external environmental factors. Interestingly, the bureaucratic model of organisation developed by Max Weber possesses many characteristics of operational control. This is because in such organisations, control over the activities of employees is exercised solely on the basis of rules, procedures and processes determined in advance.

Such bureaucratic control seeks a high degree of precision, order, discipline, reliability and stability. They are mechanistic in nature and are not affected by other environmental factors. Personal likes, dislikes and prejudices of the manager who is exercising such control does not interfere with it. Bureaucratic controls are suitable for routine types of activities carried out at the lower level of an organisation when productivity can be expressed in terms of the relationship between input and output. But performance of higher level managers on more complex activities which requires the use of creativity, innovativeness and managerial knowledge cannot be made subject to such bureaucratic controls. Such controls do not provide any scope to use creativity and managerial judgement. Nor does it make any provision for adjusting the performance as per the changing environment.

Management Control

As stated earlier, management control is broader in scope and is applied to the organisation as a whole. In the words of Robert Anthony, it is a "process by which the managers assure that resources are obtained and used effectively and efficiently for the accomplishment of the organisation's objectives." According to this definition, management control is more inclusive and aggregative. It is concerned with the mobilisation and utilisation of all resources of organisation to achieve objectives efficiently. It includes and integrates those activities that are to be performed both for obtaining and using the resources. Basically, management control represents and ensures efficient control of all resources of the organisation. But the basic point of difference between operational control and management control is that the former deals with a specific operation and that too at a lower level of the organisation. The latter is concerned with a set of operations to be performed to obtain and use resources. Thus, it is more aggregative and broader in scope.

Management controls basically aim at preserving and promoting identity and existence of the organisation in the middle of both the internal as well as the external environment. These controls are exercised to make the organisation more adaptive, dynamic and self-regulatory against the complexities, uncertainties, disturbances and distortions that are imposed by the external environment. It is only by generating and transmitting the required information to all levels of management through the process of feedback can the situation be brought under control. In management control, attempts are made to make the organisation an ongoing and dynamic system through the process of learning. This is because the organisation keeps on getting experience in exercising control. Such experience may, at a later stage, be used to change the behaviour of the organisation and make it responsive to the external environment. So, management control involves feedback to the planning stage to translate the implications of environmental factors into revised planning assumptions which provide the base for subsequent control.

Management control is generally marked by the following distinct features:

(1) Management control is broad, aggregative, all-inclusive and more global in nature. It is applied to a system or to an organisation as a whole.

(2) It requires the application of creativity, innovativeness and managerial judgement on the part of the manager to exercise it.

(3) It covers higher level activities which are key or critical for the existence and survival of the organisation. Therefore, the base of such control is a higher level plan such as objectives, strategies, etc.

(4) For a set of activities to be controlled, the manager uses policies which are generally non-repetitive, closely related and interacting with each other.

(5) In exercising management control, the principles of social psychology are also followed. This is because social and psychological factors greatly influence the working behaviour of employees.

(6) While exercising management control, due care is taken about the principle of exception and strategic point control. This has been discussed earlier.

(7) It involves more use of subjective judgements and discretion because the standards of performance are not amenable to the relationship between input and output.

(8) Management controls are more adaptive and dynamic in nature. They are based on past learning and feedback from the planning stage so as to make necessary changes in the control process.

(9) Management control takes full care of external environmental factors. It is designed to cope with the complexities and diversities of a changing environment. It helps in protecting the organisation from external threats and disturbances.

BEHAVIOURAL EFFECTS OF CONTROL

Business organisations are man-made systems which are formed and operated by individuals. The functioning of these organisations is subject to imperfection, distortions and disturbances. This is because all sub-systems involved in an organisation cannot work in complete harmony, cooperation and in a flawless manner.

These inadequacies which are involved in man-made organisations affect its functioning in an adverse manner. Surprisingly enough, the advocates of the traditional approach of management strongly believed that the individual should work in these organisations in a totally machine-like manner. His working behaviour should be marked with a high degree of rationality.

The rationality is always far from realities and human origination cannot work as super human on the concept of rationality. But attempts are made to make the control system as rational as possible by using scientific methods and norms in it. For example, in a bureaucratic organisation, to make control more objective, certain rules and procedures are laid down to control situations. In doing so, the personal bias, likes and dislikes of the manager do not interfere in the process of controlling. However, the behaviour of the organisation is very complex. In addition to economic and technical factors, its functioning is greatly influenced by social and psychological factors. Therefore due consideration is given to beliefs, values, aspirations and needs of employees working in an organisation.

Thus, while designing a control system for an organisation, it should be recognised and appreciated that the performance of employees and their working behaviour cannot be made fully mechanised. The control system without a human face cannot control human behaviour and performance. Therefore, a control system should be realistic and a 'semi-rational instrument with a human face.'

In addition, all traditional forms of an organisation are strictly based on the concept of hierarchy and authority which implies a superior-subordinate relationship, although, for many reasons, this relationship seems to be desirable for the smooth functioning of the organisation. But totally authoritative attitudes on the part of the superior to deal with subordinates may not necessarily bring the desired results in all situations. Authority relations and authority-based control systems are considered to be coercive which implies the force of authority to control the activities of subordinates. It should, however, be remembered that excessive use of authority on the part of the superior represents close supervision and control that has outlived its utility.

Instead of forcing the subordinates to fall in line with the standards of performance and behaviour, they should be persuaded to comply voluntarily or with less use of authority. It is also true that every organisation operates on the basis of some predetermined rules, methods, policies and norms. The application of these organisational plans should be intended to ensure the smooth functioning of the organisation.

On the other hand, the use of rules and norms to control working behaviour of employees should be free from regulating, dominating, oppressing and policing. Obviously a set of rules will bring order and discipline in an organisation. At the same time, misuse or discretionary application of these may lead to a more complicated and harmful situation. In this connection, it has been rightly pointed out that in a traditional controls system which is based on the use of authority, conformity is at a premium and creativity is at a discount and innovativeness and imagination have little place in it.

The control systems that are marked by high degrees of rationality, rigidity and impersonality create a suffocative and tense environment for employees. Under such systems, initiative is not encouraged, creativity is not appreciated, innovativeness does not develop and imagination is not used. In these circumstances, employees are bound to behave in a defensive and over-cautious manner and tend to keep performance at a low level. Besides, such control systems give rise to many other unwanted and destructive forces such as stress, tension, resentment and dissatisfaction among employees. It does not affect only their level of performance but also hampers their career development. This is because they do not get any opportunity to interact freely with their superiors and to discuss work-related problems. They always work in a stressful and fearful environment. Due to a punishment-oriented control system, the performance of an employee may decrease.

On the basis of the above discussion regarding the basic nature of traditional control it is inferred that control should not be exercised to ensure conformity with standards by using force. It should be directed upon the employees in such a manner so as to make them self-regulated and controlled. It should also make them more competent and capable of handling situations and taking decisions to solve work-related problems. Thus, it calls for more freedom to be granted to them so that they may develop initiative, creativity and other constructive faculties to discharge assumed responsibility in a satisfactory manner. To make the control system more effective and responsive, it should be backed with supportive and dynamic leadership, proper motivation, cordial interpersonal relationship, persuasion, reformative attitude, facilitative role, effective communication system and conducive organisational climate. Further, a culture of self-direction, self-discipline and self-control should be allowed to grow so that each employee working in an organisation can play a more effective role by developing his career and contributing the maximum for the accomplishment of organisational goals.

SUMMARY

The managing process is incomplete without controlling. On the one hand, the process of managing comes to an end at controlling and on the other hand, it restarts from there. Controlling may be defined as a process of ensuring that each activity in the organisation is being performed in a planned manner.

It also involves regulating, checking and moulding working behaviour of the employees to make it more desirable. Controlling is a basic function of management which ensures that all management functions are performed to achieve planned goals. It is a continuous process which aims at taking corrective measures to bring the actual results closer to the desired results.

Controlling facilitates the effective utilisation of resources to achieve objectives. It brings order and discipline in the organisation and promotes and preserves the identity of the organisation against internal as well as external threats.

There is a close relationship between planning and controlling. These are considered as inseparable management twins which are interdependent, interacting and supplementary to each other.

A control cycle mainly consists of objectives, action plan, allocation of resources, delegation of authority, performance comparison with objectives, performance evaluation and feedback. It is slightly different from the controlling process.

The controlling process mainly involves the setting of standards of performance for employees, monitoring and measuring their actual performance, making comparison between these two to identify differences, analysing the causes of differences and finally taking corrective measures to improve performance or check recurrence of the event.

There are two important dimensions of control, namely 'critical point control' and 'control by exception'. If the operative system to be controlled is very complex and involves a large number of activities, the manager, instead of controlling each and every activity, concentrates on the more critical or important activities and through them the whole system is controlled.

According to the principle of 'control by exception', the manager takes care of those activities whose deviation is below or above permissible limits. Thus, if activities are performed according to standards it is not reported to the manager.

Control may be of three types, namely, post, current and pre-control. Post control is also known as feedback control which includes bringing future performance in line with standards on the basis of past performance. Control starts when the event has happened.

In current control there is a little gap between the occurrence of an event and the taking of remedial measures. As the event occurs simultaneously, instant corrective action is taken. Rather, such action is built in within the system and applied automatically if the situation starts going beyond permissible limits.

Pre control or feed forward control aims at taking preventive measures before the event occurs. At an early signal about the occurrence of the event, a set of preventive measures is kept ready. If the event starts occurring these measures are used to minimise losses arising out of the situation.

To perform control functions efficiently, a proper network of communication in the organisation is required. It plays an important role in all types of control. The effectiveness of a control system to a large extent depends on the availability of accurate information on time regarding the actual performance or on the occurrence of the event.

To control efficiently, continuous monitoring is required so that timely action can be taken before the situation goes out of control. This is possible only with the help of the required relevant and reliable information. Similarly, on the completion of a job or happening or event, the results are communicated to the manager through the process of feedback. The effectiveness of remedial measures depends on the availability of such information.

The control system in an organisation, to be more effective, must possess some features. It must be understandable, flexible, economical, appropriate, forward looking and interactive in nature. It must be focussed on the objectives, concentrated on serious exceptions and aim at taking remedial action to improve performance.

On the basis of area of application, controls may be divided into categories such as operational control and management control.

Operational control is applied to specific operations such as quality control, stock control, etc. Such controls are programmed beforehand and generally have similar stages involved as pointed out earlier. Operational controls are simple, routine type and based on rules, procedures and processes determined in advance.

Management control aims at mobilisation and utilisation of all resources of the organisation efficiently to achieve common goals. Such controls are broader in scope, aggregative in nature and applied to the entire organisation. Management control aims at promoting and preserving an identity of organisation against internal and external threats, uncertainties and other disturbances. It requires a lot of creativity, managerial knowledge and experience on the part of the manager who exercises it.

Organisations are man-made systems full of complexities and imperfections. It is therefore desirable that while designing and installing a control system in an organisation, norms of rationality, rigidity of relationships and the social and psychological aspects of the organisation are taken into account. Instead of imposing control on employees and forcing them to fall in line with it, more emphasis should be placed on self-regulatory control which may be enforced through education, environment, dynamic leadership, guidance of superiors and a set of sound plans and procedures.

TEST QUESTIONS

1. Define controlling and explain the various elements involved in the controlling process.
2. Define control and enumerate the requirements of an effective control system.
3. Discuss the importance of controlling in an organisation.
4. Describe the relationship between planning and controlling.
5. How would you measure and evaluate performance of a business school?
6. Explain the role of information in controlling.
7. Briefly discuss the various elements of a control cycle.
8. Distinguish between operational control and management control.
9. What would be recommended to make employees' response more positive or neutral in an organisational control system?
10. "If you start controlling everything, you will be controlling nothing". Comment.
11. Explain the role and significance of communication in controlling.
12. Write short notes on
    - (a) Pre-control and post-control
    - (b) Critical point control
    - (c) Control by exception
    - (d) Management information system
    - (e) Current control.
13. What do you mean by management control? Explains its important features.

OBJECTIVE TYPE QUESTIONS

Which of the following statements are correct and which are incorrect? Give reasons to support your answers.

1. Feed forward control is preventive control.
2. Real time control aims at instant corrective action.
3. Operational control is mostly routine and standardised.
4. An effective control system is always backward looking.
5. Feed forward control is the same as post-control.
6. Critical point control does not focus on key result areas of performance.

7. Operational control does not involve much managerial judgement and discretion to handle the system.
8. Preventive control is superior to post-control and current control.
9. Current control is also known as 'steering' control.
10. Feedback control implies corrective action before the event occurs.
11. "No news is good news" is a theme of critical point control.
12. Controlling also involves the motivational aspect.

REFERENCES

Abegglen, J. C. *The Japanese Factory: Aspect of its Social Organisation*. Glencoe, Ill., U.S.A.: Free Press, 1958.

Arens, Alvin A.and Loebbelke, James K. *Auditing and Integrated Approach*. Englewood Cliffs, N.J., U.S.A.: Prentice Hall, 1984.

Berger, F. J., Roethlis and Dickson, W. J. *Management and the Workers*. Cambridge, U.S.A.: Harvard University Press, 1939.

Flamholtz, Eric. 'Organisational Control Systems as Managerial Tool'. *California Management Review*. 22, Winter, 1979.

Koontz, Harold and Bradspies, Robert W. 'Managing Through Feed Forward Control'. *Business Horizons*. 15, June, 1972.

Kreintner, Robert. *Management*. Delhi, India: A.I.T.B.S. Publishers and Distributors, 1996.

Mockler, Robert J. *The Management Control Process*. Englewood Cliffs, N.J., U.S.A.: Prentice-Hall, 1984.

Moshal, B. S. *Management: Theory and Practice*. New Delhi, India: Galgotia Publishing Company, 2002.

Pinches, George E. *Essentials of Financial Management*. New York, U.S.A.: Harper and Row, 1990.

Selznick, C. F. Philip. *The Organisational Weapon*. New York, U.S.A.: McGraw-Hill, 1952.

Smith, Jack I., Keith, Robert M. and Stephens, William I. *Accounting Principles*. New York, U.S.A.: McGraw-Hill, 1989.

Stoner, A. F. and Freeman, R. Edward. *Management*. New Delhi, India: Prentice Hall of India Private Limited, 1995.

Trice, Harrison M. and Beyer, Janice M. *The Cultures of Work Organisations*. Englewood Cliffs, N.J., U.S.A.: Prentice-Hall, 1998.

EXPERIENCE I

Quality Control in Arvind Mills

For Arvind Mills, global quality is not just a buzzword; it is a target that must be met 365 days a year, 24 hours a day, 60 minutes an hour and 60 seconds to the minute to ensure that every millimetre of the 1.90 metres of denim it spins out every second conforms to specifications laid down by Arvind's global customers. Actually, Arvind's planning for quality began in 1987 when it chose globalisation as a survival strategy. In 1987, when Arvind sent its first sample to Levi Strauss, the jeans maker subjected it to its specifications criteria that related to the diameter of the yarn, the moisture content, etc., and rejected it. Arvind was thus forced to spend the next six years in creating a new infrastructure, redesigning its sourcing, shop and processes radically to meet Levi Strauss' requirements.

They set up a quality goal for themselves of 'building quality into the process rather than on inspection'. The company formalised its quality vision in a statement that appears on every table and wall of Arvind's plants. "We are committed to implementing all actions necessary to ensure letting the customer dictate quality standards." Managers went directly to them to find out requirements. They have built up global quality into all four components of its production process: sourcing raw material, manufacturing the product, monitoring for flaws and shipping it to the customer. All people of the organisation, senior experienced ones as well as freshers, committed themselves to the global quality goal. Arvind Mills uses automated check, regular off-line laboratory analyses of the material produced (a second line of quality control) as well as manual checks by trained people to ensure that only good quality fabric is manufactured at Arvind Mills. To back its quality systems, the company has chosen a quality focused recruitment and training policy.

To activate its quality control devices, Arvind empowers its workforce to shut down machines themselves whenever the output goes out of control. So, training courses are designed to encourage participation and process ownership. Unlike the usual classrooms, where trainees face the trainer, Arvind's training centre comprises a cluster of round tables, each with own presentation kits—a seating design which promotes teamwork. The company has also realised that the multi-skilling of its people is important.

These quality measures taken up seriously have fetched rich dividends for Arvind Mills with an 85 per cent repeat buying rate. The last time when the company had a consignment returned on quality control was in 1991; it is six years hence that no Arvind fibre has been rejected on quality basis. Its denim quality has been rated in the top percentile on the basis of independent validation by the Swiss company, Uster, which monitors the performance ratings of yarns from companies across the world.

Because of its quality standards, its Arrow range of premium shirts received ISO 9002 certification in March 1992.

CASE STUDY I

Control out of Bounds

In the machine age, control was of utmost importance. Executives used a set of rigid control devices. They focused on comprehensive reporting systems and never ending review meetings. They were allergic to sudden developments in work settings. They were capable of controlling all the resources needed for corporate success. Attempts were made to precisely specify boundaries of different business units to eliminate the interdependence of resources across the portfolio. Critical inputs were controlled through backward integration.

In the new age, boundaries of control have disappeared. It is not possible to control what is now critical for corporate success (that is, competitors' intentions, emerging market needs, etc.) Executives have no longer any control over other factors such as emerging crises and opportunities. At the most what they can do is to utilise over-the-horizon radar system and build flexibility in everything they do. They have eventually lost their ability to control 'things' for varied reasons. On the one hand, there are factors as speed and unpredictability of 'things' taking place around them. On the other hand, the resources that are critical for corporate survival and growth are beyond their direct control. Network has replaced hierarchy. There is no compulsion for enhanced dependence on suppliers. Attempts must be made to look for suitable alliance partners to share risk in R&D investment. There is an urgent need to find ways to encash emerging opportunities across the business unit. Today's executives are required to exert influence rather than control.

A reputed multinational food processing unit, with an annual turnover of Rs. 30 crore, set up an apple juice concentrate plant in a remote and backward area in Kashmir. The area was very close to the 'apple belt' and the company was being supplied pre-falls and culls at a cheap rate. The plant, being of a seasonal nature, was operational for a maximum of four months in a year. Consequently, there was a heavy pressure on the production personnel to produce the maximum during that period. The company was equipped with a well-organised control department to ensure that the product conformed to the highest quality standards. The quality control and production departments were headed by a qualified and experienced food technologist, Mr. Sudhir, who was assisted by a team of well qualified and experienced production foremen and quality control chemists. Mr. Sudhir reports to the factory manager, Mr. Goyal, who apart from being a mechanical engineer from IIT, had a management degree from the U.K.

Strict Quality Control

The chemists working in the quality control department were very strict and possessed a fair degree of integrity. They would reject truckloads of apples

Case Study I continued

Case Study I continued

of inferior quality. The apple purchase department personnel, who reported to Mr. Goyal directly often protested to the factory manager that the rejection was unwarranted on the plea of non-availability of good quality prefalls. However, such protests were more due to lack of 'quality consciousness' among the apple purchase personnel. As a result, while the plant was able to produce concentrates of high quality, the quantity produced was not even half the planned target. The concentrate was exported to America where it found acceptance in the face of stiff quality competition.

During the second season, Mr. Sudhir was transferred to another plant and the production department was put under the engineering in charge, Mr. Koul, who was an engineering graduate without any experience of production. The quality control department was now put under Mr. Goyal directly. Further, a fresh management trainee, Mr. Raju, (an engineering graduate from IIT), was recruited and asked to look after the apple purchase department. Both Mr. Koul and Mr. Raju were young and 'over-enthusiastic'. They were given targets to be achieved and were clearly told that quality should be given top priority.

To begin with, Mr. Goyal decided to commence production early in the season against the advice of quality control personnel. Because of the high acidity of the apples in the early part of the season, the concentrate produced was sub-standard. Subsequently, the suggestions given by quality control personnel were either neglected or not implemented by Mr. Goyal on the plea that the production target had to be realised at any cost. Thus, even low-grade apples were accepted and crushed. This lack of quality consciousness on the part of Mr. Goyal demoralised the quality control chemists and they started losing interest in their jobs. Both Mr. Koul and Mr. Raju achieved the targets, which exceeded the planned targets. Once again, the concentrate was exported to America despite the fact that the laboratory had certified its low quality. Not surprisingly, the concentrate was rejected in that country. The management took a serious view of the situation and Mr. Goyal was finally transferred and demoted.

Questions

1. Was it a wise step to transfer Mr. Sudhir considering his qualifications and experience as also the importance of maintaining high quality standards?
2. Should the factory manager have initiated steps towards better coordination between the purchase and quality control departments?
3. Was Mr. Goyal justified in ignoring the suggestions of the quality control personnel?
4. What was expected from Mr. Goyal as factory manager?

—oo(O)oo—

CHAPTER 16

CONTROLLING TECHNIQUES AND COORDINATION

LEARNING OBJECTIVES

1. To know traditional techniques of controlling, particularly budgetary control.
2. To know modern techniques of controlling, especially MIS, management audit and network techniques.
3. To understand coordination and its nature and its significance as an essence of management.

Managers have many controlling techniques at their disposal. They use them according to their needs and suitability of a particular technique. But in practice, a combination of two or more than two techniques may be used to exercise efficient control and to get better results. It is because no single technique is complete in itself. These techniques may be placed in two groups.

TRADITIONAL TECHNIQUES

(1) Direct supervision and personal observation

(2) Budgetary control

(3) Financial statements

(4) Breakeven analysis.

MODERN TECHNIQUES

(1) Management information systems
(2) Management audit
(3) Control by return on investment techniques
(4) Self control
(5) Network techniques
    (a) Project evaluation and review technique (PERT)
    (b) Critical path method (CPM)

TRADITIONAL TECHNIQUES

(1) Direct Supervision and Personal Observation

In an organisation with various techniques of control, one should not overlook the importance of direct supervision because much of the control in an organisation is attempted through this technique. Under this controlling technique, the manager or supervisor ensures that each employee performs his work as per given standards or norms by on-the-spot overseeing and observation.

The physical presence of the manager and his deep involvement in the work-situation regarding the progress of work has a definite influence over the performance and behaviour of subordinates.

Observing the actual performance of work done by employees at the work place is considered to be one of the oldest control techniques that seems to be very effective also. The manager can seek more important first-hand information on various aspects of the work performance through face-to-face contact. Sometimes the manager takes corrective action just on the spot without any loss of time. Although managers working at higher levels do not find enough time to visit the work site, in view of the growing significance of personal observation every manager plans some visits to the various work units to ascertain how things are going on. Through direct supervision, the manager can maintain work discipline among subordinates and in turn, they also get an opportunity to express their problems and difficulties and offer suggestions regarding the work and physical working conditions under which it is being performed. This controlling technique also helps the manager to understand the various dynamics of the work being performed.

This kind of information may prove to be useful for him at the time of planning the work because if he remains in direct touch with various work units and subordinates working therein he may prepare a plan that can be implemented without any problems and hardship. However, the technique of personal observation is very time-consuming but no other device can substitute it. Unscheduled visits of the manager to the work site may also put psychological pressure on employees to comply with prescribed norms. It also boosts the morale of the work force because they can freely interact with the manager or supervisor.

(2) Budgetary Control

Budgetary device has two aspects, preparation of the budget that is concerned more with planning and implementation which seems to be more related to control. Budgets are a useful tool of control because they facilitate measurement comparison, monitoring and evaluation of organisational activities, which have been expressed in monetary terms as against budgetary estimates.

Budgetary control is considered as one of the most important traditional control devices. However, to exercise control over day-to-day operations of the organisation by way of preparing various budgets and getting them executed is known as budgetary control.

The Institute of Cost and Management Accountants of England and Wales has defined budgetary control as "the establishment of objective relating to the responsibility of execution to the requirement of a policy and the continuous comparison of actual and budgetary results either to secure by individual action the objective of that policy or provide a basis for its revision."

Though the elements or essentials of budgetary control remain almost similar relatively in big organisations the entire budgetary system may be more complex as per their requirements. In many organisations, only important activities are planned and controlled by means of budgets. In brief, budgets are formal quantitative statements of resources set aside to carry out planned activities over a given period. As such, they are commonly used to plan and control activities at every level of the organisation.

Elements of Budgetary Control

Basically, the process of budgetary control involves the following essential elements.

(1) As usual as in other controlling devices, at the first stage of budgetary control, the overall corporate objectives of the organisation have to be broken down into departmental goals and these goals are further narrowed down into specific targets which can easily be translated into standards of performance. In other words, long-term objectives are converted into short-term objectives such as sales volume, market share, production level, profit, etc. These are known as budgeted standards.

(2) At the second stage of budgetary control, to achieve standards of performance or short-term or operational goals, a proper estimation of the required physical and human resources is prepared.

(3) Allocation of budget is sought for various activities which are to be performed to achieve these budgetary goals.

(4) Responsibility centres are designed at various levels of the organisation and accountability is fixed on the concerned executive who has authority to perform that operation. For example, in a sales budget, the sales manager who has authority over physical and human resources may be made accountable to generate a specific volume of sale of a particular product over a period.

(5) Constant monitoring, measuring, and evaluation of actual results to be obtained through budgets is made to facilitate comparison of actual results with budgeted results and to discover any gap between them.

(6) At the final stage, deviations which are alternatively known as 'budgetary variations' are studied and analysed to find out possible causes and thereby devising suitable remedial measures to bring actual results closer to budgeted standards.

Advantages

Budgetary control offers the following advantages:

(1) Since budgets are prepared in monetary units, they can directly convey information on key organisational goals such as profit. Therefore, they are considered more useful for profit organisations.

(2) Budgets establish a clear and unambiguous standard of performance for a set period of time, usually a year. At periodic intervals during that period actual performance may be compared with the budgeted figure, deviations can quickly be detected and acted upon for improvements.

(3) It also establishes a clear relationship and balance between inputs such as material, labour, capital and time and output such as production, profit and performance.

(4) Budgeting is also used for coordinating the activities of various departments of the organisation. Thus, production should bear a logical relation with sales and the sales budget cannot be prepared without knowing production programmes and schedules. Not only the act of preparing a budget but integrating it into the master budget facilitates coordination.

(5) Like other controlling techniques, budgetary control is also a source of motivation for personnel involved in its execution, because to execute it, adequate authority is given to them, necessary resources are allocated and budgetary sanctions are made within which they act with a higher degree of freedom.

(6) It is an effective device of control for management. It enables the manager to compare and measure actual performance against predetermined budgetary standards and act accordingly to control the situation or performance.

(7) Budgetary control facilitates management by exception because it helps to attract attention on the efforts of the manager on those operations which deviate in a significant way from budgeted standards.

(8) It can also be used as an important device for fixing responsibility on managers working at different levels. In case actual results do not conform to budgetary goals, they will be accountable to higher level managers.

(9) Budgets provide allocation of resources for various operations and departments according to their requirements. They also indicate the direction in which these resources have to be utilised to lead to maximum effective use of the resources of the organisation.

(10) Budgets are important instruments of managerial planning and control. They prescribe time-bound targets or results and determine the future course of action to achieve those targets and the state of future uncertainty is tackled in an effective way.

3. Financial Statements

Annual financial statements prepared by organisations at the end of each financial year may be used as important tools of control. These statements include trading and profit-and-loss account, and the balance sheet provides a means to monitor three major financial conditions of the organisation. These are

1. Liquidity of the organisation, that is, the ability of the organisation to convert assets into cash to meet current financial needs and obligations.
2. Profitability, that is, the ability of the organisation to earn profit regularly over an extended period of time.
3. Financial position, that is, long-term balance between debt and equity capital.

Financial statements are usually prepared at the end of each financial year on the basis of transactions and events which have occurred during that period. Thus, these statements cannot be used to influence transactions and events that have occurred in the past. By analysing the information given in the statements of the previous years, the dynamics of revenue generation and incidence of expenditure and trends of change in the assets and liabilities may be uncovered. On the basis of such information, a projected financial statement can be prepared for the next year. The information contained in these statements can be used by the management, creditors, investors and prospective investors and others to form their judgement regarding the operating performance and financial position of the organisation. The various parties use the information given in these statements to get a better insight into the financial strengths and weaknesses of the organisation. Further, the information given in financial statements also facilitates ratio analysis to be conducted by managers. These financial ratios, in fact, have predictive power as to whether a business will survive or not. The financial ratios are generally categorised as under.

(i) Liquidity

How well the organisation can meet its short-term obligations.

(ii) Assets Management

How effectively the organisation has been managing its assets.

(iii) Debt Management

To what extent debt capital has been used by the organisation.

(iv) Profitability

What the combined effects of assets management, debt management and liquidity on the profitability of the organisation are.

(v) Market Value

How investors consider the past performance of the organisation and its future prospects.

By calculating various ratios in each area of operation and then comparing them with standard ratios, managers can exercise feed forward and feedback financial controls.

In brief, an analysis of financial statement represents the process of identifying financial strengths and weaknesses of the organisation by establishing a relationship between the items of the balance sheet and the profit and loss account. It can be undertaken either by the management itself or by an outside party hired for the purpose. To add to the value of the financial statement as a tool to be used for financial control, various accounting software packages have been developed.

4. Break-even Analysis

In order to ascertain and control the behaviour of cost, revenue and profit at various levels of activities, the break-even technique is commonly used. In well managed businesses, the concept of profit is a forethought rather than an afterthought. Break-even analysis is often considered as cost, volume profit analysis. By using the algebraic or graphic method, managers can calculate the break even point, the level of sales or production at which the organisation neither earns a profit nor suffers a loss. In fact, the break-even point is a profit-making threshold because every additional unit sold or produced above this point will fetch a margin of profit for the organisation. The organisation generally incurs two types of costs to the effect of production or sales.

These are fixed cost and variable cost. Fixed cost includes those costs which are incurred by the organisation irrespective of the level of production or sale. It remains fixed regardless of how much the organisation produces, a single unit or the maximum capacity available. Such cost includes all contractual costs like rent, utilities, insurance premium, managerial and professional staff salaries, property taxes and licences.

Variable costs are those costs which vary directly with the volume of production or sales such as labour, material overheads, sales commission, transport expense, etc.

The following algebraic method is commonly used to calculate the break-even point:

$$\text{BEP} = \frac{\text{fixed cost}}{\text{p} - \text{Variable cost}}$$

$$\text{(p)} = \text{is price per unit}$$

The difference between the price per unit and variable cost per unit is technically referred to as a contribution margin. Above the break-even point, the margin of contribution contributes to the profit of the firm.

The technique of BE analysis may profitably be used for price planning and profit planning. On the one hand, it helps the manager to know what impact price change will have on the profit and on the other, it seeks to determine the required level of output to earn a specific amount of profit. But the major problem associated with this technique is that, in practice, it is very difficult to make a clear distinction between fixed costs and variable costs. Moreover, because of the complex factors involved in the demand and supply of a product, the technique remains more important only for general planning and decision making thereby having less scope of being used as a control device.

MODERN TECHNIQUES

1. Management Information Systems

Information is not only an important input for the process of planning and decision making but it also plays a significant role in the process of control because it is only on the basis of reliable and relevant information can a standard of performance be set up and the performance of subordinates be regularly monitored, evaluated and measured. Feedback of information helps in revising standards and making the controlling system more effective. To provide the necessary information to the manager on a regular basis a 'management information system' is installed. This system may be defined as an assemblage of personnel and facilities for collecting, processing, storing, retrieving and transmitting information that is required by one or more managers in the performance of their functions. The managers working at various levels such as higher, middle and lower require information on both the internal as well as the external environment for a better understanding of the problems faced by them and for finding appropriate solutions for them. These sets of required information may be generated by the management information system both from internal as well as external sources. It enables managers to make timely and factual decisions on various strategic and operational matters and problems. A management information system provides information to managers on past, current and projected estimates prepared for the future. It also increases the alertness and awareness of the managers by supplying information in the form of progress reports and review reports on various ongoing operations. Systematic collection, supply and storage of information through this system avoids duplication and overload of information, because only that information is supplied to managers that is required by them.

To make the system cost effective and responsive to the requirements of the organisation, it is designed by applying the system approach in consultation with the various managers because to develop and process the information economically, all activities regarding information generation, flow, storage and distribution of information have to be made in a proper system.

Managers at all levels find that the management information system provides information necessary for effective operation. These information systems are rapidly becoming indispensable for planning, decision making and controlling because the promptness and accuracy with which managers receive information about what is going on correctly and what is going on wrongly largely determines the effectiveness of a controlling system.

In view of the growing importance of information, particularly in planning and controlling, managers consider it as a valuable asset that needs to be carefully managed and protected. Although, managers might use the information for different objectives, they evaluate information on the basis of the following factors:

(i) Quality of Information

The more precise and accurate the information, the higher will be the quality of decisions made by managers relying on it. However, the cost of obtaining information keeps on increasing as the quality of information becomes superior. Therefore, if information of superior quality does not help managers significantly in decision making, it will not be considered an asset.

(ii) Timeliness of Information

To exercise effective control, corrective action must be taken and applied before major deviations take place. Therefore, the required information must be provided to the right person at the right time for appropriate action to be taken.

(iii) Quantity of Information

Managers cannot make accurate and timely decisions if sufficient information is not made available to them. If they receive more information, which is known as information overload, they may overlook important information on serious problems or may engage in irrelevant information.

(iv) Relevance of Information

The information supplied to the managers must be relevant to their jobs, responsibilities, tasks and positions. For example, the personnel manager does not need to know the levels of inventories and the information supplied to the finance manager about matters related to the personnel department will be irrelevant to his job and position.

Though management information systems may be manual and mechanised, in view of its central role, most organisations prefer to computerise it since in such a setting the role of the information system becomes more meaningful and significant in terms of its scope and quality. Computer systems are more useful and cost effective

(i) where there is a large volume of routine data to be processed;

(ii) when tasks and activities are repetitive;

(iii) when it is necessary to store and have quick access to a large volume of data and information;

(iv) when speedy processing and up-to-the minute business records are essential; and

(v) when there is a need to perform complex computation.

Modern managers become effective and comfortable with the use of computers for the following reasons:

(i) It facilitates the collection, management and communication of information up and down the hierarchy as well as between managers at the same level.

(ii) It leads to automatic operations both in the factory and in the office.

(iii) It supports decision making, planning and controlling at all levels.

(iv) It simplifies management control.

(v) It gives an edge over competitors.

(vi) It improves the quality of information.

(vii) It ensures cost effectiveness in managing information.

2. Management Audit

In connection with the control of overall performance, management audits are becoming increasingly important and popular. These audits are different from those performed by external auditors which concentrate on the verification of financial data. A management audit provides a device to survey and evaluate how effectively and efficiently organisational operations and activities have been managed. The management audit may also be defined as a systematic evaluation of the functioning, performance and effectiveness of the management of an organisation. Management audit is generally conducted at the instance of top management to ascertain and review the quality of management. It may also be known as internal audit because it is conducted by a team of experts drawn from relevant areas of the organisation. It is, however, to be noted that it starts from where the balance sheet audit leaves off. Broadly, it is an independent appraisal of various operations and systems within an organisation to determine whether acceptable policies and procedures are being followed, standards are being met, resources are being used efficiently and economically, planned objectives are being accomplished effectively and, finally, organisational goals are being achieved. The management audit is intended to serve the interest of the organisation as a whole. Generally, a management audit team consisting of various experts and specialists forms its opinions and conclusions based on the analysis of evidence and information against a set of criteria of performance and effectiveness. On the basis of such evaluation, recommendations to improve the quality of management may be made.

The management audit mainly covers the following areas which are known as 'searchlight areas':

(i) Determination of corporate objectives, formulation of other corporate plans such as strategies, policies, programmes, procedures, rules, etc. The extent to which they have been pursued and observed and the extent to which they have been achieved.

(ii) Design of organisational structure consisting of role, relationship, authority and responsibility.

(iii) Degree of effectiveness and efficiency with which organisational resources have been allocated, mobilised and utilised to seek objectives.

(iv) The manner in which and the degree of co-ordination with which all sub-systems of the organisation are functioning and contributing to the overall functioning of the organisation.

(v) Internal environment including work culture and climate and its contribution to cooperation, harmony, productivity, satisfaction, etc.

(vi) Quality and timeliness of managerial decisions made by managers to solve problems.

(vii) Detailed appraisal of various control systems installed and operating in the organisation.

(viii) Operational efficiency of the organisation.

(ix) Effectiveness in handling environmental threats and problems.

Advantages

Management audit offers the following advantages:

(i) It helps in pointing out inadequacies and deficiencies in the entire process of management. On its basis, necessary attempts may be made to improve the overall efficiency of the management process.

(ii) It seeks to improve communication and control systems installed in an organisation to increase its operational efficiency.

(iii) It promotes and protects organisations from outside threats and challenges by initiating timely and appropriate strategies to deal with the changing environment.

(iv) By improving coordination in the functioning of various subsystems it helps to secure effective organisational functioning.

(v) It ensures updating of the existing set of managerial policies, strategies and other important plans to make them responsive to the existing situation.

(vi) Management audit encourages creativity and innovativeness among the managerial personnel working in the organisation.

3. Control by Return on Investment

This controlling technique is mainly used in large organisations. It provides the basic yardstick to measure whether invested capital has been used effectively or not to generate a reasonable amount of return. In every organisation, the ownership group that takes risks associated with business intends to get a reward for it in the form of return on investment. The rate of return on investment is an overall measure of the financial performance of the organisation or of its individual departments or divisions. It can be calculated as under.

$$\text{ROI} = \frac{\text{Net income}}{\text{Sales}} \times \frac{\text{Sales}}{\text{Total Investment}}$$

In other words, net income is the residue of revenue generated through sales and cost of sales. Net income before or after corporate tax may be used for making a comparison. Total investment includes both working as well as fixed capital invested in business. It provides top management an effective means of control and measures to compare the activities and performance of departmental managers. This technique also permits managers to find out the source of difficulty and problems which affect the return on investment in an adverse manner. This technique does not look at profit as an absolute criterion but as a return on capital employed in business. The objective of business is to optimise return from capital employed in business rather than to optimise profits only. It recognises the importance of capital in the business, by considering capital as a scarce resource which may limit the further growth and development of an organisation if it is not employed and used effectively and efficiently. To ensure its optimal utilisation, points of spoilage, leakage, inefficiency and mis-utilisation are to be taken care of and plugged promptly. According to this technique, return on capital can be increased either by increasing sales volume proportionately more than the total investment or by reducing total investment without having any reduction in sales volume. It can also be done by increasing the sales volume proportionately more than the cost of sales or by reducing the cost of sales proportionately more than the decrease in sales volume. This has been a key technique in the control system of Dupont Company, U.S.A., during 1919 and subsequently many other organisations in the U.S.A. have also accepted the relevance and appropriateness of this technique. Nowadays, it is still considered a very powerful technique of control because it focuses attention on the utilisation of resources of an organisation. It highlights inefficiency and inadequacies in relation to the utilisation of resources and necessitates timely action to improve it.

4. Self-Control

In the context of modern management, the self-control approach is considered very effective. Behavioural scientists also recognize that control is more effective when it is self-directed. In fact, self control is a part of 'auto-management' which provides the conditions and environment in which employees feel more homely in the organisation while performing assigned jobs. The concept of self-control is in contrast to the traditional approach of 'close supervision and control' in which the manager hardly grants any freedom to his subordinates; rather they are forced to obey all orders and instructions given to them. This is also known as imposed control in which generally employees feel uncomfortable, stressed and tensed which ultimately affects their level of performance in an adverse manner. This type of rigid and close control is exercised by managers who adopt an autocratic style of leadership. They expect that their subordinates carry out each directive and instruction given to them without questioning their relevance and need. As against this, in self-control, enough operational freedom is granted to subordinates to set standards of performance to decide the pace and speed of the work to be performed, evaluation of performance, comparison, analysis of deviation and taking corrective action. Self-control which is considered more effective and long-lasting helps in creating a sense of responsibility among employees towards the standard of performance and results as expected of them. Employees working under self-control feel highly committed and work more efficiently on a voluntary basis. However, to make self-control more effective and contributive, willingness among employees is to be created and they are trained and capable of assuming responsibility and work with least interference from their superior. They keep on consulting their superior only in case of complicated situations which they cannot handle on their own. In doing so, the superior simply acts as a watchdog concentrating more on strategic planning, controlling and coordination. In practice, the concept of self-control is not used completely in isolation of close control since in every situation of close control there seems to be some degree of self-control also and similarly all employees working in the organisation cannot be totally left to self-control since some degree of control is to be exercised by managers to control the activities of subordinates. The concept of self-control is more related to the behaviour of employees since it is just a matter of thinking that they are given more freedom by their superior to perform an assigned work. Even in such a situation, they do not hesitate in obtaining necessary directives on some more difficult problems from their superiors and they take such directives only as supportive and not as coercive measures. By creating conditions for self-control, the manager controls every thing but without imposing control on subordinates. Rather, in self-control they are induced voluntarily to comply with standard of performance and behaviour. Such types of controls are very common in a free-form of organisation in which employees do not work in the hierarchy of authority and assume joint responsibility and authority for performing work. Self-control not only grants operational freedom to employees but also seeks career development on their part by encouraging the use of creativity and innovativeness. It also provides greater satisfaction to them because the need for self-fulfilment and achievement is satisfied.

5. Network Techniques

In order to introduce an element of precision in planning and control, the network techniques, PERT (Project evaluation and review technique) and CPM (Critical path method) are used. These techniques are especially useful for planning, scheduling and implementing time-bound projects involving the performance of a variety of complex, diverse and interrelated activities. These techniques deal with time scheduling and resource allocation for activities involved in the project and aim at efficient execution of projects within a given time schedule and structure of costs. These techniques have their origin in the U.S.A. PERT was developed by a team of management consultants for the U.S. Navy special projects in 1958 and CPM was developed by Du Pont and Remington Rand.

Programme Evaluation and Review Technique

Although PERT was developed to plan and control Polaris submarine programmes, it contributed not only to the development of submarine projects but also helped to bring the system to a stage of readiness nearly two years ahead of schedule. It ultimately caught the attention of managers and since then has been regularly applied for planning, controlling and coordinating various activities of projects. The techniques of PERT and CPM involve the following steps:

(i) At the first stage, the project which comprises complex, diverse and specialised activities is broken into various identifiable activities. The term 'activity' may be defined as an operation or a job to be carried out for completing the project. These activities consume time and resources.

(ii) After having identified the various activities to be performed, they are arranged in a logical sequence. In order to arrange them in a network, their interrelationship is analysed because these activities may be interlinked with each other in several ways. For example, two activities may be related to each other in terms of a type of resource required. On the other hand, one activity may be of such a nature that it cannot be performed without having performed another activity. This kind of interdependence is known as precedence requirement.

(iii) Once various activities are arranged in a logical sequence, time estimates for each activity are prepared. These estimates consist of determination and assignment of timings at which the activity will start and finish. The duration of each activity is known as activity time. On the basis of the nature of the activity time, the projects may be classified into two groups:

- Projects in which activity time can be estimated with sufficient certainty such as building a house, erecting a plant, etc.
- Projects in which there is a high degree of uncertainty regarding activity time such as developing a new product, launching a space vehicle, etc.

In PERT, three estimates of time for each activity are calculated and then estimates of the expected time for each activity is determined. These estimates are

- Most likely time (TM): The time that is generally taken by the activity.
- Optimistic time (TO): The time by which an activity can be completed if everything is normal.
- Pessimistic time (TP): The time by which an activity will get completed even under adverse conditions.
- Expected time of activity (TE).

$$= \frac{TO + 4TM + TP}{6}$$

(iv) At this stage, in order to determine the total time required for completing a project, the sequence of these activities, completion of which is critical for the timely completion of the entire project, is discovered which is known as the critical path. The critical path tends to be the longest path in the network because it allows that certain activities cannot be started unless other related activities known as 'preceders' have been completed. If any activity in a critical path is delayed, the entire project will be delayed accordingly.

In PERT, the following key terms are used which must be properly understood to apply this technique:

Event

Event is a performance milestone representing the start to finish of an activity. Handling examinations is an event.

Activity

Activity is a time and resource consuming job that begins and ends with an event such as studying for an examination and taking an examination.

Time

Times are estimated times (which have been discussed in stage No. 3) for the completion of activities.

Critical Path Method

The critical path is the most time consuming chain or sequence of activities. In other words, it is the longest path critical in the sense that if any of the activities is delayed, the entire project is bound to be delayed.

POSITIVE AND NEGATIVE ASPECTS OF NETWORK TECHNIQUES

With a wide application of these techniques in business organisations, the positive and negative sides of these have become apparent.

(i) Application of these techniques for planning, controlling and executing big and complex projects is beneficial because with the help of this technique the project as a whole is broken up into various sequential activities that can be managed efficiently.

(ii) PERT is of great help to managers in planning because it forces them to visualise the project and its various activities in totality.

(iii) It also helps managers as a tool for predicting resource needs, potential problem areas and the impact of delay on the completion of the project. On the basis of it, they can initiate timely action.

(iv) The PERT technique is considered very useful, particularly in a situation which requires the project to be completed in time; especially when completion time is very important as otherwise it may attract some penalty, managers are left with no option but to use it.

(v) Efficient management of time and resources in respect of big projects leads to various economies and ultimately reduces its cost.

(vi) Identification of critical activities and their sequence indicates and ensures timely completion of projects even in an adverse situation. It also gives an opportunity to managers to calculate various time estimates in the context of the realities of uncertainties.

However, PERT is beset with the following limitations and drawbacks:

(i) It is a time-consuming technique and by the time the network of activities is developed it may become obsolete.

(ii) In practice, it has been found that estimates of time for various activities cannot be prepared on the basis of any scientific method; rather it is based on intuition and guesswork.

(iii) The PERT technique cannot be applied with regard to assembly line operations in which scheduling of operations is more guided by the speed of machines.

(iv) False and imaginary assumptions regarding activities and events may render the technique ineffective.

Although PERT and CPM have common characteristics in terms of the stages involved and application as a planning and control technique, they differ from each other on the following counts:

- The critical path method is invariably used in those projects that involve activities for which deterministic estimates can be prepared whereas PERT is used for those projects in which estimates are probable because of more uncertainties.
- The PERT technique may be used more profitably to execute those projects in which competition time is an essence, but CPM can be used for those projects in which the cost factor remains more important.

COORDINATION

Introduction and Meaning

An organisation is a large system consisting of many sub-systems that contribute to its functioning. In order to seek smooth and effective functioning of the entire organisation, these sub-systems are to be integrated and coordinated with each other and with a larger system. By coordinating them rationally their role may be made more meaningful. The term 'coordination' may be defined as the process of bringing about unity and harmony in the functioning of all departments or divisions or diverse sub-systems involved in the organisation. Thus, coordination is a conscious and rational managerial function of pulling together various components of organised activity and weaving them into a unified and integrated whole to achieve predetermined goals. Broadly, coordination is the process of integrating objectives and activities of separate work units or functional departments in order to realise organisational goals. Without coordination, people and departments will lose sight of their role in the organisation and may be tempted to pursue their own interests and goals at the cost of organisational goals. The process of coordination aims at forging unity of purpose and implementation of plans in a harmonious manner to seek common goals. The process of co-ordination is inevitable and imperative in group efforts as common goals can be achieved only by integrating, unifying and coordinating efforts made by the various members. In this connection, Luther Gulick has rightly pointed out that "if subdivision of work is inescapable, coordination becomes mandatory." However, it is to be remembered that coordination is not spontaneous but rather some deliberate efforts are to be made to achieve and maintain it. In the words of Ordway Tead coordination is "the efforts to ensure the smooth interplay of the functions and forces of all the different components and parts of an organisation to the end that its purpose will be realised with a minimum of function and maximum of collaborative effectiveness." Tead also made it clear that the functions and forces of various departments or sub-systems are brought together in such a way so as to achieve the goals of the organisation effectively.

Many authors belonging to the classical approach of management have given a lot of attention to coordination. James Mooney considered it as the first principle of an organisation; Fayol defines it as a means of using and correlating organisational activities and Urwick considers that the purpose of organisation is itself a coordination.

There has been a controversy regarding the scope and nature of coordination among various authors of management and organisation. Henri Fayol considered it as one of the functions of management but Theo Haimann considers it a part of all managerial functions. Newman has also described coordination as a part of all phases of administration. However, coordination is often regarded as an 'essence of management' or as the epitome of management. Because, it is spread over the entire process of management. Each managerial function is an exercise in coordination. All management functions need coordination and are to be performed in a co-ordinated manner to achieve organisational goals. In other words, the manager brings about the process of co-ordination as he performs the five basic functions of management. Therefore, more precisely, co-ordination should be viewed as an orderly synchronisation of efforts of subordinates to provide proper timing and quality of execution so that their unified efforts lead to objectives, namely the common purpose of the organisation.

By making a careful analysis of the definitions of coordination given above, the following features may be drawn:

(i) Coordination is basically a responsibility of every manager since he performs management functions and he is in an authoritative position to maintain coordination.

(ii) It is a rational and conscious process since for maintaining coordination the manager has to make deliberate efforts on his part.

(iii) A continuous process as it is spread over the entire process of management which is to be repeated in a continuous manner.

(iv) Also regarded as a part of the classical approach of management as a lot of attention has been given to it by classical authors like Mooney, Urvick, Fayol, Luther Gluick, etc.

(v) Aims at securing smooth functioning of an organisation with the help of its sub-systems and thereby to achieve organisational goals.

(vi) May also be recognised as a 'system'.

(vii) May be regarded as the mother function of management in which all other functions like planning, organising, staffing, directing and controlling are embedded.

NEED AND SIGNIFICANCE OF COORDINATION

The necessity of coordinating individual activities arises out of differences of opinion as to how common goals can be achieved and how individual goals and organisational goals can be integrated since common goals can be accomplished effectively only when activities performed by members through various departments are harmonised. The extent to which coordination is needed in an organisation depends on the communication requirements of the tasks performed and the degree of interdependence of the various departments performing them. If the performance of tasks requires an information flow between departments, then a high degree of coordination is needed. Broadly, the need and significance of coordination may be understood on the basis of the following factors:

(i) Core of Group Efforts

Coordination is more imperative and indispensable in group efforts, that is, where two or more individuals are working together to accomplish common goals and their activities have to be synchronised. Without integrating and unifying them, common goals cannot be realised effectively.

(ii) Unification of Activities

To create a structure of the organisation, activities are divided and sub-divided into smaller jobs and tasks making them distinct and different. Thus, unless these tasks and jobs are harmonised by bringing them into related groups, organisational goals cannot be achieved. Diversity among various work units, departments and individual employees is reduced through coordination.

(iii) Interdependence of Work Units

The various work units created in an organisation normally have interdependence. They require frequent interaction to be made with each other. It is possible only through coordination devices since they are a means of managing these interdependences and interactions.

(iv) Integration of Goals

Through the process of coordination, it is ensured that individual goals are integrated with departmental goals and departmental goals are well merged and harmonised with overall organisational goals. This is done in such a way so that the goals at a lower level contribute to the goals at a higher level.

(v) Key to other Managerial Functions

The importance of coordination also lies in the fact that it is a key for other management functions like planning, organising, staffing, directing and controlling. As coordination helps in making plans more purposeful and meaningful, an organisation is more well knit, direction is more effective and control more regulative and efficient.

(vi) Resolution of Conflicts

In an organisation, conflicts or clashes may frequently arise due to roles, relationships, contributions, positions, values and norms. If they are not resolved in time, organisational functioning may be adversely affected. Coordination becomes imperative to reduce and resolve such conflicts and thereby secure unity of action in the pursuit of common goals.

(vii) Harmonising Organisational Flows

To maintain the smooth functioning of an organisation, various flows involved in it such as flow of information, authority and resources should be harmonised. This is done in a predetermined manner taking into account timing, volume and direction of these flows. For example, if the required information is not provided in time to the manager, it may hamper the process of decision making. Similarly, if enough authority and resources are not provided in time it may adversely affect the implementation of the plan.

According to Henri Fayol, in a well coordinated enterprise the following facts are to be observed:

(i) Each department works in harmony with the others. The store knows what has to be supplied and at what time, production knows its target, maintenance keeps equipment and tools in good order, finance procures the necessary funds, and security sees to the protection of goods and services, personnel. All these activities are carried on in a sure orderly fashion.

(ii) Each department, division and sub-division is precisely informed as to its share in the joint task and reciprocal aid they are to afford each other.

(iii) The working schedule of various departments and subdivisions thereof is constantly attuned to circumstances.

TECHNIQUES OF ACHIEVING COORDINATION

The task of achieving coordination is very difficult. It may be further complicated if the jobs and tasks are highly specialised, interdependence is greater and difference of opinion and perceptions regarding the role, relationship and goals of the organisation are very sharp. It should, however, be noted that coordination is not subject to executive command and directives; rather some meaningful attempts should be made by managers to achieve it. The following techniques may help in achieving co-ordination:

(i) Authority Relationship

Well-organised formal groups of employees represent the authority relationship of superiors and subordinates. This relationship which also implies vertical structure or authority structure of an organisation greatly helps in maintaining coordination. Every superior having authority exercises it to control the activities of subordinates and to bring about coordination in their functioning.

(ii) Clearly Defined and Well-understood Objectives

For effective coordination, it is desirable that every department and individual employee working therein understands the organisational objectives. The knowledge of these objectives will result in commonness of purpose and activities being performed in various departments may be unified in the light of these objectives.

(iii) Use of Standing Plans

To guide decision-making and action on the part of the manager, several standing plans such as policies, procedures, rules and methods are made. These plans are used to solve routine and repetitive problems faced by different departments. It ultimately brings uniformity and consistency in decision-making and action on the part of every managerial and non-managerial employee.

(iv) Communication Network

Coordination requires an effective network of communications in an organisation. Through vertical, horizontal and diagonal channels of communication various managerial positions are well connected with each other. Free flow of required information resulting in interaction between related departments becomes a means of achieving coordination because through these channels, the managers of such departments can exchange information and keep each other well-informed about the working of their respective departments which facilitates effective co-ordination.

(v) Committees and Group Decision Making

The committee system of management and group decision-making are also considered important devices for achieving co-ordination in the functioning of various departments. The committees are formed by members of several departments to solve problems which involve the interest of those departments. The members representing their departments express their opinions, exchange information, and solve the problem collectively . Similarly, group decision making which involves many employees to participate in decision making further unifies and integrates their activities.

(vi) Horizontal Relationship

A horizontal relationship between managers working at the same levels but heading different departments also serves as an important device of coordination. Such relationships may be formal or informal in nature but very often an informal relationship may prove more effective to achieve co-ordination among them. Through horizontal relationships managers of equal rank and status make free and fair exchange of the required information on departmental matters without any hesitation, fear and complex of authority.

(vii) Co-ordination through Leadership

In the words of McFarland, the "concept of coordination is basically inseparable from that of leadership so that to speak of either is to imply the existence of the other." It is through effective leadership that communication takes place among members, group decision making is encouraged and participative approaches to management are used which go a long way to achieve effective co-ordination.

(viii) Special Co-ordinator

Apart from the above devices, sometimes managers may be appointed or may be given the responsibility of maintaining coordination either in group efforts, project work or in other programmes to be implemented to perform certain functions or activities.

PRINCIPLES OF COORDINATION

Mary Parker Follet pointed out four broad rules or principles which may be used as guidelines by managers to achieve co-ordination. These principles are listed below:

(i) The Principle of Direct Control

The first and foremost principle of co-ordination is direct personal contact between members of the organisation which should be encouraged and maintained. Through such relationships they can communicate with each other, exchange views and develop mutual understanding among themselves regarding various problems and matters. Such direct personal contacts cut across authority relationships and may be informal in nature.

(ii) Principle of Early Stage of Co-ordination

According to this principle, coordination should be achieved at the early stage of planning and policy making since as time passes in the process of planning, the task of achieving coordination may become more difficult and complicated. On the other hand, if the manager of a particular department who is formulating policy and making plans frequently meets and discusses with other heads, effective coordination may be achieved.

(iii) Principle of Reciprocal Relations

This principle states that organisation is a system of interrelated elements and each element is closely related with the others, and therefore, they must pull together because each element affects the other and all elements affect the organisation. In this connection, Mary Follet pointed out that all factors in a situation are reciprocally related. For example, when A works with B and he in turn works with C and D, each of the four finds himself influenced by the others, and influenced by all the persons in the total situation.

(iv) Co-ordination as a Continuous Process

According to this principle, coordination is a continuous process. It is something which must go on all the time. It has no definable end. Coordination should not be left to chance and it is the duty of the manager to make regular efforts to achieve it constantly so that organisational goals can be achieved effectively.

In selecting an appropriate mechanism of co-ordination, managers in the 21st century need to recognise that organisational coordination capabilities are improving rapidly because of electronic information processing systems. These systems are simple, inexpensive and readily available. It is practical and cost effective even for small organisations to buy these systems and maintain a well coordinated flow of information in the organisation for its effective functioning.

TEST QUESTIONS

1. What is budgetary control? Explain the essential elements of budgetary control.
2. What do you understand by management audit? State a few major areas which could be the searchlight of management audit.
3. Comment. 'Co-ordination and control are inseparable twins of management.'
4. 'Coordination is regarded as the epitome and essence of the entire range of managerial functions'. Comment.
5. 'Control and coordination are related but are different functions.' Comment.
6. Explain the term 'coordination'. What are the various mechanisms of achieving coordination?
7. 'Coordination is an essence of managerial function'. Comment.
8. Write short notes on
   (a) Management audit
   (b) Break-even analysis
   (c) Critical point control
   (d) Budgetary control
   (e) Self-regulatory control
   (f) Control by exception
   (g) Pre-control and post-control.
9. Write short notes on:
   (a) Features of coordination
   (b) Importance of coordination
   (c) Principles of coordination.
10. Explain the merits and demerits of activities network techniques.
11. 'Self control involves part of imposed control.' Comment.
12. 'Control is not a use of force but a process of exerting influence on others.' Discuss.

—oo(O)oo—

CHAPTER 17

MANAGEMENT OF ORGANISATIONAL CHANGE AND DEVELOPMENT

LEARNING OBJECTIVES

1. To know the concept of change.
2. To develop understanding about planned change and internal and external factors.
3. To know about the process of change and resistance to it.
4. To develop understanding of the management of change.
5. To learn about emerging horizons of management and challenges facing managers.
6. To get an idea about action research.
7. To identify the basic assumptions of organisational development.
8. To remember the key elements to the success of change.

MEANING AND CONCEPT

An organisation is a man-made system. It works through individuals to achieve objectives. While working in an organisation, these individuals come into contact with each other and develop personal and social relations. These relations give rise to informal groups. These informal groups become a part of the formal organisation and affect its functioning. The individuals who are members or employees of the organisation, the informal groups that are formed by them and the organisation in which they work for a long period of time develop a particular way of corporate life. When variations take place due to internal or external forces, it is known as organisational change. This may also be defined as an alteration in the status quo of the organisation.

The change is inevitable and, to some extent, desirable for the organisation. It is because every organisation has to succeed, develop and grow. Growth and development of the organisation will force it to change. An organisation that fails to change is sure to fail. Change is required not only for growth but also to help the organisation to maintain a relative degree of stability in its functioning.

In a modern high-tech industrial society, an organisation is considered as an open adaptive system. It interacts with the external environment on a regular basis. The external environment which mainly consists of many socio-cultural, economic, legal, political and technological factors is dynamic and ever changing. The changes taking place in the external environment may bring new opportunities or create new problems for the organisation. Therefore, the managers of the organisation continuously monitor the external environment and discover new ways of utilising the resources of the organisation. Thus, the survival and growth of the organisation depends on its capability to reconcile or adjust with the rapidly changing environment. In order to adapt to the changing environment, managers have to make changes in the existing structure, processes and goals of the organisation. These changes have a direct reflection on the entire corporate life.

The changes may be minor or major depending on the requirement of the situation. For example, there may be a change in a particular work procedure which is minor and may affect only a few or particular employees. On the other hand, if the existing technology being used in production is changed it may revolutionise the entire production system and a large number of employees are bound to be affected. Hence, it is known as a major change taking place in the organisation. It is however to be noted that the dimension and nature of organisational change depend on how the changing environment has been affecting it. How many sub-systems or organisations are going to be affected and to what extent and finally how capable is the organisation to cope with the changes taking place in the environment. Thus, the organisation has to learn to change and live and develop in a state of change.

TYPES OF CHANGES

Mintberg has concluded that in every organisation there are periods of continuity in which established strategies remained unchanged and there are periods of change. These changes may be of four types, namely, incremental change, piecemeal change, transformational change and flux change.

'Incremental' changes take place frequently and in a gradual manner. These changes are logical and involve little deviation from the past, for example, upgradation of existing technology, expansion of existing markets, etc. Piecemeal changes imply a change only in some strategies while others remain unchanged. For example, the marketing strategy of the organisation is being changed because of growing competition without affecting other functional strategies. While the strategies of an organisation are changed without any clear direction it is known as a 'period of flux'. For example, some new product has been added to the existing product line so as to broaden it.

Transformational changes take place rarely but they are major and involve a significant departure from the past, for example, adoption of new technology, diversification of organisational operations, etc. The economic liberalisation in India during 1991 resulted in transformational changes in many organisations.

David Nadler and management professor Michael Tushman developed a typology of organisational changes. According to them, organisational changes may be of four types:

(1) Anticipatory change

(2) Reactive change

(3) Incremental change

(4) Strategic change.

Anticipatory changes are made with the intention to take advantage of situations that are expected to arise. Such changes are systematically planned because the manager monitors the situation regularly and whenever he expects a change, he attempts to make a change in the organisation to get its benefit.

Reactive changes are those that are forced on to the organisation by unexpected environmental pressures. In other words, if there is a change in the external environment, reactive changes are made to cope with the situation arising from it. Sometimes, these changes are also made to exploit new opportunities as provided by the changing environment.

Incremental changes are those that are made with the intention to maintain functioning of an organisation on its chosen path. Since the organisation has many sub-systems, these are to be adjusted from time to time so as to secure smooth functioning of the whole organisation. Such adjustments are known as incremental changes.

Strategic changes are more basic in nature. These changes have great influence on the overall functioning of the organisation. They alter the overall shape and direction of the organisation, for example, change in technology, change in location of the plant, diversification of organisational operations, etc.

CONCEPT OF PLANNED CHANGE

After having extensively discussed the various aspects of organisational changes, it becomes easy to understand the basic concept of planned change. Planned change may be considered as a systematic and deliberate change which the manager attempts to introduce in the organisation to face an expected situation. It is a systematic attempt to redesign an organisation in a way that will enable it to cope with the changing environment and achieve new goals. It may also be defined as "the deliberate design and implementation of a structural innovation, a new policy or goal or a change in the operating philosophy, climate or style."

The planned change aims at preparing the entire organisation to change its process, structure, technology or goals to adapt to a changing situation. In a planned change, the manager keeps an eye on and monitors the external environment. He makes an assessment of the impact of change in the environment. Accordingly, he introduces changes in the organisation to cope with the changing environment. Planned change has the following characteristics:

1. Planned change is always deliberate, systematic and rational in nature. These changes are the result of innovative and creative thinking on the part of the manager.
2. Planned change aims at coping with a changing environment and achieving a new set of goals for the organisation.
3. These changes may arise both from internal as well as external environments. For example, if the organisation grows, planned changes are made to keep in the right direction and to maintain continuity. Similarly, if there is change in the competition, the manager has to develop a suitable course of action to deal with it effectively.
4. Planned changes are natural and inevitable. An organisation faces this problem regardless of its size. Every organisation makes some structural changes in response to the changing environment.
5. Planned changes are broader in scope and magnitude. They may affect the whole organisation or a substantial part of it in a significant way. Thus these changes aim at preparing the entire organisation to adapt to change.
6. Planned changes may have both positive as well as negative aspects. If they have a positive aspect, they are more readily accepted by the employees; otherwise, the employees may resist the changes.
7. Planned changes are difficult, expensive and painful also. Due to these changes, employees may be compelled to surrender their comfortable and convenient work habits. Similarly, some local employees may lose their jobs.
8. Planned change may focus on the structure, processes, technology, people and organisational goals, depending on the nature and magnitude of change.

FORCES OF CHANGE

Change may be of any nature or magnitude but it is necessary for the manager to identify the forces of change. These forces may act as stimulants to change and may be internal or external.

1. External Forces

External forces of change include all those factors of macro-environment and task environment which directly or indirectly affect the functioning of an organisation. The organisation hardly has any control on these factors. If there is any change in these factors, the organisation has to align with them.

There are many external forces that may bring change in an organisation and some of them are:

(a) Socio-Cultural Forces

These forces mainly include changing cultural values and norms, social objectives, pattern of education, population dynamics, rate of urbanisation, social tradition and customs, etc.

(b) Economic Forces

These forces are very complex. They include the general economic conditions of the country or region to which the organisation belongs. In addition, economic forces also include market dynamics like demand, competition, price mechanism, buying capacity, distribution of income, cost, quality and availability of various resources and their distribution among various sectors of the economy.

(c) Political and Legal Forces

The functioning of organisations is guided by a wide range of political and legal factors. They include the political system, ideology of the ruling and major opposition parties, political stability, morality and values. Governmental intervention in business and various legislative actions made by it and policies towards labour, foreign trade and other fiscal matters are also included in it.

(d) Technological Forces

New techniques of production, innovation of new processes and products, growing emphasis on research and development are some of the major technological forces which may bring about changes in an organisation. In addition, transfer of technology, rate of obsolescence and laws regulating its use are also included in technological terms.

(e) Work Environment Forces

There are some work environment forces that may also necessitate change in an organisation. These forces may include customers, suppliers, community, society, etc. Customer loyalty, regularity of suppliers, community attitude, recognition of society are the major forces of a work environment.

2. Internal Forces

These forces may either be derived from the change in the external environment or may be management induced forces. For example, if the management decides to provide a day care service for the children of working women to motivate them, it may be regarded as a management induced force. And if, as per an agreement with the trade union, the management is forced to construct houses for its employees, it may be considered as a derivative force. Internal forces mainly include the following:

(1) Top management and its philosophy and corporate policy.

(2) Retirement, promotion, resignation and transfer of key functionaries of the organisation.

(3) Change in the perception, attitude, feelings, beliefs and expectations of the employees working in the organisation.

(4) Change in work schedule, allocation of duties, job content, duty hours, composition of work group, etc.

(5) Change in the internal environment of the organisation.

PROCESS OF PLANNED CHANGE

The organisation has many forces for change as described above. Some of these forces act for maintaining the status quo and support stability in the organisation and take the organisation to its original position. These are known as 'restraining forces'. Another set of forces known as 'driving force' or force for change compels the organisation to deviate from its original position (Figure 17.1).

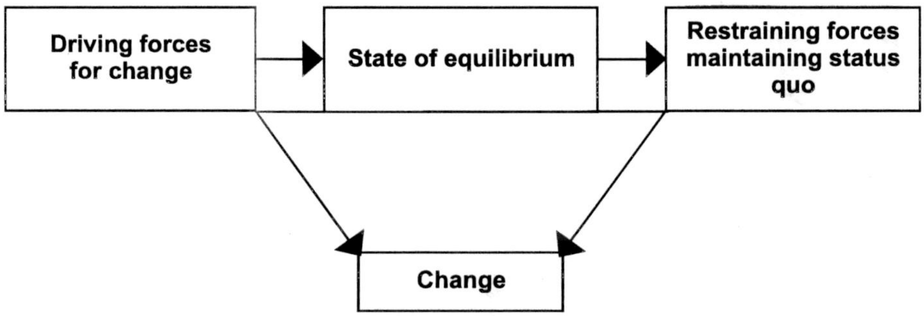

Figure 17.1. Figure showing process of planned change

Source: Stoner, James A. F. and Freeman, Reward, *Management*, p. 415

The model of change process has been developed by Kurt Lewin. In this model, he stated that the driving force or force for change moves in one way and restrains forces or a force to maintain the status quo in another and wherever these two forces reconcile, that emerges as performance. He also proposed the following three phases of change process to move the organisation from the present situation to the future.

1. Unfreezing the situation
2. Changing or moving to a new situation
3. Reflecting the situation.

(1) Unfreezing the Situation

The phase of unfreezing creates awareness among individuals and the organisation about the change and prepares them for it. If the change comes suddenly, the members of the organisation may discard it. Thus, through this phase they are gradually prepared to discard conventional methods and accept new alternatives. The main object of unfreezing the situation is to make the members willing and ready to accept change and if there is any resistance to it, to neutralise it. In the words of Scherin, unfreezing is the process of breaking down the old attitude and behaviour, customs and traditions so that they may start with a clean slate. This can be done by making announcements, holding meetings and promoting ideas throughout the organisation via bulletins, notice boards, personal contacts and group conferences. Unfreezing the situation mainly involves the following steps:

(a) Identification and recognition of driving force or forces for change.

(b) To increase these driving forces.

(c) To restrict the restraining force or forces for maintaining the status quo so that if there is any resistance to change, it can be neutralised.

(2) Changing or Moving to a New Situation

Once the members of the organisation have identified the need for change and they have been prepared to accept it, there is a need to redefine their behaviour pattern. In the changing or moving phase, the members learn and acquire a new pattern of behaviour. It involves the following elements:

(a) Compliance

In order to change the behaviour of a member, the reward and punishment strategy is strictly enforced. Fear of punishment or expectation of a reward may force a member to change his behaviour for the better.

(b) Identification

Members of the organisation are induced to identify themselves with some given role models whose behaviour they would like to adopt.

(c) Internalisation

In order to get an individual adjusted to a new situation, some changes (internal) are made in his thought process. They are left alone to think of themselves and to search their hearts to bring about a change in the existing pattern of behaviour and adopt a new one.

(3) Refreezing the Situation

During this phase, members replace their old patterns of behaviour completely for a successful change to take place. This occurs when the new behaviour becomes a normal way of life. In order to make a new behaviour a permanent one, it must be continuously reinforced so that newly acquired behaviour does not diminish.

In addition to the above phases of the change process, the managers of an organisation should make continuous attempts to balance the 'driving forces and restraining forces'. This is done by strengthening the driving forces or by weakening the restraining forces so that change may occur in the organisation.

TYPES OF PLANNED CHANGE

On the basis of the above discussion on planned change, it becomes clear that both external as well as internal forces are equally responsible for bringing about a change in the organisation. Planned change can be introduced in the organisation with regard to its mission or objective, its structure, its process and the technology being used in the organisation.

(1) Change in the Mission or Objective

The organisation may be forced to change its mission either by dropping some of them or adding some new ones due to the rapidly changing environment. Once the mission objective is changed, the entire future course of action of the organisation is bound to be changed to pursue a new mission. For example, if a hospital primarily aimed at providing health care service in the community also starts research work on some important human diseases, it has to change its focus and has to make many changes in the existing structure and technology used in the organisation. Such changes are known as strategic changes because they are basic in nature and affect the entire organisation.

(2) Structural Change

Structural change implies redistribution of authority and responsibility among the members. It also includes rearranging of its internal systems such as work flow, management hierarchy, line of communication, decentralised operations, participative management, etc. As a result of such changes, the status quo of the employees is bound to be changed and they have to learn how to solve work-related problems, how to make decisions and acquire additional skills for that.

For example, decentralisation may give them more authority and responsibility. A change in the work flow may improve their efficiency and a change in the managerial style may force them to develop a new attitude and perception.

(3) Technological Change

These changes are related to products being produced and the process being used in the organisation. Such changes involve a change in equipment, production process and methods and applications of statistical and computer-aided production devices. Technological changes may bring about change in other components of the organisation and in its culture and working environment.

Similarly, the use of modern sophisticated technology in the production process may force the organisation to provide training to employees or hire skilled employees for that purpose. F. W. Taylor made a valuable contribution to improve the technological aspect of job performance to raise the efficiency of workers. For this purpose, he suggested a mental revolution to bring about necessary changes in the attitude of employees.

(4) People-oriented Change

An organisation is a man-made system and is operated by people. When they join the organisation they carry some values, beliefs, needs, expectations, attitudes, etc. To get better results and higher performance, some desirable changes are made in their working behaviour and morale. Their skills are developed and attempts are made to realise their potential. To make a change in the working behaviour of members, the scheme of management by objective may be introduced, development programmes may be conducted and training may be provided to them.

RESISTANCE TO CHANGE

As stated earlier, change is inevitable and desirable to achieve a higher level of performance and make more profitable use of organisational resources. The change in the external environment may bring new opportunities or may pose a serious threat to the survival of the organisation. The organisation has to make some internal adjustments or changes to use the opportunity profitably or to counter threats to maintain its survival. When changes are introduced in the organisation, they force members to make necessary changes and modifications in the attitude, perception and working behaviour. Since members have to shift from their established way of life, they resent it and follow a path of resistance.

If the changes brought into the organisation are more positive and beneficial for the members, the degree of resistance on their part will be on the lower side and if the change is less beneficial or has a more negative aspect, the degree of resistance will be higher. It is interesting to note that change is a law of nature and to resist change is a natural tendency of human behaviour. However, it is easy to prepare for it and get adjusted to the change if the potential reward to be given to employees is adequate to persuade them to change. Such changes can be implemented with the least resistance.

WHY DO EMPLOYEES RESIST CHANGE?

Employees resist change for many reasons. Some of the most common ones are:

(a) Insecurity

Insecurity among the affected employees regarding the impact of change is one of the major reasons for resistance. They feel insecure about loss of employment. The insecurity arises in their minds because they feel that due to change, new technology, methods and systems may be introduced in the organisation, which perhaps they do not know.

The sense of insecurity may also be created among them because at times the change, on the face of it. seems to be leading to unemployment. For example, introduction of computers in a manual work setting gives an impression to the employees that some of them may be retrenched which may not be necessary actually.

(b) Change in Status Quo

A change introduced in the organisation may involve the redistribution of authority and responsibility, redefining the job and reallocation among employees. In these cases, their status quo or existing position is bound to be changed. They may be forced to give up their familiar habits, people, place and practices. They have to adjust to a new situation which they may find inconvenient and uncomfortable.

(c) Communication Gap

One of the major reasons for resistance is a communication gap among employees about the change to be introduced, its impact on them and the required adjustment on their part. If the need for change is not communicated to the employees in time and in an acceptable manner, they may be anxious about the impact and therefore may resist it. Thus, to reduce such resistance, they must be taken into confidence. For this, exchange of required information should be done and they should be given participation in the process of implementation of the change.

(d) Socio-psychological Reasons

Resistance to change may also arise due to some social and psychological reasons. Change may place the employees in a new work setting in which they face a new superior and new fellow employees. On the one hand they are deprived of their usual set of superiors and subordinates and on the other they are forced to work with unknown people. In such a situation, they become psychologically weak and feel socially displaced. Thus, it tends to be opposed by those who are affected by the change in a negative way.

(e) Group Pressure

At times, members of a group oppose change because the group to which they belong is not in favour of it. This is because individual members may be more loyal, committed and sincere towards group norms, values and objectives. They may be prepared to sacrifice their individual interest for the interest of the group. For example, the call for a strike given by the union is to be followed by all members, though some of them may not be in favour of it. But because of group pressure, they prefer to go along with it.

(f) Loss of Power and Control

Although the change may be good for improving the overall performance of the organisation, it may erode the power base of the individual employee or of a group. Due to change, they may lose some power and influence and therefore they resist it. Apart from this, the change may reduce the power of the employees and they may be forced to accept a new power position. To enjoy a new power position they may be required to establish new relationships which may not be possible for some time.

(g) Nature of Change

If the changes are minor and do not affect the members significantly, resistance to them may be at a minimum. On the other hand, if the change is introduced suddenly without any warning about the imbalance or problems that may arise in the workplace, it faces more resistance from the members of the organisation.

(h) Rigid Organisational Structure

Lack of adequate flexibility in the structure of the organisation may also become a source of resistance. The change, even for betterment, may not be implemented due to rigidity in the structure. It is, therefore, preferred to have a modern form of organisation, such as free form, project or matrix form which have a greater degree of flexibility and changes can be made without any problem.

(i) Past Experience of Employees

If the change had not been handled by the organisation efficiently and the members of the organisation had a bitter experience about it in the past, they will oppose the new change also. Due to lack of trust among the employees, the importance of the change may be misinterpreted and they may oppose it. Thus, the emotional response of the employees should be properly diagnosed and should be taken care of at the time of introducing the change.

STRATEGIES TO OVERCOME RESISTANCE TO CHANGE

Resistance to change on the part of employees is a signal that something is wrong in the process of introducing and implementing the change. The manager therefore must determine the real cause of the resistance and then develop a suitable strategy to overcome it efficiently.

Without full acceptance from the employees, change cannot be implemented successfully though it may be extremely beneficial for the organisation. Some of the alternative strategies of ways to overcome resistance to change are:

(1) Participation and Involvement

Employees are part and parcel of the organisation. Any change to be introduced may affect them. Thus, to reduce their resistance to change, it is desirable to associate and involve them in the change process. They should be made party to the change so to to get their maximum cooperation and commitment. Due care should be taken with regard to their participation and involvement in the change.

Managers should be willing to seek the active participation of the employees. If the change results in personal benefit, it would be easier to seek their active participation. By participating in the implementation of change, employees take a personal interest in its success.

(2) Education and Communication

It is necessary to educate the employees about the change so as to reduce their resistance. They can be educated through training, seminars, conferences and meetings. One of the simplest ways of preparing the employees to accept change is through the process of education. They may be made familiar with the change, its effect on them and its implementation process. They may be persuaded about the need and importance of the change. Similarly, communication also plays an important role in diffusing the resistance of the employees. By way of providing the required information on the change, they may be taken into confidence and their doubts and confusions can be removed to create a favourable impression in their minds.

(3) Leadership

Leadership qualities on the part of the manager may help in getting the affected employees involved in the process of change. Through the leadership process, the manager may use his informal relationship with subordinates to seek their cooperation to implement the change. The manager who is an efficient leader may also put great influence on the subordinates and may alter their unfavourable attitude towards the change. Thus, the leadership process which is basically aimed at influencing the behaviour of others may prove helpful in the successful implementation of the change.

(4) Facilitation and Support

If members resist change because of their adjustment problems, the process of facilitation and support may help to reduce the degree of resistance. The manager can assure them all types of help that they require for their adjustment in the new situation. It may include removing their difficulties, helping them to acquire new skills and develop a new relationship which they require in the new situation. But it is a time-consuming as well as an expensive way to minimize resistance.

(5) Negotiation and Agreement

If a particular group of members which is very powerful in the organisation is losing significantly due to the change, the negotiation process may be used to overcome this resistance. It is considered as one of the most effective ways to avoid major resistance. The group members or their trade union leaders may be invited to bargain on behalf of the members. In the process of negotiation both the parties, employees' representative and the manager, find some way to diffuse the resistance. At the end of the bargaining process, an agreement is entered into to make it binding on the employees.

(6) Timing of Change

As stated earlier, a sudden and untimely change may result in strong opposition from the employees. The timing of introducing change may have a great impact on the resistance. If the change is introduced at an appropriate time, and in a gradual manner, resistance of the affected employees may be reduced significantly. Thus, the manager must be careful to select the right time for the change to be introduced.

(7) Use of Group Pressure

The functioning of informal groups in the organisation plays an important role in modifying the working behaviour of the members. In a cohesive group in particular members accept the change because the group is in its favour. In such a situation, the manager should place emphasis on the group and through it, the members may be prepared to accept the change. By convincing the group, which has considerable influence on its members, the task of introducing change may be made simple.

(8) Use of Power by a Change Agent or Initiator

If change agents hold a powerful position in the organisation, they may coerce the employees to accept the change. By facing the threat of demotion, suspension or termination they may be forced to fall in line with the change. This strategy can be used to overcome any kind of resistance, but it seems to be very risky.

MANAGEMENT OF CHANGE

It is necessary for the organisation to change for its successful growth and development. It is only through planned change and its efficient management can the organisation cope with the changing environment and may seek a profitable use of its resources. The process of management of change is really very difficult. It requires a lot of resources and effort on the part of the manager. The following steps are involved in the process of management of change:

1. To Identify Need for Change

At the first stage of the management of the change process, the manager attempts to identify the need for change. This need is identified in terms of those internal as well as external factors which necessitate the change. The manager may get the required information regarding the need for change either from the feedback process in the control system or he may monitor the situation on a regular basis to get such information. In addition to this, the manager has also to ascertain that the change is 'strategic' or 'process oriented' or 'people oriented' or 'a very minor one'.

2. To Develop New Objectives and Goals

The changed situation may demand a review of organisational goals. Thus, the manager has to modify the existing set of goals in the light of the changing internal and external environments. At times, rapid and drastic changes taking place in the external environment may force the organisation for a strategic change. Because of the changing environment, the existing goals of the organisation may become outdated and it can survive only with a new set of goals.

3. To Determine Type of Change

Once the need and objective of the change has been determined, it is necessary to decide about the type of change to be introduced and implemented in the organisation. The change may be introduced in relation to the objectives of the organisation. Or it may be made on the organisational structure. Besides, it may also be a process oriented or people oriented change (These have been discussed in detail earlier).

4. To Prepare a Detailed Plan for Change

This step involves preparing a plan and deciding when, how, and by whom the change is to be introduced. For the successful implementation of change, first of all an appropriate time is to be chosen. Detailed methodology is also to be chalked out to highlight how the change may be introduced. Similarly, an agent for change is also to be selected.

In this regard, it is to be decided whether the change will be introduced by the manager of the organisation or should the responsibility be given to outside specialists or management consultants. The main purpose of preparing such a plan is to facilitate the proper and smooth implementation of change with the least resistance from affected employees. The role of balancing the driving forces and restraining forces is very important in this connection.

5. To Implement the Change

Once the change plan has been prepared, it is necessary to communicate it to all within the organisation. This is done with the purpose of convincing the members about the need, objective, nature and possible benefits of the proposed change. Proper communication may help in reducing resistance and in seeking necessary support to implement the change.

Along with communication, resources may be allocated and all other administrative arrangements may be made to execute the plan of change. Successful implementation of the plan is greatly influenced by the commitment, devotion and leadership qualities of the manager or specialist who is to implement the plan.

6. Review and Feedback

To smoothen the implementation of the change in the given direction, it is necessary to review and evaluate the progress of the implementation of change. Continuous review and feedback may provide the necessary information to the manager to enable him to take action to speed up the implementation process in the desired direction.

EMERGING HORIZONS OF MANAGEMENT IN A CHANGING ENVIRONMENT

Management is a dynamic process. It becomes more interesting and challenging when a situation changes. The change in the external environment may bring new opportunities and may also pose new threats and challenges. Both have an impact on the development and application of management knowledge. As change takes place or is likely to take place, the manager takes action and develops new ways to cope with change as efficiently as possible.

Although changes in a business environment are not within the control of a manager, he has to monitor and analyse them and take suitable action to overcome them and maintain the survival of the organisation and facilitate its growth and development. To survive and grow in the middle of so complex and diverse changes is not an easy task. Every kind of change in the environment does make the job of a manager more challenging. On the one hand, these changes cannot be predicted precisely and on the other they may be random, casual, complex and unstructured.

ACTION RESEARCH

It is a systematic way of studying 'change' and collecting data on the various aspects of it to take suitable action. It refers to a change process which is based on the systematic collection of data, analysing it and selecting change action to correct the situation. It is also considered as a scientific methodology to manage change in the organisation. It has the following steps:

(1) Diagnosis

At the very outset of the action research process, the management consultant would diagnose the problem within the organisation. He would collect information on the problem from various employees who are more affected and concerned about it.

To gather information on the problem, he may interview the employees through questionnaires, review past records and may secure the viewpoints of employees by listening to them. The diagnosis part is considered very important because with the help of it the problem situation may be precisely identified and defined.

(2) Analysis

After obtaining the required information on the problem from the employees and past records, it is to be studied and analysed. Through analysis a deep understanding about the various aspects of the problem may be developed. In the process of analysis the problem situation may be broken into components and the relationship of each component may be studied. Analysis is done mainly to discover the pattern or tendency of the problem situation.

(3) Feedback

To make the action process more effective, feedback of information on the problem is necessary. In the process of feedback, the management consultant who is conducting the action research shares information and exchanges it with the employees from whom it is gathered. The main objective of the feedback process is to seek the participation of the employees to solve the problem. Through feedback the consultant tells the employees what he has discovered from the information supplied by them.

(4) Action

The action part of the research process is very important because at this stage the management consultant chooses and prepares a suitable action plan. By implementing such an action plan, the problem situation may be solved and corrected. The action plan developed by the consultant may be in the form of new policies, plans and other management practices. It may also take the form of an altogether new approach to be introduced in the organisation such as management by objective programme, quality circles, team approach, flexitime approach, etc.

(5) Evaluation

The action plan developed and implemented by the management consultant is to be evaluated in terms of cost effectiveness and other relevant factors. The main idea of evaluating it is to revise it as per the requirement of the situation and finally make it more effective. While evaluating it, it is also ensured that the action plan is consistent with other plans of the organisation. At this stage, the outcome of the implementation of the action plan is also judged on the basis of information gathered at the initial stage of the action research process.

The action research process may generally be conducted by a management consultant hired from outside the organisation. This is because they may conduct the whole process with a high degree of objectivity and independence. Sometimes managers working in the organisation may also be deputed for this purpose. The action research process is considered beneficial for the organisation. This is because it totally focuses on the problem situations being faced by employees. At the same time, it is solved with the active cooperation and participation of the employees. Such participation would certainly help in implementing the change in the organisation. It may rather reduce resistance on the part of the employees for the change.

Thus, successful managers always anticipate and adjust to the changing environment rather than being passive and unprepared to face it. The real test of knowledge, skill and others capabilities of the manager lies in how efficiently he works in the disturbed new situation and how comfortably he adapts to it. Today's managers cannot afford the luxury of ignoring environmental changes.

Due to rapid changes in the economic, socio-cultural, legal, political and technological environment all around the world, management knowledge is affected in the following ways:

(a) Management theory has been greatly affected by these changes. The development of new principles and generalisations have rendered traditional management techniques less effective. The validity and application of these techniques have been questioned. Development of new approaches has put a big question mark on the relevance and utility of these traditional principles of management.

(b) Due to many uncertainties and complexities associated with the external environment, the application of management knowledge in practice has also become more difficult. Mere experience and knowledge of management is not enough. To overcome a challenging situation one has to have creativity, innovativeness, adaptability and other required capabilities because rapid changes have rendered past experience and precedents less important and sometimes irrelevant also. The manager not knowing about the past may be of little use for the future.

(c) As a result of drastic changes in the theory as well as practice of management, the successful manager is bound to acquire new skill and talent which is more useful in meeting new situations. It is very interesting to note that management knowledge provides a career to only those who are capable of managing challenging situations efficiently. In this regard, the manager has to integrate theory and practice of management in such a way so as to develop a meaningful and useful manner of managing (Figure 17.2).

Figure 17.2. Acquiring new skills and abilities by integrating theory and practice of management

1. Environmental Changes

Before discussing new trends that are likely to be witnessed in future management it is desirable to take stock of the wide-ranging changes that have taken place in the external environment.

(i) Socio-Cultural Changes

Society is always in transition. The change in social values, objectives, population dynamics, immigration to cities, etc., have really created new challenges for managers. Some of the important changes taking place and that affect the various functions of a manager are as under:

(a) Emerging Strong Middle Income Group

Our society is likely to be dominated by the newly emerging middle income group. This group consists of mostly salaried people and self-employed professionals having enough buying capacity and ability to consume. This segment of society is highly educated, well aware and extraordinarily vocal. Better quality of goods, status symbol, more consumption situation, demand for semi-luxury goods, better working conditions, more salary and perks and a desire to earn more are some of the common features of this group.

(b) Higher Rate of Literacy

The more emphasis on education and its level may affect management in two ways. On the one hand, the increasing trend in education will create awareness among customers and they will occupy central place in the organisation. The management of consumer relationships and consumer orientation of business are to be given top priority. On the other hand, a high rate of literacy along with professional skill among the people who join the organisation may also force the manager to make drastic changes in the internal environment of the organisation.

(c) Interface of Industry with Educational Institutions

In order to make better utilisation for business purposes, there is great pressure on industry to interface with higher educational institutions by sharing the cost of education and making it more meaningful to be utilised in business. Such interface may help in developing human resources as per the need of business organisations.

(d) Change in Life Style

Because of the factors mentioned above and other important social changes including the unitary family system, continuing pressure of equal employment opportunities for men and women have changed the working behaviour of people in the organisation. On the one hand, higher buying capacity and growing needs are posing great difficulties for managers in developing a suitable motivation mechanism. On the other hand, they are giving lower priority to security because both spouses are working and they can afford to change jobs.

2. Economic Changes

There has been a drastic change in the economic environment of the country after the initiation of economic liberalisation during 1991. The shift in the approach of the organisation from an inward to an outward approach, growing competition, disinvestment in the public sector, entry of multinational organisations, changing credit policy, more operational autonomy to banking institutions, redefining the government's relationship with industry and weeding out various outdated regulations governing trade and industry are part of the environment. In the recent past, growth, more growth and still more growth aiming at generating about 10 million additional jobs every year has changed the complexion of the economic environment for tomorrow's business organisations.

These economic changes have added a new dimension to management. For example, due to rapid changes in the environment and growing competition, especially from multinational organisations, Indian managers have been forced to think and act upon strategic management and control.

3. Globalisation of Business Operations

The global economy has been the need of every country. Intentions of making optimal utilisation of local resources and the expanding market outside the boundaries of the country have also created new challenges for managers. These challenges arise out of cross-country culture. Working for foreign-owned companies, meeting world standards, pressure of free trade, etc., are giving new exposure to managers.

4. Technological Changes

Technology is regarded as the key to economic and social progress. The development of sophisticated modern technology has extended the natural, physical and mental reach of human beings. It has also facilitated the gradual development of the 'industrial age' into an 'information age'. Nowadays an organisation having easy access to required information develops and enjoys competitive advantages over rival organisations because the information is recognised as an important strategic resource and input of business.

Managerial ability is greatly influenced and depends on how successfully the manager generates the required, relevant and reliable information and how he uses it in decision making and performing other managerial functions. Technology basically is an output of the innovation process. It is a systematic development of a new product and process and its application in practice. Thus a proper understanding of the innovation process on the part of the manager may help to translate new ideas into concrete goods and services. The role of technology and information in the future will assume an important place in managing the organisation efficiently. It is only the team of well informed and innovative managers who will prove valuable assets for the organisation in a fast-changing environment.

5. Ecological and Environmental Changes

Ecological balance and environment-friendly use of business resources has become a major concern of the 21st century. Every country in the race of economic development is bound to face the problem of ecological imbalances. More industrialisation would lead to a higher degree of pollution along with increased industrial output. Growing environmental degradation, reckless use of natural resources, growing consumerism, etc., have forced the government to make suitable legislation, particularly to control growing pollution and the consumption of natural resources. The manager of today and tomorrow will have to develop a suitable strategy to make environment-friendly use of resources to produce eco-friendly products. Ecology has assumed an important place in social marketing. Thus, to restore the ecological balance, the manager has to cooperate with the government to use natural resources in a cautious manner and to prevent all types of pollution. Ecological and environmental factors can influence the location decision of a manager in a significant way.

6. Political and Legal Changes

The relationship between the government and business is changing rapidly. Political commitment of regulating and controlling business operations in the larger interest of the nation is increasing day by day. Although, as per recent trends, the government attempts to liberalise the economy and grant more freedom to business organisations, these organisations are also expected to uphold public interest in an acceptable manner. Managers, who are considered custodians of socially, economically and politically powerful organisations, are greatly influenced by the changing political situation. Due to many relevant pieces of legislation made by the government, personal and legal accountability of the manager has increased and the whole process of management seems to be politicalised. It is in this sense that decision making on the part of managers is affected not only by economic considerations but also by social, political and legal implications. The orderly political process contributes to business growth and development and it is adversely affected by the instability and low morality of politics. Thus the need of the hour is that managers should be politically conscious and active in their approach so as to preserve the identity of the organisation and to seek its growth and prosperity.

NEW TRENDS AFFECTING MANAGEMENT OF ORGANISATIONS IN THE FUTURE

On the basis of the discussion above on environmental changes, the one fact that emerges is that managers have to keep pace with changes to survive and grow. In the recent past many changes have taken place all over the world, but no one could predict them. At the most, on the basis of past changes, one can have some idea about the shape of things to come and can plan tentatively for that. An analysis of the above changes indicates the following trends to follow in the coming days:

1. Growth of International Business

There has been tremendous growth in international business. It is providing new opportunities to many organisations for further expansion and diversification of activities. Earlier, it used to be the monopoly of a few developed countries like the U.S.A., the U.K., Germany, Japan, etc., to have their multinational corporations in each other's country. The trend has changed. On the one hand, these multinationals are having their subsidiaries in less developed countries. On the other hand, many organisations from developing countries like Brazil, Taiwan, South Korea, Singapore and India are making their presence felt in international business. In view of this changing situation, managers have become global players.

2. Information Explosion

The development of communication technology and the information explosion has reduced the work to a global village. It has become very simple to disseminate information all over the world promptly and accurately. It has reduced physical distance and ignorance of knowledge. Because of these development, new opportunities have arisen which can be exploited profitably if managers know how to understand, measure and manage the knowledge. Thus, more efficient managers have to learn more and more about the world and develop a global vision.

3. Growing Relevance of Research and Development Work

To get a competitive edge over others, it is widely accepted that the organisation must spend a part of its earnings on research and development work. It is only through a proper R&D set-up in the organisation can scientific and technological advancements be translated into products and services that are more useful and cheap for customers. One of the major reasons for the domination of the U.S.A., Japan, Germany and other European countries in the international business is their strong R&D base. Now it is shifting to developing nations also.

4. Reawakening of Ethical and Moral Values

The social responsiveness and general conduct of a business organisation even in developed countries is being questioned. In many countries, suitable legislation has been made to raise the ethical and moral values of business organisations. India is no exception. Through such legislation, managers have been made legally accountable not only to customers and employees but the nation as a whole.

There is a growing realisation among managers that high ethical and moral values observed by them will help in the long run to raise the level of profitability of the organisation. In this regard it is interesting to note that ethical training is being provided to managers, a specific code of conduct is being enforced on them and they are expected to make the functioning of the organisation more transparent.

5. Theme of Customer Satisfaction

Although customer satisfaction is not a new concept in management, it has been in the limelight in the recent past. It is widely acknowledged that only those organisations that are firmly committed to customer satisfaction can face competition and survive. To increase customer satisfaction, managers have to formulate various plans and courses of action to produce and distribute goods and services that are customer friendly. In view of its growing significance, the management of relationships with customers is becoming popular and would be important in the 21st century.

6. Productivity Improvement

Productivity has become a central challenge in all organisations of all sizes. Managers are expected to produce more with less inputs. By increasing productivity, prices are reduced, salary and wages are increased, more profits are earned, growth and development takes place and more jobs are created. The chief executive of the U.S.-based General Electric Company, John F. Welch has rightly said that "for a company or for a nation, productivity is a matter of survival." The productivity of an organisation is considered as a threat to its global competitiveness. To overcome this problem, managers are bound to rethink and redefine their relationships with subordinates and discover new ways to tap their potential and talent to increase productivity.

NEW CHALLENGES FOR MANAGERS

In the light of the environmental changes mentioned above and the new trends that are emerging, the job of managers has become more challenging and tomorrow's managers have to face the following challenges to survive and grow:

1. Strategic Management

In the context of global operations, a new dimension has been added to management, that is, 'strategic management'. In the fast-changing environment and growing competition, no organisation can survive without relating its strengths and weaknesses to newly arising opportunities and threats. Managers have to think and act strategically. The strategic management process ensures competitively superior match between an organisation and its changing environment. It helps in mobilising the resources and efforts of the organisation in the direction and destination that are more profitable. Managers who think and act strategically are capable of visualising their organisation in the light of world trends and events and discovering important interdependencies in various areas. They mainly emphasise on how an organisation should act and react to newly-emerging opportunities and threats. It is clear that those who succeed in thinking and acting strategically would move ahead in the organisation.

2. Creative Decision Making

Rapid, random, unpredicted and unstructured changes in the environment have forced managers to switch over to creative decision making because no set procedures, rules and techniques may be applicable to solve such problems. Moreover, management theory may prove inadequate to deal with such problems. It is only creativity, innovativeness, foresightedness and other required qualities of managers that can help them solve such problems.

They reformulate, redefine and apply their experience and talent to such a problem situation.

3. Restructuring and Re-engineering of the Organisation

The traditional forms of an organisation have outlived their utility and to meet future challenges, managers have to focus on modern forms that are more flexible, open, transparent and adaptive. These organisations will be based on knowledge and information. In order to bring about dramatic improvement in the existing level of performance, organisations are restructured and re-engineered as per the demands of the situation. The care of customers, spirit of team work, auto-management, total quality management (TQM) and application of various human resource development processes are to be made a part of organisational functioning.

4. Using the Power of People by Empowering Them

Human resources is the most important asset of an organisation. If employees are fully involved in their work setting and are provided a congenial internal environment, there is no limit to their contributions to achieve organisational objectives. This can be done by providing an opportunity to them to work in self-managed teams. Recognising their contribution, giving them a patient hearing and providing them full support to perform their jobs along with proper training and development may create a situation of empowerment. By simplifying the organisation, re-defining the role of middle-level managers, ensuring autonomy, using prompt action, and eliminating bureaucratic procedures, the process of empowerment can be further promoted.

5. Seeking Strategic Alliances and to Manage Them

One step ahead of globalisation, multinational corporations are seeking strategic alliances. These alliances are sought to get the benefits of complementary competences of organisations in different countries. For example, Indian organisations are seeking such alliances through (50:50) equity arrangement and joint ventures with organisations working in developed countries so as to get more advantage of their research work and highly sophisticated technology. This had added a new dimension to the existing knowledge of management. Managers need to develop the required competence to understand the mutual interest of both partners and to manage it in the long run for their mutual benefit.

6. Visionary Leadership

Tomorrow's manager is expected to have a clear vision of the future of the organisation and mobilise resources in that direction. Visionary leadership demands more authority to be given to lower level employees to improve the quality of the product and productivity. He puts people first to generate a congenial work environment in the work place. Such leaders do not control the activities of subordinates but attempt to modify their behaviour.

7. Managing Relationships

Many parties have a stake in the organisation, such as customers, employees, society, government, financiers, etc. When these parties transact business, some kind of a relationship is established between an organisation and these parties. There is a need for a manager to maintain better relationships and improve them regularly.

It is by improving relationships that the smooth functioning of an organisation can be maintained. To improve the relationship, quality of goods and services is to be upgraded, mutual rapport is to be established and the required information on various related aspects is to be supplied to them. Further, a spirit of teamwork is created among employees, greater emphasis is placed on social responsibility and ultimately the organisation becomes a source of satisfaction for these parties.

ORGANISATIONAL DEVELOPMENT

Introduction

An organisation is a collective entity of people. It is formed to seek a common goal by performing a variety of activities and operations within the framework of an external environment. Environment is dynamic in nature, beyond the control of the organisation. Therefore, an organisation has to develop capabilities to respond to the changing environment.

Organisational development is a way in which organisations develop and change. The change is an integral part of its functioning. This is because the organisation functions in an ever-changing external environment. Its success to a large extent depends on the ability to cope with the changing environment. The organisation that fails to change may decay or die. It is only through organisational development that an organisation learns to change, to adjust and to reconcile with the rapidly changing world. The main objective of organisational development is to help in formulating suitable strategy to make the organisation more effective, viable and a continuing entity.

In organisational development, by applying the principles of practices of behavioural science, the overall functioning of the organisation is improved to achieve goals efficiently. The basic concept underlying organisational development is to improve the efficiency of the organisation by suitably modifying its human aspect. It is obvious that technology is also an important aspect, but it would have little meaning without a team of dedicated and committed employees.

Organisational Development Defined

The term 'organisational development' was coined and used by Richard Beckhard in the mid 1950s as a response to the need for integrating organisational needs with individual needs. He defined the term in a broader sense as an effort, which is

(a) planned,
(b) organisation wide,
(c) managed from the top,
(d) increases organisational effectiveness and health, through
(e) planned intervention in the processes of organisation.

Thus, organisational development is a programme of planned changes that aims at helping people and the organisation to work more efficiently. It may be considered as an intervention strategy that uses the various processes of the organisation to focus on the whole organisation. It seeks to change beliefs, values, attitudes, practices and the entire organisational culture, so as to adopt modern technology and to live with the fast pace of change.

Organisational development may also be defined as long term, more encompassing, more complex and more costly approach to change. It aims at pushing the whole organisation to a higher level of functioning. It also affects and increases the existing performance level of its members and the degree of their satisfaction at the work place.

According to Kreitner, "Organisation development consists of planned effect to help persons and work to live together more effectively over a time in their organisation. These goals are achieved by applying the behaviourial science approach, principles, methods and theories adopted from the fields of psychology, sociology, management and education."

In the words of Pareek and Rao "Organisational development is a planned effort, initiated by process specialists to help an organisation develop its diagnostic skill, coping capabilities and linkage strategies in the form of temporary and semi-permanent systems and a culture of mutuality."

According to Warner Burke, consultant in organisational development "O.D. is a process of fundamental changes in an organisation's culture. By fundamental changes, as opposed to fixing a problem and/or improving a procedure some significant aspect of the organisation will never be the same."

Keith Davis pointed out three basic causes which are related to the origin of the concept of organisational development:

(1) Reward structure on the job did not reinforce training. As a result, the momentum of training becomes slow. Even well-designed training and development programmes could not yield because the internal environment of the organisation did not support training programmes. Under such conditions, organisational development programmes were considered necessary.

(2) Rapidly changing business environment which requires that the organisation must respond effectively to survive and prosper. It was possible only through development of the whole organisation and improving the culture and problem-solving capabilities.

(3) Approach of organisational development was also considered necessary to make training programmes more effective and result-oriented. This is because through such programmes of organisational development, trainees learn to work on real problems and in real situations. It leads to more experience and training on their part as compared to traditional programmes such as lectures, discussions, etc.

In brief, organisational development is a process of planned change and improvement of the organisation through an application of knowledge of the behavioural sciences.

Characteristics of Organisational Development

On the basis of the above definitions, the following characteristics may be drawn:

1. It Involves the Whole Organisation

Organisational development is more comprehensive, encompassing and broad which covers the entire organisation. It focuses on required changes to be made on all components or sub-systems of organisation. It implies a total change in the organisation in view of the rapidly changing environment.

2. It is System Oriented

Organisational development is a system-oriented programme. It views the organisation as a system which consists of many sub-systems. The major components or sub-systems of the organisation are structural design which consists of major departments, the work flow consisting of decision-making, flow of material, etc. The human aspect which consists of individual groups, interpersonal relations, etc., are also included in it.

3. It is Result Oriented

Organisational development programmes are functional and result-oriented. These programmes focus on real problems and situations and find solutions. It facilitates increased learning and experience on the part of members of the organisation.

4. It Involves Top Management

All development programmes are initiated and implemented with the active and full support of top management. Therefore, top management must be sensitive enough to have awareness and commitment of these programmes.

5. It Involves the Use of Knowledge of the Behavioural Sciences

Organisational development programmes are based on a knowledge of the behaviourial sciences such as psychology, sociology, management, education, etc. By using the knowledge, practices and principles of these fields, the functioning of the human aspect is improved. The manager learns how to improve individual and group behaviour, interpersonal relations, manage conflicts, etc.

6. It Relates with Organisational Culture

Mostly, organisational development strategies are related to organisational culture. Such programmes deal with the existing set of values, beliefs and perceptions so as to make them high performing as per environmental changes.

7. It Makes the Organisation Healthier

By implementing planned change in various components or sub-systems of an organisation, the overall health of the organisation is improved. It includes all techniques and processes that make a sick organisation healthy and a healthy organisation healthier. But using such programmes, the organisation becomes more viable, effective and an ongoing entity to achieve its goals.

8. It Improves Organisational Effectiveness

The main objective of implementing organisational development programmes is to cope with the changing environment. These programmes aim at improving the overall work culture and climate so as to increase the efficiency of individual employees. By re-designing and redefining human resource policies, people working in the organisation are made more efficient and contributive. By improving group processes the overall effectiveness of the organisation tends to improve.

9. It Improves the Quality of Employees

Organisational development mainly focuses on various problem areas and aims at solving problems in those areas. This is because OD deals with real problems in a real situation. Through these programmes, employees are made capable of handling situations and solving problems efficiently and intelligently. It ultimately leads to more experience and training on their part as compared to the lecture and discussion methods.

10. It is a Systematic Process

Organisational development programmes involve the use of the 'action research process'. It aims at diagnosing the problem, sharing information with employees, involving them in the process and finally seeking their participation in the implementation of OD programmes. By associating them in the process their resistance is reduced to a minimum.

Objectives of Organisational Development

A programme of organisational development is designed and implemented according to specific requirements of the individual organisation. But more commonly, the basic objective of these programmes is to increase organisational effectiveness by developing a new organisational culture and competencies. More specifically, programmes of organisational development may be pursued with the following objectives:

1. To create awareness among the employees about the objectives of the organisation and integrate individual goals with that of the organisation.
2. To strengthen mutual trust, cooperation, communication and mutual support among members.
3. To develop satisfying work experience which may further build enthusiasm among the employees.
4. To encourage the culture of problem solving and developing the necessary skills for it rather than avoid problems.
5. To supplement the use of formal authority with an authority based on personal knowledge and skill.
6. To develop more effective work groups by improving the work environment and interpersonal relations among members.
7. To develop a suitable reward system which recognise profit and service and growth and people.
8. To encourage and facilitate openness of communication among the members of the organisation.
9. To increase the personal responsibility of managers to make plans and implement them and encourage self-control and self-direction.
10. To encourage personal willingness to change.

Basic Assumptions of Organisational Development

In order to make organisation development programmes more effective and utilise them fully, the following basic assumptions must be taken into account:

1. Generally, individuals have drive and desire for personal growth and development. Their work habits are in response to the work environment. Thus, to change work habits, necessary modifications and adjustments are to be made in the work environment.
2. The highest productivity can be achieved by integrating and coordinating individual goals with organisational goals.

3. A feeling of cooperation among members is more effective and desirable than conflict. This is because mutual cooperation tends to bring them closer, creates mutual trust and avoids disagreement.
4. Openness of communication seems to be desirable so that every member can freely express and exchange ideas and knowledge. The suppression of feelings would create dissatisfaction and hamper personal growth.
5. To facilitate the growth of individual members, the environment of openness, mutual trust and support should be built around the organisation.
6. The difference between commitment and agreement must be made at the time of initiating and implementing change. This is because if employees do agree with the change it does not mean that they will be committed to it. It is commitment that is required to implement change.
7. In order to sustain the effectiveness and success of organisational development programmes, the human resources system should be strengthened and made responsive to change.

Process of Organisational Development

Organisational development is a systematic and planned approach to improve organisational effectiveness. It is primarily concerned with problems faced by members and finding out solutions of those problems. By solving the problems, the operational efficiency at every level of the organisation is increased. The commonly used process of organisational development comprises the following elements:

1. Diagnosis Phase

Organisational development aims at solving the problems faced by employees. In order to solve the problem it has to be identified and defined precisely. This is done at the diagnosis phase. This phase refers to identification.

The diagnosis may be carried out either by a team of managers or by some OD consultant hired from outside. It attempts to analyse the internal current profile of the organisation in terms of structure, systems and processes to identify problems and strengths. It indicates that aspect of the organisation that needs to be improved and how such improvements can be made. It consists of the following steps:

(a) preliminary diagnosis of the problem.

(b) collection of required data to support and facilitate diagnosis.

(c) Feedback of data to members of the organisation.

(d) Evaluation of the data by members.

(e) Planning a tentative course of action.

2. Intervention Phase

After having identified and defined the problem, an intervention phase begins. It includes all techniques and approaches that are used to take action so as to bring about the desired change in the organisation. Intervention programmes may be used to improve the effectiveness of individuals, their inter-personal relations, functioning of informal groups or organisational effectiveness. These programmes aim at correcting organisational deficiencies that have been diagnosed. Such actions may be focused either on individuals or on the groups formed by them or on the organisation as a whole.

(a) intervention programmes for individuals include career planning and development, sensitivity training, assertiveness training and transactional analysis.

(b) intervention programmes of a group may include team building, process consultation, confrontation training and managerial grids.

(c) Intervention programmes for the whole organisation include survey and feedback. It helps members to know where they stand in relation with others on important matters and issues that are related to the organisation. This is done by sharing information on these with them.

3. Follow-up Phase

After the completion of the intervention phase, the follow-up starts. It basically aims at:

(a) evaluating the effectiveness of intervention programmes.

(b) taking necessary measures to sustain change which has been introduced in the organisation through intervention programmes. To evaluate these programmes, a comparison is made between two situations of absenteeism, turnover, grievance and work satisfaction before and after the implementation of the programmes. Similarly, to maintain the change brought about in the organisation it is necessary to install a reward and punishment system. This is because with its help changes brought in the working behaviour and level of commitment of the members may be raised and maintained for a longer period of time.

(c) Discussing with managers on the stress and strains in the implementation of programmes and modifying them as per the requirements of the current situation (Figure 17.3).

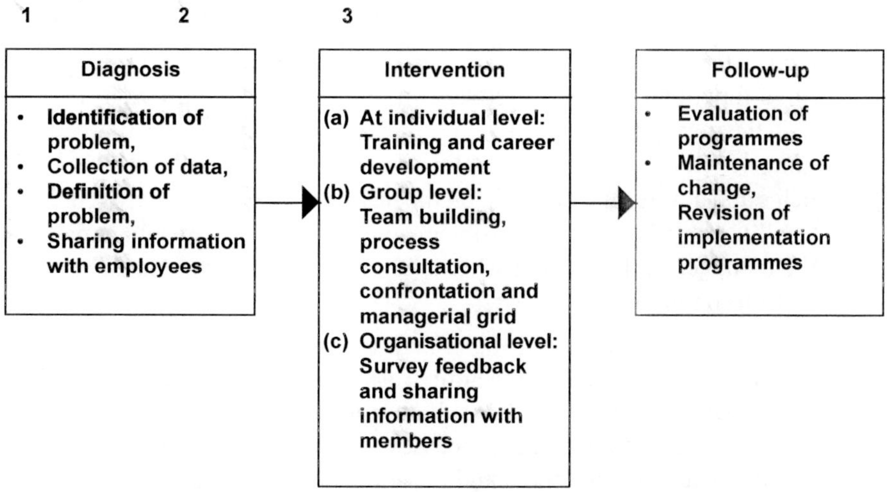

Figure 17.3. Process of organisational development

O.D. INTERVENTION PROGRAMMES

OD intervention is a set of planned activities designed to improve the overall functioning of an organisation. It increases organisational effectiveness mainly at three levels (individual, group, organisation). To bring about the desired changes, various OD programmes are initiated and implemented. Some of these intervention programmes are discussed as under:

1. Survey Feedback

This is one of the most popular OD programmes that is used at the organisation level. It may be considered as part of 'action research'. In this programme, the whole organisation in terms of structure, components and processes is surveyed either by a team of managers or by an outside consultant. The main purpose of a survey feedback is to evaluate the attitude of the members, to identify deficiencies in the perception of members and rectify them. In this programme, either all the members of an organisation or a unit or department participates.

Information on various important organisational matters such as leadership styles, communication effectiveness, reward system, quality of interpersonal relationships, decision-making practices and coordination among the various units or sub-systems of the organisation is sought from members. The idea is to ascertain their attitude and perception.

After processing the information, discussion is initiated by the manager of the unit among the members. This is done to identify possible implications of the findings based on that information.

2. Process Consultation

An organisation is a man-made system. It may develop many inadequacies in its functioning. Managers may find it difficult to improve it. In order to help the manager, information is supplied to him on what is going on around him, within him and between him and other people. The consultant guides, helps and advises the manager on the process that is to be improved. It would finally enable him to solve problems on his own. The consultant works with the manager in diagnosing what is to be improved. The manager develops skills to improve the process.

These processes might be related to work flow, informal relationships among the members of the unit, formal communication channels, etc. Participation of both the consultant and the manager of the unit in the evaluating and diagnosing processes, events and developing alternatives would create greater understanding of the process. This facilitates decision-making to solve the problem on the part of the manager.

3. Team Building

Team building is also a very useful OD programme which aims at improving intra and inter-group effectiveness and success. This programme is usually used at the group level where the activities of the group are interdependent. The main purpose of team building is to increase trust and openness among the members by using high interaction group activities.

These activities may include a better interaction model, sharing resources more effectively, forming task forces, etc. Team building places more emphasis on increasing togetherness, sharing and a spirit of cooperation among the members. It may be used to achieve the following goals:

(a) to determine team goals and priority of goals.

(b) to determine the way it is to be performed in the group.

(c) to analyse how the group is functioning.

(d) to evaluate relationships among members of the team.

Team building is a continuous process which may take years to learn how members pull together and function as members of a team. The main activities that are undertaken in team building may include goal setting, developing interpersonal relations among members, coordinating their functions, role analysis and team process analysis.

4. Sensitivity Training

This is also known as laboratory training encounter group or T groups (training group). This is a method of modifying and changing the working behaviour of members through unstructured group interaction. Under this programme, members are brought together in a free and open environment to discuss themselves and their interactive processes. Individual members learn through observing and participating what is the style of functioning, communicating and how they are perceived by other members.

The main objective of sensitivity training is to increase awareness of their own behaviour to secure greater sensitivity about the behaviour of others and increase their understanding of group processes. By providing such training, the listening skill of the trainee is improved, greater openness is created, tolerance is raised and conflict-resolving skill is enhanced.

5. Inter-Group Development

In the functioning of an organisation, many groups may be involved. These groups may be interdependent and their activities are coordinated to achieve common goals. As there may be problems within a group, the interdependent groups may also have problems with each other. Generally, these groups may develop unhealthy competition, conflict of goals and overlapping of responsibility. These problems, if not tackled properly, may adversely affect the smooth functioning of an organisation. Through inter-group development programmes necessary changes are made in the attitude and perception of the group for each other. This is mainly done by improving inter-group solutions through 'problem-solving'. In this method, each group meets independently to develop a list of perceptions about other groups. These groups share such lists with each other and differences are identified and discussed. Mutual rapport is built to look into and resolve such differences. By improving inter-group relations, conflict and competition is transformed into cooperation and disagreement into coordination.

6. Grid Organisational Development

This is a systematic programme of organisational development which has been developed by Robert Blake and Jane Mouton. It has the following phases:

(a) **Introduction:** Blake and Mouton state that the two styles of management leadership, one concerned with people and the other concerned with production are not mutually exclusive. Rather, these styles are complementary to each other. Thus, the manager must have high concern for both.

(b) **Team Building:** The manager should focus on the team instead of on individuals. Team members should determine standards and develop ways to achieve organisational goals.

(c) **Inter-group Development:** At this phase, the main focus is placed on the organisation. Conflicts among various groups involved in the functioning of the organisation should be reduced. They should be made to work together in a coordinated manner.

(d) **Organisational Goal Setting:** Managers at the top decide about the aims and mission of the organisation and formulate basic corporate strategy to achieve such aims. Middle level managers should be involved in making policies.

(e) **Implementation of Strategic Model:** This phase involves the measuring and evaluation of what has been done. The idea is to know the achievements as well as mistakes made in the previous phases. The new opportunities and challenges arising out of the changing environment are also taken care of in this phase.

SUCCESS OF CHANGE EFFORTS

17 Key Elements to Successful Change

1. Is the sponsor of change high up enough to have power to deal with resistance effectively?
2. Is day to day leadership supportive to change and committed to it?
3. Is there a strong sense of urgency from senior management about the need of change and is it shared by the rest of the organisation?
4. Does the management have a clear vision of how the future will look different from the present?
5. Are there objective measures to evaluate change efforts and are reward systems designed to reinforce them?
6. Is the particular change effort consistent with other changes going on in the organisation?
7. Are functional managers willing to sacrifice their personal interest for the good of the organisation?
8. Does management pride itself on closely monitoring changes and actions of competitors?
9. Is the importance of the customer and knowledge of his needs well accepted by every one in the work force?
10. Are managers and employees rewarded for taking risk, being innovative and looking for new solutions?
11. Is the organisational structure flexible?
12. Are communication channels open both downward and upward?
13. Is the organisation's hierarchy relatively flat?
14. Has organisation successfully implemented major change in the recent past?
15. Is employee satisfaction and trust in management high?
16. Is there a high degree of cross-boundary interactions and cooperation between units in the organisation?
17. Are decisions made quickly taking into account a wide variety of suggestions?

The success of a change programme to a large extent depends on the readiness of the organisation. The key elements mentioned in the box and identified by Symmetrix, a consultancy firm, are considered as guides to implement change in the organisation. The more affirmative answers to the questions in the box, the greater possibility that change efforts will succeed.

SUMMARY

An organisation is an open adaptive system. Its functioning is greatly influenced by the rapidly changing environment. To remain a goal-seeking entity and grow further, it has to change as per the requirements of the situation. If it fails to generate the required strength to cope with change it may collapse. Organisational change may be defined as a variation or alteration in the status quo of the organisation.

The change may be minor or major depending on the impact of the changing environment on various sub-systems of the organisation and its ability to reconcile with it. But a major change takes place at the level of the organisation and affects many departments and employees. The change may be anticipatory, reactive, incremental and strategic in nature.

The planned change may be defined as a systematic and deliberate change which managers introduce in the organisation to face an expected situation. Such change affects the organisation, its processes, structure, goals and technology, and finally the organisation is prepared to cope with change. These changes may be natural, inevitable, rational and deliberate. They are more expensive and broader in scope.

Change may be forced upon an organisation either by internal or external factors including a change in the internal working environment and culture, change in socio-cultural, economic, legal, political and technological factors.

The process of planned change has three important elements. The first is unfreezing the situation which creates an awareness about the change among members of the organisation. The second is changing or moving to a new situation which includes learning a new pattern of behaviour to cope with change. Similarly, the third element is refreezing the situation which makes a new pattern of behaviour a normal way of life.

Planned change may be of various types including change in mission or objectives, structural change, technological and people-oriented changes.

Change to be implemented in the organisation may force employees to make necessary changes in their attitude, perception and working behaviour and skill. Due to the change, they have to modify their present way of corporate life which they may not accept easily. Employees normally have a tendency to resist it. They resist change due to a variety of reasons including job insecurity, change in status quo, communication gap, group pressure, loss of power and control, rigid organisational change and other socio-psychological reasons.

But the organisation makes necessary attempts to overcome resistance. The strategies adopted by the organisation may include seeking more participation of employees, educating, communicating, negotiating with them, using group pressure, change agents and dynamic leadership.

The change being implemented may have serious implications on the overall functioning of the organisation. Therefore, the change is to be managed properly to get the maximum benefit out of it. In the process of managing it, first of all, the need for change is identified, a new set of objectives and goals is developed, type of change required is determined, detailed plan is prepared and finally the change is implemented.

To make the managing process more systematic, action research is conducted. This refers to the collection of data, analysing it and selecting change action to correct the situation.

To change according to the changing environment, the organisation has to learn to change. One of the common ways is organisational development. This is a programme of planned change which aims at helping people and the organisation to work more efficiently. It is a long-term, lengthy, costly and comprehensive approach to change.

Organisational development programmes generally involve the whole organisation, are initiated by top management, need the knowledge of the behavioural sciences and relate with culture. The basic objective of such a programme is to increase organisational effectiveness by developing a new organisational culture and competencies.

The process of organisational development has three stages including the diagnosis phase, intervention phase and follow-up phase. Through this process, many intervention programmes are conducted to implement change. Such programmes may be designed and used either for individual employees or at the group level or at the level of the entire organisation. These programmes may include survey feedback, process consultation, team building, sensitivity training, inter-group development and grid organisational development.

In order to ensure the success of a change programme, a conducive environment is built around the organisation. In this regard 17 key elements to successful change have been identified by a consultancy firm.

TEST QUESTIONS

1. Define the term 'change'. Discuss the various types of change.
2. What is meant by 'planned change'? Explain the internal and external factors that force an organisation to change.
3. 'Organisations that fail to change are sure to fall'. Comment.
4. Discuss the elements that are involved in the process of planned change.

5. 'Change in an organisation should be implemented with the cooperation of the affected employees'. Comment.
6. Why is change inevitable and desirable? Can an organisation survive without change? Give reasons to support your answer.
7. Why do employees resist change? Explain the various reasons for it.
8. 'Resistance to change is an irrational response'. Give reasons in favour and against this statement.
9. Describe the various elements of the action research process.
10. Give a complete account of future challenges to be faced by managers in the 21st century to manage organisations.
11. What is organisational development? Bring out its main characteristics.
12. Discuss the various objectives of a development programme.
13. Explain the various elements that are involved in the process of organisational development.
14. Describe the various organisational development assumptions.
15. Explain the various organisational development intervention programmes.
16. Write short notes on
    (a) Kurt Lewin's model of change process
    (b) Planned change
    (c) Management of change
    (d) Resistance to change
    (e) Action research
    (f) Process of organisational development
    (g) Sensitivity training
    (h) Grid organisational development
17. Suggest at least 10 prerequisite factors for successful change.

REFERENCES

Freeman, R. Edward, Stoner, A. F. and Gilbert, Daniel R. *Management*. New Delhi, India: Prentice-Hall of India Private Limited, 2001.

Jaeger, Alfred M. 'Organisation Development and National Culture: Where is the Fit'? *Academy of Management Review*, January, 1986.

Katz, Daniel and Kahn, Robert L. *The Social Physicology of Organisation*. New York, U.S.A.: Wiley, 1978.

Koontz, Harold and Weihrich, Heinz. *Essentials of Management*. New Delhi, India: Tata McGraw-Hill Publishing Company Limited, 1998.

Lawrence, Paul R. and Lorsch. Jay W. *Organisation and Environment: Managing Differentiation and Integration.* Homewood, Ill., U.S.A.: Irwin, 1967.

Moorhead and Griffin. *Organisational Behaviour*. Delhi, India: A.I.T.B.S. Publishers and Distributors, 1999.

Moshal, B. S. *Organisation and Management: Text and Cases.* New Delhi, India: Galgotia Publishing Company, 2002.

Quick, James C. and Quick, Jonathan D. *Operational Stress and Preventive Management.* New York, U.S.A.: McGraw-Hill, 1984.

Vicars, William M. and Hartke, Darrel D. 'Evaluating O.D. Evaluations: A Status Report'. *Group and Organisation Studies*, June, 1984.

EXPERIENCE I

Application of Process Consultation Approach to a Conference

BACKGROUND

An international conference was held in India in December 1974 for 20 days in which process consultation help was provided for the entire conference period, except for a few days when some members did their personal work and sight-seeing. There were participants from 12 different parts of the world. The proceedings and discussions were conducted in two languages, English and French. A voluntary service agency, established in 1997, sponsored the conference. This agency has about 140 local units in different parts of the world and has a total membership of about 1,400. The organisation is divided into 12 divisions, the largest having 16 local units and 320 members and the smallest having four local units with 16 members. The agency held its annual meeting with 21 members; 12 representatives of the 12 divisions, four members of the top governing body and five observers. The agency has collective leadership with four members. (We shall call it the top team).

The request for process consultation was received from the top team, which, with other representatives had experienced dissatisfaction during the previous international conference. Decisions had been influenced by only a few members; participation was very low; conflicts occurred, but were soothed by emotional appeals, more task-oriented and less development-oriented decisions were made; a sense of futility pervaded; and the conference ended in tension. The top team then decided to have some specialist advice for planning the next conference, as well as help during the conference to conduct the proceedings to achieve better understanding, wider participation, critical but supportive discussions and joint decision-making.

Experience I continued

Experience I continued

After receiving the invitation, but before deciding whether it would be worthwhile to undertake this assignment, a detailed discussion was held with the top team in their office in Europe on their expectations from this help of process consultation. After detailed discussions, it was agreed that such help may be useful for the success of the conference.

Objectives

The objectives of the process consultation to the international conference were discussed at the initial meeting in Europe. They were further spelt out and agreed on in the first meeting with the top teams. These objectives were as follows:

1. To bring about the maximum amount of mutual openness in the conference so that the members may be able to talk freely and help each other.
2. To ensure more widespread and better quality participation of the members.
3. To improve the quality of decision-making so that decisions are taken faster and seek more commitment on the part of members to execute and carry out these decisions.
4. To resolve differences that may arise during the conference more creatively and in such a way that the differences in points of view may enrich the conference.
5. To provide the necessary feedback and help in the improvement of the conference process as the conference proceeds. In other words, to help develop a monitoring and self-corrective system during the conference.

The Client

It was clarified and agreed upon by the top team that the client for the conduct of the conference would be the top team and not the total conference so that the consultant would provide help to the top team in designing as well as conducting the conference. However, in due course he would also provide feedback to the total conference and the total group would become a client at that stage on several aspects. It was also agreed that this arrangement should be made clear from the beginning to the total conference.

Experience I continued

Experience I continued

PROCESS CONSULTATION IN ACTION

The client group wanted help in designing the conference, process facilitation in the conference and reviewing the progress in order to monitor the conference design and procedure. As will be evident from the discussion on the various dimensions of process consultation below, the role of the consultant becomes less active as the conference progressed. One whole day was spent on preliminary discussions and it was decided that the consultant(s) and client group (four members of the top team) would spend two full days, prior to the conference, in talking about the purposes of the conference, the expectations from process consultation, if such information was available, and to establish certain norms for process consultation. Two days immediately before the conference were therefore earmarked for this purpose.

There were long discussions on various aspects, such as working relationships between the consultant and the client. It was agreed that every day after the meetings were over, the process analysis group, consisting of the four members of the top team and the consultant, would sit together for at least two hours to review the day's activities. It was also agreed that the consultant would give feedback and raise issues and that the client group would increasingly make notes and share their own feedback. This was to be a crucial meeting where the roles and design for the next day were to be prepared in the light of the understanding of the process of that day. It was also decided that such meetings might become necessary even during lunch and other breaks, and provision for that was also made. This arrangement was honoured throughout the conference, and this led to a healthier understanding between the consultant and the client and among the client group as well.

The objectives, as stated earlier, were worked out during these two days and alternative ways to achieve them were also discussed. The following dimensions were attended to as part of the process consultation.

THE MAIN ACTIVITIES

Initial Unfreezing Activities

Although the client did not know what it meant operationally, it was agreed between the client group and the consultant(s) that it was necessary to do something to create a climate of openness, trust and mutual understanding from the very beginning. It was also agreed that there should be enough opportunity for the members attending the conference to interact with

Experience I continued

Experience I continued

each other from the beginning and that a norm of asking questions without feeling embarrassed may be established. It was also agreed that individual members may be helped to get some idea about their own orientation so that the norms of critical self-examination may be established. All this was done through a three-day programme which was separately prepared as an initial unfreezing intervention.

The programme consisted of

(1) Micro lab, designed to stimulate participants think about the various objectives of the conference by performing simple tasks in unconventional ways.
(2) Structured exercises to stimulate some dimensions of group life which were identified after discussion with the top team in the beginning.
(3) Structured ways of collecting data about the orientation and styles of the members of the conference in order to help them develop insight into them and the relationship with their effectiveness.
(4) Discussion of six reports prepared by representatives of various divisions to share and increase empathy.

The programme began with the micro lab and it was followed by structured feedback on orientation and interpersonal styles of individual members. The structured exercises and discussion of reports were taken up after these two activities.

Issues in Focus

The following issues were focussed during the three-day programme:

(1) Insight into Behavioural Orientations

Behavioural orientations as revealed by some psychological tests each individual took, were discussed in the total group, taking examples from individual profiles. A general interpretation of the total culture of the organisation was also given, based on the patterns of scores of the total group. It was, for example, pointed out that the members, out of their eagerness not to hurt each other, tended to avoid being closer and establish meaningful personal relationships. The need for such relationships was quite high in the group. The implications of such trends were discussed.

Experience I continued

Experience I continued

(2) Empathy

A non-verbal test on empathy was given and scores interpreted. The implications of the extreme scores were discussed. Persons with low scores could be insensitive and therefore not understand the problems of others, whereas persons with high scores could be too sensitive and could avoid taking the risk of expressing themselves freely. It was discussed how persons can continue to have high empathy and at the same time retain spontaneity of behaviour.

(3) Use of Group Sources

Through an exercise, the conditions under which the group resources are used were discussed. Individuals over-concerned with their own achievement tend to neglect group resources which can help individuals have synergetic achievements—the group achieving more than the total potentiality of its individual members.

(4) Collaboration

Emphasis was put on collaborative efforts to resolve issues. One important dimension was the perception of goals; whether the individual perceived the goal as his own, or as that of the total group to which he belonged made a difference in his strategy of achieving it. Thus, it was brought out by comparing the behaviour of some individuals who were more effective in solving group problems with that of other individuals who were not so effective. During this exercise, a peculiar phenomenon was observed. Whenever the members had an opportunity to meet and discuss a strategy, they collaborated on work without such a previous meeting. It appeared that collaboration was not a problem when they were working in a face-to-face situation, but they became individualistic when they were working alone.

(5) Developing People

One major issue which seemed important was how new members were developed. Through an exercise, data was generated to demonstrate how expectations by important persons like senior executives influenced performance and motivation. It was also demonstrated how over-concern indicates a lack of trust in one's ability, and that help is useful when it is sought on specific aspects. Encouragement and genuine positive reinforcement was seen in the exercise producing better effects on performance than detailed guidance.

Experience I continued

Experience I continued

ASPECTS COVERED

As stated above, the main work of the process consultant was to provide process consultation to the chief executive group. Several kinds of consultations were provided during this time. The following aspects were covered:

(1) Feedback on the Behaviour of the Client

This was done to improve the conference ability and decision-making capacity of the top team. Usually, two members of the top team chaired meetings during the day.

(2) Feedback on the Day's Programme and Design

The consultant also made notes on why certain aspects of the programmes did or did not go through well. Notes were also taken on several aspects, such as members' need to participate and influence decisions, visible conflicts in the group and among some members over certain items and clique formation in the discussions. The consultant shared these notes with the top team and asked them to react to them and used as feedback to prepare the next day's programme.

Such feedback was found to be useful both for increasing the insight of the client group as well as for giving them training in keeping such notes; as a result more process notes were prepared by all the four members of the top team; and were shared at these meetings. This helped to increase their confidence in their ability to take notes and make observations.

(3) Designing of the Programme

The consultant made no comments on the substantial discussions and issues but helped the client group in designing the next day's programme. In the initial stages, the consultant was active in giving suggestions and generating alternatives so that the client group could choose from among these alternatives with several considerations. Later, he deliberately became less active in generating such alternatives and encouraged the client group to do their own thinking. The consultant's attempt was to help the client to make it more flexible and creative in generating alternatives and then take decisions. On several occasions, the meetings were very exhaustive and it was felt that there was no time and energy for such process work. However, fortunately, this was a very rewarding experience and in spite of such exhaustion, the process discussion meetings were regularly held, and the analysis led to a more mutually satisfying experience.

Experience I continued

Experience I continued

Help to the Total Group

Although the consultant initially worked with the top team, as he came to be accepted and become a part of the total conference group, his role in giving process feedback to the total group was encouraged and welcomed by the conference members and was seen as useful. When the group was engaged in some conflict and some members of the group wanted the consultant to make comments on what was happening, or when he felt that his comments on the process might help the group, he made such process feedback available to the group. His style was more in raising questions, making observations available, giving certain facts and data to the group as he observed it, and leaving it there. He did not get into an argument on how that feedback could be used. It was left to the members of the group to use or not to use the feedback. Rarely did the feedback either threaten the conference or leave it neglected. Mostly, the feedback was used. The consultant was very careful to see that this did not happen frequently, otherwise the group, instead of depending on the expertise of the top team or on their own, would continue to depend on the consultant's help. However, the consultant also did not shy away from making some significant observations to the total group when, in his judgement, the observations might be too late if not at that particular point of time.

Help of Working Methodology

The consultant also provided help to the top team on the methodology of working. This was, in fact, the main thrust of the process consultant throughout the duration of the conference. As stated earlier, the main focus of the help was on wider participation and distribution of decision-making among most of the members of the conference. The consultant helped the top team to think of a variety of ways of achieving these goals. His main attempt was to raise questions and help them search several methodologies, come out with new ideas and finally take a decision themselves. In the process analysis meeting, the working of different methodologies was reviewed. In working out a methodology, the objectives were discussed and alternative methodologies reviewed in the light of the objectives. For example, the various advantages and disadvantages of using the small groups or the large groups were discussed before a decision was taken by the top team on how to use these groups. The client groups themselves suggested on one occasion that smaller groups would provide more opportunity to an individual to think. It was suggested and agreed on the basis of experience of a day that in the smaller groups there was much more understanding and less commitment to an idea so that the ownership of the idea was lost, but the tendency to own up to the responsibility of

Experience I continued

Experience I continued

ideas and feelings was promoted. It was certainly observed and agreed that there was much more participation of members in smaller groups.

The consultation on methodology was essentially in terms of raising questions on the design of the groups, on timing of the various discussions, building and sequencing the various events, building process analysis in between and so on. Close attention to the design was found to be most helpful as was revealed by a sense of solidarity and mutuality reflected in the group, and noticed not only by the top team but by other members of the conference also.

Evaluation of Methodology

It was decided to have a mid-conference evaluation in order to know how the conference was going on and to plan corrective action to make the rest of the conference more productive. The consultant helped the top team in designing the methodology of evaluation. Long discussion was held on the purpose and methodology of evaluation. The discussion was spread over four days and various aspects were taken up. Finally, it was decided that evaluation should involve all the members of the conference to be forward-looking and thorough and that it should not become a ritual. In order to achieve these objectives, it was decided to divide the entire working of the conference into four different aspects; and the members were divided into four groups, each group discussing one aspect for which a broad routine of the items to be considered was given to them. These groups met for one hour simultaneously and prepared written reports which were then shared in the total community and members of the community could comment on and discuss the various aspects. These dimensions of the conference were:

(1) objectives of the first half of the conference and to what extent they had been achieved;

(2) resources and means used including the outside behavioural science consultant, other outside resources, small group work, total group meetings, visits, etc.;

(3) specific items of the programme, including the process activities, initial unfreezing programme, reports, specific session on substantial issues; and

(4) physical and other facilities.

A different method was adopted at the end of the conference. One member was requested to interview as many members as considered necessary and prepare a report. The member presented an excellent critical report which was highly admired. Then other members added any other remarks that they personally wanted to make.

Experience I continued

EXPERIENCE II

Organisation Falls to External Change

GAMMA CONSULTANTS

A division of Gamma Consultants, which was providing accounting services to client organisations had recently lost a number of important clients. There was a steady decline in the division's volume of business and profitability, but attempts at reorientation had met with little success.

Senior employees of the division territorialized much of the office work. For example, the secrets of accounts receivable were the province of one senior employee; the mysteries of discount rates and accounts payable belonged to another. Even the employees who performed the specialised functions did not fully comprehend the reasons for some of the actions they executed. Much of the office work reflected the reasoning of the long tenured office manager whose style did not include explanation of his directions.

Like following religious rituals whose original significance had been lost in the midst of history, the office personnel performed countless tasks withoutt understanding their relevance but unwilling, unable and even frightened to change them. Not understanding the goals of their activities, they could not evaluate and modify their behaviour. The employees were threatened by even minor changes. In such a context, the division was going down steadily in performance and yet all attempts to bring about a strategic outlook were proving to be futile.

EXPERIENCE III

Ranbaxy Charts 10-year Roadmap to Fuel Growth

Ranbaxy Laboratories has prepared a new pill for growth. Christened 'Vision Garuda' it is a 10-year roadmap to attain significant growth, positioning Ranbaxy as a research-based global pharmaceutical company.

The vision statement, a brainchild of the company CEO and MD, D. S. Brar, targets to scale turnover of $ 5 billion by 2012, company sources said. In 2002, Ranbaxy had notched up a turnover of Rs. 2,768.6 crore posting a 42.6 per cent rise over 2001.

The plan envisages the development of two to three patented new drugs (from new molecules) over and above the existing molecules under development. Sources said these drugs would be in the areas of urology, metabolic disorders and anti-infectives.

Experience III continued

Experience III continued

The drug development will be coupled with an alliance-making strategy in areas of strength and non-strength with global pharma majors. Alliances would be made in various areas like identifying target (protein) for drug development, phase-III clinical trials (areas of non-strength) and also in the stages of pre-clinical phase-I and phase-II of trials (areas of strength).

Ranbaxy has already entered into a co-licensing alliance with Schwarz Pharma for development of RBS-2258, a drug to treat benign prostatic hyperplasia (BPH). Other molecules under study/development are: RBX 6198 (second) BPH molecule) RBX 9841 (antagonists for overactive urinary bladder), RBX 7796 (respiratory infections) and RBX 7644 (anti-bacteria) among others.

The pharma major has also decided to set up a R&D unit in North America. The facility will come into place by June 2004. Rashmi Barbhajya, president R&D, said: "The unit in North America will not be as big as the Indian facility and the quantum of investment and number of scientists to be recruited are yet to be worked out. However, it would be a key facility for critical factors like conducting phase-III clinical trials (which no company can afford to do outside the U.S.A. and Europe) and preparatory work for regulatory approval."

'Vision Garuda' will also focus on novel drug delivery systems (a unique method to lower dosage and increase the efficacy of a drug), expansion of manufacturing facilities in India and strategic locations overseas. It will also revamp organisational structures to cater to a wider span of operations and standardise business processes.

The sources added that the U.S. business is poised to contribute significantly to Ranbaxy's revenue growth.

CASE STUDY I

The New England Arts Project had its headquarters above an Italian restaurant in Portsmouth, New Hampshire. The project had five full-time employees and during the busy times of the year, particularly the month before Christmas, it hired as many as six part-time workers to type, address envelopes and send out mailings. Although each of the full-timers had a title and formal job description, an observer would have had trouble telling their positions apart. Suzanne Clammer, for instance, was the executive director, the head of the office, but she could be found typing or licking envelopes just as often as Martin Weld, who has been

Case Study I continued

Case Study I continued

working for less than a year as office coordinator, the lowest position in the project's hierarchy.

Despite a constant sense of being a month behind, the office ran relatively smoothly. No outsider would have had a prayer of finding a mailing list or a budget in the office, but project employees knew where almost everything was, and after a quiet fall they did not mind having their small space packed with workers in November. But a number of federal funding agencies on which the project relied began to grumble about the cost of the part-time workers, the amount of time the project spent handling routine paperwork, and the change was on. Finally, Martin Weld said it: "May be we should get a customer."

To Welk, fresh out of college, where he had written his papers on a word processor, computers were just another tool to make a job easier. But his belief was not shared by the others in the office, the youngest of whom had 15 years more seniority than he. A computer would eat the project's mailing list, they said, destroying any chance of raising funds for the year. It would send the wrong things to the wrong people, insulting them and convincing them that the project had become another faceless organisation that did not care. They swapped horror stories about computers that had charged them thousands of dollars for purchases they had never been made or had assigned the same airplane seat to five people.

"We'll lose all control," Suzanne Clammer complained. She saw some kind of office automation as inevitable, yet she kept thinking she would probably quit before it came about. She liked hand-addressing mailings to arts patrons whom she had met, and she felt sure that the recipients contributed more because they recognised her neat blue printing. She remembered the agonies of typing class in high school and believed she was too old to take on something new and bound to be much more confusing. Two other employees, with whom she had worked for a decade, called her after work to ask if the prospect of a computer in the office meant they should be looking for other jobs. "I have enough trouble with English grammar," one of them wailed. "I'll never be able to learn Pascal or Lotus or whatever these new languages are."

One morning Glammer called Martin Welk into her office, shut the door, and asked him if he could recommend any computer consultants. She had read an article that explained how a company could waste thousands of dollars by adopting integrated office automation in the wrong way, and she figured the project would have to hire somebody for at least six months to get the new machines working and to teach the staff how to use them.

Case Study I continued

Case Study I continued

Welk was pleased because Clammer had evidently accepted the idea of a computer in the office. But he also realised that as the resident authority on computers, he had a lot of work to do before they went shopping for machines.

Questions

1. Is organisation development appropriate in this situation? Why is it and why is it not?
2. What kinds of resistance to change have the employees of the project displayed?
3. What can Martin Welk do to overcome the resistance?

—oo(O)oo—

CHAPTER 18

MANAGEMENT CASE STUDY METHOD

LEARNING OBJECTIVES

1. To develop conceptual clarity regarding management or business cases and relate them with "medical" cases.
2. To learn various objectives of management case study.
3. To bring out various factors on the basis of which cases can be analysed and written.
4. To remember Raymond's question-based approach and Schnelle's 10-point model to be used to writing case studies.

CONCEPT AND DEFINITION

The basic responsibility of a manager is to solve problems, to tackle situations and to resolve crises as effectively as possible. While managing an organisation, these situations are far and again what makes the job of a manager more difficult and challenging. The real test of managerial skill and talent lies in solving these problems in time and thereby taking the organisation ahead to achieve its objectives.

Thus, in order to develop the required managerial skill among management students and trainees to solve wide-ranging problems, they are exposed to real-life situations and very similar situations through the management case study method. This method aims at developing the required talent on the part of the manager needed for applying managerial knowledge and thoughts in practical situations. In other words, the case method helps managers to translate thoughts into concrete decisions and action. It is through management case studies that they can develop the necessary skill for it.

Management of business cases represents a problem situation which involves many events occurring around it in a definite chronological sequence. These events associated with the problem situation may also be considered as the facts of the case. They are mixed with each other making the problem situation more difficult. Such cases, by and large, may resemble 'medical cases'. This is because business cases are identified, defined and diagnosed with the help of symptoms just like medical cases. These are to be solved by a developing a suitable course of action.

The case study method was initially developed in 1871 by Christopher Longdel at Harvard Law School, U.S.A., for developing practical know-how on the part of law trainees. Gradually, this method received prominence in the field of management which is a combination of science and art. Management cases may be programmed or non-programmed which may be routine and repetitive or may be new or unique. Similarly, they may further be classified as problematic, descriptive and illustrative. This is because some times they involve complex problems which are to be analysed and solved or they may be describing the situation as to how and when various events related to the case have occurred, which helps in solving the problem. In addition, these cases may be illustrative or exemplary involving new and more effective practice or stating the general law of management. It is widely accepted that management cases should represent real-life situations and must be factual. At the initial stage, the management student or trainee may be first exposed to less complicated and simple problems which may be very 'similar' to the real situation. Gradually, they may be prepared to cope with more complicated problems that have many dimensions.

The management case study method primarily involves decision making. This is because to solve the problem or a case, the manager has to decide among the available alternatives as to which one is appropriate and has a close association with the problem or which one is more valid in a given situation. Thus, this method basically aims at developing decision-making skills and analytical abilities on the part of the manager. It also helps in providing information training and communication skills required to establish proper and effective interpersonal relations with subordinates, peers and superiors.

OBJECTIVES OF THE CASE METHOD

To under the usefulness of this method in the managing process, it is desirable to know and discuss its objectives. The major objectives of the case method are:

1. It develops and enhances confidence among managers to solve problems effectively. In every sphere of management, they have to face and solve a wide range of problems and the case method prepares them for it.
2. It trains managers for decision making by developing the required skill and talent on their part. Through the management case method, they keep on learning how to identify problems, analyse them, develop alternative solutions and finally, solve them.

3. Through the management case method, managers learn how to handle and use data and information available on various aspects of the problem. Such ability is necessary to be developed among managers for encouraging factual decision making.
4. The management case method also provides systematic and scientific training to managers to translate knowledge of management into concrete decisions and action. Through this method, they become familiar with practical real-life situations. They also get an opportunity to match it with theoretical frame-up of management knowledge.
5. One of the most important objectives of this method is to broaden the horizon of knowledge of managers by exposing them to a wide range of situations. In this way, they acquire the necessary skill to observe and analyse situations minutely and formulate different sets of management policies and strategies to deal with different situations.

According to Schnelle, the case method has the following objectives:

1. To provide a description of real business situations so as to acquaint students with the principles and practices obtaining and involved in various work settings.
2. Introduction of realism into formal instruction by matching their theoretical knowledge and its relevance to practical solutions.
3. Demonstrate various types of goals, problems, facts, conditions, conflicts and personalities involved in organisational settings.
4. Develop decision-making ability on the part of managers.
5. Develop independent thinking but a cooperative approach to work in group situations.

Careful analysis of the above objectives of the case method reveals that it is an integral part of the management process. It would help managers to make effective use of theoretical knowledge to seek optimal utilisation of resources to achieve the objectives of the organisation. Interestingly, it provides an insight into the problems, thereby enabling managers to handle different situations in different ways.

HOW TO WRITE AN ANALYSIS OF A CASE STUDY

Although many management experts and authors have suggested certain guidelines to analyse and write case studies, a stereotype or predetermined procedure cannot be followed for this purpose. This is because every situation may be made of a different set of variables calling upon the manager to treat them differently and then formulate a suitable strategy for them. Besides, the case study method represents an application of management knowledge in practice which may vary from manager to manager. Thus, the exact manner or procedure to be followed by the manager to a large extent depends on the degree of involvement and exposure on the part of the manager and the nature of the problem faced by him. With the passage of time, an individual manager comes across a variety of problems which he attempts to solve as effectively as possible by devising his own procedure taking into account organisational, environmental and his individual constraints. However, certain basic guidelines may be suggested to students to write an analysis of the case. The process of writing an analysis involves three major elements:

1. Identification of a problem situation.
2. Analysis and evaluation of a problem situation.
3. Making recommendations to solve the problem.

According to the Harvard system of case study, the following five steps are involved in case analysis:

1. Defining the central base involved in the case.
2. Selecting relevant areas of consideration.
3. Analysing relevant areas of consideration and ascertaining their relative significance.
4. Surveying other possibilities.
5. Drawing a final conclusion.

Similarly, Schnelle suggested the following 10-point complex problem-solving device:

1. Identifying a problem.
2. Determining the facts on various aspects of the problem.
3. Ascertaining and developing alternative courses of action.
4. Analysing of advantages and disadvantages of each alternative course.
5. Assessment of advantages and disadvantages.
6. Predicting the occurrence of advantages and disadvantages.
7. Selecting the best alternative (decided upon).
8. Executing the decision.
9. Filing the solution of the problem.
10. Comparing the expected result with the real result of the decision.

T. J. Raymond pointed out the following questions which should be raised by the case analyst to analyse the case:

1. What are the actual problems involved in the case?
2. What are the relevant facts?
3. What are the crucial unknown aspects of the case?

4. What are the major critical questions related to each specific event?
5. In what ways are logic and reasoning used to determine crucial inferences, connections and relationships?
6. In what manner can contradictory facts and arguments be weighted in making decisions?
7. What should be the proper timing of a decision?
8. In what ways can those decisions be best executed?

In the above approach, Raymond has given more emphasis on the fact that while analysing a problem situation, unknown and suspected aspects of the problem should also be taken into account. Significantly, to make a balanced decision, he also pointed out that an analyst should take note of those facts and arguments that are contrary to a given situation. In addition, the analyst should also visualise how he can apply logic and reasoning to derive inferences and relationships.

Although Raymond's question-based approach and Schnelle's 10-point mode differ on certain counts, but by analysing them carefully a more integrated and simplified approach for analysing a case may be suggested as under:

1. To identify a problem situation in terms of its origin, causes, symptoms and effects.
2. To take stock of the existing set of managerial policies and strategies of the organisation since these may pose constraints to arrive at a particular situation.
3. To unfold all possible unknown and suspected aspects of a given problem and collect relevant information on the various aspects of the problem.
4. By applying reasoning to derive both implicit and explicit inferences, associations and relationships and to study them thoroughly.
5. To evaluate all the possible inferences and relationships providing alternative solutions.
6. To narrow down the choice to an appropriate solution having close association with the given problem.
7. To give necessary arguments in favour of the recommended solution taking into account the contrary side of it.

In order to help the student in writing a case study, the following solved case exercise may prove useful.

CASE STUDIES

Case Study I

Ashok, a senior sales executive, had been working with ABC Sons, a reputed publishing firm, for the last 15 years. The firm has a wide range of publications of textbooks for school and college students. The firm is owned by a family having four brothers and the eldest one, who is about 55 years old, is a bachelor and looks after all the activities of production and distribution. The role of the other brothers is 'follow-up' in nature and supportive. About 100 employees are working in the firm including 15 in the sales department having no line of authority and all of them are accountable to the owner. Most of the employees working in the organisation are not satisfied with the behavioural pattern of the owner, barring a few who are considered faithful to him. Mr. Ashok, who has been for a longer period of time with the same clientele, has developed good relations. He supplies specimen copies of books to teachers in time and follows them up by getting the books recommended for students. He is very popular among the teachers because of his good behaviour, professional knowledge and other qualities of salesmanship. He is 35 years old, not very ambitious but concerned about his future. He has a feeling that he has not been given any recognition by the owner for his sincerity and hard work. Recently, he had an argument with the owner over the distribution of specimen copies to teachers, because the owner suspected some wastage and leakage on the part of Ashok. Though he had clarified his position in this regard, the owner kept on suspecting his integrity without sufficient grounds. Finally, when Ashok came to know about the owner's suspicions through some others in the office, he decided to leave. Within a couple of months, he left the firm and joined another one the owner of which is young and dynamic and seriously interested to broaden the product line with new publications, especially in the field of management. It is reliably learnt that within a short span of about one year, the sales volume of ABC and Sons has declined considerably. The owner is greatly worried about it and he appointed Shyam Verma, who has the same experience, in place of Ashok. But he is finding it very difficult to cope with the situation and check the decline.

Questions

Read the above case and answer the following questions:

(1) What is wrong with ABC and Sons?

(2) Enumerate all the possible reasons for which Ashok left the firm.

(3) Give suggestions to control the decline in the sales volume of ABC and Sons.

Suggested Analysis

After having gone through the whole case, it is discovered that the main problem of ABC and Sons is the decline in sales volume and growing dissatisfaction among the employees mainly due to bad management, lack of human relations approach, unhealthy internal environment, and lack of mutual trust and confidence.

In the second part of the case, all the possible causes due to which Ashok has left the firm are enumerated. And in the third part, it is concluded that lost sales will result in decreased market share which cannot be regained easily. Therefore, the firm has to review the entire range of the existing set of marketing strategies.

The entire case analysis is to be written in three parts.

1. Identification of the Problems of ABC and Sons

(a) lack of professionalism in management.

(b) conservative approach of the owner.

(c) lack of proper control system to exercise control over the activities of the sales people, particularly with regard to the distribution of specimen copies of books.

(d) lack of proper work culture in the firm.

(e) lack of mutual trust and confidence creating confusion, chaos and suspicion.

(f) Non-application of various systems of human resource development such as recruitment, selection, performance appraisal, training and transfer, promotion, etc.

(g) lack of human relations approach.

(h) lack of proper departmentalisation of activities and working relationships among the employees.

(i) Highly centralised organisation retaining more authority at the top level by the owner.

2. Causes of the Problem

(a) Due to lack of a chain of command in the firm, the employees tend to be indisciplined which may reduce their efficiency.

(b) The non-availability of the required feedback from the teachers to whom specimen copies of the books are given is the immediate cause for Ashok to leave the firm.

(c) Lack of adequate promotional avenues in the firm which might be causing frustration among the employees as a result of which Ashok left the firm.

(d) The owner of the firm has unjustifiable behaviour and completely lacks a scientific approach and recognition of the human factor in the functioning of the organisation.

(e) The performance of Ashok had never been evaluated and recognised as a result of which he could not get suitable rewards for it. Rather, he was treated at par with less efficient employees.

(f) Non-existence of informal organisation has also caused problems for the employees. Under one-man rule, they feel strained and stressed and do not have any outlet to release their tensions.

3. Solution and Recommendations

(a) Induction of qualified professional managers in the organisation, especially to handle key positions like marketing executive and editor looking after production.

(b) Chain of command should be established by creating various departments and working relationships of superiors and subordinates should be created among the employees to discipline them and control their activities.

(c) To develop the efficiency level of employees for which scientific selection should be made and proper training be given to them.

(d) A control system should be installed to ensure that every concerned teacher gets specimen copies and there is no wastage and leakage.

(e) To evaluate the level of performance, a suitable device of performance appraisal should be adopted. This may be done on a quarterly or half-yearly basis. On the basis of performance, employees performing efficiently must be rewarded adequately and necessary measures should be taken to improve their performance.

(f) The internal environment of the organisation should be improved by encouraging the development of informal groups leading to more socialisation and a relaxed atmosphere for the employees.

CASE STUDY II

Nawal had just graduated from the Indian Institute of Management, Bangalore, and joined his father's small business which employed 28 semi-skilled workers. After one week, his father, a retired government officer, called him and said, "Nawal, I have had a chance to observe your working with the men and women for the past few days. Although I hate to, I must say some thing. You are just too nice to people. I know they taught you human relations stuff at IIM, but it just does not work here. I remember when the Hawthorne studies were first reported every one in the academic field got all excited about them. But believe me, there is more to managing people than just being nice to them."

Questions

Read the above case carefully and answer the following questions:

1. Do you think Nawal's father understood the Hawthorne studies correctly?
2. If you were Nawal what would your reaction be to your father's comment?

Suggested Analysis

Careful analysis of the above case reveals that the central problem involved regards human relations in the organisation. Since Nawal had graduated in management, he seems to be well convinced regarding the importance of the human relations approach in management. This approach advocates that employees working in an organisation cannot be treated like cogs in a machine or like other resources. They have certain needs, wants, expectations, beliefs and values which interfere with their working. It is indisputable that if they are given proper treatment they will be more satisfied which may lead to not only work for money but they also need recognition, appreciation, warm treatment and congenial interpersonal relations.

In the light of these factors, Nawal must have believed in maintaining warmth, interpersonal relations with employees by reducing the social distance, listening to their viewpoints and helping them in every respect by being nice to them.

But it is clear from the arguments of his father that he knows something about the findings of the Hawthorne experiment but his viewpoint is highly influenced and dominated by the weak points or lacunae associated with that experiment. He firmly believes that these findings are purely academic in nature and managing the men in the organisation is much more than that. It can be safely inferred from the case that Nawal is on the positive side of the approach whereas his father is more guided by the negative aspects of the human relations approach.

Nevertheless, the relevance of the Hawthorne studies and its conclusions cannot be reduced only up to keeping the employees happy but these conclusions go a long way to raise the level of satisfaction of employees and thereby enhance productivity. To understand the implications of these conclusions it is desirable to discuss them.

In the first phase, Elton Mayo highlighted that the psychological, social and other factors besides the economic factor have a definite impact on the level of satisfaction and productivity of employees. Thus, their needs, feelings and expectations should be taken care of.

The second set of conclusions indicated and emphasised the role and importance of informal relations upon the working behaviour of the employees. Through informal relations they communicate freely and frankly even on official matters, their social needs are fulfilled, and they feel relaxed and comfortable in their work setting.

In addition, a third set of conclusions deals with the human side of organisation thus creating a need and importance of humanising relations between the management and workers. This can possibly be done by adopting a supportive style of supervision, improving physical working conditions, creating effective and proper interpersonal relations and encouraging informal relations among them. By doing this the employees would not only feel happy, and comfortable and more satisfied but ultimately a sense of belonging will be created among them, they can be made more loyal and sincere towards the organisation which may further contribute to higher efficiency.

At the same time, Nawal's father has long experience in managing people in government departments. His views should also be respected. He may be right in his approach to the extent of not only believing that efforts need to be made by an organisation for keeping employees happy in their work setting, it should also be ensured that happiness and more satisfaction contribute to higher productivity. Thus, in a nutshell, the humanisation of the organisation, socialisation of the employees, cordial human relations and happiness of the employees should be treated as a means to raise their productivity in the organisation.

Case Study III

Vikas Automobiles Ltd. is engaged in the business of repairing and overhauling automobiles. It has about 50 employees working in the workshop. Current practices have led to an extreme amount of customer dissatisfaction due to a very lengthy waiting time, discourteous work force, poor quality of workmanship and the high cost of repairing automobiles. As a result, customers have started getting their services elsewhere. The owner is very keen to improve the situation but he finds his people are not motivated by a spirit of service basically because of poor wages and indifferent supervision. This is located in an environmentally alert community and they have also been complaining to the local municipal authority that the nasty way in which operations are handled and wastewater disposed off, is causing a lot of inconvenience in the locality. The owner-manager wants your help in raising the level of productivity of the employees and effectiveness of the operation.

You have been asked to look into the operations of the company, analyse the whole situation and make necessary recommendations.

Suggested Analysis

1. Identification of the Problems

(a) Customers' dissatisfaction

(b) Decline in the volume of business

(c) Reduced market share

(d) High waiting time

(e) Poor quality of workmanship

(f) Discourteous behaviour of employees

(g) Unfavourable attitude of the community

2. Causes of the Problems

(a) Lack of motivation

(b) Lack of required training to employees

(c) Dissatisfactory wage system

(d) Indifferent supervision

(e) Environmental awareness among the people of the community

(f) Ineffective waste disposal system

3. Solutions and Recommendations

(a) Scientific training should be provided to the employees to improve their workmanship as well as behavioural pattern.

(b) Motivation system should be designed by studying and analysing the needs and wants of the employees.

(c) Incentive wage system should be installed to provide reasonable wages to employees and incentives should be linked to productivity, for example, more incentives for higher productivity.

(d) Supporting supervision should be provided to the workers. They should be helped, guided and inspired to work efficiently. Their work-related problems should be promptly looked into and solved.

(e) To make the attitude of the community favourable, local people should be given priority in employment and the company should contribute to promote the overall welfare of the community.

(f) Responsibility should be fixed on each supervisor to complete jobs in time.

(g) Interpersonal relations with customers need to be improved by creating mutual trust and confidence and improving the quality of service rendered to them.

CASE STUDY IV

Economy Transport Ltd. is a transport company plying more than 1,000 passenger buses in Delhi on different routes. There are about 1,500 employees working in the company. Out of these, 300 crewmen (drivers and conductors) are working on the routes. The behaviour of these crewmen while dealing with the public and daily commuters is not satisfactory. So far as the salary structure of these crewmen is concerned they are paid reasonably well. In spite of this, they have become lethargic, lazy and careless. Their productivity level is also very low as compared to the crewmen of other transport companies. After having surveyed their behaviour pattern it came to light that they are little interested in their jobs and that it has lost its meaning for them.

Questions

Read the above case and answer the following questions:

(a) As a manager of this company, what kind of job design would you suggest for these crewmen? Why?

(b) Is it possible to modify their behaviour by imparting training to them? Explain.

(c) Is it necessary to motivate them by giving monetary incentives? Give reasons?

Case Study V

Manoj has a small factory producing plastic goods. There are 100 employees working in the factory. At present, it is solely managed by his father. Manoj has jointed his father recently after completing post-graduation in management.

He discovers that the authority to manage all the affairs in the factory has been retained by his father who is the owner. There hardly seems to be any line of authority in the factory. Some of his relatives and trustworthy senior employees have been empowered to look after various operations like purchase, sale, accounting and finance. Manoj is not fully satisfied with the present set-up of distribution of authority. He wants to decentralise part of the authority still being retained by his father. He believes that through delegation of authority he will be able to establish a cordial and healthy relationship among the senior subordinates.

Questions

Read the above case and answer the following questions:

(a) What is the need to delegate authority as felt by Manoj and what should be the base of delegation?

(b) You are requested to suggest some guidelines to make the delegation of authority more effective.

(c) Does it help in motivating the employees? Explain.

Case Study VI

Sohan Lal started a music cassette company in 1980 on a very small scale. In a short span of five years, his company's sales almost equalled the combined sales of the three other leading music recording companies in India. This was possible because of Mr. Lal's business acumen, extraordinary managerial skills, imaginative sales promotion programmes and, above all, his interest in good music and lower overhead expenses. Encouraged by the enormous success of his music recording company, Mr. Sohan Lal ventured into other manufacturing activities. Throughout this period, he found it difficult to delegate authority and continues making all the final decisions on new product plans, capital budgeting, advertising, pricing policies, sales plans, hiring of staff and labour union and other matters. Some of the newly set up units that turned out to be unprofitable were closed down after a few years.

Questions

Carefully examine the above case and answer the following questions.

(a) What could have been the possible reason of Mr. Lal's reluctance to delegate authority?

(b) How would you have convinced Mr. Lal about the utility of delegating authority?

Case Study VII

Ritesh is vice-president (finance) in a company having more than 5,000 employees on its rolls. He had been working as finance manager in a multinational company. He is highly ambitious, bold and courageous in his approach. He is result-oriented and practical in his approach. He does not respect rules and formalities and moves in a direct manner adopting short cuts. He seeks a high degree of compliance to orders and instructions given by him.

The use of rationality and intellect is on the low side and his decisions are based on intuition. But in this new company, most of the middle-level managers are equipped with knowledge of modern management. They are unhappy with the working style of the vice-president (finance).

Questions

Read the above case and answer the following questions.

(a) What managerial style is being used by Ritesh and how is it different from other styles of management?

(b) Why are the young professionally qualified middle-level managers not happy with him?

(c) Give suggestions to improve the working style being followed by Ritesh.

Case Study VIII

Mr. Malhotra has been working in X-company as finance manager for the last two years. Though he had a very long and rich experience of working in the finance department of the same company and dealing with various types of financial problems faced by the company, he is facing many new problems in this new assignment. He has a heavy work load of departmental activities and sometimes he has to stay late in the office even up to 10 p.m. Besides, he has been unable to cope with the problem he is facing with regard to the vice-president (finance) because the latter assumes that Mr. Malhotra is well-versed in finance functions and therefore a new kind of assignment, though related to finance, that is, evaluation of finance and investment projects, has been assigned to him.

In view of this situation, Mr. Mayank, who is a chartered accountant working at a lower level in the finance department had been appointed as a staff specialist to Mr. Malhotra to help, guide and advise him on specialised matters such as project evaluation, etc. Since then, the efficiency level of Mr. Malhotra has come down and he does not feel comfortable with Mr. Mayank.

Questions

(a) Why is Mr. Malhotra not comfortable with his staff specialist, Mr. Mayank.

(b) How can he cope with the situation of a heavy workload requiring a variety of skills and expertise?

(c) Give suggestions to make the situation healthy and comfortable for Mr. Malhotra.

Case Study IX

Mr. Rastogi has been working as a senior foreman in an automobile company manufacturing two-wheeler scooters. He has a long experience of assembly line operations. There are 1,200 skilled and semi-skilled workers working in two shifts on the assembly line. Due to the increasing demand of scooters in the market, Mr. Rastogi has been asked by the production manger to increase the daily production by raising the efficiency level of the workers. In this connection, the production manager is of the opinion that to increase the level of efficiency, minor adjustments and changes should be made in the production process. But senior foreman Rastogi is not convinced by the suggestion of the production manager. He firmly believes that in addition to changes to be made in the production process, it is more important to develop team spirit among the workers by providing a monetary incentive to them.

Questions

Read the above case and answer the following questions.

(a) Why does senior foreman Rastogi differ with the production manager? In the difference based on approach? If so, explain those approaches.

(b) What considerations should be taken into account to make the monetary incentive scheme effective?

Case Study X

ABC Ltd. is a Delhi-based company producing a variety of products such as electrical goods, chemicals, footwear, detergent powder, washing soap, etc. These products are being produced in Delhi and distributed throughout the country with the help of dealers. The company is facing many problems which are but natural in the process of growth and development. Moreover, it is facing cut-throat competition from local manufacturers of these products in different parts of the country, as a result of which sales volume has come down. In view of this, the managing director of the company feels that to make the products of the company more competitive in terms of price, quality and consumer need, the manufacturing operations of the company should be decentralised to various parts of the country so as to get the benefits of localised products.

Questions

Study the whole case carefully and answer the following questions.

(a) Is the proposal of decentralising production operations feasible? Give reasons.

(b) Which form of decentralisation or combination of several forms should be adopted by the company?

(c) Will mere delegation of authority to local production centres be enough? Comment on this keeping in view the difference between delegation and decentralisation of authority.

Case Study XI

Paul Samuel is a financial manager in XYZ company producing and distributing consumer goods. He has been heading the finance department for the last five years. The finance department consists of more than 100 employees. He has two deputy and four assistant finance managers to help in the day-to-day functioning of the department. Recently, the company diversified its operations into production and distribution of consumer durables. The workload of the finance department increased consequently both in terms of quality and in quantity. Besides performing managerial functions with regard to the finance department, the financial department has to attend various meetings at a higher level. He is also given the responsibility of preparing project reports and conducting feasibility studies of various proposals given to him from higher levels. He feels overburdened and consequently his efficiency is on the decline. He is unable to cope with the increased multidimensional workload. To help him directly, a chartered accountant having experience of 10 years has been appointed as his staff specialist. But the finance manager, due to many reasons, does not feel comfortable with the specialist. Often, they disagree with each other.

Questions

Study the case carefully and answer the following questions.

(a) What may be the possible reasons that the finance manager does not feel comfortable with the chartered accountant?

(b) Why do they disagree? Explain the various causes.

(c) How to resolve the disagreement between the two? Give suggestions.

Case Study XII

Subhash has been working as an operator in the assembly line of an automobile company manufacturing two-wheeler scooters and bikes for the last 10 years. He has been working very honestly and sincerely and meets the standard of performance determined for him. He has a creative mind and even at home discusses various work-related matters with his wife. He tells her that he is capable of making certain improvements in the overall functioning of a motor bike. But when he takes his ideas to his superior he makes fun of it and does not give serious though to it.

Gradually, the level of Subhash came down. Though he knows it, yet he is unable to cope with the situation. Sometimes, he feels frustrated at not getting monetary hikes every year. He is finding it difficult to meet the standards of performance. He has already started losing interest in the job.

Questions

You are required to study the whole case and answer the following questions.

(a) What are the possible causes of Subhash's changing pattern of working behaviour?

(b) How is it possible for the superior to make him more efficient and maintain his existing level of efficiency?

(c) What exact scheme should the superior introduce in the assembly line to tap the creativity of his operators?

Case Study XIII

A firm having a roaring business of leather goods intends to decentralise its operations. In this regard, six manufacturing plants of more or less similar nature have been installed in different places within the country. But the board of directors of the company is indecisive on how much authority should be delegated to managers heading the plants. More specifically, the board of directors seeks your advice on the question whether the power to appoint supervisory and middle-level managerial staff should be at the plant level or with the head office.

Questions

You are required to study the case and answer the following questions.

(a) How should the head office share authority with its plant managers?

(b) On what matters should the head office retain authority and what matters should be left to plant managers?

(c) Give suggestions to maintain coordination between the head office and its plants located in various places.

Case Study XIV

The managing director of a company is very serious and worried about increasing costs of production and resultant losses. He intends to appoint some management consultant to enquire into the matter. For this purpose, he has asked his private secretary to type a letter. It was around 5 p.m. and in a hurry, the private secretary could not file it and put it up to the managing director. Rather, he left it on the table. Next morning, a messenger from the branch office came to the head office to deliver a letter. He saw the letter and went through it. When he returned to the branch office, he narrated the contents of the letter to his superior. Soon the news spread among the middle-level managerial, clerical and lower level staff that the company is likely to retrench employees. Immediately, union leaders held a meeting on the matter. By the time the letter was despatched, it was known to every one in the organisation.

Questions

You are required to study this case and answer the following questions.

(a) What is a 'grapevine' and how does it help in communication?

(b) 'Only half truths and rumours are spread through informal relations'. Do you agree with this? Give reasons.

(c) How to make informal communication more effective? Give suggestions.

CASE STUDY XV

We assume that monetary incentives are very strong and widely accepted motivators for employees, because one can satisfy all his level of needs with money. Not only are the physical needs of food, clothing and shelter satisfied by it, the need for security, social and other higher level needs are also partially met with it. But in some cases, managers are less inclined to give these incentives and on the contrary they give high value to non-monetary incentives such as more authority, promotion, recognition, appreciation, self-achievement, etc.

Questions

Read the above statement carefully and answer the following questions.

(a) Monetary incentives have a strong motivating appeal. Why and to what extent? Discuss.

(b) Non-monetary incentives are equally or more important motivators for employees. Discuss with the help of Maslow's need hierarchy.

(c) People are motivated when they are given more freedom. Discuss.

CASE STUDY XVI

Raghavan is a senior financial manager in a reputed consultancy organisation. He reports directly to the vice-president (finance). He is heading a department consisting of 100 employees. He has been recently promoted to this position. He has been working in the same department for a long time. After having worked for some time, he comes to know that middle-level managers such as deputy and assistant managers and foreman and superiors do not fully cooperate with him to implement his decisions. He analyses the entire situation and arrives at the conclusion that middle-level and lower-level managers should be associated with the decision-making process to get their maximum cooperation and contribution. He takes the entire matter to the vice-president (finance) and discusses it with him.

Questions

Read the case carefully and answer the following questions.

(a) How should Mr. Raghavan convince the vice-president that individual decision are less effective than group decisions?

(b) Which scheme of participation of middle and lower level managers should be suggest to the vice-president (finance).

(c) What would be the overall implication of this move on the level of satisfaction and efficiency of lower-level managers?

CASE STUDY XVII

"I expect every manager in my department to be completely rational in every decision he makes," declared Mr. Ishwar Dayal, Director (Marketing) in Overseas Plastic Ltd. "Every one of us, irrespective of his position in the organisation has to be a professional rationalist and I expect him not only to know what he is doing but also to be right only in more than half his decisions. But that is not good enough for me. However, one may be excused for occasional mistakes especially in matters beyond one's control but no one can be pardoned for acting irrationally."

"I endorse your view, sir," says Ms Indu Ahluwalia, his advertising manager. "And I always try to be rational and logical in my decisions but would you mind helping me to be sure of this by explaining what rational decisions are."

Questions

Read and analyse the above case and answer the following questions.

(a) Explain how Mr. Ishwar Dayal might describe what is involved in making rational decisions.

(b) If Ms Indu Ahluwalia declares that there is no way she can be completely rational, what would you suggest?

Case Study XVIII

Mr. Ashok, a professionally qualified engineer, has been working in one of the production plants of the company as assistant plant manager. After having worked for five years, he gets an opportunity for promotion. He is promoted to the position of plant manager and transferred to another plant which is facing difficulty in meetings its production targets and budgetary standards. He is highly ambitious and an authority-oriented energetic person. He strongly believes that to solve the problem, rigid and close control should be exercised. He should make decisions on his own and get them implemented by exercising his authority. After joining the new plant, he gives directives to each work station to increase production by 10 per cent and reducing the budget by 5 per cent. He monitors the situation closely, finally dismisses five supervisors who fail to meet their production targets without giving a patient hearing to them. He promotes senior operators to the positions of the dismissed supervisors. Ultimately, this style of functioning yielded the desired results. Productivity increases and budgetary deviations are brought under control.

Questions

Read the above case and answer the following questions.

(a) What kind of organisational behaviour has Mr. Ashok followed? Discuss the type of organisational climate created by him.

(b) Give suggestions to improve the existing organisational climate considering relaxed control and self control.

Case Study XIX

Campa-Cola Ltd. is a great Indian company producing and distributing cold drinks in India. The company has been in existence for the last 15 years. It has a large manufacturing plant in Delhi and a fleet of trucks for the purpose of controlled and efficient distribution of cold drinks in the neighbouring states as well. Employees working in the company are fully satisfied with the service conditions, promotional avenues and welfare schemes launched by the company for them. Customers also feel comfortable and satisfied with the drink both in terms of quality and price. But after the entry of two big multinational companies, Coca-Cola and Pepsi, the entire situation has changed. Campa-Cola has lost 90 per cent of its market to these companies and it has become very difficult to compete with them.

Questions

Read the above case carefully and answer the following questions.

(a) Make out a SWOT analysis of Campa-Cola Ltd.

(b) Suggest a suitable strategy to maintain the survival and profitability of Campa-Cola in the light of competition from multinational companies.

(c) How can Campa-Cola utilise its strengths to regain its lost market share?

Case Study XX

In 1990, Mr. Sanjay Kataria, a chartered accountant, was elected as the chairman of Promising Life Insurance Company which was at that time the third largest life insurance company in the country. During the next five years, however, while its business increased, it did not grow as fast as its major competitors and Promising Company dropped from third to sixth place.

This naturally perturbed Sanjay Kataria as it did the board of directors of the company. Finally, after deliberations, the board of directors concluded that lack of leadership in the sales of both ordinary life policies and group life insurance was the major cause of the company's comparatively slow progress. It was also generally concluded that the two directors in charge of sales in these two major areas with district managers working under them were not very competent leaders.

Sanjay Kataria called these two directors and asked them to ensure strong leadership at the regional and district level or else quit their jobs. As these directors left the meeting with the chairman, one of them told the other: "Now, just how do we make people leaders? How can we be sure whether a person is a leader or not? You know this is a tough job."

Questions

Read and analyse the above case and answer the following questions:

(a) If you were one of the directors, how would you answer the question that the other director raised?

(b) What would you do about developing strong leaders?

Case Study XXI

As a result of economic reforms initiated in the recent past, the Indian economy has been globalised. Regulations and controls have been relaxed. Many more multinationals have been inclined to make their entry in India. Consequently, market dynamics, specially the nature of competition, has changed drastically. Indian organisations are finding it difficult to compete with their counterparts coming from outside. You are a manager in one of the well-established pharmaceutical companies already working in India for the last 20 years. To compete with multinational companies, you personally feel that production as well as the distribution systems are to be made cost effective so that better quality of medicines can be produced and distributed at reasonable cost. To improve the cost-effectiveness of the system you believe that the organisation is over-staffed. You bring this fact to the knowledge of the managing director. He discusses this problem with you in the light of human resources planning and development. The managing director asks you the following questions.

Questions

(a) How to proceed with manpower planning? Discuss the various steps involved in it.

(b) How will you convince your managing director that human resources planning and development would help in making the production and distribution systems cost effective?

CASE STUDY XXII

India's economy is going through a radical change. After initiation of many economic reforms during 1991, the business environment in the country has changed a lot. We have definitely moved towards a free market economy. As a result of this, many new opportunities have been created and at the same time new challenges and threats have also arisen. There were more than half a dozen organisations engaged in the production and distribution of cola drinks under different brand names. When two giant multinationals, namely Coca-Cola and Pepsi-Cola, entered the Indian market, the existence and survival of domestic organisations came into jeopardy because of the cut-throat competition. Some local organisations have disappeared and others are surviving on the border line.

Questions

Read the above case and answer the following questions.

(a) How can domestic organisations cope with the changing environment?

(b) What have been their strengths and weaknesses and how can they penetrate the cold drinks market further?

(c) Suggest suitable strategies to be followed by them.

—oo(O)oo—